A-Level Year 1 & College

Mathematics

Exam Board: Edexcel

When it comes to AS-Level Maths, all you need is love. No, hang on —
all you need is this massive CGP Student Book. We always mix those up.

But there's still plenty in here to fall in love with. Crystal-clear study notes,
tips, examples and a huge helping of practice questions for every topic...
all perfectly matched to the latest Edexcel course. Dreamy.

It even includes a free Online Edition to read on your PC, Mac or tablet!

CGP

How to get your free Online Edition

Go to **cgpbooks.co.uk/extras** and enter this code...

3103 1512 5572 7482

Contents

About this Book

In this book you'll find...

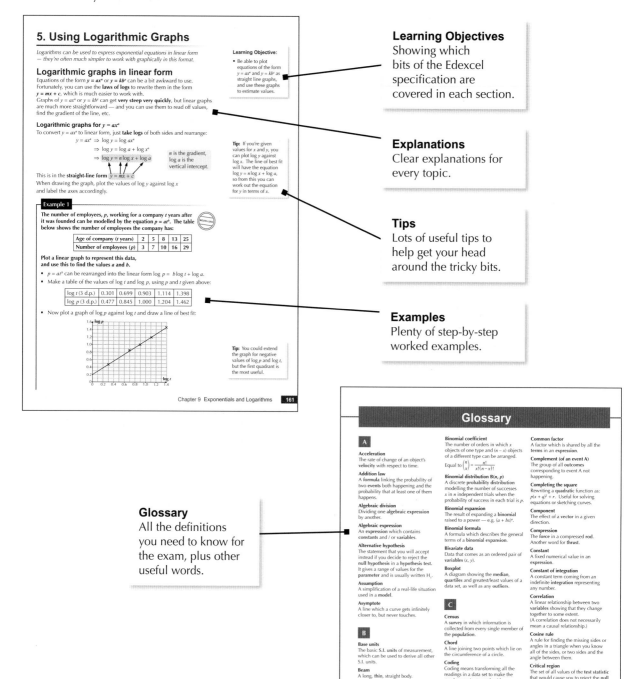

5. Using Logarithmic Graphs

Logarithms can be used to express exponential equations in linear form — they're often much simpler to work with graphically in this format.

Learning Objective:
- Be able to plot equations of the form $y = ax^n$ and $y = kb^x$ as straight line graphs, and use these graphs to estimate values.

Logarithmic graphs in linear form

Equations of the form $y = ax^n$ or $y = kb^x$ can be a bit awkward to use. Fortunately, you can use the **laws of logs** to rewrite them in the form $y = mx + c$, which is much easier to work with.

Graphs of $y = ax^n$ or $y = kb^x$ can get **very steep very quickly**, but linear graphs are much more straightforward — and you can use them to read off values, find the gradient of the line, etc.

Logarithmic graphs for $y = ax^n$

To convert $y = ax^n$ to linear form, just **take logs** of both sides and rearrange:

$$y = ax^n \Rightarrow \log y = \log ax^n$$
$$\Rightarrow \log y = \log a + \log x^n$$
$$\Rightarrow \log y = n \log x + \log a$$

n is the gradient, $\log a$ is the vertical intercept.

This is in the **straight-line form** $y = mx + c$.
When drawing the graph, plot the values of $\log y$ against $\log x$ and label the axes accordingly.

Tip: If you're given values for x and y, you can plot $\log y$ against $\log x$. The line of best fit will have the equation $\log y = n \log x + \log a$, so from this you can work out the equation for y in terms of x.

Example 1

The number of employees, p, working for a company t years after it was founded can be modelled by the equation $p = at^b$. The table below shows the number of employees the company has:

Age of company (t years)	2	5	8	13	25
Number of employees (p)	3	7	10	16	29

Plot a linear graph to represent this data, and use this to find the values a and b.

- $p = at^b$ can be rearranged into the linear form $\log p = b \log t + \log a$.
- Make a table of the values of $\log t$ and $\log p$, using p and t given above:

$\log t$ (3 d.p.)	0.301	0.699	0.903	1.114	1.398
$\log p$ (3 d.p.)	0.477	0.845	1.000	1.204	1.462

- Now plot a graph of $\log p$ against $\log t$ and draw a line of best fit:

Tip: You could extend the graph for negative values of $\log p$ and $\log t$, but the first quadrant is the most useful.

Chapter 9 Exponentials and Logarithms   161

Learning Objectives
Showing which bits of the Edexcel specification are covered in each section.

Explanations
Clear explanations for every topic.

Tips
Lots of useful tips to help get your head around the tricky bits.

Examples
Plenty of step-by-step worked examples.

Glossary
All the definitions you need to know for the exam, plus other useful words.

Glossary

A

Acceleration
The rate of change of an object's **velocity** with respect to time.

Addition law
A **formula** linking the probability of two **events** both happening and the probability that at least one of them happens.

Algebraic division
Dividing one **algebraic expression** by another.

Algebraic expression
An **expression** which contains **constants** and / or **variables**.

Alternative hypothesis
The statement that you will accept instead if you decide to reject the **null hypothesis** in a **hypothesis test**. It gives a range of values for the **parameter** and is usually written H_1.

Assumption
A simplification of a real-life situation used in a **model**.

Asymptote
A line which a curve gets infinitely closer to, but never touches.

B

Base units
The basic S.I. **units** of measurement, which can be used to derive all other S.I. units.

Beam
A long, **thin**, straight body.

Bearing
A direction, given as an angle measured clockwise from north.

Biased sample
A **sample** which does not fairly represent the **population** it is taken from.

Binomial
A **polynomial** with only two terms e.g. $a + bx$.

Binomial coefficient
The number of orders in which x objects of one type and $(n - x)$ objects of a different type can be arranged.

Equal to $\binom{n}{x} = \dfrac{n!}{x!(n-x)!}$

Binomial distribution B(n, p)
A discrete **probability distribution** modelling the number of successes x in n independent trials when the probability of success in each trial is p.

Binomial expansion
The result of expanding a **binomial** raised to a power — e.g. $(a + bx)^n$.

Binomial formula
A formula which describes the general terms of a **binomial expansion**.

Bivariate data
Data that comes as an ordered pair of **variables** (x, y).

Boxplot
A diagram showing the **median**, **quartiles** and greatest/least values of a data set, as well as any **outliers**.

C

Census
A **survey** in which information is collected from every single member of the **population**.

Chord
A line joining two points which lie on the circumference of a circle.

Coding
Coding means transforming all the readings in a data set to make the numbers easier to work with.

Coefficient
The **constant** multiplying the **variable**(s) in an algebraic **term** e.g. 4 in the term $4x^2y$.

Collinear points
Three or more points are collinear if they all lie on the same straight line.

Common denominator
A denominator (i.e. bottom of a fraction) which is shared by all fractions in an **expression**.

Common factor
A factor which is shared by all the **terms** in an **expression**.

Complement (of an event A)
The group of all **outcomes** corresponding to event A not happening.

Completing the square
Rewriting a **quadratic** function as: $p(x + q)^2 + r$. Useful for solving equations or sketching curves.

Component
The effect of a **vector** in a given direction.

Compression
The **force** in a compressed rod. Another word for **thrust**.

Constant
A fixed numerical value in an expression.

Constant of integration
A constant term coming from an indefinite **integration** representing any number.

Correlation
A linear relationship between two **variables** showing that they change together to some extent. (A correlation does not necessarily mean a causal relationship.)

Cosine rule
A rule for finding the missing sides or angles in a triangle when you know all of the sides, or two sides and the angle between them.

Critical region
The set of all values of the **test statistic** that would cause you to reject the **null hypothesis**.

Critical value
The value of the **test statistic** at the edge of the **critical region**.

Cubic equation
An **equation** that can be written $ax^3 + bx^2 + cx + d = 0$ (where $a \neq 0$).

Cumulative distribution function
A function, F(x), which gives the probability that a **random variable**, X, will be less than or equal to a particular value, x.

Glossary   477

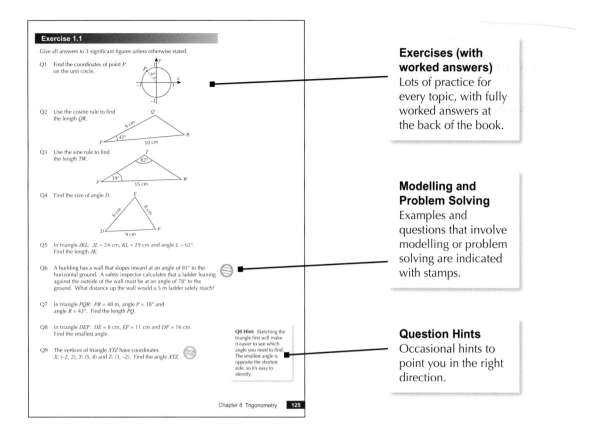

Exercises (with worked answers)
Lots of practice for every topic, with fully worked answers at the back of the book.

Modelling and Problem Solving
Examples and questions that involve modelling or problem solving are indicated with stamps.

Question Hints
Occasional hints to point you in the right direction.

Formula Sheet
Contains all the formulas you'll be given in the AS exams.

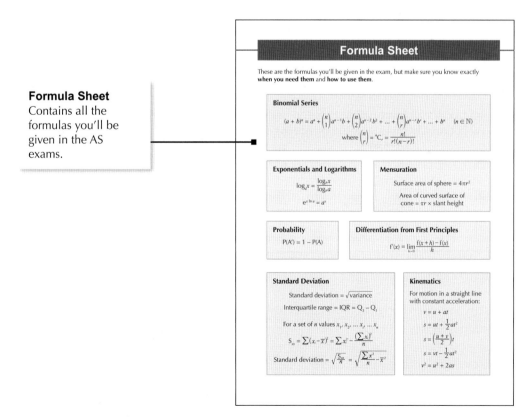

Published by CGP

Editors:
Chris Corrall, Sammy El-Bahrawy, Will Garrison, Paul Jordin, Caley Simpson, Ben Train.

Contributors:
Katharine Brown, Michael Coe, Claire Creasor, Alastair Duncombe, Anna Gainey, Phil Harvey,
Barbara Mascetti, Alan Mason, Mark Moody, James Nicholson, Andy Pierson, Rosemary Rogers, Janet West

ISBN: 978 1 78294 717 2

With thanks to Mona Allen, Janet Dickinson, Allan Graham, Frances Knight, Alison Palin, Andy Park,
David Ryan and Dawn Wright for the proofreading.
With thanks to Jan Greenway for the copyright research.

Printed by Elanders Ltd, Newcastle upon Tyne.
Clipart from Corel®

1. Modelling

A mathematical model is a mathematical description of a real-life situation. Modelling involves simplifying the situation so that you can understand its behaviour and predict what is going to happen.

Using mathematical models

Modelling in maths generally boils down to using an **equation** or a set of equations to **predict** what will happen in real life. You'll meet them in all areas of this course. For example:

- In **algebra**, formulas involving exponentials are used to model things like population growth (see pages 157-159).

- In **mechanics**, equations are used to model how the speed and acceleration of a moving object changes over time (see Chapter 19).

- In **statistics**, probability distributions are models which are used to predict the probability of a particular outcome in a trial (see pages 311-312).

Learning Objectives:

- Understand the mathematical modelling process.
- Be able to describe some examples of mathematical modelling.
- Understand why mathematical modelling involves making assumptions.
- Understand the process of refining a mathematical model.

Example 1

A company predicts that its latest product will sell 500 units in its first month on sale, and that sales will gradually increase by an average of 250 units per month. Write an equation to model the predicted sales, s, of the product during its mth month on sale.

s is the mth term of an arithmetic sequence with first term $a = 500$ and common difference $d = 250$.

So $s = a + (m-1)d = 500 + 250(m-1) = 250 + 250m = \boxed{250(m+1)}$

This is a model, because it's based on a prediction of how the sales will go. The actual sales might end up being much higher or lower if the company has got its predictions wrong.

Tip: You should have met arithmetic sequences at GCSE. They also come up in Year 2 of A-Level Maths.

Modelling assumptions

Models are always **simplifications** of the real-life situation. When you construct a model, you have to make **assumptions**. In other words, you **ignore** or **simplify** some factors that might affect the real-life outcome, in order to keep the maths simpler. For example:

- A population growth model might ignore the fact that the population will eventually run out of **food**, because that won't happen in the **time period** you're modelling.

- A model for the speed of a moving object might ignore **air resistance**, because that would make the maths much **more complicated**, or because you might only want a **general result** for objects of all shapes and sizes.

- Probability distributions based on past data often assume the **conditions** in future trials will be the **same** as when the past data was recorded.

Tip: There are many possible reasons for making assumptions — e.g. a factor might only have a small effect, it might be hard to predict, or you might not have enough data to model its effect accurately.

Tip: There are lots of special terms to describe the assumptions you might make in mechanics — there's a list of them on p.333.

Example 2

Leon owns a gooseberry farm. This week, he had 5 workers picking fruit, and they picked a total of 1000 punnets of gooseberries. Leon wants to hire more workers for next week. He predicts that next week, if the number of workers on his farm is w, the farm will produce p punnets of gooseberries, where $p = 200w$.

Suggest three assumptions Leon has made in his model.

Leon's model predicts that the mean number of punnets produced per worker next week will be the same as this week. That means he's assumed all the conditions next week will be the same as the conditions this week. For example:

- Leon has assumed all the new workers he employs next week will work at the same speed on average as the ones he employed this week.

- He has assumed that the weather next week will be good enough to allow each worker to work as many hours as this week.

- He has assumed that there will be enough gooseberries to fill 200 punnets per worker, however many workers he employs.

Tip: In modelling questions, don't forget to link your answers back to the original context of the question.

Refining models

An important part of the modelling process is **refining** a model. This usually happens after the model has been **tested** by comparing it with real-world outcomes, or if you find out some **extra information** that affects the model.

Refining a model usually means changing some of the **assumptions**. For example:

- You might adjust a population growth model if you found that **larger populations** were more susceptible to **disease**, so grew more slowly.

- You might decide to refine a model for the speed of an object to take into account the **friction** from the surface the object is travelling over.

- You might adjust a probability distribution if you collect **more data** which changes the **relative frequency** of the outcomes.

Tip: You could be asked to criticise or evaluate a model — e.g. you might need to assess if any assumptions are unrealistic. There's more on this on page 159.

Example 2 (cont.)

Leon discovers that the weather forecast for next week is bad, and his workers are only likely to be able to pick gooseberries for half the number of hours they did this week. How should he refine his model?

Leon's original model was $p = 200w$, based on all the workers next week picking at the same average weekly rate as this week. If his workers can only pick for half the time, they can only pick half as many gooseberries.

So the refined model would be $p = 200w \div 2 \implies \boxed{p = 100w}$

Tip: In this example, the model is refined because there's new information. Leon might also refine his model at the end of next week, for example if he found that his new workers were a lot slower or faster than his current ones.

Modelling is one of the **overarching themes** of the AS and A-Level Maths courses. In other words, it could come up within any other topic — you might be given a model to use, or be asked to create one yourself.

Throughout this book, examples and questions involving modelling are marked with stamps like this:

2. Problem Solving

Some maths questions can be straightforward to answer — you're told what maths you need to use, then you use it to get a solution. 'Problem solving' questions are those tricky ones where you have to work out for yourself exactly what maths you need to do.

Learning Objectives:

- Understand the problem solving cycle.
- Be able to apply problem solving skills to maths questions.

The problem solving cycle

Whenever maths is used to solve a real-life problem, the process used can be described using a **problem solving cycle**. The basic cycle looks like this:

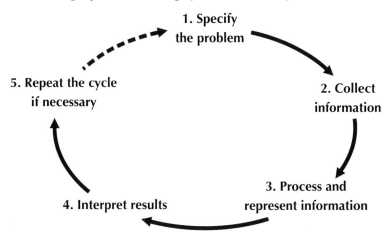

Tip: Problem solving questions include: questions that don't have 'scaffolding' (i.e. they're not broken down into parts a), b), c) etc.), 'wordy' questions with a real-life context, questions that need more than one area of maths, and questions that test if you actually understand the maths as well as being able to use it.

These steps apply to pretty much anything you can use maths for.

1. **Specify the problem**

   The **problem** is the actual question you want to answer.
   It could be anything from "What's the probability I roll a 6 on this dice?" to "How long will it take this ball to fall 10 m?" to "What's the angle of elevation from here to the top of that lighthouse?".

2. **Collect information**

   You'll need some **numbers** to solve the problem. This step might involve taking measurements, carrying out surveys or looking up data.

3. **Process and represent information**

   Once you've got the information you need, you can do the **calculations**. Representing the information might involve drawing a **graph** or **diagram**.

4. **Interpret results**

   Once you've done the calculation, you might need to **interpret** it to work out what the numerical answer means in terms of the original question.

5. **Repeat the cycle if necessary**

   You might decide to **repeat** the process. E.g. if you collected your information via a survey, you might want to repeat it with a larger or more representative sample. If your calculations involved modelling, you might want to **refine** your model (see previous page).

Tip: Like modelling, problem solving is an overarching theme that will come up throughout the course. (There's also a third one — 'proof and mathematical language', which is covered in Chapter 2.)

Problem solving in maths questions

You can apply a version of the problem solving cycle to any maths question where it's not immediately obvious what you're supposed to do.

1. Specify the problem

The first thing to do is work out what the question is actually asking. The question might be phrased in an unusual way to try to throw you, or it might be written in a 'wordy' context, where you need to turn the words into maths.

2. Collect information

Write down what you know. All the information you need to answer the question will either be given in the question somewhere, or it'll require facts that you should already know.

Tip: When you're doing a maths question, it's unlikely you'll need to consider repeating the problem solving cycle once you've calculated the answer — just be aware that it's part of the real-world problem solving process.

3. Process and represent information

When you know what you're trying to find out, and what you already know, you can do the calculation to answer the question.

4. Interpret results

Don't forget to give your answer in terms of the original context. The result of your calculation won't necessarily be the final answer.

Tip: Of course, you wouldn't normally need to do so much writing for a problem solving question — it's written out like this here as an example of how the problem solving thought process might work.

Example

Armand cuts out a semicircle of cardboard from a rectangular sheet of cardboard measuring 20 cm by 40 cm and throws the rest away. The cardboard he throws away has an area of 398.08 cm². How long is the straight side of the semicircle? (Use $\pi = 3.14$.)

- **Specify the problem.** What are you trying to find?

  The length of the straight side of a circle is the diameter of the full circle, which is twice the radius. So that's what you're looking for here.

- **Collect information.** What do you know?

  The total area of the sheet of cardboard is 20 cm × 40 cm.
  398.08 cm² was thrown away, the rest is the area of the semicircle.
  The area of a semicircle = $\frac{1}{2}$ × area of a circle = $\frac{1}{2}\pi r^2$

- **Process and represent information.** Do the maths.

  Area of semicircle = $20 \times 40 - 398.08 = 800 - 398.08 = 401.92$ cm²
  So $401.92 = \frac{1}{2}\pi r^2 = \frac{1}{2} \times 3.14 \times r^2 = 1.57 \times r^2$

  $\Rightarrow r^2 = 401.92 \div 1.57 = 256$

  $\Rightarrow r = \sqrt{256} = 16$ cm

  $\qquad d = 2r = 2 \times 16 = 32$ cm

- **Interpret results.** Give the answer in the context of the question.

  The length of the straight side of the semicircle is $\boxed{32 \text{ cm.}}$

 Throughout the rest of this book, if you see a stamp like this, it means there's an example that shows some of these problem solving skills in action, or a question where you'll probably need them.

1. Proof

Mathematical proof is a logical argument that shows that a statement is true (or false). There are a few different types of proof that you need to be familiar with, but first there's a bit of notation to learn that will come up often throughout the course of A-Level maths.

Notation

Set notation

In maths, a '**set**' is just a **collection** of objects or numbers (called **elements**) — a set is often represented by a capital letter. To show something is a set you put **curly brackets** around it — e.g. A = {0, 1, 2}.

- You can write out the **complete list** of elements:
  {1, 3, 5, 7, 9, 11, 13, 15, 17, 19, 21, 23, 25, 27, 29}

- Or you can write out the **rule** that connects the elements:
  {odd numbers between 0 and 30}

- The rule can also be written out using numbers and symbols: $\{x : x < 0\}$.
  In words, this means "the set of values of x such that x is less than 0".

- A set containing **no elements** is called the **empty set**, written as: $\varnothing = \{\}$.

If you have more than one set you can talk about their **union** and **intersection**.

> The **union** of two sets A and B is the combination of both sets — so it contains **all the elements** of **both sets**. It is written $A \cup B$.

> The **intersection** of two sets A and B is a smaller set that contains only the elements present in **both** sets. It is written $A \cap B$.

For example, if A = {1, 3, 5, 7, 9} and B = {1, 4, 9, 16},
then $A \cup B$ = {1, 3, 4, 5, 7, 9, 16} and $A \cap B$ = {1, 9}.

Function notation

- A **function** of x, written **f(x)**, takes a value of x, does something to it, and then outputs another value — it's just like an **equation** of x, but y is replaced with **f(x)**.

- For example, the function f(x) = x^2 + 1 takes a value of x, squares it and then adds 1. So if x = 4, f(4) = $(4)^2$ + 1 = 17.

Logical notation

The symbols $\Rightarrow$ and $\Leftrightarrow$ crop up all over the place.
These are logic symbols — they show when one thing **implies** another.

> '$p \Rightarrow q$' means 'p implies q'. You can read it as '**if** p, **then** q' — so **if** p is true, **then** q must also be true — e.g. $x = 2 \Rightarrow x^2 = 4$.

> '$p \Leftrightarrow q$' means 'p implies q and q implies p'. This means that p is true **if and only if** (or **iff**) q is true — e.g. $x^2 = 4 \Leftrightarrow x = \pm 2$

Learning Objectives:

- Be comfortable with mathematical notation for sets, functions, logical arguments and equivalence.
- Be able to show that sums and products of integers are odd or even (as required).
- Be able to use proof by exhaustion and proof by deduction to show that statements are true.
- Be able to use disproof by counter-example to show that statements are false.

Tip: Have a look at p.56-58 to see how set notation is used to show solutions to inequalities.

Tip: You'll see function notation used a lot in the chapters on quadratics (Chapter 4) and differentiation (Chapter 10).

Tip: You might also see an arrow like this $\Leftarrow$. It works in the same way as the other implication arrow — it just goes the opposite way.
E.g. $p \Leftarrow q$ means 'q implies p'.

Equivalence notation

There are three variations on the equals sign that you also need to know.

> $\neq$ means **not equal to**
> — e.g. sin 90° $\neq$ cos 90°

> $\approx$ means **approximately equal to**
> — e.g. 1 ÷ 3 $\approx$ 0.33.

> $\equiv$ is the **identity symbol**. It means that two things are **identically equal** to each other. So $(a + b)(a - b) \equiv a^2 - b^2$ is true for **all values** of a and b (unlike an equation like $a^2 = 9$, which is only true for certain values of a).

Tip: Identities crop up in trigonometry — see Chapter 8.

Proof

Simple proofs — odd and even numbers

Before you get onto the trickier proofs, there are some nice simple proofs about **odd** and **even numbers** that are really useful. But first you need to know these 'proper' definitions for them:

Tip: Remember, integers are just whole numbers. They can be positive, negative or 0.

> Any **even** number can be written as $2a$, where a is an integer.

> Any **odd** number can be written as $2b + 1$, where b is an integer.

In the proofs below, $2j + 1$ and $2k + 1$ represent any two **odd numbers**, and $2l$ and $2m$ represent any two **even numbers** (where j, k, l and m are integers).

Example 1

a) **Prove that the sum of two even numbers is even.**

> **Proof:** $2l + 2m = 2(l + m) =$ even
> so even + even = even

Tip: You've shown that it can be written as 2 × something. This means it's divisible by two, so is an even number.

b) **Prove that the sum of an odd number and an even number is odd.**

> **Proof:** $(2j + 1) + (2l) = 2j + 2l + 1 = 2(j + l) + 1 =$ odd
> so odd + even = odd

c) **Prove that the product of two odd numbers is odd.**

> **Proof:** $(2j + 1)(2k + 1) = 4jk + 2j + 2k + 1 = 2(2jk + j + k) + 1 =$ odd
> so odd × odd = odd

Tip: You can prove that e.g. the product of two even numbers is even in a similar way.

Proof by deduction

A **proof by deduction** is when you use **known facts** to build up your argument and show a statement **must** be true.

Example 2

Tip: A quotient is what you get when you divide one number by another.

A definition of a rational number is 'a number that can be written as a **quotient of two integers, where the denominator is non-zero'**.

Use this definition to prove that the following statement is true:
   "The product of two rational numbers is always a rational number."

- Take **any two** rational numbers and call them a and b.

- By the **definition** of rational numbers you can write them in the form $a = \dfrac{p}{q}$ and $b = \dfrac{r}{s}$, where p, q, r and s are all integers, and q and s are non-zero.

- The **product** of a and b is $ab = \dfrac{p}{q} \times \dfrac{r}{s} = \dfrac{pr}{qs}$.

- pr and qs are the products of integers, so they must also be integers, and because q and s are non-zero, qs must also be non-zero.

- We've shown that ab is a quotient of two integers and has a non-zero denominator, so by definition, ***ab* is rational**.

- Hence the original statement is **true**.

Tip: Here, the "known facts" are the definition of a rational number, the fact that the products of integers are integers, and the fact that the products of non-zero integers are also non-zero.

Proof by exhaustion

In **proof by exhaustion** you break things down into two or more **cases**. You have to make sure that your cases cover **all possible situations**, then prove separately that the statement is true for **each case**.

Example 3

Prove the following statement:
"For any integer *x*, the value of f(*x*) = *x*³ + *x* + 1 is an odd integer."

- To prove the statement, split the situation into **two cases**:

    (i) x is an **even number**, and (ii) x is an **odd number**.

- (i)   If x is an **even integer**, then it can be written as $x = 2n$, for some integer n. Substitute $x = 2n$ into the function:
  $f(2n) = (2n)^3 + 2n + 1 = 8n^3 + 2n + 1 = 2(4n^3 + n) + 1$
  n is an integer $\Rightarrow (4n^3 + n)$ is an integer
  $\phantom{n \text{ is an integer}} \Rightarrow 2(4n^3 + n)$ is an even integer
  $\phantom{n \text{ is an integer}} \Rightarrow 2(4n^3 + n) + 1$ is an **odd integer**
  So f(*x*) is **odd** when x is **even**.

Tip: These two cases cover all possible situations, because an integer is always either odd or even.

- (ii) If x is an **odd integer**, then it can be written as $x = 2m + 1$, for some integer m. Substitute $x = 2m + 1$ into the function:
  $f(2m + 1) = (2m + 1)^3 + 2m + 1 + 1$
  $ = (8m^3 + 12m^2 + 6m + 1) + 2m + 1 + 1$
  $ = 8m^3 + 12m^2 + 8m + 3 = 2(4m^3 + 6m^2 + 4m + 1) + 1$

  m is an integer $\Rightarrow (4m^3 + 6m^2 + 4m + 1)$ is an integer
  $\phantom{m \text{ is an integer}} \Rightarrow 2(4m^3 + 6m^2 + 4m + 1)$ is an even integer
  $\phantom{m \text{ is an integer}} \Rightarrow 2(4m^3 + 6m^2 + 4m + 1) + 1$ is an **odd integer**

  So f(*x*) is **odd** when x is **odd**.

Tip: Again, you need to use the definitions of odd and even numbers — and the fact that sums and products of integers are also integers.

- You have shown that f(*x*) is **odd** when x is even **and** when x is odd. As any integer x **must** be either odd or even, you have therefore shown that f(*x*) is **odd** for **any** integer x, so the statement is **true**.

Disproof by counter-example

Disproof by **counter-example** is the easiest way to show a mathematical statement is **false**. All you have to do is find **one case** where the statement doesn't hold.

Tip: You might have to try a few different numbers before you come up with an example that doesn't work.

> ### Example 4
>
> **Disprove the following statement:**
>   *"For any pair of integers x and y, if x > y, then $x^2 + x > y^2 + y$."*
>
> - To **disprove** the statement, it's enough to find just **one example** of x and y where $x > y$, but $x^2 + x \leq y^2 + y$.
>
> - Let $x = 2$ and $y = -4$.
>   Then $2 > -4 \Rightarrow x > y$
>   but $x^2 + x = 2^2 + 2 = 6$
>   and $y^2 + y = (-4)^2 + (-4) = 12$,
>   so $x^2 + x < y^2 + y$
>
> - So when $x = 2$ and $y = -4$, the first part of the statement holds, but the second part of the statement **doesn't**.
>
> - So the statement is **not true**.

Tip: A good way to find counter-examples to inequalities containing a squared term is to try negative numbers — often the inequality doesn't work for numbers less than 0.

Exercise 1.1

Q1 Hint: These proofs are similar to the ones on p.6.

Q1 a) Prove that the sum of two odd numbers is even.

    b) Prove that the product of two even numbers is even.

    c) Prove that the product of an odd number and an even number is even.

Q2 By finding a counter-example, disprove the following statement:
"If p is a non-zero integer, then $\dfrac{1}{p^2} < \dfrac{1}{p}$."

Q3 Hint: To show a number is divisible by 4, you need to be able to write it as 4 × an integer.

Q3 Prove that, for any integer x, $(x + 5)^2 + 3(x - 1)^2$ is always divisible by four.

Q4 Prove by exhaustion that the product of any three consecutive integers is even.

Q5 Disprove the following statement:
"$n^2 - n - 1$ is a prime number for any integer $n > 2$."

Q6 Disprove the following: $\sqrt{x^2 + y^2} < x + y$.

Q7 Hint: Use the definition of rational numbers from p.6 — and have a look at p.14-15 for more on adding fractions.

Q7 Prove that the sum of two rational numbers is also a rational number.

Q8 a) Prove the statement below:
"For any integer n, $n^2 - n - 1$ is always odd."

    b) Hence prove that $(n^2 - n - 2)^3$ is always even.

1. Algebraic Expressions

This chapter will cover some of the basic algebra skills that you'll need again and again throughout the course — so you'll need to make sure you're completely comfortable with everything here. The good news is you should have seen a lot of it before.

Learning Objectives:

- Be able to use and expand brackets.
- Be able to identify common factors and take them outside the brackets.
- Be able to simplify complicated expressions including algebraic fractions.

Expanding brackets

Single brackets

When you've got just **one set of brackets** multiplied by a single number or letter, multiply each term in the brackets by the term outside the brackets.

$$a(b + c + d) = ab + ac + ad$$

Double brackets

For **two sets** of brackets multiplied together (where there are **two terms** in each), multiply **each term** in one set of brackets by **each term** in the other. You should **always** get **four terms** from multiplying out double brackets (though sometimes two of the terms will **combine**).

$$(a + b)(c + d) = ac + ad + bc + bd$$

Tip: Remember **FOIL**: First Outside Inside Last as a rule for multiplying out double brackets. It's just an easy way to remember it.

Squared brackets

Squared brackets are just a **special case** of double brackets where both brackets are the **same**. Write them out as two sets of brackets until you're comfortable with it.

$$(a + b)^2 = (a + b)(a + b) = a^2 + ab + ba + b^2 = a^2 + 2ab + b^2$$

A common **mistake** is to write $(a + b)^2 = a^2 + b^2$ — you must remember that $(a + b)^2$ is actually $(a + b)(a + b)$ to avoid this trap.

Long brackets

Long brackets are brackets with **many terms**. Just like with double brackets, you need to multiply every term in the first set of brackets by every term in the second — you'll just need to do it with more terms.

Write out the expression again with each term from the first set of brackets separately multiplied by the second set of brackets. Always use this middle step so that you don't get confused by all the terms.

$$(x + y + z)(a + b + c + d)$$
$$= x(a + b + c + d) + y(a + b + c + d) + z(a + b + c + d)$$

Then multiply out each of these single brackets, **one at a time**.

Many brackets

When you've got **many sets** of brackets multiplied together, multiply them out **two at a time**, treating each set of two as double brackets or long brackets.

Multiply out the first **two** sets of brackets...

$$(a + b)(c + d)(e + f) = (ac + ad + bc + bd)(e + f)$$

...then multiply out the remaining **two sets**.

$$= ac(e + f) + ad(e + f) + bc(e + f) + bd(e + f)$$

Now multiply out each of these single brackets, **one at a time**.

Tip: Once you've multiplied out the first pair, the resulting terms may cancel or simplify — making the second step easier.

Examples

Single Brackets **Expand $3xy(x^2 + 2x - 8)$.**

Multiply each term inside the brackets by the bit outside — separately.

$$(3xy \times x^2) + (3xy \times 2x) + (3xy \times (-8))$$
$$= (3x^3y) + (6x^2y) + (-24xy)$$
$$= 3x^3y + 6x^2y - 24xy$$

Multiply the numbers first, then put the letters together.

Tip: Putting brackets round each bit makes it easier to read.

Squared Brackets **Expand $(2y^2 + 3x)^2$.**

Either write it as two sets of brackets and multiply it out...

$$(2y^2 + 3x)(2y^2 + 3x)$$
$$= 2y^2 \cdot 2y^2 + 2y^2 \cdot 3x + 3x \cdot 2y^2 + 3x \cdot 3x$$
$$= 4y^4 + 6xy^2 + 6xy^2 + 9x^2$$
$$= 4y^4 + 12xy^2 + 9x^2$$

...or do it in one go.

$$(2y^2)^2 + 2(2y^2)(3x) + (3x)^2$$

$a^2 \qquad 2ab \qquad b^2$

$$= 4y^4 + 12xy^2 + 9x^2$$

Tip: The dots used here mean 'multiplied by' — just like the $\times$ sign.

Tip: Don't forget to **collect like terms** here: $6xy^2 + 6xy^2 = 12xy^2$

Long Brackets **Expand $(2x^2 + 3x - 6)(4x^3 + 6x^2 + 3)$**

Multiply each term in the first set of brackets by the whole second set of brackets:

$$(2x^2 + 3x - 6)(4x^3 + 6x^2 + 3)$$
$$= 2x^2(4x^3 + 6x^2 + 3) + 3x(4x^3 + 6x^2 + 3) + (-6)(4x^3 + 6x^2 + 3)$$

Now multiply out each of these sets of brackets and simplify it all:

$$= (8x^5 + 12x^4 + 6x^2) + (12x^4 + 18x^3 + 9x) + (-24x^3 - 36x^2 - 18)$$
$$= 8x^5 + 24x^4 - 6x^3 - 30x^2 + 9x - 18$$

> **Many Brackets** | **Expand** $(2x + 5)(x + 2)(x - 3)$
>
> Start by multiplying the first two sets of brackets.
>
> $$(2x + 5)(x + 2)(x - 3) = (2x^2 + 4x + 5x + 10)(x - 3)$$
> $$= (2x^2 + 9x + 10)(x - 3)$$
>
> Now multiply the long bracket by the final set of brackets.
> $$= 2x^2(x - 3) + 9x(x - 3) + 10(x - 3)$$
>
> Expand the single brackets and simplify.
> $$= (2x^3 - 6x^2) + (9x^2 - 27x) + (10x - 30) = \boxed{2x^3 + 3x^2 - 17x - 30}$$

Exercise 1.1

Q1 Expand the brackets in these expressions:

a) $5(x + 4)$ b) $a(4 - 2b)$ c) $-2(x^2 + y)$

d) $6mn(m + 1)$ e) $-4ht(t^2 - 2ht - 3h^3)$ f) $7z^2(2 + z)$

g) $4(x + 2) + 3(x - 5)$ h) $p(3p^2 - 2q) + (q + 4p^3)$ i) $7xy(x^2 + z^2)$

Q2 Expand and simplify:

a) $(x + 5)(x - 3)$ b) $(2z + 3)(3z - 2)$ c) $(u + 8)^2$

d) $(ab + cd)(ac + bd)$ e) $(10 + f)(2f^2 - 3g)$ f) $(7 + q)(7 - q)$

g) $(2 - 3w)^2$ h) $(4rs^2 + 3)^2$ i) $(5k^2l - 2kn)^2$

Q3 Expand and simplify the following expressions:

a) $(l + 5)(l^2 + 2l + 3)$ b) $(2 + q)(3 - q + 4q^2)$

c) $(m + 1)(m + 2)(m - 4)$ d) $(r + s)^3$

e) $(4 + x + y)(1 - x - y)$ f) $(2c^2 - cd + d)(2d - c - 5c^2)$

Q4 Carole's garden is a square with sides of length x metres. Mark's garden is a rectangle. One side of the rectangle is 3 metres longer than the side of the square and the other is twice as long as the side of the square, plus an extra metre. Find the difference in area between Mark's garden and Carole's. Give your answer in terms of x.

(PROBLEM SOLVING)

Factorising
Common Factors

The **factors** of a term are all the bits that **multiply together** to make it up — if something is a factor of a term, the term will be **divisible** by it.

For example, consider the term **$12xy^2$** — it has many factors including:

- All the **factors of 12** — 1, 2, 3, 4, 6 and 12.

- The variable x.

- The variable y (and also y^2).

- Any combinations of these multiplied together e.g. $3xy$, $12y^2$, $6x$ etc.

Tip: The definition of a **term** is a collection of numbers, letters and brackets all multiplied or divided together.

Example 1

Find all the factors of 6x.

A good way to do this is to break it up as much as you can:
$$6x = 1 \times 2 \times 3 \times x$$

None of these have any other factors so we can't break it down further.

Now list all possible combinations of 1, 2, 3 and x:

$$1, \quad 2, \quad 3, \quad 6, \quad x, \quad 2x, \quad 3x, \quad 6x.$$

1 is always a factor.

The term itself is also a factor.

A factor which is in every term of an expression is a called a **common factor**. They can be '**taken out**' and put outside brackets to simplify the expression. When you've taken out **all** possible factors, the expression is **factorised**.

Example 2

Factorise $2x^3z + 4x^2yz + 14x^2y^2z$ completely.

Look for any factors that are in each term.
$$2x^3z + 4x^2yz + 14x^2y^2z$$

<u>Numbers:</u>   There's a common factor of 2 here because 2 divides into 2, 4 and 14.

<u>Variables:</u>   There's at least an x^2 in each term...
... and there's a z in each term.

Tip: The key here is the phrase '**at least**'. There is an x^3 in one term but only an x^2 in the other two, so each term has at least an x^2 in it.

So there's a common factor of $2x^2z$ in this expression.

This can be seen more easily if you write each term as $2x^2z \times$ 'something':

$$2x^3z + 4x^2yz + 14x^2y^2z = 2x^2z \cdot x + 2x^2z \cdot 2y + 2x^2z \cdot 7y^2$$

Write the common factor outside a set of brackets...

$$= 2x^2z(x + 2y + 7y^2)$$

...and put what's left of each term inside the brackets.

The three terms in the brackets have no common factors — so this expression is completely factorised.

Tip: After factorising, you should always check that your answer multiplies out to give the original expression. (You can do this in your head — if you trust it.)

You can check that you did it right by multiplying it out again and checking you get the original expression:

$$2x^2z(x + 2y + 7y^2) = 2x^3z + 4x^2yz + 14x^2y^2z$$

It's not just numbers and variables that you need to look for — you can sometimes take out **whole sets of brackets** as factors of an expression.

Example 3

Express $(y + a)^2(x - a)^3 + (x - a)^2$ as a product of factors.

This can be written:
$$(y + a)^2(x - a)(x - a)^2 + (x - a)^2$$

$(x - a)^2$ is a common factor — so write the common factor outside a set of brackets and put what's left of each term inside the brackets:

$$(x - a)^2[(y + a)^2(x - a) + 1]$$

This term will give $(x - a)^2$.

This term will multiply to give $(y + a)^2(x - a)^3$.

The two terms in the brackets share no common factors so the expression is factorised.

Tip: 'Expressing as a product of factors' just means writing it as numbers, variables or sets of brackets multiplied together. The things you multiply together are the **factors** of the expression.

Difference of two squares

If you expand brackets of the form $(a - b)(a + b)$ the 'ab' terms cancel and you're left with one square minus another:

$$(a - b)(a + b) = a^2 + ab - ba - b^2 = a^2 + ab - ab - b^2 = a^2 - b^2$$

This result is called the **difference of two squares**:

$$a^2 - b^2 = (a - b)(a + b)$$

Watch out for it when factorising — if you spot that an expression is just 'something squared' minus 'something else squared', you can use this result to rewrite the expression as a pair of brackets, i.e. to factorise it.

Tip: When dealing with lots of terms in brackets, you might find it easier to use square brackets for some of them.

Tip: For more on factorising quadratics see pages 24-27.

Example 4

a) Factorise $x^2 - 36y^2$.

36 is a square number so $36y^2$ can be written as a square:
$$x^2 - 36y^2 = x^2 - 6^2y^2$$
$$= x^2 - (6y)^2$$
$$= (x - 6y)(x + 6y)$$

This is a difference of two squares.

b) Factorise $x^2 - 5$.

5 isn't a square number but you can still write it as a square:
$$x^2 - 5 = x^2 - \left(\sqrt{5}\right)^2$$
$$= \left(x - \sqrt{5}\right)\left(x + \sqrt{5}\right)$$

Also a difference of two squares.

Tip: Any number can be written as the square of its root — see pages 20-23 for more on surds.

Exercise 1.2

Q1 Factorise the following expressions completely:

a) $9k + 15l$

b) $u^2 - uv$

c) $10w + 15$

d) $2x^2y - 12xy^2$

e) $f^2g^2 - fg$

f) $3u^2v^2 + 5u^4v^4 + 12u^2v$

g) $p^3 + 3pq^3 + 2p$

h) $abcde - bcdef - cdefg$

i) $11xy^2 - 11x^2y - 11x^2y^2$

j) $mnp^2 + 7m^2np^3$

Q2 Hint: Remember to look for a difference of two squares.

Q3d) Hint: Remember that $(b - a) = -(a - b)$

Q5 Hint: Look for common factors first — if you can't see any, try to multiply out the brackets and see if it simplifies that way.

Tip: This equals sign with 3 lines $\equiv$ means it's true for all values of a, b, c or x — this is called an **identity** (see page 6).

Q2 Write the following expressions as products of factors:
a) $x^2 - y^2$
b) $9a^2 - 4b^2$
c) $25x^2 - 49z^2$
d) $a^2c - 16b^2c$
e) $y^2 - 2$
f) $4x^2 - 3$

Q3 Express the following as the product of factors.
a) $(4 - z)^2(2 - z) + p(2 - z)$
b) $(r - d)^3 + 5(r - d)^2$
c) $(b + c)^5(a + b) - (b + c)^5$
d) $l^2m(a - 2x) + rp^2(2x - a)$

Q4 Simplify each expression, leaving your answer in its factorised form.
a) $(p + q)^2 + 2q(p + q)$
b) $2(2x - y)^2 - 6x(2x - y)$
c) $(r + 6s)^2 - (r + 6s)(r - s)$
d) $(l + w + h)^2 - l(l + w + h)$

Q5 Simplify these expressions by expanding brackets, factorising or both.
a) $(m + 5)(m^2 - 5m + 25)$
b) $(p - 2q)(p^2 + 2pq + 4q^2)$
c) $(u - v)(u + v) - (u + v)^2$
d) $(c + d)^3 - c(c + d)^2 - d(c + d)^2$

Algebraic fractions

You should have seen all these methods before when working with numerical fractions — but you need to learn them for **algebraic fractions** too.

Adding and subtracting

If you're **adding fractions** together and they all have the same **denominator**, you can just add the **numerators**.

$$\frac{a}{x} + \frac{b}{x} + \frac{c}{x} \equiv \frac{a+b+c}{x}$$

x is the **common denominator**

If the fractions you want to add don't have a common denominator you can 'find' one — **rewrite** the fractions so that the denominators are the same by multiplying **top** and **bottom** by the same thing.

Example 1

a) **Express** $\frac{1}{2x} - \frac{1}{3x} + \frac{1}{5x}$ **as a single fraction.**

- You need to rewrite these so that all the **denominators** are **equal**. What you want is something that all these denominators **divide into**.

- **30** is the lowest number that 2, 3 and 5 all go into and each denominator contains an x. So make the common denominator **30x**.

- **Multiply** the top and bottom lines of each fraction by whatever makes the bottom line 30x.

$$\frac{1}{2x} - \frac{1}{3x} + \frac{1}{5x} = \frac{1}{2x} \cdot \frac{15}{15} - \frac{1}{3x} \cdot \frac{10}{10} + \frac{1}{5x} \cdot \frac{6}{6}$$
$$= \frac{15}{30x} - \frac{10}{30x} + \frac{6}{30x}$$
$$= \frac{15 - 10 + 6}{30x}$$
$$= \frac{11}{30x}$$

Always check that these cancel down to give what you started with.

b) Simplify $\dfrac{3}{x+2} + \dfrac{5}{x-3}$.

- Again, the first step is to rewrite the fractions so that they have a **common denominator**.

- You need an expression that both **(x + 2)** and **(x − 3)** divide into — you can get one by multiplying the denominators together to give a common denominator of **(x + 2)(x − 3).**

- Make the denominator of **each fraction** into the common denominator.

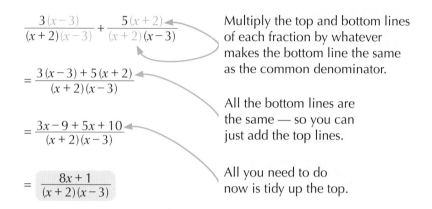

$$\frac{3\,(x-3)}{(x+2)(x-3)} + \frac{5\,(x+2)}{(x+2)(x-3)}$$

Multiply the top and bottom lines of each fraction by whatever makes the bottom line the same as the common denominator.

$$= \frac{3\,(x-3) + 5\,(x+2)}{(x+2)(x-3)}$$

All the bottom lines are the same — so you can just add the top lines.

$$= \frac{3x - 9 + 5x + 10}{(x+2)(x-3)}$$

$$= \boxed{\frac{8x + 1}{(x+2)(x-3)}}$$

All you need to do now is tidy up the top.

c) Simplify $\dfrac{3}{2x^2} + \dfrac{6}{5x}$.

- Finding a common denominator here is a bit more tricky. You could still **multiply** the two denominators together to get $10x^3$ — but this wouldn't give the **simplest** one.

- You have $2x^2 = 2 \times x \times x$ and $5x = 5 \times x$ and you need to find a term which **both** of them divide into. You must include each different factor **at least once** in your term — but some **more than once**.

- The different factors are **2**, **5** and x so you need **at least one** of each — there are **two** x's in the first denominator so you'll need an x^2, but you **don't** need another for the x in the second denominator since this is accounted for by multiplying by the x^2.

- So the common denominator is $2 \times 5 \times x \times x = \mathbf{10x^2}$.

$$\frac{3}{2x^2} + \frac{6}{5x} = \frac{3 \times 5}{2x^2 \times 5} + \frac{6 \times 2x}{5x \times 2x}$$

$$= \frac{15}{10x^2} + \frac{12x}{10x^2}$$

Rewrite fractions with a common denominator.

$$= \frac{15 + 12x}{10x^2}$$

Add the numerators.

$$= \boxed{\frac{3\,(5 + 4x)}{10x^2}}$$

Factorise the numerator.

Tip: Finding any old common denominator is easy — just multiply all the denominators together. But if you're careful and don't include any bits twice, you'll have a lot less simplifying to do at the end.

Simplifying

Algebraic fractions can sometimes be simplified by cancelling **factors** that appear in both the numerator and denominator.

You can do this in **two ways**. Use whichever you prefer — but make sure you understand the ideas behind both.

Example 2

Simplify $\dfrac{ax + ay}{az}$.

You can either...

① Factorise — then cancel.

Factorise the top line.

$$\frac{ax + ay}{az} = \frac{a(x + y)}{az} = \frac{\cancel{a}(x + y)}{\cancel{a}z} = \frac{x + y}{z}$$

Cancel the 'a'.

... Or

② Split into two fractions — then cancel.

$$\frac{ax + ay}{az} = \frac{ax}{az} + \frac{ay}{az}$$

This is just the rule from page 14 for adding fractions — but backwards.

$$= \frac{\cancel{a}x}{\cancel{a}z} + \frac{\cancel{a}y}{\cancel{a}z} = \frac{x}{z} + \frac{y}{z} = \frac{x + y}{z}$$

Exercise 1.3

Q1 Express each of these as a single fraction.

a) $\dfrac{x}{3} + \dfrac{x}{4}$

b) $\dfrac{2}{t} + \dfrac{13}{t^2}$

c) $\dfrac{1}{2p} - \dfrac{1}{5q}$

d) $\dfrac{ab}{c} + \dfrac{bc}{a} + \dfrac{ca}{b}$

e) $\dfrac{2}{mn} - \dfrac{3m}{n} + \dfrac{n^2}{m}$

f) $\dfrac{2}{ab^3} - \dfrac{9}{a^3 b}$

Q2 Express the following as single fractions in their simplest form.

a) $\dfrac{5}{y - 1} + \dfrac{3}{y - 2}$

b) $\dfrac{7}{r - 5} - \dfrac{4}{r + 3}$

c) $\dfrac{8}{p} - \dfrac{1}{p - 3}$

d) $\dfrac{w}{2(w - 2)} + \dfrac{3w}{w - 7}$

e) $\dfrac{z + 1}{z + 2} - \dfrac{z + 3}{z + 4}$

f) $\dfrac{1}{q + 1} + \dfrac{3}{q - 2}$

Q3 Simplify these expressions.

a) $\dfrac{2x + 10}{6}$

b) $\dfrac{6a - 12b - 15c}{3}$

c) $\dfrac{np^2 - 2n^2 p}{np}$

d) $\dfrac{4st + 6s^2 t + 9s^3 t}{2t}$

e) $\dfrac{10yz^3 - 40y^3 z^3 + 60y^2 z^3}{10z^2}$

f) $\dfrac{12cd - 6c^2 d + 3c^3 d^2}{12c^2 de}$

2. Laws of Indices

The laws of indices are just a set of simple rules for manipulating expressions involving indices (powers). They'll be used regularly throughout this course for simplifying expressions, equations and formulas.

Learning Objective:

- Be able to use the laws of indices to simplify expressions.

Laws of indices

You should already know that the expression x^n just means n **lots** of x multiplied together. The n is called the **index** or power of x.
So when you square a number (e.g. x^2), the index or power is 2.

OK, now you're ready to see the laws.
Here are the first **three** you need to know:

> If you multiply two numbers, you **add** their powers.
> $$a^m \times a^n = a^{m+n}$$

> If you divide two numbers, you **subtract** their powers.
> $$\frac{a^m}{a^n} = a^{m-n}$$

> If you have a power to the power of something else, you **multiply** the powers together.
> $$(a^m)^n = a^{mn}$$

Tip: Don't forget — index and power mean the same thing. We'll use power for the rest of the section.

There are also laws for manipulating **fractional** and **negative** powers...

$$a^{\frac{1}{m}} = \sqrt[m]{a}$$

$$a^{-m} = \frac{1}{a^m}$$

$$a^{\frac{m}{n}} = \sqrt[n]{a^m} = \left(\sqrt[n]{a}\right)^m$$

Tip: $\sqrt[m]{a}$ is the mth root of a.

...and one simple law for **zero** powers, which works for any non-zero number or letter.

$$a^0 = 1$$

Now, let's see the laws in action in some worked examples.

Example 1

Simplify the following:

a) (i) $a^2 a$ (ii) $x^{-2} \cdot x^5$ (iii) $(a + b)^2 (a + b)^5$ (iv) $ab^3 \cdot a^2 b$

> (i) $a^2 a = a^{2+1} = a^3$ $\boxed{a^m \times a^n = a^{m+n}}$
>
> (ii) $x^{-2} \cdot x^5 = x^{-2+5} = x^3$
>
> (iii) $(a + b)^2 (a + b)^5 = (a + b)^{2+5} = (a + b)^7$
>
> (iv) $ab^3 \cdot a^2 b = a^{1+2} b^{3+1} = a^3 b^4$ ← Add the powers of a and b separately.

Tip: Note that $x = x^1$.

Tip: To understand part b) (iii), remember that:

$$(ab^2)^4 = (ab^2) \cdot (ab^2) \cdot (ab^2)$$
$$\cdot (ab^2)$$
$$= a \cdot a \cdot a \cdot a \cdot b^2$$
$$\cdot b^2 \cdot b^2 \cdot b^2$$
$$= a^4 \cdot (b^2)^4 = a^4 b^8$$

b) (i) $(x^2)^3$ (ii) $\{(a + b)^3\}^4$ (iii) $(ab^2)^4$

(i) $(x^2)^3 = x^6$ $\boxed{(a^m)^n = a^{mn}}$

(ii) $\{(a + b)^3\}^4 = (a + b)^{12}$

(iii) $(ab^2)^4 = a^4(b^2)^4 = a^4 b^8$ This power of 4 applies to both bits inside the brackets.

c) (i) $\dfrac{x^{\frac{3}{4}}}{x}$ (ii) $\dfrac{x^3 y^2}{xy^3}$

Tip: For part c) (i), you could simplify further to $\dfrac{1}{\sqrt[4]{x}}$.

(i) $\dfrac{x^{\frac{3}{4}}}{x} = x^{\frac{3}{4} - 1} = x^{-\frac{1}{4}} = \dfrac{1}{x^{\frac{1}{4}}}$ $\boxed{\dfrac{a^m}{a^n} = a^{m-n}}$

(ii) $\dfrac{x^3 y^2}{xy^3} = x^{3-1} y^{2-3} = x^2 y^{-1} = \dfrac{x^2}{y}$ Subtract the powers of x and y separately.

d) (i) $4^{\frac{1}{2}}$ (ii) $125^{\frac{1}{3}}$

(i) $4^{\frac{1}{2}} = \sqrt{4} = 2$ $\boxed{a^{\frac{1}{m}} = \sqrt[m]{a}}$

(ii) $125^{\frac{1}{3}} = \sqrt[3]{125} = 5$

e) (i) $9^{\frac{3}{2}}$ (ii) $16^{\frac{3}{4}}$

(i) $9^{\frac{3}{2}} = (9^{\frac{1}{2}})^3 = (\sqrt{9})^3 = 3^3 = 27$ $\boxed{a^{\frac{m}{n}} = \sqrt[n]{a^m} = (\sqrt[n]{a})^m}$

(ii) $16^{\frac{3}{4}} = (16^{\frac{1}{4}})^3 = (\sqrt[4]{16})^3 = 2^3 = 8$ It's often easier to work out the root first, then raise it to the power.

f) (i) 2^{-3} (ii) $(x + 1)^{-1}$

(i) $2^{-3} = \dfrac{1}{2^3} = \dfrac{1}{8}$ $\boxed{a^{-m} = \dfrac{1}{a^m}}$

(ii) $(x + 1)^{-1} = \dfrac{1}{x + 1}$

g) (i) 2^0 (ii) $(a + b)^0$

(i) $2^0 = 1$ $\boxed{a^0 = 1}$

(ii) $(a + b)^0 = 1$

Example 2

Express $\dfrac{(7^{\frac{1}{3}})^6 \times (7^{-1})^4}{(7^{-4})^{-2}}$ **as** 7^k**, where** k **is an integer.**

This one looks really complicated but it's just a series of easy steps. Make sure to work through it slowly and don't jump ahead.

$$\frac{\left(7^{\frac{1}{3}}\right)^6 \times \left(7^{-1}\right)^4}{\left(7^{-4}\right)^{-2}} = \frac{7^{\frac{6}{3}} \times 7^{-1\times 4}}{7^{-4\times -2}}$$

$(a^m)^n = a^{mn}$

$$= \frac{7^2 \times 7^{-4}}{7^8}$$

$$= \frac{7^{2-4}}{7^8}$$

$a^m \times a^n = a^{m+n}$

$$= \frac{7^{-2}}{7^8}$$

$$= 7^{-2-8}$$

$\dfrac{a^m}{a^n} = a^{m-n}$

$$= 7^{-10}$$

Tip: You could also write this as $\frac{1}{7^{10}}$.

Exercise 2.1

Q1 Simplify the following, leaving your answer as a power:

a) 10×10^4

b) $y^{-1} \times y^{-2} \times y^7$

c) $5^{\frac{1}{2}} \times 5^3 \times 5^{\frac{-3}{2}}$

d) $6^5 \div 6^2$

e) $3^4 \div 3^{-1}$

f) $\dfrac{6^{11}}{6}$

g) $\dfrac{r^2}{r^6}$

h) $(3^2)^3$

i) $(k^{-2})^5$

j) $(z^4)^{-\frac{1}{8}}$

k) $(8^{-6})^{-\frac{1}{2}}$

l) $\dfrac{p^5 q^4}{p^4 q}$

m) $\dfrac{c^{-1} d^{-2}}{c^2 d^4}$

n) $(ab^2)^2$

o) $\dfrac{12yz^{-\frac{1}{2}}}{4yz^{\frac{1}{2}}}$

Q2 Evaluate:

a) $4^{\frac{1}{2}} \times 4^{\frac{3}{2}}$

b) $\dfrac{2^3 \times 2}{2^5}$

c) $\dfrac{7^5 \times 7^3}{7^6}$

d) $(3^2)^5 \div (3^3)^3$

e) $\left(4^{-\frac{1}{2}}\right)^2 \times \left(4^{-3}\right)^{-\frac{1}{3}}$

f) $\dfrac{\left(2^{\frac{1}{2}}\right)^6 \times \left(2^{-2}\right)^{-2}}{\left(2^{-1}\right)^{-1}}$

g) 1^0

h) $\left(\dfrac{4}{5}\right)^0$

i) $(-5.726324)^0$

Q3 Express the following as negative or fractional powers or both:

a) $\dfrac{1}{p}$

b) $\sqrt{q}$

c) $\sqrt{r^3}$

d) $\sqrt[4]{s^5}$

e) $\dfrac{1}{\sqrt[3]{t}}$

Q4 Evaluate:

a) $9^{\frac{1}{2}}$

b) $8^{\frac{1}{3}}$

c) $4^{\frac{3}{2}}$

d) $27^{-\frac{1}{3}}$

e) $16^{-\frac{3}{4}}$

Q5 If $p = \dfrac{1}{16}q^2$, write the following expressions in terms of q:

a) $p^{\frac{1}{2}}$

b) $2p^{-1}$

c) $p^{\frac{1}{2}} \div 2p^{-1}$

Q6 Find the value of x for each of the following:

a) $4^x = \sqrt[3]{16}$

b) $9^x = \dfrac{1}{3}$

c) $\sqrt{5} \times 5^x = \dfrac{1}{25}$

3. Surds

Learning Objectives:

- Be able to simplify expressions containing surds.
- Be able to rationalise denominators.

This section will cover how to simplify expressions containing square roots. There are laws for simplifying these expressions just like the ones for powers.

The laws of surds

Put $\sqrt{2}$ into a calculator and you'll get 1.414213562...
But square 1.414213562 and you get 1.999999999.

No matter how many decimal places you use, you'll never get exactly 2. This is because $\sqrt{2}$ is an **irrational number** — its decimal expansion **continues forever**.

Tip: A rational number is a number that can be expressed as $\frac{p}{q}$ where p and q are integers and $q \neq 0$. An irrational number is just one which is not rational.

The only way to express a number like this **exactly** is to leave it as a root. Numbers like $\sqrt{2}$ that can only be written exactly using roots are called **surds**. The number $\sqrt{3}$ is a surd because it can't be written exactly without a root — $\sqrt{9}$ is **not** a surd because it can be simplified to 3.

Tip: Remember that $\sqrt{x} = x^{\frac{1}{2}}$ (see p.17).

There are three rules you'll need to know to be able to use surds properly:

$$\sqrt{ab} = \sqrt{a}\sqrt{b}$$
$$\sqrt{\frac{a}{b}} = \frac{\sqrt{a}}{\sqrt{b}}$$
$$a = (\sqrt{a})^2 = \sqrt{a}\sqrt{a}$$

Simplifying surds usually just means making the number in the $\sqrt{}$ sign smaller or getting rid of a fraction inside the $\sqrt{}$ sign.

Examples

a) Simplify $\sqrt{12}$

$$\sqrt{12} = \sqrt{4 \times 3} = \sqrt{4} \times \sqrt{3} = \boxed{2\sqrt{3}}$$

$$\sqrt{ab} = \sqrt{a}\sqrt{b}$$

b) Simplify $\sqrt{\frac{3}{16}}$

$$\sqrt{\frac{a}{b}} = \frac{\sqrt{a}}{\sqrt{b}}$$

$$\sqrt{\frac{3}{16}} = \frac{\sqrt{3}}{\sqrt{16}} = \boxed{\frac{\sqrt{3}}{4}}$$

c) Find $\left(2\sqrt{5} + 3\sqrt{6}\right)^2$

You'll need to multiply out squared brackets here. Remember:

$$(a + b)^2 = (a + b)(a + b) = a^2 + 2ab + b^2$$

$$\left(2\sqrt{5} + 3\sqrt{6}\right)^2 = \left(2\sqrt{5} + 3\sqrt{6}\right)\left(2\sqrt{5} + 3\sqrt{6}\right)$$
$$= \left(2\sqrt{5}\right)^2 + \left(2 \times \left(2\sqrt{5}\right) \times \left(3\sqrt{6}\right)\right) + \left(3\sqrt{6}\right)^2$$
$$= \left(2^2 \times \sqrt{5^2}\right) + \left(2 \times 2 \times 3 \times \sqrt{5} \times \sqrt{6}\right) + \left(3^2 \times \sqrt{6^2}\right)$$
$$= 20 + 12\sqrt{30} + 54$$
$$= \boxed{74 + 12\sqrt{30}}$$

$= 4 \times 5 = 20$

$= 9 \times 6 = 54$

$= 12\sqrt{5}\sqrt{6} = 12\sqrt{30}$

Tip: Multiply surds very carefully — it's easy to make a silly mistake.

d) Express $\sqrt{63} - \sqrt{28}$ in the form $k\sqrt{x}$ where k and x are integers.

Try to write both numbers as 'a square number' $\times x$. Here x is 7.

$$\sqrt{63} - \sqrt{28} = \sqrt{9 \times 7} - \sqrt{4 \times 7}$$
$$= \sqrt{9}\sqrt{7} - \sqrt{4}\sqrt{7}$$
$$= 3\sqrt{7} - 2\sqrt{7}$$
$$= \boxed{\sqrt{7}}$$

The square root of a square number simplifies.

Tip: An integer is just a positive or negative whole number, including 0.

Tip: So in this case, k is just 1.

Exercise 3.1

Q1 Simplify the following surds:

a) $\sqrt{8}$ b) $\sqrt{24}$ c) $\sqrt{50}$ d) $\sqrt{63}$

e) $\sqrt{72}$ f) $\sqrt{\dfrac{5}{4}}$ g) $\sqrt{\dfrac{7}{100}}$ h) $\sqrt{\dfrac{11}{9}}$

Q2 Evaluate the following.
Give your answer as either a whole number or a surd.

a) $2\sqrt{3} \times 4\sqrt{3}$ b) $\sqrt{5} \times 3\sqrt{5}$

c) $\left(\sqrt{7}\right)^2$ d) $2\sqrt{2} \times 3\sqrt{5}$

e) $\left(2\sqrt{11}\right)^2$ f) $5\sqrt{8} \times 2\sqrt{2}$

g) $4\sqrt{3} \times 2\sqrt{27}$ h) $2\sqrt{6} \times 5\sqrt{24}$

i) $\dfrac{\sqrt{10}}{6} \times \dfrac{12}{\sqrt{5}}$ j) $\dfrac{\sqrt{12}}{3} \times \dfrac{2}{\sqrt{27}}$

Q3 Express the following in the form $k\sqrt{x}$, where k and x are integers and x is as small as possible.

a) $\sqrt{20} + \sqrt{5}$ b) $\sqrt{32} - \sqrt{8}$

c) $\sqrt{27} + 4\sqrt{3}$ d) $2\sqrt{8} - 3\sqrt{2}$

e) $3\sqrt{10} + \sqrt{250}$ f) $4\sqrt{27} + 2\sqrt{48} + 5\sqrt{108}$

Q3 Hint: To add two or more surds, you'll need to make sure the $\sqrt{x}$ bit is the same in each term.

Q4 Expand the following expressions.
Give your answers in the simplest form.

a) $(1 + \sqrt{2})(2 + \sqrt{2})$

b) $(3 + 4\sqrt{3})(2 - \sqrt{3})$

c) $(\sqrt{11} + 2)(\sqrt{11} - 2)$

d) $(9 - 2\sqrt{5})(9 + 2\sqrt{5})$

e) $(\sqrt{3} + 2)^2$

f) $(3\sqrt{5} - 4)^2$

Q5 Triangle ABC is right-angled with angle ABC = 90°.
Side AC has length $5\sqrt{2}$ cm and side AB has length $\sqrt{2}$ cm.
Find the length of side BC in the form $k\sqrt{3}$ cm,
where k is an integer.

Rationalising the denominator

Surds are pretty complicated — they're probably the last thing you want on
the bottom of a fraction. You can remove surds from the denominators of
fractions by **rationalising the denominator**.

To rationalise the denominator you multiply **top and bottom** of the fraction
by an **expression** that will get rid of surds in the denominator.

Tip: Multiplying a
fraction by the same thing
on the top and bottom
won't change its value.

Examples

a) **Show that** $\dfrac{9}{\sqrt{3}} = 3\sqrt{3}$.

To get rid of the surd multiply top and bottom by $\sqrt{3}$.

$$\frac{9}{\sqrt{3}} = \frac{9 \times \sqrt{3}}{\sqrt{3} \times \sqrt{3}} = \frac{9\sqrt{3}}{3} = \boxed{3\sqrt{3}}$$

Cancelling 3 from top and bottom.

Tip: The method in
b) is an example of
the difference of two
squares rule (page 13):
$(a + b)(a - b) = a^2 - b^2$
If you replace the b
with $\sqrt{b}$ on both sides
you get the following:
$(a + \sqrt{b})(a - \sqrt{b}) = a^2 - (\sqrt{b})^2$
$= a^2 - b$
This no longer contains
a surd ($\sqrt{\ }$), so it is
rationalised.

If you also replace
a with $\sqrt{a}$ you get:
$(\sqrt{a} + \sqrt{b})(\sqrt{a} - \sqrt{b}) = a - b$
This can be used to
rationalise a denominator
that contains a sum or
difference of two surds.

b) **Rationalise the denominator of** $\dfrac{1}{1 + \sqrt{2}}$.

If a fraction is of the form $\dfrac{1}{a + \sqrt{b}}$, multiply top and bottom by $a - \sqrt{b}$
— the denominator with the opposite sign in front of the surd.

$$\frac{1}{1 + \sqrt{2}} \times \frac{1 - \sqrt{2}}{1 - \sqrt{2}} = \frac{1 - \sqrt{2}}{(1 + \sqrt{2})(1 - \sqrt{2})}$$

$$= \frac{1 - \sqrt{2}}{1^2 - \sqrt{2} + \sqrt{2} - \sqrt{2}^2}$$

$$= \frac{1 - \sqrt{2}}{1 - 2}$$

$$= \frac{1 - \sqrt{2}}{-1}$$

$$= -1 + \sqrt{2}$$

The surds cancel
each other out.

c) **Rationalise the denominator of** $\dfrac{7+\sqrt{5}}{3+\sqrt{5}}$.

$$\frac{7+\sqrt{5}}{3+\sqrt{5}}\times\frac{3-\sqrt{5}}{3-\sqrt{5}}=\frac{(7+\sqrt{5})(3-\sqrt{5})}{(3+\sqrt{5})(3-\sqrt{5})}$$

$$=\frac{(7\times3)-7\sqrt{5}+3\sqrt{5}-(\sqrt{5})^{2}}{3^{2}-3\sqrt{5}+3\sqrt{5}-(\sqrt{5})^{2}}$$

Multiply top and bottom by $3-\sqrt{5}$.

$$=\frac{21-4\sqrt{5}-5}{9-5}$$

The surds cancel each other out.

$$=\frac{16-4\sqrt{5}}{4}$$

Now cancel 4 from each term.

$$=\ 4-\sqrt{5}$$

Exercise 3.2

Q1 Simplify the following, giving your answers in the form $p\sqrt{q}$, where p and q are integers:

a) $\dfrac{6}{\sqrt{3}}$
b) $\dfrac{21}{\sqrt{7}}$
c) $\dfrac{30}{\sqrt{5}}$

d) $\sqrt{45}+\dfrac{15}{\sqrt{5}}$
e) $\dfrac{\sqrt{54}}{3}-\dfrac{12}{\sqrt{6}}$
f) $\dfrac{\sqrt{300}}{5}+\dfrac{30}{\sqrt{12}}$

Q2 Express the following in the form $a+b\sqrt{k}$, where a, b and k are integers:

a) $\dfrac{4}{1+\sqrt{3}}$
b) $\dfrac{8}{-1+\sqrt{5}}$
c) $\dfrac{18}{\sqrt{10}-4}$

Q3 Express the following in the form $p+q\sqrt{r}$, where r is an integer, and p and q are integers or fractions:

a) $\dfrac{\sqrt{2}+1}{\sqrt{2}-1}$
b) $\dfrac{\sqrt{5}+3}{\sqrt{5}-2}$
c) $\dfrac{3-\sqrt{3}}{4+\sqrt{3}}$

d) $\dfrac{3\sqrt{5}-1}{2\sqrt{5}-3}$
e) $\dfrac{\sqrt{2}+\sqrt{3}}{3\sqrt{2}-\sqrt{3}}$
f) $\dfrac{2\sqrt{7}-\sqrt{5}}{\sqrt{7}+2\sqrt{5}}$

Q4 Express the following in the form $k(\sqrt{x}\pm\sqrt{y})$, where x and y are integers and k is an integer or fraction.

a) $\dfrac{4}{\sqrt{7}-\sqrt{3}}$
b) $\dfrac{24}{\sqrt{11}-\sqrt{17}}$
c) $\dfrac{2}{\sqrt{13}+\sqrt{5}}$

Q4 Hint The $\pm$ symbol suggests that the answer could be either $+$ or $-$.

Q5 Solve the equation $8=(\sqrt{5}-1)x$ giving your answer in the form $a+b\sqrt{5}$ where a and b are integers.

Q6 Solve the equation $5+\sqrt{7}=(3-\sqrt{7})y$ giving your answer in the form $p+q\sqrt{7}$ where p and q are integers.

Q7 A rectangle has an area of $(2+\sqrt{2})$ cm² and a width 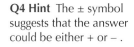 of $(3\sqrt{2}-4)$ cm. Find the length of the rectangle. Give your answer in the form $a+b\sqrt{2}$ where a and b are integers.

1. Quadratic Equations

In this section, you'll learn three methods that are used for solving quadratic equations — factorising, completing the square and the quadratic formula. These methods will also help you to sketch graphs of quadratic functions later in the chapter.

Factorising a quadratic

Quadratic equations are equations of the general form:

$$ax^2 + bx + c = 0$$

where a, b and c are constants (i.e. numbers) and $a \neq 0$.

Factorising a quadratic means putting it into two brackets called **factors** — the **solutions** to the equation can be easily worked out from these factors.

There are **two cases** that you need to know: when $a = 1$, and when $a \neq 1$.

Factorising when $a = 1$

Fortunately, there's a step-by-step method you can follow when factorising this sort of quadratic:

Tip: All quadratics can be rearranged into this standard form — but not all will factorise. Methods of solving quadratics that don't factorise are covered later in this chapter.

> To factorise a quadratic with $a = 1$:
>
> - Rearrange into the standard $ax^2 + bx + c$ form.
> - Write down the two **brackets**:
> $$(x \quad)(x \quad)$$
> - Find two numbers that **multiply** to give 'c' and **add/subtract** to give 'b' (ignoring signs).
> - Put the numbers in the brackets and choose their **signs**.

This will all make more sense once you've seen a worked example...

Example 1

Solve $x^2 - 8 = 2x$ by factorising.

(1) Rearrange into standard $ax^2 + bx + c = 0$ form.

Subtract $2x$ from both sides to give...

$$x^2 - 2x - 8 = 0$$

So $a = 1$, $b = -2$, $c = -8$.

Tip: Be careful with the values of b and c — don't let the minus signs catch you out.

---

(2) Write down the two brackets with x's in:

$x^2 - 2x - 8 = (x \quad)(x \quad)$

Since $a = 1$, you know that there will be an x in each bracket, which will multiply together to give x^2.

(3) Find the numbers.

Find two numbers that **multiply** together to make c but which also **add or subtract** to give b (you can ignore any minus signs for now).

1 and 8 multiply to give 8 — and add / subtract to give 9 and 7.

2 and 4 multiply to give 8 — and add / subtract to give 6 and 2.

These are the values for c and b you're after — so this is the right combination: 2 and 4.

(4) Find the signs.

So far you've got: $x^2 - 2x - 8 = (x \quad 2)(x \quad 4)$

Now all you have to do is put in the plus or minus signs.

It must be +2 and –4 because $2 \times (-4) = -8$ and $2 + (-4) = 2 - 4 = -2$

$$x^2 - 2x - 8 = (x + 2)(x - 4)$$

If c is negative, then the signs must be opposite.

Tip: If two things multiplied together give a negative answer, they must have opposite signs.

(5) Now that you've factorised using the step by step method — you can use the factors to solve the equation.

$$(x + 2)(x - 4) = 0$$

The factors (brackets) multiply to give 0, so one of them **must** be 0.

$\Rightarrow x + 2 = 0$ or $x - 4 = 0$

$\Rightarrow x = -2$ or $x = 4$

Don't forget this last step. The factors aren't the answer.

Tip: If two things multiply together to give 0, one of them must be equal to 0.

Example 2

Solve $x^2 + 4x - 21 = 0$ by factorising.

- It's already in the standard form, so start by writing down the brackets:
  $$x^2 + 4x - 21 = (x \quad)(x \quad)$$

- 1 and 21 multiply to give 21 — and add / subtract to give 22 and 20.
  3 and 7 multiply to give 21 — and add / subtract to give 10 and 4.

These are the values you need, so 3 and 7 are the right numbers:
$$x^2 + 4x - 21 = (x \quad 3)(x \quad 7)$$

- c is negative so we must need opposite signs.
  The signs must be -3 and $+7$ because $7 - 3 = 4$ and $7 \times (-3) = -21$

So...
$$x^2 + 4x - 21 = (x - 3)(x + 7)$$

And solving the equation to find x...
$$(x - 3)(x + 7) = 0$$
$$\Rightarrow x = 3 \ \text{ or } \ x = -7$$

Factorising when $a \neq 1$

The basic method's the same as before — but it can be a bit more awkward.

> To factorise a quadratic with $a \neq 1$:
>
> - Rearrange into the standard $ax^2 + bx + c$ form.
>
> - Write down the two brackets, but instead of just having x in each, you need two things that will multiply to give ax^2:
> $$(nx \quad)(mx \quad)$$
> where n and m are two numbers that multiply to give a.
>
> - Find two numbers that multiply to give 'c' but which will give you bx when you multiply them by nx and mx, and then add / subtract them.
>
> - Put the numbers in the brackets and choose their **signs**.

Tip: In practice, this third step is a case of working through all possible cases until you get it right.

Again, a worked example will help.

Example 3

Factorise $3x^2 + 4x - 15$.

(1)   This quadratic's already in the standard form so you don't need to rearrange it.

(2)   As before, write down two brackets — but instead of just having x in each, you need two things that will multiply to give $3x^2$. It's got to be $3x$ and x here.
$$3x^2 + 4x - 15 = (3x \quad)(x \quad)$$

(3)   Work out the numbers. You need to find two numbers that multiply together to make 15 — but which will give you $4x$ when you multiply them by x and $3x$, and then add / subtract them.

$(3x \quad 1)(x \quad 15) \Rightarrow x$ and $45x$
which then add or subtract to give $46x$ and $44x$.

$(3x \quad 15)(x \quad 1) \Rightarrow 15x$ and $3x$
which then add or subtract to give $18x$ and $12x$.

$(3x \quad 3)(x \quad 5) \Rightarrow 3x$ and $15x$
which then add or subtract to give $18x$ and $12x$.

$(3x \quad 5)(x \quad 3) \Rightarrow 5x$ and $9x$
which then add or subtract to give $14x$ and $4x$.

Tip: It's a good idea to write out the brackets for each possible number combination — it makes it easier to see if you've got the right numbers.

This is the value you're after — so this is the right combination.

(4) Add the signs.
You know the brackets must be like these...

$$(3x \quad 5)(x \quad 3) = 3x^2 + 4x - 15$$

'c' is negative — that means the signs in the brackets are opposite.
The numbers must be -5 and $+3$ since $9x - 5x = 4x$ and $-5 \times 3 = -15$.
So...

$$(3x - 5)(x + 3) = 3x^2 + 4x - 15$$

Tip: You've only got two choices for the signs of the numbers, -5 and 3 or 5 and -3. If you're unsure which it is, just multiply each case out to see which is right.

Exercise 1.1

Q1 Factorise the following expressions.
    a) $x^2 - 6x + 5$ b) $x^2 - 3x - 18$
    c) $x^2 + 22x + 121$ d) $x^2 - 12x$
    e) $y^2 - 13y + 42$ f) $x^2 + 51x + 144$
    g) $x^2 - 121$ h) $x^2 - 35x + 66$

Q1 Hint: If b or c is zero, use the factorising methods from Chapter 3.

Q2 Solve the following equations.
    a) $x^2 - 2x - 8 = 0$ b) $2x^2 + 2x - 40 = 0$
    c) $p^2 + 21p + 38 = 0$ d) $x^2 - 15x + 54 = 0$
    e) $x^2 + 18x = -65$ f) $x^2 - x = 42$
    g) $x^2 + 1100x + 100\,000 = 0$ h) $3x^2 - 3x - 6 = 0$

Q2 Hint: Look out for questions where the equation can be simplified before factorising — for example by dividing through by a number.

Q3 Factorise the following expressions.
    a) $4x^2 - 4x - 3$ b) $2x^2 + 23x + 11$
    c) $7x^2 - 19x - 6$ d) $-x^2 - 5x + 36$
    e) $2x^2 - 2$ f) $3x^2 - 3$

Q4 Solve the following equations.
    a) $-5x^2 - 22x + 15 = 0$ b) $32x^2 + 60x + 13 = 0$
    c) $5a^2 + 12a = 9$ d) $8x^2 + 22x + 15 = 0$

Q5 Solve $(x - 1)(x - 2) = 37 - x$.

Q6 $f(x) = -x^2 + 7x + 30$. Find the x coordinates of the point or points at which the graph of $f(x)$ meets the x-axis.

Q7 In a scientific experiment, the temperature, $T\,°C$, is modelled by the equation $T = -2h^2 + 13h - 20$, where h is the time in hours from the start of the experiment. Find both times at which the temperature is $0\,°C$.

Q8 Factorise $x^2 + 6xy + 8y^2$.

The quadratic formula

You should now be comfortable with solving quadratics by factorising. But there are two important points to bear in mind:

- The expression **won't** always factorise.

- Sometimes factorising is so messy that it's **easier** to just use other methods.

So if the question doesn't tell you to factorise, **don't assume** it will factorise.

Example 1

Solve $6x^2 + 87x - 144 = 0$.

This will actually factorise, but there are 2 possible bracket forms to try:

$$(6x \quad)(x \quad) \text{ or } (3x \quad)(2x \quad)$$

And for each of these, there are 8 possible ways of making 144 to try.

If you tried to factorise this example, you'd be going all day.

Luckily, there's a formula which will work out the **solutions** of a quadratic equation, even when you can't factorise — it's known as **the quadratic formula**.

$$\text{If } ax^2 + bx + c = 0 \text{ then:}$$
$$x = \frac{-b \pm \sqrt{b^2 - 4ac}}{2a}$$

Example 2

Solve the quadratic equation $3x^2 - 4x = 8$, leaving your answer in surd form.

The mention of surds in the answer suggests that the quadratic will be too hard to factorise, so we'll use the quadratic formula instead.

- Get the equation in the standard $ax^2 + bx + c = 0$ form.

$$3x^2 - 4x = 8$$

So... $3x^2 - 4x - 8 = 0$

- Write down the coefficients a, b and c — making sure you don't forget minus signs.

$$a = 3 \quad\nearrow \quad 3x^2 - 4x - 8 = 0$$

$$b = -4 \qquad c = -8$$

Tip: If the question asks you to give your answer in surd form or as a decimal, that's a big hint to use the quadratic formula instead of trying to factorise.

Tip: If any of the **coefficients** (i.e. if a, b or c) in your quadratic equation are **negative**, be especially careful.

- Very carefully, plug these numbers into the formula. It's best to write down each stage as you do it.

$$x = \frac{-b \pm \sqrt{b^2 - 4ac}}{2a}$$

$$x = \frac{-(-4) \pm \sqrt{(-4)^2 - 4 \times 3 \times (-8)}}{2 \times 3}$$

These minus signs multiply together to get a plus.

$$x = \frac{4 \pm \sqrt{16 + 96}}{6}$$

- Simplify your answer as much as possible, using the rules of surds.

Tip: See p.20 for a reminder of these rules.

$$x = \frac{4 \pm \sqrt{112}}{6}$$

$$x = \frac{4 \pm \sqrt{16}\sqrt{7}}{6}$$

$$x = \frac{4 \pm 4\sqrt{7}}{6}$$

$$x = \frac{2 \pm 2\sqrt{7}}{3}$$

The $\pm$ sign means that you actually have two different expressions for x, which you get by replacing the $\pm$ with $+$ and $-$.
Doing this gives you the two solutions to the quadratic equation.

$$x = \frac{2 + 2\sqrt{7}}{3} \quad \text{or} \quad x = \frac{2 - 2\sqrt{7}}{3}$$

Example 3

Solve the quadratic equation $2x^2 = 4x + 3$, leaving your answer in the form $p \pm q\sqrt{r}$ where p, q and r are whole numbers or fractions.

Rearranging $2x^2 = 4x + 3$ you get $2x^2 - 4x - 3 = 0$
and so $a = 2$, $b = -4$ and $c = -3$

So plugging these values into the quadratic formula, you get:

$$x = \frac{-b \pm \sqrt{b^2 - 4ac}}{2a}$$

$$x = \frac{-(-4) \pm \sqrt{(-4)^2 - 4 \times 2 \times (-3)}}{2 \times 2}$$

$$x = \frac{4 \pm \sqrt{16 + 24}}{4} = \frac{4 \pm \sqrt{40}}{4} = \frac{4 \pm 2\sqrt{10}}{4} = \frac{2 \pm \sqrt{10}}{2}$$

$$= \frac{2}{2} \pm \frac{1}{2}\sqrt{10} = 1 \pm \frac{1}{2}\sqrt{10}$$

Using a calculator

You can also use a **graphical calculator** to solve quadratic equations. There are two different ways to do this:

■ Use the calculator to **plot** the graph of the quadratic, then work out where it crosses the x-axis — these values of x are the solutions to f(x) = 0 (there's more about this on pages 41-45).

■ Some calculators will allow you to **solve** quadratic equations directly — enter the values for a, b and c, and it'll give you the solutions.

In each case, you'll have to make sure your equation is in the **standard form** ($ax^2 + bx + c$). Be careful though — sometimes your calculator will only give you one solution (even if there are two), and it won't usually give answers in surd form.

> **Tip:** Different calculators work in different ways — make sure you know how to do this on your calculator.

Exercise 1.2

Q1 Solve the following equations using the quadratic formula, giving your answers in surd form where necessary.

    a) $x^2 - 4x = -2$ b) $x^2 - 2x - 44 = 0$

    c) $x^2 - 14x + 42 = 0$ d) $4x^2 + 4x - 1 = 0$

    e) $x^2 - \frac{5}{6}x + \frac{1}{6} = 0$ f) $x^2 - x - \frac{35}{2} = 0$

> **Q1 Hint:** Have a go at solving these equations using a calculator too.

Q2 a) Multiply out $(x - 2 + \sqrt{5})(x - 2 - \sqrt{5})$.

    b) Solve the equation $x^2 - 4x - 1 = 0$ using the quadratic formula.

    c) How does your answer to b) relate to the expression given in a)?

Q3 The roots of the equation $x^2 + 8x + 13 = 0$ can be written in the form $x = A \pm \sqrt{B}$ where A and B are integers. Find A and B.

Q4 Solve the following equations, giving your answers in surd form where necessary.

    a) $x^2 + x + \frac{1}{4} = 0$ b) $25x^2 - 30x + 7 = 0$

    c) $60x - 5 = -100x^2 - 3$ d) $2x(x - 4) = 7 - 3x$

Completing the square

You could be asked to **solve** a quadratic equation by **completing the square** so you need to know this method just as well as the others. And what's more — it gives you loads of **useful information** about the quadratic.

> Completing the square just means writing a quadratic expression $ax^2 + bx + c$ in the form $a(x + \text{something})^2 + d$.
>
> ■ Basically, the '**square**' is this bit: $a(x + \text{something})^2$
> The 'something' is chosen so that it will produce the correct x^2 and x terms when the square is multiplied out.
>
> ■ But this square won't always give the right constant term — so you need to '**complete**' it by adding a number to the square to make it the **same** as the original quadratic: $a(x + \text{something})^2 + d$

The method can seem complicated at first, but is actually very simple when you get it. As always, working through examples is the best way to learn it.

When $a = 1$

We'll start with the slightly easier case of $a = 1$...

Example 1

Rewrite $x^2 + 6x + 3$ by completing the square.

First, write down a square of the form $(x + \text{something})^2$. Choose it so that when you multiply it out you get the correct x^2 and x terms.

$$(x + 3)^2$$

> This number is just half the coefficient of x i.e. $\frac{b}{2}$.

Now complete the square:

$$(x + 3)^2 - 6$$

> This square multiplies out to give $x^2 + 6x + 9$ but we need the constant term to be $+3$...

> ...so subtract 6 from the square to match the original quadratic.

So... $\quad x^2 + 6x + 3 = (x + 3)^2 - 6$

Check that your answer multiplies out to give what you started with.

$$(x + 3)^2 - 6 = x^2 + 3x + 3x + 9 - 6 = x^2 + 6x + 3 \checkmark$$

Example 2

Rewrite $x^2 - 5x - 1$ by completing the square.

Again, start by writing down the square:

This example has a negative coefficient of x — so make sure you have a minus sign in the brackets.

$$\left(x - \frac{5}{2}\right)^2$$

> Remember, this is just $\frac{b}{2}$.

Now complete the square....

$$\left(x - \frac{5}{2}\right)^2 - \frac{25}{4} - 1$$

> The square multiplies out to give $x^2 - 5x + \frac{25}{4}$ but we need the constant term to be -1...

> ...so subtract the $\frac{25}{4}$ and then 'add' -1.

$$x^2 - 5x - 1 = \left(x - \frac{5}{2}\right)^2 - \frac{29}{4}$$

> Simplify the number.

Tip: You can always find the number that completes the square by subtracting off the number term you get from the bracket and adding on the number term from the original quadratic.

Check your answer...

$$\left(x - \frac{5}{2}\right)^2 - \frac{29}{4} = x^2 - \frac{5}{2}x - \frac{5}{2}x + \frac{25}{4} - \frac{29}{4} = x^2 - 5x - 1 \checkmark$$

When $a \neq 1$

It's a little more complicated in cases where a is not 1. You have to put a outside of the squared bracket, and allow for this when choosing the number to go inside the bracket — basically by dividing by a.

Tip: The formula for completing the square for the general quadratic $ax^2 + bx + c$ is:
$$a\left(x + \frac{b}{2a}\right)^2 + \left(c - \frac{b^2}{4a}\right)$$

Example 3

Rewrite $2x^2 + 3x - 5$ by completing the square.

Start by writing the square —
$a = 2$ so it will be of the form $2(x + \text{something})^2$:

$$2\left(x + \frac{3}{4}\right)^2$$

This number is always the coefficient of x divided by $2a$, i.e. $\frac{b}{2a}$.

Now complete the square:

$$2\left(x + \frac{3}{4}\right)^2 - \frac{9}{8} - 5$$

The square multiplies out to give $2x^2 + 3x + \frac{9}{8}$, but we need the constant term to be -5...

...so subtract the $\frac{9}{8}$ and then 'add on' -5.

Tip: If the constant terms are fractions, don't forget to put them over a common denominator before you try to add / subtract them.

So... $2x^2 + 3x - 5 = 2\left(x + \frac{3}{4}\right)^2 - \frac{49}{8}$

Simplify the number.

Check your answer...

$$2\left(x + \frac{3}{4}\right)^2 - \frac{49}{8} = 2\left(x^2 + \frac{3}{2}x + \frac{9}{16}\right) - \frac{49}{8}$$

$$= 2x^2 + 3x + \frac{9}{8} - \frac{49}{8} = 2x^2 + 3x - 5 \checkmark$$

Example 4

Rewrite $3 - 4x - x^2$ by completing the square.

Again, start by writing the square. Here $a = -1$:

$$-(x + 2)^2$$

This number is just $\frac{b}{2a}$ again.

Tip: If it helps, rewrite the expression in the standard form $ax^2 + bx + c$.

Now complete the square:

$$-(x + 2)^2 + 7$$

The square multiplies out to give $-x^2 - 4x - 4$ but we want the constant to be $+3$...

...so add 7 to the square to make it match the original quadratic.

So... $3 - 4x - x^2 = -(x + 2)^2 + 7$

Check your answer...

$$-(x + 2)^2 + 7 = -(x^2 + 4x + 4) + 7 = -x^2 - 4x - 4 + 7$$

$$= -x^2 - 4x + 3 \quad (= 3 - 4x - x^2) \checkmark$$

Once you've completed the square, a quadratic equation becomes very easy to **solve**:

- Take the **constant term** to the other side of the equals sign.

- Take the square root of both sides — don't forget the **negative** square root.

- **Rearrange** to find the solutions.

Example 5

Solve $3 - 4x - x^2 = 0$ by completing the square.

From Example 4, you can write $3 - 4x - x^2$ as $-(x + 2)^2 + 7$ by completing the square.

So now all you need to do is set this equal to zero and rearrange.

$-(x + 2)^2 + 7 = 0$ ⟵ Take the constant to the other side.

$-(x + 2)^2 = -7$

$(x + 2)^2 = 7$ ⟵ Take a square root — don't forget the ± sign.

$x + 2 = \pm\sqrt{7}$

$x = -2 \pm\sqrt{7}$ ⟵ Subtract 2 from both sides.

So $x = -2 + \sqrt{7}$ or $x = -2 - \sqrt{7}$

Tip: When you take the square root of something, you need to put a ± sign in front of the $\sqrt{}$ sign.

Exercise 1.3

Q1 Solve the following equations, leaving your answer in surd form where appropriate:

a) $(x + 4)^2 = 25$

b) $(5x - 3)^2 = 21$

Q1 Hint: In these questions you don't need to complete the square — they'll just give you practice at the 'solving' bit.

Q2 Rewrite the following expressions in the form $p(x + q)^2 + r$:

a) $x^2 + 6x + 8$ b) $x^2 + 8x - 10$

c) $x^2 - 3x - 10$ d) $x^2 - 20x + 15$

e) $x^2 - 2mx + n$ f) $3x^2 - 12x + 7$

Q3 Solve the following equations by completing the square:

a) $x^2 - 6x - 16 = 0$ b) $p^2 - 10p = 200$

c) $x^2 + 2x + k = 0$ d) $9x^2 + 18x = 16$

e) $x^2 + 4x - 8 = 0$ f) $2x^2 - 12x + 9 = 0$

g) $2x^2 - 12x - 54 = 0$ h) $5x^2 - 3x + \dfrac{2}{5} = 0$

Q4 By completing the square, show that the expression $3x^2 - 12x + 14$ is positive for all x.

Q5 By completing the square, show that the solutions to $ax^2 + bx + c = 0$ are found at $x = \dfrac{-b \pm \sqrt{b^2 - 4ac}}{2a}$.

Quadratics involving functions of x

Sometimes you'll be asked to solve an equation that doesn't look like a quadratic — it might involve different powers of x, or functions like $\sin x$ or e^x. However, as long as it's in the form $a(\textbf{something})^2 + b(\textbf{something}) + c$, you can solve it like a normal quadratic. Instead of '$x = $', you'll be left with 'something $= $', which you'll then have to solve.

Tip: There's more on solving trig equations in Chapter 8, and on solving exponential equations in Chapter 9.

The way to solve these equations is:

- Identify the function of x, and replace it with a different letter, say u.

- Solve the resulting quadratic equation for u.

- Replace u with the original function, and solve it to find x.

This will make more sense with a worked example:

Example

Solve the equation $x^{\frac{2}{3}} + 3x^{\frac{1}{3}} - 40 = 0$.

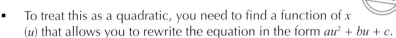

- To treat this as a quadratic, you need to find a function of x (u) that allows you to rewrite the equation in the form $au^2 + bu + c$.

- If you take $u = x^{\frac{1}{3}}$, then u^2 would be $x^{\frac{2}{3}}$ — this fits with the equation.

- So the equation can be written as $u^2 + 3u - 40 = 0$, where $u = x^{\frac{1}{3}}$.

- Now solve this quadratic — luckily it factorises:
$$u^2 + 3u - 40 = 0$$
$$(u + 8)(u - 5) = 0$$
$$\text{So } u = -8 \text{ or } u = 5.$$

- Finally, substitute $x^{\frac{1}{3}}$ back into the equations and solve for x:
$$x^{\frac{1}{3}} = -8, \text{ so } x = (-8)^3 = \boxed{-512} \quad \text{or} \quad x^{\frac{1}{3}} = 5, \text{ so } x = 5^3 = \boxed{125}$$

Exercise 1.4

Q1 Find an expression for u, in terms of x, that allows you to write each equation below in the form $au^2 + bu + c = 0$. You do **not** need to solve the resulting equations.

    a) $2x + 4x^{\frac{1}{2}} - 7 = 0$ b) $e^x(e^x - 6) = 8$

    c) $5^x + 5^{2x} = 4$ d) $2\cos^2 x + 3 = 5\cos x$

Q2 a) Rewrite the equation below in the form $(x + m)^2 + n$:
$$x^2 + 6x + 7$$

    b) Hence solve the equation $(2x + 1)^2 + 6(2x + 1) + 7 = 0$. Leave your answers in surd form.

Q3 Find all four solutions to the equation $x^4 - 17x^2 + 16 = 0$.

Q4 Solve the equation $\dfrac{3}{(5x + 2)^2} + \dfrac{1}{5x + 2} = 10$.

2. Quadratic Functions and Roots

The roots of a quadratic function f(x) are just the solutions to the equation f(x) = 0. But you don't actually need to solve the equation to find out how many roots there are.

Learning Objectives:

- Be able to identify the number of real roots of a quadratic function.

- Be able to calculate the discriminant of a quadratic function.

- Be able to use the discriminant to solve problems involving quadratics with unknown coefficients.

The roots of a quadratic function

Quadratic functions are just functions of the form $f(x) = ax^2 + bx + c$. Their graphs all have the same **general shape**, no matter what the values of a, b and c are. This general shape is called a **parabola**. Parabolas are either **'u'**-shaped or **'n'**-shaped:

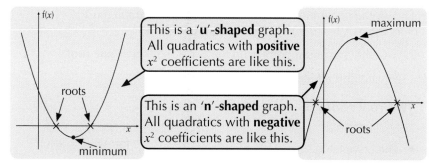

This is a **'u'-shaped** graph. All quadratics with **positive** x^2 coefficients are like this.

This is an **'n'-shaped** graph. All quadratics with **negative** x^2 coefficients are like this.

Tip: You'll see how to draw graphs of quadratic functions later in the chapter.

The **roots** of a quadratic function are the values of x where the function $f(x)$ is equal to **zero** — i.e. where the graph **crosses the x-axis**. They are the same as the **solutions** to the quadratic equation $f(x) = 0$. The functions shown above each have 2 roots because their graphs cross the x-axis twice.

A quadratic function may have **0**, **1** or **2 roots**. You'll see two methods for finding out which it is — **completing the square** and using the **discriminant**.

Using the completed square

If you've already **completed the square**, you can easily work out the number of roots by examining the completed square. The function will look like this:

$$f(x) = p(x + q)^2 + r$$

The key to this method is remembering that anything squared is ≥ 0.

So, let's assume for now that p is positive:

- Since p is **positive**, the graph will be **u-shaped** and have a **minimum**.

- The smallest value that $f(x)$ can take will occur when the bracket is 0 (since the square is ≥ 0). At that point $f(x)$ is just r, and x must be $-q$.

- So the minimum is $(-q , r)$. This also tells you that the graph of $f(x)$ has a **line of symmetry** at $x = -q$.

Now the **value of r** tells us the number of roots...

- If $r < 0$, the minimum is below the x-axis, so the graph must cross the axis twice — meaning there are **two roots**.

- If $r > 0$, the graph is always above the x-axis — so there are **no roots**.

- If $r = 0$, the minimum point is on the x-axis, so there's **one root**.

So that covers cases where p is positive, i.e. u-shaped graphs.

Tip: Just picture what the graph looks like — remember, it's u-shaped. The number of times the graph crosses the x-axis depends on whether the minimum is above, below or on the axis.

Next, we'll see what happens when p is negative:

$$f(x) = p(x + q)^2 + r$$

- Since p is **negative**, the graph will be **n-shaped** and have a **maximum**.
- And also because p is negative, the highest value of $p(x + q)^2$ will be when the bracket is 0. At that point $f(x)$ is just r, and x is $-q$.
- So the maximum is **($-q$, r)**. Again, this tells you that the graph has a **line of symmetry** at $x = -q$.

Tip: The coordinates of the maximum are actually just the same as those we found for the minimum: $(-q, r)$.

Look at the **value of r** to work out the number of roots...

- If $r < 0$, the graph is always below the x-axis — so there are **no roots**.
- If $r > 0$, the maximum is above the x-axis, so the graph must cross the axis twice, meaning there are **two roots**.
- If $r = 0$, the maximum point is on the x-axis, so there's **one root**.

Let's see what this all means for a few functions.

Tip: Remember, real numbers are just all the rational and irrational numbers. Have a look at p.38 for an explanation of what is meant by 'real' roots.

Two real roots

$y = x^2 - 6x + 8$

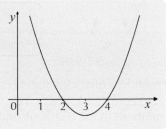

- The completed square is $(x - 3)^2 - 1$.
- The minimum is $(3, -1)$ which is below the x-axis.
- So there are two roots ($x = 2$ and $x = 4$).

One real root

$y = x^2 - 6x + 9$

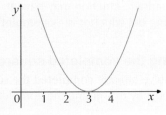

Tip: When you're factorising a quadratic equation, if both factors come out the same, in this case $(x - 3)(x - 3)$, the function has one root. We call this one **repeated** root.

- The completed square is $(x - 3)^2$.
- The minimum is $(3, 0)$, so the graph just touches the x-axis.
- $x = 3$ is the only root.

No real roots

$y = x^2 - 6x + 10$

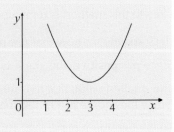

- The completed square is $(x - 3)^2 + 1$.
- The minimum is $(3, 1)$ which is above the x-axis.
- So the graph never touches the x-axis, and there are no roots.

All the different cases we've covered can actually be summarised in these three simple rules:

> For a quadratic function of the form $f(x) = p(x + q)^2 + r$:
> - If p and r have **different signs**, the function has **two** real roots.
> - If $r = 0$ then the function has **one** real root.
> - If p and r have the **same sign**, the function has **no** real roots.

How many real roots does the quadratic function f(x) = x² + 4x + 7 have?

- Completing the square, you can rewrite the function in the form
  $f(x) = p(x + q)^2 + r$: $f(x) = (x + 2)^2 + 3$

- $p = 1$ and $r = 3$ are of the same sign, so the function has no real roots.

- You can see why this works using the following argument:

$$f(x) = (x + 2)^2 + 3 \longleftarrow \text{This number's positive.}$$

The smallest this bit
can be is zero (at $x = -2$).

$(x + 2)^2$ is never less than zero
so f(x) is never less than three.

- This means that:
  a) f(x) can never be negative.
  b) The graph of f(x) never crosses the x-axis — so there are no real roots.

Exercise 2.1

Q1 How many real roots does each quadratic function have?

a)

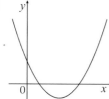

b)

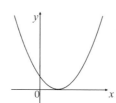

c)

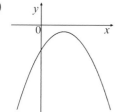

d)

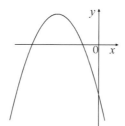

Q2 Express $f(x) = x^2 + 6x + 10$ in the form $f(x) = (x + q)^2 + r$,
where q and r are positive or negative constants.
Using your answer, state whether f(x) has any real roots
and give the equations of any lines of symmetry of the graph of f(x).

Q2 Hint: Complete
the square.

Q3 The function $f(x) = -x^2 - 7x - 6$ can be expressed in the form
$$f(x) = -\left(x + \frac{7}{2}\right)^2 + \frac{25}{4}$$

Does this function have any real roots? Explain your answer.

Using the discriminant

Remember the **quadratic formula** for solving an equation of the form $ax^2 + bx + c = 0$:

$$x = \frac{-b \pm \sqrt{b^2 - 4ac}}{2a}$$

The **$b^2 - 4ac$** bit is called the **discriminant**.

- If the discriminant is **positive**, the formula will give you **two** different values for x — when you **add** and **subtract** the $\sqrt{b^2 - 4ac}$ bit.

- If it's **zero**, you'll only get **one** value for x, since adding and subtracting zero gets the same value.

- If it's **negative**, you don't get any (real) values for x because you can't take the square root of a negative number.

To picture what this means, recall the examples from page 36:

Tip: In some areas of maths, you can actually take the square root of negative numbers and get 'imaginary' or 'complex' numbers. That's why we say no 'real' roots.

Two real roots	One real root	No real roots
$b^2 - 4ac > 0$	$b^2 - 4ac = 0$	$b^2 - 4ac < 0$

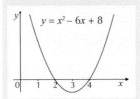

$y = x^2 - 6x + 8$

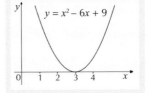

$y = x^2 - 6x + 9$

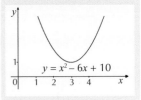

$y = x^2 - 6x + 10$

When working out the **discriminant**, the first thing you have to do is to work out what a, b and c are. Make sure you get them the right way round — it's easy to get mixed up if the quadratic's in a different order.

Example 1

Find the discriminant of $15 - x - 2x^2$.
How many real roots does the function $f(x) = 15 - x - 2x^2$ have?

- First, identify a, b and c by rewriting as $-2x^2 - x + 15$:
$$a = -2, \ b = -1 \text{ and } c = 15$$

- Then put these values into the formula for the discriminant:
$$b^2 - 4ac = (-1)^2 - (4 \times -2 \times 15) = 1 + 120 = \boxed{121}$$

- The discriminant is > 0, so $15 - x - 2x^2$ has $\boxed{\text{two distinct real roots.}}$

Tip: Watch out — don't make the mistake of writing $a = 15$, $b = -1$ and $c = -2$ (this would be the function $15x^2 - x - 2$).

You may need to work with a quadratic where one or more of a, b and c are given in terms of an **unknown**. This means that you'll end up with an equation or inequality for the discriminant in terms of the unknown — you might have to solve it to find the **value** or **range of values** of the unknown.

Example 2

Find the range of values of k for which the function
$f(x) = 3x^2 + 2x + k$:
a) has 2 distinct roots,   b) has 1 root,   c) has no real roots.

- First, decide what a, b and c are: $a = 3, b = 2, c = k$

- Then work out what the discriminant is: $b^2 - 4ac = 2^2 - 4 \times 3 \times k$
$$= 4 - 12k$$

a) Two distinct roots means:

$\boxed{b^2 - 4ac > 0}$ $\Rightarrow 4 - 12k > 0$
$\Rightarrow 4 > 12k$
$\Rightarrow k < \dfrac{1}{3}$

b) One root means:

$\boxed{b^2 - 4ac = 0}$ $\Rightarrow 4 - 12k = 0$
$\Rightarrow 4 = 12k$
$\Rightarrow k = \dfrac{1}{3}$

The working is exactly the same in all three cases. The only difference is the equality / inequality symbol.

c) No roots means:

$\boxed{b^2 - 4ac < 0}$ $\Rightarrow 4 - 12k < 0$
$\Rightarrow 4 < 12k$
$\Rightarrow k > \dfrac{1}{3}$

Tip: The discriminant often comes up in exam questions — but sometimes they'll be sneaky and not actually tell you that's what you have to find. Any question that mentions **roots** of a quadratic will probably mean that you need to find the **discriminant**.

Example 3

The equation $kx^2 + 12x + 9k = 0$ has two distinct roots.
Find the range of possible values for k.

- First, decide what a, b and c are: $a = k, b = 12, c = 9k$

- Then work out what the discriminant is: $b^2 - 4ac = 12^2 - 4 \times k \times 9k$
$$= 144 - 36k^2$$

- Two distinct roots means

$\boxed{b^2 - 4ac > 0}$ $\Rightarrow 144 - 36k^2 > 0$
$\Rightarrow 36k^2 < 144$
$\Rightarrow k^2 < 4$
$\Rightarrow -2 < k < 2$

Tip: You'll learn more about quadratic inequalities in Chapter 5 — but here you just need to notice that if $k^2 < 4$, then k must be between 2 and –2.

Q1 Find the discriminant, and hence the number of real roots, for each of the following:

Q1 Hint: Make sure the equation is written in the form $ax^2 + bx + c$ before trying to calculate the discriminant.

a) $x^2 + 8x + 15$

b) $x^2 + 2\sqrt{3}x + 3$

c) $(2x + 1)(5x - 3)$

d) $-3x^2 - \frac{11}{5}x - \frac{2}{5}$

e) $9x^2 + 20x$

f) $\frac{19}{16}x^2 - 4$

Q2 The discriminant of the equation $15x^2 + bx = 2$ is 169, where b is a positive number. Find all possible values of b.

Q3 The equation $0 = ax^2 + 7x + \frac{1}{4}$ has one real root. Find a.

Q4 Determine the number of real roots of the following equations, without solving them:

a) $13x^2 + 8x + 2 = 0$

b) $\frac{x^2}{3} + \frac{5}{2}x + 3 = 0$

Q5 Find the range of values of p for which $x^2 - 12x + 27 + p = 0$ has two distinct real roots.

Q6 Find the range of values of q for which $10x^2 - 10x + \frac{q}{2} = 0$ has two distinct real roots.

Q7 The equation $2x^2 + (10p + 1)x + 5 = 0$ has no real roots. Show that p satisfies:
$$p(5p + 1) < \frac{39}{20}$$

Q8 Find the range of values of k for which $-2x^2 - 2x + k = 0$ has:

a) two distinct roots.

b) one real root.

c) no roots.

Q9 The equation $x^2 + (k + 5)x + \frac{k^2}{4} = 0$, where k is a constant, has no real roots.

a) Show that k satisfies $10k + 25 < 0$.

b) Find the range of possible values of k.

Q10 a) Find the discriminant of $\left(k - \frac{6}{5}\right)x^2 + \sqrt{k}x + \frac{5}{4}$.

b) For what values of k would the equation
$$\left(k - \frac{6}{5}\right)x^2 + \sqrt{k}x + \frac{5}{4} = 0$$
have:

(i) one real root?

(ii) no real roots?

(iii) two distinct real roots?

3. Quadratic Graphs

Using the methods you've learnt for finding roots of quadratic functions, you'll be able to draw the graph of any quadratic function at all.

Sketching a quadratic graph

There are two pieces of information you **always need** to know about a quadratic function before you can sketch it.

■ The **shape** — u-shaped or n-shaped.

■ The coordinates of the **points of intersection** with the x- and y-axes.

Sometimes, there will be two **different** graphs which have the same points of intersection and shape — in this case you'll need to work out the location of the **vertex point** (maximum or minimum) to decide which graph is right.

Tip: The **vertex** of a quadratic graph is just the point where the graph changes direction. It is either a maximum point or a minimum point depending on the shape of the graph.

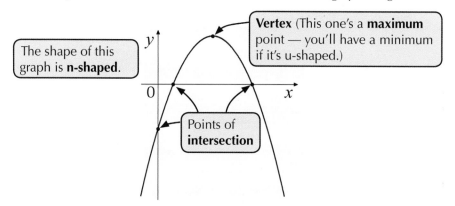

The shape of this graph is **n-shaped**.

Vertex (This one's a **maximum** point — you'll have a minimum if it's u-shaped.)

Points of **intersection**

Shape

The first thing you need to decide is the **shape** of the graph — look at the coefficient of the x^2 term.

■ If the coefficient of x^2 is **positive** — the graph will be **u-shaped**.

■ If the coefficient of x^2 is **negative** — the graph will be **n-shaped**.

Intercepts

The next bit of information you need is where the graph **intersects the axes** — set x or y equal to zero and work out the other coordinate.

If you're sketching the function $y = ax^2 + bx + c$:

■ To find the **y-intercept** — let $x = 0$ and calculate the value of y.

■ To find the **x-intercepts** — let $y = 0$ and solve the equation $0 = ax^2 + bx + c$ to find the value or values of x.

Don't forget the x-intercepts correspond to the roots of the quadratic function — bear in mind that there may be only **one** root, or **no** roots.

Tip: Use one of the methods of solving quadratics from earlier in the chapter to work out the x-intercepts — they're just the solutions of the equation.

Example 1

Sketch the graph of the quadratic function $f(x) = x^2 - 4x + 3$, including any points of intersection with the axes.

- The coefficient of x^2 is positive...

$$f(x) = x^2 - 4x + 3$$

...so the graph's u-shaped.

- Let $x = 0$ in the function to find the y-intercept.
$$f(0) = (0)^2 - 4(0) + 3 = 3$$

So the y-intercept is at 3.

- Solve $f(x) = 0$ to find the x-intercepts.
This equation will factorise:
$$x^2 - 4x + 3 = 0$$
$$\Rightarrow (x - 3)(x - 1) = 0$$
$$\Rightarrow x - 3 = 0 \text{ or } x - 1 = 0$$
$$\Rightarrow x = 3 \text{ or } x = 1$$

So the x-intercepts are at 1 and 3.

- Put all this information together to sketch the graph.

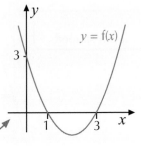

Vertex points

You'll sometimes need to find the minimum or maximum of the graph — which one it is depends on whether your graph is u-shaped or n-shaped.

One way to find the vertex is to **complete the square** and then interpret this. You actually did this back on pages 35-36 when finding the number of roots of a quadratic. Have a look back at those pages to remind yourself of the method. But here's the key result you need...

A graph with an equation of the form $y = p(x + q)^2 + r$ has a vertex at $(-q, r)$.

If $p > 0$, the graph is u-shaped, so the vertex is a minimum.

If $p < 0$, the graph is n-shaped, so the vertex is a maximum.

Tip: This comes from the fact that a square is always positive and so can never be less than 0.

Example 2

a) Find the vertex of the graph of $y = f(x)$, where $f(x) = 3x^2 - 6x - 7$, stating whether it is a maximum or minimum.

- As it's a quadratic function and the coefficient of x^2 is positive, it's a **u-shaped** graph so it has a minimum.

- Completing the square gives $f(x) = 3x^2 - 6x - 7 = 3(x - 1)^2 - 10$.

This is a square — it can never be negative. The smallest it can be is 0.

- When the squared bit is zero, f(x) reaches its minimum value. So find the value of x that makes the squared bit zero.

$f(x) = 3(x - 1)^2 - 10$ ← This bracket is 0 when $x = 1$...

$f(1) = 3(1 - 1)^2 - 10$

$f(1) = 3(0)^2 - 10 = -10$ ← ...so the minimum is -10.

> **Tip:** $f(1)$ means using $x = 1$ in the function

The vertex is $(1, -10)$.

b) **Find where the graph of $y = f(x)$ crosses the axes and hence sketch the graph.**

- $y = f(x)$ crosses the y-axis when $x = 0$ which gives:

$$y = 3(0)^2 - 6(0) - 7 = -7$$

- $y = f(x)$ crosses the x-axis when $f(x) = 0$ so...

$$3x^2 - 6x - 7 = 0$$

$$\Rightarrow 3(x - 1)^2 - 10 = 0 \quad \longleftarrow \text{ Complete the square.}$$

$$\Rightarrow (x - 1)^2 = \frac{10}{3} \quad \longleftarrow \begin{array}{l}\text{Solve it to find where} \\ y = f(x) \text{ crosses the } x\text{-axis.}\end{array}$$

$$\Rightarrow x - 1 = \pm\sqrt{\frac{10}{3}}$$

$$\Rightarrow x = 1 \pm\sqrt{\frac{10}{3}}$$

- So $y = f(x)$ crosses the x-axis when $x = 1 + \sqrt{\frac{10}{3}}$ or $x = 1 - \sqrt{\frac{10}{3}}$

- Now use this information to sketch the graph...

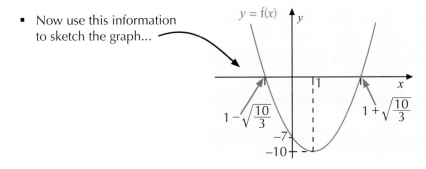

If a function has **no real roots**, the shape and the axis intercepts won't be **enough** to draw the graph. In these cases you'll **have** to find the coordinates of the **vertex point**, even if the question doesn't ask you to.

Example 3

Sketch the graph of the equation $y = 2x^2 - 4x + 3$, showing any intersection points with the axes.

- The coefficient of x^2 here is positive...

$$y = 2x^2 - 4x + 3$$

...so the graph's u-shaped.

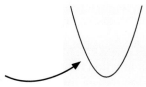

- Now find the places where the graph crosses the axes (both the y-axis and the x-axis).

  (i) Put $x = 0$ to find where it meets the y-axis.

  $$y = 2x^2 - 4x + 3$$

  $$y = (2 \times 0)^2 - (4 \times 0) + 3$$

  so $\boxed{y = 3}$ is where it crosses the y-axis.

Tip: You could use the quadratic formula to try to solve the equation:

$$x = \frac{-b \pm \sqrt{b^2 - 4ac}}{2a}$$

But if you did you'd quickly realise that there are no solutions.

  (ii) Solve $y = 0$ to find where it meets the x-axis (or show that it doesn't).

  Let $2x^2 - 4x + 3 = 0$

  The discriminant $b^2 - 4ac = -8 < 0$

  So it has $\boxed{\text{no real roots,}}$ and doesn't cross the x-axis.

- Now the information we have so far isn't enough to say exactly what the graph will look like — it could be either of these...

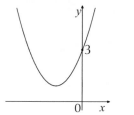 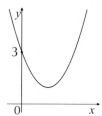

...so we need to find the minimum to tell us which it is.

By completing the square...

$$y = 2(x - 1)^2 + 1$$

...the minimum value is $y = 1$, which occurs at $x = 1$.

Putting all this together — the sketch looks like this:

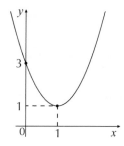

So we've seen a couple of examples of finding the vertex by completing the square. But if you've already worked out the roots, and found that there are **one** or **two** real roots, you can work out the vertex more easily like this:

Tip: You can also find the vertex of a quadratic function using differentiation — see p.177-178.

<u>If the function has **two distinct roots** — use symmetry of quadratic graphs</u>

- The graph of a quadratic function is **symmetrical**, so the x-coordinate of the vertex is **halfway** between the roots of the function

- Work out the x-value halfway between the two roots and put it into the function to find the corresponding y-value of the vertex.

<u>If the function has **one root** — the vertex is at the root</u>

- If a function has one root, then its graph just **touches** the x-axis at the root — this point will always be the vertex.

Example 4

A rocket is launched from the ground.
Its height, h m, is modelled by the equation $h = 30t - 5t^2$,
where t is the time in seconds.

Sketch a graph to show the rocket's flight, and hence find its maximum
height above the ground and the total duration of its flight.

- The coefficient of t^2 is negative so the graph is n-shaped.

- Now find the places where the graph crosses the axes.

    (i)   Putting $t = 0$ gives $h = 0$ as the h-intercept.

    (ii) Putting $h = 0$ gives:

    $$30t - 5t^2 = 0 \Rightarrow 5t(6 - t) = 0$$

    $$\Rightarrow \boxed{t = 0 \text{ and } t = 6} \text{ as the } t\text{-intercepts}$$

- Putting all this together,
  the sketch looks like this:

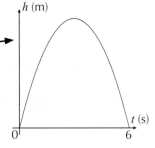

- Now use your graph to answer the questions.

- First find the maximum height of
  the rocket — to do this, you need
  to find the vertex of the graph.

- You know the two roots of the equation and you know the graph is
  symmetrical, so you can work out the maximum by finding the t-value
  halfway between the two roots.

  The maximum point is at $t = 3$. ◄——— Halfway between 0 and 6

- The maximum height of the rocket is just the h-value at the maximum
  point — $t = 3$ gives $h = 30(3) - 5(3)^2 = 90 - 45 = \boxed{45 \text{ m.}}$

- The total duration of the flight is the time from when the rocket was
  launched to when it hit the ground — i.e. the two times at which $h = 0$.
  These points are $t = 0$ and $t = 6$, so the flight lasted for $6 - 0 = \boxed{6 \text{ s.}}$

Tip: Don't let the
different letters put
you off — y has been
replaced by h, and x has
been replaced by t.

Tip: Just ignore the parts
of the graph where t and
h are less than 0 — time
and height can't be
negative in this example.

Tip: So the coordinates
of the maximum point
are (3, 45).

Exercise 3.1

Q1   Sketch the following graphs on the same set of axes,
indicating the x-intercepts of each.

a) $y = x^2 - 1$ b) $y = x^2 - 9$

Q2   a) Factorise the expression $f(x) = x^2 - 10x + 9$.

b) Use your answer to a) to sketch the graph of $f(x)$,
showing the points where it crosses both axes.

c) Sketch the graph of $-f(x)$ on the same axes.

Q2c) Hint:
Remember that the
graph of $y = -f(x)$ is just
$y = f(x)$ reflected in the
x-axis (see page 94 for
more on this).

Q3   For each of the following quadratic functions:

   (i)   Describe its shape.

   (ii)   Find the value of the y-intercept.

   (iii) Find the number of real roots.

Q3(iii) Hint: See pages 35-38 for a recap on finding the number of roots of a quadratic.

   (iv)   Find the values of x at which the graph intersects the x-axis — if it does.

   (v)   Find the coordinates of the vertex.

   (vi)   Sketch the graph of the function, marking on all the information you've found.

   a) $y = -x^2 + 2x + 1$ b) $y = x^2 - 7x + 15$ c) $y = 2x^2 + 4x - 9$

Q4   The graph on the right shows the quadratic function $y = f(x)$.

   a) $f(x)$ can be written in the form $f(x) = (x + q)^2 + r$, where q and r are integers. Use the graph to find the values of q and r.

   b) Copy the sketch, and on the same axes, sketch the function $g(x) = (x + 4)^2$.

   c) How many real roots does each function have?

Q5   a) Complete the square of the expression $x^2 - 6x + 5$.

   b) Use part a) to solve the equation $x^2 - 6x + 5 = 0$

   c) Draw a graph of $y = x^2 - 6x + 5$ showing any intersections with the axes and marking the vertex.

Q6   Sketch the following graphs, showing any intersections with the axes:

   a) $y = x^2 - 2x + 1$ b) $y = x^2 + x - 1$

   c) $y = x^2 - 8x + 18$ d) $y = -x^2 + 3$

Q7   a) What are the roots of the quadratic function shown in the graph on the right?

   b) The quadratic can be written in the form $y = -x^2 + px + q$ where p and q are integers. Use your answer to part a) to find p and q.

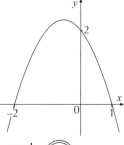

Q8   A theme park is designing a new roller coaster that starts on a raised platform then goes underground. The first 10 seconds of the roller coaster's vertical path are modelled by the equation $h = 0.25t^2 - 2.5t + 4$, where h is the height in metres above the ground and t is the time in seconds.

   a) Sketch a graph showing height of the roller coaster during the first 10 seconds of the ride.

Q8a) Hint: This might look tricky to factorise, but you can multiply through by 4 to give you integer coefficients.

   b) For the first 10 seconds of the ride, use your graph to find:

      (i)   the height of the raised platform.

      (ii) the lowest point of the roller coaster.

      (iii) how long the roller coaster is underground for.

4. Factorising Cubics

So far in this chapter you've seen lots of ways to solve quadratic equations. Cubic equations (ones with an x^3 term) are a bit trickier. Luckily, there are some useful tools to help, such as the Remainder Theorem and the Factor Theorem, as well as algebraic division.

Learning Objectives:

- Be able to factorise cubic expressions.

- Be able to use the Remainder Theorem and Factor Theorem to find remainders and factors of polynomials.

- Be able to carry out simple algebraic division.

Factorising a cubic (when x is a factor)

Factorising a **cubic** means exactly what it meant with a quadratic — writing it as a product of **factors** in **brackets**. Let's start with factorising cubics that have an x in **every term**.

For a cubic of the form $ax^3 + bx^2 + cx$, **take out x** as your first factor as follows:

$$ax^3 + bx^2 + cx = x(ax^2 + bx + c)$$

Now you can just factorise the **quadratic** inside the brackets to get the other factors using the methods given earlier in the chapter. Once you've factorised, you can solve a cubic equation just as you would solve a quadratic.

Tip: Cubic equations can have one, two or three real solutions. So unlike quadratics, they always have at least one real root.

Example 1

Factorise and solve the following cubic equations.

a) $x^3 - 2x^2 - 24x = 0$

Start by taking out a factor of x...

$$\begin{aligned}
x^3 - 2x^2 - 24x &= x(x^2 - 2x - 24) \quad \text{— This quadratic will factorise.}\\
&= x(x\quad)(x\quad)\\
&= x(x\quad 6)(x\quad 4)\\
&= x(x - 6)(x + 4)\\
&\Rightarrow x(x - 6)(x + 4) = 0
\end{aligned}$$

Put in the x's, work out the numbers then choose the signs.

So either $x = 0$, $x - 6 = 0$ or $x + 4 = 0$ $\Rightarrow$ $x = 0$, $x = 6$ or $x = -4$

b) $-x^3 - 2x^2 + 3x = 0$

If the x^3 coefficient is negative, take out a factor of $-x$...
...but don't forget these signs change.

$$\begin{aligned}
-x^3 - 2x^2 + 3x &= -x(x^2 + 2x - 3)\\
&= -x(x\quad)(x\quad)\\
&= -x(x\quad 3)(x\quad 1)\\
&= -x(x + 3)(x - 1)\\
&\Rightarrow -x(x + 3)(x - 1) = 0
\end{aligned}$$

Factorise the quadratic in the brackets using the normal method.

So either $x = 0$, $x + 3 = 0$ or $x - 1 = 0$ $\Rightarrow$ $x = 0$, $x = -3$ or $x = 1$

Example 2

Solve the cubic equation $-4x^3 - 4x^2 + x = 0$.

- The first thing you need to do is factorise. The x^3 coefficient is negative, so take out a factor of $-x$ again...

$$-4x^3 - 4x^2 + x = 0$$
$$-x(4x^2 + 4x - 1) = 0$$

- Now $-x(4x^2 + 4x - 1) = 0$ so either $x = 0$ or $4x^2 + 4x - 1 = 0$. $x = 0$ is one solution and solving the quadratic equation will give the other two.

- This quadratic $4x^2 + 4x - 1$ won't factorise so use the quadratic formula.

$$x = \frac{-b \pm \sqrt{b^2 - 4ac}}{2a}$$

$$= \frac{-4 \pm \sqrt{4^2 - 4 \times 4 \times (-1)}}{2 \times 4}$$

$$= \frac{-4 \pm \sqrt{32}}{8} = \frac{-4 \pm 4\sqrt{2}}{8}$$

$$= -\frac{1}{2} \pm \frac{1}{2}\sqrt{2}$$

- So the solutions are $\boxed{x = 0,\ x = -\frac{1}{2} + \frac{1}{2}\sqrt{2} \text{ and } x = -\frac{1}{2} - \frac{1}{2}\sqrt{2}.}$

Exercise 4.1

Q1 Factorise the following cubic expressions:

a) $x^3 + 5x^2 + 6x$

b) $x^3 + 6x^2 - 7x$

c) $x^3 - 18x^2 + 81x$

d) $x^3 + 7x^2 + 10x$

e) $-x^3 + 4x^2 - 3x$

f) $2x^3 + 15x^2 + 25x$

g) $x^3 - 49x$

h) $x^3 - \frac{9}{4}x$

Q2 Hint: Some of the quadratics may not factorise — use the quadratic formula to get the remaining solutions.

Q2 Solve the following cubic equations:

a) $-x^3 + 2x^2 + 24x = 0$

b) $x^3 - \frac{7}{9}x^2 + \frac{10}{81}x = 0$

c) $2x^3 + 9x^2 + 4x = 0$

d) $3x^3 - 3x^2 + 4x = 0$

e) $x^2(4x + 3) = x$

f) $2x^3 + 8x^2 = -3x$

The Remainder Theorem

When x **isn't** a factor of the cubic, factorising it becomes a lot trickier. First, you'll need to **find a linear factor** (i.e. of the form $(ax + b)$), and then you need to **divide** the cubic by that factor (there are a couple of ways of doing this, which are covered later in this section).

Before you can do that, there are a couple of useful theorems to learn. The first of these is the **Remainder Theorem**. The Remainder Theorem gives you a quick way of **working out** the **remainder** from a division, but **without** actually having to do the division.

Tip: A polynomial is an algebraic expression made up of the sum of constant terms and variables raised to positive integer powers, such as quadratics and cubics.

For a polynomial f(x), the Remainder Theorem says:

> When you divide **f(x)** by **($x - a$)**, the remainder is **f(a)**.

So just stick $x = a$ into the polynomial.

Dividing a polynomial by divisors that are **multiples** of each other, e.g. $(x + 2)$ and $(3x + 6)$, will produce the **same remainder**. This means you can **simplify** the divisor to get it in the form $x - a$ and the Remainder Theorem still holds.

Example 1

Use the Remainder Theorem to work out the remainder when $(2x^3 - 3x^2 - 3x + 7)$ is divided by $(x - 2)$.

- So: $f(x) = 2x^3 - 3x^2 - 3x + 7$

- You're dividing by $(x - 2)$, so $a = 2$

- So the remainder must be:
$$f(a) = f(2) = (2 \times 8) - (3 \times 4) - (3 \times 2) + 7 = \boxed{5}$$

> **Tip:** Be careful if you're dividing by something like $(x + 7)$, as a will be negative. In this case, you'd get $a = -7$.

If you want the remainder after dividing by something like $(ax - b)$, there's an extension to the Remainder Theorem:

> When you divide **f(x)** by **$(ax - b)$**, the remainder is $f\left(\dfrac{b}{a}\right)$.

> **Tip:** Note, $\dfrac{b}{a}$ is just the value of x that would make the bracket 0.

Example 2

Find the remainder when you divide $(2x^3 - 3x^2 - 3x + 7)$ by $(2x - 1)$.

- So: $f(x) = 2x^3 - 3x^2 - 3x + 7$

- You're dividing by $(2x - 1)$, so comparing it to $(ax - b)$ we get:
$$a = 2 \quad \text{and} \quad b = 1$$

- So the remainder must be:
$$f\left(\frac{b}{a}\right) = f\left(\frac{1}{2}\right) = 2\left(\frac{1}{8}\right) - 3\left(\frac{1}{4}\right) - 3\left(\frac{1}{2}\right) + 7 = \boxed{5}$$

If you're given the remainder when a polynomial is divided by something, you can use the Remainder Theorem to work **backwards** to find an **unknown coefficient** in the original polynomial.

Example 3

When $(x^3 + cx^2 - 7x + 2)$ is divided by $(x + 2)$, the remainder is –4. Use the Remainder Theorem to find the value of c.

- The polynomial was divided by $(x + 2)$, so: $a = -2$

- When you divide f(x) by $(x - a)$, the remainder is f(a), so:
$$f(-2) = -4 \quad \Rightarrow \quad (-2)^3 + c(-2)^2 - 7(-2) + 2 = -4$$
$$-8 + 4c + 14 + 2 = -4$$
$$4c = -12$$
$$\boxed{c = -3}$$

Q1 Use the Remainder Theorem to work out the remainder in each of the following divisions:

a) $2x^3 - 3x^2 - 39x + 20$ divided by $(x - 1)$

b) $x^3 - 3x^2 + 2x$ divided by $(x + 1)$

c) $6x^3 + x^2 - 5x - 2$ divided by $(x + 1)$

d) $x^3 + 2x^2 - 7x - 2$ divided by $(x + 3)$

e) $4x^3 - 6x^2 - 12x - 6$ divided by $(2x + 1)$

f) $x^3 - 3x^2 - 6x + 8$ divided by $(2x - 1)$

Q2 Find the remainder when $f(x) = x^4 - 3x^3 + 7x^2 - 12x + 14$ is divided by:

a) $x + 2$ b) $2x + 4$ c) $x - 3$ d) $2x - 6$

Q3 The remainder when $x^3 + cx^2 + 17x - 10$ is divided by $(x + 3)$ is -16. Use the Remainder Theorem to find the value of c.

Q4 The remainder when $x^3 + px^2 - 10x - 19$ is divided by $(x + 2)$ is 5. Use the Remainder Theorem to find the value of p.

Q5 When $x^3 - dx^2 + dx + 1$ is divided by $(x + 2)$ the remainder is -25. Use the Remainder Theorem to find the value of d.

Q6 When $x^3 - 2x^2 + 7x + k$ is divided by $(x + 1)$ the remainder is -8. Find the value of k.

Q7 $f(x) = x^4 + 5x^3 + px + 156$. The remainder when $f(x)$ is divided by $(x - 2)$ is the same as the remainder when $f(x)$ is divided by $(x + 1)$. Use the Remainder Theorem to find the value of p.

The Factor Theorem

If you get a **remainder of zero** when you divide $f(x)$ by $(x - a)$, then $(x - a)$ must be a **factor** of $f(x)$. This is the **Factor Theorem**.

The **Factor Theorem** states:

> If **f(x)** is a polynomial, and **f(a) = 0**, then **(x – a)** is a factor of **f(x)**.

This also works the other way round — if $(x - a)$ is a factor of $f(x)$, then **f(a) = 0**. From the Remainder Theorem, you know that dividing by **multiples** of a divisor gives the **same remainder**. So, as a factor has a remainder of 0, any multiple of that factor will also have a remainder of 0, so must also be a factor.

Tip: Remember, a root is just a value of x that makes $f(x) = 0$. So if you know the roots of $f(x)$, you also know the factors of $f(x)$ — and vice versa.

Tip: This also means that $f\left(\dfrac{b}{a}\right) = 0 \iff (ax - b)$ is a factor of $f(x)$.

Example 1

Use the Factor Theorem to show that $(x - 2)$ is a factor of $(x^3 - 5x^2 + x + 10)$.

- $a = 2$, so work out $f(a)$: $f(a) = f(2) = 8 - (5 \times 4) + 2 + 10 = 0$

- The remainder is 0, so that means $(x - 2)$ divides into $x^3 - 5x^2 + x + 10$ **exactly**. So $(x - 2)$ must be a **factor** of $x^3 - 5x^2 + x + 10$.

Example 2

Show that $(2x + 1)$ is a factor of $f(x) = 2x^3 - 3x^2 + 4x + 3$.

- Notice that $2x + 1 = 0$ when $x = -\frac{1}{2}$. So plug this value of x into $f(x)$.

- If you show that $f\left(-\frac{1}{2}\right) = 0$, then the Factor Theorem says that $\left(x + \frac{1}{2}\right)$ is a factor — which means that $2\left(x + \frac{1}{2}\right) = (2x + 1)$ is also a factor.

- $f\left(-\frac{1}{2}\right) = 2\left(-\frac{1}{8}\right) - 3\left(\frac{1}{4}\right) + 4\left(-\frac{1}{2}\right) + 3 = \boxed{0}$

- So, by the Factor Theorem, $(2x + 1)$ is a factor of $f(x)$.

Just one more useful thing to mention about polynomials and factors:

> If the **coefficients** in a polynomial **add up to 0**, then $(x - 1)$ is a **factor**.

This works for all polynomials — there are no exceptions.

Tip: If you put $x = 1$ into a polynomial $f(x)$, x^2, x^3 etc. are all just 1, so $f(1)$ is the sum of the coefficients.

Example 3

Factorise the polynomial $f(x) = 6x^2 - 7x + 1$.

- The coefficients (6, –7 and 1) add up to 0, which means $f(1) = 0$, and so $(x - 1)$ is a factor.

- Then just factorise it like any quadratic to get this:
$$f(x) = 6x^2 - 7x + 1 = \boxed{(6x - 1)(x - 1)}$$

Tip: Have a look back at page 26 for a reminder of how to factorise quadratics when $a \neq 1$.

Exercise 4.3

Q1 Use the Factor Theorem to show that:
   a) $(x - 1)$ is a factor of $x^3 - x^2 - 3x + 3$
   b) $(x + 1)$ is a factor of $x^3 + 2x^2 + 3x + 2$
   c) $(x + 2)$ is a factor of $x^3 + 3x^2 - 10x - 24$

Q2 Use the Factor Theorem to show that:
   a) $(2x - 1)$ is a factor of $2x^3 - x^2 - 8x + 4$
   b) $(3x - 2)$ is a factor of $3x^3 - 5x^2 - 16x + 12$

Q2 Hint: Be careful with the fractions here.

Q3 a) Use the Factor Theorem to show that $(x - 3)$ is a factor of $x^3 - 2x^2 - 5x + 6$.
   b) Show, by adding the coefficients, that $(x - 1)$ is also a factor of this cubic.

Q4 $f(x) = 3x^3 - 5x^2 - 58x + 40$. Use the Factor Theorem to show that the following are factors of $f(x)$:
   a) $(x + 4)$ b) $(3x - 2)$

Q5 $(x - 3)$ is a factor of the cubic $qx^3 - 4x^2 - 7qx + 12$. Find the value of q.

Q6 The polynomial $f(x) = x^3 + cx^2 + dx - 2$ has factors $(x - 1)$ and $(x - 2)$. Using the Factor Theorem, find the values of c and d.

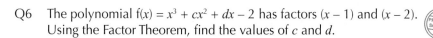

Factorising a cubic (when x isn't a factor)

Now that you've seen the Remainder Theorem and the Factor Theorem, you can use them to factorise cubics that **don't** have an x in every term. First, you need to use the **Factor Theorem** (and a bit of trial and error) to find one of the factors of the cubic:

> ▪ First, **add up** the **coefficients** to check if $(x - 1)$ is a factor.
>
> ▪ If that doesn't work, keep trying small numbers (find $f(-1)$, $f(2)$, $f(-2)$, $f(3)$, $f(-3)$ and so on) until you find a number that gives you **zero** when you put it in the **cubic**. Call that number k. $(x - k)$ is a **factor of the cubic**.

Once you've found one of the factors, here's how to **factorise the cubic**:

> 1) Write down the **factor** you know **($x - k$)**, and another set of brackets: $(x - k)(\qquad)$.
>
> 2) In the brackets, put the x^2 **term** needed to get the right x^3 term.
>
> 3) In the brackets, put in the **constant** (that when multiplied by k gives the constant in the cubic).
>
> 4) Put in nx as the **x term** and then **multiply** to find the x^2 terms.
>
> 5) **Equate the coefficients** of the x^2 terms you've just found with the coefficient of x^2 from the question, then **solve** to find n.
>
> 6) **Factorise** the quadratic you've found — if that's possible.

Tip: Once you've found n, you should check that it gives you the correct x term as well.

Tip: If the quadratic can't be factorised, just leave it as it is.

Examples

a) Factorise $x^3 + 6x^2 + 5x - 12$.

▪ Check to see if the coefficients add up to 0: $1 + 6 + 5 - 12 = 0$.

▪ They do, so: $(x - 1)$ is a factor.

▪ Then factorise your cubic to get:

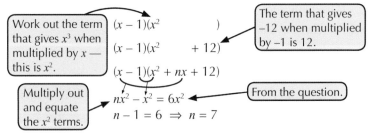

| Work out the term that gives x^3 when multiplied by x — this is x^2. | $(x - 1)(x^2 \qquad)$ | The term that gives −12 when multiplied by −1 is 12. |

$(x - 1)(x^2 \qquad + 12)$

$(x - 1)(x^2 + nx + 12)$

Multiply out and equate the x^2 terms.

$nx^2 - x^2 = 6x^2$ ← From the question.

$n - 1 = 6 \Rightarrow n = 7$

▪ Check that this gives you the right x term: $(x - 1)(x^2 + nx + 12)$

$$12x - nx = 12x - 7x = 5x \checkmark$$

▪ So you have: $x^3 + 6x^2 + 5x - 12 = (x - 1)(x^2 + 7x + 12)$

▪ You can factorise this quadratic: $x^2 + 7x + 12 = (x + 3)(x + 4)$

▪ So your final answer is:

$$x^3 + 6x^2 + 5x - 12 = (x - 1)(x + 3)(x + 4)$$

b) $f(x) = 2x^3 - 3x^2 - 12x + 20$.
   Factorise $f(x)$ and find all the solutions of $f(x) = 0$.

- Check to see if the coefficients add up to 0: $2 - 3 - 12 + 20 = 7$.

- They don't — so use trial and error for values of x, until you find a number that gives you a value of zero...

$$f(-1) = (2 \times -1) - (3 \times 1) - (12 \times -1) + 20 = 27 \text{ ✗}$$

$$f(2) = (2 \times 8) - (3 \times 4) - (12 \times 2) + 20 = 0 \text{ ✓} \implies (x - 2) \text{ is a factor}$$

- Factorise the cubic: $(2x^3 - 3x^2 - 12x + 20) = (x - 2)(2x^2 + x - 10)$
$$= (x - 2)(x - 2)(2x + 5)$$
$$= (x - 2)^2(2x + 5)$$

- So the solutions of $f(x) = 0$ are: $x = 2$ and $x = -\dfrac{5}{2}$

Tip: If you've added the coefficients and they don't add up to zero, then you don't need to do f(1), as you already know that $(x - 1)$ isn't a factor.

c) $f(x) = 4x^3 + 9x^2 - 30x - 8$.
   Given that $x = -\dfrac{1}{4}$ is one solution of $f(x) = 0$, fully factorise $f(x)$.

- If $-\dfrac{1}{4}$ is a root, that means $(4x + 1)$ is a factor.

- Then factorise your cubic: $f(x) = (4x + 1)(x^2 + 2x - 8)$

- And then... $f(x) = (4x + 1)(x - 2)(x + 4)$

Tip: You could also use $\left(x + \dfrac{1}{4}\right)$ as the factor, but it's a lot harder to find the quadratic when you have fractions in the expression.

Exercise 4.4

Q1 Factorise the following:
   a) $x^3 - 3x^2 + 2x$
   b) $2x^3 + 3x^2 - 11x - 6$
   c) $x^3 - 3x^2 + 3x - 1$
   d) $x^3 - 3x^2 + 4$
   e) $x^3 - 3x^2 - 33x + 35$
   f) $x^3 - 28x + 48$

Q2 $f(x) = x^3 + 4x^2 - 8$
   a) Write $f(x)$ as the product of a linear factor and a quadratic factor.
   b) Find the solutions of $f(x) = 0$. Give your answers in surd form where appropriate.

Q2b) Hint: The mention of surds suggests that you'll need to use the quadratic formula.

Q3 Find the roots of the cubic equation $x^3 - x^2 - 3x + 3 = 0$.

Q4 $f(x) = 6x^3 + 37x^2 + 5x - 6$
   Use the fact that $(3x - 1)$ is one factor of $f(x)$ to fully factorise $f(x)$.

Q5 $f(x) = x^3 - px^2 + 17x - 10$, where $(x - 5)$ is a factor of $f(x)$.
   a) Find the value of p.
   b) Factorise $f(x)$.
   c) Find all the solutions to $f(x) = 0$.

Q6 Factorise the following cubic equations:
   a) $3x^3 + 2x^2 - 7x + 2$
   b) $5x^3 - 13x^2 + 4x + 4$

Q7 Show that $x = 2$ is the only real root of the cubic equation $2x^3 - x^2 - 2x - 8 = 0$.

Algebraic division

Once you've found one linear factor of a cubic, you can use **algebraic long division** to find the quadratic factor.

The best way to explain how this works is with a worked example:

Tip: This is an alternative method for factorising cubics — use the method on p.52 if you prefer.

Tip: If the cubic is missing one of the terms (e.g. $ax^3 + bx^2 + c$), you'll need to add in a term in the correct place with a coefficient of 0 (so here you'd write $ax^3 + bx^2 + 0x + c$), otherwise you might miss out some terms in the division.

Tip: The bit you're dividing by is called the divisor.

Tip: Note that we only divide each term by 'x', not '$x - 2$'. The -2 bit is dealt with in the steps in between.

Example

$x - 2$ is a factor of the cubic $f(x) = 2x^3 - 5x - 6$. Use algebraic long division to write $f(x)$ as the product of a linear factor and a quadratic factor.

- This cubic doesn't have an x^2 term, so write $0x^2$ where it should be.

$$x - 2 \overline{) 2x^3 + 0x^2 - 5x - 6}$$

- Start by dividing the first term in the cubic ($2x^3$) by the first term of the divisor (x): $2x^3 \div x = 2x^2$. Write this answer above the cubic:

$$\begin{array}{r} 2x^2 \\ x - 2 \overline{) 2x^3 + 0x^2 - 5x - 6} \end{array}$$

- Multiply the divisor ($x - 2$) by this answer ($2x^2$) to get $2x^3 - 4x^2$ and write this under the first two terms of the cubic:

$$\begin{array}{r} 2x^2 \\ x - 2 \overline{) 2x^3 + 0x^2 - 5x - 6} \\ 2x^3 - 4x^2 \end{array}$$

- Subtract this from the main expression to get $4x^2$. Bring down the $-5x$ term just to make things clearer for the next subtraction.

$$\begin{array}{r} 2x^2 \\ x - 2 \overline{) 2x^3 + 0x^2 - 5x - 6} \\ - (2x^3 - 4x^2) \\ \hline 4x^2 - 5x \end{array}$$

- Now divide the first term of the remaining polynomial ($4x^2$) by the first term of the divisor (x) to get $4x$ (the second term in the answer).

$$\begin{array}{r} 2x^2 + 4x \\ x - 2 \overline{) 2x^3 + 0x^2 - 5x - 6} \\ - (2x^3 - 4x^2) \\ \hline 4x^2 - 5x \end{array}$$

- Multiply $(x - 2)$ by $4x$ to get $4x^2 - 8x$, then subtract again and bring down the -6 term.

$$
\begin{array}{r}
2x^2 + 4x \phantom{{}+3} \\
x - 2 \overline{)\, 2x^3 + 0x^2 - 5x - 6} \\
-\underline{(2x^3 - 4x^2)} \phantom{{}-5x-6} \\
4x^2 - 5x \phantom{{}-6} \\
-\underline{(4x^2 - 8x)} \phantom{{}-6} \\
3x - 6
\end{array}
$$

- Divide $3x$ by x to get 3 (the third term in the answer). Then multiply $(x - 2)$ by 3 to get $3x - 6$.

$$
\begin{array}{r}
2x^2 + 4x + 3 \\
x - 2 \overline{)\, 2x^3 + 0x^2 - 5x - 6} \\
-\underline{(2x^3 - 4x^2)} \phantom{{}-5x-6} \\
4x^2 - 5x \phantom{{}-6} \\
-\underline{(4x^2 - 8x)} \phantom{{}-6} \\
3x - 6 \\
-\underline{(3x - 6)} \\
0
\end{array}
$$

- After subtracting, you're left with 0 — this means there's no remainder.

- Don't forget the final step — writing f(x) as a product of a linear factor and a quadratic factor.

$$\text{So } f(x) = (x - 2)(2x^2 + 4x + 3)$$

Tip: This quadratic won't factorise, so f(x) is fully factorised. Sometimes you'll have to factorise the quadratic as well to fully factorise the cubic equation.

Exercise 4.5

Q1 Use algebraic long division and the given factors to fully factorise the following cubic equations:

a) $x^3 - 2x^2 - 15x + 36$, factor: $(x - 3)$

b) $x^3 - x^2 - 11x - 10$, factor: $(x + 2)$

c) $2x^3 + 11x^2 - 23x - 14$, factor: $(x - 2)$

Q2 Write $x^3 - 5x + 4$ as the product of a linear factor and a quadratic factor using long division.

Q3 $f(x) = x^3 + 2x^2 - 7x - 2$. Use algebraic long division to express f(x) in the form $(x - 2)g(x)$, where g(x) is a quadratic.

Q4 $f(x) = x^3 - 7x - 6$ and $f(-2) = 0$. Use algebraic long division to find all the solutions of $f(x) = 0$.

Q2, 4 Hint: Remember to add in any missing terms, giving them a coefficient of 0.

1. Inequalities

Solving an inequality is very similar to solving an equation. But when multiplying or dividing both sides of an inequality, you've got to make sure that you keep the inequality sign pointing the right way.

Linear inequalities

Solving where the inequality sign doesn't change direction

Solve inequalities like you'd solve equations — whatever you do to one side, you have to do to the other.

- If you **add** or **subtract** something from both sides of an inequality, the inequality sign **doesn't** change direction.

- Multiplying or dividing both sides of an inequality by a **positive** number **doesn't** affect the direction of the inequality sign.

You might be asked to give your answers in **set notation** — take a look back at page 5 if you need a reminder of what this means.

Tip: You can also give inequalities in **interval notation**. For example, $1 < x \leq 2$ can be written as $(1, 2]$ — the round bracket means that 1 is not included, while the square bracket means that 2 is included. Intervals such as $x \geq 3$ are written as $[3, \infty)$.

Example 1

Find the set of values for x which satisfy:

a) $x - 3 < -1 + 2x$

$$x - 3 + 1 < -1 + 2x + 1$$

Adding 1 to both sides leaves the inequality sign pointing in the same direction.

$$x - 2 < 2x$$

$$x - 2 - x < 2x - x$$

Subtracting x from both sides doesn't affect the direction of the inequality sign.

$$\boxed{-2 < x}$$

And this is the same as... $\boxed{x > -2}$

b) $2(4x + 1) \geq 2x + 17$

$$8x + 2 \geq 2x + 17 \qquad \longleftarrow \text{ First, expand the brackets...}$$

$$8x + 2 - 2 \geq 2x + 17 - 2 \qquad \longleftarrow \text{ ... then subtract 2...}$$

$$8x \geq 2x + 15$$

$$8x - 2x \geq 2x + 15 - 2x \qquad \longleftarrow \text{ ...and then } 2x, \text{ from both sides...}$$

$$6x \geq 15$$

$$\frac{6x}{6} \geq \frac{15}{6} \qquad \longleftarrow \text{ ...then finally, dividing by 6...}$$

$$\boxed{x \geq \frac{5}{2}} \qquad \longleftarrow \text{ ...leaves the inequality sign pointing in the same direction.}$$

Solving where the inequality sign does change direction

When solving inequalities, multiplying or dividing by **negative** numbers **changes** the direction of the inequality sign.

Example 2

Find the set of values of x for which $4 - 3x \leq 16$.

$4 - 3x - 4 \leq 16 - 4$ ◄——— Subtract 4 from both sides.

$-3x \leq 12$

$\dfrac{-3x}{-3} \geq \dfrac{12}{-3}$ ◄——— Then divide both sides by –3 — but change the direction of the inequality sign.

$x \geq -4$

Tip: The reason for the sign changing direction is because it's just the same as swapping everything from one side to the other:

$-3x \leq 12$

$0 \leq 12 + 3x$

$-12 \leq 3x$

$-4 \leq x$ or $x \geq -4$

Example 3

Find the set of values of x for which $\dfrac{2 - 4x}{3} > \dfrac{5 - 3x}{4}$.
Give your answer in set notation.

$4(2 - 4x) > 3(5 - 3x)$ ◄——— Multiply both sides by 12 to remove the fractions.

$8 - 16x > 15 - 9x$ ◄——— Multiply out the brackets.

$-16x > 7 - 9x$ ◄——— Subtract 8 from both sides.

$-7x > 7$ ◄——— Add 9x to both sides.

$x < -1$ ◄——— Then divide both sides by –7 and change the direction of the inequality sign.

$\{x : x < -1\}$ ◄——— Don't forget to write the answer in set notation

---

Finding the solution to two inequalities

You may be given two inequalities and be asked to find a solution which satisfies **both** of them.

Example 4

Find the set of values for x which satisfy both the inequalities
$x - 5 < -3 + 2x$ and $2x > 4x - 6$.

▪ Solve both inequalities separately.

$x - 5 < -3 + 2x$ $2x > 4x - 6$

$x - 2 < 2x$ $2x + 6 > 4x$

$-2 < x$ $6 > 2x$

                           $3 > x$

Tip: You can write these solutions as $x > -2$ and $x < 3$ if you prefer.

- Show both solutions on a number line.
  Each line has an open circle at the end to show that this number isn't equal to x.

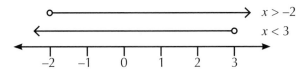

- Look where the two lines overlap to find the set of values that satisfy **both** inequalities.
  They overlap between –2 and 3, so:

$$-2 < x < 3$$

- Or, in set notation, this is:

$$\{x : -2 < x < 3\}$$

Exercise 1.1

Q1 Find the set of values for x which satisfy:

  a) $2x - 1 < x + 4$ b) $4 - 3x \geq 10 - 5x$

  c) $5x + 7 > 3x + 1$ d) $3 - 2x \leq 5x - 4$

  e) $9 - x \geq 7x + 5$

Q2 Find the set of values for x which satisfy the inequalities below. Give your answers in set notation.

  a) $2(x + 3) > 3(x + 2)$ b) $5(1 + 3x) \leq 7$

Q3 Find the set of values for x which satisfy:

  a) $\dfrac{6 - 5x}{2} < \dfrac{4 - 8x}{3}$ b) $\dfrac{3x - 1}{4} \geq 2x$

  c) $\dfrac{x - 2}{2} - \dfrac{2x + 3}{3} < 7$

Q4 Find the set of values for x which satisfy the inequalities below. Give your answers in set notation.

  a) $-5 < 2x - 3 < 15$ b) $-5 \leq 4 - 3x < 19$

Q5 Solve the following inequalities, and represent the solutions on a number line:

  a) $2x \geq 3 - x$ b) $5x - 1 < 3x + 5$

  c) $2x + 1 \geq 3x + 2$ d) $3(x - 3) \leq 5(x - 1)$

  e) $9 - x \leq 3 - 4x$ f) $\dfrac{2(x - 3)}{3} + 1 < \dfrac{2x - 1}{2}$

Q6 a) Find the set of values of x for which $7 \leq 3x - 2 < 16$.

  b) Show your solution to part a) on a number line.

Q7 Find the set of values for x which satisfy **both** $4 - 2x < 10$ and $3x - 1 < x + 7$. Give your answer in set notation.

Q8 Find the values of x which satisfy both inequalities:

    a) $2x \geq 3x - 5$ and $3x - 2 \geq x - 6$

    b) $5x + 1 \leq 11$ and $2x - 3 < 5x - 6$

    c) $2x - 1 \leq 3x - 5$ and $5x - 6 > x + 22$

    d) $3x + 5 < x + 1$ and $6x - 1 \geq 3x + 5$

Quadratic inequalities

When solving inequalities, it's important that you **don't divide** or **multiply** by **variables** (anything you don't know the value of, e.g. x or y).

- The variable might be **negative** — so the inequality sign may end up pointing in the wrong direction.

- The variable could be equal to **zero** — you can't divide something by zero.

Tip: If you have an x on the bottom of a fraction (e.g. $\frac{2}{x} < 1$), you'd have to multiply both sides by x^2 (as this is always positive). So $\frac{2}{x} < 1$ would become $2x < x^2$ (see the following examples for how to solve questions like this).

Example 1

Simplify the quadratic inequality $36x < 6x^2$.

- Start by dividing by 6.

- Dividing by 6 is okay because 6 is definitely positive.

$$\Rightarrow 6x < x^2$$

- It's tempting to divide both sides by x now — but x could be negative (or zero).

- So instead take $6x$ from both sides.

$$\Rightarrow \quad \boxed{0 < x^2 - 6x} \quad \text{which is...} \quad \boxed{x^2 - 6x > 0}$$

The best way to **solve** a **quadratic inequality** is to do the following:

> - Rewrite the inequality with zero on one side.
> - Sketch the graph of the quadratic function.
> - Use the graph to find the solution.

Example 2

Find the values of x which satisfy $-x^2 + 2x + 4 \geq 1$.

- First rewrite the inequality with zero on one side.

$$-x^2 + 2x + 3 \geq 0$$

- Then you need to draw the graph of $y = -x^2 + 2x + 3$.

Tip: See pages 41-45 for more on drawing graphs of quadratic functions.

- So find where it crosses the x-axis (i.e. where $y = 0$), by factorising to find the roots:

$$-x^2 + 2x + 3 = 0 \Rightarrow x^2 - 2x - 3 = 0$$

$$\Rightarrow (x + 1)(x - 3) = 0$$

$$\Rightarrow x = -1 \quad \text{and} \quad x = 3$$

Tip: See pages 24-27 if you need a refresher on how to factorise a quadratic.

- The coefficient of x^2 is negative, so the graph is n-shaped. So it looks like this:

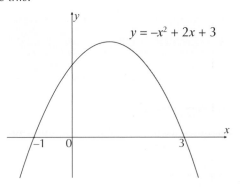

$y = -x^2 + 2x + 3$

- Now you're trying to solve the inequality $-x^2 + 2x + 3 \geq 0$, so you're interested in when the graph is **positive or zero**, i.e. when it's **above the x-axis**.

- From the graph, this is when x is between -1 and 3 (including those points).

- So the solution is: $-1 \leq x \leq 3$

Tip: Look at the inequality sign to tell you which bit of the graph you want — it'll either be the range(s) of x where the graph is below the x-axis or the range(s) where it's above.

Tip: Here you're looking for when it's positive **or** zero because the inequality sign in the quadratic equation tells us it's "greater than or equal to" zero.

Example 3

Find the values of x which satisfy $2x^2 + 2x - 5 > 3x - 2$. Give your answer in set notation.

- First rewrite the inequality with zero on one side.
$$2x^2 - x - 3 > 0$$

- Then draw the graph of $y = 2x^2 - x - 3$.

- So factorise the quadratic equation to find where it crosses the x-axis:
$$2x^2 - x - 3 = 0$$
$$\Rightarrow \quad (2x - 3)(x + 1) = 0$$
$$\Rightarrow \quad x = \frac{3}{2} \quad \text{and} \quad x = -1$$

- The coefficient of x^2 is positive, so the graph is u-shaped. So it looks like this:

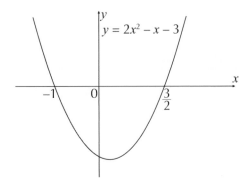

$y = 2x^2 - x - 3$

- Now you're trying to solve $2x^2 - x - 3 > 0$, so you need to say when the graph is **positive**.

- Looking at the graph, there are two parts of the x-axis where this is true — when x is less than -1 and when x is greater than $\frac{3}{2}$.

- So the solution is:
$$x < -1 \quad \text{or} \quad x > \frac{3}{2}$$

- In set notation, this is:
$$\{x : x < -1\} \cup \left\{x : x > \frac{3}{2}\right\}$$

Tip: You're only looking for when it's positive (rather than zero too) because the inequality sign in the quadratic inequality is a "greater than" sign.

Example 1 revisited

- On page 59 you had to simplify $36x < 6x^2$.
$$36x < 6x^2$$
$$\Rightarrow \quad 6x < x^2$$
$$\Rightarrow \quad 0 < x^2 - 6x$$

- To **solve** this, draw the graph of $y = x^2 - 6x = x(x - 6)$:

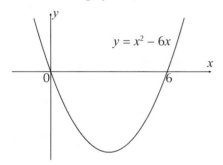

- You're looking for when it is positive.
- And this is positive when:
$$x < 0 \quad \text{or} \quad x > 6$$

Tip: In this case, the solution is $x < -1$ **or** $x > \frac{3}{2}$, so you want the **union** ($\cup$) of the two sets. If the inequality was the other way around (i.e. $2x^2 - x - 3 < 0$), you would end up with the **intersection** ($\cap$) of two sets — the values of x that satisfy both $x > -1$ **and** $x < \frac{3}{2}$.

Tip: If you'd divided the inequality $6x < x^2$ by x you'd only get half the solution — you'd miss the $x < 0$ part.

You may be asked to find the set of values for x which satisfy **both** a quadratic inequality and a linear inequality. To do this, you just work out the solution of each inequality separately and then use a **graph** to help you find the solution that satisfies both.

Example 4

Find the set of values of x which satisfy:

a) $5x - 10 > 4x - 7$

- Solve in the usual way.
$$5x - 10 > 4x - 7$$
$$\Rightarrow \quad 5x > 4x + 3$$
$$\Rightarrow \quad \boxed{x > 3}$$

b) $2x^2 - 11x + 5 < 0$

- You've already got zero on one side, so just factorise the quadratic to find where the graph crosses the x-axis:

$$2x^2 - 11x + 5 = 0$$

$$\Rightarrow \quad (2x - 1)(x - 5) = 0$$

$$\Rightarrow \quad x = \frac{1}{2} \quad \text{and} \quad x = 5$$

- The coefficient of x^2 is positive, so the graph is u-shaped. It looks like this:

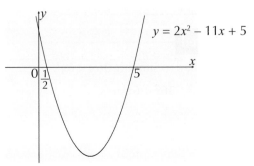

Tip: You're looking for when it is negative as the inequality sign tells us it is less than zero.

- You're interested in when this is negative, i.e. when it's below the x-axis.

- From the graph, this is when x is between $\frac{1}{2}$ and 5.

- So $2x^2 - 11x + 5 < 0$ when:

$$\frac{1}{2} < x < 5$$

c) both $5x - 10 > 4x - 7$ <u>and</u> $2x^2 - 11x + 5 < 0$

- You already know the solutions to both inequalities — and the graph above shows the solution to the quadratic inequality.

- So add the line $x = 3$ to your graph.

- You're now interested in when the curve is negative, **and** when the x values are greater than 3.

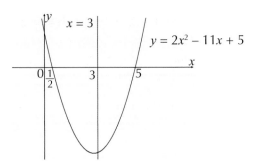

- So both inequalities are satisfied when:

$$3 < x < 5$$

Solving a quadratic inequality to find k

On page 39, you came across a quadratic containing an unknown constant (k) and used the formula for the **discriminant** to form a **linear inequality** in terms of k. The example below is similar, but it results in a **quadratic inequality**.

Tip: The discriminant is just the $b^2 - 4ac$ part of the quadratic formula — see page 38 for more.

Example 5

The equation $kx^2 + (k + 3)x + 4 = 0$ has two distinct real solutions. Show that $k^2 - 10k + 9 > 0$, and find the set of values of k which satisfy this inequality.

- The original equation has two distinct real solutions, so the discriminant must be greater than 0 — i.e. $b^2 - 4ac > 0$.

- Identify a, b and c: $a = k$, $b = (k + 3)$ and $c = 4$

- Then put these values into the formula for the discriminant:

$$b^2 - 4ac = (k + 3)^2 - (4 \times k \times 4) = k^2 + 6k + 9 - 16k = k^2 - 10k + 9$$

- So:

$$\boxed{k^2 - 10k + 9 > 0} \text{ as required}$$

- Now, to find the set of values for k, you have to factorise the quadratic:

$$k^2 - 10k + 9 = (k - 1)(k - 9)$$

- So, the graph of the quadratic will cross the horizontal axis at $k = 1$ and $k = 9$, and it's u-shaped.

- Sketching the graph, you can see that the quadratic is > 0 when:

$$\boxed{k < 1 \quad \text{or} \quad k > 9}$$

- Or you can give the answer in set notation:

$$\boxed{\{k : k < 1\} \cup \{k : k > 9\}}$$

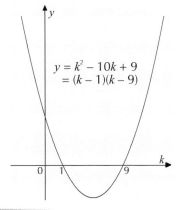

$$y = k^2 - 10k + 9$$
$$= (k - 1)(k - 9)$$

Tip: This question doesn't mention finding the discriminant — but that's what you've got to do first, to get that quadratic inequality in terms of k.

Exercise 1.2

Q1 Use the graphs given to solve the following quadratic inequalities:

   a) $x^2 + 2x - 3 < 0$ b) $4x - x^2 < 0$

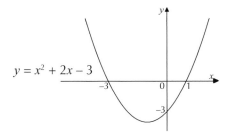

$y = x^2 + 2x - 3$

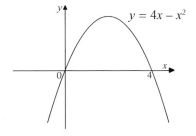

$y = 4x - x^2$

c) $2x^2 \geq 5 - 9x$

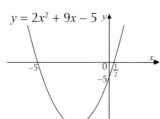

$y = 2x^2 + 9x - 5$

d) $x^2 - 2x - 5 > 0$

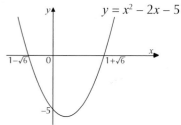

$y = x^2 - 2x - 5$

Q2 Hint: Here, you're given the graphs but you'll have to calculate where the x-intercepts are yourself.

Q2 Use the graphs given to help you solve the quadratic inequalities below. Give your answers in set notation.

a) $x^2 \leq 4$

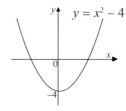

$y = x^2 - 4$

b) $13x < 3x^2 + 4$

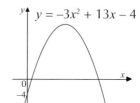

$y = -3x^2 + 13x - 4$

c) $x^2 + 4 < 6x$

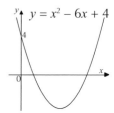

$y = x^2 - 6x + 4$

Q3 Find the ranges of values of x which satisfy the following quadratic inequalities. Include a sketch of the graph for each answer.

a) $x^2 + 5x - 6 \geq 0$
b) $x^2 - 3x + 2 < 0$
c) $6 - 5x > 6x^2$
d) $x^2 - 5x + 24 \leq 5x + 3$
e) $36 - 4x^2 \leq 0$
f) $x^2 - 6x + 3 > 0$
g) $x^2 - x + 3 > 0$
h) $6 \geq 5x^2 + 13x$

Q4 Hint: See the tip on p.59 for a hint on how to solve these.

Q4 Find the values of x which satisfy the following inequalities, giving your answers in set notation:

a) $\dfrac{1}{x} > 5$

b) $7 > \dfrac{3}{x}$

Q5 A rectangular office is to be built, measuring $(x - 9)$ metres wide and $(x - 6)$ metres long. Given that at least 28 m² of floor space is required, find the set of possible values of x.

Q6 a) Find the set of values of k for which $kx^2 - 6x + k = 0$ has two distinct real solutions.

b) Find the set of values for k which gives the equation $x^2 - kx + k = 0$ no real roots. Give your answer in set notation.

Q7 Find the values of x which satisfy both $4(3 - x) \geq 13 - 5x$ and $7x + 6 \geq 3x^2$.

Graphing inequalities

You've seen on the last few pages how **graphs** can be used to solve quadratic inequalities. You can also show **regions** on a graph that satisfy **more than one inequality** in **two variables** (x and y) — whether they're linear or quadratic. The method has four steps:

> 1) **Write each inequality as an equation.**
>
>   Just put = wherever you have an inequality sign, and **rearrange** so that it's in the form "$y = ...$". You might have to **split up** any inequalities that are of the form $a < x < b$ into two separate bits — i.e. $a = x$ and $x = b$.

> 2) **Draw the graph for each equation.**
>
>   If the original inequality was **<** or **>**, draw a **dotted line**, and draw a **solid line** for ≤ or ≥.

> 3) **Work out which side of each line you want.**
>
>   Look back at each inequality and **substitute** in the coordinates of a point to see whether or not it **satisfies** the inequality (usually the **origin** is an easy point to use). If it does, you want the side of the line that the point is on, and if not, you want the other side.

> 4) **Label the correct region.**
>
>   Once you know which side of each line you need, shade the **other side** (the side that does **not** satisfy the inequality). Once you've done this for each inequality, **label** the **unshaded** area. This will be the region that satisfies **all** of the inequalities.

Tip: If the origin lies on one of the lines, you might have to use a different point — but the method is the same.

Tip: Make sure you read the question carefully — you could be asked to shade the region that **satisfies** the inequalities rather than the regions that don't. For the following examples, the correct region will be unshaded.

Example 1

Draw the following inequalities on a graph and label the region that satisfies all three:

$$2x + y > 4 \qquad x - y < 1 \qquad y \le 3$$

① The first step is to change these into equations:
$$y = 4 - 2x \qquad y = x - 1 \qquad y = 3$$

② Now you can plot the lines on your graph — use **dotted lines** for the first two, and a **solid line** for $y = 3$.

Tip: Don't forget to rearrange the equations into the form "$y = ...$" at this point.

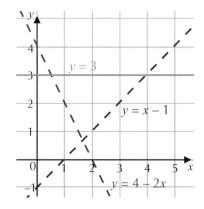

③ Now you have to decide which side of each line you want. Try the origin (0, 0) in each inequality.

- $2x + y > 4 \Rightarrow 0 + 0 > 4$ which is **false**. The origin is on the **wrong** side of the line, so shade this side.

- $x - y < 1 \Rightarrow 0 - 0 < 1$ which is **true**. The origin is on the **correct** side of the line, so shade the other side.

- $y \leq 3 \Rightarrow 0 \leq 3$ which is **true**. The origin is on the **correct** side of the line, so shade the other side.

④ Finally, the shaded graph looks like this:

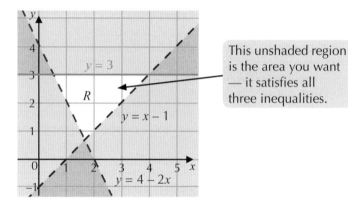

This unshaded region is the area you want — it satisfies all three inequalities.

Tip: You can check your answer by testing a point — for example, the point (2, 2) lies in the unshaded region and satisfies all three inequalities here.

Don't forget to label the correct region — this one is labelled R.

Example 2

Draw and label the region that satisfies the following inequalities:
$$y > x^2 - x - 2 \qquad\qquad y \geq 4 + 7x - 2x^2$$

① First, write the inequalities as equations:

$$y = x^2 - x - 2 \qquad\qquad y = 4 + 7x - 2x^2$$
$$= (x + 1)(x - 2) \qquad\qquad = (4 - x)(1 + 2x)$$

② Now draw the graphs of these equations, using a **dotted line** for $y = x^2 - x - 2$ and a **solid line** for $y = 4 + 7x - 2x^2$:

Tip: Try and sketch the quadratics as accurately as you can (by finding the x- and y-intercepts and vertices — see pages 41-45).

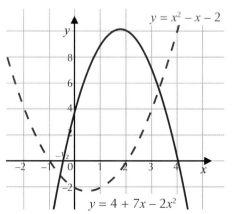

③ Now try the origin in each inequality:

- $y > x^2 - x - 2 \Rightarrow 0 > 0 - 0 - 2$ which is **true**. The origin is on the **correct** side of the line, so shade the other side.

- $y \geq 4 + 7x - 2x^2 \Rightarrow 0 \geq 4 + 0 - 0$ which is **false**. The origin is on the **wrong** side of the line, so shade this side.

④ So you get an unshaded region that looks like this:

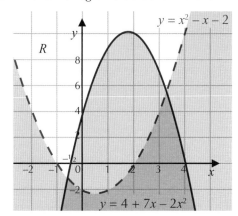

Tip: The region is not enclosed, so it continues upwards to infinity — that's fine.

Exercise 1.3

Hint: Use graph paper or squared paper for this exercise.

Q1 Draw and shade the regions that satisfy the following sets of inequalities:

a) $x + y < 5$, $\quad 2x + y \geq 4$, $\quad x + 2y > 6$

b) $x \leq 4$, $\quad y \leq 7$, $\quad x + y > 4$

c) $y > x^2$, $\quad x - y \geq -3$

d) $y - 2 \leq x^2$, $\quad 2x^2 - y < 2$

Q1 Hint: Be careful — this question asks you to shade the region that satisfies the inequalities, not the region that doesn't.

Q2 Regions A and B are described by the sets of inequalities below:

A: $x + 2y \leq 12$, $\quad 2y - 3x \leq 4$, $\quad y \geq 2$

B: $x \geq 3$, $\quad 2x \leq y + 9$, $\quad x + 3y \leq 15$

Which region has the greater area?

Q3 A bakery is running out of ingredients and wants to see how many sponge cakes and baguettes they can make.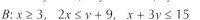

A cake requires 1 lb of flour and 3 eggs, and a baguette requires 2 lb of flour and 1 egg. The bakery can make x cakes and y baguettes. They have 24 lb of flour remaining, which can be represented by the inequality $x + 2y \leq 24$.

a) They only have 42 eggs left. Use this information to form another inequality in x and y.

b) On a graph, draw and label the region that satisfies both of these inequalities.

c) A customer requests 8 cakes and 10 baguettes for a fête. Can the bakery meet their order? If not, what ingredient(s) do they not have enough of?

Q3b) Hint: Note that x and y can't be negative (since they can't make a negative number of cakes/baguettes). So $x \geq 0$ and $y \geq 0$ have to be satisfied as well.

2. Simultaneous Equations

Learning Objectives:

- Be able to solve two linear simultaneous equations using elimination or substitution.

- Be able to solve simultaneous equations where one is linear and one is quadratic using substitution.

Solving simultaneous equations just means finding the answers to two equations at the same time — i.e. finding values for x and y for which both equations are true.

Simultaneous equations — both linear

Solving by elimination

Simultaneous equations are just a pair of equations containing two unknown quantities, usually x and y.

This is how simultaneous equations are often shown:

$$3x + 5y = -4$$

$$-2x + 3y = 9$$

But they'll look different sometimes, maybe like this:

$$4 + 5y = -3x$$

$$-2x = 9 - 3y$$

You can solve two linear simultaneous equations by **elimination**. Before you can use the method, you need to **rearrange** them as '$ax + by = c$'.

$$4 + 5y = -3x \qquad\qquad\longrightarrow\qquad\qquad 3x + 5y = -4$$

$$-2x = 9 - 3y \qquad\qquad\qquad\qquad\qquad -2x + 3y = 9$$

Tip: You can also solve two linear simultaneous equations by substitution — see page 70.

The elimination method involves **four** steps:

1) **Match the coefficients**

   Multiply the equations by numbers that will make either the x's or the y's **match** in the two equations (ignoring minus signs).

2) **Eliminate to find one variable**

   If the coefficients are the **same** sign, you'll need to **subtract** one equation from the other. If the coefficients are **different** signs, you need to **add** the equations.

3) **Find the other variable (that you eliminated)**

   When you've found one variable, put its value into one of the **original equations** so you can find the **other** variable.

4) **Check your answer**

   By putting these values into the **other original equation**.

Example

Solve the simultaneous equations $3x + 5y = -4$ and $-2x + 3y = 9$.

- Number your equations 1 and 2.

$$\textcircled{1} \quad 3x + 5y = -4$$

$$\textcircled{2} \quad -2x + 3y = 9$$

Tip: It's a good idea to label them as equation $\textcircled{1}$ and equation $\textcircled{2}$ — so you know which one you're working with.

- Match the coefficients:
  To get the x's to match, you need to multiply the first equation by 2 and the second by 3:

Tip: Go for the lowest common multiple (LCM), e.g. the LCM of 2 and 3 is 6.

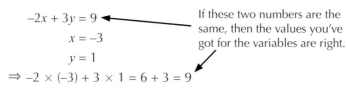

Number these new equations.

- Eliminate to find one variable:
  Add the new equations together to eliminate the x's.

$$③+④ \quad 19y = 19$$
$$y = 1$$

- Find the variable you eliminated:
  So $y = 1$. Now stick that value for y into one of the equations to find x:

$$y = 1 \text{ in } ① \Rightarrow 3x + 5 = -4$$
$$3x = -9$$
$$x = -3$$

- So the solution is $x = -3, y = 1$

- Check your answer:
  Put these values into the other equation

$$-2x + 3y = 9$$
$$x = -3$$
$$y = 1$$
$$\Rightarrow -2 \times (-3) + 3 \times 1 = 6 + 3 = 9$$

If these two numbers are the same, then the values you've got for the variables are right.

Tip: You should always check your answer to make sure you've worked out x and y correctly. Then pat yourself on the back if you have. You deserve it.

If you drew the **graph** of each equation you'd get two straight lines.

- The point where these two lines **intersect** gives the **solution** to the two simultaneous equations.

- For the last example, the graph of the two lines $3x + 5y = -4$ and $-2x + 3y = 9$ would look like this:

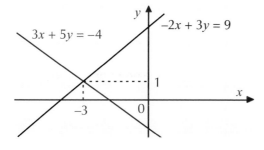

Tip: See Chapter 6 for more on straight line graphs.

- The point where the two lines intersect is $(-3, 1)$
  — which is the same as the answer worked out above.

- However, **not all** simultaneous equations have solutions that work in both equations — for example, no values of x and y satisfy both $2x + 3y = 5$ and $4x + 6y = 7$. This would be obvious if you **sketched the graphs** — the lines are **parallel** so they never intersect.

Tip: If you're asked to find the coordinates of the point of intersection, you should find them using an algebraic method rather than reading off the graph.

Q1   Solve the following simultaneous equations:

a) $2x - 3y = 3$
     $x + 3y = 6$

b) $3x + 2y = 7$
     $7x - y = -12$

c) $4x + 3y = -4$
     $6x - 4y = 11$

d) $7x - 6y = 4$
     $11x + 9y = -6$

e) $6x + 2y - 8 = 0$
     $4x + 3 = -3y$

f) $2x + 18y - 21 = 0$
     $-14y = 3x + 14$

g) $2x + 16y = 10$
     $64y - 5 + 3x = 0$

Q1 Hint: Don't forget to rearrange the equations so they're in the form $ax + by = c$. It makes life much easier.

Q2   Find the point of intersection of each pair of straight lines.

a) $y = 2x - 3$
     $y = \frac{1}{2}x + 3$

b) $y = -\frac{2}{3}x + 7$
     $y = \frac{1}{2}x + \frac{21}{2}$

c) $x + 2y + 5 = 0$
     $3x - 5y - 7 = 0$

d) $2x - 3y = 7$
     $5x - \frac{15}{2}y = 9$

e) $8x = -3y + 10$
     $9y = 3 - 6x$

f) $7x - 5y = 15$
     $2x - 9 = 3y$

Q2 Hint: Although this question is phrased differently to Q1, it's still asking you to do the same thing — but remember, not all simultaneous equations have solutions (see previous page).

Q3   Three roads on a map are modelled (in (x, y) coordinates) by the following equations:

     A: $5x + 2y = -11$ B: $2x = y + 1$ C: $5y = 13 + x$

     Signposts are placed at every intersection of the roads. Find the coordinates of all of these signposts.

Simultaneous equations — if one is not linear

Solving by substitution

Elimination is great for simple equations, but it won't always work. Sometimes one of the equations has not just x's and y's in it — but bits with x^2 and y^2 as well. When one of the equations has quadratic terms, you can **only** use the **substitution** method. The substitution method involves **four** steps:

1) **Isolate variable in linear equation**
    Rearrange the linear equation to get either x or y on its own.

2) **Substitute into the quadratic equation**
    — to get a quadratic equation in just one variable.

3) **Solve to get values for one variable**
    — either by factorising or using the quadratic formula.

4) **Stick these values in the linear equation**
    — to find corresponding values for the other variable.

Tip: Always check your answer at the end too, by putting the values back into the original equations.

Example 1

Solve the simultaneous equations $-x + 2y = 5$ and $x^2 + y^2 = 25$.

- Start by labelling the two equations. Here the linear equation is labelled ①, and the equation with quadratic terms is labelled ②.

$$① \quad -x + 2y = 5$$
$$② \quad x^2 + y^2 = 25$$

Tip: The linear equation is the one with only x's and y's in. The quadratic is the one with x^2 or y^2 terms.

- Rearrange the linear equation so that either x or y is on its own on one side of the equals sign.

$$① \quad -x + 2y = 5$$
$$\Rightarrow \quad x = 2y - 5$$

- Substitute this expression into the quadratic...

$$\text{Sub into } ② : \qquad x^2 + y^2 = 25$$
$$\Rightarrow (2y - 5)^2 + y^2 = 25$$

- ...and then rearrange this into the form $ax^2 + bx + c = 0$, so you can solve it — either by factorising or using the quadratic formula.

$$\Rightarrow (4y^2 - 20y + 25) + y^2 = 25$$
$$\Rightarrow 5y^2 - 20y = 0$$
$$\Rightarrow 5y(y - 4) = 0$$
$$\Rightarrow y = 0 \text{ or } y = 4$$

Tip: You'll often, but not always, get a pair of solutions if one of the equations is quadratic.

- Finally put both these values back into the linear equation to find corresponding values for x:

When $y = 0$:

$$① \quad -x + 2y = 5$$
$$\Rightarrow x = -5$$

When $y = 4$:

$$① \quad -x + 2y = 5$$
$$-x + 8 = 5$$
$$\Rightarrow x = 3$$

- So solving these simultaneous equations has actually produced a **pair** of solutions:

$$x = -5, y = 0 \quad \text{and} \quad x = 3, y = 4$$

- Now, **check your answers** by putting each set of values back into the original equations.

$x = -5, y = 0$:

$$-(-5) + 2 \times 0 = 5 \checkmark$$
$$(-5)^2 + 0^2 = 25 \checkmark$$

$x = 3, y = 4$:

$$-(3) + 2 \times 4 = 5 \checkmark$$
$$3^2 + 4^2 = 25 \checkmark$$

Tip: The solutions to simultaneous equations are just the points where their graphs meet. If there are 2 solutions, the graphs will cross in 2 places. If there are no solutions, the graphs will never meet.

- The equation $x^2 + y^2 = 25$ is actually a circle about the origin with radius 5 and the linear equation is just a standard straight line.

- So by solving the simultaneous equations you're actually finding the two points where the line passes through the circle — the points $(-5, 0)$ and $(3, 4)$.

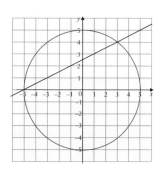

Tip: Circles are covered in more detail in Chapter 6.

Example 2

Find any points of intersection of the following graphs:

a) $y = x^2 - 4x + 5$ **and** $y = 2x - 4$

- Label the two equations:

$$\text{①} \quad y = x^2 - 4x + 5$$
$$\text{②} \quad y = 2x - 4$$

- Substitute ② in ① :

$$2x - 4 = x^2 - 4x + 5$$

- Rearrange and solve:

$$x^2 - 6x + 9 = 0$$
$$(x - 3)^2 = 0$$
$$x = 3 \quad \longleftarrow \quad$$

Double root — i.e. you only get 1 solution from the quadratic equation.

- In Equation ② this gives:

$$y = 2 \times 3 - 4$$
$$y = 2$$

- So there's one solution: $x = 3$, $y = 2$

- Since the equations have only one solution, the two graphs only meet at one point: (3, 2).

- The straight line is actually a **tangent** to the curve.

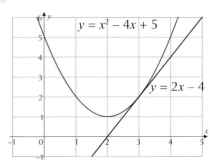

b) $y = x^2 - 4x + 5$ **and** $y = 2x - 5$

- Label the two equations:

$$\text{①} \quad y = x^2 - 4x + 5$$
$$\text{②} \quad y = 2x - 5$$

- Substitute ② in ① :

$$2x - 5 = x^2 - 4x + 5$$

- Rearrange and try to solve with the quadratic formula (since it won't factorise). Start by finding the discriminant:

$$x^2 - 6x + 10 = 0$$
$$b^2 - 4ac = (-6)^2 - 4 \times 1 \times 10$$
$$= 36 - 40 = -4$$

Tip: Page 38 has all you need to know about the discriminant.

- $b^2 - 4ac < 0$, so the quadratic has no real roots.

  > So the simultaneous equations have no solutions.

- This means the graphs never meet:

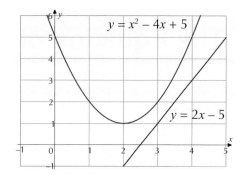

Exercise 2.2

Q1 Solve the following simultaneous equations using substitution:

a) $y = 4x + 3$
$2y - 3x = 1$

b) $5x + 2y = 16$
$2y - x - 4 = 0$

Q2 Solve the following simultaneous equations:

a) $y = 2x + 5$
$y = x^2 - x + 1$

b) $y = 2x^2 - 3$
$y = 3x + 2$

c) $2x^2 - xy = 6$
$y - 3x + 7 = 0$

d) $xy = 6$
$2y - x + 4 = 0$

e) $y = x^2 - 2x - 3$
$y + x + 8 = 0$

f) $y = 2x^2 - 3x + 5$
$5x - y = 3$

g) $2x^2 + 3y^2 + 18x = 347$
$4x + y = 7$

Q3 Find the points of intersection of the following curves and straight lines:

a) $y = \frac{1}{2}x^2 + 4x - 8$
$y = 4 + \frac{3}{2}x$

b) $y = 2x^2 + x - 6$
$5x - y + 10 = 0$

c) $x^2 + y^2 = 50$
$x + 2y = 5$

d) $2x^2 - y + 3x + 1 = 0$
$y - x - 5 = 0$

Q4 a) Solve the simultaneous equations $x^2 + y^2 = 10$ and $x - 3y + 10 = 0$.

b) Say what your answer to part a) means geometrically.

> **Q4b) Hint:** Here, you don't need to draw a graph, just describe what your answer to part a) means.

Q5 Without drawing the graphs, determine whether the following curves and lines intersect at one or two points, or do not intersect at all:

a) $y = x^2 + 6x - 7$ and $y = 2x - 3$

b) $3x^2 + 4y^2 + 6x = 9$ and $x + 2y = 3$

c) $xy + 2x - y = 8$ and $x + y = 1$

1. The Equation of a Straight Line

Learning Objectives:

- Be able to find the equation of a straight line passing through two given points, or through one point with a certain gradient.

- Write straight line equations in any of the three forms:
  $y - y_1 = m(x - x_1)$,
  $y = mx + c$ and
  $ax + by + c = 0$.

Any straight line can be described by an equation made up of an x term, y term and constant term (though one of these may be zero). There are three standard ways of arranging straight line equations that you need to learn.

$$y - y_1 = m(x - x_1)$$

This is the first form you need to know.

$$y - y_1 = m(x - x_1)$$

m is the **gradient**
x_1 and y_1 are the **coordinates** of one of the points on the line.

If you're told **two points** that a straight line passes through, this is probably the easiest one to use. You do need to be a little careful using the formula, so here's a method to follow:

1) **LABEL** the points (x_1, y_1) and (x_2, y_2).

2) **GRADIENT** — find this using $m = \dfrac{y_2 - y_1}{x_2 - x_1}$.

3) **WRITE DOWN THE EQUATION** $y - y_1 = m(x - x_1)$.

4) **SUBSTITUTE** in your values for m, x_1 and y_1.

Tip: Remember that the gradient just means the steepness of the line, and in its simplest form is just $m = \dfrac{\text{change in } y}{\text{change in } x}$ for two points.

Example

Find the equation of the line that passes through the points (−3, 10) and (1, 4), and write it in the form $y - y_1 = m(x - x_1)$.

- Label the points.

$$\text{Point 1} \longrightarrow (x_1, y_1) = (-3, 10)$$
$$\text{Point 2} \longrightarrow (x_2, y_2) = (1, 4)$$

- Find the gradient of the line using $m = \dfrac{y_2 - y_1}{x_2 - x_1}$.

$$m = \frac{4 - 10}{1 - (-3)} = \frac{-6}{4} = -\frac{3}{2}$$

- Write down the equation of the line.

$$y - y_1 = m(x - x_1)$$

- Now just substitute in the values for m, x_1 and y_1.

$$x_1 = -3,\ y_1 = 10,\ m = -\frac{3}{2} \longrightarrow y - 10 = -\frac{3}{2}(x - (-3))$$

$$y - 10 = -\frac{3}{2}(x + 3)$$

Tip: Make sure you subtract the same way round on the top and bottom of the fraction. In other words, $\dfrac{y_2 - y_1}{x_1 - x_2}$ **don't** do this:

Tip: This would work fine if you used x_2 and y_2 instead. The equation would look different, but still represent the line.

$y = mx + c$

This form for the straight line equation is probably the most popular — it's certainly the easiest form to make sense of.

$$y = mx + c$$

m is the **gradient** of the line

c is the **y-intercept** (where it crosses the y-axis).

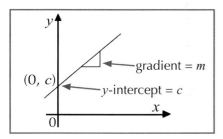

When in $y = mx + c$ form, you can simply read off the values of m and c — and together these give you a fairly good idea of what the graph will look like.

Tip: This diagram shows a straight line with positive values for m and c. A negative value for m would make the graph slope downwards.

As well as being easy to interpret, it's fairly easy to find the equation of a line in $y = mx + c$ form. Here are a couple of examples — you're given different information in each case.

Examples

A straight line has a gradient of –2 and passes through the point (3, 1). Find the equation of the line.

- To find c, sub in the values of m, x and y given in the question.

$$y = mx + c$$
$$1 = (-2 \times 3) + c$$
$$7 = c$$

- Then put your values of m and c into the equation $y = mx + c$.

$$y = -2x + 7$$

Tip: It's a good idea to put the x- and y-values of your given point into your final equation to check it's right.

Find the equation of the straight line that passes through the points (–18, 16) and (10, 2).

- Start by finding m.

$$m = \frac{2-16}{10-(-18)} = \frac{-14}{28} = -\frac{1}{2}$$

- Write down the equation with $m = -\frac{1}{2}$:

$$y = -\frac{1}{2}x + c$$

- Using one of the given points, substitute in values for x and y — this will find c.

$x = 10$, $y = 2$ gives:
$$2 = -\frac{1}{2}(10) + c$$
$$c = 7$$

Tip: This method is very similar to that on the previous page — find the gradient, then put in the x and y values of one of the points.

- So the equation is:

$$y = -\frac{1}{2}x + 7$$

Q1 Give the gradient and y-intercept of the following straight lines:

a) $y = -4x + 11$ 　　　 b) $y = 4 - x$ 　　　 c) $y = 1.7x - 2.3$

Q2 Give equations for the following straight lines in the form $y = mx + c$:

a) gradient -3, y-intercept $(0, 2)$

b) gradient 5, y-intercept $(0, -3)$

c) gradient $\frac{1}{2}$, y-intercept $(0, 6)$

d) gradient 0.8, y-intercept $(0, 1.2)$

Q3 Use the information in the diagrams to the find the equation of each straight line in the form $y = mx + c$.

a)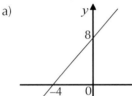

b)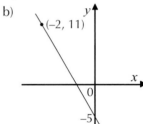

Q4 Find the equations of the lines that pass through the following pairs of points. Give each answer in these forms:

(i) $y - y_1 = m(x - x_1)$ 　　　　 (ii) $y = mx + c$.

a) $(4, 1)$, $(0, -3)$ 　　　　　　 b) $(12, -3)$, $(14, 1)$

c) $(5, 7)$, $(-2, 5)$ 　　　　　　 d) $(-3, 6)$, $(4, -2)$

Q5 Find the equation of the straight line which passes through the point $(-4, -3)$ and has a gradient of $\frac{1}{4}$. Give your answer in the form $y = mx + c$.

Q6 A straight line has gradient 3 and passes through the point $(2, -7)$. State which of the following coordinates are points on the line. (PROBLEM SOLVING)

a) $(1, -10)$ 　　　　　　　 b) $(-2, -7)$

c) $(5, 2)$ 　　　　　　　　 d) $(0.5, 2.5)$

e) $(7, 8)$ 　　　　　　　　 f) $(0, -12)$

Q7 Hint: In this question, x and y have been replaced with t and d respectively.

Q7 The distance travelled by a car is modelled by a straight line graph. At time $t = 0$ hours, it starts at distance $d = 0$ kilometres, and its (MODELLING) speed (the gradient) is a constant 32 km/h throughout the journey.

a) Give the equation of the line in the form $d = mt + c$

b) How long does it take the car to travel a distance of 9.6 km? Give your answer in minutes.

c) Give one criticism of this model.

$ax + by + c = 0$

This is the last form you need to know for straight line equations.

$$ax + by + c = 0 \qquad \text{Where } a, b \text{ and } c \text{ are integers.}$$

Note that this form doesn't involve m. As a result, it's not as easy to work with. So if you're asked to give an equation in this form, it's often easiest just to find it in one of the previous two forms, then rearrange it at the end.

One important thing to remember when using this form is that a, b and c are integers, so you must get rid of any fractions.

Example 1

Find the gradient and y-intercept of the line $7x + 3y - 6 = 0$.

- The easiest way to answer this question is to rearrange the equation into the form $y = mx + c$.

$$7x + 3y - 6 = 0$$
$$\Rightarrow 3y = -7x + 6$$
$$\Rightarrow y = -\frac{7}{3}x + 2$$

- Now compare the equation with $y = mx + c$: $m = -\frac{7}{3}$ and $c = 2$

- So for the line $7x + 3y - 6 = 0$:

$$\text{gradient} = -\frac{7}{3} \text{ and the } y\text{-intercept is } (0, 2)$$

Example 2

Find the equation of the line that passes through the point $(2, -15)$ and has gradient $-\frac{3}{2}$, giving your answer in the form $ax + by + c = 0$, where a, b and c are integers.

- Start by finding the equation in one of the easier forms. We'll use $y - y_1 = m(x - x_1)$ this time, but $y = mx + c$ would be just as easy...

$$m = -\frac{3}{2} \text{ gives: } \quad y - y_1 = -\frac{3}{2}(x - x_1)$$

- Now sub in $x_1 = 2$ and $y_1 = -15$:

$$y + 15 = -\frac{3}{2}(x - 2)$$

- Now you can start rearranging into $ax + by + c = 0$ form:

$$y + \frac{3}{2}x + 15 - 3 = 0$$
$$y + \frac{3}{2}x + 12 = 0$$
$$\Rightarrow 3x + 2y + 24 = 0$$

Tip: If you end up with an equation like $\frac{3}{2}x - \frac{4}{3}y + 6 = 0$, where you've got a 2 and a 3 on the bottom of the fractions — multiply everything by the lowest common multiple of 2 and 3, i.e. 6.

Q1 Write the following equations in the form $ax + by + c = 0$, where a, b and c are integers.

   a) $y = 5x + 2$ b) $3y = -\frac{1}{2}x + 3$

   c) $2(x - 1) = 4y - 1$ d) $7x - 3 = 2y + 6$

   e) $\frac{1}{2}(4x + 3) = 3(y - 2)$ f) $3(y - 4) = 4(x - 3)$

Q2 Hint: You'll need to convert to a different form so that you can interpret the equations.

Q2 Find the gradient and y-intercept of the following lines:

   a) $6x - 2y + 3 = 0$ b) $-9x + 3y - 12 = 0$

   c) $-x - 4y - 2 = 0$ d) $7x + 8y + 11 = 0$

Q3 Find the equation of the line that passes through the following points. Write your answer in the form $ax + by + c = 0$, where a, b and c are integers.

   a) $(5, 2)$, $(3, 4)$ b) $(9, -1)$, $(7, 2)$

   c) $(-6, 1)$, $(4, 0)$ d) $(-12, 3)$, $(5, 7)$

Q4 Hint: Again, it's easiest to find the equation in a different form, then convert it at the end.

Q4 Find the equation of the lines below in the form $ax + by + c = 0$, where a, b and c are integers.

   a)

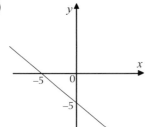

   b)

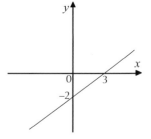

Q5 At a cafe, a small cup of coffee costs £x and a large cup of coffee costs £y. Robert buys 3 small cups and 4 large cups for £18.

   a) Write this as an equation in the form $ax + by + c = 0$, where a, b and c are all integers.

Q5b) Hint: Draw, not sketch — you might want to use graph/squared paper for this.

   b) Draw the straight line graph of this equation.

   c) Amani buys 1 small cup and 2 large cups for £8. Write a second equation (in the same form) to represent this and plot the graph on the same set of axes.

Q5d) Hint: Here you're really just solving the simultaneous equations graphically.

   d) Write down the cost of a small cup of coffee and the cost of a large cup of coffee.

2. Parallel and Perpendicular Lines

You can work out the equation of a line, if 1) it is parallel or perpendicular to a line you already know the equation of, and 2) you know a point that the line passes through. The first thing you need to do is find the gradient of the line.

Learning Objectives:

- Be able to find the equation of a line parallel or perpendicular to a given line through a given point.

- Know the conditions for two straight lines to be parallel or perpendicular to each other.

Parallel lines

Parallel lines have **equal gradient** — that's what makes them parallel. So when finding the equation of a line parallel to a line with a given equation, you know the gradient will be the same for both.

Example 1

Find the line parallel to $y = \frac{3}{4}x - \frac{7}{4}$ that:

a) **has a y-intercept of (0, 4)**

- Parallel lines have the same gradient, so the gradient of the line you want is also $\frac{3}{4}$.

- You then need to find c — this is just the y-intercept which we already know is at 4.

- So putting m and c into the equation $y = mx + c$ gives: $\boxed{y = \frac{3}{4}x + 4}$

b) **passes through the point (3, –1).**

- The gradient is $\frac{3}{4}$. So the new equation will be: $\boxed{y = \frac{3}{4}x + c}$

- You then need to find c. We know that the line passes through point $(3, -1)$, so stick $x = 3$ and $y = -1$ into the equation to find c:

$$-1 = \frac{3}{4}(3) + c \quad \Rightarrow \quad c = -\frac{13}{4}$$

- So the equation of the line is: $\boxed{y = \frac{3}{4}x - \frac{13}{4}}$

Example 2

Find the line parallel to $2x - 8y + 11 = 0$ that passes through the point (3, –1). Give your equation in the form $ax + by + c = 0$, where a, b and c are integers.

- First, put the given line in a more useful form, i.e. $y = mx + c$...

$$2x - 8y + 11 = 0$$
$$-8y = -2x - 11$$
$$y = \frac{1}{4}x + \frac{11}{8}$$

- The gradient of the given line is $\frac{1}{4}$, so that's also the gradient of the parallel line you want.

$$y = \frac{1}{4}x + c$$

$$x = 3 \text{ and } y = -1 \longrightarrow -1 = \frac{1}{4}(3) + c \quad \Rightarrow \quad c = -\frac{7}{4}$$

- So $y = \frac{1}{4}x - \frac{7}{4}$ which rearranges to $\boxed{x - 4y - 7 = 0}$

You may be asked whether two lines are parallel or not. To work this out you need to **compare** their gradients. This is easiest when both equations are in the **same form** — so one or both equations may need **rearranging**.

Example 3

Line l_1 is given by the equation $y = \frac{1}{2}x + 6$ and line l_2 is given by the equation $3x + 6y - 1 = 0$. Find out whether the lines are parallel.

- To compare the gradients you want both lines in the form $y = mx + c$. So rearrange line l_2 into this form:

$$3x + 6y - 1 = 0$$
$$\Rightarrow 6y = -3x + 1$$
$$\Rightarrow y = -\frac{3}{6}x + \frac{1}{6}$$
$$\Rightarrow y = -\frac{1}{2}x + \frac{1}{6}$$

- Then compare the two equations:

$$y = \frac{1}{2}x + 6 \quad \longleftarrow \quad \text{Line } l_1$$
$$y = -\frac{1}{2}x + \frac{1}{6} \quad \longleftarrow \quad \text{Line } l_2$$

- You are only concerned about the gradient so look at the bit before the x. Here line l_1 has a gradient of $\frac{1}{2}$ and line l_2 has a gradient of $-\frac{1}{2}$.

- So:

  The lines l_1 and l_2 are NOT parallel.

Tip: Rearranging the equations into the form $y = mx + c$, rather than $ax + by + c = 0$, makes it a hundred million times* easier to compare the gradients.   *Approximately.

Exercise 2.1

Q1 State which of the following straight lines are parallel to $y = -3x - 1$.

a) $2y = -6x + 2$

b) $y - 3x - 1 = 0$

c) $6y + 18x = 7$

d) $\frac{1}{3}(y + 1) = x$

e) $-9y - 2 = 27x$

f) $4y = 12x$

Q2 Find the equations of the parallel lines shown in blue.
Write them in the form $ax + by + c = 0$, where a, b and c are integers.

a) $y = 4x - 1$
(3, 2)

b) (-4, -5)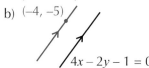
$4x - 2y - 1 = 0$

Q3 State whether the following pairs of lines are parallel.

a) $y = 2x + 1$

$y + \frac{1}{2}x = 1$

b) $2x - 3y + 1 = 0$

$y = \frac{2}{3}x + 2$

c) $-5x + 4y + 3 = 0$

$8y = 10x$

Q4 Line A passes through the point (4, 3) and is parallel to the line $2x - 4y + 3 = 0$. Find the equation of line A in the form:

a) $y = mx + c$,

b) $ax + by + c = 0$.

Perpendicular lines

Finding the equations of **perpendicular** lines (or '**normals**') is just as easy as finding the equations of parallel lines — you just need to know one key fact:

> The gradients of perpendicular lines **multiply to give –1**.

Tip: Remember, 'perpendicular' just means 'at right angles'.

Which means:

> Gradient of the perpendicular line = –1 ÷ **the gradient of the other one**.

Tip: So if a line has a gradient of m, a line perpendicular to it will have a gradient of $-\dfrac{1}{m}$.

Example 1

Find the equation of the line perpendicular to $y = \dfrac{1}{3}x - 1$ that passes through (–2, 4).

- Use the gradient rule:

Gradient of perpendicular line = –1 ÷ gradient of the other one

$$= -1 \div \frac{1}{3} = -3$$

So: $y = -3x + c$

Tip: Remember, to divide by a fraction, turn it upside down and then multiply by it.

- To find c, put the coordinates (–2, 4) into the equation

$$4 = (-3) \times (-2) + c$$

$$\Rightarrow c = 4 - 6 = -2$$

- So the equation of the line is: $\boxed{y = -3x - 2}$

Example 2

Find the equation of the line perpendicular to $7x - 3y + 5 = 0$ that passes through the point (–3, –11).

- Start by converting the equation into a more useful form:

$$7x - 3y + 5 = 0$$

$$-3y = -7x - 5$$

$$y = \frac{7}{3}x + \frac{5}{3} \quad \longleftarrow \text{ So the gradient is } \frac{7}{3}.$$

- Now use the gradient rule:

Gradient of perpendicular line = $-1 \div \dfrac{7}{3} = -\dfrac{3}{7}$

So we have: $y = -\dfrac{3}{7}x + c$

- Substitute in the coordinates (–3, –11) to find c:

$$-11 = -\frac{3}{7}(-3) + c$$

$$c = -11 - \frac{9}{7} = -\frac{86}{7}$$

- So the perpendicular line has equation:

$$y = -\frac{3}{7}x - \frac{86}{7} \quad \Rightarrow \quad \boxed{3x + 7y + 86 = 0}$$

You can use the fact that the gradients of perpendicular lines **multiply** to give **–1** to work out whether two lines are perpendicular.

Example 3

Show that the line $2x + 5y + 3 = 0$ is perpendicular to $y = \frac{5}{2}x + 5$.

- To work out if they are perpendicular, first find the gradient of both lines.

- Rearrange $2x + 5y + 3 = 0$ into the form $y = mx + c$ to find its gradient:

$$2x + 5y + 3 = 0$$
$$\Rightarrow 5y = -2x - 3$$
$$\Rightarrow y = -\frac{2}{5}x - \frac{3}{5}$$

- So the gradient of this line is $-\frac{2}{5}$.

- Comparing $y = \frac{5}{2}x + 5$ to $y = mx + c$, its gradient is $\frac{5}{2}$.

- The two lines are perpendicular if the gradients of the two lines **multiply** together to make **–1**.

$$-\frac{2}{5} \times \frac{5}{2} = -1$$

The two lines are perpendicular.

Example 4

The points A (2, 5) and B (6, 0) lie on the line l_1. The line l_2 is perpendicular to l_1 and passes through point A.

a) Find an equation for l_2 in the form $ax + by + c = 0$, where a, b and c are integers.

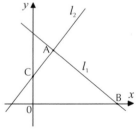

- To find the equation of l_2 we need to find its gradient. We know two points on the line l_1, so work out its gradient first.

$$(x_1, y_1) = (2, 5), (x_2, y_2) = (6, 0)$$
$$m = \frac{0 - 5}{6 - 2} = -\frac{5}{4}$$

- The gradient of a perpendicular line is: $-1 \div$ the other one. So the gradient of l_2 is:

$$m = -1 \div -\frac{5}{4}$$
$$\Rightarrow m = \frac{4}{5}$$

- So l_2 is:
$$y = \frac{4}{5}x + c$$

- To find c, put the coordinates for point A (2, 5) into $y = \frac{4}{5}x + c$.

$$5 = \frac{4}{5} \times 2 + c$$
$$\Rightarrow c = \frac{17}{5}$$

- So the equation of the line l_2 is:

$$y = \frac{4}{5}x + \frac{17}{5} \quad \Rightarrow \quad \boxed{4x - 5y + 17 = 0}$$

b) Find the coordinates of point C.

- At C, $x = 0$. So put $x = 0$ into the equation $y = \frac{4}{5}x + \frac{17}{5}$:

$$\Rightarrow y = \frac{4}{5} \times 0 + \frac{17}{5} = \frac{17}{5}$$

So the coordinates of point C are $\left(0, \frac{17}{5}\right)$.

Tip: This is actually the value of c you just found.

Exercise 2.2

Q1 Find the equations of the dotted lines.
Give your answers in the form $y = mx + c$

a)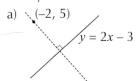

b)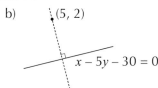

Q2 Find the equations of the lines which are perpendicular to each of the following lines and pass through the points given. Give your answers in the form $ax + by + c = 0$, where a, b, and c are integers.

a) $y = \frac{1}{4}x - 1$ $\quad(-1, 2)$
b) $2x + 3y - 1 = 0$ $\quad(-3, -1)$
c) $5x - 10y + 1 = 0$ $\quad(6, -5)$
d) $y = \frac{3}{2}x + 2$ $\quad(2, 1)$

Q3 Work out which of the following pairs of lines are perpendicular.

a) $y = \frac{4}{3}x - 2$ and $3x + 4y - 1 = 0$

b) $y = \frac{3}{2}x - 1$ and $3x + 2y - 3 = 0$

c) $4x - y + 3 = 0$ and $2x + 8y + 1 = 0$

Q4 Triangle ABC has vertices at A(0, 2), B(4, 3) and C(5, –1).
   a) Find the equations of the lines AB, BC and AC in the form $y = mx + c$.
   b) What type of triangle is ABC? Explain why.

Q5 Line A passes through the point (a, b) and is perpendicular to the line $3x - 2y = 6$. Find an equation of line A in terms of a and b.

Q6 The perpendicular bisector of a line segment AB is the line that is perpendicular to AB, passing through its midpoint. Find the equation of the perpendicular bisector of the line AB, where A = (1, 4) and B = (5, 2).

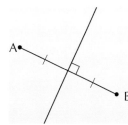

3. Proportion

Learning Objectives:

- Be able to interpret direct proportion and convert a statement of proportion into an algebraic equation.
- Be able to use proportion to find values and calculate the constant of proportionality.

Proportion is just a way of describing how two variables are related. There are a few different types of proportion, but the main one you need to know about is direct proportion.

Direct proportion

If two variables are in **direct proportion**, it means that changing one variable will change the other by the same scale factor. So doubling one variable will result in the other variable doubling, and the same for tripling, halving, etc. In fact, multiplying or dividing by **any** constant will have the same effect on both.

To say that "y is directly proportional to x", you can write:

$$y \propto x$$

This is equivalent to writing:

$$y = kx$$

where k is a constant. k is sometimes called the **constant of proportionality**.

If you compare this equation to $y = mx + c$, you can see that the graph of two variables in direct proportion is a straight line. The gradient of the line is the constant of proportionality, k, and the y-intercept is 0 — i.e. the line passes through the origin (0, 0).

Example 1

The circumference of a circle, C, is directly proportional to its radius, r.

a) What is the constant of proportionality linking C and r?

- The question says that $C \propto r$, which is the same as saying $C = kr$.
- You know that the circumference of a circle is given by $2\pi r$.
- So $kr = 2\pi r \implies \boxed{k = 2\pi}$

b) A circle with a radius of p cm has a circumference of 13 cm. Find the circumference of a circle with a radius of 2.5p cm.

- You could use the formula to find p, but you don't need to.
- The radius of the second circle is 2.5 times the size of the original, so the circumference will be 2.5 times the original as well.
- So $C = 2.5 \times 13 = \boxed{32.5 \text{ cm}}$

c) Sketch the graph of C against r.

- The equation of the line is $C = 2\pi r$, which is a straight line through the origin with gradient 2π:

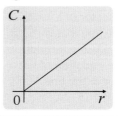

Tip: Any time you have two variables in direct proportion, the graph will be a straight line through the origin.

Example 2

The amount of money that Tina earns, y, is directly proportional to the number of hours that she works, x. Given that $y = £91$ when $x = 7$:

a) **Find the constant of proportionality.**

$y \propto x$, so first write this as $y = kx$, then substitute $y = 91$ and $x = 7$:

$91 = k \times 7 \Rightarrow k = 91 \div 7 = \boxed{13}$

b) **Find how much she would earn if she worked for 4 hours.**

Substitute $x = 4$ into your equation $y = kx$:

$y = 13x \Rightarrow y = 13 \times 4 = \boxed{£52}$

c) **How many hours does she need to work in order to earn £104?**

Now, $y = 104$, so:

$104 = 13x \Rightarrow x = 104 \div 13 = \boxed{8 \text{ hours}}$

Proportion can also be used for relationships that are **not linear**. These are not 'direct' proportion, but they do work in a similar way. For example:

$$y \propto \frac{1}{x} \Rightarrow y = \frac{k}{x}$$
$$V \propto r^3 \Rightarrow V = kr^3$$
$$\omega \propto \frac{1}{\sqrt{m}} \Rightarrow \omega = \frac{k}{\sqrt{m}}$$

You might see these written as e.g. "y is proportional to the cube root of x" instead of $y \propto \sqrt[3]{x}$. In any case, you can always replace the $\propto$ with "$= k \times$" to convert a proportion statement into an equation.

Tip: When $y \propto \frac{1}{x}$, this is known as **inverse proportion** — when one doubles, the other halves (and so on). Similarly, "y is inversely proportional to x^2" means $y \propto \frac{1}{x^2}$.

Exercise 3.1

Q1 Given that $y \propto x$ in each case, find the value of a if:

a) $y = 24$ when $x = 8$ and $y = a$ when $x = 5$

b) $y = 13$ when $x = 26$ and $y = a$ when $x = 14$

c) $y = 28$ when $x = 7$ and $y = 96$ when $x = a$

d) $y = a$ when $x = 3$ and $y = 21$ when $x = 6$

e) $y = 36$ when $x = a$ and $y = a$ when $x = 9$ $(a > 0)$

Q2 Prove that if $y \propto x$ and $y \propto z$, then $x \propto z$.

Q3 For each equation below, explain whether $y \propto x$:

a) $y = 7x + 2$

b) $y = ax - bx$ (a and b constants)

c) $y = 2x + 2x^2 - 2 - x - 2x^2$

d) $y = (x + 3)^2 - (x - 3)^2$

Q4 Siobhan is modelling the motion of a sliding box. She finds that the frictional force on the box is directly proportional to its mass. If the frictional force, F, is 15 N when its mass, m, is 12 kg, estimate the frictional force when the mass of the box is increased to 18 kg.

Chapter 6 Coordinate Geometry, Graphs and Circles   85

4. Curve Sketching

Learning Objectives:

- Be able to sketch the graphs of simple cubic and quartic functions.

- Be able to sketch the graphs of reciprocal functions and functions with other negative powers.

- Know what the term asymptote means.

Being able to sketch the graph of a curve is an important skill at A-Level. It can help you get your head round tricky questions. Usually, you only need a rough sketch of a graph — so just knowing the basic shapes of these graphs will do.

Cubic and quartic functions

Cubic functions are **polynomials** that have an x^3 term in them as the highest power of x. They can be written $y = ax^3 + bx^2 + cx + d$ (for $a \neq 0$). Similarly, **quartics** go up to x^4 — they can be written $y = ax^4 + bx^3 + cx^2 + dx + e$.

Here are the graphs for some cubic and quartic functions:

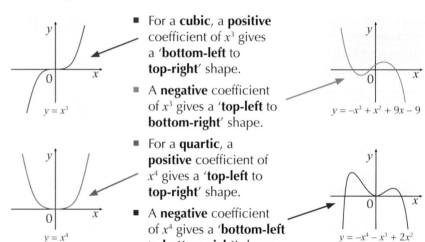

- For a **cubic**, a **positive** coefficient of x^3 gives a '**bottom-left** to **top-right**' shape.

- A **negative** coefficient of x^3 gives a '**top-left** to **bottom-right**' shape.

- For a **quartic**, a **positive** coefficient of x^4 gives a '**top-left** to **top-right**' shape.

- A **negative** coefficient of x^4 gives a '**bottom-left** to **bottom-right**' shape.

Tip: The other terms in the polynomial determine whether the graph has 'dips' in it. The constant term is the y-intercept — just like c in the equation of a straight line ($y = mx + c$ — see page 75).

In general, for any graph in the form $y = kx^n$ (when n is positive):

EVEN

- When n is **EVEN**, you get a u-shape or an n-shape.

- If k is **POSITIVE**, you get a u-shape above the x-axis.

- And if k is **NEGATIVE**, you get an n-shape below the x-axis.

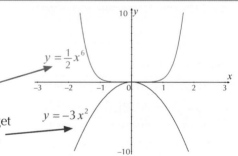

Tip: The graphs for negative values of n are covered on pages 89-90.

ODD

- When n is **ODD**, you get a 'corner-to-corner' shape.

- If k is **POSITIVE**, you get a 'bottom-left to top-right' shape.

- And if k is **NEGATIVE**, you get a 'top-left to bottom-right' shape.

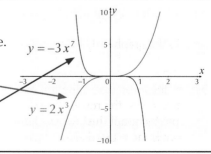

Tip: Remember, this is the basic shape for $y = kx^n$ — if there are other terms in the polynomial, the graph might have 'dips' in it, like the ones above.

You may be asked to sketch some simple cubic and quartic graphs.
The key to this is finding where the graph **crosses the axes**.

- To find where a graph crosses the y-axis, just set $x = 0$ and find the value of y.

- The easiest way to find where it crosses the x-axis is to **factorise** the polynomial — it crosses the x-axis when **each bracket** is set equal to **0**.

When you're sketching cubics and quartics, watch out for any **repeated roots**. Repeated roots occur when a **factor** is repeated (i.e. when a bracket is squared, cubed, etc.).

- A **squared** bracket means it's a **double root**, and the graph will only **touch** the x-axis, not cross it, at this point (see part b of the example below).

- A **cubed** bracket means a **triple root**, which still crosses the x-axis, but **flattens out** as it does so (see part c on the next page).

Examples

Sketch the graphs of the following cubic functions.

a) $f(x) = x(x - 1)(2x + 1)$

- If you multiplied out the brackets, you'd get $2x^3 - x^2 - x$. But it's just the $2x^3$ term we're interested in for deciding the rough shape.

- Since the coefficient of x^3 is positive, the graph will have a **bottom-left** to **top-right** shape.

- The graph crosses the y-axis at $f(0) = 0(-1)(1) = 0$.

- Now we need to find where the graph crosses the x-axis, i.e. where $f(x) = 0$. The cubic is actually given in factorised form here, so we can simply read off the solutions.

$$x(x - 1)(2x + 1) = 0 \implies x = 0, 1 \text{ and } -\frac{1}{2}$$

- So the curve crosses the x-axis **three times** and will look like this:

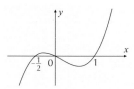

Tip: You might have to factorise the cubic yourself to find the roots — see pages 47-55.

Tip: The dip means the graph crosses the x-axis 3 times, creating the 3 roots.

b) $g(x) = (x - 3)^2(x + 1)$

- Multiplying out the brackets gives $x^3 - 5x^2 + 3x + 9$.

- Again, the coefficient of x^3 is positive here, so this graph will also have a bottom-left to top-right shape.

- Now find where it crosses both axes:

$g(0) = (0 - 3)^2 \times (0 + 1) = 9$, so the y-intercept is $(0, 9)$.

- For the x-intercepts, find where $g(x) = 0$. Again, the function is helpfully factorised...

$$(x - 3)^2(x + 1) = 0 \implies x = 3 \text{ and } x = -1$$

- So the graph only crosses the x-axis **twice** and looks like this:

Tip: Again you don't actually need to multiply out the whole function — you only need to know what the x^3 term will be.

The $(x - 3)$ bracket is **squared**, so the cubic has a **double root** at $x = 3$ — the result of this is that the graph **just touches** the x-axis there but doesn't cross it.

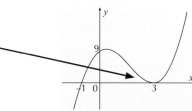

c) $h(x) = (2 - x)^3$

Expanding the brackets gives $h(x) = 8 - 12x + 6x^2 - x^3$.

- This time, the coefficient of x^3 is **negative**, so the graph will have a **top-left to bottom-right** shape.

- $x = 0$ gives a y-intercept of 8.

- The function is zero **only once,** at $\boxed{x = 2}$ — this is a **triple root** (you know this because the $(2 - x)$ bracket is cubed).

- The graph looks like this:

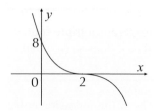

Tip: This graph is actually just the graph of $y = -x^3$ shifted 2 to the right. Graph transformations like this are covered a little later in the chapter.

Exercise 4.1

Q1 Hint: If you're not sure exactly what the graph will do, stick some values for x into the function. Some good places to start are numbers near to the roots, or very large positive and negative numbers (which help to check what happens at the extremes).

Q1   The diagram shows four graphs A, B, C and D.
State which graph would represent each of the following functions.

a) $y = -1.5x^4$ b) $y = 0.5x^3$ c) $y = 2x^6$ d) $y = -3x^3$

A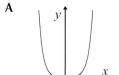

B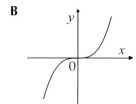

C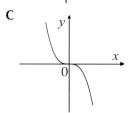

D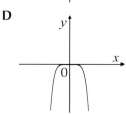

For Questions 2-4, sketch the graphs of the functions, showing clearly where they meet the x-axis.

Q2   a) $y = x(x + 2)(x - 3)$

   b) $y = (x + 1)(2x - 1)(x - 3)$

   c) $y = x(x + 1)(2 - x)$

Q3   a) $y = x^2(2x - 5)$

   b) $y = x(5 - x)^2$

   c) $y = (1 - x)(2 - x)^2$

Q4   a) $y = -5x^2(3x - 2)$

   b) $y = (7 - x)(9 - 2x)(3 - x)$

   c) $y = (4 + x)^3$

Q5 a) Factorise completely $x^3 - 7x^2 + 12x$.

b) Use your answer to part a) to sketch the graph of $y = x^3 - 7x^2 + 12x$, showing clearly where the graph meets the coordinate axes.

Q5a) Hint: Take a look at pages 47-55 for help with factorising cubics.

Q6 Sketch the graphs of these functions, showing clearly where the graph meets the coordinate axes.

a) $y = x^3 - 16x$ b) $y = 2x^3 - 12x^2 + 18x$

Q7 Sketch the graph of $y = f(x)$, where:

a) $f(x) = 3x(x - 4)^2(2x - 1)$ b) $f(x) = -3x^2(2x - 7)^2$

Q8 Sketch the graphs of the following quartics:

a) $y = x^2(x^2 - 9x + 14)$

b) $y = (x + 1)(2 - 3x)(4x^2 - 9)$

c) $y = (x - 5)(2x^3 + 5x^2 - 3x)$

Q8 Hint: Factorise the quartic, then work out the coefficient of the x^4 term to see if it's positive or negative.

Reciprocal functions and negative powers

Reciprocal functions are those of the form $y = \dfrac{k}{x}$, where k is a constant. The graph of a reciprocal function always has **asymptotes**.

> An **asymptote** of a curve is a **line** which the curve gets infinitely close to, but **never** touches.

You need to be able to sketch the graphs of reciprocal functions. Here are some examples:

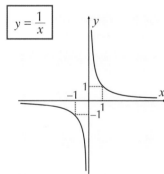

- The graph never crosses the x- or y-axes, as you can't divide by zero.

- So the y-axis is a vertical asymptote $(x = 0)$ and the x-axis is a horizontal asymptote $(y = 0)$.

Tip: Normally, to find where the graph crosses the x- and y-axes, you'd set $y = 0$ and $x = 0$, respectively. Doing that here means you'd end up with a zero as the denominator.

Tip: For reciprocal graphs of the form $y = \dfrac{1}{x + a} + b$, the asymptotes will be at $y = b$ and $x = -a$ (see Example 2 on page 92).

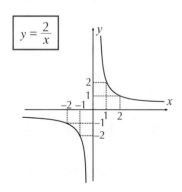

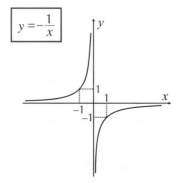

Tip: As always with curve sketching, it's a good idea to pop in some real values of x to see what happens.

For these graphs, try very small positive and negative numbers, e.g. 0.001 and –0.001, and very large positive and negative numbers, e.g. 10 000 and –10 000.

The function $y = \dfrac{k}{x}$ can also be written as $y = kx^{-1}$. In general, **negative powers** of x (i.e. functions of the form $y = kx^{-n}$, such as $y = 2x^{-3}$) can also be written in the form $y = \dfrac{k}{x^n}$. You need to be familiar with functions written in either form.

For any graph in the form $y = \dfrac{k}{x^n}$ or kx^{-n}:

EVEN

- When n is EVEN, you get a graph with two bits next to each other.

- If k is POSITIVE, both parts of the graph are above the x-axis

- And if k is NEGATIVE, the graph is below the x-axis.

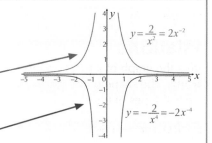

$y = \dfrac{2}{x^2} = 2x^{-2}$

$y = -\dfrac{2}{x^4} = -2x^{-4}$

Tip: All these graphs have asymptotes of $x = 0$ and $y = 0$.

ODD

- When n is ODD, you get a graph with two bits opposite each other.

- If k is POSITIVE, the graph is in the top-right and bottom-left quadrants.

- And if k is NEGATIVE, it's in the top-left and the bottom-right.

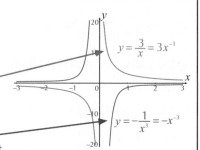

$y = \dfrac{3}{x} = 3x^{-1}$

$y = -\dfrac{1}{x^3} = -x^{-3}$

Exercise 4.2

Q1 Hint: You could work this out easily by popping in a positive and negative value of x into each function and seeing what you get.

Q1 The diagram shows four graphs A, B, C and D.
State which graph would represent each of the following functions:

   a) $y = x^{-2}$ b) $y = -3x^{-3}$ c) $y = -\dfrac{3}{x^4}$ d) $y = 2x^{-5}$

Q2 Sketch the graphs of the following reciprocal functions, showing the points where $x = 1$ and $x = -1$:

   a) $y = 1.5x^{-5}$ b) $y = 7x^{-2}$ c) $y = -\dfrac{6}{x}$ d) $y = -1.2x^{-4}$

Q3 a) Sketch the graphs of $y = 3x^{-2}$ and $y = -x^3 - 2x^2$ on the same axes.
    b) Find the number of real roots of $3x^{-2} = -x^3 - 2x^2$.

Q3-4 Hint: Two graphs $y = f(x)$ and $y = g(x)$ will intersect at the points where $f(x) = g(x)$.

Q4 a) Use graph paper to draw the graphs of $y = -\dfrac{2}{x}$ and $y = 4 - x^2$ on the same axes for $-3 \leq x \leq 3$. Use a scale of 2 cm for 1 unit.
    b) Use your answer to part a) to estimate the solutions to $-\dfrac{2}{x} = 4 - x^2$.

5. Graph Transformations

If you have a function f(x), you can transform its graph in three different ways — by translating it, stretching it or reflecting it.

Translations

Translating the graph of a function means moving it either **horizontally** or **vertically**. The shape of the graph itself doesn't change, it just moves. There are two types of translation:

$y = f(x) + a$

Adding a number to the **whole function** translates the graph in the **y-direction**.

- If $a > 0$, the graph goes **upwards**.
- If $a < 0$, the graph goes **downwards**.
- This can be described by a column vector: $\begin{pmatrix} 0 \\ a \end{pmatrix}$.

$y = f(x + a)$

Writing '$x + a$' instead of 'x' means the graph moves **sideways** ("translated in the **x-direction**").

- If $a > 0$, the graph goes to the **left**.
- If $a < 0$, the graph goes to the **right**.
- As a **column vector**, this would be $\begin{pmatrix} -a \\ 0 \end{pmatrix}$.

Learning Objectives:

- Know the effect of the transformations $y = f(x) + a$, $y = f(x + a)$, $y = af(x)$, $y = f(ax)$.
- Apply any of these transformations to quadratic, cubic and reciprocal functions.
- Given the graph of a function f(x), sketch the graph resulting from any of the above transformations.

Tip: Function notation is used a lot in this section. Remember, if $f(x) = 3x^2$ then:

- $f(5)$ means $3(5)^2 = 75$
- $f(x - 2)$ means $3(x - 2)^2$
- $af(x)$ means $a \times 3x^2$

Tip: You might see translation vectors with either round brackets or square brackets — they mean the same thing.

Example 1

Shown below is the graph of $y = f(x)$, where $f(x) = x(x + 2)(x - 2)$.

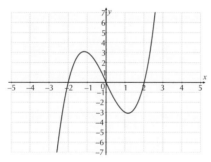

a) **Sketch the graph $y = f(x) + 2$.**

- 2 has been added to the **whole function**, i.e. $a = 2$.
- So the graph will be translated 2 units in the y-direction, i.e. shifted **upwards** by 2.

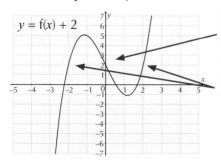

The point (0, 0) on f(x) has become the point (0, 2).

The other roots of f(x), (–2, 0) and (2, 0), have become (–2, 2) and (2, 2).

Tip: When sketching a transformed graph, you need to show what happens to its **key points**, e.g. where it crosses the axes, max / min points, etc.

Tip: The equation of the transformed function is:
$y = x(x + 2)(x - 2) + 2$,
$= x^3 - 4x + 2$.

But you don't need to know this to sketch the transformed function.

Tip: This is a translation by the vector $\begin{pmatrix} 0 \\ 2 \end{pmatrix}$.

b) Sketch the graph $y = f(x - 1)$.

- Here, it's of the form $y = f(x + a)$ so it's a translation in the x-direction.
- $a = -1$ which is negative, so it's a translation to the **right** by 1 unit.

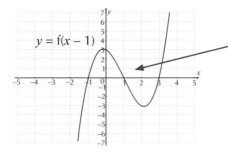

1 is added to the x-coordinate of every point.

E.g. $(-2, 0)$ becomes $(-1, 0)$.

Example 2

Given that $f(x) = \dfrac{1}{x}$:

a) Sketch the graph of $y = f(x) + 2$ and state the equations of the asymptotes.

- First, sketch the graph of $f(x) = \dfrac{1}{x}$. The graph $y = f(x) + 2$ is a translation of the graph upwards by 2.

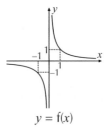 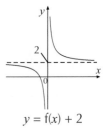

$y = f(x)$ $y = f(x) + 2$

- For $f(x) = \dfrac{1}{x}$, the horizontal asymptote is $y = 0$ and the vertical asymptote is $x = 0$. So for $y = f(x) + 2$, the horizontal asymptote becomes $y = 2$ (as it has moved up 2) but the vertical asymptote is still $x = 0$.

b) Sketch the graph of $y = f(x + 2)$ and state the equations of the asymptotes.

- The graph of $f(x + 2)$ is a translation to the left by 2.

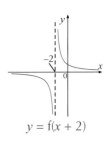

- This time, the horizontal asymptote remains at $y = 0$ but the vertical asymptote moves to $x = -2$.

$y = f(x + 2)$

c) What column vectors describe the translations in parts a) and b)?

- In part a), the graph is translated by 2 units in the positive y-direction, so the translation vector is $\begin{pmatrix} 0 \\ 2 \end{pmatrix}$.
- For part b), the translation is in the negative x-direction (again by 2 units), giving a translation vector of $\begin{pmatrix} -2 \\ 0 \end{pmatrix}$.

Q1 The diagram shows the graph of $y = f(x)$. The curve has a maximum at (2, 4) and meets the x-axis at (0, 0) and (5, 0).

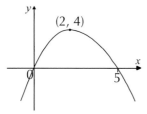

a) Sketch the graph of $y = f(x) + 2$, labelling the coordinates of the maximum and where the curve meets the y-axis.

b) Sketch the graph of $y = f(x + 2)$, labelling the points where the curve meets the x-axis and the maximum.

Q2 If $g(x) = -\dfrac{2}{x}$, sketch these graphs and write down the equations of the asymptotes for each.

a) $y = g(x)$ b) $y = g(x + 3)$ c) $y = g(x) + 3$

Q3 Given that $y = x^2(x - 4)$, describe how you would translate the graph to give the graph of $y = (x - 2)^2(x - 6)$. Include a column vector in your answer.

Q4 Explain how the graph of $y = x^3 + 3x + 7$ can be translated to give the graph of $y = x^3 + 3x + 2$. Include a column vector in your answer.

Q5 The graph of $y = x^2 - 3x + 7$ is translated by the vector $\begin{pmatrix} -1 \\ 0 \end{pmatrix}$. Write down the equation of the new graph. Give your answer in as simple a form as possible.

Q6 The diagram shows the graph of $y = f(x)$.

The graph has a maximum at (5, 3), crosses the x-axis at (3, 0) and (6, 0) and crosses the y-axis at (0, –1).

a) Sketch the graph of $y = f(x) - 2$.

b) Label the coordinates of the maximum and the point where the graph meets the y-axis.

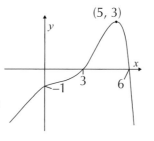

Q7 a) Sketch the graph of $y = (x - 1)(2x - 3)(4 - x)$ and label the points where the graph meets the coordinate axes.

b) The graph in part a) is translated by the vector $\begin{pmatrix} 2 \\ 0 \end{pmatrix}$.

Give the equation of the translated graph in its simplest form.

c) On separate axes, sketch the graph of the equation from part b), labelling all the points where the graph meets the x-axis.

Stretches and reflections

The graph of a function can be stretched, squashed or reflected by **multiplying** the whole function or the x's in the function by a number. The result you get depends on what you multiply and whether the number is positive or negative.

Tip: Remember that all these stretches or squashes are in the **vertical** direction (i.e. parallel to the y-axis).

$y = af(x)$

Multiplying the **whole function** by a, stretches the graph **vertically** by a scale factor of a.

- If $a > 1$ or $a < -1$, the graph is **stretched**.
- If $-1 < a < 1$, the graph is **squashed**.
- If a is **negative**, the graph is **also reflected** about the x-axis.

For every point on the graph, the x-coordinate stays the same and the y-coordinate is multiplied by a.

Tip: Don't describe a transformation as a "squash" in the exam — call it a "stretch with a scale factor of...".

Example 1

The diagram shows the graph of a function f(x).

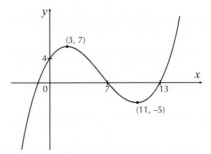

Tip: There are 5 key points marked on the graph that you'll need to keep track of:
(0, 4), (3, 7), (7, 0), (11, −5) and (13, 0)

a) **Sketch the graph $y = \frac{1}{3}f(x)$.**

- The graph above will be stretched vertically by a scale factor of $\frac{1}{3}$.
- As $\frac{1}{3}$ is less than 1, the 'stretch' will actually be a squash.
- The diagram gives a number of key points on the graph — you need to show where each of these points has moved to on the transformed graph:

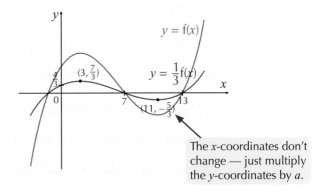

Tip: The graph still crosses the x-axis at the same points as the original graph — this is true for all $y = af(x)$ transformations.

The x-coordinates don't change — just multiply the y-coordinates by a.

b) Sketch the graph $y = -2f(x)$.

- Here the **whole function** has been multiplied by -2.

- So the graph will be stretched vertically by a factor of 2, but also reflected in the x-axis because of the minus sign.

- Again, you need to show what has happened to each key point.

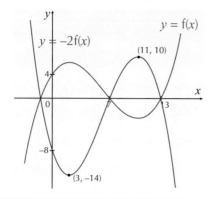

So that's vertical stretches covered. Next up are horizontal stretches:

$y = f(ax)$

Writing 'ax' instead of 'x' stretches the graph **horizontally** by a scale factor of $\dfrac{1}{a}$.

- If $a > 1$ or $a < -1$, the graph is **squashed**.

- If $-1 < a < 1$, the graph is **stretched**.

- **Negative** values of a **reflect** the basic shape in the **y-axis**.

For these transformations, the y-coordinate of each point stays the same and the x-coordinate is multiplied by $\dfrac{1}{a}$.

Tip: Notice that a being bigger or smaller than 1 has the **opposite effect** for horizontal stretches compared to vertical stretches.

Example 2

The diagram below shows the graph of $y = f(x)$ again.

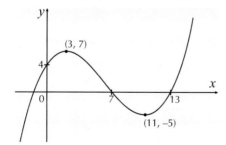

a) Sketch the graph $y = f\left(\dfrac{1}{2}x\right)$.

- $\dfrac{1}{2}$ is positive and between -1 and 1, so the graph will be stretched horizontally by a scale factor of 2.

- For each point given, the x-coordinate is multiplied by 2 but the y-coordinate doesn't change.

- The graph looks like this (this time, the y-intercept doesn't change, but the two x-intercepts do).

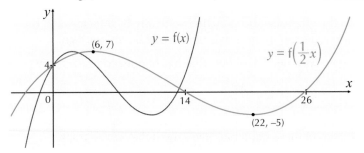

b) **Sketch the graph y = f(–3x).**

- The transformation has the form $y = f(ax)$, so it's a horizontal stretch.

- $a = -3$, so the graph will be 'stretched' by a scale factor of $\frac{1}{3}$, i.e. squashed...

- ... and also **reflected** in the y-axis since a is negative.

- Find the new position of key points by multiplying their x–coordinate by $-\frac{1}{3}$ (and leaving the y-coordinate the same.)

- So the graph looks like this:

Tip: As always, label any key points, e.g. (3, 7) has become (–1, 7), and (11, –5) has become $\left(-\frac{11}{3}, -5\right)$.

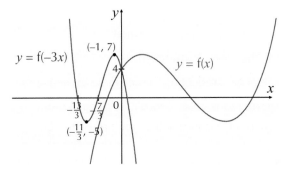

Exercise 5.2

Q1   The diagram shows the graph of $y = g(x)$. The graph has a minimum at (–2, –3), a maximum at (2, 3) and crosses the x-axis at (0, 0), (–4, 0) and (4, 0).

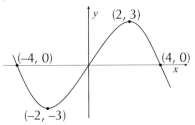

Sketch the graphs of these functions, labelling clearly the coordinates of any maximums, minimums and intersections with the axes:

a) $y = 2g(x)$ b) $y = g(2x)$ c) $y = -2g(x)$ d) $y = g(-2x)$

Q2 The diagram shows the graph of f(x) and Graph A of a function that is a transformation of f(x).

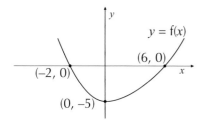 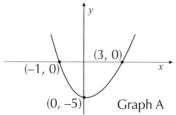

Which of these equations gives the transformed graph?

a) $y = 2f(x)$ b) $y = f(2x)$ c) $y = f(0.5x)$ d) $y = 0.5f(x)$

Q3 The diagram shows the graph of f(x) and Graph A of a function that is a transformation of f(x).

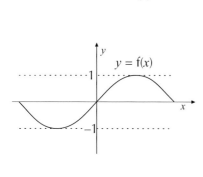 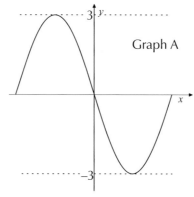

Graph A

Q3 Hint: There are actually two transformations that could give Graph A, but only one of them is listed.

Which of these equations could give the transformed graph?

a) $y = 3f(x)$ b) $y = -3f(x)$ c) $y = f(-3x)$ d) $y = f(3x)$

Q4 Given that $f(x) = x^3 - x$, sketch the graphs of the following functions:

a) $y = f(x) + 2$ b) $y = f(x - 2)$ c) $y = f(-2x)$ d) $y = -2f(x)$

Q5 Describe clearly the transformation that is required to take the graph of $y = x^3 + 2x + 4$ to the graph of $y = 3x^3 + 6x + 12$.

Q6 Describe clearly the transformation that is required to take the graph of $y = x^2 + x + 4$ to the graph of $y = 4x^2 - 2x + 4$.

Q6 Hint: The terms which contain x's are different to the original, but the constant term is not.

Q7 a) Sketch the graph of $f(x) = x^2 - 6x - 7$ showing clearly the coordinates of any maximum or minimum points and where the curve meets the coordinate axes.

b) Write down the equation of the graph obtained by stretching the graph of f(x) vertically with a scale factor of –2.

c) Sketch the graph with equation you found in part b) showing clearly the coordinates of any maximum or minimum points and where the curve meets the coordinate axes.

Q7a) Hint: Complete the square — see pages 30-33 and 42-43 for a recap.

6. Circles

- Know and be able to find the equation of a circle with radius r and centre (a, b), in the form: $(x - a)^2 + (y - b)^2 = r^2$.
- Be able to find the radius and coordinates of the centre of a circle, given the equation of the circle.
- Know the three main circle properties, and apply them to find lengths, angles and coordinates.

If you've survived maths this long, you'll be very familiar with circles — you're probably a dab hand at working out their circumference and area. Now we're going to have a look at using equations to describe a circle. An equation of a circle can tell you its radius and where its centre is.

The equation of a circle
Circles with centre (0, 0)

The diagram to the right shows a circle centred on the origin $(0, 0)$ and with radius r.

You can describe a circle centred on the origin, with radius r, using the equation:

$$x^2 + y^2 = r^2$$

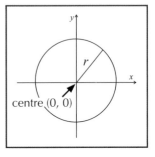

Even though you're dealing with circles, you get the equation above using **Pythagoras' theorem**. Here's how:

- The **centre** of the circle is at the origin, labelled **C**.

- **A** is any point on the circle, and has the coordinates (x, y).

- **B** lies on the x-axis and has the same x-coordinate as A.

- So the length of line **CB** $= x$, and **AB** $= y$.

- Therefore, using Pythagoras' theorem to find the radius r, we get:

$$CB^2 + AB^2 = r^2$$

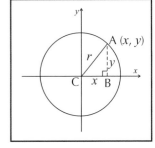

Which is... $x^2 + y^2 = r^2$

If you're given the equation of a circle in the form $x^2 + y^2 = r^2$, you can work out the radius of the circle in the following way:

Tip: You can use the equation of a circle to find out if it intersects a line — have a look at the example on p.71.

Example

A circle has the equation $x^2 + y^2 = 4$. Find the radius of the circle.

- **Compare** the equation $x^2 + y^2 = 4$ to $x^2 + y^2 = r^2$.

- Equating the two equations gives: $r^2 = 4$

$$r = 2$$

Tip: Ignore the negative square root as the radius will be positive.

Circles with centre (a, b)

Unfortunately, circles aren't always centred at the origin.
This means we need a general equation for circles that
have a centre somewhere else — the point (a, b).

The general equation for circles with **radius r** and **centre (a, b)** is:

$$(x - a)^2 + (y - b)^2 = r^2$$

Notice that if the circle had a centre at (0, 0), then you'd get $a = 0$ and $b = 0$,
so you'd just get $x^2 + y^2 = r^2$ (the equation for a circle centred at the origin).

The example below shows how you get the equation of a circle when
the coordinates of the centre and the value of the radius are given.

Example 1

Find the equation of the circle with centre (6, 4) and radius 3.

- If we draw a point P (x, y) on the **circumference** of the circle and
  join it to the centre (6, 4), we can create a **right-angled triangle**.

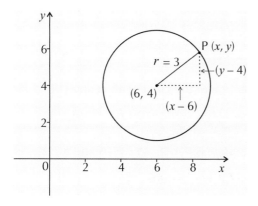

- The **sides** of this right-angled triangle are made up of the radius r
  (the hypotenuse), and sides of length $(x - 6)$ and $(y - 4)$.

- Now let's see what happens if we use **Pythagoras' theorem**:

$$(x - 6)^2 + (y - 4)^2 = 3^2$$

or: $$(x - 6)^2 + (y - 4)^2 = 9$$

This is the equation for the circle.

> **Tip:** For the circle
> centred at the origin, the
> side lengths were r, x
> and y. Make sure you're
> happy with why the side
> lengths here are r, $(x - 6)$
> and $(y - 4)$.

Example 2

**What is the centre and radius of the circle with equation
$(x - 2)^2 + (y + 3)^2 = 16$?**

- **Compare** $(x - 2)^2 + (y + 3)^2 = 16$ with the general form:

$$(x - a)^2 + (y - b)^2 = r^2$$

- So, $a = 2$, $b = -3$ and $r = 4$.

> So the centre (a, b) is $(2, -3)$ and the radius (r) is 4.

- On a set of axes, the circle would look like this:

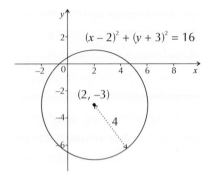

If you're given the centre and radius of a circle and you're asked to find the equation of the circle, just put the values of a, b and r into the equation $(x - a)^2 + (y - b)^2 = r^2$.

Example 3

Write down the equation of the circle with centre (–4, 2) and radius 6.

- The question says, 'Write down...', so you know you **don't** need to do any working.

- The **centre** of the circle is $(-4, 2)$, so $a = -4$ and $b = 2$.

- The **radius** is 6, so $r = 6$.

- Using the **general equation** for a circle $(x - a)^2 + (y - b)^2 = r^2$ you can write:

> $(x + 4)^2 + (y - 2)^2 = 36$

- On a set of axes, the circle would look like this:

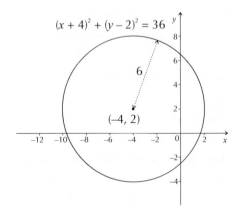

Q1 A circle has centre (0, 0) and radius 5.
Find an equation for the circle.

Q2 A circle C has radius 7 and centre (0, 0).
Find an equation for C.

Q3 Find the equation for each of the following circles:
a) centre (2, 5), radius 3
b) centre (–3, 2), radius 5
c) centre (–2, –3), radius 7
d) centre (3, 0), radius 4

> **Q3 Hint:** Be careful here with the +/– signs.

Q4 Find the centre and radius of the circles with the following equations:
a) $(x - 1)^2 + (y - 5)^2 = 4$
b) $(x - 3)^2 + (y - 5)^2 = 64$
c) $(x - 3)^2 + (y + 2)^2 = 25$

Q5 A circle has centre (5, 3) and radius 8.
Find an equation for the circle.

Q6 A circle has centre (3, 1) and a radius of $\sqrt{31}$.
Find an equation for the circle.

Q7 The equation of the circle C is $(x - 6)^2 + (y - 4)^2 = 20$
a) Find the coordinates of the centre of the circle.
b) Find the radius of the circle and give your answer in the form $p\sqrt{5}$.

Q8 A circle has radius $\sqrt{5}$ and centre (–3, –2).
Find an equation for the circle.

Rearranging circle equations

Sometimes you'll be given an equation for a circle that doesn't look much like $(x - a)^2 + (y - b)^2 = r^2$ — e.g. $x^2 + y^2 + 8x + 6y + 3 = 0$.

The general form of this type of equation is:

$$x^2 + y^2 + 2fx + 2gy + c = 0$$

- In this form, you can't immediately tell what the **radius** is or where the **centre** is.

- All you'll need to do is a bit of **rearranging** to get the equation into the form $(x - a)^2 + (y - b)^2 = r^2$.

- To do this, you'll normally have to **complete the square** — this is shown in the examples on the next couple of pages.

> **Tip:** Completing the square was covered in Chapter 4. It might be useful to take a look back at pages 30-33 before you move on to the following examples

Example 1

The equation of a circle is $x^2 + y^2 - 6x + 4y + 4 = 0$.
Find the centre of the circle and the radius.

- You need to get the equation $x^2 + y^2 - 6x + 4y + 4 = 0$
  into the form $(x - a)^2 + (y - b)^2 = r^2$.

- To do this, we need to **complete the square**.

- So, first **rearrange** the equation to group the x's and the y's together:

$$x^2 + y^2 - 6x + 4y + 4 = 0$$
$$x^2 - 6x + y^2 + 4y + 4 = 0$$

Tip: To complete the square, write down the squared bracket that will produce the x^2 and x terms, then take off the number term that the bracket will also produce.

- Then **complete the square** for the x-terms and the y-terms.

$$x^2 - 6x + y^2 + 4y + 4 = 0$$
$$(x - 3)^2 - 9 + (y + 2)^2 - 4 + 4 = 0$$

Tip: Collect all the number terms to find r^2.

- Then **rearrange** to get it into the form $(x - a)^2 + (y - b)^2 = r^2$.

$$(x - 3)^2 + (y + 2)^2 = 9$$

- This is the recognisable form, so we can use this equation to find:

the centre is $(3, -2)$ and the radius is $\sqrt{9} = 3$

Example 2

a) Show that the circle with equation $x^2 + y^2 + 2fx + 2gy + c = 0$,
where f, g and c are constants, has its centre at $(-f, -g)$
and a radius of $\sqrt{f^2 + g^2 - c}$.

- As before, you want to rearrange $x^2 + y^2 + 2fx + 2gy + c = 0$
  into in the form $(x - a)^2 + (y - b)^2 = r^2$.

- Rearrange and complete the square for the x-terms and y-terms:

$$x^2 + y^2 + 2fx + 2gy + c = 0$$
$$x^2 + 2fx + y^2 + 2gy + c = 0$$
$$(x + f)^2 - f^2 + (y + g)^2 - g^2 + c = 0$$
$$(x + f)^2 + (y + g)^2 = f^2 + g^2 - c$$

- Now compare this to the general equation of a circle (given above) to find a, b and r:

$$a = -f, \quad b = -g, \quad r^2 = f^2 + g^2 - c$$

- So the circle's centre is at $(-f, -g)$ and its radius is $\sqrt{f^2 + g^2 - c}$
  as required.

b) Use this result to find the centre and radius of the circle given by the equation $x^2 + y^2 - 5x - 5y + 10 = 0$.

- If you write the equation $x^2 + y^2 - 5x - 5y + 10 = 0$ into the form $x^2 + y^2 + 2fx + 2gy + c = 0$ you get:

$$x^2 + y^2 + 2\left(-\tfrac{5}{2}x\right) + 2\left(-\tfrac{5}{2}y\right) + 10 = 0$$

- So f and g are both $-\tfrac{5}{2}$ and $c = 10$.

- Using the result from part a), the centre of the circle is at $(-f, -g) = \left(\tfrac{5}{2}, \tfrac{5}{2}\right)$.

- The radius of the circle is $\sqrt{f^2 + g^2 - c}$:

$$r = \sqrt{\left(-\tfrac{5}{2}\right)^2 + \left(-\tfrac{5}{2}\right)^2 - 10}$$
$$= \sqrt{\tfrac{25}{4} + \tfrac{25}{4} - 10}$$
$$= \sqrt{\tfrac{50}{4} - \tfrac{40}{4}}$$
$$= \sqrt{\tfrac{10}{4}} = \sqrt{\tfrac{5}{2}}$$

- So: the centre is $\left(\tfrac{5}{2}, \tfrac{5}{2}\right)$ and the radius is $\sqrt{\tfrac{5}{2}}$

Tip: You could write the radius as $\dfrac{\sqrt{10}}{2}$ instead.

Exercise 6.2

Q1 For each of the following circles find the radius and the coordinates of the centre.

a) $x^2 + y^2 + 2x - 6y - 6 = 0$

b) $x^2 + y^2 - 2y - 4 = 0$

c) $x^2 + y^2 - 6x - 4y = 12$

d) $x^2 + y^2 - 10x + 6y + 13 = 0$

Q2 A circle has the equation $x^2 + y^2 + 2x - 4y - 3 = 0$.

a) Find the centre of the circle.

b) Find the radius of the circle. Give your answer in the form $k\sqrt{2}$.

Q3 A circle has the equation $x^2 + y^2 - 3x + 1 = 0$.

a) Find the coordinates of the centre of the circle.

b) Find the radius of the circle.
    Simplify your answer as much as possible.

Using circle properties

Here is a reminder of some of the most useful properties of circles. Although it might not be obvious when you first look at a question, these rules could help you answer some tricky-sounding circle questions.

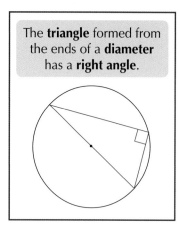

The **triangle** formed from the ends of a **diameter** has a **right angle**.

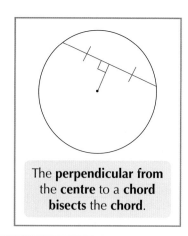

Tip: A chord is a line joining two points which lie on the circumference of a circle.

Tip: Bisecting means dividing into two equal parts.

The **perpendicular from** the **centre** to a **chord** **bisects** the **chord**.

A **tangent** to the circle **meets** a **radius** at a **right angle**.

Tip: So the tangent and the radius at a point are perpendicular.

Example 1

The circle shown is centred at C. Points A and B lie on the circle. Point B has coordinates (6, 3). The midpoint, M, of the line AB has coordinates (4, 4). Line *l* passes through both C and M.

Find an equation for the line *l*.

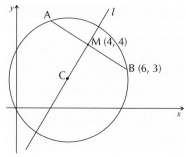

Tip: In the exam, after a question like this, they might then give you a bit more info and ask you to work out the equation for the circle.

- AB is a **chord**. *l* goes through the centre of the circle and **bisects** the chord. So we can say that the line *l* is **perpendicular** to the chord.

- We know two points on AB, so start by finding its **gradient**: $\dfrac{3-4}{6-4} = -\dfrac{1}{2}$

- The gradients of perpendicular lines multiply to give –1 (see page 81), so the gradient of *l* will be –1 divided by the gradient of the chord:

$$\text{Gradient of } l = \frac{-1}{-\frac{1}{2}} = 2$$

- Then substitute the gradient, 2, and the point on *l* that you know, (4, 4), into one of the equations for a **straight line** to work out the equation:

$$y - y_1 = m(x - x_1)$$
$$y - 4 = 2(x - 4)$$
$$y - 4 = 2x - 8$$
$$y = 2x - 4$$

Tip: See pages 74-77 for a recap on straight line equations.

Example 2

Point A (6, 4) lies on a circle with the equation $x^2 + y^2 - 4x - 2y - 20 = 0$.

a) **Find the centre and radius of the circle.**

- Get the equation into the form: $(x - a)^2 + (y - b)^2 = r^2$.
  First, **rearrange** the equation to group the *x*'s and the *y*'s together:

$$x^2 + y^2 - 4x - 2y - 20 = 0$$
$$x^2 - 4x + y^2 - 2y - 20 = 0$$

- Then **complete the square** for the *x*-terms and the *y*-terms, and **rearrange** to get it into the form $(x - a)^2 + (y - b)^2 = r^2$.

$$(x - 2)^2 - 4 + (y - 1)^2 - 1 - 20 = 0$$
$$(x - 2)^2 + (y - 1)^2 = 25$$

- This shows: the centre is (2, 1) and the radius is 5.

b) **Find the equation of the tangent to the circle at A.**

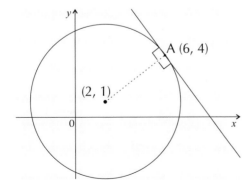

- The **tangent** is at **right angles** to the radius at (6, 4).
- Gradient of radius at (6, 4) = $\dfrac{4-1}{6-2} = \dfrac{3}{4}$

- Gradient of tangent $= \dfrac{-1}{\frac{3}{4}} = -\dfrac{4}{3}$

Tip: The question doesn't ask for the equation in a particular form, so pick whatever's easiest.

- Using $y - y_1 = m(x - x_1)$

$$y - 4 = -\dfrac{4}{3}(x - 6)$$

$$3y - 12 = -4x + 24$$

$$4x + 3y - 36 = 0$$

Example 3

The points A $(-2, 4)$, B $(n, -2)$ and C $(5, 5)$ all lie on the circle shown below. AB is a diameter of the circle.

Show that $n = 6$.

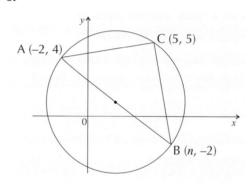

- The line AB is a **diameter** of the circle. So the angle ACB is an angle in a semicircle and must be a **right angle**.

- This means the lines AC and BC are **perpendicular** to each other.

- The gradients of two perpendicular lines multiply to give **–1**, so use this to work out n.

- First, find the gradient of AC: $\quad m_1 = \dfrac{5-4}{5-(-2)} = \dfrac{1}{7}$

- Then find the gradient of BC: $\quad m_2 = \dfrac{-2-5}{n-5} = \dfrac{-7}{n-5}$

Tip: Alternatively, you could use the gradient of AC to find the equation of the line BC in the form $y = mx + c$ (it will pass through $(5, 5)$ and have gradient -7), and then substitute in the point $(n, -2)$ to find n.

- Use the gradient rule: $\quad m_1 \times m_2 = -1$

$$\dfrac{1}{7}\left(\dfrac{-7}{n-5}\right) = -1 \quad \longleftarrow \boxed{\text{Cancel the 7s.}}$$

$$\dfrac{-1}{n-5} = -1$$

$$1 = n - 5$$

$$n = 6 \text{ as required}$$

A circle that passes through all three vertices of a triangle is called the **circumcircle** of the triangle. Finding the equation of a circumcircle involves using properties of circles, perpendicular lines and lots of algebra.

Example 4

Find the equation of the circumcircle of the triangle ABC where:
   A = (3, 9)   B = (6, 0)   C = (10, 8)

Tip: This is the same as asking you to find the equation of the circle through these points.

- The best way to begin is to sketch the triangle and its circumcircle:

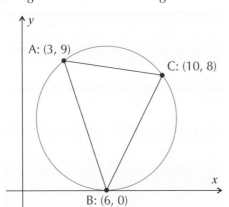

- To find the equation of a circle, you need to know its centre and radius. Start by finding the centre.

- The sides of the triangle are **chords** of the circle. You know from the circle properties that a line from the centre of the circle that meets one of these chords at right angles also bisects it.

Tip: The perpendicular bisector of a line passes through its midpoint at right angles to the line.

- So, if you can find the **perpendicular bisectors** of the sides of the triangle, they will all meet at the centre of the circle. In practice, you only need to find where two of the lines meet, so consider the perpendicular bisectors of AB and BC.

Tip: The coordinates of the point halfway between (x_1, y_1) and (x_2, y_2) are $\left(\frac{x_1 + x_2}{2}, \frac{y_1 + y_2}{2} \right)$.

- AB: Midpoint $= \left(\frac{3+6}{2}, \frac{9+0}{2} \right) = \left(\frac{9}{2}, \frac{9}{2} \right)$

    Gradient $= \frac{0-9}{6-3} = \frac{-9}{3} = -3$

So the perpendicular bisector of AB has a gradient of $\frac{-1}{-3} = \frac{1}{3}$ and passes through the point $\left(\frac{9}{2}, \frac{9}{2} \right)$ — its equation is $y - \frac{9}{2} = \frac{1}{3}\left(x - \frac{9}{2} \right)$

$$y = \frac{1}{3}x - \frac{3}{2} + \frac{9}{2}$$

$$y = \frac{1}{3}x + 3$$

- BC: Midpoint $= \left(\frac{6+10}{2}, \frac{0+8}{2} \right) = (8, 4)$

    Gradient $= \frac{8-0}{10-6} = \frac{8}{4} = 2$

So the perpendicular bisector of BC has a gradient of $-\frac{1}{2}$ and passes through the point (8, 4) — its equation is $y - 4 = -\frac{1}{2}(x - 8)$

$$y = -\frac{1}{2}x + 4 + 4$$

$$y = -\frac{1}{2}x + 8$$

- With these two lines, you can find the centre of the circle by seeing where they cross.

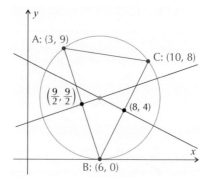

- Now find the centre by solving the simultaneous equations:

$$\frac{1}{3}x + 3 = -\frac{1}{2}x + 8$$

$$\frac{1}{3}x + \frac{1}{2}x = 5$$

$$2x + 3x = 30$$

$$5x = 30 \ \text{ so } \ x = 6$$

- Substitute this value of x into one of the equations to find y:

$$y = \frac{1}{3}(6) + 3 = 2 + 3$$

$$y = 5$$

- So the centre of the circle is (6, 5).

- The radius is the distance from the centre to a point on the edge. The distance from the centre (6, 5) to point B (6, 0) is easy to read off — you can see that the radius is 5.

- So the equation of the circumcircle is:

$$(x - 6)^2 + (y - 5)^2 = 25$$

Exercise 6.3

Q1 The circle shown below has the equation $(x - 3)^2 + (y - 1)^2 = 10$. The line shown is a tangent to the circle and touches it at point A (4, 4).

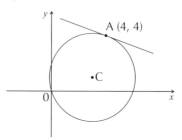

a) Find the centre of the circle, C.

b) Work out the gradient of the radius at (4, 4).

c) Find the equation of the tangent at A in the form $ax + by = c$.

Q2 A circle has the equation $(x + 1)^2 + (y - 2)^2 = 13$.
The circle passes through the point A $(-3, -1)$.
Find the equation of the tangent at A in the form $ax + by + c = 0$.

Q2 Hint: Do this in the same way as Q1. First find the centre of the circle, then the gradients of the radius and tangent.

Q3 The circle C has the equation $x^2 + y^2 + 2x - 7 = 0$.
Find an equation of the tangent to the circle at the point $(-3, 2)$.

Q4 A circle has the equation $x^2 + y^2 + 2x + 4y = 5$.
The point A $(0, -5)$ lies on the circle.
Find the tangent to the circle at A in the form $ax + by = c$.

Q5 A circle with centre $(-2, 4)$ passes through the point A $(n, 1)$.
Given that the tangent to the circle at A has a gradient of $\frac{5}{3}$, find the value of n.

Q6 The circle shown is centred at C. Points A and B lie on the circle.
Point A has coordinates $(-3, 7)$. The midpoint of the line AB, M, has coordinates $(-1, 1)$. Line l passes through both C and M.

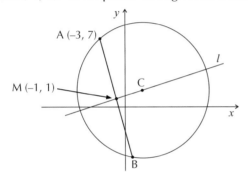

Q6 Hint: AB is a chord.

a) Use the information above to find an equation for the line l.

b) The coordinates of C are $(2, 2)$.
Find an equation for the circle.

Q7 The points A $(-2, 12)$, B $(4, 14)$ and C $(8, 2)$ all lie on the circle shown below.

a) Prove that the line AC is a **diameter** of the circle.

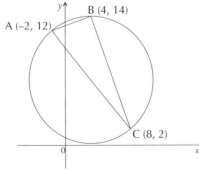

b) Hence find the equation of the circle.

Q8 Find the equation of the circle that passes through the points A $= (2, 11)$, B $= (6, 5)$ and C $= (-9, 0)$.

1. Binomial Expansions

Binomials are just polynomials that only have two terms (the 'bi' and 'poly' bits come from the Greek words for 'two' and 'many'). Binomial expansions are all about multiplying out brackets with two terms. This section has a few methods you can use on different types of expansions.

Learning Objectives:

- Be able to use Pascal's triangle to find the coefficients of a binomial expansion.
- Be able to find binomial coefficients using factorials and using the notation $\binom{n}{r}$ or ^nC_r.
- Be able to use the formula to expand binomials of the form $(1 + x)^n$ and $(1 + ax)^n$.
- Be able to use the formula to expand binomials of the form $(a + bx)^n$.

Binomial expansions — $(1 + x)^n$

Pascal's triangle

- A **binomial expansion** is what you get when you **multiply out the brackets** of a polynomial with two terms, like $(1 + x)^5$ or $(2 - 3x)^8$.

- It would take ages to multiply out a bracket like this by hand if the power was really big — fortunately, binomial expansions **follow a pattern**:

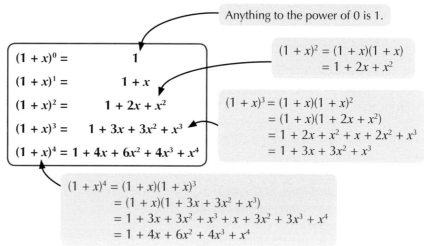

Anything to the power of 0 is 1.

$$(1 + x)^0 = 1$$
$$(1 + x)^1 = 1 + x$$
$$(1 + x)^2 = 1 + 2x + x^2$$
$$(1 + x)^3 = 1 + 3x + 3x^2 + x^3$$
$$(1 + x)^4 = 1 + 4x + 6x^2 + 4x^3 + x^4$$

$$(1 + x)^2 = (1 + x)(1 + x)$$
$$= 1 + 2x + x^2$$

$$(1 + x)^3 = (1 + x)(1 + x)^2$$
$$= (1 + x)(1 + 2x + x^2)$$
$$= 1 + 2x + x^2 + x + 2x^2 + x^3$$
$$= 1 + 3x + 3x^2 + x^3$$

$$(1 + x)^4 = (1 + x)(1 + x)^3$$
$$= (1 + x)(1 + 3x + 3x^2 + x^3)$$
$$= 1 + 3x + 3x^2 + x^3 + x + 3x^2 + 3x^3 + x^4$$
$$= 1 + 4x + 6x^2 + 4x^3 + x^4$$

Tip: When you expand a binomial you usually write it in increasing powers of x, starting with x^0 and going up to x^n.

Tip: For the moment we're just looking at $(1 + x)^n$. Binomials of the form $(a + bx)^n$, like $(2 - 3x)^8$, are covered on pages 116-118.

A French man called Blaise Pascal spotted the pattern in the **coefficients** and wrote them down in a **triangle**, so it's imaginatively known as '**Pascal's triangle**'. The pattern's easy — each number is the **sum** of the two above it:

```
              1
           1     1
        1     2     1
     1     3     3  + 1
  1     4     6   = 4     1
```

Tip: The triangle is symmetrical, so once you've got the first half of the coefficients you don't need to work out the rest.

So the next line is: **1   5   10   10   5   1**
Giving: $(1 + x)^5 = 1 + 5x + 10x^2 + 10x^3 + 5x^4 + x^5$.

If you're expanding a binomial with a power that's not too huge, writing out a quick **Pascal's triangle** is a good way to **find the coefficients**.

Example

Find the binomial expansion of $(1 + x)^6$.

Draw **Pascal's triangle** — you're raising the bracket to the **power of 6**, so go down to the **7th row**.

Write the answer out, using the **coefficients** from the 7th row, and increasing the power of x:

```
              1
           1     1
         1    2    1
       1    3    3    1
      1   4    6    4   1
    1   5   10   10   5   1
  1   6   15   20   15   6   1
```

Tip: Make sure you go down to the correct row — you need one more row than the power you're raising the bracket to.

$$(1 + x)^6 = 1 + 6x + 15x^2 + 20x^3 + 15x^4 + 6x^5 + x^6$$

The binomial formula

For expansions with higher powers you don't need to write out Pascal's triangle — there's a formula you can use instead:

$$(1 + x)^n = 1 + \frac{n}{1}x + \frac{n(n-1)}{1 \times 2}x^2 + \frac{n(n-1)(n-2)}{1 \times 2 \times 3}x^3 + \dots + x^n$$

At first glance this looks a bit awful, but each term follows a pattern:

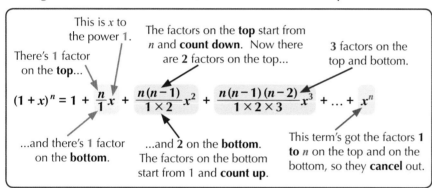

This is x to the power 1.

The factors on the **top** start from n and **count down**. Now there are **2** factors on the top...

3 factors on the top and bottom.

There's **1** factor on the **top**...

...and there's **1** factor on the **bottom**.

...and **2** on the **bottom**. The factors on the bottom start from 1 and **count up**.

This term's got the factors **1** to n on the top and on the bottom, so they **cancel** out.

Tip: Try to remember the patterns from term to term — it should sink in if you get plenty of practice using it.

Once you get **halfway** along, the **factors** on the top and bottom start to **cancel**, and the coefficients repeat themselves (they're symmetrical):

$$(1 + x)^5 = 1 + \frac{5}{1}x + \frac{5 \times 4}{1 \times 2}x^2 + \frac{5 \times 4 \times \cancel{3}}{1 \times 2 \times \cancel{3}}x^3 + \frac{5 \times 4 \times \cancel{3} \times \cancel{2}}{1 \times \cancel{2} \times \cancel{3} \times 4}x^4 + \frac{\cancel{5} \times \cancel{4} \times \cancel{3} \times \cancel{2} \times 1}{1 \times \cancel{2} \times \cancel{3} \times \cancel{4} \times \cancel{5}}x^5$$

$$= 1 + \frac{5}{1}x + \frac{5 \times 4}{1 \times 2}x^2 + \frac{5 \times 4}{1 \times 2}x^3 + \frac{5}{1}x^4 + x^5$$

$$= 1 + 5x + 10x^2 + 10x^3 + 5x^4 + x^5$$

Examples

a) Expand $(1 + x)^{20}$, giving the first four terms only.

- The binomial formula is:

$$(1 + x)^n = 1 + \frac{n}{1}x + \frac{n(n-1)}{1 \times 2}x^2 + \frac{n(n-1)(n-2)}{1 \times 2 \times 3}x^3 + \dots + x^n$$

- You're looking for $(1 + x)^{20}$, so $n = 20$:

$$(1 + x)^{20} = 1 + \frac{20}{1}x + \frac{20 \times 19}{1 \times 2}x^2 + \frac{20 \times 19 \times 18}{1 \times 2 \times 3}x^3 + \dots + x^{20}$$

Tip: Make sure you write down your working — if you just bung the numbers straight into your calculator, you won't be able to spot if you've made a mistake.

- The first 4 terms are:

$$(1+x)^{20} = 1 + \frac{20}{1}x + \frac{\cancel{20}^{10} \times 19}{1 \times \cancel{2}}x^2 + \frac{\cancel{20}^{10} \times 19 \times \cancel{18}^{6}}{1 \times \cancel{2} \times \cancel{3}}x^3 + \ldots$$

$$= 1 + 20x + (10 \times 19)x^2 + (10 \times 19 \times 6)x^3 + \ldots$$

$$= 1 + 20x + 190x^2 + 1140x^3 + \ldots$$

b) **What is the term in x^7 in this expansion?**
   Give your answer in its simplest form.

- The term in x^7 has 7 factors on the top and bottom of the coefficient.

- In this expansion n is 20, so on the top you count down from 20.

- Term in $x^7 = \dfrac{\cancel{20}^{?} \times 19 \times \cancel{18} \times 17 \times 16 \times 15 \times \cancel{14}}{1 \times \cancel{2} \times \cancel{3} \times \cancel{4} \times \cancel{5} \times \cancel{6} \times \cancel{7}}x^7$

$$= (19 \times 17 \times 16 \times 15)x^7$$

$$= \boxed{77\ 520x^7}$$

There are a few bits of **notation** you need to know that will make writing out the binomial formula a bit easier.

Factorials

- The product on the **bottom** of each binomial coefficient is $1 \times 2 \times \ldots \times r$, where r is the **power x is raised to** in that term.

Tip: $r! = 1 \times 2 \times \ldots \times r$ is said 'r factorial'. By convention, $0! = 1$.

- This product can be written as a **factorial**: $r! = 1 \times 2 \times \ldots \times r$.
  E.g. in the binomial expansion of $(1 + x)^{20}$, the coefficient of the term in x^3 is:

$$\frac{20 \times 19 \times 18}{1 \times 2 \times 3} = \frac{20 \times 19 \times 18}{3!}$$

- In fact, you can write the **whole** coefficient using **factorials**.
  For example, the coefficient of x^3 above is:

Tip: Here you've multiplied top and bottom by 17! — this is just so you can write the factors on the top as a factorial (you need to multiply all the way down to 1 to do this).

$$\frac{20 \times 19 \times 18}{1 \times 2 \times 3} = \frac{20 \times 19 \times 18 \times 17 \times \ldots \times 2 \times 1}{1 \times 2 \times 3 \times 1 \times 2 \times \ldots \times 17}$$

$$= \frac{20 \times 19 \times \ldots \times 1}{(1 \times 2 \times 3)(1 \times 2 \times \ldots \times 17)}$$

$$= \frac{20!}{3!17!}$$

- For a general binomial expansion of $(1 + x)^n$, the coefficient of x^r is:

$$\frac{n \times (n-1) \times \ldots \times (n-(r-1))}{1 \times 2 \times \ldots \times r}$$

Tip: The two numbers on the bottom of the factorial fraction always add up to the number on the top.

$$= \frac{n \times (n-1) \times \ldots \times (n-(r-1)) \times (n-r) \times \ldots \times 2 \times 1}{1 \times 2 \times \ldots \times r \times 1 \times 2 \times \ldots \times (n-r)}$$

$$= \frac{n \times (n-1) \times \ldots \times 1}{(1 \times 2 \times \ldots \times r)(1 \times 2 \times \ldots \times (n-r))}$$

$$= \frac{n!}{r!(n-r)!}$$

- So each term in a **binomial expansion** of $(1 + x)^n$ is of the form:

$$\boxed{\frac{n(n-1)(n-2)\ldots(n-(r-1))}{1 \times 2 \times 3 \times \ldots \times r}x^r = \frac{n!}{r!(n-r)!}x^r}$$

Tip: You'll use these coefficients again in the binomial distribution in Chapter 16.

n is the power you're raising the **bracket** to,
r is the power of x in the **term** the coefficient belongs to.

^nC_r notation

There are a couple of even **shorter ways** of writing the **binomial coefficients**:

$$\boxed{\frac{n!}{r!\,(n-r)!}} \;=\; \boxed{\binom{n}{r}} \;=\; \boxed{^nC_r}$$

There's a button on your calculator for finding this.

Tip: This is in the formula booklet.

For example, going back to the coefficient of x^3 in the expansion of $(1 + x)^{20}$:

$$\frac{20 \times 19 \times 18}{1 \times 2 \times 3}x^3 = \frac{20!}{3!17!}x^3 = \binom{20}{3}x^3 = {}^{20}C_3 x^3$$

Tip: The C in ^nC_r stands for 'choose' — you say these coefficients 'n choose r', e.g. $\binom{3}{2}$ is '3 choose 2'.

So the **binomial formula** can be written using **any** of these notations, and you need to be familiar with **all** of them:

$$\boxed{(1 + x)^n = 1 + \frac{n!}{1!\,(n-1!)}x + \frac{n!}{2!\,(n-2)!}x^2 + \frac{n!}{3!\,(n-3)!}x^3 + \dots + x^n}$$

$$\boxed{(1 + x)^n = 1 + \binom{n}{1}x + \binom{n}{2}x^2 + \binom{n}{3}x^3 + \dots + x^n}$$

$$\boxed{(1 + x)^n = 1 + {}^nC_1 x + {}^nC_2 x^2 + {}^nC_3 x^3 + \dots + x^n}$$

Tip: These coefficients will always come out as a whole number that's at least 1 — if you get a coefficient that isn't, then you know you've made a mistake somewhere.

Tip: $^nC_0 = {}^nC_n = 1$.

- Most **calculators** will have an '**nCr**' button for finding binomial **coefficients**. To use it you put in n, press '**nCr**', then put in r.

- This is particularly handy if you're just looking for a **specific term** in a **binomial expansion** and you don't want to write the whole thing out.

Tip: If you get confused with which number's which, remember $n \geq r$.

Example

Find the 6ᵗʰ term of the expansion of $(1 + x)^8$.

- You're raising the **bracket** to the power of **8**, so $n = 8$.

- The **6ᵗʰ term** is the x^5 term (the first term is $1 = x^0$, the second is $x = x^1$ term and so on), so $r = 5$.

- So put '**8 nCr 5**' into your calculator: $^8C_5 = 56$.

- The question asks for the **whole term** (not just the coefficient) so the answer is: $56x^5$

Exercise 1.1

Q1 Use Pascal's triangle to expand $(1 + x)^4$.

Q2 Use your calculator to work out the following:

    a) $^6C_2$ b) $\binom{12}{5}$ c) $\dfrac{30!}{4!26!}$ d) $^8C_8$

Q3 Without using a calculator, work out the following:

    a) $\dfrac{9!}{4!5!}$ b) $^{10}C_3$ c) $\dfrac{15!}{11!4!}$ d) $\binom{8}{6}$

Q4 Find the first 4 terms, in ascending powers of x, of the binomial expansion of $(1 + x)^{10}$. Give each term in its simplest form.

Q5 Write down the full expansion of $(1 + x)^6$.

Q6 Find the first 4 terms in the expansion of $(1 + x)^7$.

Binomial expansions — $(1 + ax)^n$

When the **coefficient of x** in your binomial **isn't 1** (e.g. $(1 + 2x)^6$) you have to substitute the **whole x term** (e.g. $2x$) into the **binomial formula**:

$$(1 + ax)^n = 1 + \binom{n}{1}(ax) + \binom{n}{2}(ax)^2 + \binom{n}{3}(ax)^3 + \dots + (ax)^n$$

When a is **–1** (i.e. $(1 - x)^n$) the formula looks just like the formula for $(1 + x)^n$, but the **signs** of the terms **alternate**:

$$(1 - x)^n = (1 + (-x))^n$$

$$= 1 + \frac{n}{1}(-x) + \frac{n(n-1)}{1 \times 2}(-x)^2 + \frac{n(n-1)(n-2)}{1 \times 2 \times 3}(-x)^3 + \dots + (-x)^n$$

$$= 1 - \frac{n}{1}x + \frac{n(n-1)}{1 \times 2}x^2 - \frac{n(n-1)(n-2)}{1 \times 2 \times 3}x^3 + \dots \pm x^n$$

So for $(1 - x)^n$ you just use the usual binomial **coefficients**, but with **alternating signs**:

$$(1 - x)^n = 1 - \binom{n}{1}x + \binom{n}{2}x^2 - \binom{n}{3}x^3 + \dots \pm x^n$$

Tip: The sign of the last term is **plus** if n is **even** and **minus** if n is **odd**.

Examples

a) **What is the term in x^5 in the expansion of $(1 - 3x)^{12}$?**

The **general** binomial formula for $(1 - 3x)^n$ is:

$(1 - 3x)^n = (1 + (-3x))^n$

$= 1 + \frac{n}{1}(-3x) + \frac{n(n-1)}{1 \times 2}(-3x)^2 + \frac{n(n-1)(n-2)}{1 \times 2 \times 3}(-3x)^3 + \dots + (-3x)^n$

So for **$n = 12$** this is:

$(1 - 3x)^{12} = 1 + \frac{12}{1}(-3x) + \frac{12 \times 11}{1 \times 2}(-3x)^2 + \frac{12 \times 11 \times 10}{1 \times 2 \times 3}(-3x)^3 + \dots + (-3x)^{12}$

The **term in x^5** is: $\frac{12!}{5!7!}(-3)^5 x^5 = \binom{12}{5}(-3x)^5 = (792 \times -243)x^5$

$$= -192\,456x^5$$

b) **Find the coefficient of x^2 in the expansion of $(1 + 6x)^4(1 - 2x)^6$.** (PROBLEM SOLVING)

To find the x^2 term in the combined expansion you'll need to find all the **terms up to x^2** in both expansions (because these will form the x^2 term when they're multiplied) and then **multiply** together:

- $(1 + 6x)^4 = 1 + \binom{4}{1}(6x) + \binom{4}{2}(6x)^2 + \dots = 1 + 24x + 216x^2 + \dots$

- $(1 - 2x)^6 = 1 + \binom{6}{1}(-2x) + \binom{6}{2}(-2x)^2 = 1 - 12x + 60x^2 - \dots$

- So: $(1 + 6x)^4(1 - 2x)^6 = (1 + 24x + 216x^2 + ...)(1 - 12x + 60x^2 - ...)$
$$= 1 - 12x + 60x^2 - ... + 24x - 288x^2 + 1440x^3 - ...$$
$$+ 216x^2 - 2592x^3 + 12\ 960x^4 - ...$$
$$= 1 + 12x - 12x^2 + (higher\ power\ terms) + ...$$

- So the coefficient of x^2 is: $\boxed{-12}$

Tip: Most of this line of working isn't needed — you only really need to pick out the terms in the brackets which will multiply to give x^2. These are just $(1 \times 60x^2)$, $(24x \times -12x)$ and $(216x^2 \times 1)$ which give $60x^2$, $-288x^2$ and $216x^2$.

Approximations

- You can use a binomial expansion to expand **longer expressions** or to find **approximations** of a number raised to a power.

- Approximating usually involves taking a really small value for x so that you can **ignore high powers** of x (because they'll be really, really small).

- For example, if you're asked to approximate 1.001^9, then you just stick $x = 0.001$ into the expansion of $(1 + x)^9$. Because 0.001 is small, 0.001^2 is really small and adding on really small terms won't make much difference, so just the **first few terms** will give a good approximation.

Example 1

a) **Expand $(1 + 2x)^7$ to find the first 4 terms in ascending powers of x.**
$$(1 + 2x)^7 = 1 + {}^7C_1(2x) + {}^7C_2(2x)^2 + {}^7C_3(2x)^3 + ...$$
$$= 1 + 7(2x) + 21(4x^2) + 35(8x^3) + ...$$
$$= \boxed{1 + 14x + 84x^2 + 280x^3 + ...}$$

Tip: You can find the binomial coefficients using any of the methods from pages 110-114 — just pick whichever one you prefer.

b) **When x is small, x^3 and higher powers can be ignored.**
Hence show that for small x: $(2 - x)(1 + 2x)^7 \approx 2 + 27x + 154x^2$
Multiply your expansion of $(1 + 2x)^7$ through by $(2 - x)$:
$$(2 - x)(1 + 2x)^7 \approx (2 - x)(1 + 14x + 84x^2)$$
$$= 2 + 28x + 168x^2 - x - 14x^2 - 84x^3$$
$$= 2 + 27x + 154x^2 - 84x^3 \approx \boxed{2 + 27x + 154x^2}\ \text{as required}$$

Tip: You only need to include the terms up to the one in x^2 as you're told to ignore terms in x^3 and above in the question.

Example 2

a) **Find the first 3 terms of the expansion of $\left(1 - \dfrac{x}{4}\right)^9$.**
Use the **formula**, but replace x with $\left(-\dfrac{x}{4}\right)$:
$$\left(1 - \frac{x}{4}\right)^9 = 1 + \binom{9}{1}\left(-\frac{x}{4}\right) + \binom{9}{2}\left(-\frac{x}{4}\right)^2 + ... = 1 - 9\left(\frac{x}{4}\right) + 36\left(\frac{x^2}{16}\right) - ...$$
$$= \boxed{1 - \frac{9}{4}x + \frac{9}{4}x^2 - ...}$$

Tip: For approximations like these, you're only expected to use the terms of the expansion you've already found the coefficients for (unless you're told otherwise).

b) **Use your expansion to estimate $(0.998)^9$.**

$(0.998)^9 = (1 - 0.002)^9 = \left(1 - \dfrac{x}{4}\right)^9$ when $x = 0.008$.

So **substitute** $x = 0.008$ into the expansion you've just found — the first three terms are enough as 0.008^3 and higher powers will be very small:
$$(0.998)^9 = \left(1 - \frac{0.008}{4}\right)^9 \approx 1 - \frac{9}{4}(0.008) + \frac{9}{4}(0.008)^2$$
$$= 1 - 0.018 + 0.000144 = \boxed{0.982144}$$

Tip: If you do 0.998^9 on your calculator you get 0.98214333... so this is a pretty good approximation.

Q1b) Hint: You'll find some of the terms vanish when you subtract the second expansion.

Q1   Find the full expansions of:

   a) $(1 - x)^6$ b) $(1 + x)^9 - (1 - x)^9$ c) $(1 - 2x)^5$

Q2   Find the first 3 terms in the expansion of $(1 + x)^3(1 - x)^4$.

Q3   Find the coefficient of x^3y^2 in the expansion of $(1 + x)^5(1 + y)^7$.

Q2 Hint: You'll need to go up to x^2 in both expansions, then multiply the expansions together to find all the terms up to x^2 in the combined expansion.

Q4   Find the first 4 terms, in ascending powers of x, of the binomial expansion of $(1 + kx)^8$, where k is a non-zero constant.

Q5   In the expansion of $(1 - kx)^6$, the coefficient of x^2 is 135. Use this information to find the value of k, given that k is positive.

Q6   If x is small, so that x^2 and higher powers can be ignored, show that $(1 + x)(1 - 3x)^6 \approx 1 - 17x$.

Q7   a) Find, in their simplest form, the first 5 terms in the expansion of $\left(1 + \frac{x}{2}\right)^{12}$, in ascending powers of x.

   b) Use the expansion to work out the value of 1.005^{12} to 7 d.p.

Binomial expansions — $(a + b)^n$

When your binomial is of the form $(a + b)^n$ (e.g. $(2 + 3x)^7$, where $a = 2$ and $b = 3x$) you can use a slightly **different formula**:

$$\boxed{(a + b)^n = a^n + \binom{n}{1}a^{n-1}b + \binom{n}{2}a^{n-2}b^2 + \dots + \binom{n}{n-1}ab^{n-1} + b^n}$$

Tip: The powers of a decrease (from n to 0) as the powers of b increase (from 0 to n). The sum of the powers of a and b in each term is always n.

This formula is in the **formula booklet** and you don't need to know the proof, but seeing where it comes from might make things a bit clearer. You can find it from the binomial formula you've already seen:

- First rearrange so the binomial is in a form you can work with:

$$(a + b)^n = \left(a\left(1 + \frac{b}{a}\right)\right)^n = a^n\left(1 + \frac{b}{a}\right)^n$$

- You expand this by putting '$\frac{b}{a}$' into the **binomial formula** for $(1 + x)^n$, just like in the previous section:

$$= a^n\left(1 + \binom{n}{1}\left(\frac{b}{a}\right) + \binom{n}{2}\left(\frac{b}{a}\right)^2 + \dots + \binom{n}{n-1}\left(\frac{b}{a}\right)^{n-1} + \left(\frac{b}{a}\right)^n\right)$$

$$= a^n\left(1 + \binom{n}{1}\frac{b}{a} + \binom{n}{2}\frac{b^2}{a^2} + \dots + \binom{n}{n-1}\frac{b^{n-1}}{a^{n-1}} + \frac{b^n}{a^n}\right)$$

- **Multiply** through by a^n:

$$= a^n + \binom{n}{1}a^{n-1}b + \binom{n}{2}a^{n-2}b^2 + \dots + \binom{n}{n-1}ab^{n-1} + b^n$$

This is a general formula that works for any a and b, including 1 and x. So given **any binomial** you can pop your values for a, b and n into this formula and you'll get the **expansion**.

Example 1

Give the first three terms, in ascending powers of x, of the expansion of $(4 - 5x)^7$.

Use the **formula** from the previous page, with $a = 4$, $b = -5x$ and $n = 7$.

$$(4 - 5x)^7 = (4 + (-5x))^7 = 4^7 + \left(\binom{7}{1} \times 4^6 \times (-5x)\right) + \left(\binom{7}{2} \times 4^5 \times (-5x)^2\right) + \dots$$

$$= 16\,384 + (7 \times 4096 \times -5x) + (21 \times 1024 \times 25x^2) + \dots$$

$$= \boxed{16\,384 - 143\,360x + 537\,600x^2 + \dots}$$

> **Tip:** Be careful with b here — there's a minus sign that might catch you out.

Your other option with expansions of $(a + b)^n$ is to **factorise** the binomial so you get $a^n\left(1 + \dfrac{b}{a}\right)^n$, then plug $\dfrac{b}{a}$ into the **original binomial formula** (as you did with $(1 + ax)^n$ expansions in the last section).

Example 2

What is the coefficient of x^4 in the expansion of $(2 + 5x)^7$?

- Factorise: $(2 + 5x) = 2\left(1 + \dfrac{5}{2}x\right)$, so $(2 + 5x)^7 = 2^7\left(1 + \dfrac{5}{2}x\right)^7$.

- So the expansion $(2 + 5x)^7$ is the same as the expansion of $\left(1 + \dfrac{5}{2}x\right)^7$ multiplied by 2^7.

- Find the coefficient of x^4 in the expansion of $\left(1 + \dfrac{5}{2}x\right)^7$.

  The term is: $\binom{7}{4} \times \left(\dfrac{5}{2}x\right)^4 = \dfrac{7 \times 6 \times 5 \times 4}{1 \times 2 \times 3 \times 4} \times \dfrac{5^4}{2^4}x^4 = 35 \times \dfrac{5^4}{2^4}x^4 = \dfrac{21875}{16}x^4$

  So the coefficient is: $\dfrac{21875}{16}$

- Multiply this by 2^7 to get the coefficient of x^4 in the original binomial:
  $$2^7 \times \dfrac{21875}{16} = \boxed{175\,000}$$

> **Tip:** If you do it this way, make sure you don't forget to multiply back through by a^n when you give your final answer.

You can find an **unknown** in a binomial expansion if you're given some information about the coefficients:

Example 3

a) **The coefficient of x^5 in the binomial expansion of $(4 + kx)^7$ is 81 648. Find k.**

- From the $(a + b)^n$ formula, the term in x^5 of this expansion is:
  $${}^7C_5 4^2 (kx)^5 = 21 \times 16 \times k^5 \times x^5 = 336k^5 x^5$$

- So the coefficient of x^5 is $336k^5$.

- $336k^5 = 81\,648 \implies k^5 = 243 \implies \boxed{k = 3}$

> **Tip:** Just as with the $(1 + x)^n$ formula, you need to be familiar with all the ways of writing the binomial coefficients.

b) **In the expansion of $(1 + x)^n$, the coefficient of x^5 is twice the coefficient of x^4. What is the value of n?**

(PROBLEM SOLVING)

- The coefficient of x^5 is $\dfrac{n!}{5!(n-5)!}$, the coefficient of x^4 is $\dfrac{n!}{4!(n-4)!}$.

- The coefficient of x^5 is twice the coefficient of x^4, so:

$$\frac{n!}{5!\,(n-5)!} = 2 \times \frac{n!}{4!\,(n-4)!}$$

$$\frac{1}{5!\,(n-5)!} = 2 \times \frac{1}{4!\,(n-4)!} \quad \longleftarrow \boxed{\text{Cancel the } n!}$$

$$\frac{1}{5 \times 4! \times (n-5)!} = 2 \times \frac{1}{4! \times (n-4) \times (n-5)!}$$

$$\frac{1}{5} = 2 \times \frac{1}{(n-4)}$$

$$n - 4 = 10$$

$$n = 14$$

Tip: $5! = 5 \times 4!$ and $(n-4)! = (n-4) \times (n-5)!$

$\boxed{\text{Cancel the } 4! \text{ and the } (n-5)!}$

- To check: $^{14}C_5 = 2002$, $^{14}C_4 = 1001$, so $^{14}C_5 = 2 \times {}^{14}C_4$

Tip: It's really easy to check your answer for questions like this on a calculator — so make sure you do.

$\boxed{\text{The value of } n \text{ is } 14}$

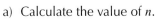

Exercise 1.3

Q1 Find the first 4 terms of the binomial expansion of $(3 + x)^6$.

Q2 Find the full expansion of $(2 + x)^4$.

Q3 In the expansion of $(1 + \lambda x)^8$, the coefficient of x^5 is 57 344.
 a) Work out the value of λ.
 b) Find the first 3 terms of the expansion.

Q4 a) Find the first 5 terms in the expansion of $(2 + x)^8$.
 b) Use this expansion to find an approximation for 2.01^8 to 5 d.p.

Q4b) Hint: This is the same method as the approximation example for $(1 + ax)^n$ expansions on page 115.

Q5 Find the first 4 terms in the expansion of $(3 + 5x)^7$.

Q6 Find the first 5 terms, in ascending order, of $(1 + x)(3 + 2x)^6$.

Q7 The term in x^2 for the expansion of $(1 + x)^n$ is $231x^2$.
 a) What is the value of n?   b) What is the term in x^3?

Q8 In the expansion of $(a + 3x)^8$, the coefficient of x^2 is $\frac{32}{27}$ times bigger than the coefficient of x^5. What is the value of a?

Q9 In the expansion of $(1 + 2x)^5(3 - x)^4$, what is the coefficient of x^3?

Q10 In the expansion of $(1 + x)^n$, the coefficient of x^3 is 3 times larger than the coefficient of x^2.
 a) Calculate the value of n.
 b) If the coefficient of x^2 is $a \times$ (the coefficient of x), what is a?

Q11 In the expansion of $(2 + \mu x)^8$, where μ is a constant, the coefficient of x^2 is 87 808. What are the possible values of μ?

1. The Sine and Cosine Rules

In this section you'll see how SOHCAHTOA and the sine and cosine rules can be used to find the length of each side and the size of each angle in a triangle, as well as its area. You might have seen some of this at GCSE, so parts of this chapter will just be a recap.

Trig values from triangles

You need to know the values of **sin**, **cos** and **tan** at 30°, 60° and 45°, and there are two **triangles** that can help you remember them. It may seem like a long-winded way of doing it, but once you know how to do it, you'll always be able to work them out — even without a calculator.

The idea is you draw the triangles below, putting in their angles and side lengths. Then you can use them to work out special trig values like **sin 45°** or **cos 60°** with exact values instead of the decimals given by calculators.

First, make sure you can remember SOHCAHTOA:

$$\sin = \frac{\text{opp}}{\text{hyp}} \qquad \cos = \frac{\text{adj}}{\text{hyp}} \qquad \tan = \frac{\text{opp}}{\text{adj}}$$

These are the two triangles that you'll use:

Half an equilateral triangle with sides of length 2:

- You can work out the height using Pythagoras' theorem: height $= \sqrt{2^2 - 1^2} = \sqrt{3}$.

- Then you can use the triangle to work out sin, cos and tan of 30° and 60°.

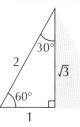

$$\sin 30° = \frac{1}{2} \qquad \cos 30° = \frac{\sqrt{3}}{2} \qquad \tan 30° = \frac{1}{\sqrt{3}}$$

$$\sin 60° = \frac{\sqrt{3}}{2} \qquad \cos 60° = \frac{1}{2} \qquad \tan 60° = \sqrt{3}$$

Right-angled triangle with two sides of length 1:

- You can work out the hypotenuse using Pythagoras' theorem: hypotenuse $= \sqrt{1^2 + 1^2} = \sqrt{2}$.

- Then you can use the triangle to work out sin, cos and tan of 45°.

$$\sin 45° = \frac{1}{\sqrt{2}} \qquad \cos 45° = \frac{1}{\sqrt{2}} \qquad \tan 45° = 1$$

Learning Objectives:

- Be able to find the values of sin, cos and tan of 30°, 60° and 45° without a calculator.

- Use the unit circle to find values of sin and cos.

- Know the sine and cosine rules and be able to use them on any triangle.

- Be able to work out the area of a triangle using the formula $\frac{1}{2}ab \sin C$.

Tip: Make sure you're confident with these values as they often pop up.

Trig values from the unit circle

You can also find trig values from the **unit circle** — a circle with **radius 1**, centred on the **origin**.
Take a point on the unit circle and make a right-angled triangle:

Tip: The hypotenuse is always the radius — so it's always 1.

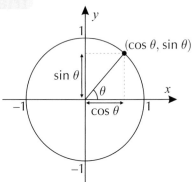

From this you know that:

$$\sin \theta = \frac{\text{opp}}{1} = \text{opp} = y$$

$$\cos \theta = \frac{\text{adj}}{1} = \text{adj} = x$$

Tip: You can use the unit circle to easily find sin and cos of 0° and 90° — they're just the points on the axes.
So at the point (1, 0):
cos 0° = 1, sin 0° = 0.
And at the point (0, 1):
cos 90° = 0, sin 90° = 1.

So on the unit circle, the y-coordinate is **sin θ** and the x-coordinate is **cos θ**.

For any point on the unit circle, the coordinates are $(\cos \theta, \sin \theta)$, where θ is the angle measured from the **positive** x-axis in an **anticlockwise** direction.

This is true for **all** values of θ, including values greater than 90°.

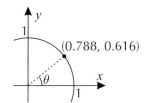

Example 1

The coordinates of a point on the unit circle, given to 3 s.f., are shown on the diagram to the right. Find θ to the nearest degree.

- The point is on the unit circle, so you know that the coordinates are $(\cos \theta, \sin \theta)$. So $\cos \theta = 0.788$ and $\sin \theta = 0.616$.

Tip: For the second step, you could do $\sin^{-1}$ (0.616) instead.

- You only need one of these to find the value of θ.
  $\cos \theta = 0.788 \quad \Rightarrow \quad \theta = \cos^{-1} (0.788) = 38°$ (to the nearest degree).

Example 2

Find the coordinates of the point A on the unit circle, shown on the diagram to the right. Give your answer to 2 d.p.

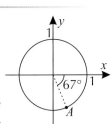

- To work out the coordinates of A, you need the angle from the positive x-axis in an **anticlockwise** direction. This is $360° - 67° = 293°$.

- $\cos 293° = 0.3907...$, and $\sin 293° = -0.9205...$
  So the coordinates of A are $(0.39, -0.92)$ to 2 d.p.

The sine and cosine rules

There are three useful formulas you need to know for working out information about a triangle. There are **two** for finding the **angles** and **sides** (called the **sine rule** and **cosine rule**) and one for finding the **area**.

Tip: These rules work on any triangle, not just right-angled triangles.

a, b and c are the lengths of the sides

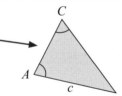

A, B and C are the angles opposite the sides with the same letters (so angle C is opposite side c).

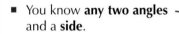

The Sine Rule

$$\frac{a}{\sin A} = \frac{b}{\sin B} = \frac{c}{\sin C}$$

The Cosine Rule

$$a^2 = b^2 + c^2 - 2bc \cos A$$

Area of any triangle

$$\text{Area} = \frac{1}{2} ab \sin C$$

Tip: You can use any two bits of the sine rule to make a normal equation with just one = sign. The sine rule also works if you flip all the fractions upside down: $\frac{\sin A}{a} = \frac{\sin B}{b} = \frac{\sin C}{c}$.

To decide which rule to use, look at what you know about the triangle:

You can use the **sine rule** if:

- You know **any two angles** and a **side**.

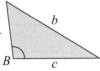

You can **sometimes** use the **sine rule** if:

- You know **two sides** and an **angle that isn't between them**.

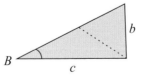

This doesn't always work though — sometimes there are **2 possible** triangles:

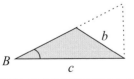

Tip: Remember, if you know two angles you can work out the third by subtracting them from 180°.

You can use the **cosine rule** if:

- You know **all three** sides...

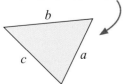

- ...or you know **two sides** and the **angle** that's **between** them.

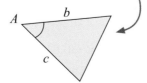

Tip: You can also rearrange the cosine rule into the form $\cos A = \frac{b^2 + c^2 - a^2}{2bc}$ to find an angle.

Example 1

Find the missing sides and angles for $\triangle ABC$, in which $A = 40°$, $a = 27$ m and $B = 73°$. Then find the area of the triangle.

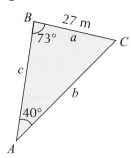

- Start by **sketching** the triangle. It doesn't have to be particularly accurate, but it can help you decide which rule(s) you need.

- Here you have 2 angles and a side, so you can use the **sine rule**.

- First, though, start by finding angle C (using the fact that the angles in a triangle add up to 180°).

$$\angle C = 180° - 73° - 40° = 67°$$

- Now use the sine rule to find the other sides one at a time:

$$\frac{a}{\sin A} = \frac{b}{\sin B} \Rightarrow \frac{27}{\sin 40°} = \frac{b}{\sin 73°} \qquad \frac{c}{\sin C} = \frac{a}{\sin A} \Rightarrow \frac{c}{\sin 67°} = \frac{27}{\sin 40°}$$

$$\Rightarrow b = \frac{27 \times \sin 73°}{\sin 40°} \qquad\qquad \Rightarrow c = \frac{27 \times \sin 67°}{\sin 40°}$$

$$= 40.2 \text{ m} \ (1 \text{ d.p.}) \qquad\qquad = 38.7 \text{ m} \ (1 \text{ d.p.})$$

- Now you've found the missing values, you can find the area using the formula:

$$\text{Area of } \triangle ABC = \frac{1}{2} ab \sin C$$

Tip: Use the unrounded value for b here (rather than just 40.2).

$$= \frac{1}{2} \times 27 \times 40.169... \times \sin 67°$$

$$= 499.2 \text{ m}^2 \ (1 \text{ d.p.})$$

Example 2

Find the values of X, Y and Z.

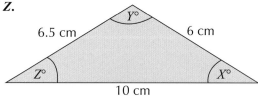

Tip: One of the hardest things about using the sine and cosine rules is matching the sides and angles given in the question to the ones in the formula. If it helps, label your triangle with A, B, C, a, b and c each time.

- You've been given all three sides but none of the angles, so start by using the **cosine rule** to find angle Z (you'll have to rearrange the formula a bit first).

$$a^2 = b^2 + c^2 - 2bc \cos A \Rightarrow \cos A = \frac{b^2 + c^2 - a^2}{2bc}$$

$$\Rightarrow \cos Z = \frac{10^2 + 6.5^2 - 6^2}{(2 \times 10 \times 6.5)}$$

Tip: Just use the $\cos^{-1}$ button on your calculator to work out the value of Z from $\cos Z$.

$$\Rightarrow \cos Z = 0.817... \Rightarrow Z = 35.183...°$$

$$\Rightarrow Z = 35.2° \ (1 \text{ d.p.})$$

- Use the cosine rule **again** to find the value of another angle. It doesn't matter which one you go for (using Y here).

$$a^2 = b^2 + c^2 - 2bc \cos A$$

$$\Rightarrow \cos Y = \frac{6^2 + 6.5^2 - 10^2}{2 \times 6 \times 6.5}$$

$$\Rightarrow \cos Y = -0.278... \Rightarrow Y = 106.191...$$

$$\Rightarrow \boxed{Y = 106.2°} \ (1 \text{ d.p.})$$

- Now that you have two of the angles, you can find the other by subtracting them from 180°:

$$X = 180° - 35.183...° - 106.191...° = 38.624...°$$

$$= \boxed{38.6°} \ (1 \text{ d.p.})$$

Tip: You could try using the sine rule here, but it would give you a value of 73.8° for Y — and you can see from the diagram that angle Y is obtuse. So here you'd have to subtract 73.8° from 180° to get the actual value of Y — there's more on this later in the chapter.

- You can find the areas of more **complicated** shapes by turning them into **multiple triangles** stuck together, then using the **sine** and **cosine rules** on each individual triangle.

- This method can be used for working out angles and sides in real-life problems, such as calculating distances travelled or areas covered. Sometimes you'll see a problem that uses **bearings**.

Example 3

Rasmus the trawlerman has cast his nets between buoys in the North Sea (shown on the diagram below).

a) **Find the area of sea his nets cover to 2 s.f.**

Tip: Rasmus's boat is called the Sea Beast.

- You can start by finding the distance between X and Z (let's call it y) — this will split the area into 2 triangles.
  Do this by treating XYZ as a triangle and using the **cosine rule**:

$$a^2 = b^2 + c^2 - 2bc \cos A$$

$$\Rightarrow y^2 = 400^2 + 350^2$$
$$- 2 \times 400 \times 350 \times \cos 45°$$

$$\Rightarrow y^2 = 84\,510.1...$$

$$\Rightarrow \boxed{y = 290.7 \text{ m}} \ (1 \text{ d.p.})$$

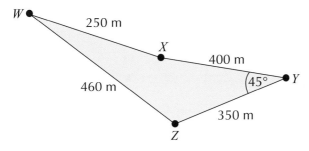

- Now you have all three sides for the left-hand triangle, so you can find an angle (let's say W) with the **cosine rule**.

$$a^2 = b^2 + c^2 - 2bc \cos A$$

$$\Rightarrow \cos W = \frac{460^2 + 250^2 - 290.70...^2}{2 \times 460 \times 250}$$

$$\Rightarrow \cos W = 0.824...$$

$$\Rightarrow \boxed{W = 34.5°} \text{ (1 d.p.)}$$

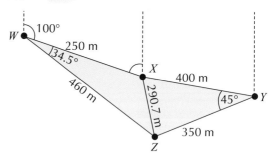

Tip: You could have found the area of the right-hand triangle at the start as you had all the info you needed.

- Now you have enough information to find the **area** of each triangle with the formula on page 121.

Left-hand triangle:

$$A = \frac{1}{2} ab \sin C$$

$$= \frac{1}{2} \times 250 \times 460 \times \sin 34.48...°$$

$$= \boxed{32\ 600 \text{ m}^2} \text{ (3 s.f.)}$$

Right-hand triangle:

$$A = \frac{1}{2} ab \sin C$$

$$= \frac{1}{2} \times 400 \times 350 \times \sin 45°$$

$$= \boxed{49\ 500 \text{ m}^2} \text{ (3 s.f.)}$$

- So the total area of sea covered is:

$$32\ 600 + 49\ 500 = \boxed{82\ 000 \text{ m}^2} \text{ (2 s.f.)}$$

b) If X is on a bearing of 100° from W, on what bearing does Rasmus have to sail to get from X to Y (to 3 s.f.)?

Tip: This comes from the rules of parallel lines — you did this at GCSE.

- To find the bearing, find all the other angles round X and subtract them from 360°. The unknown angle marked below is $180° - 100° = 80°$.

- To find the angle $\angle WXZ$, use the cosine rule on the left-hand triangle:

$$a^2 = b^2 + c^2 - 2bc \cos A \Rightarrow \cos \angle WXZ = \frac{250^2 + 290.70...^2 - 460^2}{2 \times 250 \times 290.70...}$$

$$\Rightarrow \angle WXZ = \cos^{-1}(-0.444...)$$

$$\Rightarrow \angle WXZ = 116.38° \text{ (2 d.p.)}$$

- Then do the same for angle $\angle YXZ$, using the right-hand triangle:

$$a^2 = b^2 + c^2 - 2bc \cos A \Rightarrow \cos \angle YXZ = \frac{400^2 + 290.70...^2 - 350^2}{2 \times 400 \times 290.70...}$$

$$\Rightarrow \cos \angle YXZ = 0.524...$$

$$\Rightarrow \angle YXZ = 58.36° \text{ (2 d.p.)}$$

- Now just subtract all the angles from 360° to find the bearing Rasmus should sail on to get from X to Y:

$$360° - 80° - 116.38° - 58.36° = 105.26° = \boxed{105°} \text{ (3 s.f.)}$$

Give all answers to 3 significant figures unless otherwise stated.

Q1 Find the coordinates of point P
    on the unit circle.

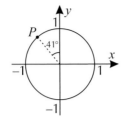

Q2 Use the cosine rule to find
    the length QR.

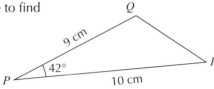

Q3 Use the sine rule to find
    the length TW.

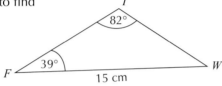

Q4 Find the size of angle D.

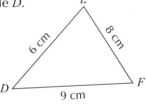

Q5 In triangle JKL: JL = 24 cm, KL = 29 cm and angle L = 62°.
    Find the length JK.

Q6 A building has a wall that slopes inward at an angle of 81° to the
    horizontal ground. A safety inspector calculates that a ladder leaning
    against the outside of the wall must be at an angle of 78° to the
    ground. What distance up the wall would a 5 m ladder safely reach?

Q7 In triangle PQR: PR = 48 m, angle P = 38° and
    angle R = 43°. Find the length PQ.

Q8 In triangle DEF: DE = 8 cm, EF = 11 cm and DF = 16 cm.
    Find the smallest angle.

Q9 The vertices of triangle XYZ have coordinates
    X: (–2, 2), Y: (5, 8) and Z: (3, –2). Find the angle XYZ.

Q8 Hint: Sketching the
triangle first will make
it easier to see which
angle you need to find.
The smallest angle is
opposite the shortest
side, so it's easy to
identify.

Q10 Find the area of this triangle.

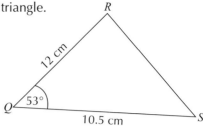

Q11 Find the area of this triangle to 2 d.p.

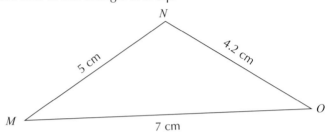

Q12 Two points, A and B, are both at sea level and on opposite sides of a mountain. The distance between them is 5 km. From A, the angle of elevation of the top of the mountain (M) is 21°, and from B, the angle of elevation is 17°.

a) Find the distance BM.

b) Hence find the height of the mountain to the nearest metre.

Q13 Hint: Bearings are measured clockwise from the vertical (North).

Q13 A ship sails 8 km on a bearing of 070° and then changes direction to sail 10 km on a bearing of 030°.

a) Draw a diagram to represent the situation.

b) What is the ship's distance from its starting position?

c) On what bearing must it now sail to get back to its starting position?

Q14 Find the area of the quadrilateral $ABCD$ shown in the diagram below.

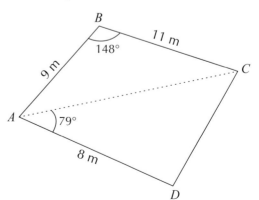

2. Trig Identities

Trig identities are really useful for simplifying expressions, and they can make equations easier to solve by replacing one term with another.

Trig identities

There are **two trig identities** you need to know — they're really useful, and also fairly straightforward to find using results you already know.

You know that $\sin = \dfrac{\text{opp}}{\text{hyp}}$, $\cos = \dfrac{\text{adj}}{\text{hyp}}$ and $\tan = \dfrac{\text{opp}}{\text{adj}}$ (see p.119).

So $\sin \div \cos = \dfrac{\text{opp}}{\text{hyp}} \div \dfrac{\text{adj}}{\text{hyp}} = \dfrac{\text{opp}}{\text{hyp}} \times \dfrac{\text{hyp}}{\text{adj}} = \dfrac{\text{opp}}{\text{adj}} = \tan$. So for all values of θ:

$$\tan \theta \equiv \frac{\sin \theta}{\cos \theta}$$

On page 120 you saw that the coordinates (x, y) of a point on the unit circle can be written as $(\cos \theta, \sin \theta)$ — i.e. $x = \cos \theta$ and $y = \sin \theta$.

The equation of the unit circle is $x^2 + y^2 = 1$.
Substituting in $\cos \theta$ and $\sin \theta$ gives the equation $\cos^2 \theta + \sin^2 \theta = 1$.

This is true for all values of θ, so you can write it as an identity:

$$\sin^2 \theta + \cos^2 \theta \equiv 1$$

This can be rearranged into $\sin^2 \theta \equiv 1 - \cos^2 \theta$ or $\cos^2 \theta \equiv 1 - \sin^2 \theta$.

You can use these identities to **prove** that two expressions are equivalent.

Example 1

Show that $\dfrac{\cos^2 \theta}{1 + \sin \theta} \equiv 1 - \sin \theta$.

- A good way of doing this kind of question is to play around with **one side** of the equation until it's the same as the other side.

- Start with the left-hand side: $\quad \dfrac{\cos^2 \theta}{1 + \sin \theta}$

- There are usually "clues" that you can pick up to help you decide what to do next. You know there's a trig identity for $\cos^2 \theta$, so start by **replacing** it in the fraction:

$$\frac{\cos^2 \theta}{1 + \sin \theta} \equiv \frac{1 - \sin^2 \theta}{1 + \sin \theta}$$

- The next step isn't quite as obvious, but if you look at the top of the fraction it might remind you of something — it's a **difference of two squares** (see p.13).

$$\frac{1 - \sin^2 \theta}{1 + \sin \theta} \equiv \frac{(1 + \sin \theta)(1 - \sin \theta)}{1 + \sin \theta}$$

Learning Objectives:

- Know the trig identities $\tan \theta \equiv \dfrac{\sin \theta}{\cos \theta}$ and $\sin^2 \theta + \cos^2 \theta \equiv 1$.

- Be able to use trig identities to prove other relations.

- Be able to use trig identities to find the exact values of an expression.

Tip: The '$\equiv$' means that the relation is true for all values of θ. An identity is just a relation which contains a '$\equiv$' sign — see page 6.

Tip: Have a look back at p.98-100 for a reminder of circle equations.

Tip: $\sin^2 \theta$ is another way of writing $(\sin \theta)^2$.

Tip: The replacements aren't always easy to spot — look out for things like differences of two squares, or 1's that can be replaced by $\sin^2 \theta + \cos^2 \theta$.

- Now you can just cancel the $1 + \sin \theta$ from the top and bottom of the fraction, and you get the answer you were looking for:

$$\frac{(1 + \sin \theta)(1 - \sin \theta)}{1 + \sin \theta} \equiv 1 - \sin \theta \quad \text{This is the right-hand side.}$$

Example 2

Find the exact value of sin θ if cos $\theta = \dfrac{2}{3}$, given that θ is an acute angle.

- The identity to use here is $\sin^2 \theta + \cos^2 \theta \equiv 1$

- Rearranging this gives $\sin^2 \theta \equiv 1 - \cos^2 \theta$

- Then put in the value of $\cos \theta$ in the question and square root each side:

$$\sin \theta = \sqrt{1 - \left(\frac{2}{3}\right)^2} = \sqrt{\frac{5}{9}} = \frac{\sqrt{5}}{3}$$

Tip: You're told that θ is acute here, which means that $\sin \theta$ is positive (check out the graph on the next page), so you can ignore the negative square root.

Exercise 2.1

Q1 Use the identity $\tan \theta \equiv \dfrac{\sin \theta}{\cos \theta}$ to show that $\dfrac{\sin \theta}{\tan \theta} - \cos \theta \equiv 0$.

Q2 Use the identity $\sin^2 \theta + \cos^2 \theta \equiv 1$ to show that $\cos^2 \theta \equiv (1 - \sin \theta)(1 + \sin \theta)$.

Q3 Given that x is acute, find the exact value of $\cos x$ if $\sin x = \dfrac{1}{2}$.

Q3, 5 Hint: You're told that x is acute, so ignore the negative roots.

Q4 Show that $4 \sin^2 x - 3 \cos x + 1 \equiv 5 - 3 \cos x - 4 \cos^2 x$.

Q5 Given that x is acute, find the exact value of $\tan x$ if $\sin^2 x = \dfrac{3}{4}$.

Q4 Hint: If you're not told which identity to use, just play around with the ones you know until something works.

Q6 Show that $(\tan x + 1)(\tan x - 1) \equiv \dfrac{1}{\cos^2 x} - 2$.

Q7 A student is asked to solve the equation $\sin \theta = \dfrac{1}{2} \tan \theta$, where $0° \leq \theta \leq 90°$. Their working is shown below:

$$\sin \theta = \frac{1}{2} \tan \theta \Rightarrow \sin \theta = \frac{1}{2} \times \frac{\sin \theta}{\cos \theta}$$

$$\Rightarrow \cos \theta \sin \theta = \frac{1}{2} \sin \theta \Rightarrow \cos \theta = \frac{1}{2} \Rightarrow \theta = 60°.$$

Find the error they made and explain how this has resulted in an incomplete solution.

Q8 Hint: $\dfrac{1}{\tan x} \equiv \dfrac{\cos x}{\sin x}$

Q8 Show that $\tan x + \dfrac{1}{\tan x} \equiv \dfrac{1}{\sin x \cos x}$.

Q9 Show that $4 + \sin x - 6 \cos^2 x \equiv (2 \sin x - 1)(3 \sin x + 2)$.

Q10 Show that $\sin^2 x \cos^2 y - \cos^2 x \sin^2 y \equiv \cos^2 y - \cos^2 x$.

Q11 Use the identity $\sin^2 \theta + \cos^2 \theta \equiv 1$ to prove Pythagoras' theorem.

PROBLEM SOLVING

3. Trig Functions

Being able to sketch the graphs of trig functions and their transformations is really useful — it'll come in handy later in the chapter when you have to solve equations within a given interval.

Graphs of trig functions

You should be able to draw the graphs of **sin x**, **cos x** and **tan x** without looking them up — including all the important points, like where the graphs cross the **axes** and their **maximum** and **minimum** points.

Learning Objectives:
- Be able to sketch the graphs of sin x, cos x and tan x.
- Be able to sketch the common transformations of the graphs of sin x, cos x and tan x.

---

sin x

- The graph of $y = \sin x$ is **periodic** — it repeats itself every 360°. So $\sin x = \sin (x + 360°) = \sin (x + 720°) = \sin (x + 360n°)$, where n is an integer.

- It bounces between $y = -1$ and $y = 1$, and it can **never** have a value outside this range.

- It goes through the **origin** (as $\sin 0° = 0$) and then crosses the x-axis every **180°**.

- $\sin (-x) = -\sin x$. The graph has **rotational symmetry** about the origin, so you could rotate it 180° about (0, 0) and it would look the same.

- The graph of $y = \sin x$ looks like this:

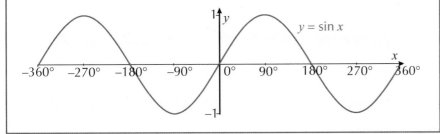

Tip: You say that sin x has a period of 360°.

---

cos x

- The graph of $y = \cos x$ is also **periodic** with period 360°. $\cos x = \cos (x + 360°) = \cos (x + 720°) = \cos (x + 360n°)$, where n is an integer.

- It also bounces between $y = -1$ and $y = 1$, and it can **never** have a value outside this range.

- It crosses the y-axis at **$y = 1$** (as $\cos 0° = 1$) and the x-axis at $\pm 90°$, $\pm 270°$ etc.

- $\cos (-x) = \cos x$. The graph is **symmetrical** about the **y-axis**, so you could reflect it in the y-axis and it would look the same.

Tip: The graphs of sin x and cos x are the same shape but shifted 90° along the x-axis. This makes them easier to remember, but make sure you don't get them mixed up.

- The graph of $y = \cos x$ looks like this:

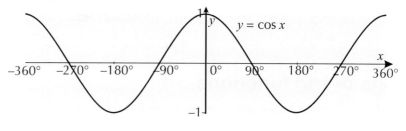

tan x

Tip: The best way to learn these functions is to practise sketching them and marking on the key points.

Tip: $y = \tan x$ is undefined at these points because you're dividing by zero. Remember from p.127 that $\tan x \equiv \dfrac{\sin x}{\cos x}$, so when $\cos x = 0$, $\tan x$ is undefined, and $\cos x = 0$ when $x = 90°$, $270°$ etc. (see the graph above).

- The graph of $y = \tan x$ is also **periodic**, but this time it repeats itself every 180°. So $\tan x = \tan (x + 180°) = \tan (x + 360°) = \tan (x + 180n°)$, where n is an integer.

- It takes values between $-\infty$ and ∞ in each **180° interval**.

- It goes through the **origin** (as $\tan 0° = 0$).

- It's **undefined** at $\pm 90°$, $\pm 270°$, $\pm 450°$...
  — at these points it **jumps** from ∞ to $-\infty$ or vice versa.

- The graph of $y = \tan x$ looks like this:

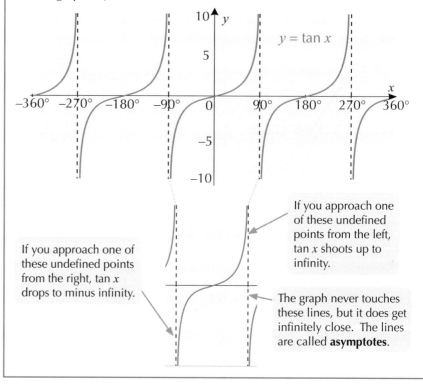

If you approach one of these undefined points from the right, tan x drops to minus infinity.

If you approach one of these undefined points from the left, tan x shoots up to infinity.

The graph never touches these lines, but it does get infinitely close. The lines are called **asymptotes**.

Transformations

You came across different types of **transformations** on pages 91-96.
A **translation** is a horizontal or vertical **shift** that doesn't change the shape of the graph. A **stretch** is exactly what it says — a horizontal or vertical **stretch** (or **squash**) of the graph. You need to be able to apply these types of transformation to **trig functions**.

1. A translation along the y-axis: $y = \sin(x) + c$

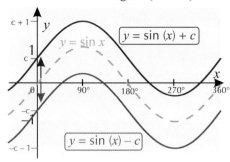

- For $c > 0$, $\sin(x) + c$ is just $\sin x$ **shifted c up**.

- Similarly, $\sin(x) - c$ is just $\sin x$ **shifted c down**.

2. A translation along the x-axis: $y = \sin(x + c)$

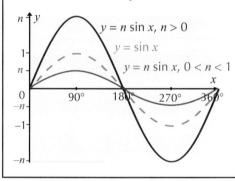

- For $c > 0$, $\sin(x + c)$ is just $\sin x$ **shifted c to the left**.

- Similarly, $\sin(x - c)$ is just $\sin x$ **shifted c to the right**.

Tip: For $y = \sin(x + c)$, the graph has a maximum where $x + c = 90°$, $450°$, etc. — i.e. when $x = 90° - c$, $450° - c$, ...
It has a minimum where $x + c = 270°$, $630°$ ... and crosses the x-axis at $x + c = 0°$, $180°$, $360°$ ...

3. A vertical stretch: $y = n \sin x$

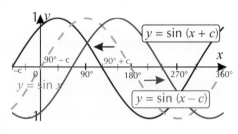

- For $y = n \sin x$, the graph of $y = \sin x$ is **stretched vertically** by a factor of n.

- If $n > 1$, the graph gets taller, and if $0 < n < 1$, the graph gets flatter.

- And if $n < 0$, the graph is also **reflected** in the x-axis.

Tip: In the diagram, n is 2 for the blue curve and 0.5 for the orange curve.

Tip: When $0 < n < 1$ it looks like a squash, but it's still called a stretch.

4. A horizontal stretch: $y = \sin nx$

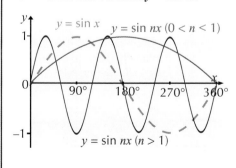

- For $y = \sin nx$, the graph of $y = \sin x$ is **stretched horizontally** by a factor of $\frac{1}{n}$.

- If $0 < n < 1$, the graph of $y = \sin x$ is **stretched horizontally outwards**, and if $n > 1$ the graph of $y = \sin x$ is **squashed inwards**.

- If $n < 0$, the graph is also **reflected** in the y-axis.

Tip: Make sure you know which way the stretch goes. The larger n is, the more squashed the graph becomes. In the diagram, n is 3 for the blue curve and 0.5 for the orange curve.

The same transformations will apply to the graphs of $y = \cos x$ and $y = \tan x$ as well.

Example 1

On the same axes, sketch the graphs of $y = \cos x$ and $y = -2 \cos x$ in the range $-360° \leq x \leq 360°$.

- Start by **sketching** the graph of $\cos x$:

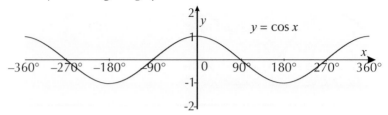

- Next, think about what the **transformed** graph will look like. It's in the form $y = n \cos x$, so it will be **stretched vertically**.

- $n = -2$, so it will be stretched by a factor of **2**. As n is negative, it will also be **reflected** in the x-axis. This is all the information you need to be able to sketch the graph.

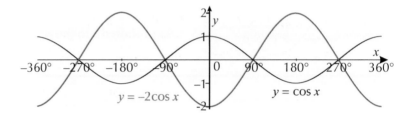

Example 2

On the same axes, sketch the graphs of $y = \tan x$ and $y = \tan 2x$ in the interval $-180° \leq x \leq 180°$.

- Again, start by sketching the graph of $y = \tan x$ (see p.130) — this is the dark red line shown below.

- This time it's in the form $y = \tan nx$, so it will be **stretched horizontally**. $n > 1$, so the graph will be stretched by a factor of $\frac{1}{2}$, which is the same as a squash by a factor of 2.

- To make it easier, draw dotted lines for the new asymptotes (divide the x-values of the old ones by 2) then draw the tan shape between them — shown in orange.

Tip: You'll have double the number of repetitions of the tan shape in the same interval because you've halved the period.

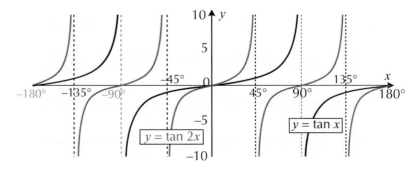

Q1 On the same set of axes, sketch the graphs of $y = \cos x$ and $y = \cos x + 3$ in the interval $-360° \leq x \leq 360°$.

Q2 On the same set of axes, sketch the graphs of $y = \cos x$ and $y = \cos (x + 90°)$ in the interval $-180° \leq x \leq 180°$.

Q3 On the same set of axes, sketch the graphs of $y = \sin x$ and $y = \frac{1}{3} \sin x$ in the interval $-180° \leq x \leq 180°$.

Q4 On the same set of axes, sketch the graphs of $y = \sin x$ and $y = \sin 3x$ in the interval $0° \leq x \leq 360°$.

Q5 On the same set of axes, sketch the graphs of $y = \cos x$ and $y = -\cos x$ in the interval $0° \leq x \leq 360°$.

Q6 a) Sketch the graph of $f(x) = \tan x$ in the interval $-90° \leq x \leq 270°$.

b) Translate this graph 90° to the left and sketch it on the same set of axes as part a).

c) Write down the equation of the transformed graph.

> **Q6c) Hint:** Just look at what's happened to the graph, then think about which type of transformation is needed to achieve it.

Q7 a) Sketch the graph of $y = \sin x$ in the interval $-360° \leq x \leq 360°$.

b) Stretch the graph horizontally by a factor of 2 and sketch it on the same set of axes as part a).

c) Write down the equation of the transformed graph.

Q8 The diagram shows the graph of $y = \sin x$ and a transformed graph.

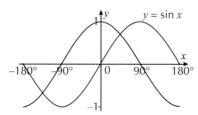

a) Describe the transformation.

b) Write down the equation of the transformed graph.

Q9 The diagram shows the graph of $y = \cos x$ and a transformed graph.

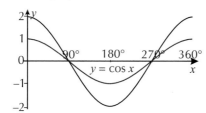

a) Describe the transformation.

b) Write down the equation of the transformed graph.

4. Solving Trig Equations

Learning Objectives:
- Be able to solve trig equations by sketching a graph.
- Be able to solve trig equations using a CAST diagram.
- Be able to solve trig equations of the form $\sin kx = n$ and $\sin (x + c) = n$.
- Be able to solve trig equations using trig identities and quadratics.

Once you know how to sketch the graphs of trig functions, you can use them to solve trig equations. Solving a trig equation just means finding the value (or values) of x that satisfies the given equation.

Sketching a graph

To solve trig equations in a **given interval** you can use one of two methods. The first is drawing a **graph** of the function and reading solutions off the graph. You'll often find that there's **more than one** solution to the equation — in every **360° interval**, there are usually **two** solutions to an equation, and if the interval is bigger (see Example 2 below), there'll be even more solutions.

Example 1

Solve $\cos x = \frac{1}{2}$ for $0° \leq x \leq 360°$.

- Start by using your **calculator** to work out the first value.
  For $\cos x = \frac{1}{2}$, $x = 60°$.

Tip: This is actually one of the common trig angles from page 119.

- Then **sketch a graph** of $\cos x$ in the interval you're interested in, and draw a horizontal line across for $y = \frac{1}{2}$. The points where the line and curve **meet** are the solutions of the equation.

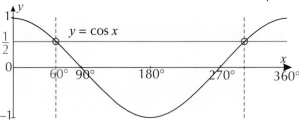

Tip: If you are dealing with sin or tan instead, use the graphs to work out the solutions in a similar way.

- Each 360° interval of the graph is symmetrical, so the second solution will be the same distance from 360° as the first is from 0°. You know one solution is 60°, so the other solution is 360° − 60° = 300°.

- You now know all of the solutions in this interval: $x = 60°, 300°$

If you had an interval that was **larger** than **one repetition** of the graph (i.e. 360° for sin and cos, and 180° for tan), you'd just add or subtract **multiples** of 360° (for sin and cos) or 180° (for tan) onto the solutions you've found until you have **all** the solutions in the **given interval**.

Example 2

Solve $\sin x = -0.3$ for $0° \leq x \leq 720°$. Give your answers to 3 s.f.

- Again, use your **calculator** to work out the first value. For $\sin x = -0.3$, $x = -17.45...°$ However, this is **outside** the given interval for x, so **add on 360°** to find a solution in the interval:
  $-17.45...° + 360° = 342.54...°$

Tip: You add on 360° because the curve repeats every 360°. For tan, you would add on 180°.

- Now **sketch a graph** of $\sin x$ in the interval you need, and draw a horizontal line across at $y = -0.3$. This time, you'll need to draw the graph between $x = 0°$ and $x = 720°$, so there'll be **2 repetitions** of the sin wave.

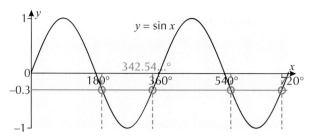

- You can see from the graph that there are **4 solutions** in the given interval (because the horizontal line crosses the curve 4 times). You've already found the one at $x = 342.54...°$ — to find the one before it, you use the **symmetry** of the graph. The solution you know is $360° - 342.54...° = 17.45...°$ away from $360°$. Now, looking at the graph, the other solution between $0°$ and $360°$ will be $17.45...°$ away from **180°**: i.e. $180° + 17.45...° = 197.45...°$

- For the next two solutions (the ones between $360°$ and $720°$), just **add 360°** onto the values you've already found:
  $197.45...° + 360° = 557.45...°$ and $342.54...° + 360° = 702.54...°$

- So the solutions to $\sin x = -0.3$ for $0 \le x \le 720°$, to 3 s.f., are:

$$x = 197°, 343°, 557°, 703°$$

Tip: If the interval is bigger, just keep on adding (or subtracting) lots of $360°$ until you have all the answers within the required interval.

Exercise 4.1

Q1 By sketching a graph, find all the solutions to the equations below in the interval $0° \le x \le 360°$. Give your answers to 1 decimal place.

    a) $\sin x = 0.75$ b) $\cos x = 0.31$ c) $\tan x = -1.5$

    d) $\sin x = -0.42$ e) $\cos x = -0.56$ f) $\tan x = -0.67$

Q2 By sketching a graph, find all the solutions to the equations below in the interval $0° \le x \le 360°$.

    a) $\cos x = \dfrac{1}{\sqrt{2}}$ b) $\tan x = \sqrt{3}$ c) $\sin x = \dfrac{1}{2}$

    d) $\tan x = \dfrac{1}{\sqrt{3}}$ e) $\tan x = 1$ f) $\cos x = \dfrac{\sqrt{3}}{2}$

Q2 Hint: All of these values relate to the common angles on p.119.

Q3 One solution of $\cos x = -0.8$ is $143.1°$ (1 d.p.). Use the graph below to find all the solutions in the interval $0° \le x \le 360°$.

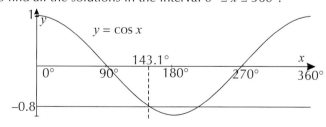

Q4 Find all the solutions of the equation $\tan x = 2.5$ in the interval $0° \le x \le 1080°$. Give your answers to 1 decimal place.

Q5 Find all the solutions of the equation $\sin x = 0.81$ in the interval $-360° \le x \le 360°$. Give your answers to 3 significant figures.

Q4-5 Hint: Be careful with the intervals here — and remember that tan repeats every $180°$.

Using a CAST diagram

The second way of finding the solutions to a trig equation is by using a **CAST diagram**. CAST stands for Cos, All, Sin, Tan, and it shows you where each of these functions is **positive** by splitting a 360° period into **quadrants**.

Tip: CAST diagrams are useful because they summarise the information from the graphs of sin, cos and tan without actually having to sketch the graphs.

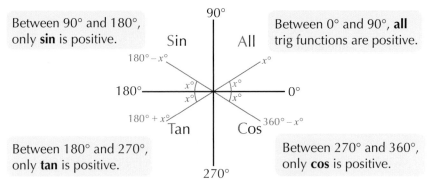

Between 90° and 180°, only **sin** is positive.

Between 0° and 90°, **all** trig functions are positive.

Between 180° and 270°, only **tan** is positive.

Between 270° and 360°, only **cos** is positive.

Tip: The angle you put into the CAST diagram should be acute (i.e. between 0° and 90°) — if you get a negative value, just put the positive value into the diagram. Or you can measure **clockwise** from 0° for negative angles.

- To use a CAST diagram, you need to use your **calculator** to find the first solution of the trig function (or, if it's a common angle, you might just be able to recognise it).

- You then make the **same angle** from the **horizontal** in each of the four quadrants (shown in the diagram above), then measure each angle **anticlockwise** from 0°. So if the first solution was 45°, the solution in the sin quadrant would be 135° (180° − 45°) measured anticlockwise from 0°, and so on.

- **Ignore** the ones that give a **negative** result (unless the given value is negative — in which case you want the two quadrants in which the trig function is **negative**).

Example 1

Find all the solutions of $\sin x = \frac{1}{2}$ for $0° \leq x \leq 360°$.

- Use a **calculator** to find the **first solution** (30°), and put this in your CAST diagram.

- Then add the **same angle** to each **quadrant**, measuring from the **horizontal** in each case.

Tip: This value is also a common angle — you don't need to use a calculator if you can remember it.

Tip: Remember, each line you mark on the diagram represents the angle being measured anticlockwise from 0°.

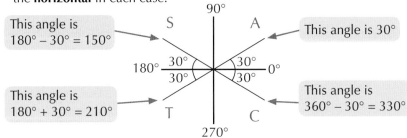

This angle is $180° - 30° = 150°$

This angle is 30°

This angle is $180° + 30° = 210°$

This angle is $360° - 30° = 330°$

- You need a **positive** value of $\sin x$ (because $\frac{1}{2}$ is positive), so you're only interested in the quadrants where $\sin x$ is positive — i.e. the first and second quadrants. There are two solutions: 30° and 150°.

- For values **outside** the interval $0° \leq x \leq 360°$, just find solutions between 0° and 360° and then **add** or **subtract multiples of 360°** to find solutions in the correct interval (there's an example of this on the next page).

Example 2

Find all the solutions of tan x = –6 for 0° ≤ x ≤ 720°.
Give your answers to 1 d.p.

- Using a **calculator**, you'll find that the first solution is x = –80.5° (1 d.p.).
  Ignore the negative and just put the value 80.5° into the CAST diagram.

- Add the **same angle** to each **quadrant**,
  measuring from the **horizontal** in each case.

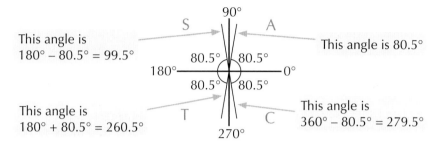

This angle is
180° – 80.5° = 99.5°

This angle is 80.5°

This angle is
180° + 80.5° = 260.5°

This angle is
360° – 80.5° = 279.5°

- You need a **negative** value of tan x (as –6 is negative), so just look at the
  quadrants where tan x is negative (i.e. the 'S' and 'C' quadrants).
  There are two solutions: 99.5° and 279.5° (the first value was **negative**,
  so you could have measured **clockwise** from 0° to find the solution 279.5°).

- To find the solutions between 360° and 720°,
  just **add 360°** to the solutions you've already found.

- The solutions of tan x = –6 for 0° ≤ x ≤ 720° are
  x = 99.5°, 279.5°, 459.5° and 639.5° (to 1 d.p.)

Tip: Adding or
subtracting 360° is
the same as going
round a full circle on
the CAST diagram (so
you end up back at
the same position).

Exercise 4.2

Q1 One solution of sin x = 0.45 is x = 26.7° (1 d.p.). Use a CAST
diagram to find all the solutions in the interval 0° ≤ x ≤ 360°.

Q2 Use a CAST diagram to find the solutions of the following equations
in the interval 0° ≤ x ≤ 360°. Give your answers to 1 d.p.

  a) cos x = 0.8   b) tan x = 2.7   c) sin x = –0.15

  d) tan x = 0.3   e) tan x = –0.6   f) sin x = –0.29

  g) 4 sin x – 1 = 0   h) 4 cos x – 3 = 0   i) 5 tan x + 7 = 0

Q2 Hint: You might
have to rearrange some
of the equations first.

Q3 Use a CAST diagram to find all the solutions to tan x = –8.4
in the interval 0° ≤ x ≤ 360°. Give your answers to 3 s.f.

Q4 Use a CAST diagram to find all the solutions to sin x = 0.75
in the interval 0° ≤ x ≤ 720°. Give your answers to 1 d.p.

Q5 Use a CAST diagram to find all the solutions to cos x = 0.31
in the interval –180° ≤ x ≤ 180°. Give your answers to 1 d.p.

Q6 Use a CAST diagram to find all the solutions to sin x = 0.82
in the interval 0° ≤ x ≤ 720°. Give your answers to 3 s.f.

Changing the interval

Sometimes you'll have to solve equations of the form **sin** $kx = n$ or **sin** $(x + c) = n$ (where n, k and c are numbers). In these situations it's usually easiest to **change the interval** you're solving for, then **solve as normal** for kx or $x + c$. You'll then need to remember to get the final solutions either by **dividing by** k or **subtracting** c at the end.

Solving equations of the form sin $kx = n$

Let's start by looking at how to solve equations of the form **sin** $kx = n$.

- First, **multiply** the **interval** you're looking for solutions in by k. E.g. for the equation sin $2x = n$ in the interval $0° \le x \le 360°$, you'd look for solutions in the interval $0° \le 2x \le 720°$. Then **solve** the equation over the new interval.

- However, this gives you solutions for kx, so you then need to **divide** each solution by k to find the values of x.

You can either **sketch the graph** over the new interval (this will show you **how many** solutions there are) or you can use the **CAST method** to find solutions between 0° and 360° then add on multiples of 360° until you have all the solutions in the new interval — use whichever method you prefer.

Example 1

Solve cos $4x = 0.6$ **for** $0° \le x \le 360°$. **Give your answers to 1 d.p.**

- First, **change** the **interval**. The interval is $0° \le x \le 360°$, and the value of k is 4, so **multiply** the whole interval by **4**: $0° \le 4x \le 1440°$.

- Then **solve** the equation to find the solutions for **4x**. I'm going to use a **CAST diagram**, but you could sketch a graph if you prefer.

- Find the **first solution** using a calculator: cos $4x = 0.6$
$$\Rightarrow 4x = 53.13° \text{ (2 d.p.)}$$

You want the quadrants where cos is **positive**, so the other solution between 0° and 360° is:
$4x = 360° - 53.13° = 306.87°$ (2 d.p.)

- Now **add on** multiples of 360° to find **all** the solutions in the interval $0° \le 4x \le 1440°$ (to 2 d.p.):
53.13°, 306.87°, 413.13°, 666.87°, 773.13°, 1026.87°, 1133.13°, 1386.87°

- Remember, these are solutions for **4x**. To find the solutions for x, **divide** through by **4**. So the solutions to cos $4x = 0.6$ in the interval $0° \le x \le 360°$ (to 1 d.p.) are:
13.3°, 76.7°, 103.3°, 166.7°, 193.3°, 256.7°, 283.3°, 346.7°

- It's a good idea to **check** your answers — just put your values of x into cos $4x$ and check that they give you 0.6. You can make sure you've got the **right number** of solutions too — there are 2 solutions to cos $x = 0.6$ in the interval $0° \le x \le 360°$, so there'll be 8 solutions to cos $4x = 0.6$ in the same interval.

Tip: If you'd sketched a graph, you could just see how many times the graph and line crossed — there's an example of this on the next page.

Example 2

Solve sin $3x = -\dfrac{1}{\sqrt{2}}$ for $0° \leq x \leq 360°$.

- This time you've got **$3x$** instead of x, which means the **interval** you need to find solutions in is $0° \leq 3x \leq 1080°$. So sketch the graph of $y = \sin x$ between 0° and 1080°.

- Use your **calculator** to find a solution. You'll get $3x = -45°$, but this is outside the interval for $3x$, so use the pattern of the graph to find a solution in the interval. As the sin curve **repeats every 360°**, there'll be a solution at $-45° + 360° = 315°$.

- Now you can use the **symmetry** of the graph to find the other solution between 0° and 360° — the graph is symmetrical in each interval of 180°, so the other solution is at $180° + 45° = 225°$.

- You know the graph repeats every 360°, so **add on** lots of 360° to the answers you've just found to find the other solutions between 0° and 1080°: $3x = 585°, 675°, 945°, 1035°$.

Tip: This is actually one of the common angles from p.119 — so you could have found it without using a calculator.

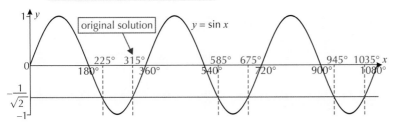

- Now you have 6 solutions for $3x$, so **divide them all by 3** to get the solutions for x: $x = 75°, 105°, 195°, 225°, 315°, 345°$.

Tip: Again, you can check your answers using a calculator — and make sure they're in the right interval.

Example 3

Find all the solutions of $0.9 + 3 \tan 2x = 5.1$ for $0° \leq x \leq 360°$. Give your answers to 1 d.p.

- First, rearrange into a more familiar format:
$0.9 + 3 \tan 2x = 5.1 \Rightarrow 3 \tan 2x = 4.2 \Rightarrow \tan 2x = 1.4$

- It's $2x$, so the interval needs to be multiplied by 2: $0° \leq 2x \leq 720°$

- Use a calculator to work out the first solution: $2x = 54.46°$ (2 d.p.)

- Then use a CAST diagram to find the other solution between 0° and 360°:

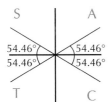

You want the quadrants where tan is **positive**, so the other solution between 0° and 360° is:
$2x = 180° + 54.46° = 234.46°$ (2 d.p.)

- To find the solutions between 360° and 720°, just **add 360°** to the solutions you've already found: $2x = 414.46°, 594.46°$ (2 d.p.)

- Finally, to find the solutions for x between 0° and 360°, just divide by 2: $x = 27.2°, 117.2°, 207.2°, 297.2°$ (1 d.p.)

Solving equations of the form sin (x + c) = n

The method for solving equations of the form **sin (x + c) = n** is similar — but instead of multiplying the interval, you have to add or subtract the value of *c*.

- **Add** (or **subtract**) the value of *c* to the **whole interval** — so the interval $0° \leq x \leq 360°$ becomes $c \leq x + c \leq 360° + c$ (you add *c* onto each bit of the interval).

- Now **solve** the equation over the **new interval** — again, you can either sketch a graph or use a CAST diagram.

- Finally, **subtract** (or **add**) *c* from your solutions to give the values for *x*.

Example 1

Solve $\cos (x + 60°) = \dfrac{3}{4}$ for $-360° \leq x \leq 360°$, giving your answers to 1 d.p.

Tip: Be careful with the interval here — the original interval isn't $0° \leq x \leq 360°$.

- You've got $\cos (x + 60°)$ instead of $\cos x$ — so **add 60°** to each bit of the interval. The new interval is: $-300° \leq x + 60° \leq 420°$.

- Use your **calculator** to get a solution:

$$\cos (x + 60°) = \frac{3}{4} \Rightarrow x + 60° = 41.4° \text{ (1 d.p.)}$$

- Use the **symmetry** of the graph to find the other solution between 0° and 360°. The first solution is 41.4° away from 0°, so the next solution will be 41.4° away from 360° — i.e. at $360° - 41.4° = 318.6°$ (1 d.p.).

- The cos graph **repeats** every 360°, so to find the other solutions, **add and subtract 360°** from the answers you've just found, making sure they're still within the interval you want: $x + 60° = 401.4°, 678.6°$ (not in interval), $-41.4°, -318.6°$ (not in interval).

Tip: You can see from the graph that there should be 4 solutions in this interval, but be careful — if your graph wasn't accurate, it would be easy to miss a solution.

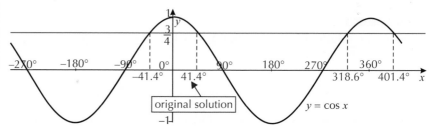

- These solutions are for $\cos (x + 60°)$ so you need to **subtract 60° from each value** to find the solutions for *x* (to 1 d.p.): $x = -101.4°, -18.6°, 258.6°$ and $341.4°$

- So there are **4 solutions**, and they're all in the required interval $(-360° \leq x \leq 360°)$. Again, you can **check** your answers by putting them back into $\cos (x + 60°)$ and making sure you get $\dfrac{3}{4}$.

Example 2

Solve tan $(x - 75°) = 2$ for $0° \leq x \leq 360°$. Give your answers to 1 d.p.

- First, find the new interval. This time you want to **subtract 75°** from each bit of the interval, so the new interval is $-75° \leq x - 75° \leq 285°$. You'll need to sketch the graph of tan x over this interval.

- Use your **calculator** to find a solution:
  tan $(x - 75°) = 2 \Rightarrow x - 75° = 63.4°$ (1 d.p.)

- Now you can use the **pattern** of the graph to find the other solution in the interval — the tan graph **repeats** every **180°**, so add on 180° to the solution you've already found: $63.4° + 180° = 243.4°$ (1 d.p.)

Tip: To see if there are any other solutions within the interval, add and subtract 180° to the values you've just found: $x - 75° = -116.6°$, 423.4°. Both of these values are outside the required interval, so there are only 2 solutions.

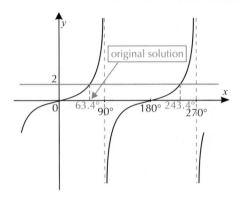

- Finally, **add on 75°** to find the solutions in the interval $0° \leq x \leq 360°$ (to 1 d.p.): $x = 138.4°, 318.4°$

Example 3

Solve $2 \sin (x + 60°) + \sqrt{3} = 0$ for $0° \leq x \leq 720°$.

- First, rearrange: $2 \sin (x + 60°) + \sqrt{3} = 0 \Rightarrow 2 \sin (x + 60°) = -\sqrt{3}$

  $$\Rightarrow \sin (x + 60°) = -\frac{\sqrt{3}}{2}$$

- This time, **add 60°** to each bit of the interval: $60° \leq x + 60° \leq 780°$

- $\frac{\sqrt{3}}{2}$ is a **common trig value** — from p.119 you know that $\sin 60° = \frac{\sqrt{3}}{2}$, so put 60° into the **CAST diagram**:

Tip: Have a look back at the example on p.137 to see how to deal with negative values.

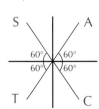

As you're finding solutions for $-\frac{\sqrt{3}}{2}$, you want the quadrants where sin is **negative** (the 3rd and 4th quadrants), so the solutions between 0° and 360° are:

$x + 60° = 180° + 60° = 240°$ and
$x + 60° = 360° - 60° = 300°$

- To find the other solutions (between 360° and 720°), just **add 360°** to the solutions you've already found: $x + 60° = 600°, 660°$

- Finally, **subtract 60°** from each solution to find the values of x:
  $x = 180°, 240°, 540°, 600°$

In this exercise, give all answers to 1 d.p.

Q1   Solve $\sin 2x = 0.6$ in the interval $0° \leq x \leq 360°$.

Q2   Solve $\tan 4x = 4.6$ in the interval $0° \leq x \leq 360°$.

Q3   Solve $\cos 3x = -0.24$ in the interval $0° \leq x \leq 360°$.

Q4   Find all the solutions to $\cos 2x = 0.72$ in the interval $0 \leq x \leq 360°$.

Q5   Find all the solutions to $\frac{1}{2}\sin 3x - 0.61 = -0.75$
in the interval $0 \leq x \leq 360°$.

Q6 Hint: Don't let the $\frac{x}{2}$ throw you — it's exactly the same method as before, except you divide the interval by 2 instead of multiplying.

Q6   Solve $\tan \frac{x}{2} = 2.1$ in the interval $0° \leq x \leq 360°$.

Q7   Find all the solutions to $\cos (x - 27°) = 0.64$
in the interval $0° \leq x \leq 360°$.

Q8   Solve $\tan (x - 140°) = -0.76$ in the interval $0° \leq x \leq 360°$.

Q9   Find all the solutions to $\sin (x + 36°) = 0.45$ in the interval $0° \leq x \leq 360°$.

Q10 Find all the solutions to $\tan (x + 73°) = 1.84$
in the interval $0° \leq x \leq 360°$.

Q11 Find all the solutions to $\sin (x - 45°) = -0.25$
in the interval $-180 \leq x \leq 360°$.

Q12 Solve $\cos (x + 22.5°) = 0.13$ in the interval $0 \leq x \leq 360°$.

Using trig identities to solve equations

Sometimes you'll be asked to find solutions to an equation that has a **tan** term as well as a sin or cos term in it.
In these situations you might need to use the **trig identity** for $\tan x$ (p.127):

$$\tan x \equiv \frac{\sin x}{\cos x}$$

This will **eliminate** the tan term, and you'll be left with an equation just in terms of sin or cos.

Similarly, if you have a **$\sin^2 x$** or **$\cos^2 x$**, you can use the other identity to rewrite one trig function in terms of the other.

$$\sin^2 x + \cos^2 x \equiv 1$$

If you're left with a quadratic equation (e.g. one that contains both $\sin^2 x$ and $\sin x$), you might need to factorise before you solve it. To do this, it's usually easiest to make a substitution (e.g. $y = \sin x$ — see p.34).

Example

Solve $6 \cos^2 x + \cos x \tan x = 5$ for $0° \leq x \leq 360°$.
Give any non-exact answers to 1 d.p.

- The equation has both cos x and tan x in it, so writing tan x as $\dfrac{\sin x}{\cos x}$ would be a good place to start:

$$6 \cos^2 x + \cos x \tan x = 5 \quad \Rightarrow \quad 6 \cos^2 x + \cos x \, \dfrac{\sin x}{\cos x} = 5$$

- Now the cos x terms will **cancel**:

$$6 \cos^2 x + \cos x \, \dfrac{\sin x}{\cos x} = 5 \quad \Rightarrow \quad 6 \cos^2 x + \sin x = 5$$

- Now the equation has both sin x and cos x in it.
So **replace** the $\cos^2 x$ with $1 - \sin^2 x$:

$$6 \cos^2 x + \sin x = 5 \quad \Rightarrow \quad 6(1 - \sin^2 x) + \sin x = 5$$

> **Tip:** Now sin x is the only trig function you need to deal with — it doesn't matter that the original equation didn't have sin in it.

- **Multiply out** the bracket and **rearrange** it so that you've got zero on one side — you get a **quadratic** in sin x:

$$6(1 - \sin^2 x) + \sin x = 5 \quad \Rightarrow \quad 6 - 6 \sin^2 x + \sin x - 5 = 0$$
$$\Rightarrow \quad 6 \sin^2 x - \sin x - 1 = 0$$

- It's easier to **factorise** the quadratic if you make the **substitution** $y = \sin x$:

$$6 \sin^2 x - \sin x - 1 = 0 \Rightarrow 6y^2 - y - 1 = 0$$
$$\Rightarrow (2y - 1)(3y + 1) = 0$$
$$\Rightarrow (2 \sin x - 1)(3 \sin x + 1) = 0$$

- Now you have two things multiplying together to make zero.
That means **one** of them must be **equal** to zero.

$$2 \sin x - 1 = 0 \quad \Rightarrow \quad \sin x = \dfrac{1}{2} \quad \text{or} \quad 3 \sin x + 1 = 0 \quad \Rightarrow \quad \sin x = -\dfrac{1}{3}$$

- For $\sin x = \dfrac{1}{2}$, the first solution is $x = 30°$.
You can use a **CAST diagram** to find the other solutions:

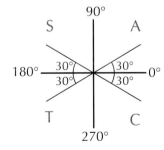

> **Tip:** You could also find the other solutions by using the graph method — sketch the curve $y = \sin x$.

- You need a **positive** solution for sin x, so look at the **1st** and **2nd** quadrants: 30° and 180° − 30° = 150°.

- For $\sin x = -\frac{1}{3}$, use your calculator to find $x = -19.47...°$.

  You can then use a CAST diagram again to find the solutions in the interval $0° \le x \le 360°$:

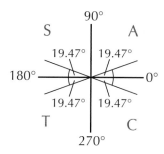

- You need a **negative** solution for $\sin x$, so look at the quadrants where sin is negative — i.e. the **3rd** and **4th** quadrants:
  $180° + 19.47...° = \boxed{199.47...°}$ and $360° - 19.47...° = \boxed{340.52...°}$.

- You now have all the solutions:
  $x = 30°, 150°, 199.5°$ and $340.5°$ (to 1 d.p.)

Exercise 4.4

In this exercise, give all non-exact answers to 1 d.p.

Q1 Solve each of the following equations for values of x in the interval $0° \le x \le 360°$:

a) $(\tan x - 5)(3 \sin x - 1) = 0$ b) $5 \sin x \tan x - 4 \tan x = 0$

c) $\tan^2 x = 9$ d) $4 \cos^2 x = 3 \cos x$

e) $3 \sin x = 5 \cos x$ f) $5 \tan^2 x - 2 \tan x = 0$

g) $6 \cos^2 x - \cos x - 2 = 0$ h) $7 \sin x + 3 \cos x = 0$

Q2 Find the solutions to each of the following equations in the given interval:

a) $\tan x = \sin x \cos x$ $0° \le x \le 360°$

b) $5 \cos^2 x - 9 \sin x = 3$ $-360° \le x \le 720°$

c) $2 \sin^2 x + \sin x - 1 = 0$ $-360° \le x \le 360°$

Q3 a) Show that the equation $4 \sin^2 x = 3 - 3 \cos x$ can be written as $4 \cos^2 x - 3 \cos x - 1 = 0$.

     b) Hence solve the equation $4 \sin^2 x = 3 - 3 \cos x$ in the interval $0° \le x \le 360°$.

Q4 Find all the solutions of the equation $9 \sin^2 2x + 3 \cos 2x = 7$ in the interval $0° \le x \le 360°$.

Q5 Find all the solutions of the equation $\frac{\cos x}{\tan x} + \sin x = 3$ in the interval $-360° \le x \le 360°$.

1. Exponentials

Exponentials are extremely useful functions — they're used in loads of different real-world scenarios, from radioactive decay to rabbit populations. So you'll be seeing lots of 'Modelling' stamps in this chapter...

Exponentials

Exponentials are functions of the form $y = a^x$ (or $f(x) = a^x$), where **$a > 0$**. **All** graphs of exponential functions have the **same basic shape**.

$y = a^x$ for $a > 1$

- All the graphs go through **1** at $x = 0$ since $a^0 = 1$ for any a.

- $a > 1$ — so y **increases as x increases**.

- The **bigger** a is, the **quicker** the graph increases (so the curve is **steeper**).

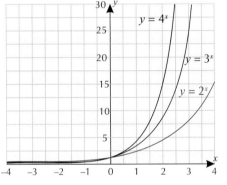

- As x **decreases**, y **decreases** at a **smaller and smaller rate** — y will approach zero, but never actually get there.

- This means as $x \to \infty$, $y \to \infty$ and as $x \to -\infty$, $y \to 0$.

Tip: Notice that the graph of $y = a^x$ is always positive — it never goes below the x-axis.

Tip: The notation $x \to \infty$ just means 'x tends to ∞' (i.e. x gets bigger and bigger). Similarly $y \to 0$ means 'y tends to 0' (gets smaller and smaller). a^x gets infinitely close to 0 but never reaches it, so $y = 0$ is an **asymptote** of the graph — see p.89.

$y = a^x$ for $0 < a < 1$

- All the graphs go through **1** at $x = 0$ since $a^0 = 1$ for any a.

- $0 < a < 1$ — so y **decreases as x increases**.

- The **smaller** a is, the **faster** the graphs decrease (so the curve is **steeper**).

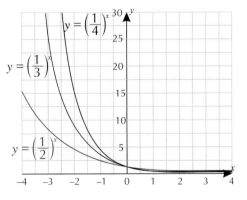

- As x **increases**, y **decreases** at a **smaller and smaller rate** — y will approach zero, but never actually get there.

- This means as $x \to \infty$, $y \to 0$ and as $x \to -\infty$, $y \to \infty$.

Tip: These graphs have the same shapes as the ones above but reflected in the y-axis. This makes sense since $\left(\frac{1}{a}\right)^x$ is the same as a^{-x} — i.e. $f(-x)$ (see p.95).

The exponential function, e^x

The main feature of **exponential graphs** or **functions** is that the **rate of increase / decrease** of the function is **proportional** to the function itself.

Tip: An **irrational number** is a real number which can't be written as a fraction $\frac{a}{b}$ (where a and b are both integers and $b \neq 0$).

You need to know about a value of 'a' for which the **gradient** of $y = a^x$ is **exactly the same** as a^x. That value is known as **e**, an **irrational number** around 2.7183 (it's stored in your calculator just like π). This **special case** of an exponential function, $y = e^x$, is called **'the' exponential function**.

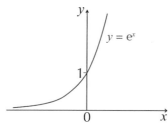

Because e is just a number, the graph of **$y = e^x$** has all the properties of $y = a^x$:

- $y = e^x$ cuts the y-axis at **(0, 1)**.
- As $x \rightarrow \infty$, $e^x \rightarrow \infty$ and as $x \rightarrow -\infty$, $e^x \rightarrow 0$.
- $y = e^x$ **does not exist** for $y \leq 0$ (i.e. $e^x > 0$ — it can't be zero or negative).

Tip: If a question asks you to give an exact solution, leave the answer in terms of e — e.g. write e^3, not 20.0855...

Tip: The graphs of Ae^{kx} and Ae^{-kx} come up a lot in modelling (see p.157-159).

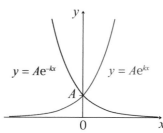

For **positive constants** A and k, the graph of Ae^{kx} looks similar to the graph of e^x, except that it cuts the y-axis at **(0, A)**. For the graph of Ae^{-kx}, you just reflect the graph of Ae^{kx} in the y-axis.

Gradient of $y = Ae^{kx}$

Tip: The gradient of a curve is the same as the gradient of the tangent to the curve at a point — for example, on the curve $y = e^x$, the gradient of the tangent to the curve at $x = 2$ is e^2 (so the gradient of the curve is also e^2 at this point).

There's more on finding the gradient of a curve on p.164-165.

As mentioned above, an interesting property of $y = e^x$ is that its gradient is e^x. This can be generalised:

> For the graph $y = e^{kx}$, where k is a constant, its gradient is ke^{kx}.
> For the graph $y = Ae^{kx}$, where A and k are constants, its gradient is kAe^{kx}.

The gradient shows the **rate of change** of the function. So the rate of change of Ae^{kx} is **directly proportional** to the function itself. This means that an **exponential model** is suitable in situations where the rate of increase/decrease of y is proportional to the value of y.

If the **signs** for A and k are **different**, (e.g. $y = -2e^{3x}$ or $y = 4e^{-x}$) then the gradient will be negative — i.e. it's a **decreasing** function (see p.182).

Example 1

Tip: You could be asked to give your answer to a certain number of decimal places or significant figures. For example, $40e^{16}$ = 355 444 420.82... = 355 000 000 (to 3 s.f.)

Find the gradient of the curve $f(x) = 5e^{8x}$ at the points $x = 0$ and $x = 2$. Leave your answers as exact solutions.

- This equation is in the form $f(x) = Ae^{kx}$, where $A = 5$ and $k = 8$

- So you can use the formula above for finding the gradient: $kAe^{kx} = 8 \times 5 \times e^{8x} = 40e^{8x}$

- At $x = 0$, the gradient of $f(x)$ is $40e^{8 \times 0} = 40e^0 = \boxed{40}$

- At $x = 2$, the gradient of $f(x)$ is $40e^{8 \times 2} = \boxed{40e^{16}}$

Example 2

The number of geese, g, at a nature reserve after t days is modelled using the formula $g = Ae^{kt}$, where A and k are constants.

After 1 day, there were 80 geese, and the gradient of the curve plotted from the data collected was 241. Find A and k, giving your answers to 1 s.f.

- "After 1 day" means $t = 1$:
  When $t = 1$, $g = 80 \Rightarrow 80 = Ae^k$.
  At this point, the gradient is $241 \Rightarrow 241 = kAe^k$.

- Solve these simultaneously (substitute $Ae^k = 80$ into $241 = kAe^k$):
  $241 = kAe^k \Rightarrow 241 = 80k \Rightarrow k = \dfrac{241}{80} = 3.0125$. So $k = 3$ (1 s.f.)

- Put this back into one of the original equations to find A:
  $80 = Ae^k \Rightarrow 80 = Ae^{3.0125} \Rightarrow A = \dfrac{80}{e^{3.0125}} = 3.933...$ So $A = 4$ (1 s.f.)

- The equation of the curve is $g = 4e^{3t}$

Tip: In real-life situations, A is called the initial value — and it's usually positive.

Tip: Use the unrounded value of k to find A.

Tip: The initial value is 4 — so there were 4 geese to start with.

Exercise 1.1

Q1 On the same axes, sketch the graphs of:

a) $y = 2^x$ b) $y = 3^{-x}$ c) $y = e^x$

Q2 Match each of the following functions to one of the graphs below:

a) $y = 3e^{3x}$ b) $y = 3^x$ c) $y = 3e^{-x}$

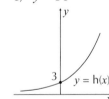

Q3 Find the gradient of each curve at the points given. Leave your answers in exact form.

a) $y = e^{3x}$ at the points $x = 0$ and $x = 1$

b) $y = 5e^{0.5x}$ at the points $x = -2$ and $x = 2$

c) $x = 2.5e^{6t}$ at the points $t = \dfrac{1}{3}$ and $t = 5$

Q4 The population of rabbits in a wood is modelled using the function $f(t)$, where t is the number of years since the population was first counted.

The gradient of the curve of $f(t)$ is always 0.4 times the value of $f(t)$. When first counted, there were 7 rabbits.

Find the function $f(t)$ and use it to estimate the number of rabbits in the wood after 5 years.

2. Logs

'Logarithm' might sound scary, but it's just a fancy way of describing the power that something has been raised to. Once you know how to use logs, you can solve all sorts of equations that involve powers.

Learning Objectives:

- Be able to convert between index and log notation.
- Know and be able to use the natural logarithm, ln.
- Understand the relationship between exponentials and logs.

Logs

A **logarithm** is just the power that a number needs to be **raised to** to produce a given value.

Before now, you've used **index notation** to represent powers, but sometimes it's easier to work with **log notation**.

In **index notation**, 3^5 means that **5** lots of **3** are multiplied together. **3** is known as the **base**. You now need to be able to **switch** from index notation into **log notation**, and vice versa.

Log notation looks like this:

$$\log_a b = c$$

... which means the **same** as the **index notation**...

$$a^c = b$$

Tip: If you're struggling to get your head round this, try putting in some numbers — e.g. $\log_3 9 = 2$ is the same as $3^2 = 9$.

- The little number 'a' after 'log' is the **base**.

- 'c' is the **power** the base is being **raised** to.

- 'b' is the answer you get when a is raised to the power c.

- Log means '**power**', so the log above really just means: "what is the power you need to raise a to if you want to end up with b?"

> As $\log_a b = c$ is the same as $a^c = b$, it means that:
>
> $$\log_a a = 1 \quad \text{and} \quad \log_a 1 = 0$$

Tip: In index notation, this is saying that $a^1 = a$, and $a^0 = 1$.

- The **base** of a log must always be a **positive number** $\neq 1$ (otherwise the log isn't defined for some, or all, values).

- For $a > 1$, if $b > 1$, then c is **positive**. And if $0 < b < 1$ then c is **negative**. For $0 < a < 1$, the **opposite** is true.

Tip: Remember from p.145 that the graph of $y = a^x$ is always positive — so you can't take the log of a negative number (i.e. there's no power you can raise a positive number to to make it negative).

- There are two bases that are more common than others: the first is **base 10**. The button marked 'log' on your calculator uses base 10.

> Index notation: $10^2 = 100$
>
> or
>
> log notation: $\log_{10} 100 = 2$

- So the **logarithm** of 100 to the **base 10** is 2, because 10 raised to the **power** of 2 is 100.

- The base goes here but it's usually left out if it's 10.

- The other common base is **base e** — this is known as the **natural logarithm** and is written 'ln':

Tip: Your calculator can probably also find logs to any base.

> Index notation: $e^3 = 20.085...$
>
> or
>
> log notation: $\ln 20.085... = 3$

- So the **natural logarithm** of 20.085... is 3, because e raised to the **power** of 3 is 20.085...

- You don't need to write the base — 'ln' tells you that it's e.

Example 1

a) **Write down the value of $\log_2 8$.**
- **Compare** to $\log_a b = c$. Here the **base** (a) is 2. And the answer (b) is 8.
- So think about the **power** (c) that you'll need to raise 2 to to get 8.
- 8 is 2 raised to the power of 3, so $2^3 = 8$ and $\boxed{\log_2 8 = 3}$

b) **Write down the value of $\log_9 3$.**
- Work out the **power** that 9 needs to be raised to to get 3.
- 3 is the square root of 9, or $9^{\frac{1}{2}} = 3$, so $\boxed{\log_9 3 = \dfrac{1}{2}}$

Tip: Don't get caught out here — the power is actually a fraction.

c) **Write $3^0 = 1$ using log notation.**
- You just need to make sure you get things in the **right place**.
- 0 is the **power** (c) or logarithm that 3 (a, the **base**) is raised to to get 1 (b).
- So sub into $\log_a b = c$ to get: $\boxed{\log_3 1 = 0}$

Inverse Functions

An **inverse function** does the **opposite** to the function. So if the function was '+ 1', then the inverse would be '− 1'. And if the function was '× 2', the inverse would be '÷ 2'. The inverse for a function f(x) is written **f^{-1}(x)**.

Tip: Not every function has an inverse. You'll learn much more about which functions have inverses if you carry on to Year 2 of the A Level course.

> For the function f(x) = a^x, its inverse is f^{-1}(x) = $\log_a x$.
> And for g(x) = e^x, its inverse is g^{-1}(x) = $\ln x$.

Doing an inverse function to the original gets you **back to x** on its own. This gives you the following very useful formulas which will help you to solve equations later in the chapter:

$$a^{\log_a x} = x$$
$$\log_a (a^x) = x$$

$$e^{\ln x} = x$$
$$\ln (e^x) = x$$

(for any positive $a \neq 1$)

Tip: $\log_a a = 1$ and $\ln e = 1$.

The graph of an inverse function is a **reflection** in the line $y = x$:

- $y = \ln x$ is the **reflection** of $y = e^x$ in the line $y = x$.

- It cuts the x-axis at **(1, 0)** (so **ln 1 = 0**).

- As $x \to \infty$, $\ln x \to \infty$, but it happens very slowly.

- As $x \to 0$, $\ln x \to -\infty$.

- $\ln x$ **does not exist** for $x \leq 0$ (i.e. x can't be zero or negative).

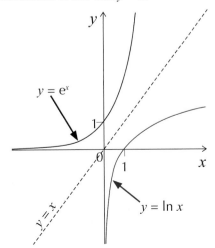

Tip: The graphs of $y = a^x$ and $y = \log_a x$ look very similar to the graphs for $y = e^x$ and $y = \ln x$ — they'll just have steeper or gentler curves, depending on the value of a.

Example 2

Solve the following equations, giving your answers as exact solutions.

a) $e^x = 10$

Apply ln to both sides to remove the e function.

$$e^x = 10$$

$\ln e^x = x$ → $\ln e^x = \ln 10$

$$x = \ln 10$$

b) $\ln x = 2$

Apply e to both sides to remove the ln function.

$$\ln x = 2$$

$e^{\ln x} = x$ → $e^{\ln x} = e^2$

$$x = e^2$$

Exercise 2.1

In this exercise, log means $\log_{10}$.

Q1 Write the following using log notation:

a) $2^3 = 8$ b) $5^4 = 625$ c) $49^{\frac{1}{2}} = 7$

d) $8^{\frac{2}{3}} = 4$ e) $10^{-2} = \dfrac{1}{100}$ f) $2^{-3} = 0.125$

g) $4^x = 9$ h) $x^3 = 40$ i) $8^{11} = x$

> **Q1 Hint:** If you're finding these tricky to get your head around, work out what a, b and c are first, and then substitute them into $\log_a b = c$.

Q2 Write the following using index notation (you don't need to work out any values):

a) $\ln a = 6$ b) $\log_5 t = 0.2$ c) $\log_4 m = 1$

d) $\ln p = 13$ e) $\log k = 5$ f) $\log_x a = m$

> **Q2 Hint:** Treat questions with 'ln' in exactly the same way as you would with any other base — e is just a number, so the base $a = e$.

Q3 Find the value of the following.
Give your answer to 3 d.p. where appropriate.

a) $\log 1000$ b) $\log 0.01$ c) $\log 3$

d) $\ln 2$ e) $\ln 1$ f) $\ln 6$

Q4 Find the value of:

a) $\log_2 4$ b) $\log_3 27$ c) $\log_5 0.2$

Q5 Find the value of x, where $x \geq 0$, by writing the following in index notation:

a) $\log_x 49 = 2$ b) $\log_x 8 = 3$ c) $\log_x 100\,000 = 5$

d) $\log_x 3 = \dfrac{1}{2}$ e) $\log_x 7 = \dfrac{1}{3}$ f) $\log_x 2 = \dfrac{1}{5}$

Q6 Solve these equations, giving
(i) an exact solution   (ii) a solution correct to 3 s.f.

a) $e^x = 5$ b) $\ln x = 8$ c) $e^{3t} = 11$

Q7 In each part, use index notation to write y in terms of x, given that:

a) $\log_a x = 2$ and $\log_a y = 4$ b) $\log_a x = 3$ and $\log_{2a} y = 3$

c) $\ln x = 5$ and $\ln y = 20$

PROBLEM SOLVING

3. Solving Equations

Once you know what logs are, you then need to learn what they can do. There are three 'laws of logs' which are really useful for simplifying nasty-looking expressions with lots of logs into expressions with just one log.

Laws of logs

You'll need to be able to **simplify** expressions containing logs in order to answer trickier questions — e.g. to **add** or **subtract** two logs you can combine them into one. To do this, you'll need to use the **laws of logarithms**. These **only work** if the **base** of each log is the **same**:

Laws of Logarithms

$$\log_a x + \log_a y = \log_a (xy) \qquad \log_a x - \log_a y = \log_a \left(\tfrac{x}{y}\right) \qquad \log_a x^k = k \log_a x$$

So $\log_a \dfrac{1}{x} = \log_a (x^{-1}) = -\log_a x$ and $\log_a \sqrt{x} = \log_a (x^{\frac{1}{2}}) = \dfrac{1}{2} \log_a x$

Tip: These laws work exactly the same for the natural log (ln) too. They're really useful, so make sure you know them off by heart.

Example 1

Simplify the following:

a) $\log_3 4 + \log_3 5$

- First check that the logs you're **adding** have the same base. They do (it's 3) so it's OK to combine them.
- You need to use the law $\log_a x + \log_a y = \log_a (xy)$.
- So here, $a = 3$ (the base), $x = 4$ and $y = 5$.

$$\log_3 4 + \log_3 5 = \log_3 (4 \times 5) = \boxed{\log_3 20}$$

b) $\log_3 4 - \log_3 5$

- You're **taking** one log from another here, and the bases are the same.
- You need to use the law $\log_a x - \log_a y = \log_a \left(\tfrac{x}{y}\right)$.
- So here, $a = 3$ (the base), $x = 4$ and $y = 5$.

$$\log_3 4 - \log_3 5 = \boxed{\log_3 \left(\tfrac{4}{5}\right)}$$

c) $3 \ln 2 + 2 \ln 5$

- The logs are being **added**, but first you must use the law $\ln x^k = k \ln x$ to get rid of the 3 and 2 in front of the logs.
- Using the law, the logs become:

$$3 \ln 2 = \ln (2^3) = \boxed{\ln 8}$$

$$2 \ln 5 = \ln (5^2) = \boxed{\ln 25}$$

- The logs both have the same base (e) so the expression becomes:

$$\ln 8 + \ln 25 = \ln (8 \times 25) = \boxed{\ln 200}$$

Tip: $\ln = \log_e$, so you can use the laws of logs in the same way.

Example 2

a) **Write the expression $2 \log_a 6 - \log_a 9$ in the form $\log_a n$, where n is a number to be found.**

- Use $\log_a x^k = k \log_a x$ to **simplify** $2 \log_a 6$:

$$2 \log_a 6 = \log_a 6^2 = \log_a 36$$

- Then use $\log_a x - \log_a y = \log_a \left(\frac{x}{y}\right)$:

$$\log_a 36 - \log_a 9 = \log_a (36 \div 9) = \boxed{\log_a 4}$$

Tip: All three of the laws are used here. And if you're not sure where the 2 in the final answer has come from, remember that $\log_a a = 1$, so $\ln e = 1$.

b) **Write the expression $\ln \dfrac{(ex)^2}{y^3}$ in terms of $\ln x$ and $\ln y$.**

Use the laws of logs to **break up** the expression:

$$\ln \frac{(ex)^2}{y^3} = \ln (ex)^2 - \ln y^3 \quad \longleftarrow \quad \text{Using } \log_a x - \log_a y = \log_a \left(\frac{x}{y}\right)$$

$$= \ln e^2x^2 - \ln y^3$$

$$= \ln e^2 + \ln x^2 - \ln y^3 \quad \longleftarrow \quad \text{Using } \log_a x + \log_a y = \log_a (xy) \text{ on the first term}$$

$$= 2 \ln e + 2 \ln x - 3 \ln y$$

$$= \boxed{2 + 2 \ln x - 3 \ln y} \quad \longleftarrow \quad \text{Using } \log_a x^k = k \log_a x \text{ on each term}$$

Exercise 3.1

Q1 Write each of the following in the form $\log_x n$ (or $\ln n$), where n is a number to be found:

a) $\log_a 2 + \log_a 5$ b) $\ln 8 + \ln 7$ c) $\log_b 8 - \log_b 4$

d) $\log_m 15 - \log_m 5$ e) $3 \log_a 4$ f) $2 \ln 7$

g) $\frac{1}{2} \log_b 16$ h) $\frac{2}{3} \log_a 125$ i) $\frac{1}{5} \ln 4^5$

Q2 Write each of the following expressions as a single log:

a) $2 \log_a 5 + \log_a 4$ b) $3 \log_m 2 - \log_m 4$ c) $3 \ln 4 - 2 \ln 8$

d) $\frac{2}{3} \ln 216 - 2 \ln 3$ e) $1 + \log_a 6$ f) $2 - \log_b 5$

Q3 If $\log_a 2 = x$, $\log_a 3 = y$ and $\log_a 5 = z$, write in terms of x, y and z:

a) $\log_a 6$ b) $\log_a 16$ c) $\log_a 60$

Q3 Hint: Rewrite the numbers as products of their prime factors.

Q4 Simplify each of the following as much as possible:

a) $\log_b b^3$ b) $\log_a \sqrt{a}$

c) $\ln 4e - 2 \ln 2$ d) $\ln 9 + \ln \frac{e}{3} - \ln 3$

Q5 Show that:

a) $\log_2 4^x = 2x$ b) $\dfrac{\ln 54 - \ln 6}{\ln 3} = 2$

Q6 Find the value of $4 + \log_c \dfrac{1}{c^2} + \log_c \sqrt{c}$.

Changing the base of a log

As well as the three laws of logs on page 151, there is another rule to learn which lets you **change bases**.

- Your calculator probably has a button that can work out any old log for you. But some scientific calculators can only work out $\log_{10}$ or **ln** — which makes it slightly trickier to calculate logs with a **different base**.

- You can **change the base** of any log to **any other base** using this formula:

$$\text{Change of Base: } \log_a x = \frac{\log_b x}{\log_b a}$$

- So $\log_a x = \dfrac{\log_{10} x}{\log_{10} a}$ or $\log_a x = \dfrac{\ln x}{\ln a}$.

- Even if your calculator **can** work out any log, you still need to **learn** this — it's quite useful when it comes to solving equations with logs.

Examples

By converting to $\log_{10}$:

a) **Find the value of $\log_7 4$ to 4 d.p.**

- **Change** the **base** of the log to **10**.

- Here, $a = 7$ and $x = 4$. And we want $b = 10$. So:

$$\log_7 4 = \frac{\log_{10} 4}{\log_{10} 7} = \boxed{0.7124 \ (4 \text{ d.p.})}$$

- You can check this on your calculator by doing:

$$7^{0.7124\ldots} = 4$$

b) **Find the value of $\log_3 2$ to 4 d.p.**

- **Change** the **base** of the log to **10**.

- Here, $a = 3$ and $x = 2$. And we want $b = 10$. So:

$$\log_3 2 = \frac{\log_{10} 2}{\log_{10} 3} = \boxed{0.6309 \ (4 \text{ d.p.})}$$

> **Tip:** You're trying to work out what power you'd need to raise 7 to to get 4.

Exercise 3.2

Q1 Write the following in terms of $\log_{10}$:

   a) $\log_9 2$
   b) $\log_4 8$
   c) $\log_{17} 16$

Q2 Find the value of the following logs to 3 s.f.:

   a) $\log_6 3$
   b) $\log_9 2$
   c) $\log_3 13$
   d) $\log_5 4$

Q3 By changing the base, write each of the following expressions as a single log:

   a) $\dfrac{\log_{10} 19}{\log_{10} 11}$
   b) $\dfrac{\log_6 2}{\log_6 7}$
   c) $\log_3 4 \times \log_4 5$

Solving equations

You saw earlier on page 149 that exponentials and logs are the **inverses** of each other, and that:

$$a^{\log_a x} = x = \log_a a^x$$

So you can use logs to **get rid** of exponentials and vice versa — including using e^x and $\ln x$ to cancel each other out, as you saw on page 149. This is useful for solving equations.

Tip: You can prove this using the laws of logs: $\log_a a^x = x \log_a a = x$.

Tip: You can also write a^x as $e^{x \ln a}$: $e^{x \ln a} = e^{\ln a^x} = a^x$

Tip: Here, a log of base 10 has been used, because it's easy to work out on your calculator. You could have used ln (i.e. base e) instead if you preferred.

Tip: Don't make the mistake of writing: $\frac{\log 3}{\log 2} = \log\left(\frac{3}{2}\right)$ as you can't cancel terms like this.

Example 1

Solve $2^{4x} = 3$ to 3 significant figures.

- To solve the equation, you want x **on its own**.

- To do this you can **take logs** of both sides:

$$\log 2^{4x} = \log 3$$

- Now use one of the **laws of logs**: $\log x^k = k \log x$:

$$4x \log 2 = \log 3$$

- You can now **divide** both sides by $4 \log 2$ to get x on its own:

$$x = \frac{\log 3}{4 \log 2}$$

- But $\frac{\log 3}{4 \log 2}$ is just a number you can find using a **calculator**:

$$x = 0.396 \text{ (to 3 s.f.)}$$

Example 2

Solve $7 \log_{10} x = 5$ to 3 significant figures.

- You want x **on its own**, so begin by **dividing** both sides by 7:

$$\log_{10} x = \frac{5}{7}$$

- You now need to **take exponentials** of both sides by doing '10 to the power of' both sides (since the log is to base 10):

$$10^{\log_{10} x} = 10^{\frac{5}{7}}$$

- Logs and exponentials are **inverse** functions, so they **cancel out**:

$$x = 10^{\frac{5}{7}}$$

- Again, $10^{\frac{5}{7}}$ is just a number you can find using a **calculator**:

$$x = 5.18 \text{ (to 3 s.f.)}$$

Tip: If you're taking exponentials, make sure you use the same base as the log (here it's 10).

Tip: You could get from $\log_{10} x = \frac{5}{7}$ to $x = 10^{\frac{5}{7}}$ just by changing from log notation to index notation — see p.148.

Problems involving exponentials and logs

In an exam, you might be asked to solve an equation where you have to use a **combination** of the methods covered in this chapter. It can be tricky to work out what's needed, but just remember that you're trying to get x **on its own** — and think about which laws will help you do that.

If you're asked to give an **exact** solution, leave your answer in exponential or log form (i.e. don't actually calculate the decimal value of it).

Example 3

Solve ln $(2x - 1) = 2$, giving your answer as an exact solution.

Apply e to both sides to remove the ln function.

$$\ln (2x - 1) = 2$$
$$e^{\ln (2x - 1)} = e^2$$

$e^{\ln x} = x$ → $$2x - 1 = e^2$$
$$2x = e^2 + 1$$
$$x = \frac{e^2 + 1}{2}$$

Example 4

Find the two exact solutions of the equation $e^x + 5e^{-x} = 6$.

- A big clue here is that you're asked for more than one solution. Think quadratics... (see page 34)

- Multiply each part of the equation by e^x to get rid of e^{-x}.
$$e^x + 5e^{-x} = 6$$
$$e^{2x} + 5 = 6e^x$$
$$e^{2x} - 6e^x + 5 = 0$$

Tip: Remember basic powers laws:
$(e^x)^2 = e^{2x}$
$e^{-x} \times e^x = e^0 = 1$.

- Substitute y for e^x to get a quadratic in y. Since you're asked for exact solutions, it will probably factorise.
$$y^2 - 6y + 5 = 0$$
$$(y - 1)(y - 5) = 0$$
$$y = 1 \quad \text{and} \quad y = 5$$

- Put e^x back in and apply the inverse function ln x to both sides.
$$e^x = 1 \quad \text{and} \quad e^x = 5$$
$$\ln e^x = \ln 1 \quad \text{and} \quad \ln e^x = \ln 5$$

$\ln e^x = x$ → $$x = \ln 1 = 0 \quad \text{and} \quad x = \ln 5$$

Example 5

Solve $6^{x-2} = 3^x$, giving your answer to 3 s.f.

- Start by taking **logs** of both sides (you can use any base, so use 10).
$$\log 6^{x-2} = \log 3^x$$

- Now use **log $x^k = k$ log x** on both sides:
$$(x - 2) \log 6 = x \log 3$$

Tip: Have a look back at page 151 if you can't remember the log laws.

- **Multiply out** the brackets and **collect** all the x terms on one side:
$$x \log 6 - 2 \log 6 = x \log 3 \Rightarrow x \log 6 - x \log 3 = 2 \log 6$$
$$\Rightarrow x (\log 6 - \log 3) = 2 \log 6$$

- Use $\log_a x - \log_a y = \log_a \left(\frac{x}{y}\right)$ on the bracket:
$$x (\log 2) = 2 \log 6 \Rightarrow x = \frac{2 \log 6}{\log 2} = 5.17 \text{ (3 s.f.)}$$

Example 6

Solve $7^{30x} = 5^{70}$, giving your answer as a single log in the form $a \log_b c$, where a is a number and b and c are integers.

Take logs of both sides:
$$7^{30x} = 5^{70}$$
$$\Rightarrow \quad \log_7 7^{30x} = \log_7 5^{70} \qquad \boxed{\text{Using } \log_a x^k = k \log_a x}$$
$$\Rightarrow \quad 30x \log_7 7 = 70 \log_7 5$$
$$\boxed{\log_a a = 1} \quad \Rightarrow \quad 30x = 70 \log_7 5$$
$$\Rightarrow \quad x = \frac{7}{3} \log_7 5$$

Tip: By taking logs of base 7, you can replace $\log_7 7$ with 1, which simplifies your working. You could take logs of a different base — but you'd have to use the change of base formula for your final answer.

Exercise 3.3

Q1 Solve each of these equations for x, to 3 s.f.

a) $2^x = 3$
b) $7^x = 2$
c) $1.8^x = 0.4$
d) $0.7^x = 3$
e) $2^{3x-1} = 5$
f) $0.4^{5x-4} = 2$

Q2 Solve each of these equations for x, giving your answers in the form $a \log_b c$, where a, b and c are all integers:

a) $2^{4x} = 3^{100}$
b) $11^{6x} = 10^{90}$
c) $6^{50-x} = 2^{50}$

Q3 Find the value of x for each case:

a) $\log 5x = 3$
b) $\log_2 (x + 3) = 4$
c) $\log_3 (5 - 2x) = 2.5$

Q4 Solve each of these equations for x:

a) $4^{x+1} = 3^{2x}$
b) $2^{5-x} = 4^{x+3}$
c) $3^{2x-1} = 6^{3-x}$

Q5 Find the value(s) of x which satisfy each of the following equations:

a) $\log_6 x = 1 - \log_6 (x + 1)$
b) $\log_2 (2x + 1) = 3 + 2 \log_2 x$

Q6 Solve these equations, giving your answers as exact solutions.

a) $5e^{3t} = 11$
b) $e^{(0.5x + 3)} = 9$
c) $10 - 3e^{(1 - 2x)} = 8$
d) $3 \ln (2x) = 7$
e) $\ln (5t - 3) = 4$
f) $6 - \ln (0.5x) = 3$

Q7 Solve these equations, giving your answers in terms of $\ln 3$.

a) $e^{3x} = 27$
b) $e^{(6x - 1)} = \frac{1}{3}$
c) $\frac{1}{3} e^{(1 - x)} - 3 = 0$

Q8 Solve these equations, giving exact answers.

a) $\ln 5 + \ln x = 7$
b) $\ln (2x) + \ln (3x) = 15$
c) $\ln (x^2 - 4) - \ln (2x) = 0$
d) $3 \ln (x^2) + 5 \ln x = 2$

Q9 Solve the equations $9^{x-2} = 3^y$ and $\log_3 2x = 1 + \log_3 y$ simultaneously.

Q10 Find, where possible, the solutions of the following equations:

a) $2^{2x} - 5(2^x) + 4 = 0$
b) $4^{2x} - 17(4^x) + 16 = 0$ 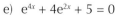
c) $3^{2x+2} - 82(3^x) + 9 = 0$
d) $2^{2x+3} - 9(2^x) + 1 = 0$
e) $e^{4x} + 4e^{2x} + 5 = 0$
f) $3e^{2x} + 10e^x + 3 = 0$

4. Modelling Exponential Growth and Decay

Modelling growth and decay means using a formula to predict how something will increase or decrease. In an exam, you'll often be given a background story to an exponential equation. There's nothing here you haven't seen before, you just need to know how to deal with all the wordy bits.

Learning Objectives:

- Understand and be able to use exponential functions as models for real-world situations, in particular growth and decay.
- Understand the limitations of models using exponential functions.

Modelling exponential growth and decay

Logs can be used to solve **real-life** problems involving **exponential growth** and **decay**.

- Exponential **growth** is when the rate of growth **increases** faster and faster as the amount gets bigger.

- Exponential **decay** is just **negative** exponential growth. The **rate** of decay gets slower and slower as the amount gets smaller.

Example 1

The exponential growth of a colony of bacteria can be modelled by the equation $B = 60e^{0.03t}$, where B is the number of bacteria and t is the time in hours from the point at which the colony is first monitored ($t \geq 0$). Use the model to:

a) **Work out the initial population of bacteria.**

The initial population of bacteria is given by the formula when $t = 0$.
$$B = 60e^{0.03t} = 60e^{(0.03 \times 0)} = 60e^0 = 60 \times 1$$
$$B = 60$$

Tip: Don't forget that $e^0 = 1$.

b) **Predict the number of bacteria after 4 hours.**

- Substitute $t = 4$ into the equation to find B after 4 hours. $\longrightarrow$ $B = 60 \times e^{(0.03 \times 4)}$
$$= 60 \times 1.1274... = 67.6498...$$
- Round down because you want to know the number of whole bacteria. $\longrightarrow$ So $B = 67$ bacteria

c) **Predict the time taken for the colony to grow to 1000.**

- You need to find the time, t, when the population is 1000. $\longrightarrow$ $B = 1000$
- Substitute in the value of B. $\longrightarrow$ $1000 = 60e^{0.03t}$
$$e^{0.03t} = 1000 \div 60 = 16.6666...$$
- Take 'ln' of both sides. $\longrightarrow$ $\ln e^{0.03t} = \ln(16.6666...)$
$$0.03t = 2.8134...$$
$$t = 2.8134... \div 0.03$$
$$= 93.8 \text{ hours to 3 s.f.}$$

Chapter 9 Exponentials and Logarithms

157

Example 2

£350 is initially paid into a bank account that pays 3% interest per year. No further money is deposited or withdrawn from the account. Create a model to show how much money will be in the account after *t* years. Use this model to calculate how many whole years it will be before there is over £1000 in the account.

- After 1 year there will be £350 × 1.03, after two years there will be £350 × 1.03², etc. So after *t* years, there will be £350 × 1.03ᵗ.

- Now use this model to find *t* when 350 × 1.03ᵗ > 1000.

$$350 \times 1.03^t > 1000$$
$$\Rightarrow \ 1.03^t > \frac{20}{7}$$

Take logs: $\log 1.03^t > \log \frac{20}{7}$

$$t \log 1.03 > \log \frac{20}{7}$$

$$t > \frac{\log \frac{20}{7}}{\log 1.03}$$

$$\Rightarrow \ t > 35.516...$$

- So there'll be over £1000 in the account after 36 years.

Tip: If your calculator allows any base, you could have used $\log_{1.03}$ here instead.

Tip: $\log 1.03 > 0$, so you can divide both sides of the inequality by it. But if $0 < x < 1$, then $\log x < 0$, so if you divide by this then you need to flip the inequality sign.

Example 3

The concentration (*C*) of a drug in the bloodstream, *t* hours after taking an initial dose, decreases exponentially according to $C = Ae^{-kt}$, where *A* and *k* are constants. If the initial concentration is 0.72, and this halves after 5 hours, find the values of *A* and *k* and sketch a graph of *C* against *t*.

- 0.72 is the initial concentration — so start by putting this information into the equation and solving for *A*.

$$\text{When } t = 0, C = 0.72$$
$$\text{So } 0.72 = A \times e^0$$
$$0.72 = A \times 1$$
$$A = 0.72$$

- After 5 hours the initial concentration has halved — so you can put in the value of *C* at *t* = 5, and then solve for *k*.

$$\text{When } t = 5, C = 0.72 \div 2 = 0.36$$

$$0.36 = 0.72 \times e^{-5k}$$

$$0.36 = \frac{0.72}{e^{5k}}$$

$$e^{5k} = \frac{0.72}{0.36} = 2$$

$\ln e^{5k} = \ln 2$ ← Apply ln to solve for *k*.

$$5k = \ln 2$$
$$k = \ln 2 \div 5$$
$$k = 0.139 \text{ to 3 s.f.}$$

So the equation is $C = 0.72e^{-0.139t}$

Tip: This is a decreasing function because you have –*k* in the equation (and *A* is positive) — see p.146.

- OK — the last thing left to do is to sketch the graph. Now whenever you're asked to draw a sketch of an exponential or logarithmic function, the key is to find any intercepts and asymptotes.

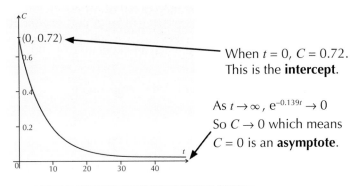

When $t = 0$, $C = 0.72$.
This is the **intercept**.

As $t \to \infty$, $e^{-0.139t} \to 0$
So $C \to 0$ which means
$C = 0$ is an **asymptote**.

Tip: You only need to draw the graph for $t \geq 0$, since time is always positive.

Limitations of modelling

The real world can't always be simplified to a couple of variables — it's usually much more **complicated** than that.
Models **ignore** most factors, leaving only the ones you're interested in.
This simplification means that models aren't spot on — they have **drawbacks**:

- Often an exponential model will match the real-world scenario for only a **short amount of time** — beyond that the numbers get too big or too small.

- A model may need tweaking for different values to reflect this — for example, there may be an **upper limit** to stop a value increasing to infinity.

Tip: You can only use the model to make predictions within the time frame of the model. If it's outside the time frame, then you're **extrapolating**, which is much less accurate.

Example 4

The penguin population of a small island is surveyed.
The population, P, can be modelled by the formula $P = 5000e^{0.1t}$,
where t is the number of years after the initial survey.

a) **What does the '5000' in the formula represent?**

5000 is the initial number of penguins (when $t = 0$).

b) **Explain why this model may not be appropriate for the long term.**

After 60 years ($t = 60$), the penguin population is over 2 million.
This seems unrealistic — it's much too large a population.
The model doesn't take into account other factors (e.g. predators, food supply) and allows the population to grow infinitely.

Exercise 4.1

Give your answers correct to 3 significant figures.

Q1 A radioactive substance has a half-life of 10 years. Its decay is modelled by the equation $A = A_0 e^{-kt}$, where A is the activity in Bq (becquerel) after t years and A_0 and k are constants.

a) After how many years will the substance be reduced to a quarter of its original activity?

b) Find the original activity if the activity after 5 years is 200 grams.

c) Find the activity remaining after 15 years.

Q1 Hint: Half-life is the length of time it takes for the activity of the sample to halve.

Q2 An oven is turned on at 12:00. After t minutes its temperature, $T\,^\circ C$, is given by the formula:
$$T = 225 - 207\,e^{-\frac{t}{8}}$$

a) What was the initial temperature of the oven?

b) What was the temperature after 5 minutes?

c) At what time does the oven reach a temperature of 190 °C?

d) Sketch the graph of T against t.

e) Explain how the model restricts the temperature from rising indefinitely.

Q2 Hint: When sketching a graph, make sure you label any significant points, e.g. where the curve meets any axes.

Q3 A fungus is being grown under controlled conditions in a laboratory. Initially, it covers an area of 4 mm². After t hours, its area is F mm², where $F = F_0 e^{gt}$ (F_0 and g are constants). After 6 hours its area is 10 mm².

a) Find the values of F_0 and g.

b) Predict the area of the fungus after 12 hours.

c) How long will it take for the fungus to grow to 15 mm²?

d) Describe one limitation of the model used.

Q4 A woman is prescribed a medicine, and the concentration of the medicine in her bloodstream is monitored. Initially the concentration in her bloodstream is 3 mg per litre of blood (mg/l). After t hours, the concentration of the drug is N mg/l, where $N = Ae^{-t}$.

a) What is the concentration after 30 minutes?

b) How long does it take for the level to reduce to 0.1 mg/l?

c) Sketch the graph of N against t.

d) What is the gradient of the graph in terms of t?

Q4a) Hint: Make sure you read the units carefully — in the question t is in hours but here you're asked about minutes, so you'll need to convert first.

Q5 The value of a car ($£V$) t years after purchase can be modelled by the formula:
$$V = 1500 + 9000\,e^{-\frac{t}{3}}.$$

a) Explain the significance of the negative coefficient of t.

b) What was its price when new?

c) What was its value after 5 years?

d) After how many whole years will it be worth less than £2500?

e) Sketch the graph of V against t.

Q6 A forest fire spreads in such a way that the burnt area (H hectares) after t hours is given by the relation $H = 20e^{bt}$. Assume that the fire burns unchecked.

a) Interpret the value 20 used in the model.

b) If $e^b = 1.8$, find b.

c) Find the area burnt after 3 hours.

d) How long would it take to burn an area of 500 hectares?

e) What constant factor is the burnt area multiplied by every hour? What percentage does the burnt area increase by each hour?

f) Describe one limitation of the model.

5. Using Logarithmic Graphs

Logarithms can be used to express exponential equations in linear form
— they're often much simpler to work with graphically in this format.

Logarithmic graphs in linear form

Equations of the form $y = ax^n$ or $y = kb^x$ can be a bit awkward to use.
Fortunately, you can use the **laws of logs** to rewrite them in the form
$y = mx + c$, which is much easier to work with.
Graphs of $y = ax^n$ or $y = kb^x$ can get **very steep very quickly**, but linear graphs
are much more straightforward — and you can use them to read off values,
find the gradient of the line, etc.

Logarithmic graphs for $y = ax^n$

To convert $y = ax^n$ to linear form, just **take logs** of both sides and rearrange:

$$y = ax^n \Rightarrow \log y = \log ax^n$$

$$\Rightarrow \log y = \log a + \log x^n$$

$$\Rightarrow \boxed{\log y = n \log x + \log a}$$

n is the gradient, log *a* is the vertical intercept.

This is in the **straight-line form** $\boxed{y = mx + c}$
When drawing the graph, plot the values of log *y* against log *x*
and label the axes accordingly.

Tip: If you're given values for x and y, you can plot log y against log x. The line of best fit will have the equation $\log y = n \log x + \log a$, so from this you can work out the equation for y in terms of x.

Example 1

The number of employees, *p*, working for a company *t* years after
it was founded can be modelled by the equation $p = at^b$. The table
below shows the number of employees the company has:

Age of company (*t* years)	2	5	8	13	25
Number of employees (*p*)	3	7	10	16	29

**Plot a linear graph to represent this data,
and use this to find the values *a* and *b*.**

- $p = at^b$ can be rearranged into the linear form $\log p = b \log t + \log a$.
- Make a table of the values of log *t* and log *p*, using *p* and *t* given above:

log *t* (3 d.p.)	0.301	0.699	0.903	1.114	1.398
log *p* (3 d.p.)	0.477	0.845	1.000	1.204	1.462

- Now plot a graph of log *p* against log *t* and draw a line of best fit:

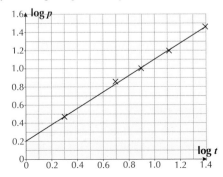

Tip: You could extend the graph for negative values of log *p* and log *t*, but the first quadrant is the most useful.

- The vertical intercept is at 0.2, so:
$$\log a = 0.2 \Rightarrow a = 10^{0.2} = \boxed{1.585} \text{ (3 d.p.)}$$

- The gradient can be found by taking two coordinates on the line of best fit, e.g. (0, 0.2) and (1.0, 1.1):
$$b = \frac{y_2 - y_1}{x_2 - x_1} = \frac{1.1 - 0.2}{1.0 - 0} = \boxed{0.9}$$

- So $\boxed{p = 1.585t^{0.9}}$

Logarithmic graphs for $y = kb^x$

Graphs of the form $y = kb^x$ can also be rearranged to be in linear form, but slightly differently:

$$y = kb^x \Rightarrow \log y = \log kb^x$$
$$\Rightarrow \log y = \log k + \log b^x$$
$$\Rightarrow \boxed{\log y = x\log b + \log k}$$

$\log b$ is the gradient, $\log k$ is the vertical intercept.

This is in the **straight-line form** $\boxed{y = mx + c}$
This time, plot $\log y$ against x.

Example 2

The populations (y) of rabbits and foxes on an island over time (t) are modelled using the graph on the right.

a) **Calculate the combined population (to 3 s.f.) when the number of rabbits and foxes are equal.**

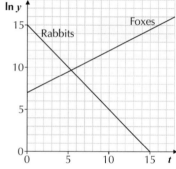

- Find the equation for each line — note the vertical axis is **ln y**, not y.
$$\text{Foxes: } \ln y = \frac{1}{2}t + 7 \qquad \text{Rabbits: } \ln y = 15 - t$$

- The populations are equal when the lines on the graph cross:
$$\frac{1}{2}t + 7 = 15 - t \Rightarrow \frac{3}{2}t = 8 \Rightarrow t = \frac{16}{3}$$

- Put this value back into one of the above equations, e.g. rabbits:
$$\ln y = 15 - t \Rightarrow \ln y = 15 - \frac{16}{3} = \frac{29}{3} \Rightarrow y = e^{\frac{29}{3}} = \boxed{15\,782.652...}$$

- This is the same as the fox population, so the combined population is
$$2 \times 15\,782.652... = \boxed{31\,600 \text{ (3 s.f.)}}$$

b) **Explain why this model may not be appropriate for an extended timescale.**

After 15 years there'll be less than 1 rabbit, and the fox population will continue to grow exponentially. This is clearly unrealistic.

Q1 The value, £V, of a large piece of machinery is modelled by the equation $V = pq^t$, where t is the age of the machinery in years, and p and q are constants. The line l below plots log V against t:

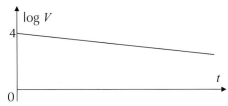

The gradient of l is $-\frac{1}{40}$. Write an equation for l, and use this to find the value of the machinery when it is 20 years old.

Q2 A tank is being filled with water. At time $s = 0$, there is already 2 mm of water in the tank. After s seconds, the height, h mm, of the water in the tank can be modelled by the equation $h = 2 \times 3^s$.

a) (i) Sketch the graph of h against s.

(ii) Sketch the graph of $\log_3 h$ against s.

(iii) Which is the more useful graph for calculations? Explain your reasoning.

b) Explain why this model is unsuitable for long time periods, and suggest an improvement to the model.

Q3 The number of bacteria, p, in a petri dish is observed over a period of time, t. The bacteria population can be modelled by the formula $p = at^b$, where a and b are constants. The results from the observations are shown in the table below.

t (days)	1	3	4	6	9
p (1000s)	2	14	22	44	88

Plot a linear graph to represent this data, and use this to find the values of a and b.

Q4 The activity, x, of a radioactive substance decreases over time, t. The activity follows the formula $x = kb^t$, where k and b are constants. The measurements from an experiment are shown in the table below.

t (days)	5	50	100	200	300
x (Bq)	80.449	32.411	11.803	1.565	0.207

Draw a linear graph of this data, and use a line of best fit to calculate the initial activity of the substance, to the nearest Bq.

Q5 The rules of a sport say that the length, l m, and the width, w m, of the rectangular playing field can be any value, as long as the area is 120 m². Use logs to model the relationship between l and w as a straight line and show this graphically.

1. The Gradient of a Curve

Differentiation is an algebraic process that finds the gradient of a curve. It is useful for finding out how fast one thing changes with respect to another.

Finding the gradient of a curve

The **gradient** of a curve is just how **steep** it is. Unlike a straight line, the steepness of a curve **changes** as you move along it — you can only give an **exact value** for the gradient at a **particular point** on the curve.

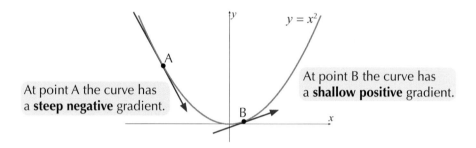

At point A the curve has a **steep negative** gradient.

At point B the curve has a **shallow positive** gradient.

At a **point**, the gradient of a curve is the same as the gradient of the **tangent line** to the curve at that point.

- The tangent line is a **straight line** which **just touches** the curve at that point, without going through it.

- Sadly, you can't work out the gradient of this tangent using the normal method of picking **two points** and finding the change in y ÷ change in x. This is because you only know **one point** on the line — the point where the tangent **meets the curve**.

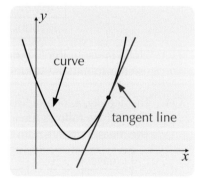

curve

tangent line

- So we need another method to find the gradient of a curve — it's known as **differentiation**.

Differentiating produces an **algebraic expression** for the gradient as a **function of x** — its numerical value **changes** as you move along the curve.

Before we get started with differentiation, there's some **notation** to learn:

- The function you get from differentiating y **with respect to x** is called the **derivative** of y with respect to x and it's written $\dfrac{dy}{dx}$.

- $\dfrac{dy}{dx}$ represents the **rate of change** of y with x. In other words, it tells you how quickly y is changing for a given value of x. This is the same as the **gradient** of the curve $y = f(x)$.

- The notation $\mathbf{f'(x)}$ means the derivative of $y = f(x)$ with respect to x. It's sometimes used instead of $\dfrac{dy}{dx}$.

Tip: $\dfrac{dy}{dx}$ is **not** a fraction, it's just notation for a derivative.

Tip: For an example involving real-life rates of change, see pages 187-190 and Chapter 19 (p.356-360).

Differentiating from first principles

To find the derivative of a function you need to find its gradient as a function of x.

You can get **close** to the gradient of the tangent (and so the curve) at a point $(x, f(x))$, by finding the gradient of the line joining $(x, f(x))$ and another point **close to** it on the curve.

- On the diagram, the point $(x + h, f(x + h))$ is a small distance further along the curve from $(x, f(x))$.

- As h gets smaller, the distance between the two points gets smaller.

- The closer the points, the **closer** the line joining them will be **to the tangent line**.

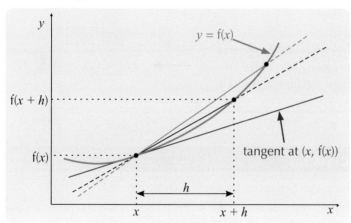

Tip: Remember, the gradient of a line which passes through points (x_1, y_1) and (x_2, y_2) is given by:
$$\frac{y_2 - y_1}{x_2 - x_1}$$

Now you can write an expression for the gradient of the **straight line** joining the two points $(x, f(x))$ and $(x + h, f(x + h))$ like this:

$$\frac{f(x + h) - f(x)}{(x + h) - x}$$

And you know that as h gets **smaller**, the gradient of the straight line gets **closer and closer** to the gradient of the **curve** at $(x, f(x))$.
So you can write an expression for the gradient of the curve $y = f(x)$ like this:

$$f'(x) = \lim_{h \to 0}\left[\frac{f(x + h) - f(x)}{(x + h) - x}\right]$$

Tip: You might also see these expressions with 'δx' instead of 'h'. You can write '$(x + h) - x$' as just 'h' to simplify the denominator.

Tip: $\lim\limits_{h \to 0}$ in front of the function just means 'what the function goes towards as h goes towards zero'.

This method of differentiation is known as differentiating from **first principles** and the formula can be used to find the gradient of a curve as a function of x.

Find an expression for the gradient of the function $f(x) = x^2$ by differentiating from first principles.

- Write down the formula for differentiating from first principles. $\longrightarrow$ $f'(x) = \lim_{h \to 0}\left[\dfrac{f(x+h)-f(x)}{(x+h)-x}\right]$

- Use the fact that $f(x) = x^2$. $\longrightarrow$ $= \lim_{h \to 0}\left[\dfrac{(x+h)^2 - x^2}{(x+h)-x}\right]$

- Multiply out and simplify. $\longrightarrow$ $= \lim_{h \to 0}\left[\dfrac{x^2 + 2xh + h^2 - x^2}{x+h-x}\right]$

    $= \lim_{h \to 0}\left[\dfrac{2xh + h^2}{h}\right]$

- Now decide what will happen as h gets close to 0. $\longrightarrow$ $= \lim_{h \to 0}[2x + h]$

- In this case $2x + h$ gets close to $2x$. $\longrightarrow$ $= \boxed{2x}$

Find the gradient of the curve $y = 0.5x$ by differentiating from first principles.

$\dfrac{dy}{dx} = \lim_{h \to 0}\left[\dfrac{f(x+h)-f(x)}{(x+h)-x}\right]$

- Use the fact that $y = f(x)$ with $f(x) = 0.5x$. $\longrightarrow$ $= \lim_{h \to 0}\left[\dfrac{0.5(x+h)-0.5x}{(x+h)-x}\right]$

    $= \lim_{h \to 0}\left[\dfrac{0.5h}{h}\right]$

Tip: A straight line will always have a constant gradient.

- Decide what will happen as h gets close to 0. There are no h's so the limit is just 0.5. $\longrightarrow$ $= \lim_{h \to 0}[0.5] = \boxed{0.5}$

Exercise 1.1

Q1 The curve C is given by $y = f(x)$ where $f(x) = x^3$.

    a) Find the gradient of the straight line joining the point on the curve where $x = 1$ and the point on the curve where:

        (i) $x = 2$ (ii) $x = 1.5$ (iii) $x = 1.1$

    b) The gradient of the curve at the point $(1, 1)$ is 3. What do you notice about the gradient of the straight lines in part a) as the value of x moves closer to 1?

Q2 Derive from first principles expressions for the gradients of the following curves:

    a) $y = x$ b) $f(x) = x^3$ c) $f(x) = 2x$

Q3 For each of the following, find the derivative of y with respect to x by differentiating from first principles.

    a) $y = 5x^2 + 1$ b) $y = x - x^2$ c) $y = 2x^3 + 3x$

2. Differentiating $y = f(x)$

Differentiating from first principles can take a long time, especially if there are large powers involved. Luckily, there's a formula that will do it quickly for you.

Differentiating x^n

Expressions are much easier to **differentiate** when they're written using **powers of x** — like writing $\sqrt{x}$ as $x^{\frac{1}{2}}$ or $\frac{3}{x^2}$ as $3x^{-2}$.

When you've done this, you can use this **formula** to differentiate:

$$\text{If } y = x^n, \text{ then } \frac{dy}{dx} = nx^{n-1}$$

It comes from differentiating x^n from **first principles**, like on the previous pages.

Example 1

Differentiate each of the following using the formula for powers of x.

a) $y = x^2$

For 'normal' powers, n is just the power of x. Here $n = 2$.

$$\frac{dy}{dx} = nx^{n-1}$$
$$= 2x^1$$
$$= \boxed{2x}$$

b) $y = \sqrt{x}$

First write the square root as a fractional power of x. $\longrightarrow \quad y = x^{\frac{1}{2}} \quad \left(n = \frac{1}{2}\right)$

$$\frac{dy}{dx} = nx^{n-1}$$
$$= \frac{1}{2}x^{\left(-\frac{1}{2}\right)}$$
$$= \boxed{\frac{1}{2\sqrt{x}}}$$

c) $y = \frac{1}{x^2}$

Write the fraction as a $\longrightarrow \quad y = x^{-2} \quad (n = -2)$
negative power of x.

$$\frac{dy}{dx} = nx^{n-1}$$
$$= -2x^{-3}$$
$$= \boxed{-\frac{2}{x^3}}$$

d) $y = 4x^3$

This is just a normal power with $n = 3$, but there's a constant (a number) in front of it.

$$y = 4x^3$$
$$\frac{dy}{dx} = 4(nx^{n-1})$$
$$= 4(3x^2)$$
$$= \boxed{12x^2}$$

If there's a number in front of the x^n term, multiply the derivative by it. Formally:

$$\text{If } y = ax^n, \frac{dy}{dx} = anx^{n-1}$$

Learning Objectives:

- Be able to differentiate powers of x.
- Be able to differentiate sums and differences of powers of x.
- Be able to differentiate more complicated functions containing powers of x.
- Be able to sketch the graph of $y = f'(x)$ by differentiating $y = f(x)$.
- Be able to find tangents and normals to a curve.

Tip: When it says 'differentiate', it actually means 'differentiate **with respect to x**' as it's a function of x you're differentiating.

Tip: Differentiation's much easier if you know the laws of indices really well. Like knowing that $x^1 = x$ and $\sqrt{x} = x^{\frac{1}{2}}$ — see page 17.

Example 2

Differentiate $y = 5$ using the formula for powers of x.

There are no powers of x in this expression for y so multiply by $x^0 = 1$.

$y = 5x^0$, $n = 0$

$\dfrac{dy}{dx} = 5(nx^{n-1})$

$= 5(0x^{-1})$

$= 0$

Tip: Differentiating $y = a$ where a is just a constant (i.e. a number) always gives zero, because the line has a gradient of 0.

You could be asked to **use** your gradient function to work out the **numerical value** of the gradient at a **particular point** on the curve.

Example 3

Find the gradient of the curve $y = x^2$ at $x = 1$ and $x = -2$.

You need the gradient of the graph of $y = x^2$, so differentiate this function to get $\dfrac{dy}{dx} = 2x$.

Now when $x = 1$, $\dfrac{dy}{dx} = 2$.

And so the gradient of the graph at $x = 1$ is 2.

And when $x = -2$, $\dfrac{dy}{dx} = -4$.

So the gradient of the graph at $x = -2$ is -4.

Exercise 2.1

Q1 Differentiate to find $\dfrac{dy}{dx}$ for:

a) $y = x^6$　　b) $y = x^3$　　c) $y = x^{-2}$　　d) $y = 3x^2$

e) $y = 7x$　　f) $y = 3$　　g) $y = 3\sqrt{x}$　　h) $y = 2x^{-1}$

Q2 Differentiate to find $f'(x)$ for:

a) $f(x) = x^5$　　b) $f(x) = x^7$　　c) $f(x) = x^{-4}$　　d) $f(x) = 4x^3$

e) $f(x) = 8\sqrt{x}$　　f) $f(x) = 3\sqrt[3]{x}$　　g) $f(x) = -7$　　h) $f(x) = 4x^{-2}$

Q3 Find the gradient of each of the following functions:

a) $y = 2x^2$ when $x = 4$　　　　　　b) $y = x^{-1}$ when $x = 2$

c) $y = -4x^5$ when $x = 1$　　　　　d) $f(x) = 2\sqrt{x}$ at the point (9, 6)

e) $f(x) = x^4$ at the point (-2, 16)　　f) $f(x) = -2x^3$ when $f(x) = -250$

Differentiating functions

Even if there are **loads** of terms in the expression, it doesn't matter.

Differentiate each bit **separately** and you'll be fine.

Formally, this means:

$$\frac{d}{dx}(x^m + x^n) = \frac{d}{dx}(x^m) + \frac{d}{dx}(x^n)$$

Example 1

a) **Differentiate $f(x) = x^4 + 3x^2 - 2$.**

Differentiate each bit separately.

$$f(x) = x^4 \quad + \quad 3x^2 \quad - \quad 2$$

$$f'(x) = 4x^3 \quad + \quad 3(2x) \quad - \quad 0 \quad = \quad \boxed{4x^3 + 6x}$$

Tip: Remember — if there's a number in front of the function, multiply the derivative by the same number.

b) **Find $\dfrac{d}{dx}\left(6x^2 + \dfrac{4}{\sqrt[3]{x}} - \dfrac{2}{x^2} + 1\right)$.**

This notation just means the derivative with respect to x of the thing in the brackets.

Rewrite the function first to get powers of x. Then differentiate each bit separately.

$$6x^2 + \frac{4}{\sqrt[3]{x}} - \frac{2}{x^2} + 1 \quad = \quad 6x^2 \quad + \quad 4x^{-\frac{1}{3}} \quad - \quad 2x^{-2} \quad + \quad 1$$

$$\frac{d}{dx}\left(6x^2 + \frac{4}{\sqrt[3]{x}} - \frac{2}{x^2} + 1\right) \quad = \quad 6(2x) \quad + \quad 4\left(-\frac{1}{3}x^{-\frac{4}{3}}\right) \quad - \quad 2(-2x^{-3}) \quad + \quad 0$$

$$= \quad \boxed{12x - \frac{4}{3\sqrt[3]{x^4}} + \frac{4}{x^3}}$$

You'll often need to **simplify** a function before you can differentiate it by multiplying out **brackets** or simplifying **fractions**. If you have a fraction to simplify, check first whether the denominator is a **factor** of the numerator, otherwise you'll need to **split it up** into terms.

Example 2

For the function $f(x) = (x + 2)^2(x - 10)$:

a) **Find $f'(x)$.**

- Multiply out the brackets and simplify.

$$f(x) = (x + 2)^2(x - 10)$$
$$= (x^2 + 4x + 4)(x - 10)$$
$$= x^3 - 10x^2 + 4x^2 - 40x + 4x - 40$$
$$= x^3 - 6x^2 - 36x - 40$$

- Differentiate term-by-term.

$$f'(x) = 3x^2 - 12x - 36 - 0$$
$$= 3x^2 - 12x - 36$$

b) Sketch the graph of $y = f'(x)$.

Tip: See page 41 for more about sketching quadratic graphs.

- $f'(x) = 3x^2 - 12x - 36$ is a quadratic with a positive coefficient of x, so the graph is u-shaped.

- $f'(0) = 3(0)^2 - 12(0) - 36 = -36$

  So the y-intercept is at $y = -36.$

- $f'(x) = 0$
  $\Rightarrow 3x^2 - 12x - 36 = 0$
  $\Rightarrow x^2 - 4x - 12 = 0$
  $\Rightarrow (x + 2)(x - 6) = 0$
  $\Rightarrow x = -2$ or $x = 6$

  So the x-intercepts are at $x = -2$ and $x = 6.$

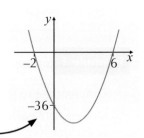

- Put all this together to draw the sketch.

Example 3

Tip: If the denominator is an expression instead of just one term, chances are the numerator will have a factor that cancels with the denominator.

a) Differentiate $y = \dfrac{x^3 - 5x^2 + 6x}{x - 2}$.

The numerator of this fraction will factorise and then one of the factors will cancel with the denominator.

$$y = \frac{x^3 - 5x^2 + 6x}{x - 2}$$

$$= \frac{x(x^2 - 5x + 6)}{x - 2}$$

$$= \frac{x(x - 3)(x - 2)}{x - 2}$$

$$= x(x - 3)$$

$$= x^2 - 3x$$

$$\frac{dy}{dx} = 2x - 3$$

b) Differentiate the function $f(x) = \dfrac{x^3 + 4x + 1}{2x^2}$.

This numerator won't factorise. Instead, split the fraction up into three fractional terms, and then write each term as a power of x.

$$f(x) = \frac{x^3 + 4x + 1}{2x^2}$$

$$= \frac{x^3}{2x^2} + \frac{4x}{2x^2} + \frac{1}{2x^2}$$

$$= \frac{x}{2} + \frac{2}{x} + \frac{1}{2x^2}$$

$$= \frac{1}{2}x + 2x^{-1} + \frac{1}{2}x^{-2}$$

Tip: For any a, b, c & d:

$$\frac{a + b + c}{d} = \frac{a}{d} + \frac{b}{d} + \frac{c}{d}$$

You can split up fractions using this rule.

Differentiating....

$$f'(x) = \frac{1}{2} + 2(-x^{-2}) + \frac{1}{2}(-2x^{-3})$$

$$= \frac{1}{2} - 2x^{-2} - x^{-3}$$

$$= \frac{1}{2} - \frac{2}{x^2} - \frac{1}{x^3}$$

Exercise 2.2

Q1 Differentiate these functions:

a) $y = 4x^3 - x^2$

b) $y = x + \dfrac{1}{x}$

c) $y = 3x^2 + \sqrt{x} - 5$

d) $f(x) = -2x^5 + 4x - \dfrac{1}{x^2}$

e) $f(x) = \sqrt{x^3} - x$

f) $f(x) = 5x - \dfrac{2}{x^3} + \sqrt[3]{x}$

Q2 Find:

a) $\dfrac{d}{dx}(x(x^6 - 1))$

b) $\dfrac{d}{dx}((x - 3)(x + 4))$

c) $\dfrac{d}{dx}(x(x - 1)(x - 2))$

d) $\dfrac{d}{dx}((x - 3)(x + 4)(x - 1))$

e) $\dfrac{d}{dx}(x^2(x - 4)(3 - x^3))$

f) $\dfrac{d}{dx}((x - 3)^2(x^2 - 2))$

> **Q2 Hint:** Remember that $\dfrac{d}{dx}(\ )$ means the derivative with respect to x of the thing in brackets.

Q3 Find the gradient of each of the following curves:

a) $y = x^4 - x^2 + 2$ when $x = 3$

b) $y = 2x^5 + \dfrac{1}{x}$ when $x = -2$

c) $y = x(x - 1)(x - 2)$ when $x = -3$

d) $y = 5(x^2 - 1)(3 - x)$ when $x = 0$

e) $y = \sqrt{x}(x - 1)$ at $(4, 6)$

f) $f(x) = x^3(x^2 - 5)$ at $(-1, 4)$

g) $f(x) = \dfrac{1}{x^2}(x^3 - x)$ at $x = 5$

h) $f(x) = \dfrac{3x^3 + 18x^2 + 24x}{x + 4}$ at $(-2, 0)$

> **Q3h) Hint:** Where there's a fraction with an expression in the denominator, try to take the denominator out of the numerator as a factor.

Q4 For the following graphs, sketch the graph of $f'(x)$ for $0 \le x \le 10$:

a)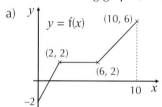

b)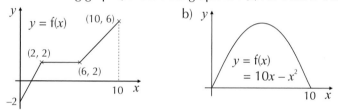

Q5 For each of the following curves, sketch the graph of $y = f'(x)$.

a) $f(x) = (x + 3)(x + 4)$

b) $f(x) = \dfrac{x^3 - 3x^2 + 2x}{x - 1}$

c) $f(x) = x^4 - 4x^3 + 4x^2 - 9$

d) $f(x) = (x - 1)^2(x + 5)$

Q6 For each of the following functions, find the coordinates of the point or points where the gradient is 0:

a) $y = x^2 - 2x$

b) $y = 3x^2 + 4x$

c) $y = 5x^2 - 3x$

d) $y = 9x - 3x^3$

e) $y = 2x^3 - x^2$

f) $y = 2x^3 + 3x^2 - 12x$

Q7 Differentiate these functions:

a) $y = \dfrac{x^2 - 3x - 4}{x + 1}$

b) $f(x) = \dfrac{x^4 - 9}{x^2 + 3}$

c) $f(x) = \dfrac{x^5 - 16x^3}{x + 4}$

d) $y = \dfrac{1}{x}(x - 3)(x - 4)$

e) $y = \sqrt{x}\left(x^3 - \sqrt{x}\right)$

f) $f(x) = \dfrac{3 - \sqrt{x}}{\sqrt{x}}$

g) $f(x) = \dfrac{x + 5\sqrt{x}}{\sqrt{x}}$

h) $f(x) = \dfrac{x - 3\sqrt{x} + 2}{\sqrt{x} - 1}$

Finding tangents and normals

Differentiation can be used to find the gradient at a point on a curve. This makes it easy to find the equation for the **tangent** or **normal** at that point.

- You already know that a **tangent** is a straight line that just **touches** the curve and has the **same gradient** as the curve at that point.

- A **normal** is a straight line that is **perpendicular** (at right angles) to the curve at a particular point.

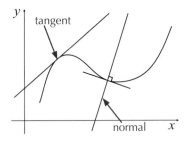

Tip: This rule for the gradients of perpendicular lines was introduced back in Chapter 6, on p.81.

Now, there's one key fact to remember for normals — tangents and normals are perpendicular, and as a result, their **gradients multiply to give –1**:

> gradient of tangent × gradient of normal = –1.
>
> $$\text{gradient of normal} = \frac{-1}{\text{gradient of tangent}}$$

Armed with this rule, we can write down a step-by-step method for finding the equation of a tangent or normal to a curve...

To find the equation of the tangent or normal to a curve at a point:
- **Differentiate** the function.
- Find the **gradient** of the curve at that point.
- Use this to deduce the gradient, m, of the tangent or normal:

  gradient of the **tangent** = gradient of the curve

  $$\text{gradient of the normal} = \frac{-1}{\text{gradient of the curve}}$$
- Write the **equation** of the tangent or normal in the form $y = mx + c$.
- Work out the **constant value c** in the equation by using the coordinates of the point (which you know lies on the tangent/normal).

Tip: The tangent and normal are always straight lines, so their equations can be written $y = mx + c$. They can also be written in the form $y - y_1 = m(x - x_1)$ or $ax + by + c = 0$ if you prefer.

Example 1

Find the equation of the tangent to the curve $y = (4 - x)(x + 2)$ at the point (2, 8), giving your answer in the form $ax + by + c = 0$, where a, b and c are integers.

- Write the curve in a form you can differentiate...

$$
\begin{aligned}
y &= (4 - x)(x + 2) \\
&= 4x + 8 - x^2 - 2x \\
&= 8 + 2x - x^2
\end{aligned}
$$

...and differentiate it.

$$
\begin{aligned}
\frac{dy}{dx} &= 0 + 2 - 2x \\
&= 2 - 2x
\end{aligned}
$$

- Find the gradient of the curve at (2, 8).

$$x = 2 \Rightarrow \frac{dy}{dx} = 2 - (2 \times 2) = 2 - 4 = -2$$

So the gradient of the curve is -2 at (2, 8).

- Gradient of the tangent = gradient of the curve, so $m = -2$.

- So the equation of the tangent is $y = -2x + c$.

- Use the point (2, 8) to work out the value of c:

$$x = 2, y = 8 \Rightarrow 8 = -4 + c \Rightarrow c = 12$$

So the tangent has equation $y = -2x + 12$.

Rearranging into the form $ax + by + c = 0$ gives:

$$2x + y - 12 = 0$$

Example 2

Find the equation of the normal to the curve $y = x(x - 3)(x + 2)$ at the point (2, –8), giving your answer in the form $y = mx + c$.

- Simplify and differentiate.

$$y = x(x - 3)(x + 2)$$
$$= x^3 - x^2 - 6x$$
$$\frac{dy}{dx} = 3x^2 - 2x - 6$$

- Find the gradient of the curve at (2, –8).

$$x = 2 \Rightarrow \frac{dy}{dx} = 3(2^2) - 2(2) - 6 = 2$$

So the gradient of the curve is 2 at (2, –8).

- Gradient of the normal at (2, –8) is

$$m = \frac{-1}{\text{gradient of the curve at (2, -8)}} = -\frac{1}{2}$$

Tip: Make sure you always check whether the question wants a normal or a tangent.

- So the equation of the normal is $y = -\frac{1}{2}x + c$.

- Use the point (2, –8) to work out the value of c.

$$x = 2, y = -8 \Rightarrow -8 = -1 + c \Rightarrow c = -7$$

So the normal has equation:

$$y = -\frac{1}{2}x - 7$$

Example 3

Find the equation of the normal to the curve $y = \dfrac{(x+2)(x+4)}{6\sqrt{x}}$ at the point (4, 4), giving your answer in the form $ax + by + c = 0$, where a, b and c are integers.

- Simplify and differentiate.

$$y = \frac{(x+2)(x+4)}{6\sqrt{x}}$$

> Denominator is one term so it'll probably need splitting up.

$$= \frac{x^2 + 6x + 8}{6x^{\frac{1}{2}}}$$

$$= \frac{x^2}{6x^{\frac{1}{2}}} + \frac{6x}{6x^{\frac{1}{2}}} + \frac{8}{6x^{\frac{1}{2}}}$$

$$= \frac{1}{6}x^{\frac{3}{2}} + x^{\frac{1}{2}} + \frac{4}{3}x^{-\frac{1}{2}}$$

$$\frac{dy}{dx} = \frac{1}{6}\left(\frac{3}{2}x^{\frac{1}{2}}\right) + \frac{1}{2}x^{-\frac{1}{2}} + \frac{4}{3}\left(-\frac{1}{2}x^{-\frac{3}{2}}\right)$$

$$= \frac{1}{4}\sqrt{x} + \frac{1}{2\sqrt{x}} - \frac{2}{3\sqrt{x^3}}$$

- Find the gradient of the curve at (4, 4).

$$x = 4 \Rightarrow \frac{dy}{dx} = \frac{1}{4}\sqrt{4} + \frac{1}{2\sqrt{4}} - \frac{2}{3\sqrt{4^3}}$$

$$= \frac{1}{2} + \frac{1}{4} - \frac{1}{12} = \frac{2}{3}$$

So the gradient of the curve is $\frac{2}{3}$ at (4, 4).

- Gradient of the normal at (4, 4) is

$$m = \frac{-1}{\text{gradient of the curve at (4, 4)}} = -\frac{3}{2}$$

- So the equation of the normal is $y = -\frac{3}{2}x + c$.

- Use the point (4, 4) to work out the value of c.

$$x = 4, \ y = 4 \Rightarrow 4 = -\frac{3}{2}4 + c \Rightarrow c = 10$$

So the tangent has equation $y = -\frac{3}{2}x + 10$.

Rearranging into the form $ax + by + c = 0$ gives:

$$3x + 2y - 20 = 0$$

Tip: Rewriting the answer in the form the question asks for will get you easy marks.

Q1 Find the equation of the tangent to each of these curves at the given point. Give your answer in the form $y = mx + c$.

a) $y = 9x - 2x^2$, $(1, 7)$
b) $y = x^3 - 2x + 3$, $(2, 7)$
c) $y = (x + 2)(2x - 3)$, $(2, 4)$
d) $y = x(x - 1)^2$, $(-1, -4)$
e) $y = x^2(x + 3) - 10$, $(2, 10)$
f) $y = x(2x + 4)(x - 3)$, $(-1, 8)$

Q2 Find the tangent to each of these curves at the given point, giving your answer in the form $ax + by + c = 0$, where a, b and c are integers.

a) $y = \frac{1}{x} + x + 3$, $\left(2, 5\frac{1}{2}\right)$
b) $y = 4x^2 - 3\sqrt{x}$, $(1, 1)$
c) $y = \frac{3}{x} + 2\sqrt{x}$, $\left(4, 4\frac{3}{4}\right)$
d) $y = \frac{1}{x} + \frac{4}{x^2}$, $\left(2, 1\frac{1}{2}\right)$
e) $y = \frac{1}{3}x^2 - 4\sqrt{x} - \frac{1}{3}$, $(4, -3)$
f) $y = x - \frac{2}{x} + \frac{3}{x^2}$, $(-3, -2)$

Q3 Find the normal to each of these curves at the given point, giving your answer in the form $ax + by + c = 0$, where a, b and c are integers.

a) $y = 3x^2 - 4x + 2$, $(2, 6)$
b) $y = x^2(x + 4) - 5x$, $(-1, 8)$
c) $y = x(x - 1)(x - 2)$, $(3, 6)$
d) $y = x(x - 3)(x + 4) - 10$, $(-2, 10)$
e) $y = \frac{x^3 - 5x^2 - 14x}{x + 2}$, $(5, -10)$

Q4 Find the normal to each of these curves at the given point, giving your answer in an appropriate form.

a) $y = \frac{2x^5 - 2x^4}{3x^3}$, $(-2, 4)$
b) $y = \frac{5x^2 - 2x + 3}{x^2}$, $\left(2, 4\frac{3}{4}\right)$
c) $y = \frac{3x - x^2}{\sqrt{x}}$, $(4, -2)$
d) $y = \frac{1}{x} - \frac{3}{x^2} - \frac{4}{x^3} + \frac{7}{4}$, $(-2, 1)$
e) $y = \frac{x^3 - 5x^2 - 4x}{x\sqrt{x}}$, $(4, -4)$

> **Q4 Hint:** This question doesn't tell you which form to use to write the equations, so you can choose whichever is easiest for each part.

Q5 Consider the curve with equation $y = f(x)$ where $f(x) = x^3 - 3x^2 + 3$.

a) Find the coordinates of the point where $f'(x) = 9$ and $x > 0$.
b) Find the equation of the tangent to the curve at this point, giving your answer in the form $y = mx + c$.
c) Find the equation of the normal to the curve at this point, giving your answer in the form $ax + by + c = 0$, where a, b and c are integers.

Q6 a) Show that the curve $y = \frac{x^3 + x^2 + x + 5}{x^2}$ passes through the point $\left(-2, -\frac{1}{4}\right)$.
b) Find the equation of the tangent to the curve at this point, giving your answer in the form $ax + by + c = 0$, where a, b and c are integers.
c) Find the equation of the normal to the curve at this point, giving your answer in the form $ax + by + c = 0$, where a, b and c are integers.

3. Using Differentiation

Learning Objectives:

- Be able to find the second derivative of functions.

- Understand that the second derivative represents the rate of change of the gradient.

- Be able to use differentiation to find all the stationary points on a curve.

- Be able to identify the nature of these stationary points.

- Be able to work out where a function is increasing or decreasing.

- Be able to use this information to make an accurate sketch of the graph of a function.

In this section you'll see some of the uses of differentiation — finding a graph's stationary points and determining their nature, finding where a function is increasing or decreasing, and using this information to make accurate sketches of functions. But first, you need to know how to find second order derivatives.

Finding second order derivatives

- If you differentiate y with respect to x, you get the derivative $\dfrac{dy}{dx}$.

- If you then differentiate $\dfrac{dy}{dx}$ with respect to x, you get the **second order derivative**, denoted $\dfrac{d^2y}{dx^2}$.

- The **second derivative** gives the **rate of change** of the **gradient** of the curve with respect to x. In other words, it tells you how quickly the **gradient** of $y = f(x)$ is changing for any given value of x.

- In function notation, the **second derivative** is written $f''(x)$.

Example

For the function $f(x) = 2x^3 + 4x^2 + x$, find $f'(x)$ and $f''(x)$.

$$f(x) = 2x^3 + 4x^2 + x$$

$$f'(x) = 2(3x^2) + 4(2x) + 1 \longleftarrow \boxed{\text{Differentiate for } f'(x).}$$

$$= 6x^2 + 8x + 1$$

$$f''(x) = 6(2x) + 8 \longleftarrow \boxed{\begin{array}{l}\text{Differentiate again to get}\\ \text{the second derivative.}\end{array}}$$

$$= 12x + 8$$

Exercise 3.1

Q1 Find $\dfrac{dy}{dx}$ and $\dfrac{d^2y}{dx^2}$ for each of these functions:

a) $y = x^3$ b) $y = x^5$ c) $y = x^4$ d) $y = x$

e) $y = \dfrac{1}{x}$ f) $y = \sqrt{x}$ g) $y = \dfrac{1}{x^2}$ h) $y = x\sqrt{x}$

Q2 Find $f'(x)$ and $f''(x)$ for each of these functions:

a) $f(x) = x(4x^2 - x)$ b) $f(x) = (x^2 - 3)(x - 4)$

c) $f(x) = \dfrac{4x^5 + 12x^3 - 40x}{4(x^2 + 5)}$ d) $f(x) = 3\sqrt{x} + x\sqrt{x}$

e) $f(x) = \dfrac{1}{x}(3x^4 - 2x^3)$ f) $f(x) = \dfrac{x^2 - x\sqrt{x} + 7x}{\sqrt{x}}$

Q3 Find the value of the second derivative at the given value for x.

a) $f(x) = x^3 - x^2$, $x = 3$ b) $y = x\sqrt{x} - \dfrac{1}{x}$, $x = 4$

c) $f(x) = x^2(x - 5)(x^2 + x)$, $x = -1$ d) $y = \dfrac{x^5 + 4x^4 - 12x^3}{x + 6}$, $x = 5$

e) $f(x) = \dfrac{9x^2 + 3x}{3\sqrt{x}}$, $x = 1$ f) $y = \left(\dfrac{1}{x^2} + \dfrac{1}{x}\right)(5 - x)$, $x = -3$

Stationary points

Stationary points occur when the **gradient** of a graph is **zero**.
There are three types of stationary point:

Maximum
When the gradient changes from positive to negative.

Minimum
When the gradient changes from negative to positive.

Point of inflection
When the gradient doesn't change sign either side of the stationary point.

Tip: Some stationary points are called **local** maximum or minimum points because the function takes on higher or lower values in other parts of the graph. The maximum and minimum points shown opposite are both local.

Because stationary points occur when the gradient is zero, you can use **differentiation** to find them:

> **1.** Differentiate f(x).
>
> **2.** Set f$'$(x) = 0.
>
> **3.** Solve f$'$(x) = 0 to find the x-values.
>
> **4.** Put the x-values back into the original equation to find the y-values.

Example 1

Find the stationary points on the curve $y = 2x^3 - 3x^2 - 12x + 5$.

- You need to find where $\frac{dy}{dx} = 0$, so start by **differentiating** the function:

$$y = 2x^3 - 3x^2 - 12x + 5 \quad \Rightarrow \quad \frac{dy}{dx} = 6x^2 - 6x - 12$$

- Then set the derivative **equal to zero**:

$$6x^2 - 6x - 12 = 0$$

- Now **solve** this equation — it's just a normal quadratic:

$$6x^2 - 6x - 12 = 0 \quad \Rightarrow \quad x^2 - x - 2 = 0$$
$$\Rightarrow \quad (x + 1)(x - 2) = 0$$
$$\Rightarrow \quad x = -1 \text{ and } x = 2$$

- You've found the x-values of the **stationary points**. To find the coordinates of the stationary points, just put these x-values into the original equation.

  This gives the coordinates $(-1, 12)$ and $(2, -15)$.

Tip: Don't forget this last step — once you've found x you need to also find y.

Example 2

Below is a sketch of the graph of $y = x^3(x^2 + x - 3)$.
One stationary point occurs at (–1.8, 9.1).
Show that the other two occur when $x = 0$
and when $x = 1$, and find their coordinates.

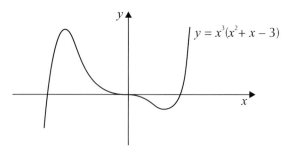

- You need to start by **differentiating** the function, but you can't do that in its current form. So first, **multiply out** the brackets:

$$y = x^3(x^2 + x - 3) = x^5 + x^4 - 3x^3$$

- Then you can just differentiate as normal:

$$y = x^5 + x^4 - 3x^3 \implies \frac{dy}{dx} = 5x^4 + 4x^3 - 9x^2$$

- Stationary points occur when the **gradient** is **equal to zero**, so set $\frac{dy}{dx}$ equal to zero and solve for x:

$$5x^4 + 4x^3 - 9x^2 = 0 \implies x^2(5x^2 + 4x - 9) = 0$$
$$\implies x^2(5x + 9)(x - 1) = 0$$
$$\implies x = 0, \ x = -\frac{9}{5} = -1.8 \text{ (given above) and } x = 1.$$

So the other two stationary points occur at $x = 0$ and $x = 1$.

- To find the **coordinates** of these points, just put the x-values into the original equation:

$$x = 0 \implies y = x^3(x^2 + x - 3)$$
$$= 0^3(0^2 + 0 - 3)$$
$$= 0(-3)$$
$$= 0$$

$$x = 1 \implies y = x^3(x^2 + x - 3)$$
$$= 1^3(1^2 + 1 - 3)$$
$$= 1(-1)$$
$$= -1$$

- So the coordinates of the stationary points are (0, 0) and (1, –1).

Q1 Without doing any calculations, say how many stationary points the graphs below have in the intervals shown.

a)

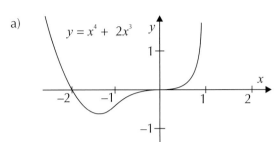

b)

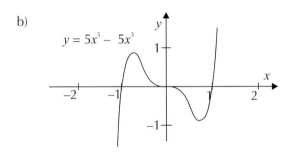

Q2 Find the x-coordinates of the stationary points of the curves with the following equations:

a) $y = x^2 + 3x + 2$ b) $y = (3 - x)(4 + 2x)$

Q3 Find the coordinates of the stationary points of the curves with the following equations:

a) $y = 2x^2 - 5x + 2$ b) $y = -x^2 + 3x - 4$

c) $y = 7 - 6x - 3x^2$ d) $y = (x - 1)(2x + 3)$

Q4 Find the coordinates of the stationary points of the curves with the following equations:

a) $y = x^3 - 3x + 2$ b) $y = 4x^3 + 5$

Q5 Show that the graph of the function given by $f(x) = x^5 + 3x + 2$ has no stationary points.

Q5 Hint: If there are no stationary points, there are no values of x for which $f'(x) = 0$.

Q6 a) Differentiate $y = x^3 - 7x^2 - 5x + 2$.

b) Hence find the coordinates of the stationary points of the curve with equation $y = x^3 - 7x^2 - 5x + 2$.

Q7 A graph is given by the function $f(x) = x^3 + kx$, where k is a constant. Given that the graph has no stationary points,  find the range of possible values for k.

Maximum and minimum points

Tip: That's what a question means when it asks you to "determine the nature of the turning points".

Once you've found where the stationary points are, you might be asked to decide if each one is a **maximum** or **minimum**. Maximum and minimum points are also known as **turning points**.

To decide whether a stationary point is a maximum or minimum, **differentiate again** to find $\frac{d^2y}{dx^2}$ or $f''(x)$ (see page 176).

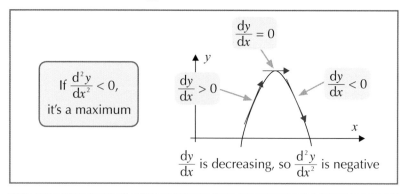

If $\frac{d^2y}{dx^2} < 0$, it's a maximum

$\frac{dy}{dx} = 0$

$\frac{dy}{dx} > 0$ $\frac{dy}{dx} < 0$

$\frac{dy}{dx}$ is decreasing, so $\frac{d^2y}{dx^2}$ is negative

Tip: If the second derivative is equal to zero, you can't tell what type of stationary point it is.

If $\frac{d^2y}{dx^2} > 0$, it's a minimum

$\frac{dy}{dx} = 0$

$\frac{dy}{dx} < 0$ $\frac{dy}{dx} > 0$

$\frac{dy}{dx}$ is increasing, so $\frac{d^2y}{dx^2}$ is positive

Example

Determine the nature of the stationary points in Example 1 on p.177 ($y = 2x^3 - 3x^2 - 12x + 5$).

- The first derivative has been found already: $\frac{dy}{dx} = 6x^2 - 6x - 12$.

  To determine the nature of the stationary points, **differentiate again**:

  $$\frac{dy}{dx} = 6x^2 - 6x - 12 \quad \Rightarrow \quad \frac{d^2y}{dx^2} = 12x - 6$$

- Then just put in the x-values of the coordinates of the **stationary points**.

Tip: You found the coordinates of the stationary points for this function on p.177. They are $(-1, 12)$ and $(2, -15)$.

- At $x = -1$, $\frac{d^2y}{dx^2} = -18$, which is **negative** — so $(-1, 12)$ is a maximum.

- And at $x = 2$, $\frac{d^2y}{dx^2} = 18$, which is **positive** — so $(2, -15)$ is a minimum.

- Since you know the **turning points** and the fact that it's a **cubic** with a positive coefficient of x^3, you can now **sketch** the graph (though the points of intersection with the x-axis would be difficult to find accurately).

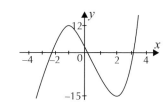

Q1 The diagram below shows a sketch of the graph of $y = f(x)$. For each turning point, say whether $f''(x)$ would be positive or negative.

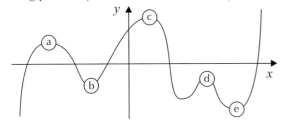

Q2 For each of the following, find the second derivative of the function and say whether the given point is a maximum or a minimum:

a) $y = x^3 - 12x + 4$ has a stationary point at $(2, -12)$.

b) $y = 2x^4 - 16x^3 + 900$ has a stationary point at $(6, 36)$.

c) $y = 4x^5 + 15x^4 - 250$ has a stationary point at $(-3, -7)$.

d) $y = x^5 - 5x^4 + 5x^2 - 40x + 400$ has a stationary point at $(4, 64)$.

Q3 A function $y = f(x)$ is such that $f(1) = 3$, $f'(1) = 0$ and $f''(1) = 7$.

a) Give the coordinates of one of the turning points of $f(x)$.

b) Determine the nature of this turning point, explaining your answer.

Q4 Find the stationary points on the graphs of the following functions and say whether they're maximum or minimum turning points:

a) $y = 5 - x^2$
b) $y = 2x^3 - 6x + 2$

c) $y = x^3 - 3x^2 - 24x + 15$
d) $y = x^4 + 4x^3 + 4x^2 - 10$

Q5 Find the stationary points on the graphs of the following functions and say whether they're maximum or minimum turning points:

a) $f(x) = 8x^3 + 16x^2 + 8x + 1$
b) $f(x) = \dfrac{27}{x^3} + x$

Q6 a) Given that $f(x) = x^3 - 3x^2 + 4$, find $f'(x)$ and $f''(x)$.

b) Hence find the coordinates of any stationary points on the graph $f(x)$ and say whether they're maximum or minimum turning points.

Q7 A function is given by $y = x^2 + \dfrac{2000}{x}$.

a) Find the value of x at which y is stationary.

b) Is this a minimum or maximum point?

Q8 The curve given by $f(x) = x^3 + ax^2 + bx + c$ has a stationary point with coordinates $(3, 10)$. If $f''(x) = 0$ at $(3, 10)$, find a, b and c. (PROBLEM SOLVING)

Q9 a) Given that a curve with the equation $y = x^4 + kx^3 + x^2 + 17$ has only one stationary point, show that $k^2 < \dfrac{32}{9}$. (PROBLEM SOLVING)

b) Find the coordinates of the stationary point and say whether it's a maximum or a minimum point.

Increasing and decreasing functions

As differentiation is about finding the gradients of curves, you can use it to find if a function is **increasing** or **decreasing** at a given point. This can help you to sketch the function and determine the nature of turning points.

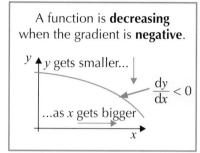

| A function is **increasing** when the gradient is **positive**. | A function is **decreasing** when the gradient is **negative**. |

You can also tell how **quickly** a function is increasing or decreasing by looking at the size of the gradient — the **bigger** the gradient (positive or negative), the **faster** the function is increasing or decreasing.

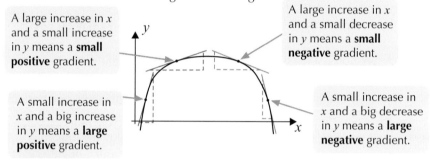

A large increase in x and a small increase in y means a **small positive** gradient.

A large increase in x and a small decrease in y means a **small negative** gradient.

A small increase in x and a big increase in y means a **large positive** gradient.

A small increase in x and a big decrease in y means a **large negative** gradient.

Example

Find the values of x for which the function $y = x^3 - 6x^2 + 9x + 3$, $x > 0$ is increasing.

- You want to know when y is increasing — so **differentiate**.

$$y = x^3 - 6x^2 + 9x + 3 \quad \Rightarrow \quad \frac{dy}{dx} = 3x^2 - 12x + 9$$

- It's an **increasing** function when the derivative is **greater** than zero, so write it down as an inequality and solve it.

$$\frac{dy}{dx} > 0 \ \Rightarrow \ 3x^2 - 12x + 9 > 0 \ \Rightarrow \ x^2 - 4x + 3 > 0 \ \Rightarrow \ (x - 3)(x - 1) > 0$$

- For the inequality to be true, either **both** brackets must be **positive** or **both** brackets must be **negative**:

$$x - 1 > 0 \ \textbf{and} \ x - 3 > 0 \ \Rightarrow \ x > 1 \ \textbf{and} \ x > 3 \ \Rightarrow \ \boxed{x > 3}$$

$$\textbf{or} \ x - 1 < 0 \ \textbf{and} \ x - 3 < 0 \ \Rightarrow \ x < 1 \ \textbf{and} \ x < 3 \ \Rightarrow \ \boxed{x < 1}$$

Tip: This is a different method for solving quadratic inequalities from the one on p.59 — use whichever one you prefer.

- $x > 0$, so the function is increasing when $\boxed{0 < x < 1 \ \text{and} \ x > 3}$.

- You could also look at the nature of the **stationary points** — this tells you where the function goes from increasing to decreasing and vice versa.

$x = 1$ and $x = 3$ at the **stationary points** (as $\frac{dy}{dx} = 0$ at these points).

$$\frac{dy}{dx} = 3x^2 - 12x + 9 \quad \Rightarrow \quad \frac{d^2y}{dx^2} = 6x - 12$$

- When $x = 1$, $\frac{d^2y}{dx^2} = -6$, so it's a **maximum**, which means the function is increasing as it approaches $x = 1$ and starts decreasing after $x = 1$.

- When $x = 3$, $\frac{d^2y}{dx^2} = 6$, so it's a **minimum**, which means the function is decreasing as it approaches $x = 3$ and starts increasing after $x = 3$.

This fits in with what you know already — that the function is increasing when $0 < x < 1$ and $x > 3$.

Exercise 3.4

Q1 For each of these functions, calculate the first derivative and use this to find the range of values for which the function is increasing.

a) $y = x^2 + 7x + 5$ 　　b) $y = 5x^2 + 3x - 2$ 　　c) $y = 2 - 9x^2$

Q2 For each of these functions, find f'(x) and find the range of values of x for which f(x) is decreasing.

a) $f(x) = 16 - 3x - 2x^2$ 　　　　b) $f(x) = (6 - 3x)(6 + 3x)$

c) $f(x) = (1 - 2x)(7 - 3x)$

Q3 Calculate $\frac{dy}{dx}$ for each of these functions and state the range of values for which the function is increasing.

a) $y = x^3 - 6x^2 - 15x + 25$ 　　b) $y = x^3 + 6x^2 + 12x + 5$

Q4 Find the first derivative of each function and state the range of values for which the function is decreasing.

a) $f(x) = x^3 - 3x^2 - 9x + 1$ 　　　b) $f(x) = x^3 - 4x^2 + 4x + 7$

Q5 Use differentiation to explain why $f(x) = x^3 + x$ is an increasing function for all real values of x.

Q5 Hint: An increasing function is one where $f'(x) > 0$ for all values of x.

Q6 Is the function $f(x) = 3 - 3x - x^3$ an increasing or decreasing function? Explain your answer.

Q7 Use differentiation to find the range of values of x for which each of these functions is decreasing:

a) $y = 2x^4 + x$ 　　　　　b) $y = x^4 - 2x^3 - 5x^2 + 6$

Q8 Differentiate these functions and find the range of values for which each function is increasing.

a) $y = x^2 + \sqrt{x}, x > 0$ 　　　b) $y = 4x^2 + \frac{1}{x}, x \neq 0$

Q9, 10 Hint: See which values of the variable satisfy the conditions of an increasing or decreasing function.

Q9 The function $y = 5 - 3x - ax^5$ is a decreasing function for all real values of x. Find the range of possible values for a.

Q10 The function $y = x^k + x$, where k is a positive integer, is an increasing function for all real values of x. Find all possible values of k.

Curve sketching

You covered some curve sketching in Chapter 6, so you should know the basic shapes of different types of graph. Now you'll see how differentiation can be used to find out more about the **shape** of the graph and to work out some **key points** like the turning points. Use the following **step-by-step** method to get all the information you need to draw an accurate sketch:

1. **Find where the curve crosses the axes.**
   - To find where it crosses the **y-axis**, just put $x = 0$ into the function and find the value of y.
   - To find where it crosses the **x-axis**, set the function equal to zero and solve for x (you'll probably have to **factorise** and find the **roots**).

2. **Decide on the shape of the graph.**
   - Look at the **highest power** of x and its **coefficient** — this determines the overall **shape** of the graph (have a look back at pages 86-90). The most common ones are **quadratics**, **cubics** and **reciprocals**.
   - A **quadratic** with a **positive** coefficient of x^2 will be **u-shaped**, and if the coefficient is **negative**, it'll be **n-shaped**.
   - A **cubic** will go from **bottom left** to **top right** if the coefficient of x^3 is **positive**, and **top left** to **bottom right** if the coefficient is **negative**. It'll also have a characteristic '**wiggle**'.
   - **Reciprocals** (e.g. $\frac{1}{x}$) and other **negative powers** have **two separate curves** in **opposite quadrants**, each with **asymptotes**.

3. **Differentiate to find the stationary points.**
   - Find the **stationary points** by **differentiating** and setting $f'(x) = 0$.
   - Then **differentiate again** to decide whether these points are **maximums** or **minimums**.

Tip: If you want, you could find where the function is increasing or decreasing as well.

Example 1

Sketch the curve of the equation $y = f(x)$, where $f(x) = x^3 - 4x^2 + 4x$.

- Start by finding where the curve **crosses the axes**. When $x = 0$, $y = 0$, so the curve goes through the origin. Find where it crosses the x-axis by solving the equation $f(x) = 0$:

$$x^3 - 4x^2 + 4x = 0 \implies x(x^2 - 4x + 4) = 0 \implies x(x-2)(x-2) = 0$$

$$\implies x = 0 \text{ and } x = 2$$

- Next find the **stationary points** on the graph by finding $f'(x)$ and solving $f'(x) = 0$:

$$f(x) = x^3 - 4x^2 + 4x \implies f'(x) = 3x^2 - 8x + 4$$

$$f'(x) = 0 \implies 3x^2 - 8x + 4 = 0 \implies (3x-2)(x-2) = 0$$

$$\implies x = 2 \implies y = 0 \quad \text{and} \quad x = \frac{2}{3} \implies y = \frac{32}{27} \ (\approx 1.2)$$

- Differentiate again to find out if these are **maximums** or **minimums**:

$$f''(x) = 6x - 8$$

At $x = 2$, $f''(x) = 4$, so this is a **minimum**.

At $x = \frac{2}{3}$, $f''(x) = -4$, so this is a **maximum**.

Tip: If you find it helpful, you can also work out where the graph is increasing and decreasing — it's increasing when $x < \frac{2}{3}$ and when $x > 2$, and decreasing when $\frac{2}{3} < x < 2$.

- It's a cubic equation with a positive coefficient of x^3, so the graph will go from bottom left to top right.
- Notice that the x-intercept $x = 2$ is also the minimum.
- Now you have all the information you need to sketch the graph:

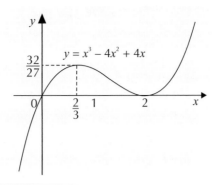

Tip: This is a cubic equation so you should know the general shape — see page 86.

Example 2

Sketch the graph of $f(x) = -8x^3 + 2x$.

- Again, start by finding where the curve **crosses the axes**. When $x = 0$, $f(x) = 0$ so the curve goes through the origin. Now solve $f(x) = 0$:

$$-8x^3 + 2x = 0 \implies 2x(-4x^2 + 1) = 0$$

So $x = 0$ or $-4x^2 + 1 = 0 \implies x^2 = \frac{1}{4} \implies x = \pm\frac{1}{2}$

- Next **differentiate** the function to find the **stationary point(s)**:

$$f(x) = -8x^3 + 2x \implies f'(x) = -24x^2 + 2$$

$f'(x) = 0$ so $-24x^2 + 2 = 0 \implies x^2 = \frac{1}{12} \implies x = \pm\sqrt{\frac{1}{12}} = \pm\frac{1}{2\sqrt{3}}$

$x = \frac{1}{2\sqrt{3}}$ gives $f(x) = \frac{2}{3\sqrt{3}}$ and $x = -\frac{1}{2\sqrt{3}}$ gives $f(x) = -\frac{2}{3\sqrt{3}}$.

- **Differentiate again** to see if these points are **maximums** or **minimums**:
$f''(x) = -48x$.

At $x = \frac{1}{2\sqrt{3}}$, $f''(x) = -\frac{24}{\sqrt{3}}$, which is negative so it's a maximum.

At $x = -\frac{1}{2\sqrt{3}}$, $f''(x) = \frac{24}{\sqrt{3}}$, which is positive so it's a minimum.

- Finally, think about the overall shape of the graph. The highest power is 3, so it's a cubic and has a negative coefficient, so the graph will go from top left to bottom right.

Tip: Don't forget the characteristic cubic 'wiggle'.

- Now you have all the information you need to sketch the graph:

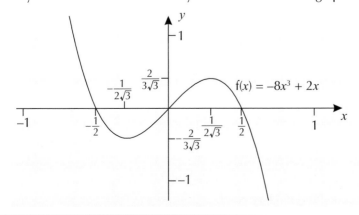

Q1 For the graph $y = x^3 - 2x^2$:
  a) Find the coordinates of the points at which it crosses each axis.
  b) Find $\dfrac{dy}{dx}$ and hence the coordinates of the points where $\dfrac{dy}{dx} = 0$.
  c) Identify whether the stationary points are maximums or minimums.
  d) Sketch the graph of $y = x^3 - 2x^2$.

Q2 a) Solve the equation $x^3 + x^2 = 0$.
  b) Find the stationary points of the graph of $f(x) = x^3 + x^2$ and say whether they're maximum or minimum points.
  c) Use your answers to parts a) and b) to sketch the graph of $f(x) = x^3 + x^2$, labelling the coordinates of the stationary points and places where the curve meets the axes.

Q3 a) Find the first and second derivatives of the function $f(x) = x^4 - x^3$.
  b) Write down the ranges of values of x for which $f(x)$ is increasing and decreasing.
  c) Sketch the graph of $y = f(x)$, labelling the coordinates of all stationary points and the points where the curve crosses the axes.

Q4 Sketch the graphs of the equations below, labelling the coordinates of any stationary points and the points where the curves cross the axes.
  a) $y = 3x^3 + 3x^2$
  b) $y = -x^3 + 9x$
  c) $y = x^4 - x^2$
  d) $y = x^4 + x^2$

Q5 Given that $x^3 - x^2 - x + 1 = (x + 1)(x - 1)^2$, sketch the graph of $y = x^3 - x^2 - x + 1$, labelling the coordinates of all the stationary points and the points where the curve crosses the axes.

Q6 a) Show that $x^3 - 4x = 0$ when $x = -2$, 0 and 2.
  b) Use first and second derivatives to show that the graph of $y = x^3 - 4x$ has a minimum at $(1.2, -3.1)$ and a maximum at $(-1.2, 3.1)$, where all coordinates are given to 1 d.p.
  c) Use your answers to parts a) and b) to sketch the graph of $y = x^3 - 4x$, labelling the coordinates of the stationary points and the points at which the curve crosses the axes.

Q7 Hint: The function is undefined at $x = 0$, so the graph won't just go straight through the y-axis (it 'jumps' from one side to the other).

The → symbol means 'tends to' or 'approaches' — you need to say what happens as x gets close to zero and to ±∞.

Q7 a) Show that the graph of $f(x) = x + \dfrac{1}{x}$, $x \neq 0$ has 2 stationary points.
  b) Calculate the coordinates of these stationary points and say whether they're maximum or minimum points.
  c) Describe what happens to $f(x)$ as $x \to 0$ from both sides.
  d) Describe what happens to $f(x)$ as $x \to \infty$ and $x \to -\infty$.
  e) Hence sketch the graph of the function $x + \dfrac{1}{x}$.

Q8 Hint: Consider what will happen as $x \to 0$ and $x \to \infty$, like you did in Q7.

Q8 a) Show that for the graph of $y = x^4 + \dfrac{8}{\sqrt{x}}$, $x > 0$, $\dfrac{dy}{dx} = 0$ when $x = 1$.
  b) Sketch the graph of $y = x^4 + \dfrac{8}{\sqrt{x}}$, $x > 0$, labelling the coordinates of the stationary point.

4. Real-Life Problems

Equations can be used to model real-life contexts. That means you can use differentiation to solve problems involving real-life rates of change (like speed or acceleration), or real-life maximum or minimum values — e.g. the maximum or minimum possible area or volume of an object.

Learning Objectives:

- Be able to solve real-life problems about rates of change.
- Be able to describe a real-life situation in mathematical terms and use differentiation to find maximum and minimum solutions.

Speed and acceleration problems

Until now, all the examples have been about differentiating functions of x to find gradients of curves. But **real-life** examples often involve a function of time, t, and you'll need to differentiate to find the **rate of change** over time. The maths is the **same**, the **letters** are just different.

The next example looks at the **distance** a car has travelled as a function of **time**.

Example

A car pulls away from a junction and travels x metres in t seconds. For the first 10 seconds, its journey is modelled by the equation $x = 2t^2$.

a) Find the speed of the car after 8 seconds.

- **Speed** is the **rate of change** of **distance** with respect to **time** — it can be found by differentiating the expression for distance with respect to time.

- So to work out the speed as a function of t, **differentiate x to find $\frac{dx}{dt}$**.

$$x = 2t^2$$
$$\frac{dx}{dt} = 4t$$

- You've got speed as a function of t, so put $t = 8$ **seconds** into the expression.

$$\text{When } t = 8, \frac{dx}{dt} = 32$$

- So the car is travelling at $32\ \text{ms}^{-1}$ after 8 seconds.

Tip: Just like in all the other questions, $\frac{dx}{dt}$ is a gradient. If you were to draw a distance–time graph, it would just be the gradient of the graph as a function of t.

Tip: You'll see more questions like this in Chapter 19.

b) Find the car's acceleration during this period.

- **Acceleration** is the **rate of change** of **speed** with respect to **time** — it can be found by differentiating the expression for speed with respect to time.

- The speed is $\frac{dx}{dt}$ so **differentiate again** to get the **second derivative** $\frac{d^2x}{dt^2}$.

$$\frac{dx}{dt} = 4t$$
$$\frac{d^2x}{dt^2} = 4$$

- This means that the car's acceleration during this period is $4\ \text{ms}^{-2}$.

Tip: Careful with the units here — acceleration is measured in metres per second².

Q1 A particle moves along a path described by the equation $x = 3t^2 - 7t$, where t is the time in seconds and x is the distance in metres.

   a) Find the speed, $\dfrac{dx}{dt}$, of the particle as a function of t.

   b) What is the speed of the particle in ms^{-1} at:

   (i) $t = 2$ seconds?   (ii) $t = 5$ seconds?

   c) Find the value of t when the speed is 17 ms^{-1}.

   d) Find the acceleration $\dfrac{d^2x}{dt^2}$ of the particle as a function of t.

Q2 A particle moves along a path described by the equation $x = 2t^3 - 4t^2$, $t > 0$, where t is the time in seconds and x is the distance in metres.

   a) Find the speed of the particle after t seconds.

   b) Find x and t when the speed is 30 ms^{-1}.

   c) Find the acceleration of the particle after t seconds.

   d) Find the acceleration at $t = 5$ seconds in ms^{-2}.

   e) Find the speed when the acceleration is 16 ms^{-2}.

Q2 Hint: For part e), use the information you've been given to work out the value of t and then put the t value into the expression for speed.

Length, area and volume problems

Because differentiation can be used to find the maximum value of a function, it can be used in **real-life problems** to maximise a quantity subject to certain factors, e.g maximising the volume of a box that can be made with a set amount of cardboard.

To find the maximum value of something, all you need is an equation **in terms of only one variable** (e.g. x) — then just **differentiate as normal**. Often there'll be too many variables in the question, so you've got to know how to manipulate the information to get rid of the unwanted variables.

Example 1

A farmer wants to build a rectangular sheep pen with length x m and width y m. She has 20 m of fencing in total, and wants the area inside the pen to be as large as possible. How long should each side of the pen be, and what will the area inside the pen be?

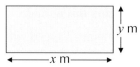

- Start by writing down an expression for the **area** of the pen:

$$\text{Area} = \text{length} \times \text{width} = xy \text{ m}^2$$

- This has **too many variables** for you to be able to work with, so you need to find an expression for y in terms of x. You know how much fencing is available, so find an expression for that in terms of x and y and rearrange it to make y the subject.

$$\text{Perimeter} = 20 \text{ m} = 2x + 2y \quad \Rightarrow \quad y = \frac{20 - 2x}{2} = 10 - x.$$

- Now you can substitute this into the expression you wrote down for the area and use **differentiation** to **maximise** it:

$$A = xy = x(10 - x) = 10x - x^2, \text{ so } A = 10x - x^2 \Rightarrow \frac{dA}{dx} = 10 - 2x$$

- Now just find when $\frac{dA}{dx} = 0$

$$\frac{dA}{dx} = 0 \Rightarrow 10 - 2x = 0, \text{ so } x = 5 \Rightarrow y = 10 - x = 5$$

- To check that this value of x gives a maximum for A, **differentiate again**:

$$\frac{d^2A}{dx^2} = -2, \text{ which is negative, so this will give a maximum for } A.$$

- So both x and y should be 5 m and the total area inside the pen will be $5 \times 5 = 25$ m².

Tip: For a given perimeter, the rectangle with the largest possible area is always a square.

Example 2

A cuboid jewellery box with a lid has dimensions $3x$ cm by x cm by y cm. It is made using a total of 450 cm² of wood.

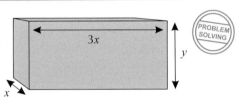

PROBLEM SOLVING

Show that the volume of the box can be expressed as $V = \dfrac{675x - 9x^3}{4}$, and use calculus to find the maximum volume.

Tip: 'Use calculus' here just means differentiate.

- You know the basic equation for volume:

$$V = \text{length} \times \text{width} \times \text{height} = 3x \times x \times y = 3x^2y$$

- This has a y that you want to **get rid of** so look for a way of **replacing** y with an equation in x (like in example 1). You can do this by finding an expression for the surface area of the box, which you know is 450 cm²:

$$\text{Surface area} = 2 \times [(3x \times x) + (3x \times y) + (x \times y)] = 450$$
$$\Rightarrow 6x^2 + 8xy = 450 \Rightarrow y = \frac{450 - 6x^2}{8x} = \frac{225 - 3x^2}{4x}$$

- Now substitute this into the expression for the volume of the box:

$$V = 3x^2y = 3x^2\left(\frac{225 - 3x^2}{4x}\right) = \frac{675x - 9x^3}{4}$$

- Now just **differentiate** and find x at the **stationary point(s)**:

$$V = \frac{675x - 9x^3}{4} \Rightarrow \frac{dV}{dx} = \frac{675 - 27x^2}{4}$$

When $\frac{dV}{dx} = 0, \frac{675 - 27x^2}{4} = 0 \Rightarrow x^2 = \frac{675}{27} = 25 \Rightarrow x = 5$

Tip: x is a length so it can't have a negative value (−5).

- Check that V is actually a maximum at $x = 5$, then just calculate V with $x = 5$:

$$\frac{d^2V}{dx^2} = -\frac{27x}{2} \quad \text{So when } x = 5, \frac{d^2V}{dx^2} = -\frac{135}{2} \text{ (so } V \text{ is a maximum)}$$

$$V = \frac{675x - 9x^3}{4} \quad \text{So when } x = 5, V = \frac{675(5) - 9(5^3)}{4} = 562.5 \text{ cm}^3$$

Differentiation isn't just limited to cuboids — it can be used on **any shape** as long as you can describe its (surface) area or volume with variables (i.e x, y).

Example 3

A cylindrical pie tin is t cm high with a diameter of d cm.
The volume of the pie tin is 1000 cm³.
Show that the surface area of the tin is given by $A = \frac{\pi}{4}d^2 + \frac{4000}{d}$
and find the minimum surface area.

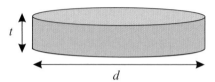

> **Tip:** The pie tin has no lid so you only need to add the surface area of one circle.

- A = area of tin's base + area of tin's curved face $= \pi\left(\dfrac{d}{2}\right)^2 + (\pi d \times t)$

$$= \frac{\pi d^2}{4} + \pi dt$$

- To get rid of the t, find an equation for the volume and **rearrange it** to make t the subject, then sub that into the equation for surface area:

$$V = \pi\left(\frac{d}{2}\right)^2 t = 1000 \quad \Rightarrow \quad t = \frac{1000}{\pi\left(\dfrac{d}{2}\right)^2} = \frac{4000}{\pi d^2}$$

$$\Rightarrow A = \frac{\pi d^2}{4} + \pi dt = \frac{\pi d^2}{4} + \left(\pi d \times \frac{4000}{\pi d^2}\right) = \frac{\pi d^2}{4} + \frac{4000}{d}$$

- Next, **differentiate** with respect to d and find the values of d that make $\dfrac{dA}{dd} = 0$:

$$\frac{dA}{dd} = \frac{\pi d}{2} - \frac{4000}{d^2} \text{ so when } \frac{dA}{dd} = 0, \ \frac{\pi d}{2} - \frac{4000}{d^2} = 0 \ \Rightarrow \ d^3 = \frac{2 \times 4000}{\pi}$$

$$\Rightarrow d = \frac{20}{\sqrt[3]{\pi}}$$

- Check to see if this value of d gives a **minimum** for A:

$$\frac{d^2 A}{dd^2} = \frac{\pi}{2} + \frac{8000}{d^3} = \frac{\pi}{2} + \frac{8000}{\left(\dfrac{8000}{\pi}\right)} = \frac{3\pi}{2}, \text{ so it's a minimum.}$$

- Now calculate the surface area for that value of d:

$$A = \frac{\pi}{4}\left(\frac{20}{\sqrt[3]{\pi}}\right)^2 + \frac{4000}{\left(\dfrac{20}{\sqrt[3]{\pi}}\right)} = \boxed{439 \text{ cm}^2} \text{ (to 3 s.f.)}$$

Exercise 4.2

> **Q1 Hint:** This is a lot like the example on p.188, but you're finding the minimum perimeter for a given area instead of the maximum area for a given perimeter.

Q1 A farmer wants to enclose a rectangular area of 100 m² with a fence. Find the minimum length of fencing he needs to use.

Q2 A ball is catapulted vertically with an initial speed of 30 m/s. After t seconds the height h of the ball, in m, is given by $h = 30t - 4.9t^2$. Use calculus to find the maximum height the ball reaches.

Q3   A rectangular vegetable patch is enclosed by a wall on one side
      and fencing on three sides as shown in the diagram.

Q3 Hint: It might look
like you're not given
enough information
here, but just call the
length x and the width y
and you're on your way.

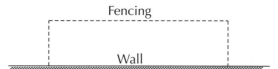

      Use calculus to show that the maximum possible area that
      can be enclosed by 66 m of fencing is 544.5 m².

Q4   A pet food manufacturer designs tins of cat food of capacity 500 cm³
      as shown. The radius of the tin is r cm and the height is h cm.

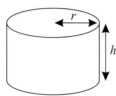

      a) Show that the surface area A of the tin is given by $A = 2\pi r^2 + \dfrac{1000}{r}$.
      b) Find the value of r which minimises the surface area (to 3 s.f.).
      c) Find the minimum possible surface area for the tin (to 3 s.f.).

Q5   A child makes a box by taking a piece of card measuring 40 × 40 cm
      and cutting squares with side length x cm, as shown in the diagram.
      The sides are then folded up to make a box.

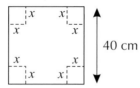

      a) Write down a formula for the volume of the box, V.
      b) Find the maximum possible volume of the box to 3 s.f.

Q6   A chocolate manufacturer designs a new box which is a triangular
      prism as shown in the diagram. The cross-section of the prism is a
      right-angled triangle with sides of length x cm, x cm and h cm.
      The length of the prism is l cm and the volume is 300 cm³.

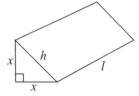

      a) Show that the surface area of the prism is given by
          $$A = x^2 + \frac{600(2 + \sqrt{2})}{x}.$$
      b) Show that the value of x which minimises the surface area of the
          box is $\sqrt[3]{600 + 300\sqrt{2}}$.

1. Indefinite Integration

Integration is just the process of getting from $\dfrac{dy}{dx}$ back to y itself.

Integration

Integration is the '**opposite**' of differentiation. When you integrate something, you're trying to find a function that returns to **what you started with** when you differentiate it. This function is called an **integral**.

The integral of a **function** $f(x)$ with respect to x is written:

$\int$ means **the integral of**. $\int f(x)\ dx$ dx means **with respect to x**.

For example, 'the integral of $2x$ with respect to x' is written $\int \mathbf{2x\ dx}$.

The answer could be **any function** which differentiates to give $2x$.

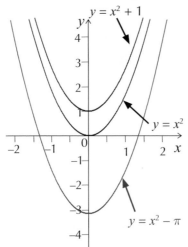

$y = x^2 + 1$

$y = x^2$

$y = x^2 - \pi$

From Chapter 10, we know that:

$$\frac{d}{dx}(x^2) = 2x$$
$$\frac{d}{dx}(x^2 + 1) = 2x$$
$$\frac{d}{dx}(x^2 - \pi) = 2x$$

If you differentiate any of these functions, you get $2x$ — they're **all possible integrals** because they all have the **same gradient**.

In fact, if you differentiate **any** function which is of the form $x^2 +$ '**a constant**' — you'll get $2x$.

So the answer to this integral is actually... $\int 2x\ dx = x^2 + C$

C is a constant representing 'any number'— it's known as the **constant of integration**.

This is an example of **indefinite integration** — a good way to remember this is that C can take an **indefinite number** of values. There are **lots of answers** to an indefinite integral, so you need to add a **constant of integration** to show that it could be **any number**.

Formally, the **Fundamental Theorem of Calculus** states that:

$$\int f(x)\ dx = F(x) + C \quad \Leftrightarrow \quad f(x) = \frac{d}{dx}(F(x))$$

Or, more simply, it says that if differentiating takes you from one function to another, then integrating the second function will take you back to the first (with a constant of integration).

Integrating x^n

The formula below tells you how to integrate **any power of x** (except x^{-1}).

$$\int x^n \, dx = \frac{x^{n+1}}{n+1} + C$$

This just says:

To integrate a power of x: (i) **Increase the power** by one
— then divide by it.

and   (ii) Add a **constant**.

Tip: You can't use this formula for $\frac{1}{x} = x^{-1}$. When you increase the power by 1 and then divide by the power you get:

$$\int x^{-1} \, dx = \frac{x^0}{0}$$

This is undefined since you can't divide by 0.

Example 1

Find the following integrals:

a) $\int x^3 \, dx$

Increase the power to 4...

$$\int x^3 \, dx = \frac{x^4}{4} + C$$

...divide by 4...   ...and add a constant of integration.

You can always check that you've got the right answer by differentiating it — you should end up with the thing you started with:

$$\frac{d}{dx}\left(\frac{x^4}{4} + C\right) = \frac{d}{dx}\left(\frac{x^4}{4}\right) + \frac{d}{dx}(C) = x^3 + 0 = x^3$$

Tip: It's easy to forget the constant of integration and lose easy marks. Make sure you get used to adding it on.

b) $\int \frac{1}{x^3} \, dx$

Increase the power by 1 to −2...

$$\int \frac{1}{x^3} \, dx = \int x^{-3} \, dx = \frac{x^{-2}}{-2} + C = -\frac{1}{2x^2} + C$$

...divide by −2...   ...and add a constant of integration.

Check your answer is correct by differentiating:

$$\frac{d}{dx}\left(-\frac{1}{2x^2} + C\right) = \frac{d}{dx}\left(-\frac{1}{2}x^{-2}\right) + \frac{d}{dx}(C) = x^{-3} + 0 = \frac{1}{x^3}$$

c) $\int \sqrt[3]{x^4} \, dx$

Add 1 to the power...

$$\int \sqrt[3]{x^4} \, dx = \int x^{\frac{4}{3}} \, dx = \frac{x^{\frac{7}{3}}}{\left(\frac{7}{3}\right)} + C = \frac{3\sqrt[3]{x^7}}{7} + C$$

...then divide by $\frac{7}{3}$ ...   ...and add a constant of integration.

Tip: Be careful when dividing by a fraction — dividing by $\frac{a}{b}$ is the same as multiplying by the fraction flipped upside-down, $\frac{b}{a}$.

Check your answer is correct by differentiating:

$$\frac{d}{dx}\left(\frac{3\sqrt[3]{x^7}}{7} + C\right) = \frac{d}{dx}\left(\frac{3}{7}x^{\frac{7}{3}}\right) + \frac{d}{dx}(C) = x^{\frac{4}{3}} + 0 = \sqrt[3]{x^4}$$

Example 2

Find $\int 4\,dx$.

There's no x^n here, but $x^0 = 1$, so you can multiply by x^0 without changing anything.

$$\int 4\,dx = \int 4x^0\,dx$$

Increase the power from 0 to 1.

$$= \frac{4x^1}{1} + C$$

Divide by the power.

$$= 4x + C$$

Tip: The integral $\int n\,dx$, where n is any constant value, will always be $nx + C$.

Exercise 1.1

Q1 Find an expression for y when $\dfrac{dy}{dx}$ is the following:

a) x^7 b) $2x^3$ c) $8x$ d) $-5x^4$ e) x^{-3}

f) $4x^{-4}$ g) $-6x^{-5}$ h) -12 i) $x^{\frac{1}{2}}$ j) $x^{\frac{1}{3}}$

Q1 Hint: When the function is multiplied by a constant, the integral of the x^n term is multiplied by the same constant — just like when you differentiate. Look at the formula and examples below if you need to.

Q2 Find the following:

a) $\int x^{\frac{2}{3}}\,dx$ b) $\int 7x^{\frac{4}{3}}\,dx$ c) $\int x^{-\frac{1}{2}}\,dx$

d) $\int 2x^{-\frac{1}{3}}\,dx$ e) $\int 14x^{0.4}\,dx$ f) $\int -1.2x^{-0.6}\,dx$

g) $\int -2x^{-\frac{5}{4}}\,dx$ h) $\int -\frac{3}{2}x^{\frac{1}{2}}\,dx$ i) $\int -\frac{4}{3}x^{\frac{4}{3}}\,dx$

Integrating functions

Like differentiating, if there are **lots of terms** in an expression, you can just integrate each bit **separately**. If the terms are multiplied by **constants**, take them **outside** the integral like this:

$$\int ax^n\,dx = a\int x^n\,dx$$

Examples

a) Find $\int \left(3x^2 - \dfrac{2}{\sqrt{x}} + \dfrac{7}{x^2} \right) dx$.

Write as powers of x.

$$\int \left(3x^2 - \frac{2}{\sqrt{x}} + \frac{7}{x^2} \right) dx = \int \left(3x^2 - 2x^{-\frac{1}{2}} + 7x^{-2} \right) dx$$

Integrate each term separately.

$$= 3\int x^2\,dx - 2\int x^{-\frac{1}{2}}\,dx + 7\int x^{-2}\,dx$$

Take the constants outside the integral.

$$= \frac{3x^3}{3} - \frac{2x^{\frac{1}{2}}}{\left(\frac{1}{2}\right)} + \frac{7x^{-1}}{-1} + C$$

Just add one constant of integration.

$$= x^3 - 4\sqrt{x} - \frac{7}{x} + C$$

Tip: When you're doing lots of separate integrations, you only need one constant of integration for the whole expression — if each integral gives a constant, you can just add them up to get a new constant.

---

b) Find y **if** $\dfrac{dy}{dx} = \dfrac{1}{2}x^3 - 4x^{\frac{3}{2}}x.$

Integrate the
derivative of
y to get y.

$$y = \int \frac{dy}{dx}\,dx = \int \left(\frac{1}{2}x^3 - 4x^{\frac{3}{2}}x\right)dx$$

$$= \int \left(\frac{1}{2}x^3 - 4x^{\frac{5}{2}}\right)dx = \frac{1}{2}\int x^3\,dx - 4\int x^{\frac{5}{2}}\,dx$$

$$= \frac{1}{2} \times \frac{x^4}{4} + (-4) \times \frac{x^{\frac{7}{2}}}{\left(\frac{7}{2}\right)} + C$$

$$= \frac{x^4}{8} - \frac{8}{7}x^{\frac{7}{2}} + C$$

c) Find $\displaystyle\int \left(\dfrac{(x-1)^2}{\sqrt{x}}\right)dx.$

$$\int \left(\frac{(x-1)^2}{\sqrt{x}}\right)dx = \int \left(\frac{x^2 - 2x + 1}{x^{\frac{1}{2}}}\right)dx = \int \left(\frac{x^2}{x^{\frac{1}{2}}} - \frac{2x}{x^{\frac{1}{2}}} + \frac{1}{x^{\frac{1}{2}}}\right)dx$$

Expand the bracket...

...split into separate terms...

...and write as powers of x.

$$= \int \left(x^{\frac{3}{2}} - 2x^{\frac{1}{2}} + x^{-\frac{1}{2}}\right)dx$$

$$= \int x^{\frac{3}{2}}\,dx - 2\int x^{\frac{1}{2}}\,dx + \int x^{-\frac{1}{2}}\,dx$$

Do each of these
bits separately.

$$= \frac{x^{\frac{5}{2}}}{\left(\frac{5}{2}\right)} - \frac{2x^{\frac{3}{2}}}{\left(\frac{3}{2}\right)} + \frac{x^{\frac{1}{2}}}{\left(\frac{1}{2}\right)} + C$$

$$= \frac{2(\sqrt{x})^5}{5} - \frac{4(\sqrt{x})^3}{3} + 2\sqrt{x} + C$$

Tip: Some expressions
will need simplifying
before you integrate
with the formula for
powers of x.

Exercise 1.2

Q1 Find $f(x)$ when $f'(x)$ is given by the following:

a) $5x + 3x^{-4}$

b) $4x(x^2 - 1)$

c) $(x-3)^2$

d) $x\left(6x + \dfrac{4}{x^4}\right)$

e) $\left(x + \dfrac{2}{x}\right)^2$

f) $x\left(3x^{\frac{1}{2}} - \dfrac{2}{x^{\frac{4}{3}}}\right)$

g) $6\sqrt{x} - \dfrac{1}{x^2}$

h) $\dfrac{2}{\sqrt{x}} - 7x^2\sqrt{x}$

i) $5(\sqrt{x})^3 - \dfrac{3x}{\sqrt{x}}$

Q1 Hint: Remember
$f'(x)$ is just another way
of saying $\dfrac{dy}{dx}$.

When you integrate $f'(x)$
you get $f(x)$ and when
you differentiate $f(x)$ you
get $f'(x)$.

Q2 Find the following integrals:

a) $\displaystyle\int (0.55x^{0.1} - 3x^{-1.5}x)\,dx$

b) $\displaystyle\int \left(8x^3 - \dfrac{2}{\sqrt{x}} + \dfrac{5}{x^2}\right)dx$

c) $\displaystyle\int \left((\sqrt{x})^5 + \dfrac{1}{2\sqrt{x}}\right)dx$

d) $\displaystyle\int \left(\sqrt{x}\left(7x^2 - 1 - \dfrac{2}{x}\right)\right)dx$

e) $\displaystyle\int (3x - 5\sqrt{x})^2\,dx$

f) $\displaystyle\int \left(\dfrac{2x^3 - \sqrt{x}}{x}\right)dx$

g) $\displaystyle\int \left(\dfrac{(5x-3)^2}{\sqrt{x}}\right)dx$

h) $\displaystyle\int (x^{\frac{1}{2}} + 1)(x^{-\frac{1}{2}} - 3)\,dx$

Q3 Given that $\dfrac{dy}{dx} = 1.5x^2 - \dfrac{4}{x^3}$, find y.

Q4 Given that $f'(x) = \dfrac{4}{3(x^{\frac{1}{3}})^4} + 5x^{\frac{3}{2}}$, find $f(x)$.

Q5 Find: a) $\displaystyle\int \left(\dfrac{(\sqrt{x} + 3)(\sqrt{x} - 1)}{\sqrt{x}}\right)dx$ b) $\displaystyle\int \left(\sqrt{x}\left(\sqrt{x} - \dfrac{1}{\sqrt{x}}\right)^2\right)dx.$

Integrating to find equations of curves

As you saw in Chapter 10, **differentiating** the equation of a curve gives its **gradient**. **Integrating** the gradient of a curve does the **opposite** — it gives you the **equation** of the curve.

But integrating actually gives you **many** possible curves because of the **constant of integration**, C. C can take any value and each different value represents a different curve (all vertically translated copies of each other).

Tip: Have a look at page 91 for more on translations of graphs.

So to find the equation of a **particular curve** by integration, you need to know the coordinates of **one point** on it, which you can use to find C.

Examples

a) The curve $y = f(x)$ goes through the point (2, 16) and $\frac{dy}{dx} = 2x^3$. Find the equation of the curve.

- You know the derivative $\frac{dy}{dx} = 2x^3$ and need to find y. So integrating gives:

$$y = \int 2x^3 \, dx = \frac{2x^4}{4} + C = \boxed{\frac{x^4}{2} + C}$$

- Check this is correct by differentiating it and making sure you get what you started with.

$$y = \frac{x^4}{2} + C$$

$$\frac{dy}{dx} = \frac{1}{2}(4x^3) + 0 = \boxed{2x^3}$$

- So this function has the correct derivative — but you haven't finished yet. You now need to find C — and you do this by using the fact that it goes through the point (2, 16). Putting $x = 2$ and $y = 16$ in the equation gives...

$$y = \frac{x^4}{2} + C$$

$$16 = \frac{2^4}{2} + C$$

$$\Rightarrow 16 = 2^3 + C$$

$$\Rightarrow C = 8$$

- So the solution you need is:

$$y = \frac{x^4}{2} + 8$$

b) The curve $y = f(x)$ goes through the point (2, 8) and $f'(x) = 6x(x - 1)$. Find $f(x)$.

- You know $f'(x)$ and need to find the function $f(x)$.

$$f'(x) = 6x(x - 1) = 6x^2 - 6x$$

- So integrate...

$$f(x) = \int (6x^2 - 6x) \, dx$$

$$\Rightarrow f(x) = \frac{6x^3}{3} - \frac{6x^2}{2} + C = 2x^3 - 3x^2 + C$$

- Check this is correct by differentiating...

$$f(x) = 2x^3 - 3x^2 + C$$

$$f'(x) = 2(3x^2) - 3(2x^1) = \boxed{6x^2 - 6x}$$

- You now need to find C using the point (2, 8).
Put $x = 2$ and $y = 8$ into $f(x) = 2x^3 - 3x^2 + C$.

$$8 = (2 \times 2^3) - (3 \times 2^2) + C$$

$$\Rightarrow 8 = 16 - 12 + C$$

$$\Rightarrow \boxed{C = 4}$$

Tip: It may seem odd to substitute the value of y into an equation without any y's, but remember that y is just the same as $f(x)$, so put the value for y wherever you see $f(x)$.

- So the answer is: $\boxed{f(x) = 2x^3 - 3x^2 + 4}$

Exercise 1.3

Q1 For each of the following, the curve $y = f(x)$ passes through the given point. Find $f(x)$.

a) $f'(x) = 4x^3$, (0, 5)

b) $f'(x) = 3x^2 - 4x + 3$, (1, –3)

c) $f'(x) = 6x(x + 2)$, (–1, 1)

d) $f'(x) = \dfrac{5}{x^2} + 2x$, (5, 4)

e) $f'(x) = 3x^2(x - 4)$, (2, –10)

f) $f'(x) = (3x + 1)(x - 1)$, (3, –3)

g) $f'(x) = x(x + \dfrac{3}{x^3})$, (–3, 5)

h) $f'(x) = \dfrac{9x^3 + 2x^{-2}}{x}$, (–1, 2)

Q2 A curve $y = f(x)$ that passes through the point (4, 9) has gradient function:

$$f'(x) = \frac{3}{\sqrt{x}} + 2x$$

Find the equation of the curve.

Q2 Hint: The gradient function is just the function which tells you the gradient — the derivative.

Q3 The gradient function of a curve is given by

$$\frac{dy}{dx} = 3\sqrt{x} + \frac{1}{x^2}$$

Find the equation of the curve if it passes through the point (1, 7).

Q4 Consider $\dfrac{dy}{dt} = (\sqrt{t} - 3)^2$.

Given that $y = 9$ when $t = 4$, find y as a function of t.

Q5 The curve $y = f(x)$ goes through the point $\left(1, \dfrac{1}{3}\right)$ and $f'(x) = \sqrt{x}\,(5x - 1)$. Find $f(x)$.

Q6 The curve $y = f(x)$ has derivative $f'(x) = x^2 + \dfrac{2}{x^{\frac{3}{2}}}$ and passes through the point $\left(1, -\dfrac{5}{3}\right)$. Find the equation of the curve.

Q7 The gradient function of a curve is given by $\dfrac{dy}{dx} = \dfrac{x - 6}{x^3} + 2$.

Find the equation of the curve if it passes through the point (3, –1).

2. Definite Integration

Learning Objectives:

- Be able to evaluate definite integrals.
- Be able to find the area between a curve and the x-axis using definite integration.

Integration can be used to find the area under a graph. In this section, you'll see how to use a definite integral to work out an area.

Evaluating definite integrals

Definite integrals have **limits** (little numbers) next to the integral sign. The limits just tell you the **range of x-values** to integrate the function between.

> The definite integral of **f(x)** with respect to x between the limits $x = a$ and $x = b$ is written:
>
> The upper limit goes here.
>
> $$\int_a^b f(x)\ dx$$
>
> The lower limit goes here.

Tip: If you're integrating with respect to a different variable, say t, then the limits tell you the range of t-values instead.

Finding a definite integral isn't really any harder than an indefinite one — there's just an **extra stage** you have to do.

- Integrate the function as normal but **don't** add a **constant of integration**.

- Once you've integrated the function, work out the **value** of the definite integral by **putting in the limits**:

> If you know that the integral of f(x) is $\int f(x)\ dx = g(x) + C$ then:
>
> $$\int_a^b f(x)\ dx = \left[g(x) \right]_a^b = g(b) - g(a)$$
>
> **Subtract** the value of g at the **lower** limit from the value of g at the **upper** limit.

Tip: The proper way to write out definite integrals is to use square brackets with the limits to the right like this.

- This is the second part of the **Fundamental Theorem of Calculus**.

Tip: You might be asked to 'evaluate' an integral — this just means find the value.

Example 1

Evaluate $\displaystyle\int_1^3 (x^2 + 2)\ dx$.

- Find the integral in the normal way — but put the integrated function in **square brackets** and rewrite the **limits** on the right-hand side.

$$\int_1^3 (x^2 + 2)\ dx = \left[\frac{x^3}{3} + 2x \right]_1^3$$

Notice that there's no constant of integration.

- Put in the limits:

Put the upper limit into the integral...

...then subtract the value of the integral at the lower limit.

$$\left[\frac{x^3}{3} + 2x \right]_1^3 = \left(\frac{3^3}{3} + 6 \right) - \left(\frac{1^3}{3} + 2 \right)$$

$$= 15 - \frac{7}{3} = \frac{38}{3}$$

Tip: A definite integral always comes out as a number.

The area under a curve

The value of a **definite integral** represents the **area** between the x-axis and the graph of the function you're integrating between the two limits.

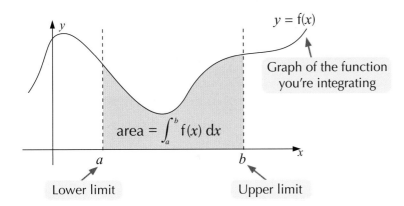

area $= \int_a^b f(x)\, dx$

Graph of the function you're integrating

$y = f(x)$

Lower limit

Upper limit

Example 2

Find the area between the graph of $y = x^2$, the x-axis and the lines $x = -1$ and $x = 2$.

You just need to integrate the function $f(x) = x^2$ between -1 and 2 with respect to x.

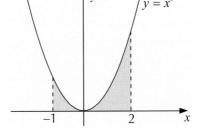

$y = x^2$

The limits of integration are -1 and 2.

$f(x) = x^2$

Put in the limits

$$\int_{-1}^{2} x^2\, dx = \left[\frac{x^3}{3}\right]_{-1}^{2}$$

$$= \left(\frac{2^3}{3}\right) - \left(\frac{(-1)^3}{3}\right) = \frac{8}{3} + \frac{1}{3} = \frac{9}{3} = 3$$

So the area is 3.

If you integrate a function to find an area that lies **below** the x-axis, it'll give a **negative** value.

If you need to find an area like this, you'll need to make your answer **positive** at the end as you can't have **negative area**.

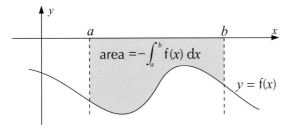

area $= -\int_a^b f(x)\, dx$

$y = f(x)$

Tip: It's important to note that you're actually finding the area between the curve and the **x-axis**, not the area under the curve (the area below a curve that lies under the x-axis will be infinite).

Example 3

Find the area between the graph of $y = 4x - 3x^2 - x^3$ and the x-axis between x = –4 and x = 0.

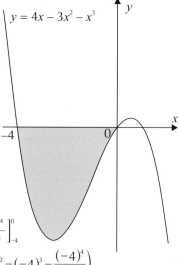

$y = 4x - 3x^2 - x^3$

- You can see from the sketch of the graph that the area you're trying to find lies **below** the x-axis.

- So all you have to do is integrate the curve between the given limits and then make the area **positive** at the end.

$$\int_{-4}^{0} (4x - 3x^2 - x^3)\, dx = \left[2x^2 - x^3 - \frac{x^4}{4} \right]_{-4}^{0}$$

$$= (0) - \left(2(-4)^2 - (-4)^3 - \frac{(-4)^4}{4} \right)$$

$$= 0 - (32 + 64 - 64)$$

$$= -32$$

- So the area between the curve and the x-axis between x = –4 and x = 0 is 32.

If you need to find the area for a portion of a curve which lies both **above** and **below** the x-axis, you'll need to find the areas above and below **separately** and add them up at the end so that the negative and positive integrals don't **cancel each other out**.

Example 4

a) **Evaluate $\int_{-2}^{2} x^3\, dx$.**

$$\int_{-2}^{2} x^3\, dx = \left[\frac{x^4}{4} \right]_{-2}^{2} = \left(\frac{2^4}{4} \right) - \left(\frac{(-2)^4}{4} \right) = \frac{16}{4} - \frac{16}{4} = 0$$

b) **Find the area between the graph of $y = x^3$, the x-axis and the lines x = –2 and x = 2.**

You'd usually just integrate the function between the limits, which gave 0 in part a). But you can see from the diagram below that the area is not 0. The 'negative area' below the axis has cancelled out the positive area.

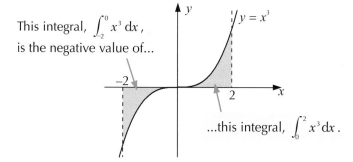

This integral, $\int_{-2}^{0} x^3\, dx$, is the negative value of...

$y = x^3$

...this integral, $\int_{0}^{2} x^3\, dx$.

- So to work out the total area, you need to work out the positive and negative areas separately and then **add** them together.

- The area **above** the x-axis is between 0 and 2, so integrate the function between these limits:

$$\int_0^2 x^3 = \left[\frac{x^4}{4}\right]_0^2 = \frac{1}{4}[x^4]_0^2 = \frac{1}{4}(2^4 - 0^4) = \frac{16}{4} = 4$$

Tip: Sometimes it's easier to take a common factor outside the square brackets — here, a factor of $\frac{1}{4}$ has been taken out.

- The area **below** the x-axis lies between -2 and 0, so integrate the function between these limits:

$$\int_{-2}^0 x^3 = \left[\frac{x^4}{4}\right]_{-2}^0 = \frac{1}{4}[x^4]_{-2}^0 = \frac{1}{4}(0^4 - (-2)^4) = -\frac{16}{4} = -4$$

The area is just the positive value of this integral, so the area is 4.

- Finally, **add** together the areas to get the total area:

$$\text{Area} = 4 + 4 = \boxed{8}$$

Some questions might give you an expression for the area in terms of an unknown and ask you to find its value (or possible values).

Example 5

Find the two possible values for A that satisfy:

$$\int_1^4 \left(\frac{3}{7}x^2 + \frac{2A}{\sqrt{x}}\right)dx = 5A^2$$

- First, you need to evaluate the integral. Treat the A as a constant for now.

$$\int_1^4 \left(\frac{3}{7}x^2 + 2Ax^{-\frac{1}{2}}\right)dx = \left[\frac{1}{7}x^3 + 4Ax^{\frac{1}{2}}\right]_1^4$$

$$= \left(\frac{64}{7} + 8A\right) - \left(\frac{1}{7} + 4A\right)$$

$$= \frac{63}{7} + 4A$$

$$= 9 + 4A$$

- You know that this is equal to $5A^2$ from the question, so form a quadratic in A and solve it:

$$9 + 4A = 5A^2$$
$$5A^2 - 4A - 9 = 0$$

- Factorise the equation: $(5A - 9)(A + 1) = 0$
  (you could use the quadratic formula here instead).

Tip: Factorising quadratics like this is covered on p.26 if you want to remind yourself of the method.

- So the solutions are:

$$5A - 9 = 0 \qquad \text{or} \qquad A + 1 = 0$$
$$5A = 9 \qquad\qquad\qquad\quad \boxed{A = -1}$$
$$\boxed{A = \frac{9}{5}}$$

Q1 Hint: Don't let minus signs catch you out. Remember you're subtracting the whole bracket so if there's a minus sign in the bracket, it'll become positive.

Q1 Find the value of the following, giving exact answers:

a) $\int_{-2}^{0} (4x^3 + 2x)\, dx$ b) $\int_{-2}^{5} (x^3 + x)\, dx$ c) $\int_{-5}^{-2} (x+1)^2\, dx$

d) $\int_{3}^{4} (6x^{-4} + x^{-2})\, dx$ e) $\int_{1}^{2} \left(x^2 + \frac{1}{x^2}\right) dx$ f) $\int_{1}^{4} (3x^{-4} + \sqrt{x})\, dx$

g) $\int_{0}^{1} ((2x+3)(x+2))\, dx$ h) $\int_{1}^{4} \left(\frac{x^2+2}{\sqrt{x}}\right) dx$ i) $\int_{4}^{9} \left(\frac{1}{x} + \sqrt{x}\right)^2 dx$

Q2 Given that $\int_{0}^{a} x^3\, dx = 64$, find a, where $a > 0$.

Q3 Calculate the exact shaded area in the following diagrams:

Q3-5 Hint: You'll need to work out where the graphs cross the x-axis.

a) 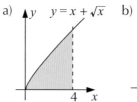   b) 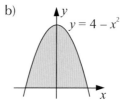   c)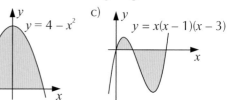

Q4-5 Hint: It may help to sketch the graph so that you can see what's happening.

Q4 Find the area enclosed by the curve with equation $y = (x - 1)(3x + 9)$, the x-axis and the lines $x = -2$ and $x = 2$.

Q5 Find the area enclosed by the graph of $y = \frac{20}{x^5}$, the x-axis and the lines $x = 1$ and $x = 2$.

Q6 Calculate the area enclosed by the line $y = 3x$, the curve $y = (x - 6)^2$ and the x-axis.

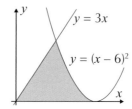

Q7 Find the possible values of A that satisfy:

a) $\int_{2}^{3} (1 - 2Ax)\, dx = 6A^2$ b) $\int_{-2}^{2} \left(\frac{21}{8}x^2 + \frac{A}{x^2}\right) dx = 3A^2$

Q8 The area under a velocity-time graph gives the distance travelled. An object's motion is tracked as it speeds up, and then slows to rest. Its velocity, v, at time t is modelled by the function below. How far does the object travel:

a) between $t = 1$ and $t = 3$?   b) in total?

Q8 Hint: All this question is asking you to do is to find the area under the graph between these limits. Remember that you're integrating with respect to t and not x.

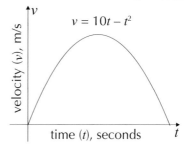

1. Vectors

You'll have seen vectors before at GCSE — they've got a size and a direction. In this section you'll see how they work and what you can do with them.

Introducing vectors

> **Scalars** are quantities **without a direction** — e.g. a speed of 2 m/s.

> **Vectors** have both **size and direction** — e.g. a velocity of 2 m/s on a bearing of 050°.

Learning Objectives:

- Understand what vectors are and how to represent them.
- Be able to add and subtract vectors and multiply them by scalars.
- Be able to show that two vectors are parallel, and that three points are collinear.
- Be able to convert between unit vector form and column vectors.

- Vectors are drawn as **lines** with **arrowheads** on them.

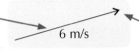

The **length** of the line represents the **magnitude** (size) of the vector.

The **direction** of the arrowhead shows the direction of the vector.

- Sometimes vectors are drawn to **scale**:

- Vectors are usually **written** using either a **lowercase bold** letter or a **lowercase underlined** letter. When the **endpoints** of a vector are labelled, the vector can also be written by putting an **arrow** over the endpoints:

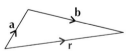

Tip: When a vector is typed it's usually bold, but if you're handwriting a vector you should always write it underlined, e.g. a.

Adding vectors

- You can **add** vectors together by drawing the arrows **nose to tail**.

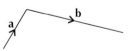

- The single vector that goes from the start to the end of the combined vectors is called the **resultant vector**.

Resultant: **r** = **a** + **b**

Tip: You might also see this referred to as the triangle rule.

- This method of adding is called the **parallelogram rule** because **a** and **b** form the sides of a parallelogram which has the resultant vector **r** = **a** + **b** as its diagonal.

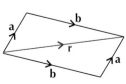

a + **b** = **r** = **b** + **a**

When you add two vectors you're really **combining** two **translations**:

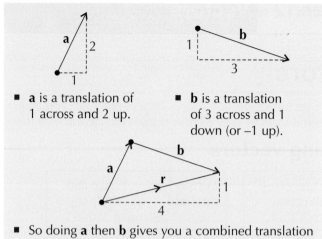

- **a** is a translation of 1 across and 2 up.
- **b** is a translation of 3 across and 1 down (or –1 up).

- So doing **a** then **b** gives you a combined translation of (1 + 3) = 4 across and (2 – 1) = 1 up.

Subtracting vectors

- The vector **–a** points in the opposite direction to the vector **a**. They're both exactly the **same size**.

- So **subtracting** a vector is the same as **adding the negative vector**:

To go from Q to P you can't just add the vectors **a** and **b** because the arrows don't run from end to end.

But replace vector **a** with **–a** (which goes in the opposite direction) and now you can add.

So: $\overrightarrow{QP} = \mathbf{b} + (-\mathbf{a}) = \mathbf{b} - \mathbf{a}$

Tip: So when you're adding, going against the arrow on a vector is the same as subtracting that vector.

You can use these rules to find a vector in terms of **other vectors**.

Example 1

Find $\overrightarrow{WZ}$ and $\overrightarrow{ZX}$ in terms of p, q and r.

- Relabel the vectors on the diagram so that they run from end to end.

- When you do this you can see that $\overrightarrow{WZ}$ is the resultant vector of **–p + q + (–r)**.

- So: $\overrightarrow{WZ} = -\mathbf{p} + \mathbf{q} - \mathbf{r}$

- Using the addition and subtraction rules in the same way to find $\overrightarrow{ZX}$ you get: $\overrightarrow{ZX} = \mathbf{r} - \mathbf{q}$

Tip: You don't have to draw this diagram out — it's enough to know that if you want your vector to go from W to X and the vector **p** goes from X to W then you need to use **–p** instead.

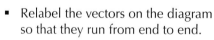
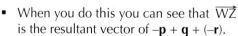
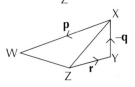

Scalar multiplication

- You can **multiply** a vector by a **scalar** (just a number).

- When you do this the **length changes** but the **direction** stays the **same**...

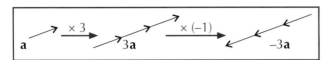

Tip: The number in these expressions is a scalar, the letter is a vector.

...unless the scalar is **negative**, then the direction's **reversed**.

- You can '**divide**' a vector by a scalar as well — you just **multiply** the vector by the **reciprocal** of the scalar. E.g. $\frac{\mathbf{a}}{3} = \frac{1}{3}\mathbf{a}$.

- **Multiplying** a vector by a **non-zero** scalar always produces a **parallel** vector.

Example 2

Show that the vector 9a + 15b is parallel to the vector 6a + 10b.

- To show that they're **parallel** you need to try and write one as a **scalar multiple** of the other.

- To do this you need to find the **scalar factor** that you multiply by:

$$\frac{9\mathbf{a}}{6\mathbf{a}} = 1.5 \quad\longleftarrow$$

$$\frac{15\mathbf{b}}{10\mathbf{b}} = 1.5 \quad\longleftarrow$$

Each **part** of the vector has the **same** scalar factor

- In this case the scalar factor is the **same** for **a** and **b**, so it's possible to write the first vector as a scalar multiple of the second.

- So $\boxed{9\mathbf{a} + 15\mathbf{b} = 1.5(6\mathbf{a} + 10\mathbf{b})}$ and the vectors are parallel.

Tip: If you're asked to find whether or not two vectors are parallel then you need to check the scalar factor for each coefficient. If they're all the same then the vectors are parallel, if not then they're not.

- All **parallel** vectors are **scalar multiples** of each other, so showing that one vector is a scalar multiple of another is the same as showing they're parallel.

Example 3

$\overrightarrow{CA} = \mathbf{p}$, $\overrightarrow{CB} = \mathbf{q}$, **point M lies halfway along $\overrightarrow{CB}$, point N lies halfway along $\overrightarrow{AB}$. Show that $\overrightarrow{MN}$ is parallel to $\overrightarrow{CA}$.**

To show that $\overrightarrow{MN}$ is parallel to $\overrightarrow{CA}$ you need to show it's a **scalar multiple** of **p**.

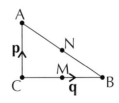

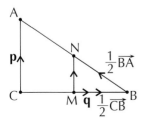

- $\overrightarrow{MN} = \overrightarrow{MB} + \overrightarrow{BN} = \frac{1}{2}\overrightarrow{CB} + \frac{1}{2}\overrightarrow{BA}$

- $\overrightarrow{BA} = -\mathbf{q} + \mathbf{p}$ and $\overrightarrow{CB} = \mathbf{q}$

- So $\overrightarrow{MN} = \frac{1}{2}\mathbf{q} + \frac{1}{2}(-\mathbf{q} + \mathbf{p}) = \frac{1}{2}\mathbf{p} = \frac{1}{2}\overrightarrow{CA}$

- $\overrightarrow{MN}$ is a scalar multiple of $\overrightarrow{CA}$, so they're **parallel**.

Tip: Vectors that have the same direction and magnitude are often called **equal vectors**.

Tip: Look out for questions where you have to recognise that two lines are parallel in order to find a vector.

- A vector can be **anywhere** in **space**.

- This means that vectors of the **same size** which are **parallel** and pointing in the **same direction** are the **same**, even if they're not in the same place.

- E.g. in a parallelogram, opposite sides have the **same vector**, so knowing one means you know the other:

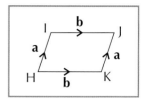

Collinear points

You can also use **vector addition** to show that three points are **collinear**.

- Three or more points are collinear if they all lie on a **single straight line**.

- If vectors $\overrightarrow{AB}$ and $\overrightarrow{BC}$ are **parallel**, then the points A, B and C must lie on a straight line, i.e. they are **collinear**.

Example 4

$\overrightarrow{AP} = $ **m**, $\overrightarrow{AQ} = $ **m + 2n**, $\overrightarrow{AR} = $ **m + 6n**. Show that P, Q and R are collinear.

First find $\overrightarrow{PQ}$ and $\overrightarrow{QR}$:

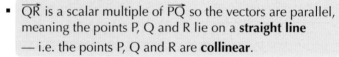

- $\overrightarrow{PQ} = -\overrightarrow{AP} + \overrightarrow{AQ}$
  $= -\mathbf{m} + \mathbf{m} + 2\mathbf{n} = 2\mathbf{n}$

- $\overrightarrow{QR} = -\overrightarrow{AQ} + \overrightarrow{AR}$
  $= -\mathbf{m} - 2\mathbf{n} + \mathbf{m} + 6\mathbf{n} = 4\mathbf{n}$

Now show that $\overrightarrow{QR}$ is a **scalar multiple** of $\overrightarrow{PQ}$:

- $\overrightarrow{QR} = 4\mathbf{n} = 2(2\mathbf{n}) = 2(\overrightarrow{PQ})$

- $\overrightarrow{QR}$ is a scalar multiple of $\overrightarrow{PQ}$ so the vectors are parallel, meaning the points P, Q and R lie on a **straight line** — i.e. the points P, Q and R are **collinear**.

Exercise 1.1

Q1 State whether each of these real world examples refers to a scalar quantity, a vector quantity or neither.

   a) A pilot flies due south for a distance of 200 kilometres.

   b) The time taken to travel from London to Exeter is 3 hours.

   c) A force of 20 newtons is required to pull a sledge up the steepest section of a hill — the slope is at an angle of 5° to the horizontal.

Q2 Vectors **a** and **b** are represented by the lines below:

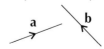

Draw and label sketches that represent the following vectors:
   a) −**a**   b) 2**b**   c) **a** + **b**   d) **a** − **b**.

Q3 For the rectangle ABCD shown on the right, write down single vectors that are equivalent to:
 a) $\overrightarrow{AB} + \overrightarrow{BC}$ b) $\overrightarrow{BC} + \overrightarrow{CD} + \overrightarrow{DA}$ c) $\overrightarrow{DC} - \overrightarrow{BC}$

Q4 In the triangle XYZ the vector **p** represents $\overrightarrow{XZ}$ and the vector **q** represents $\overrightarrow{YX}$.
 Express the following in terms of **p** or **q** or both:
 a) $\overrightarrow{XY}$ b) $\overrightarrow{YZ}$ c) $\overrightarrow{ZY}$

> **Q4 Hint:** It helps to draw the shape out before you start answering the question.

Q5 Group the following into sets of parallel vectors:

2**a** + **b**   2**p** + **q**   2**a** − **b**   4**b** + 8**a**
     10**a** − 5**b**   −**b** − 2**a** $\frac{1}{2}$**q** + **p**

Q6 In the rectangle ABCD, E is the midpoint of AD and F divides DC in the ratio 2:1.

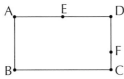

 If $\overrightarrow{AB}$ = **b** and $\overrightarrow{AD}$ = **d**, find the following vectors in terms of **b** and **d**.
 a) $\overrightarrow{DF}$ b) $\overrightarrow{BE}$ c) $\overrightarrow{EF}$

Q7 $\overrightarrow{OA}$ = **a**, $\overrightarrow{OB}$ = **b**, $\overrightarrow{OC}$ = 5**a** − 4**b**. Show that A, B and C are collinear.

> **Q7 Hint:** You need to prove that they all lie on the same straight line — which means that the vectors between them will be parallel.

Q8 In triangle DEF, J and L are midpoints of ED and FD respectively.

 Given that $\overrightarrow{EF}$ = **f** and $\overrightarrow{ED}$ = **d**, prove that $\overrightarrow{JL} = \frac{1}{2}$**f**.

Position vectors

You can use a vector to describe the **position** of a point in relation to the **origin**, O. This vector is called a **position vector**.

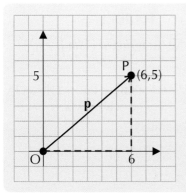

- One way of describing the position of the point P is with its **Cartesian coordinates** which are e.g. (6,5).

- This just tells you how far P is vertically and horizontally from the **origin** O.

- Another way of describing how far P is from the origin is using the **position vector** $\overrightarrow{OP}$ = **p** which has **horizontal** and **vertical** components.

> **Tip:** Position vectors always start at the origin and finish at the point they're describing the position of.

Tip: You can find the distance between two points given as position vectors using Pythagoras' theorem — see p.210.

Tip: This result will be used time after time for finding the vector from one point to another in this chapter.
Make sure you learn it in both its forms:

$$\overrightarrow{AB} = \overrightarrow{OB} - \overrightarrow{OA} = \mathbf{b} - \mathbf{a}$$

The position vector of any point A is $\overrightarrow{OA}$. It's usually called vector **a**.

> You can write the vector from one point to another in **terms** of their **position vectors**:
>
> $$\overrightarrow{AB} = -\overrightarrow{OA} + \overrightarrow{OB} = \overrightarrow{OB} - \overrightarrow{OA}$$
> $$= -\mathbf{a} + \mathbf{b} = \mathbf{b} - \mathbf{a}$$

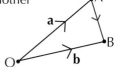

i + j units

- A **unit vector** is any vector with a **length of 1 unit**.

- The vectors **i** and **j** are **standard unit vectors**, so they each have a length of 1 unit. **i** is in the direction of the **positive x-axis**, and **j** is in the direction of the **positive y-axis**.

> **Every vector** in two dimensions is made up of **horizontal** and **vertical components**, so you can express any vector as a **sum** of **i** and **j** unit vectors:
>
> - Vector **a** goes from the origin O to the point A.
>
> - To get from O to A you move **4** units **to the right** and **3** units **up**.
>
> - So **a** is the **resultant** vector when you add a **horizontal vector** that goes **4 units** in the positive x direction and a **vertical vector** that goes **3 units** in the positive y direction.
>
> - **i** and **j** are the **standard** unit vectors we use to express horizontal and vertical components. So **a** = 4**i** + 3**j**

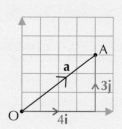

Example

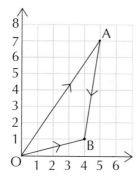

a) **Write down the position vectors of A and B in i + j form.**

- Point A lies 5 units to the right and 7 units above the origin, so the position vector of point A is: **a = 5i + 7j**

- The position vector of point B is:
  b = 4i + j

b) **Hence find $\overrightarrow{AB}$ in terms of i and j.**

To find $\overrightarrow{AB}$:

- You know $\overrightarrow{AB} = -\overrightarrow{OA} + \overrightarrow{OB} = \overrightarrow{OB} - \overrightarrow{OA}$
  $= -\mathbf{a} + \mathbf{b} = \mathbf{b} - \mathbf{a}$

- Add or subtract the **i** and **j** components **separately**:
  Vector $\overrightarrow{AB}$ = **b** – **a** = (4**i** + **j**) – (5**i** + 7**j**) = **–i – 6j**

Tip: This means that to go from A to B, you go 1 unit left and 6 units down. It's just like a translation.

Column vectors

Column vectors are another way of writing vectors in terms of their **horizontal** and **vertical components**.

- You just write the **horizontal (i) component** on **top** of the **vertical (j) component** and put a **bracket** around them:

$$x\mathbf{i} + y\mathbf{j} = \begin{pmatrix} x \\ y \end{pmatrix}$$

Tip: Using column vectors is often quicker and easier than working with sums of **i** and **j** components.

- **Calculating** with them is simple. Just add or subtract the **top** row, then add or subtract the **bottom** row **separately**:

$$\mathbf{a} = 5\mathbf{i} + 7\mathbf{j} = \begin{pmatrix} 5 \\ 7 \end{pmatrix} \qquad \mathbf{b} = 4\mathbf{i} + \mathbf{j} = \begin{pmatrix} 4 \\ 1 \end{pmatrix}$$

$$\mathbf{b} - \mathbf{a} = \begin{pmatrix} 4 \\ 1 \end{pmatrix} - \begin{pmatrix} 5 \\ 7 \end{pmatrix} = \begin{pmatrix} 4 - 5 \\ 1 - 7 \end{pmatrix} = \begin{pmatrix} -1 \\ -6 \end{pmatrix}$$

- When you're **multiplying** a column vector by a **scalar** you multiply **each number** in the column vector by the scalar:

$$2\mathbf{b} - 3\mathbf{a} = 2\begin{pmatrix} 4 \\ 1 \end{pmatrix} - 3\begin{pmatrix} 5 \\ 7 \end{pmatrix} = \begin{pmatrix} 2 \times 4 \\ 2 \times 1 \end{pmatrix} - \begin{pmatrix} 3 \times 5 \\ 3 \times 7 \end{pmatrix} = \begin{pmatrix} 8 \\ 2 \end{pmatrix} - \begin{pmatrix} 15 \\ 21 \end{pmatrix} = \begin{pmatrix} -7 \\ -19 \end{pmatrix}$$

Exercise 1.2

Q1 On a map, Jack's house has coordinates (2, 3) and his school has coordinates (4, –5). Write down the position vectors of Jack's house and Jack's school, giving your answers as column vectors.

Q2 C has position vector $-\mathbf{i} + 2\mathbf{j}$ and D has position vector $4\mathbf{i} - 3\mathbf{j}$.

a) What are the Cartesian coordinates of the points C and D?

b) Write the vectors $\overrightarrow{CD}$ and $\overrightarrow{DC}$ in unit vector form.

c) Calculate the exact distance between points C and D.

Q3 M is the midpoint of the line PQ, where P has position vector $-3\mathbf{i} + \mathbf{j}$ and M has position vector $2\mathbf{i} - 5\mathbf{j}$.

a) What is the position vector of Q?

b) Find the exact length of PQ.

Q4 Triangle ABC is shown on the right. Find the vectors $\overrightarrow{AB}$, $\overrightarrow{BC}$ and $\overrightarrow{CA}$.

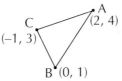

Q4 Hint: The question doesn't mention **i** and **j** components or column vectors so you can answer it using either.

Q5 A robotic vacuum cleaner models a room using a quadrilateral DEFG, with vertices at the points D (–7, –2), E (–3, –1), F (–1, 5) and G (–3, 10).

a) Give the vectors for the room's walls $\overrightarrow{DE}$, $\overrightarrow{EF}$, $\overrightarrow{FG}$ and $\overrightarrow{GD}$.

b) The vacuum cleaner follows the wall from D to E, then E to F. Give a single vector that the vacuum cleaner could have followed to get from D to F more efficiently.

2. Calculating with Vectors

Learning Objectives:

- Be able to find the magnitude of any vector in two dimensions.
- Be able to find the unit vector in the direction of any vector in two dimensions.
- Be able to find the distance between any two two-dimensional points using vectors.
- Be able to calculate the direction of any vector in two dimensions.
- Be able to use trigonometry to do calculations involving vectors.

Tip: You don't need to draw the triangle out every time, just plug the coefficients of **i** and **j** into the Pythagoras formula.

The magnitude of a vector is a scalar that tells you the vector's length. In this section you'll see how to calculate it and what you can use it for.

Calculating with vectors
Calculating the magnitude of a vector

- The **magnitude** of a vector is the **distance** between its start point and end point. It's sometimes called **modulus** instead of magnitude.

> The **magnitude** of a vector **a** is written $|\mathbf{a}|$.

> The **magnitude** of a vector $\overrightarrow{AB}$ is written $|\overrightarrow{AB}|$.

- Magnitude is a **scalar**, and it's **always positive**.

- The **i** and **j** components of a vector form a convenient **right-angled triangle**, so you can use **Pythagoras' theorem** to find a vector's magnitude.

Example 1

Find the magnitude of the vector a = 5i + 3j.

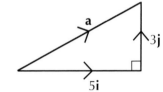

- You know the length of two sides of the right-angled triangle formed by **a** and its **horizontal** and **vertical** components.
- The magnitude of **a** is the length of the **hypotenuse** of this triangle.
- So find $|\mathbf{a}|$ using **Pythagoras**:
$$|\mathbf{a}| = \sqrt{5^2 + 3^2} = \sqrt{34} = \boxed{5.83} \text{ to 3 s.f.}$$

You can use a vector's magnitude to find the **distance** between two **points**:

Example 2

$\overrightarrow{JK} = \begin{pmatrix} 4 \\ -7 \end{pmatrix}$ **Find the distance between J and K. Give your answer in surd form.**

The distance between J and K is $|\overrightarrow{JK}| = \sqrt{4^2 + (-7)^2} = \boxed{\sqrt{65}}$

You can find **missing components** of the vector using its magnitude:

Example 3

$\overrightarrow{OP} = \begin{pmatrix} 3 \\ 5 \end{pmatrix}$, $\overrightarrow{OQ} = \begin{pmatrix} -2 \\ b \end{pmatrix}$, **given that** $|\overrightarrow{PQ}| = \sqrt{29}$ **and** $|\overrightarrow{OQ}| = \sqrt{13}$, **find** b.

- First find $\overrightarrow{PQ}$: $\overrightarrow{PQ} = \overrightarrow{OQ} - \overrightarrow{OP} = \begin{pmatrix} -2 \\ b \end{pmatrix} - \begin{pmatrix} 3 \\ 5 \end{pmatrix} = \begin{pmatrix} -5 \\ b-5 \end{pmatrix}$

- Now find the magnitude of $\overrightarrow{PQ}$ in terms of b and compare it with the value given: $|\overrightarrow{PQ}| = \sqrt{25 + (b-5)^2}$
$$\Rightarrow 29 = 25 + (b-5)^2$$
$$\Rightarrow 4 = (b-5)^2$$
$$\Rightarrow \pm 2 = b - 5$$
$$\Rightarrow b = 3 \text{ or } b = 7$$

- Do the same with $\overrightarrow{OQ}$:
$$|\overrightarrow{OQ}| = \sqrt{(-2)^2 + b^2}$$
$$\Rightarrow 13 = 4 + b^2$$
$$\Rightarrow \quad 9 = b^2$$
$$\Rightarrow \quad b = \pm 3$$

- Both statements '$b = \pm 3$' and '$b = 3$ or $b = 7$' must hold, so $\boxed{b = 3}$

- To find a **unit vector** in the direction of a particular vector you just **divide** the vector by its **magnitude** (i.e. multiply by the magnitude's reciprocal).

> **Tip:** Remember, a unit vector always has a magnitude of 1.

- So the unit vector in the direction of the vector **a** is: $\dfrac{1}{|\mathbf{a}|}\mathbf{a} = \dfrac{\mathbf{a}}{|\mathbf{a}|}$.

- Its magnitude is $\dfrac{1}{|\mathbf{a}|} \times |\mathbf{a}| = 1$.

- It's a **positive scalar multiple** of **a** (because magnitude is always positive), so it has the **same direction** as **a**.

> **Tip:** Positive scalar multiples of **a** are parallel to **a** and have the same direction as **a**. Negative scalar multiples of **a** are parallel to **a** and have the opposite direction (the direction of –**a**).

Example 4

Find the unit vector in the direction of q = 5i – 12j.

- First find the magnitude of **q**:
$$|\mathbf{q}| = \sqrt{5^2 + (-12)^2} = \sqrt{169} = 13$$

- So the unit vector is:
$$\frac{\mathbf{q}}{|\mathbf{q}|} = \frac{1}{13}(5\mathbf{i} - 12\mathbf{j}) = \boxed{\frac{5}{13}\mathbf{i} - \frac{12}{13}\mathbf{j}}$$

Calculating the direction of a vector

- The direction of a vector **a** is the **angle** between a line parallel to the x-axis and **a**. It is usually measured **anticlockwise** from the x-axis.

> **Tip:** You may see questions asking you to calculate other angles too — like the angle between a vector and the vertical y-axis.

- If you know the **i** and **j** components of a vector, then you can find the **direction** of the vector by using **trigonometry**.

Example 5

The diagram shows the vector a = 2i + 3j.
Find the magnitude and direction of the vector.

> **Tip:** This example shows how to convert a vector from component form into magnitude/direction form.

- The vector forms the hypotenuse of a right-angled triangle of height 3 units and base width 2 units:

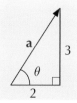

> **Tip:** It really helps to draw a diagram and make a right-angled triangle.

- Use Pythagoras' theorem as before to find the magnitude:
$$|\mathbf{a}| = \sqrt{2^2 + 3^2} = \boxed{\sqrt{13}}$$

- Use trigonometry to find the angle θ:
$$\tan \theta = \frac{3}{2} \Rightarrow \theta = \tan^{-1}\left(\frac{3}{2}\right) = \boxed{56.3° \text{ (3 s.f.)}}$$

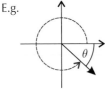
> In general, a vector $\begin{pmatrix} x \\ y \end{pmatrix}$ has magnitude $\sqrt{x^2 + y^2}$ and makes an angle of $\tan^{-1}\left(\dfrac{y}{x}\right)$ with the horizontal.

- Similarly, if you know the **magnitude** and **direction** of a vector then you can use **trigonometry** to calculate its horizontal and vertical components:

Example 6

Given a vector $\mathbf{v} = a\mathbf{i} + b\mathbf{j}$, with direction 30° and magnitude $|\mathbf{v}| = 5$, calculate a and b.

- The vector forms a right-angled triangle, with the magnitude as the length of the hypotenuse.

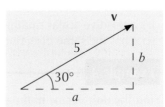

- Using trigonometry, we can find a and b:

$$\cos 30° = \frac{a}{5} \qquad \text{so } a = 5\cos 30°$$
$$\sin 30° = \frac{b}{5} \qquad \text{so } b = 5\sin 30°$$

- So, $\mathbf{v} = (5\cos 30°)\mathbf{i} + (5\sin 30°)\mathbf{j} = \dfrac{5\sqrt{3}}{2}\mathbf{i} + \dfrac{5}{2}\mathbf{j}$

Calculating the angle between two vectors

- The angle between two vectors $\mathbf{a}$ and $\mathbf{b}$ can be calculated by constructing a triangle with $\mathbf{a}$ and $\mathbf{b}$ as two of its sides.

- First calculate the **magnitude** of these vectors, and then use the **cosine rule** to find the angle between them.

Example 7

Find the angle θ between the vectors $\overrightarrow{PQ} = 3\mathbf{i} - \mathbf{j}$ and $\overrightarrow{PR} = -\mathbf{i} + 4\mathbf{j}$.

- $\overrightarrow{PQ}$ and $\overrightarrow{PR}$ form two sides of a triangle PQR.

- The length of these sides are:
$|\overrightarrow{PQ}| = \sqrt{3^2 + (-1)^2} = \sqrt{10}$
and $|\overrightarrow{PR}| = \sqrt{(-1)^2 + 4^2} = \sqrt{17}$

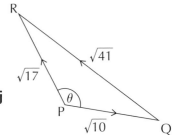

- $\overrightarrow{QR} = \overrightarrow{PR} - \overrightarrow{PQ} = -\mathbf{i} + 4\mathbf{j} - (3\mathbf{i} - \mathbf{j}) = -4\mathbf{i} + 5\mathbf{j}$
is the other side of the triangle.
It has length $|\overrightarrow{QR}| = \sqrt{(-4)^2 + 5^2} = \sqrt{41}$.

- Use the cosine rule to find angle θ:

$$\cos\theta = \frac{(\sqrt{10})^2 + (\sqrt{17})^2 - (\sqrt{41})^2}{2 \times \sqrt{17} \times \sqrt{10}} = \frac{-14}{2\sqrt{170}} = \frac{-7}{\sqrt{170}}, \text{ so:}$$

$$\theta = \cos^{-1}\left(\frac{-7}{\sqrt{170}}\right) = \boxed{122.5° \text{ (1 d.p)}}$$

Exercise 2.1

Q1 For each of the following vectors, find:
   (i) the exact magnitude
   (ii) the direction (to 2 d.p.)

Q1-3 Hint: Remember 'exact magnitude' and 'exact length' suggests some of the answers will include surds.

   a) $6\mathbf{i} + 8\mathbf{j}$ b) $12\mathbf{i} - 5\mathbf{j}$ c) $\begin{pmatrix} 2 \\ 4 \end{pmatrix}$ d) $\begin{pmatrix} -3 \\ -1 \end{pmatrix}$

   e) $\begin{pmatrix} 24 \\ -7 \end{pmatrix}$ f) $\begin{pmatrix} -\sqrt{13} \\ 6 \end{pmatrix}$ g) $3\mathbf{i} + \sqrt{7}\,\mathbf{j}$ h) $-7\mathbf{j}$

Q2 S has position vector $10\mathbf{i} + 5\mathbf{j}$.
Find the exact length of the line that joins point S to the origin.

Q3 For each of the pairs of vectors given below, find the exact magnitude of the resultant when the two vectors are added together.

   a) $\mathbf{a} = 2\mathbf{i} + \mathbf{j}$ and $\mathbf{b} = 2\mathbf{i} - 4\mathbf{j}$ b) $\mathbf{u} = -5\mathbf{i} + \mathbf{j}$ and $\mathbf{v} = 9\mathbf{i} - 5\mathbf{j}$

   c) $\mathbf{f} = \begin{pmatrix} 7 \\ 2 \end{pmatrix}$ and $\mathbf{g} = \begin{pmatrix} 17 \\ -12 \end{pmatrix}$ d) $\mathbf{d} = \begin{pmatrix} 4 \\ -2 \end{pmatrix}$ and $\mathbf{e} = \begin{pmatrix} -1 \\ -4 \end{pmatrix}$

Q4 The diagram below shows a parallelogram WXYZ.

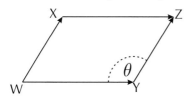

Given that $\overrightarrow{WX} = 2\mathbf{i} + 5\mathbf{j}$, and $\overrightarrow{WY} = 8\mathbf{i}$, what is angle θ (to 1 d.p.)?

Q5 $\overrightarrow{AB} = 3\mathbf{i} - 2\mathbf{j}$ and $\overrightarrow{BC} = \mathbf{i} + 5\mathbf{j}$.
Find the unit vector in the direction of $\overrightarrow{AC}$.

Q6 Point A has position vector $2\mathbf{i} - \mathbf{j}$, and point B has position vector $7\mathbf{i} - 13\mathbf{j}$. Find the unit vector in the direction of $\overrightarrow{BA}$.

Q7 The vector **c** has the same direction as vector **d**.
Given that $\mathbf{d} = 8\mathbf{i} - 6\mathbf{j}$ and $|\mathbf{c}| = 70$, find vector **c**.

Q8 Two boats set off from a harbour.
Each boat's course is modelled by a vector.

Q8 Hint: Draw a diagram to help you.

Boat A's course is given by the column vector $\mathbf{a} = \begin{pmatrix} 3 \\ 3 \end{pmatrix}$.

Boat B's course is given by the column vector $\mathbf{b} = \begin{pmatrix} -2 \\ 5 \end{pmatrix}$.

What is the angle between the two boats' courses?
Give your answer to 2 decimal places.

3. Modelling with Vectors

Learning Objectives:

- Be able to use vectors to solve problems in different contexts.
- Be able to model forces as vectors.

Vectors are really useful and can be used for modelling and solving problems. This section looks at some common uses of vectors in mathematics.

Modelling with vectors

An object's **motion** will have a **magnitude** and **direction**, so can be modelled using vectors:

- **Displacement** is the **distance** an object has travelled in a given **direction**.

- **Velocity** is the **speed** of an object with a **direction**.

- **Acceleration** is the rate at which an object's **velocity changes**.

Forces can also be modelled with vectors (see page 362).

Tip: Be careful — the word acceleration could refer to the vector **a** or its magnitude |**a**|.

Example 1

The acceleration of a particle is given by the vector
a = (6i – 2j) ms^{-2}. Find the magnitude of the acceleration,
and the angle this vector makes with the horizontal axis.

- Start with a diagram — remember, the **j**-component "–2" means "down 2".

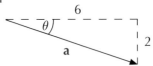

- Use Pythagoras' theorem to find the magnitude:
$$|\mathbf{a}| = \sqrt{6^2 + (-2)^2} = \sqrt{40} = \boxed{6.32 \text{ ms}^{-2} \text{ (3 s.f.)}}$$

- Use trigonometry to find the angle θ:
$$\tan \theta = \frac{2}{6} \Rightarrow \theta = \tan^{-1}\left(\frac{2}{6}\right) = \boxed{18.4° \text{ (3 s.f.)}}$$

Tip: Make sure you pay attention to whether the components are positive or negative — this tells you which direction the vector acts in.

Example 2

A ball's velocity is modelled by vector v = xi – yj ms^{-1},
with a magnitude of 4 ms^{-1} and direction of 40° below the positive x-axis.
Find the x and y components of vector v. Give your answer to 4 s.f.

- As always, draw a diagram.

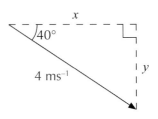

- Using trigonometry:
$$\cos 40° = \frac{x}{4} \Rightarrow x = 4 \cos 40°$$
$$= 3.064 \text{ to 4 s.f.}$$

$$\sin 40° = \frac{y}{4} \Rightarrow y = 4 \sin 40°$$
$$= 2.571 \text{ to 4 s.f.}$$

- So, $\boxed{\mathbf{v} = (3.064\mathbf{i} - 2.571\mathbf{j}) \text{ ms}^{-1}}$

Tip: You'll come across velocity and speed again in Chapter 19. Velocity can be treated as a vector, the magnitude of which gives the speed an object is moving at.

- The effect of **two forces** working together can also be modelled by vectors.
- These two vectors will probably form a triangle **without a right angle**, so you will need to use the **sine rule** and **cosine rule** (see p.121) for the trigonometry involved.

Tip: You'll see lots more about forces in Chapter 20.

Example 3

Two tug boats are pulling a ship with an angle of 30° between them. One tug boat exerts a force of 10 kN and is modelled with vector a. The other boat exerts a force of 12 kN and is modelled with vector b.

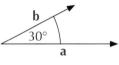

The resultant force on the ship, r, is the resultant vector of these two forces. Calculate the size of the resultant force.

Tip: The size of a force is the magnitude of the vector.

- **r** is the resultant of **a** and **b**, so **r** = **a** + **b**.
  Drawing the vectors end to end:

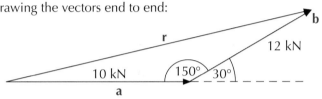

- The angle opposite **r** is 180° − 30° = 150°

- Using the cosine rule:
  $|\mathbf{r}|^2 = 10^2 + 12^2 - 2 \times 10 \times 12 \times \cos 150°$
  $= 244 - 240 \cos 150°$

Tip: The best version of the cosine rule to use here is:
$a^2 = b^2 + c^2 - 2bc \cos A$

- So, $|\mathbf{r}| = \sqrt{244 - 240 \cos 150°} = $ 21.3 kN (to 3 s.f.)

Vectors can also be used to model **lines** and the **sides of polygons** when investigating problems in geometry.

Example 4

The routes from Ayeside to Beesville ($\overrightarrow{AB}$) and to Ceeston ($\overrightarrow{AC}$) are modelled by the vectors p and q respectively. Xander's house lies between Beesville and Ceeston such that its position, X, divides the line BC in the ratio 2:5.

Find the vector $\overrightarrow{AX}$ in terms of p and q.

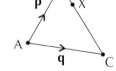

Tip: 'X divides **BC** in the ratio 2:5' means X is $\frac{2}{7}$ of the way from **B to C**.
'X divides **CB** in the ratio 2:5' would mean X is $\frac{2}{7}$ of the way from **C to B**.

- $\overrightarrow{AX} = \overrightarrow{AB} + \overrightarrow{BX}$. You know $\overrightarrow{AB}$ = **p**, so you just need to find $\overrightarrow{BX}$ in terms of **p** and **q**.

- X divides BC in the ratio 2:5, so BX is $\frac{2}{2+5} = \frac{2}{7}$ of BC.
  That means $\overrightarrow{BX} = \frac{2}{7}\overrightarrow{BC}$

- Now to find $\overrightarrow{BC}$ in terms of **p** and **q**:
  $\overrightarrow{BC} = \overrightarrow{BA} + \overrightarrow{AC} = -\overrightarrow{AB} + \overrightarrow{AC} = $ **−p + q**

Tip: You might also come across ratio questions without contexts — e.g. "P divides the vector $\overrightarrow{QR}$ in the ratio 1:3."

- Plugging all this back into your equation for $\overrightarrow{AX}$ gives:
  $\overrightarrow{AX} = \overrightarrow{AB} + \overrightarrow{BX} = \overrightarrow{AB} + \frac{2}{7}\overrightarrow{BC} = \mathbf{p} + \frac{2}{7}(-\mathbf{p} + \mathbf{q}) = \frac{5}{7}\mathbf{p} + \frac{2}{7}\mathbf{q}$

Example 5

The position vectors of the vertices of the parallelogram PQRS are:
$\overrightarrow{OP} = 2\mathbf{i} + 3\mathbf{j}$, $\overrightarrow{OQ} = 7\mathbf{i} + 4\mathbf{j}$, $\overrightarrow{OR} = 6(\mathbf{i} + \mathbf{j})$ **and** $\overrightarrow{OS} = \mathbf{i} + 5\mathbf{j}$.
What are the exact lengths of this parallelogram's diagonals?

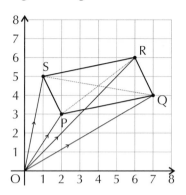

- The diagonals are:
$$\overrightarrow{PR} = \overrightarrow{OR} - \overrightarrow{OP} = 6(\mathbf{i} + \mathbf{j}) - (2\mathbf{i} + 3\mathbf{j})$$
$$= 4\mathbf{i} + 3\mathbf{j}$$

$$\overrightarrow{SQ} = \overrightarrow{OQ} - \overrightarrow{OS} = (7\mathbf{i} + 4\mathbf{j}) - (\mathbf{i} + 5\mathbf{j})$$
$$= 6\mathbf{i} - \mathbf{j}$$

- So, the lengths of the diagonals are:
$$|\overrightarrow{PR}| = \sqrt{4^2 + 3^2} = \sqrt{25} = \boxed{5} \text{ and}$$

$$|\overrightarrow{SQ}| = \sqrt{6^2 + (-1)^2} = \boxed{\sqrt{37}}$$

- Vectors are also really useful for modelling the **direction** something is **travelling** in — like the course of a ship or a plane's flight path.

- The **bearing** the vehicle travels on can be used to calculate the vector's **direction**. The **distance** it travels is the **magnitude** of its **displacement vector**, and its **speed** is the magnitude of its **velocity vector**.

Tip: Remember that bearings are always given as a 3-digit angle (e.g. 045°), measured clockwise from north (the positive y-axis). Don't get this confused with a vector's direction, which is calculated anticlockwise from the positive x-axis.
The easiest way to avoid confusion is to draw a diagram.

Example 6

A ship travels 75 km on a bearing of 140°. The ship's displacement is modelled by the vector $\mathbf{d} = \begin{pmatrix} x \\ y \end{pmatrix}$. **Calculate** x **and** y **(to 2 d.p.).**

- Draw a diagram:

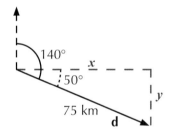

This shows you that the angle **d** makes with the positive x-axis is 50°.

- Using trigonometry:
$$\cos 50° = \frac{x}{75} \Rightarrow x = 75 \cos 50° = \boxed{48.21} \text{ (to 2 d.p.)}$$

$$\sin 50° = \frac{y}{75} \Rightarrow y = 75 \sin 50° = \boxed{57.45} \text{ (to 2 d.p.)}$$

- The y component of the vector should be negative, so:

$$\mathbf{d} = \begin{pmatrix} 48.21 \\ -57.45 \end{pmatrix} \text{ km}$$

Q1 The acceleration of a particle is given by the vector $\mathbf{a} = (\mathbf{i} + 2\mathbf{j})$ ms^{-2}.
What is the exact magnitude of the particle's acceleration?

Q2 The quadrilateral ABCD is used to model a garden.

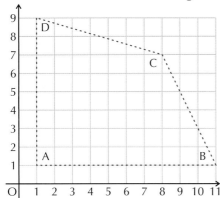

There is a straight path that crosses the garden. Its start point divides $\overrightarrow{AB}$ in the ratio 7:3, and it ends at the midpoint of $\overrightarrow{CD}$.

The path is modelled by vector $\mathbf{p} = \begin{pmatrix} x \\ y \end{pmatrix}$. Calculate x and y.

Q3 A simple mathematical model of a ball bouncing off the side of a pool table is constructed using vectors. The ball's velocity has vector $\mathbf{v}_1 = \begin{pmatrix} 3 \\ -2 \end{pmatrix}$ before it hits the side, and vector $\mathbf{v}_2 = \begin{pmatrix} 1 \\ 3 \end{pmatrix}$ afterwards.
Find the acute angle θ between $\mathbf{v}_1$ and $\mathbf{v}_2$. Give your answer to 2 d.p.

Q4 A park is modelled as a quadrilateral EFGH, with sides given by the following vectors:
$\overrightarrow{EF} = 2\mathbf{i} + 3\mathbf{j}$, $\overrightarrow{FG} = \mathbf{i} - \frac{1}{2}\mathbf{j}$, $\overrightarrow{GH} = -\mathbf{i} - \frac{3}{2}\mathbf{j}$ and $\overrightarrow{HE} = -2\mathbf{i} - \mathbf{j}$.
Show that the park is a trapezium.

Q5 An aircraft is attempting to fly due north at 600 km/h, but there is a wind from the west at 75 km/h.
The aircraft's actual course is modelled by the resultant of these two vectors. Calculate:

a) the actual bearing the plane is flying on.

b) the aircraft's resultant speed in km/h (to 2 d.p.).

> **Q5 Hint:** Due north just means a bearing of 0°. West is a bearing of 270°. Remember to calculate the resultant bearing from due north.

Q6 In the diagram below, W divides QR in the ratio $a:b$.
Given that $\overrightarrow{PW} = \frac{5}{9}\mathbf{s} + \frac{4}{9}\mathbf{t}$, find a and b.

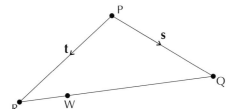

1. Populations and Samples

For all statistical experiments, you'll need some data. In this section you'll learn about populations and samples, and different ways to collect information from them — including censuses and a variety of sampling methods.

Populations and censuses
Populations
For any statistical investigation, there will be a **group** of something (it could be people, items, animals... or anything else) that you want to **find out about**.

The **whole group**, consisting of **every single** person/item/animal etc. that you want to investigate, is called the **population**. This could be:

- All the students in a maths class

- All the penguins in Antarctica

- All the chocolate puddings produced by a company in a year

A population can be either **finite** or **infinite**:

- Populations are said to be **finite** if it's possible for someone to **count** how many members there are.

- Populations are said to be **infinite** if it's **impossible** to know exactly how many members there are — there won't literally be infinitely many members... just **too many to count**.

Finite populations	Infinite populations
The number of	The number of
...fish in an aquarium.	...fish in the Atlantic Ocean.
...trees in a garden.	...leaves in a forest.
...members in a pop band.	...pop fans in the world.

Tip: This is a bit confusing — a population might have a finite number of members in theory, but if it's impossible to count them all in practice, the population is said to be infinite.

To collect information about your population, you can carry out a **survey**. This means **questioning** the people or **examining** the items.

Censuses
When you collect information from **every member** of a population, it's called a **census** — it's a **survey** of the **whole population**.

It helps if the population is fairly **small** and **easily accessible** — so that getting information from every member is a straightforward task.

You need to know the **advantages** and **disadvantages** of carrying out a **census**, so here they are:

Advantage

- It's an **accurate representation** of the population because every member has been surveyed — it's **unbiased**.

Disadvantages

- For **large** populations, it takes a lot of **time** and **effort** to carry out.
- This can make it **expensive** to do.
- It can be difficult to make sure **all** members are surveyed. If some are missed, the survey may be **biased**.
- If the tested items are **used up** or **damaged** in some way by doing a census, a census is **impractical**.

Tip: There's only really one main advantage, but it's an important one. See the next page for more on bias.

Tip: Watch out for anything that might make doing a census a silly idea.

Sampling

If doing a census is **impossible** or **impractical**, you can find out about a population by questioning or examining just a **selection** of the people or items. This selected group is called a **sample**.

Before selecting your sample, you need to identify the **sampling units** — these are the **individual members** of the population that **can be sampled**.

A **full list** of all the sampling units is called a **sampling frame**. This list must give a **unique name** or **number** to each sampling unit, and is used to represent the population when selecting a sampling method (see page 221).

Ideally, a sampling frame would be the **whole population** — but this is often **impractical**, especially with **infinite** populations.

Tip: The electoral roll of the UK is a sampling frame for the population of the UK — the sampling units are people who live in the UK. Ideally it would contain every person living in the country — but in practice it doesn't include absolutely everyone.

Example 1

For each situation described below, explain why a taking a sample is more practical than carrying out a census.

a) **A company produces 100 chocolate puddings every day, and each pudding is labelled with a unique product number. Every day, a sample of 5 puddings is eaten as a quality control test.**

   If they did a census of all the puddings, they'd have to eat all the puddings and there would be none left to sell.

b) **Mr Simson runs an online pet store. He wants to know if his customers are satisfied with the new fish food that he's selling this month. He decides to send fish-food customers an online questionnaire by collecting their email addresses during the checkout process.**

   If he emailed all customers who bought the new fish food in a month, he'd have a **lot of data** to process. A sample would be much **quicker** and **easier**.

Tip: You might be asked for a reason 'other than time or cost' for which a census would be impractical. So you do need to know all the possible problems with a census. Often there won't be a reason why a census simply **cannot** be done — it'll just be much quicker or easier to use a sample.

It's usually **more practical** to survey a **sample** rather than carry out a **census**, but your results might not be as **reliable** — make sure you can explain **why**.

Advantages

- Sample surveys are **quicker** and **cheaper** than a census, and it's easier to get hold of all the required information.

- It's the only option when surveyed items are **used up** or **damaged**.

Disadvantages

- There'll be **variability** between samples — each possible sample will give **different** results, so you could just happen to select one which doesn't **accurately reflect** the population.

- Samples can easily be affected by **sampling bias** (see below).

Tip: One way to reduce the likelihood of large variability is by using a large sample size. The larger the sample, the more reliable the information should be.

Representative and biased samples

Data collected from a sample is often used to draw **conclusions** about the **whole population**. So it's important that the sample is as similar to the population as possible — it must be a **representative sample**.

If a sample is not representative, it is **biased** and the sample **doesn't fairly represent** the population. A sample could be biased for a **number of reasons** and it can be difficult to get a completely unbiased sample — but there are a few rules you can use to **avoid** introducing bias:

To avoid sampling bias:

- Select from the correct population and make sure no member of the population is **excluded**.

  If you want to find out the views of residents from a particular street, your sample should:

  - **include only** residents from that street, and

  - be chosen from a **complete list** of all the residents.

- Select your sample at **random**.

  Non-random sampling methods include, for example, the sampler:

  - asking friends — who may all give similar answers, or

  - asking for volunteers — who may all have strong views.

- Make sure all your sample members **respond**.

  If some of your sampled residents are out when you go to interview them, it's important to go back and get their views another time.

Simple random sampling

Taking a random sample is important for avoiding bias — one way to make sure your sample is completely random is to use **simple random sampling**:

- Every person or item in the population has an **equal chance** of being in the sample.

- Each selection is **independent** of every other selection.

To choose a simple random sample:

- Give a **number** to each population **member**, from a **full list** of the population.

- Generate a list of **random numbers** and **match** them to the numbered members to select your sample.

Tip: Getting a truly random sample may not always be possible — some people in the sample may not respond, may not be possible to contact etc. However, this sampling method means every single possible combination of population members is equally likely.

Here's an example of **simple random sampling** using a **random-number table**.

Example 2

A zoo has 80 cottontop tamarins. Describe how the random-number table opposite could be used to select a sample of five of them, for a study on tail lengths.

8330	3992	1840
0330	1290	3237
9165	4815	0766

- First, draw up a **sampling frame** (a list of the 80 cottontop tamarins), giving each cottontop tamarin a **2-digit** number between **01** and **80**.

- Then use the **random-number table** to choose five numbers — you can use each 4-digit number in the table as two 2-digit numbers next to each other.

- Start at the beginning and find the first five numbers that are between 01 and 80.   These are too big.

     The first five numbers are: 83, 30, 39, 92, 18, 40, 03

- So choose the numbers 30, 39, 18, 40 and 03. Select the cottontop tamarins with the matching numbers.

Tip: You can generate random numbers from a calculator or from random-number tables.

Tip: You should reject any numbers that are bigger than the number in your sample.

To decide whether a simple random sample is suitable for investigating a real-world problem, you need to know its advantages and disadvantages.

Advantage   Every member of the population has an **equal chance** of being selected, so it's **completely unbiased**.

Disadvantage   It can be **inconvenient** if the population is spread over a **large area** — it might be difficult to track down the selected members (e.g. in a nationwide sample).

Systematic sampling (sampling every n^{th} member)

To make choosing a sample faster, you could use a **systematic sample** — this chooses **every n^{th} member** from the population to be sampled.

To choose a systematic sample:

- Give a **number** to each population **member**, from a **full list** of the population.

- Calculate a **regular interval** to use by dividing the population size by the sample size.

- Generate a **random** starting point that is less than or equal to the size of the interval. The corresponding member of the population is the **first member** of your sample.

- Keep **adding** the interval to the starting point to select your sample.

Tip: A regular interval could be every 10th member of the population, for example.

Tip: You could roll a dice or use a random-number generator to choose a suitable starting point.

Example 3

50 000 fans attended a football match. Describe how a systematic sample could be used to select a sample of 100 people.

- Give each fan a 5-digit number between **00 001** and **50 000**. This could be done by ticket number.

- $50\,000 \div 100 = 500$, so the interval is 500 — you select **every 500th** fan.

- Use a calculator to randomly generate a number between 1 and 500. E.g. if 239 is randomly generated, the starting point will be 00 239.

- Keep adding 500 to 00 239 to find the rest of the sample.
  So sample: 00 239, 00 739, 01 239, ... , 48 739, 49 239, 49 739
  $+500$ $+500$ ...

- Select the fans with the matching ticket numbers.

Tip: If the starting point was above 500 then the final number selected would be over 50 000, which is more than the population size — e.g. starting at 00 623 would give a final sampling unit of 50 123.

You could be asked about the pros and cons of systematic sampling.

Advantages
- It can be used for quality control on a production line — a **machine** can be set up to sample every nth item.
- It should give an **unbiased sample**.

Disadvantage The regular interval could coincide with a **pattern** — e.g. if every 10th item produced by a machine is faulty and you sample every 10th item, your sample will appear to show that **every item** produced is faulty, or that **no items** are faulty. Either way, your sample will be **biased**.

Stratified sampling

If a population is divided into **categories** (e.g. age or gender), you can use a **stratified sample** — this uses the same proportion of each category in the sample as there is in the population.

> To choose a stratified sample:
> - Divide the population into **categories**.
> - Calculate the **total** population.
> - Calculate the number needed for each category in the sample, using:
> $$\text{Size of category in sample} = \frac{\text{size of category in population}}{\text{total size of population}} \times \text{total sample size}$$
> - Select the sample for each category at **random**.

Tip: You can define your categories using more than one characteristic — e.g. age and gender (so the categories could be females under 18, males under 18, females aged 18-25 etc.).

Example 4

A teacher takes a sample of 20 pupils from her school, stratified by year group. The table shows the number of pupils in each year group.

Calculate how many pupils from each year group should be in her sample.

- The population is already split into five categories, based on year group.

Year Group	No. of pupils
7	120
8	80
9	95
10	63
11	42

- Total population = 120 + 80 + 95 + 63 + 42 = 400
- Calculate the number needed for each category in the sample.

$$\text{Year } 7 = \frac{120}{400} \times 20 = \boxed{6}$$
$$\text{Year } 8 = \frac{80}{400} \times 20 = \boxed{4}$$

$$\text{Year } 9 = \frac{95}{400} \times 20 = 4.75 \approx \boxed{5}$$
$$\text{Year } 10 = \frac{63}{400} \times 20 = 3.15 \approx \boxed{3}$$

$$\text{Year } 11 = \frac{42}{400} \times 20 = 2.1 \approx \boxed{2}$$

You can't have decimal amounts of pupils, so the answers for Years 9, 10 and 11 are rounded to the nearest whole number.

Tip: Your answers should add up to the sample size: 6 + 4 + 5 + 3 + 2 = 20

Tip: Now the teacher would use simple random sampling to select the pupils from each year group.

Stratified sampling is useful in certain situations.

Advantages
- If the population has **disjoint categories** (where there is no overlap), this is likely to give you a **representative** sample.
- It's useful when results may **vary** depending on categories.

Disadvantage It can be **expensive** because of the extra detail involved.

Tip: For example, opinions on a film may vary depending on gender — a stratified sample of girls and boys would be useful here.

Quota sampling

Quota sampling also involves dividing the population into categories — however, it's different from stratified sampling.

> To choose a quota sample:
> - Divide the population into **categories**.
> - Give each category a **quota** (number of members to sample).
> - Collect data until the quotas are met in **all** categories (**without** using random sampling).

Tip: The main difference between quota and stratified sampling is that no effort is made to be random in quota sampling.

This method is often used in market research. An interviewer will be told the quotas to fulfil, but can choose who to interview within each quota.

Example 5

A video-game company wants to gather opinions on a new game. The interviewer is asked to interview 65 people aged under thirty and 35 people aged thirty or above.

Give one advantage and one disadvantage of this quota sample.

- Advantage: the company doesn't have a full list of everyone who has played the game, so random sampling isn't possible.
- Disadvantage: people with strong views on the game are more likely to respond to the interviewer, which causes sampling bias.

Tip: The company have divided the population into two age groups. One reason for this could be that they know people aged under thirty are more likely to play their video games.

Once again, you need to know the advantages and disadvantages.

Advantages
- It can be done when there **isn't** a full list of the population.
- The interviewer continues to sample until all the quotas are met, so **non-response** is less of a problem.

Disadvantage It can be **easily biased** by the interviewer — within the quotas the interviewer could **exclude** some of the population (e.g. they could choose to interview only sporty-looking people, which might accidentally lead to a biased sample).

Opportunity sampling

Tip: Opportunity sampling is also known as **convenience sampling**.

The final sampling method you need to know about is **opportunity sampling**. This is where the sample is chosen from a section of the population that is **convenient** for the sampler.

Example 6

Mel thinks that most people watch her favourite television programme. She asks 20 friends whether they watch the television programme.

a) Name the sampling method Mel used.

Opportunity (or convenience) sampling — Mel asks her friends because they are easily available to sample.

b) Give a reason why Mel's sample may be biased.

Mel's friends could be of a similar age or the same gender, which is not representative of the whole population.

or...

Because this is Mel's favourite television programme, she might have encouraged her friends to watch it too.

Tip: There is no one right answer in b) — any sensible comment will do.

Here's the final set of advantages and disadvantages you need to know.

Advantage   Data can be gathered very **quickly** and **easily**.

Disadvantage It **isn't random** and can be **very biased** — there's no attempt to make the sample representative of the population.

Exercise 1.1

Q1 For each population described say whether it is finite or infinite.
   a) The members of the Ulverston Musical Appreciation Society.
   b) The population of Australia.
   c) The stars in the Milky Way galaxy.
   d) The 2016 Olympic gold medallists.
   e) The jalapeño chilli plants on sale at Church Lane Garden Centre.
   f) The cells in a human body.

Q2 Members of a local book club have to be consulted about the next book they'll read.
   a) What is the population?
   b) Explain whether a sample or a census should be used.

Q3 A teacher is investigating whether a student's ability to memorise a random string of letters is related to their ability to spell. He plans to ask students from his school, which has 1200 pupils, to do a standard spelling test and then to memorise a random string of 20 letters.
   a) What is the population?
   b) Give two reasons why he should use a sample rather than carry out a census.

Q4 For each of the following situations, explain whether it would be more sensible to carry out a census or a sample survey:

    a) Marcel is in charge of a packaging department of 8 people. He wants to know the average number of items a person packs per day.

    b) A toy manufacturer produces batches of 500 toys. As part of a safety check, they want to test the toys to work out the strength needed to pull them apart.

    c) Tara has a biased dice. She wants to find the proportion of dice rolls that will result in a 'three'.

Q5 All dogs which are admitted to the Graymar Animal Sanctuary are microchipped with a unique identification number. Between 2015 and 2016, 108 dogs were admitted. A sample of 12 dogs which were admitted between 2015 and 2016 is selected for long-term monitoring.

    a) What is the population?

    b) Explain how to carry out a systematic sample of 12 dogs.

Q6 The houses on Park Road are numbered from 1 to 173. Forty households are to be chosen to take part in a council survey. Describe a method for choosing an unbiased sample.

Q7 Pooja is doing a survey on whether people buy ethically-sourced products. She asked her mother to hand out questionnaires to 20 of her friends. Pooja's teacher said this sample was biased. What reasons might he give for saying this?

Q8 Explain why it is a good idea to use simple random sampling to select a sample.

Q9 For each of the following situations, name the sampling method used and give one disadvantage of using this sampling method:

    a) A tea company is investigating tea-drinking habits of its customers. The interviewer is asked to sample exactly 60 women and 40 men using a non-random sampling method.

    b) After a concert, a band is looking for feedback from their fans. Using the ticket numbers, they select every 100th fan to complete a survey.

    c) A student is researching shopping habits in the UK. He records how many people enter his local shopping centre between 9 am and 5 pm on a Monday.

Q10 A sports centre selects a sample of 10 members, stratified by age. The table shows the total number of members in each age group.

Age (a)	Under 20	20 to 40	41 to 60	Over 60
No. of members	45	33	15	57

Calculate how many people from each age group should be sampled.

1. Representing Data

Data is to statistics what fuel is to a car — without data, all the statistics knowledge in the world won't be much use. This chapter covers the essentials about data — from graphs, through to measures of location and dispersion.

Learning Objectives:

- Be able to recognise different types of variables.
- Be able to interpret frequency tables and grouped frequency tables.
- Be able to draw and interpret histograms.

Data basics

A lot of the subject of **statistics** involves analysing **data**.

The exam board will provide you with a **large data set**.

- You need to be **familiar** with this data, and be able to carry out all the techniques you'll meet in this section on your data.

- As there is a lot of data, you'll have to use a **calculator** or **computer** to carry out some of the analysis — but the basic techniques are covered in this chapter.

- Some **examples** in this chapter will use data from the large data set.

Data consists of a number of **observations** (or **measurements**). Each observation records a value of a particular **variable**.

There are different kinds of variables.

- Variables that take **non-numerical** values (i.e. they're not numbers) — these are called **qualitative** variables.

- Variables that take **numerical** values (i.e. they're numbers) — these are called **quantitative** variables.

There are then two different types of **quantitative** variables.

- A **discrete** variable can take only **certain values** within a particular range (e.g. shoe sizes) — this means there are 'gaps' between possible values (you can't take size 9.664 shoes, for example).

- A **continuous** variable can take **any value** within a particular range (e.g. lengths or masses) — there are no gaps between possible values.

Tip: Or you can think of a discrete variable changing 'in steps'.

Example 1

An employer collects information about the computers in his office. He gathers observations of the four variables shown in this table.

1. Manufacturer	Bell	Banana	Deucer	Deucer
2. Processor speed (in GHz)	2.6	2.1	1.8	2.2
3. Year of purchase	2014	2015	2016	2014
4. Colour	Grey	Grey	Grey	Black

a) **Which of the four variables are qualitative?**

- The variables 'Manufacturer' and 'Colour' take non-numerical values.

- So there are two qualitative variables: 'Manufacturer' and 'Colour'

---

b) Which of the four variables are quantitative?

- The variables 'Processor speed' and 'Year of purchase' take values that are numbers.

- So there are two quantitative variables: 'Processor speed' and 'Year of purchase'

Example 2

The variables below are all quantitative.
(i) length, (ii) weight, (iii) number of brothers, (iv) time,
(v) total value of 6 coins from down the back of my sofa

a) Which of these 5 quantitative variables are continuous?

- 'Length', 'weight' and 'time' can all take any value in a range.

- So the continuous variables are: 'length', 'weight' and 'time'

b) Which of these 5 quantitative variables are discrete?

- 'Number of brothers' and 'total value of 6 coins' can only take certain values.

- So there are two discrete variables — these are: 'number of brothers' and 'total value of 6 coins'

Tip: 'Number of brothers' can take only whole-number values.

'Total value of 6 coins' can only take particular values. For example, they could be worth 12p or 13p, but not 12.8p.

Data is often shown in the form of a **table**.
There are two types you need to be really familiar with.

- **Frequency tables** show the number of observations of various values.

  For example, this frequency table shows the number of bananas in thirty 1.5 kg bags.

Number of bananas	8	9	10	11	12
Frequency	3	7	10	6	4

  Tip: Frequency just means 'the number of times something happens'.

- **Grouped frequency tables** show the number of observations whose values fall within certain **classes** (i.e. **ranges** or **groups of values**). They're often used when there is a large range of possible values.

  For example, this grouped frequency table shows the number of potatoes in thirty 25 kg sacks.

Number of potatoes	50-55	56-60	61-65	66-70	71-75
Frequency	1	8	12	7	2

  - Notice how grouped frequency tables **don't** tell you the **exact** value of the observations — just the most and the least they **could** be.

  - And notice how the different classes **don't overlap**. In fact, there are 'gaps' between the classes because this is **discrete** data.

  Tip: Frequency tables and grouped frequency tables can also be drawn 'vertically', like this:

Number of bananas	Frequency
8	3
9	7
10	10
11	6
12	4

Grouped frequency tables are also used for **continuous** data. Since there are no 'gaps' between possible data values for continuous variables, there can be no gaps between classes in their grouped frequency tables either.

For example, this grouped frequency table shows the masses of 50 potatoes.

- **Inequalities** have been used to define the **class boundaries** (the upper and lower limits of each class). There are no 'gaps' and no overlaps between classes.
- The smallest class doesn't have a **lower limit** — so very small potatoes can still be put into one of the classes. Similarly, the largest class doesn't have an **upper limit**.

Mass of potato (m, in g)	Frequency
$m < 100$	7
$100 \le m < 200$	8
$200 \le m < 300$	16
$300 \le m < 400$	14
$m \ge 400$	5

This grouped frequency table shows the lengths (to the nearest cm) of the same 50 potatoes.

- The shortest potato that could go in the 6-7 class would actually have a length of 5.5 cm (since 5.5 cm would be rounded up to 6 cm when measuring to the nearest cm). So the **lower class boundary** of the 6-7 class is 5.5 cm
- The **upper class boundary** of the 6-7 class is the same as the lower class boundary of the 8-9 class — this is 7.5 cm. This means there are never any **gaps** between classes.

Length of potato (l, in cm)	Frequency
4-5	5
6-7	11
8-9	15
10-11	16
12-13	3

- For each class, you can find the **class width** using this formula:

$$\text{class width} = \text{upper class boundary} - \text{lower class boundary}$$

- And you can find the **mid-point** of a class using this formula:

$$\text{mid-point} = \frac{\text{lower class boundary} + \text{upper class boundary}}{2}$$

Tip: You don't always need to leave the top and bottom classes without a lower and upper limit — e.g. if you know for a fact that very small or very large data values are impossible.

Tip: A class with a lower class boundary of 50 g and upper class boundary of 250 g can be written in different ways. So you might see:
- '100-200, to the nearest 100 g'
- '$50 \le \text{mass} < 250$'
- '50-', followed by '250-' for the next class, and so on.

They all mean the same.

Tip: Even though a potato of length 7.5 cm would go in the 8-9 class, this is still the upper class boundary of the 6-7 class. The upper class boundary of the 12-13 class will be 13.5 cm.

Tip: 355 cm must be the upper class boundary for the 250-350 class, because no number less than this would work.

For example, the upper class boundary can't be 354.99 cm, because then a car of length 354.999 cm wouldn't fit into any of the classes. And the upper class boundary can't be 354.999 cm, because then a car of length 354.9999 cm wouldn't fit into any of the classes. And so on.

Example 3

A researcher measures the length (to the nearest 10 cm) of 40 cars. Her results are shown in the table.
Add four columns to the table to show:
(i)   the lower class boundaries
(ii) the upper class boundaries
(iii) the class widths
(iv) the class mid-points

Length (cm)	Frequency
250-350	5
360-410	11
420-450	17
460-500	7

- The shortest car that measures 250 cm (to the nearest 10 cm) is 245 cm long. So the lower class boundary of the 250-350 class is 245 cm.
- The upper class boundary of the 250-350 class is 355 cm (even though a car measuring 355 cm would actually go into the 360-410 class).

- Once you have the class boundaries, use the formulas on the previous page to find the class widths and the mid-points.

Length (cm)	Frequency	Lower class boundary (cm)	Upper class boundary (cm)	Class width (cm)	Mid-point (cm)
250-350	5	245	355	110	300
360-410	11	355	415	60	385
420-450	17	415	455	40	435
460-500	7	455	505	50	480

You can represent data from a frequency table with a **frequency polygon**.

Example 4

The table shows the maximum daily temperature (°C) in Hurn between May and October 2015. Draw a frequency polygon to show the data.

Tip: This uses a sample of the large data set.

Maximum daily temperature, t (°C)	Frequency	Mid-point
$10 < t \leq 15$	22	12.5
$15 < t \leq 20$	100	17.5
$20 < t \leq 25$	58	22.5
$25 < t \leq 30$	4	27.5

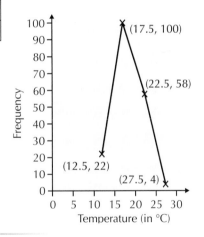

- Calculate the **mid-points** of each class using the formula from page 228.

Tip: Adding a column for mid-points makes it easier to plot the coordinates.

- Plot the **mid-points** on the horizontal (x) axis and the **frequencies** on the vertical (y) axis.
So plot the points
(12.5, 22), (17.5, 100),
(22.5, 58) and (27.5, 4).

- Join the points with a **straight line** (not a curve).

Tip: There are lots of other ways of representing data that you'll have come across at GCSE. If you're asked to draw a 'suitable' diagram, think about which will be most appropriate to represent the data you're given — for example, certain types of diagram are better for discrete or continuous variables.

Exercise 1.1

Q1 A mechanic collects the following information about cars he services:
Make, Mileage, Colour, Number of doors, Cost of service
Write down all the variables from this list that are:
a) qualitative
b) quantitative

Q2 Amy is an athletics coach. She records the following information about each of the athletes she trains:
Number of medals won last season, Height, Mass, Shoe size
Write down all the variables from this list that are examples of:
a) discrete quantitative variables
b) continuous quantitative variables

Q3   The heights of the members of a
history society are shown in the table.

a) Explain why 'height' is a
continuous variable.

b) For each class, write down:
(i)   the lower class boundary
(ii) the upper class boundary
(iii) the class width
(iv) the class mid-point

Height, h (cm)	Number of members
$140 \leq h < 150$	3
$150 \leq h < 160$	9
$160 \leq h < 170$	17
$170 \leq h < 180$	12
$180 \leq h < 190$	5
$190 \leq h < 200$	1

c) Show the information in the table in a frequency polygon.

Histograms

Tip: The formula for
frequency density (f.d.)
can actually be written:

$$\text{f.d.} = \frac{1}{k} \times \frac{\text{frequency}}{\text{class width}},$$

where k can be any
number.

However, it usually
makes sense to use $k = 1$
when drawing your own
histograms.

You'll see on the next
page how to interpret
histograms where
different values for k
have been used.

Histograms look like bar charts. However, because they're used to show
frequencies of **continuous variables**, there are **no gaps** between the bars.

To plot a histogram, you plot the **frequency density** rather than the frequency
(as you would in a bar chart). Use this formula to find frequency density:

$$\text{Frequency density} = \frac{\text{frequency}}{\text{class width}}$$

■ Here's some data showing the heights of 24 people.

Height (cm)	Lower class boundary (cm)	Upper class boundary (cm)	Class width (cm)	Frequency	Frequency density
$130 \leq h < 150$	130	150	20	3	0.15
$150 \leq h < 160$	150	160	10	4	0.4
$160 \leq h < 165$	160	165	5	5	1
$165 \leq h < 170$	165	170	5	6	1.2
$170 \leq h < 190$	170	190	20	6	0.3

Tip: If you just plotted
the **frequency** (rather
than the frequency
density), then your graph
would look like this:

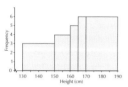

It looks like there are
lots of tall people but
this is just an illusion
created by the width
of the final class. If
this data was split into
classes all the same
width, then the graph
would look a lot more
like the histogram on
the left.

■ Here's the same data
plotted as a histogram.

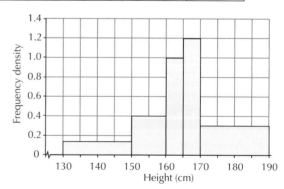

Notice how:

(i)   The vertical axis shows **frequency density.**

(ii) The horizontal axis has a **continuous** scale like an ordinary graph,
and there are **no gaps** between the columns.

(iii) A bar's left-hand edge corresponds to the **lower class boundary**.
A bar's right-hand edge corresponds to the **upper class boundary**.

Example 1

The table shows maximum daily windspeed in knots (kn) in Leuchars, over 30 days in 1987. Draw a histogram to show the data.

Tip: This uses a sample of the large data set.

Maximum gust, g (kn)	$5 < g \leq 15$	$15 < g \leq 20$	$20 < g \leq 30$	$30 < g \leq 45$
Frequency	8	9	10	3

- First draw a table showing the class width and the frequency density:

Maximum gust, g (kn)	Class width	Frequency	Frequency density
$5 < g \leq 15$	10	8	0.8
$15 < g \leq 20$	5	9	1.8
$20 < g \leq 30$	10	10	1
$30 < g \leq 45$	15	3	0.2

- Now you can draw the histogram.

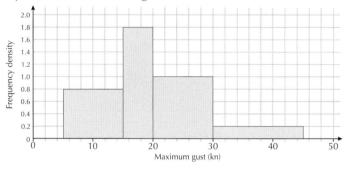

On a histogram, the frequency in a class is proportional to the **area** of its bar. In other words, **frequency = k × area of bar** (where k is a number).

Tip: If you divide the area of a bar by the total area of all of the bars in the histogram, you get the **probability** of a given class.

Example 2

This histogram shows the heights of a group of people.

There were 6 people between 155 cm and 160 cm tall.

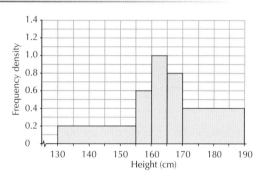

a) How many people in the group are between 130 cm and 155 cm tall?

Before looking at the 130-155 class, you need to use the information you have about the 155-160 class.

- Work out the area of the bar for 155 cm to 160 cm to find how area and frequency are related.
  Width of bar = 160 – 155 = 5
  Height of bar = 0.6
  So area of bar = 5 × 0.6 = 3

- An area of 3 represents a frequency of 6 — so '**frequency = 2 × area**'.

Tip: You always need to go through an initial stage of working out how area and frequency are related — basically, you're working out the value of k that's been used (see the 'Tip' about the frequency density formula on the previous page).

Tip: Or you can say that 1 square unit represents 2 people.

- Now you need to find the area of the bar from 130 cm to 155 cm.
  Width of bar = 155 − 130 = 25
  Height of bar = 0.2
  So area of bar = 25 × 0.2 = 5

- Remember, frequency = 2 × area.

  So 10 people are between
  130 cm and 155 cm tall.

b) **How many people in the group are over 165 cm tall?**

- There are two bars representing people over 165 cm tall.
  You need to find the frequencies represented by both of them.

  165-170 cm: 170-190 cm:
  Area of bar = 5 × 0.8 = 4   Area of bar = 20 × 0.4 = 8
  This represents 8 people.   This represents 16 people.

- Add the individual frequencies to find the total frequency.

  So 8 + 16 = 24 people are over 165 cm tall.

Example 3

The histogram below shows the speeds of cars along a stretch of road.
There were 26 cars travelling between 50 and 60 mph.

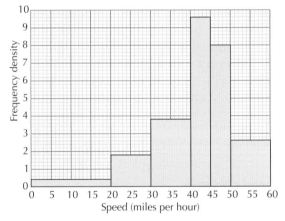

Estimate the number of cars travelling at 25 mph or less.

- Work out the area of the bar from   Width of bar = 60 − 50 = 10
  50 mph to 60 mph to find how   Height of bar = 2.6
  area and frequency are related.   So area of bar = 10 × 2.6 = 26

- An area of 26 represents a frequency of 26 — so '**frequency = area**'.

You now need to find the area of the bars to the **left** of 25 mph on the
horizontal axis (you need the frequency of cars travelling at 25 mph or **less**).

- First, find the area of   Width of bar = 20 − 0 = 20
  the 0-20 mph bar.   Height of bar = 0.4
                                   So area of bar = 20 × 0.4 = 8

                                   This represents 8 cars.

Tip: You can only
estimate the number of
cars travelling at 25 mph
or less because you
don't know exactly what
the speeds in the group
20-30 mph were.

Tip: Or you can say
that 1 square unit
represents 1 car.

- Now find **half** the area of the 20-30 mph bar — this represents speeds from 20 mph up to 25 mph.

  Width of bar = 30 – 20 = 10
  Height of bar = 1.8
  Total area of bar = 10 × 1.8 = 18
  So half the bar's area = 18 ÷ 2 = 9
  This represents 9 cars.

- Add these figures together to estimate the total number travelling at 25 mph or less.

  Total travelling at 25 mph or less
  = 8 + 9 = 17 cars

Tip: Finding half of the area under the 20-30 bar makes an **assumption** that half the cars travelling at 20-30 mph were going 25 mph or less while the other half were travelling faster than 25 mph.

Exercise 1.2

Q1 The table shows maximum daily humidity (%) in Heathrow, over 20 days in 2015.
Draw a histogram to show the data.

Humidity, h (%)	Frequency
$60 < h \le 80$	2
$80 < h \le 90$	9
$90 < h \le 95$	5
$95 < h \le 100$	4

Q2 The histogram below shows the audition times (in seconds) for contestants applying for a place on a television talent show.
The auditions for 54 contestants lasted between 30 and 45 seconds.

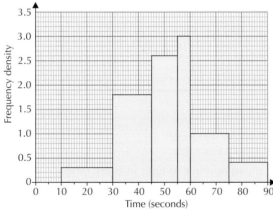

a) Work out the number of contestants whose auditions lasted less than 30 seconds.

b) Work out the total number of contestants who auditioned.

Q3 A butterfly enthusiast measures the wingspans (w, in mm), to the nearest millimetre, of a sample of tortoiseshell butterflies. She groups her measurements and displays the data in a histogram.

The group containing butterflies with a wingspan of 45-47 mm has a frequency of 12. This group is represented on the histogram by a bar of width 1.5 cm and height 9 cm.

Q3 Hint: The wingspans are measured to the nearest mm, so you need to use upper and lower class boundaries for the class widths (see page 228).

a) Show that each butterfly is represented on the histogram by an area of 1.125 cm².

b) The bar representing the butterflies with a wingspan of 52-53 mm has an area of 22.5 cm². Work out the frequency for this group.

c) The frequency for butterflies with a wingspan of 54-58 mm is 14. Work out the width and the height of the bar used to represent this group.

2. Location: Mean, Median & Mode

The mean, median and mode are measures of location (also called central tendency) — they summarise where the 'centre' of the data lies. Measures of location are sometimes referred to as averages.

The mean

The most common measure of location is called the **mean** (and is often just called 'the average' — but not while you're doing A-level Maths).

The formula for the mean ($\overline{x}$, said 'x-bar') is:

$$\text{Mean} = \overline{x} = \frac{\sum x}{n} \text{ or } \frac{\sum fx}{\sum f}$$

where each x is a **data value**, f is the **frequency** of each x (the number of times it occurs), and n is the **total number** of data values.

Tip: The $\sum$ (sigma) just means you add things together — so $\sum x$ means you add up all the values of x, and $\sum f = n$.

If you see $\sum x_i$ you have to imagine there are x-values $x_1, x_2, x_3...$ — then $\sum x_i$ means 'add up the values of x_i, for all the different values of i,' (which is just another way of telling you to add up all the different values of x).

So $\sum x$ and $\sum x_i$ mean exactly the same thing.

Example 1

Find the mean of the following list of data: 2, 3, 6, 2, 5, 9, 3, 8, 7, 2

- First, find $\sum x = 2 + 3 + 6 + 2 + 5 + 9 + 3 + 8 + 7 + 2 = 47$

- Then divide by $n = 10$ (since there are 10 values).

  This gives: $\overline{x} = \dfrac{\sum x}{n} = \dfrac{47}{10} = 4.7$

Example 2

A scientist counts the number of eggs in some song thrush nests. His data is shown in this table.

Number of eggs, x	2	3	4	5	6
Number of nests, f	4	9	16	8	3

Calculate the mean number of eggs in these nests.

- This time you have frequencies. It's best to add to the table:
  (i) a row showing the values of fx,
  (ii) a column showing the totals $\sum f$ and $\sum fx$.

Number of eggs, x	2	3	4	5	6	Total
Number of nests, f	4	9	16	8	3	40
fx		8	27	64	40	18	157

- Now use the formula for the mean: $\overline{x} = \dfrac{\sum fx}{\sum f} = \dfrac{157}{40} = 3.925$ eggs

---

Sometimes you have to work backwards from the mean.

Example 3

The mean of seven numbers is 9. When an extra number is added the mean becomes 9.5. Find the value of the extra number.

- Total of the first seven numbers = $7 \times 9 = 63$

- Call the extra number a. Then the total of all eight numbers = $63 + a$

- The mean of all eight numbers is 9.5, so
$$9.5 = \frac{63 + a}{8} \Rightarrow 76 = 63 + a \Rightarrow 13 = a$$
- So the extra number is 13 .

If you know a data set of size n_1 has mean $\overline{x_1}$ and another data set of size n_2 has mean $\overline{x_2}$, then the combined mean is $\overline{x}$, where:

$$\overline{x} = \frac{n_1 \overline{x_1} + n_2 \overline{x_2}}{n_1 + n_2}$$

Example 4

A scientist is looking at the amount of rainfall over a week in Hurn in 1987. The mean of the first 5 days is $\overline{x_1} = 5.38$ mm and the mean of the next 2 days is $\overline{x_2} = 22.45$ mm.

Find the combined mean ($\overline{x}$) of the rainfall over the week.

Tip: This uses a sample of the large data set.

- Here, $n_1 = 5$ and $n_2 = 2$.
- Using the formula: $\overline{x} = \dfrac{n_1 \overline{x_1} + n_2 \overline{x_2}}{n_1 + n_2} = \dfrac{(5 \times 5.38) + (2 \times 22.45)}{5 + 2}$

$$= \frac{71.8}{7} = 10.25714\ldots = 10.3 \,\text{mm} \text{ (to 3 s.f.)}$$

Exercise 2.1

Q1 Katia visits 12 shops and records the price of a loaf of bread. Her results are shown in the table below.

£1.08	£1.15	£1.25	£1.19	£1.26	£1.24
£1.15	£1.09	£1.16	£1.20	£1.05	£1.10

Work out the mean price of a loaf of bread in these shops.

Q2 The number of hours of sunshine per day in Camborne is recorded. The total number of hours of sunshine over 20 days is 99.8 hours. Find the mean number of hours of sunshine per day.

Q3 The numbers of goals scored by 20 football teams in their most recent match are shown in the table.

Number of goals, x	0	1	2	3	4
Frequency, f		5	7	4	3	1

Calculate the mean number of goals scored by these teams in their most recent match.

Q4 A drama group has 15 members. The mean age of the members is 47.4 years.

(PROBLEM SOLVING)

A 17-year-old joins the drama group. Find the new mean age.

The mode and the median

There are two other important measures of location you need to know about — the **mode** and the **median**.

Tip: The mode is often called the **modal value**.

> **Mode** = most frequently occurring data value.

Example 1

Find the modes of the following data sets.

a) **2, 3, 6, 2, 5, 9, 3, 8, 7, 2**

The most frequent data value is 2, appearing three times.

So the mode is $\boxed{2}$

Tip: If a data set has two modes, then it is called **bimodal**.

b) **4, 3, 6, 4, 5, 9, 2, 8, 7, 5**

This time there are two modes — the values 4 and 5 both appear twice.

So the modes are $\boxed{4 \text{ and } 5}$

c) **4, 3, 6, 11, 5, 9, 2, 8, 7, 12**

This time there is $\boxed{\text{no mode}}$ — each value appears just once.

The median is slightly trickier to find than the mode.

> **Median** = value in the middle of the data set when all the data values are placed in order of size.

First put your n data values **in order**, then find the **position** of the median in the ordered list. There are two possibilities:

(i) if $\frac{n}{2}$ is a **whole number** (i.e. n is even), then the median is halfway between the values in this position and the position above.

(ii) if $\frac{n}{2}$ is **not** a **whole number** (i.e. n is odd), **round it up** to find the position of the median.

Example 2

Find the medians of the following data sets.

a) **2, 3, 6, 2, 6, 9, 3, 8, 7**

- Put the values in order first: 2, 2, 3, 3, 6, 6, 7, 8, 9

Tip: Be careful — $\frac{n}{2}$ is the median **position**, so the median is the 5th value, **not** 5.

- There are 9 values, and $\frac{n}{2} = \frac{9}{2} = 4.5$. Rounding this up to 5 means that the median is the 5th value in the ordered list — median = $\boxed{6}$

b) **4, 3, 11, 4, 10, 9, 3, 8, 7, 8**

- Put the values in order first: 3, 3, 4, 4, 7, 8, 8, 9, 10, 11

- There are 10 values, and $\frac{n}{2} = \frac{10}{2} = 5$.

Tip: The value halfway between two numbers is their mean.

- The median is halfway between the 5th value in the ordered list (= 7) and the 6th value (= 8). So the median = $\boxed{7.5}$

If your data is in a **frequency table**, then the mode and the median are still easy to find as long as the data **isn't grouped**.

Example 3

The number of letters received one day in a sample of houses is shown in this table.

Number of letters	Number of houses
0	11
1	25
2	27
3	21

Tip: Frequency means the number of times a data value occurs.

Here, the data values are the 'numbers of letters' received in a house. So the frequencies are the 'numbers of houses' (that received that many letters).

a) **Find the modal number of letters.**
- The modal number of letters just means the mode.
- The highest frequency is for 2 letters — so the mode is 2 letters.

b) **Find the median number of letters.**
- It's useful to add a column to show the **cumulative frequency** (see p.247) — this is just a **running total** of the frequency column.

No. of letters	No. of houses (frequency)	Cumulative frequency
0	11	11
1	25	36
2	27	63
3	21	84

- The total number of houses is the last cumulative frequency, so $n = 84$.
- Since $\frac{n}{2} = \frac{84}{2} = 42$, the median is halfway between the 42nd and 43rd data values.
- Using the cumulative frequency, you can see that the data values in positions 37 to 63 all equal 2. So the median is 2 letters.

Tip: All the data values between positions 37 and 63 equal 2. Because the 42nd and 43rd data values are within this range, they also equal 2.

Exercise 2.2

Q1 The amount of money raised by seventeen friends is shown below.

£250	£19	£500	£123	£185	£101
£45	£67	£194	£77	£108	£110
£187	£216	£84	£98	£140	

a) Find the median amount of money raised by these friends.

b) Explain why it is not possible to find the mode for this data.

Q2 The maximum daily humidity (%) in Leeming was recorded over 12 days in 1987. The values are below.

80	95	88	95	82	84
80	91	86	97	93	89

a) Write down the mode of this data.

b) Find the median humidity recorded.

Q3 An online seller has received the ratings shown in this table.

a) Write down the modal customer rating.

b) Work out the median customer rating.

Rating	Number of customers
1	7
2	5
3	25
4	67
5	72

Averages of grouped data

If you have **grouped data**, you can only **estimate** the mean and median. This is because the grouping means you no longer have the exact data values. And instead of a mode, you can only find a **modal class**.

Modal class

Tip: See page 230 for more about frequency density.

- The **modal class** is the class with the **highest frequency density**.

- If all the classes are the same width, then this will just be the class with the **highest frequency**.

Example 1

Find the modal class for this data showing the heights of various shrubs.

Height of shrub to nearest cm	11-20	21-30	31-40	41-50
Number of shrubs	11	22	29	16

- In this example, all the classes are the same width (= 10 cm). So the modal class is the class with the highest frequency.

- This means the modal class is 31-40 cm

Mean

- To find an estimate of the **mean**, you assume that every reading in a class takes the value of the class **mid-point**.

Tip: This is the formula from page 234.

- Then you can use the formula $\overline{x} = \dfrac{\sum fx}{\sum f}$.

Example 2

The heights of a number of trees were recorded. The data collected is shown in this table.

Tip: The frequency (f) is the 'Number of trees'.

Height of tree to nearest m	0-5	6-10	11-15	16-20
Number of trees	26	17	11	6

Find an estimate of the mean height of the trees.

Tip: Questions with a large set of data may give **summation** statistics instead of a full set of data — in other words, you'll be given $\sum f$ and $\sum fx$.

- It's best to make another table. Include extra rows showing:
  (i) the class mid-points (x),
  (ii) the values of fx, where f is the frequency.

- And add an extra column for the totals $\sum f$ and $\sum fx$.

Tip: For the first class:
Lower class boundary = 0
Upper class boundary = 5.5
So the class mid-point = (0 + 5.5) ÷ 2 = 2.75
(See page 228 for more information.)

Height of tree to nearest m	0-5	6-10	11-15	16-20	**Total**
Class mid-point, x	2.75	8	13	18	
Number of trees, f	26	17	11	6	60 (= $\sum f$)
fx	71.5	136	143	108	458.5 (= $\sum fx$)

- Now you can use the formula given above to find the mean.

$$\text{Mean} = \overline{x} = \frac{\sum fx}{\sum f} = \frac{458.5}{60} = 7.64 \text{ m (to 2 d.p.)}$$

Median

To find an estimate for the median, use **linear interpolation**.

This table shows the tree data from the second example on the previous page, with an extra row showing the **cumulative frequency**.

Height of tree to nearest m	0-5	6-10	11-15	16-20
Number of trees	26	17	11	6
Cumulative frequency	26	43	54	60

Tip: 'Linear interpolation' is sometimes just called 'interpolation'.

- First, find **which class** the median is in.

  Since $\frac{n}{2} = \frac{60}{2} = 30$, there are 30 values less than or equal to the median. This means the median must be in the 6-10 class.

Tip: In this method, you **only** need to find $\frac{n}{2}$ — you **don't** then need to follow the rules described on page 236. However, the two ways of using $\frac{n}{2}$ turn out to be **equivalent**.

- Now, the idea behind **linear interpolation** is to **assume** that all the readings in this class are evenly spread. So divide the class (whose width is 5) into 17 intervals of equal width (one interval for each of the data values in the class), and assume there's a reading in the middle of each interval.

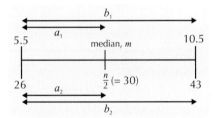

Tip: The red crosses in the diagram aren't the **actual** data values — they're **interpolated** data values (we've made an **assumption** about them being at these points).

- The numbers **on the top** of the scale are **heights** (measured in metres). The **upper and lower class boundaries** are shown, and the **median** (m) is also marked (but you don't know its value yet).

- The numbers **underneath** the scale are **cumulative frequencies**. The cumulative frequency at the lower class boundary is 26, while the cumulative frequency at the upper class boundary is 43.

- In fact, you don't need to draw the small intervals and the data points every time — a simplified version like the one on the right is enough to find a median.

- To find the **median**, m, you need to solve: $\boxed{\dfrac{a_1}{b_1} = \dfrac{a_2}{b_2}}$

Example 3

Estimate the median height for the trees recorded in this table.

Height of tree to nearest m	0-5	6-10	11-15	16-20
Number of trees	26	17	11	6

Tip: This is the same data as in the explanation above — so you already know which class contains the median.

- First draw the picture of the class containing the median (m) — just show the important numbers you're going to need.

- Then solve the equation $\dfrac{a_1}{b_1} = \dfrac{a_2}{b_2}$.

- Substituting in the numbers gives: $\dfrac{m-5.5}{10.5-5.5} = \dfrac{30-26}{43-26}$

- And so $\dfrac{m-5.5}{5} = \dfrac{4}{17}$, or $m = 5 \times \dfrac{4}{17} + 5.5 = \boxed{6.68 \text{ m (to 2 d.p.)}}$

Tip: Work out the values of a_1, b_1, a_2, b_2 from the diagram:
$a_1 = m - 5.5$
$b_1 = 10.5 - 5.5$
$a_2 = 30 - 26$
$b_2 = 43 - 26$ (b_2 is just the class frequency from the original table).

Example 4

Estimate the median length of the newts shown in the table below.

Length (to nearest cm)	0-2	3-5	6-8	9-11
Number of newts	3	18	12	4

- There are $n = 3 + 18 + 12 + 4 = 37$ data values in total.
  So $\frac{n}{2} = 18.5$ — meaning the median will be in the 3-5 class.

- Now draw the picture of the class containing the median.

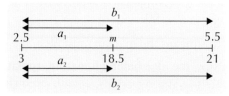

- So you need to solve:
  $$\frac{m - 2.5}{5.5 - 2.5} = \frac{18.5 - 3}{21 - 3}$$

- This gives $\frac{m - 2.5}{3} = \frac{15.5}{18}$, or $m = 3 \times \frac{15.5}{18} + 2.5 = \boxed{5.1 \text{ cm (to 1 d.p.)}}$

Exercise 2.3

Q1 The time that 60 students took to change after PE is shown below.

Time (t, mins)	Frequency, f	Mid-point, x	fx
$3 \leq t < 4$	7	3.5	24.5
$4 \leq t < 5$	14	4.5	
$5 \leq t < 6$	24		
$6 \leq t < 8$	10		
$8 \leq t < 10$	5		

a) Copy and complete the table.

b) Use the table to work out an estimate of the mean time it took these students to change.

Q2 A postman records the number of letters delivered to each of 50 houses one day.

The results are shown in this table.

Number of letters	Number of houses
0-2	20
3-5	16
6-8	7
9-11	5
12-14	2

a) State the modal class.

b) Estimate the mean number of letters delivered to these houses.

c) Write down the interval containing the median.

Q3 The table shows the maximum daily temperature t (°C) recorded in Leuchars in June 2015.

Use linear interpolation to estimate the median maximum daily temperature in Leuchars.

Temperature (t, °C)	Frequency
$10 \leq t < 13$	1
$13 \leq t < 16$	12
$16 \leq t < 19$	9
$19 \leq t < 22$	5
$22 \leq t < 25$	3

Q4 The table below shows the times that a random sample of 60 runners took to complete a marathon.

a) Estimate the mean time of these runners. (You may use $\sum fx = 16740$, where x is the mid-point of a class.)

b) Calculate an estimate for the median time it took these runners to complete the marathon.

Time (t,mins)	Frequency, f
$180 \leq t < 240$	8
$240 \leq t < 270$	19
$270 \leq t < 300$	21
$300 \leq t < 360$	9
$360 \leq t < 480$	3

Comparing measures of location

You've seen three different measures of location — the mean, the median and the mode. Each of them is useful for different kinds of data.

Mean

- The mean's a good average because you use **all** your data in working it out.

- But it can be heavily affected by **extreme values / outliers** and by distributions of data values that are **not symmetric**.

- It can only be used with **quantitative** data (i.e. numbers).

Tip: There's more about outliers on page 249.

Tip: A symmetric data set is one where the distribution of data values above the mean is the mirror image of the distribution of values below the mean.

Median

- The median is **not** affected by extreme values — so this is a good average to use when you have **outliers**.

- This also makes it a good average to use when the data set is **not symmetric**.

Mode

- The mode can be used with **qualitative** (non-numerical) data.

- But some data sets can have **more than one** mode (and if every value in a data set occurs just once, then the mode isn't very helpful at all).

Tip: You saw a bimodal data set (with two modes) on page 236. Other data sets may have more than two modes or even no mode.

Exercise 2.4

Q1 Explain whether the mean, median or mode would be most suitable as a summary of each of the following data sets.

a) Salaries of each employee at a company.

b) Length of adult female adder snakes.

c) Make of cars parked in a car park.

d) Weight of all newborn full-term babies born one year at a hospital.

e) Distance a firm's employees travel to work each morning.

Q2 Hosi records the number of bedrooms in the houses lived in by a sample of 10 adults. His results are shown in the table.

Number of bedrooms	1	2	3	4	5	6	7	8
Frequency	1	2	4	2	0	0	0	1

Explain why the mean may not be the most suitable measure of location for the data.

Q1 Hint: Think about the shape of the histogram you might expect for each data set. For example, in part a), think about how many people you might expect to earn quite a low salary, and how many you might expect to earn a very high salary.

3. Dispersion

- Be able to calculate the range, interquartile range and interpercentile range.
- Be able to draw and interpret cumulative frequency diagrams.
- Be able to determine whether a reading is an outlier.
- Be able to draw and interpret box plots.
- Be able to calculate and interpret variance and standard deviation (including with the use of coding).

A measure of location tells you roughly where the centre of the data lies. Dispersion, on the other hand, tells you how spread out the data values are.

Range, interquartile range and interpercentile range

Range

The **range** is about the simplest measure of dispersion you can imagine.

$$\boxed{\text{Range} = \text{highest value} - \text{lowest value}}$$

But the range is heavily affected by **extreme values**, so it isn't really the most useful way to measure dispersion.

Interquartile range

A more useful way to measure dispersion is to use the **interquartile range** — but first you have to find the **quartiles**. You've already seen how the median divides a data set into two halves. The quartiles are similar — there are three quartiles altogether (usually labelled Q_1, Q_2 and Q_3) and they divide the data into **four parts**.

- Q_1 is the **lower quartile** — 25% of the data is less than or equal to the lower quartile.

- Q_2 is the **median** — 50% of the data is less than or equal to the median.

- Q_3 is the **upper quartile** — 75% of the data is less than or equal to the upper quartile.

For example, the values in the data set below have been sorted so that they're in numerical order, starting with the smallest. The three quartiles are shown.

$$1 \quad 2 \quad 3 \quad | \quad 4 \quad 4 \quad 5 \quad | \quad 5 \quad 5 \quad 6 \quad | \quad 7 \quad 7 \quad 9$$
$$Q_1\quad Q_2 \quad Q_3$$

$$Q_1 = 4$$
$$Q_2 = 5$$
$$Q_3 = 6$$

The quartiles are worked out in a similar way to the median — by first finding their **position** in the ordered list of data values.

Tip: There are various ways you can find the quartiles, and they sometimes give different results. But if you use the methods below, you'll be fine.

> To find the position of the **lower quartile** (Q_1), first work out $\frac{n}{4}$.
>
> - If $\frac{n}{4}$ is a **whole number**, then the **lower quartile** is halfway between the values in this position and the position above.
>
> - If $\frac{n}{4}$ is **not** a whole number, **round it up** to find the position of the lower quartile.

Tip: This is the same as the method used on page 236 for finding the median, only with $\frac{n}{2}$ replaced by $\frac{n}{4}$.

> To find the position of the **upper quartile** (Q_3), first work out $\frac{3n}{4}$.
>
> - If $\frac{3n}{4}$ is a **whole number**, then the **upper quartile** is halfway between the values in this position and the position above.
>
> - If $\frac{3n}{4}$ is **not** a whole number, **round it up** to find the position of the upper quartile.

Tip: This is the same as the method used on page 236 for finding the median, only with $\frac{n}{2}$ replaced by $\frac{3n}{4}$.

Once you've found the upper and lower quartiles, you can find the
interquartile range (IQR).

> Interquartile range (IQR) = upper quartile (Q_3) – lower quartile (Q_1)

- The interquartile range is a measure of **dispersion**.

- It actually shows the range of the 'middle 50%' of the data.

- This means it's not affected by **extreme values**, but it still tells you something about how spread out the data values are.

Tip: You don't need to know the median (Q_2) to calculate the interquartile range.

Example 1

a) **Find the median and quartiles of the following data set:**
   2, 5, 3, 11, 6, 8, 3, 8, 1, 6, 2, 23, 9, 11, 18, 19, 22, 7

- First put the list in order:
  1, 2, 2, 3, 3, 5, 6, 6, 7, 8, 8, 9, 11, 11, 18, 19, 22, 23

- You need Q_1, Q_2 and Q_3, so find $\frac{n}{4}$, $\frac{n}{2}$ and $\frac{3n}{4}$, where $n = 18$.

- $\frac{n}{4} = \frac{18}{4} = 4.5$. This is **not** a whole number, so round up to 5.
  This means the lower quartile is equal to the 5th term: $\boxed{Q_1 = 3}$

- $\frac{n}{2} = \frac{18}{2} = 9$ is a **whole number**. The median is halfway
  between the 9th term (= 7) and the 10th term (= 8). So $\boxed{Q_2 = 7.5}$

- $\frac{3n}{4} = \frac{54}{4} = 13.5$ is **not** a whole number, so round up to 14.
  This means the upper quartile is equal to the 14th term: $\boxed{Q_3 = 11}$

b) **Find the interquartile range for the above data.**
   Interquartile range = $Q_3 - Q_1 = 11 - 3 = \boxed{8}$

When your data is **grouped**, you'll need to use **linear interpolation** to find an **estimate** for the lower and upper quartiles.

Tip: You don't have the exact data values with grouped data, so like with the median you can only estimate the lower and upper quartiles.

Example 2

a) **Estimate the lower and upper quartiles for the tree heights in this table.**

Height of tree to nearest m	0-5	6-10	11-15	16-20
Number of trees	26	17	11	6

Tip: This is the same data as on p.238-239.

- First add a row to the table showing cumulative frequency.

Height of tree to nearest m	0-5	6-10	11-15	16-20
Number of trees	26	17	11	6
Cumulative frequency	26	43	54	60

Now find the quartiles, starting with the **lower quartile** (Q_1).

- First calculate $\frac{n}{4} = \frac{60}{4} = 15$.

- Using the cumulative frequency, Q_1 is in the class 0-5.

Tip: The method is the same as the method on p.239 for estimating the median of grouped data.

- Now draw a picture of the class containing Q_1 — just show the important numbers you're going to need.

Put heights one side of the line (here, they're on top) and cumulative frequencies on the other side.

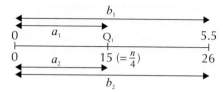

Tip: Remember, b_2 should match the class frequency from the original frequency table.

- Then solve the equation $\frac{a_1}{b_1} = \frac{a_2}{b_2}$.

- Substituting in the numbers gives: $\dfrac{Q_1 - 0}{5.5 - 0} = \dfrac{15 - 0}{26 - 0}$

- And so $\dfrac{Q_1}{5.5} = \dfrac{15}{26}$, or $Q_1 = 5.5 \times \dfrac{15}{26} = \boxed{3.2 \text{ m (to 1 d.p.)}}$

Find the **upper quartile** (Q_3) in the same way.

- First, calculate $\dfrac{3n}{4} = \dfrac{3 \times 60}{4} = 45$.

- So Q_3 is in the class 11-15.

- Now draw your picture of the class containing Q_3.

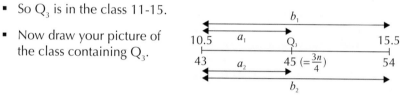

- Substituting numbers into $\frac{a_1}{b_1} = \frac{a_2}{b_2}$ gives: $\dfrac{Q_3 - 10.5}{15.5 - 10.5} = \dfrac{45 - 43}{54 - 43}$

- And so $\dfrac{Q_3 - 10.5}{5} = \dfrac{2}{11}$, or $Q_3 = 10.5 + 5 \times \dfrac{2}{11} = \boxed{11.4 \text{ m (to 1 d.p.)}}$

b) **Estimate the interquartile range for this data.**

Interquartile range (IQR) = $Q_3 - Q_1$
$$= 11.4 - 3.2 = \boxed{8.2 \text{ m (to 1 d.p.)}}$$

Interpercentile range

You've seen how the quartiles divide the data into four parts, where each part contains the same number of data values. **Percentiles** are similar, but they divide the data into **100 parts**.

Tip: The median is the 50th percentile and Q_1 is the 25th percentile, and so on.

> The **position** of the xth percentile (P_x) is $\dfrac{x}{100}$ × total frequency (n).

For example, to find the 11th percentile in a data set containing a total of 200 values:

- Calculate $\dfrac{11}{100} \times 200 = 22$.

Tip: When you're finding percentiles, the data set is usually large, and will probably be grouped.

- Use linear interpolation to estimate the value in this position in the **ordered** list of data values.

You can find **interpercentile ranges** by subtracting two percentiles.

> The $a\%$ to $b\%$ **interpercentile range** is $P_b - P_a$.

- For example, the 20% to 80% interpercentile range is $P_{80} - P_{20}$.

Example 3

A reptile specialist records the mass (*m*, in kilograms) of 150 tortoises. Her results are shown in the table.

Mass (kg)	Frequency
$0.2 \le m < 0.6$	27
$0.6 \le m < 1.0$	43
$1.0 \le m < 1.4$	35
$1.4 \le m < 1.8$	31
$1.8 \le m < 2.2$	14

a) **Estimate the 10th percentile for this data.**

- It'll help to add a column showing cumulative frequency.

- Now calculate $\frac{10}{100} \times 150 = 15$

- Using the cumulative frequency, you can see that this will be in the '$0.2 \le m < 0.6$' class.

Mass (kg)	Frequency	Cumulative frequency
$0.2 \le m < 0.6$	27	27
$0.6 \le m < 1.0$	43	70
$1.0 \le m < 1.4$	35	105
$1.4 \le m < 1.8$	31	136
$1.8 \le m < 2.2$	14	150

- So draw a picture of this class showing the important masses and cumulative frequencies.

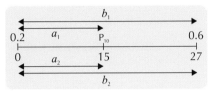

Tip: As always with linear interpolation, solve $\frac{a_1}{b_1} = \frac{a_2}{b_2}$.

- The equation $\frac{a_1}{b_1} = \frac{a_2}{b_2}$ gives $\frac{P_{10} - 0.2}{0.6 - 0.2} = \frac{15 - 0}{27 - 0}$, which means:

$$P_{10} = 0.2 + 0.4 \times \frac{15}{27} = \boxed{0.42 \text{ kg (to 2 d.p.)}}$$

b) **Estimate the 90th percentile for this data.**

- $\frac{90}{100} \times 150 = 135$

- So the 90th percentile will be in the class '$1.4 \le m < 1.8$'.

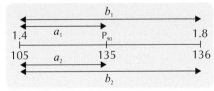

- The equation $\frac{a_1}{b_1} = \frac{a_2}{b_2}$ gives $\frac{P_{90} - 1.4}{1.8 - 1.4} = \frac{135 - 105}{136 - 105}$

This means: $P_{90} = 1.4 + 0.4 \times \frac{30}{31} = \boxed{1.79 \text{ kg (to 2 d.p.)}}$

c) **Find the 10% to 90% interpercentile range for this data.**

10% to 90% interpercentile range $= P_{90} - P_{10}$
$$= 1.79 - 0.42 = \boxed{1.37 \text{ kg (to 2 d.p.)}}$$

Q1 The diameters (in miles) of the eight planets in the Solar System are given below:

3032, 7521, 7926, 4222, 88 846, 74 898, 31 763, 30 778

For this data set, calculate:

a) the range

b) (i) the lower quartile (Q_1)
   (ii) the upper quartile (Q_3)
   (iii) the interquartile range (IQR)

Q2 Each of the three data sets below shows the speeds (in mph) of 18 different cars observed at a certain time and place.

In town at 8:45 am:
14, 16, 15, 18, 15, 17, 16, 16, 18, 16, 15, 13, 15, 14, 16, 17, 18, 15

In town at 10:45 am:
34, 29, 36, 32, 31, 38, 30, 35, 39, 31, 29, 30, 25, 29, 33, 34, 36, 31

On the motorway at 1 pm:
67, 76, 78, 71, 73, 88, 74, 69, 75, 76, 95, 71, 69, 78, 73, 76, 75, 74

For each set of data, calculate:

a) the range

b) the interquartile range (IQR)

Q3 The maximum temperature (°C) at Heathrow airport was recorded each day for 150 days in 1987. The results are shown in the table below.

For this data, estimate:

a) the lower quartile (Q_1)

b) the upper quartile (Q_3)

c) the interquartile range (IQR)

d) the 10th percentile

e) the 90th percentile

f) the 10% to 90% interpercentile range

Maximum temperature (t)	Frequency
$10 \leq t < 15$	19
$15 \leq t < 20$	66
$20 \leq t < 25$	49
$25 \leq t < 30$	16

Q4 The lengths (l) of a zoo's beetles measured to the nearest mm are shown in this table.

Length (l)	Number of beetles
0-5	82
6-10	28
11-15	44
16-30	30
31-50	16

For this data, estimate:

a) the 20% to 80% interpercentile range

b) the 5% to 95% interpercentile range

Cumulative frequency diagrams

Cumulative frequency means 'running total' — i.e. adding up the frequencies as you go along. A **cumulative frequency diagram** plots this running total so you can estimate the **median** and the **quartiles** easily (see p.236 and p.242).

- Here's some data showing the weights of 24 sixteen-year-old boys.

Weight (kg)	Frequency	Upper class boundary	Cumulative Frequency
$w \leq 40$	0	40	0
$40 < w \leq 50$	3	50	$0 + 3 = 3$
$50 < w \leq 60$	4	60	$3 + 4 = 7$
$60 < w \leq 70$	8	70	$7 + 8 = 15$
$70 < w \leq 80$	6	80	$15 + 6 = 21$
$80 < w \leq 90$	3	90	$21 + 3 = 24$

First number = 0

This is the sum of all the frequencies ≤ 70.

Last number = total frequency

Tip: The first number must be zero — this shows there are no people who weigh less than 40 kg. You might need to add a row to the table to show this. The last reading should always equal the total number of data values.

- Here's the same data plotted as a cumulative frequency diagram.

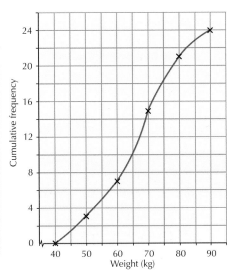

Notice how:

(i) The vertical axis shows **cumulative frequency**.

(ii) The horizontal axis has a **continuous** scale like an ordinary graph.

(iii) Points are plotted at the **upper class boundary**.

(iv) The line should start at **0** on the vertical axis.

Tip: With cumulative frequency diagrams, you usually join the points with a curve. To draw a cumulative frequency polygon, use straight lines to join the points.

Tip: Plotting points at the upper class boundary makes sense if you remember that a cumulative frequency graph shows how many data values are less than the value on the x-axis.

Example

a)   Draw a cumulative frequency diagram for the data below.

Age in completed years	11-12	13-14	15-16	17-18
Number of students	50	65	58	27

- To find the coordinates to plot, extend the table and calculate the upper class boundaries and cumulative frequencies.

Upper class boundary	11	13	15	17	19
Cumulative frequency	0	50	115	173	200

- There are 0 students under the age of 11, so the first coordinate is (11, 0).

Tip: The upper class boundary of the class 11-12 is 13 because people are '12' right up until their 13th birthday. The same reasoning also applies to the rest of the classes.

- So you draw the cumulative frequency diagram with the coordinates:
        (11, 0), (13, 50), (15, 115), (17, 173) and (19, 200).

Tip: You can only **estimate** the median and interquartile range because the data is grouped — you don't know how the ages are spread within each group.

Tip: If you drew the graph as a cumulative frequency **curve**, your estimates might be slightly different.

Tip: There's more information about the interquartile range on pages 242-243.

b) Estimate the median and interquartile range from the graph.

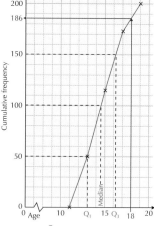

- To estimate the median from a graph go to the median position on the vertical scale and read off the value from the horizontal axis.

- Median position $= \frac{1}{2} \times 200$
$$= 100$$
So median = 14.5 years (see graph).

- You can estimate the quartiles in the same way by finding the position first.

Q_1 position $= \frac{1}{4} \times 200 = 50$, Q_3 position $= \frac{3}{4} \times 200 = 150$,
so Q_1 = **13 years** (see graph).   so Q_3 = **16.2 years** (see graph).

- Find the interquartile range:
IQR = $Q_3 - Q_1$ = **16.2 – 13** = 3.2 years

c) Estimate how many students have already had their 18th birthday.

Go up from 18 on the horizontal (age) axis and read off the number of students younger than 18 (= 186 — the blue line on the graph).

Then the number of students aged 18 or over is 200 – 186 = 14

Exercise 3.2

Q1 Draw a cumulative frequency diagram for the data given below. Use your diagram to estimate the median and interquartile range.

Distance walked, d (km)	$0 < d \leq 2$	$2 < d \leq 4$	$4 < d \leq 6$	$6 < d \leq 8$
Number of walkers	1	10	7	2

Q2 Using the cumulative frequency diagram for weight (page 247), estimate how many sixteen-year-old boys weigh:
a) Less than 55kg   b)   More than 73kg.
c) Explain why your answers are estimates.

Q3 The cumulative frequency diagram below shows the monthly earnings of some sixteen-year-olds.

a) How many people were sampled?

b) Estimate the median earnings.

c) Estimate how many earned between £46 and £84.

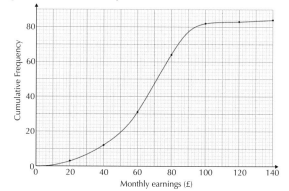

Outliers and box plots

Outliers

An **outlier** is a freak piece of data that lies a long way from the majority of the readings in a data set.

To decide whether a reading is an outlier, you have to **test** whether it falls **outside** certain limits, called **fences**.

A common way to test for outliers is to use the following values for the fences:

> - for the **lower fence**, use the value $Q_1 - (1.5 \times IQR)$
> - for the **upper fence**, use the value $Q_3 + (1.5 \times IQR)$

So using these fences, x is an outlier if:

> **either:** $x < Q_1 - (1.5 \times IQR)$
> **or:** $x > Q_3 + (1.5 \times IQR)$

Tip: There are various ways to calculate the values of the fences, but in an exam you will always be told which method to use. There's another way of finding outliers using the mean and standard deviation on p.254.

Tip: Cleaning data involves finding outliers, dealing with missing values and sorting out data that hasn't been given in the correct format.

Example 1

The lower and upper quartiles of a data set are 70 and 100. Use the fences $Q_1 - (1.5 \times IQR)$ and $Q_3 + (1.5 \times IQR)$ to decide whether the data values 30 and 210 are outliers.

- First work out the IQR: $Q_3 - Q_1 = 100 - 70 = 30$

- Then you can find where your **fences** are.

- Lower fence: $Q_1 - (1.5 \times IQR) = 70 - (1.5 \times 30) = 25$

- Upper fence: $Q_3 + (1.5 \times IQR) = 100 + (1.5 \times 30) = 145$

- 30 is **inside** the lower fence, so it is **not** an outlier.
  210 is **outside** the upper fence, so it **is** an outlier.

Box plots

A **box plot** is a kind of 'visual summary' of a set of data. Box plots show the **median**, **quartiles** and **outliers** clearly.

They look like this:

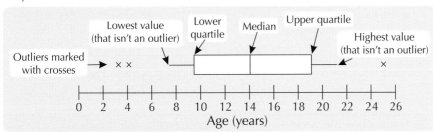

Tip: Box plots are sometimes called 'box and whisker diagrams' (where the whiskers are the horizontal lines at either end of the box).

- The **scale** is really important — always include one.

- The box extends from the **lower quartile** to the **upper quartile**.

- A vertical line drawn on the box marks the **median**.

- A horizontal line is drawn from each end of the box. These lines extend in each direction as far as the last data value that **isn't** an outlier.

- **Outliers** are marked with **crosses**.

Tip: So the box shows the 'middle 50%' of the data — the interquartile range.

Example 2

The data below shows the IQs of Year 11 students at two schools, Blossom Academy and Cherry High School.

Cherry High School 93, 105, 108, 109, 110, 112, 113, 115, 116, 118, 119, 120, 120, 121, 123, 124, 126, 128, 132, 134, 144

Blossom Academy 98, 101, 103, 105, 106, 106, 107, 108, 109, 111, 112, 114, 116, 118, 122, 124, 127, 131, 136, 140

a) **Draw a box plot to represent the data from Cherry High School. Use $Q_1 - 1.5 \times$ IQR and $Q_3 + 1.5 \times$ IQR as your fences for identifying outliers.**

- First work out the quartiles (Q_1, Q_2 and Q_3) and the fences.

  - Find the number of data values (n) for Cherry High School. Here, $n = 21$.

  - Since $\frac{n}{2} = 10.5$, the median is the 11th data value. So the **median (Q_2) = 119**

  - Since $\frac{n}{4} = 5.25$, the lower quartile is the 6th data value. So Q_1 = **112**

  - Since $\frac{3n}{4} = 15.75$, the upper quartile is the 16th data value. So Q_3 = **124**

  - The interquartile range is IQR = $Q_3 - Q_1 = 124 - 112 =$ **12**

  - This gives a **lower fence** of $Q_1 - (1.5 \times$ IQR$) = 112 - (1.5 \times 12) =$ **94**

  - And an **upper fence** of $Q_3 + (1.5 \times$ IQR$) = 124 + (1.5 \times 12) =$ **142**

- Now you can decide if you have any outliers.

  - The value 93 is **outside** the lower fence (94), so 93 is an outlier.

  - And the value 144 is **outside** the upper fence (142), so 144 is also an outlier, but there are no other outliers.

  - Now you can draw the box plot itself.

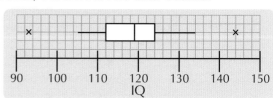

b) **Draw a box plot to represent the data from Blossom Academy.**

- For Blossom Academy:
  - $n = 20$.

  - $\frac{n}{2} = 10$, so the median is halfway between the 10th and 11th data values — **median (Q_2) = 111.5**

  - $\frac{n}{4} = 5$, so the lower quartile is halfway between the 5th and 6th data values — Q_1 = **106**

Tip: Here, the data is already in order, but you should always check.

Tip: Remember, only extend a line as far as the biggest or smallest data value that **isn't** an outlier.

- $\frac{3n}{4} = 15$, so the upper quartile is halfway between the 15th and 16th data values — $\mathbf{Q_3 = 123}$

  - The interquartile range, IQR is $Q_3 - Q_1 = 123 - 106 = \mathbf{17}$

- This gives a **lower fence** of $Q_1 - (1.5 \times IQR) = 106 - (1.5 \times 17) = \mathbf{80.5}$ and an **upper fence** of $Q_3 + (1.5 \times IQR) = 123 + (1.5 \times 17) = \mathbf{148.5}$ This means there are **no outliers** at Blossom Academy.

- So the box plot for Blossom Academy looks like this:

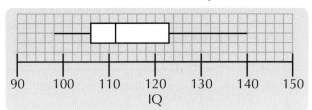

Tip: You might be asked to compare two box plots. There's more about this on pages 260-261.

Exercise 3.3

In this exercise use the fences $Q_1 - (1.5 \times IQR)$ and $Q_3 + (1.5 \times IQR)$ to test for outliers

Q1 The lower and upper quartiles of a data set are 19 and 31. Decide whether the data values 4 and 52 are outliers.

Q2 A set of data was analysed and the following values were found.
$$\text{minimum value} = 4, \text{maximum value} = 49$$
$$Q_1 = 16, \text{median} = 24, Q_3 = 37$$
a) Find the interquartile range.
b) Are there any outliers in this data set?
c) Draw a box plot to illustrate the data set.

Q3 A meteorologist is analysing the daily maximum humidities (%) from Camborne over 41 days in 2015. The data values are shown below:

95, 100, 100, 99, 99, 90, 91, 99, 98, 99, 99, 95, 97, 99, 99, 100, 92, 100, 82, 90, 97, 100, 100, 100, 100, 100, 99, 96, 92, 99, 99, 98, 99, 97, 99, 99, 90, 88, 85, 86, 74

a) Use the results to calculate the median and interquartile range.
b) Find any data values which are outliers.
c) Draw a box plot to illustrate the data.

Q4 The numbers of items of junk mail received in six months by people living in the towns of Goossea and Pigham are shown below:

Goossea 0, 2, 6, 13, 15, 17, 19, 24, 27, 28, 28, 31, 32, 35, 41, 44, 50, 75

Pigham 14, 17, 20, 20, 23, 26, 32, 33, 35, 35, 39, 41, 42, 46, 48, 52, 54, 55

a) Are any of the data values from Pigham outliers?
b) Draw a box plot to illustrate the data from Pigham.
c) Draw a box plot to illustrate the data from Goossea.

Variance and standard deviation

Variance and standard deviation are two related measures of **dispersion** — they show **how spread out** the data values are from the mean. The bigger the variance (or standard deviation), the more spread out the readings are.

Variance

- There are two ways to write the formula for the **variance**. The second one in the box below is usually much easier to use.

$$\text{variance} = \frac{\sum(x-\overline{x})^2}{n} \quad \text{or} \quad \text{variance} = \frac{\sum x^2}{n} - \overline{x}^2$$

- Here, the x-values are the data, $\overline{x}$ is the mean, and n is the total number of data values.

- The two formulas above are equivalent to each other — you can rearrange one to get the other (although you **won't** be asked to do this in the exam).

$$\frac{\sum(x-\overline{x})^2}{n} = \frac{1}{n}\sum(x^2 - 2x\overline{x} + \overline{x}^2) \qquad \text{(multiplying out brackets)}$$

$$= \frac{1}{n}\sum x^2 - 2\cdot\frac{1}{n}\cdot\overline{x}\sum x + \frac{1}{n}\sum\overline{x}^2 \qquad \text{(writing as 3 summations)}$$

$$= \frac{1}{n}\sum x^2 - 2\cdot\frac{1}{n}\cdot n\overline{x}^2 + \frac{1}{n}\sum\overline{x}^2 \qquad \left(\text{since } \sum x = n\overline{x}\right)$$

$$= \frac{1}{n}\sum x^2 - 2\cdot\frac{1}{n}\cdot n\overline{x}^2 + \frac{1}{n}\cdot n\overline{x}^2 \qquad \left(\text{since } \sum\overline{x}^2 = n\overline{x}^2\right)$$

$$= \frac{1}{n}\sum x^2 - \overline{x}^2 = \frac{\sum x^2}{n} - \overline{x}^2$$

- Variance is measured in **units²**. For example, if the data values are measured in metres (m), then the variance is measured in metres² (m²).

Standard deviation

The **standard deviation** (s.d.) is equal to the **square root** of the variance.

$$\text{standard deviation} = \sqrt{\text{variance}}$$

The standard deviation is measured in the **same units** as the data values — this can make it a more useful measure of dispersion than the variance.

> **Tip:** The formula on the right basically says:
> 'The variance is equal to the mean of the squares $\left(\frac{\sum x^2}{n}\right)$ minus the square of the mean $(\overline{x}^2)$.' The formula on the left makes it easier to understand what the variance actually is — it's 'the average of the squared deviations from the mean'.

> **Tip:** $\overline{x}$ is just a number, so you can 'take it outside the summation' — i.e. $\sum x\overline{x} = \overline{x}\sum x$.

> **Tip:** You might see the variance formula written like this: variance $= \frac{S_{xx}}{n}$, where $S_{xx} = \sum(x-\overline{x})^2$.
> S_{xx} can also be written as $\sum x^2 - \frac{(\sum x)^2}{n}$.
> Using this notation, s.d. $= \sqrt{\frac{S_{xx}}{n}}$.

> **Tip:** The first variance formula is a bit more fiddly — once you've worked out the mean, you then have to subtract it from each individual data value, before squaring and adding the results, and then dividing by n.
> So it's usually best to use the formula that involves only a single subtraction.

Example 1

Find the variance and standard deviation of the following data set:
$$2, 3, 4, 4, 6, 11, 12$$

- Find the **sum of** the numbers first: $\sum x = 2 + 3 + 4 + 4 + 6 + 11 + 12 = 42$

- Then finding the **mean** is easy: $\overline{x} = \dfrac{\sum x}{n} = \dfrac{42}{7} = 6$

- Next find the **sum of the squares**: $\sum x^2 = 4 + 9 + 16 + 16 + 36 + 121 + 144 = 346$

- Now finding the '**mean of the squares**' is easy: $\dfrac{\sum x^2}{n} = \dfrac{346}{7}$

- The **variance** is the 'mean of the squares minus the square of the mean':

$$\text{variance} = \frac{\sum x^2}{n} - \bar{x}^2 = \frac{346}{7} - 6^2 = 13.428... = \boxed{13.4 \text{ (to 3 s.f.)}}$$

- Take the **square root** of the variance to find the **standard deviation**:

$$\text{standard deviation} = \sqrt{13.428...} = \boxed{3.66 \text{ (to 3 s.f.)}}$$

Example 2

x, **the mean daily windspeed in knots, was calculated for 10 days in June 1987 in Leeming. The data is summarised as follows:**

$$\sum x = 38 \text{ and } \sum x^2 = 154$$

Find the variance and standard deviation of the data.

Tip: This uses summary statistics from a sample of the large data set.

- Find the mean: $\bar{x} = \dfrac{\sum x}{n} = \dfrac{38}{10} = 3.8$ knots

- Variance $= \dfrac{\sum x^2}{n} - \bar{x}^2 = \dfrac{154}{10} - 3.8^2 = 15.4 - 14.44 = \boxed{0.96 \text{ knots}^2}$

- Standard deviation $= \sqrt{\text{variance}} = \sqrt{0.96} = \boxed{0.980 \text{ knots (to 3 s.f.)}}$

If your data is given in a **frequency table**, then the variance formula can be written like this, where f is the frequency of each x.

$$\text{variance} = \frac{\sum fx^2}{\sum f} - \bar{x}^2, \text{ where } \bar{x} = \frac{\sum fx}{\sum f}$$

Tip: Remember, $n = \sum f$ and fx^2 means $f \times (x^2)$ — not $(fx)^2$. You could also write the formula as

$$\text{variance} = \frac{\sum f(x - \bar{x})^2}{\sum f}$$

This is trickier to use though.

Example 3

Find the variance and standard deviation of the data in this table.

x	2	3	4	5	6	7
frequency, f	2	5	5	4	1	1

- It's best to start by adding an extra row to the table showing the values of fx.

x	2	3	4	5	6	7
frequency, f	2	5	5	4	1	1
fx	4	15	20	20	6	7

- The **number** of values is: $\sum f = 2 + 5 + 5 + 4 + 1 + 1 = 18$

- The **sum** of the values is: $\sum fx = 4 + 15 + 20 + 20 + 6 + 7 = 72$

- So the **mean** of the values is: $\bar{x} = \dfrac{\sum fx}{\sum f} = \dfrac{72}{18} = 4$

- Now add two more rows to your table showing x^2 and fx^2.

x^2	4	9	16	25	36	49
fx^2	8	45	80	100	36	49

- So $\sum fx^2 = 8 + 45 + 80 + 100 + 36 + 49 = 318$

- And now you can find the variance:

$$\text{variance} = \frac{\sum fx^2}{\sum f} - \bar{x}^2 = \frac{318}{18} - 4^2 = 1.666... = \boxed{1.67 \text{ (to 3 s.f.)}}$$

- Then take the **square root** of the variance to find the **standard deviation**:

$$\text{standard deviation} = \sqrt{1.666...} = \boxed{1.29 \text{ (to 3 s.f.)}}$$

Tip: This is the same assumption you used when you found the mean of grouped data on page 238.

If your data is **grouped**, then you can only **estimate** the variance and standard deviation (because you don't know the actual data values — see page 238).

In this case, assume that each data value is equal to the **class mid-point**. Then go through the same steps as in the example on the previous page.

Tip: The variance is sometimes labelled σ^2 (where σ is the Greek letter 'sigma'), or sometimes s^2. There is a difference, although you **don't** need to know about it right now.

But if you're curious...
The symbol σ^2 is used when you have information about an entire **population**, and the symbol s^2 is used when you only have information about a **sample**.

σ^2 and s^2 are actually worked out slightly differently too. (The method in this book is the one for working out σ^2.)

Example 4

The heights of sunflowers in a garden were measured, and are recorded in the table below.

Height of sunflower, h (cm)	$150 \leq h < 170$	$170 \leq h < 190$	$190 \leq h < 210$	$210 \leq h < 230$
Frequency, f	5	10	12	3

Estimate the variance and the standard deviation of the heights.

- Start by adding extra rows for the class mid-points, x, as well as fx, x^2 and fx^2:

Height of sunflower, h (cm)	$150 \leq h < 170$	$170 \leq h < 190$	$190 \leq h < 210$	$210 \leq h < 230$
Frequency, f	5	10	12	3
Class mid-point, x	160	180	200	220
fx	800	1800	2400	660
x^2	25 600	32 400	40 000	48 400
fx^2	128 000	324 000	480 000	145 200

- The **number** of values is: $\sum f = 5 + 10 + 12 + 3 = 30$

- The **sum** of the values is: $\sum fx = 800 + 1800 + 2400 + 660 = 5660$

- So the **mean** of the values is: $\bar{x} = \dfrac{\sum fx}{\sum f} = \dfrac{5660}{30}$

Tip: Remember, variance takes 'squared' units.

- $\sum fx^2 = 128\ 000 + 324\ 000 + 480\ 000 + 145\ 200 = 1\ 077\ 200$

$$\text{variance} = \frac{\sum fx^2}{\sum f} - \bar{x}^2 = \frac{1\ 077\ 200}{30} - \left(\frac{5660}{30}\right)^2 = 311.5555...$$

$$= 312 \text{ cm}^2 \text{ (to 3 s.f.)}$$

- And standard deviation $= \sqrt{311.5555...} = 17.7$ (to 3 s.f.)

Outliers (see page 249) are freak pieces of data — you can use the mean and standard deviation to define them. Outliers are data values that lie more than **3 standard deviations** away from the mean. So value x is an outlier if:

Tip: On page 249, outliers were defined using Q_1, Q_3 and the interquartile range.

> **either:** $x < \bar{x} - 3$ standard deviations
> **or:** $x > \bar{x} + 3$ standard deviations

Outliers **affect** the mean, variance and standard deviation so being able to find them is important — this is known as '**cleaning data**'.

Example 5

x, the mean daily windspeed in knots (kn), was calculated for 10 days in 2015 in Hurn. The data is summarised as follows:

$$\sum x = 63 \text{ and } \sum x^2 = 441$$

The highest x-value is 10 knots. Use the fences $\bar{x} - 3$ standard deviations and $\bar{x} + 3$ standard deviations to decide whether this is an outlier.

Tip: This uses summary statistics from a sample of the large data set.

- Find the mean: $\bar{x} = \dfrac{\sum x}{n} = \dfrac{63}{10} = 6.3 \text{ kn}$

- Variance $= \dfrac{\sum x^2}{n} - \bar{x}^2 = \dfrac{441}{10} - 6.3^2 = 44.1 - 39.69 = 4.41 \text{ kn}^2$

- Standard deviation $= \sqrt{\text{variance}} = \sqrt{4.41} = 2.1 \text{ kn}$

- $\bar{x} - 3$ standard deviations $= 6.3 - (3 \times 2.1) = 0$
  $\bar{x} + 3$ standard deviations $= 6.3 + (3 \times 2.1) = 12.6$

  The x-value 10 kn is inside the lower and upper fences, so it is not an outlier.

Tip: Windspeed cannot be negative, so only values $x > 12.6$ would be classed as outliers.

On page 241, you saw that different measures of **location** (such as the mean) can be useful in different ways.

Now it's time to do the same for measures of **dispersion** — the range, interquartile range, variance and standard deviation.

Range

- The range is the **easiest** measure of dispersion to calculate.

- But it's heavily affected by even a **single** extreme value / outlier. And it depends on only **two** data values — it **doesn't** tell you anything about how spread out the rest of the values are.

Interquartile range

- It's **not** affected by **extreme values** — so if your data contains **outliers**, then the interquartile range is a good measure of dispersion to use.

- It's fairly **tricky** to work out.

Variance

- The variance depends on **all** the data values — so no values are 'ignored'.

- But it's **tricky** to work out, and is affected by **extreme values** / **outliers**.

- It's also expressed in **different units** from the actual data values, so it can be difficult to interpret.

Standard deviation

- Like the variance, the standard deviation depends on **all** the data values.

- But it is also **tricky** to work out, and affected by **extreme values** / **outliers**.

- It has the **same units** as the data values so it is easier to interpret.

In the exam, you might be asked why a particular measure of dispersion (or location) is **suitable** for that data. You'll have to use these pros and cons and **relate** them to the data, as well as saying what they mean **in the context** of the situation.

Q1 The attendance figures (x) for Wessex Football Club's first six matches of the season were: 756, 755, 764, 778, 754, 759.

   a) Find the mean ($\bar{x}$) of these attendance figures.

   b) Calculate the sum of the squares of the attendance figures, $\sum x^2$.

   c) Use your answers to find the variance of the attendance figures.

   d) Hence find the standard deviation of the attendance figures.

   e) Explain why the standard deviation is a reasonable measure of dispersion to use with this data.

Q2 The figures for the number of TVs (x) in the households of 20 students are shown in the table below.

x	1	2	3	4
frequency, f	7	8	4	1

   a) Find the mean number of TVs ($\bar{x}$) in the 20 households.

   b) By adding rows showing x^2 and fx^2 to the table, find $\sum fx^2$.

   c) Calculate the variance for the data above.

   d) Hence find the standard deviation.

Q3 Hint: Use the full fraction (or your calculator's memory function) to make sure your answer is accurate.

Q3 x, the daily total rainfall in mm, was measured for 100 days in 1987 in Heathrow. The data is summarised as follows:
$$\sum x = 290.7 \text{ and } \sum x^2 = 6150.83$$

   a) Find the standard deviation for this data.

   b) Decide whether the x-value 35.5 mm is an outlier or not.

Q4 The yields (w, in kg) of potatoes from a number of allotments is shown in the grouped frequency table on the right.

Yield, w (kg)	Frequency
$50 \leq w < 60$	23
$60 \leq w < 70$	12
$70 \leq w < 80$	15
$80 \leq w < 90$	6
$90 \leq w < 100$	2

   a) Estimate the variance for this data.

   b) Estimate the standard deviation.

   c) Explain why your answers to a) and b) are estimates.

Q5 Hint: Find the combined mean using the method on p.235, then use a similar process to find the combined sum of squares (you'll have to substitute the values you know into the variance formula).

Q5 Su and Ellen are collecting data on the durations of the eruptions of the volcano in their garden. Between them, they have recorded the duration of the last 60 eruptions.

   • Su has timed 23 eruptions, with an average duration of 3.42 minutes and a standard deviation of 1.07 minutes.

   • Ellen has timed 37 eruptions, with an average duration of 3.92 minutes and a standard deviation of 0.97 minutes.

They decide to combine their observations into one large data set.

   a) Calculate the mean duration of all the observed eruptions.

   b) Find the variance of the set of 60 durations.

   c) Find the standard deviation of the set of 60 durations.

Coding

Coding means doing something to all the readings in your data set to make the numbers easier to work with. That could mean:

- **adding** a number to (or **subtracting** a number from) all your readings,

- **multiplying** (or **dividing**) all your readings by a number,

- **both** of the above.

For example, finding the mean of 1831, 1832 and 1836 looks complicated. But if you subtract 1830 from each number, then finding the mean of what's left (1, 2 and 6) is much easier — it's 3. So the mean of the original numbers must be 1833 (once you've 'undone' the coding).

- You have to change your original variable, x, to a different one, such as y (so in the example above, if $x = 1831$, then $y = 1$).

- An **original** data value x will be related to a **coded** data value y by an equation of this form: ➙ $\boxed{y = \dfrac{x-a}{b}}$ where a and b are numbers you choose.

- The mean and standard deviation of the **original** data values will then be related to the mean and standard deviation of the **coded** data values by the following equations:

  - $\overline{y} = \dfrac{\overline{x}-a}{b}$, where $\overline{x}$ and $\overline{y}$ are the means of variables x and y

  - standard deviation of $y = \dfrac{\text{standard deviation of } x}{b}$

Tip: Code the data by choosing what to add/subtract and multiply/divide by based on what makes your data easiest to work with. Then work out what you're asked to find using the coded data. Finally 'undo' the coding — that's coding in a nutshell.

Tip: Because 'a' in the coding formula shifts the entire data set, it doesn't affect the spread. So the formula connecting the coded and uncoded standard deviations depends only on 'b'.

Note that if you don't multiply or divide your readings by anything (i.e. if b = 1), then the dispersion isn't changed.

Example 1

Find the mean and standard deviation of:
1 862 020, 1 862 040, 1 862 010 and 1 862 050.

- All the **original** data values (call them x) start with the same four digits (1862) — so start by subtracting 1 862 000 from every reading to leave 20, 40, 10 and 50.

- You can then make life even simpler by dividing by 10 — giving 2, 4, 1 and 5. These are the **coded** data values (call them y).

- So putting those steps together, each x-value is related to a corresponding y-value by the equation: $y = \dfrac{x - 1862\,000}{10}$

- Now work out the **mean** and **standard deviation** of the (easy-to-use) coded values. $\overline{y} = \dfrac{2+4+1+5}{4} = \dfrac{12}{4} = 3$

$$\text{standard deviation of } y = \sqrt{\dfrac{2^2 + 4^2 + 1^2 + 5^2}{4} - 3^2}$$
$$= \sqrt{\dfrac{46}{4} - 9} = \sqrt{2.5} = 1.58 \text{ to 3 s.f.}$$

Tip: This means a = 1 862 000 and b = 10.

Tip: Remember, standard deviation
$$= \sqrt{\dfrac{\sum x^2}{n} - \overline{x}^2}$$

- Then find the mean and standard deviation of the original values using the formulas above.

- $\overline{y} = \dfrac{\overline{x}-a}{b}$, so $\overline{x} = a + b\overline{y}$. So $\overline{x} = 1\,862\,000 + 10\overline{y}$
$$= 1\,862\,000 + (10 \times 3) = \boxed{1\,862\,030}$$

- And standard deviation of $y = \dfrac{\text{standard deviation of } x}{b}$

So standard deviation of $x = b \times$ standard deviation of y
$$= 10 \times 1.58 = \boxed{15.8 \text{ (to 3 s.f.)}}$$

Carry out the method in exactly the same way with **grouped** data. However, with grouped data, you assume that all the readings equal the **class mid-point**, and so this is the x-value that you use with the coding equation $y = \dfrac{x - a}{b}$.

Tip: So here, a = 15.5 and b = 10.

Example 2

Estimate the mean and standard deviation of this data concerning job interviews using the coding $y = \dfrac{x - 15.5}{10}$.

Length of interview, to nearest minute	11-20	21-30	31-40	41-50
Frequency, f	17	21	27	15

- Make a new table showing the class mid-points (x) of the original data, and the coded class mid-points (y). Also include rows for fy, y^2 and fy^2.

Length of interview, to nearest minute	11-20	21-30	31-40	41-50
Frequency, f	17	21	27	15
Class mid-point, x	15.5	25.5	35.5	45.5
Coded value, y	0	1	2	3
fy	0	21	54	45
y^2	0	1	4	9
fy^2	0	21	108	135

Now use your table to find the mean of the **coded** values ($\bar{y}$).

- The **number** of coded values is: $\sum f = 17 + 21 + 27 + 15 = 80$

- The **sum** of the coded values is: $\sum fy = 0 + 21 + 54 + 45 = 120$

- So the **mean** of the coded values is: $\bar{y} = \dfrac{\sum fy}{\sum f} = \dfrac{120}{80} = \mathbf{1.5}$

Now for the standard deviation:

- $\sum fy^2 = 0 + 21 + 108 + 135 = 264$

- So variance $= \dfrac{\sum fy^2}{\sum f} - \bar{y}^2 = \dfrac{264}{80} - 1.5^2 = 1.05$

- This gives a standard deviation for the **coded** data of:
standard deviation of $y = \sqrt{1.05} = \mathbf{1.02}$ (to 3 s.f.)

And now you can use these figures to find the mean and standard deviation of the **original** data.

- $\bar{y} = \dfrac{\bar{x} - a}{b}$, so $\bar{x} = a + b\bar{y} = 15.5 + 10 \times 1.5 = \boxed{30.5 \text{ minutes}}$

- And standard deviation of $y = \dfrac{\text{standard deviation of } x}{b}$

So standard deviation of $x = b \times$ standard deviation of y
$$= 10 \times 1.02 = \boxed{10.2 \text{ minutes (to 3 s.f.)}}$$

Sometimes, you won't have the data itself — just some **summations**.

Example 3

A travel guide employee collects some data on the cost (c, in £) of a night's stay in 10 hotels in a particular town. He codes his data using $d = 10(c - 93.5)$, and calculates the summations below.
$$\sum d = 0 \quad \text{and} \quad \sum d^2 = 998\,250$$

Calculate the mean and standard deviation of the original costs.

First find the **mean** of the coded values:

- The **number** of values (n) is 10.
- So the **mean** of the coded values is: $\bar{d} = \dfrac{\sum d}{n} = \dfrac{0}{10} = 0$

Now for the **standard deviation** of the coded values:

- variance $= \dfrac{\sum d^2}{n} - \bar{d}^2 = \dfrac{998\,250}{10} - 0^2 = 99\,825$
- This gives a standard deviation for the **coded** data of:
  standard deviation $= \sqrt{99\,825} = 316.0$ (to 4 s.f.).

Now you can find the mean and standard deviation of the **original** data.

- $\bar{d} = 10(\bar{c} - 93.5)$, so $\bar{c} = 93.5 + \dfrac{\bar{d}}{10} = 93.5$, i.e. $\bar{c} = £93.50$

- standard deviation of $d = 10 \times$ standard deviation of c,

  so standard deviation of $c = \dfrac{\text{standard deviation of } d}{10} = \dfrac{316.0}{10} = 31.6$

That is, standard deviation of $c = £31.60$ (to the nearest penny).

Tip: You might see this given as
$$\sum 10(c - 93.5) = 0 \text{ and}$$
$$\sum [10(c - 93.5)]^2$$
$$= 998\,250.$$
You could then simplify these summations using $d = 10(c - 93.5)$.

Tip: The variables aren't x and y this time, but you can still go through exactly the same steps as before.

Exercise 3.5

Q1 A set of data values (x) are coded using $y = \dfrac{x - 20\,000}{15}$.
The mean of the coded data ($\bar{y}$) is 12.4, and the standard deviation of the coded data is 1.34.
Find the mean and standard deviation of the original data set.

Q2 The widths (in cm) of 10 sunflower seeds in a packet are given below.
0.61, 0.67, 0.63, 0.63, 0.66, 0.65, 0.64, 0.68, 0.64, 0.62

a) Code the data values above (x) to form a new data set consisting of integer values (y) between 1 and 10.

b) Find the mean and standard deviation of the original values (x).

Q3 The table below shows the weight, x, of 12 items on a production line.

Weight (to nearest g)	100-104	105-109	110-114	115-119
Frequency	2	6	3	1

Use the coding $y = x - 102$ to estimate the mean and standard deviation of the items' weights.

Q4 Twenty pieces of data (x) have been summarised as follows:
$$\sum (x + 2) = 7 \quad \text{and} \quad \sum (x + 2)^2 = 80.$$
Calculate the mean and standard deviation of the data.

Q4 Hint: Code the data using $y = x + 2$.

Comparing distributions

In the exam you might be asked to **compare** two distributions.

To do this, there are different kinds of things you can say, depending on what information you have about the distributions. You can:

- Compare measures of **location**, such as the mean, median or mode.
  - You'll need to say which distribution has the higher mean/median/mode, and by how much.
  - Then say what this means **in the context of the question**.
- Compare measures of **dispersion**, such as variance, standard deviation, range, interquartile range or interpercentile range.
  - You'll need to say which distribution's data values are more 'tightly packed', or which distribution's values are more spread out.
  - Then say what this means **in the context of the question**.

Tip: '...in the context of the question' means you need to use the same 'setting' in your answer as the question uses.

For example, if the question is all about the weights of tigers in a zoo, then you need to talk about the weights of tigers in the zoo in your answer as well.

Example 1

This table summarises the marks obtained by a group of students in Maths 'Calculator' and 'Non-calculator' papers.

Comment on the location and dispersion of the distributions.

Calculator paper		Non-calculator paper
58	Median, Q_2	42
30	Interquartile range	21
55	Mean	46
21.2	Standard deviation	17.8

Location:
- The mean and the median are both higher for the Calculator paper (the mean is 9 marks higher, while the median is 16 marks higher).
- So scores were generally higher on the Calculator paper.

Dispersion:
- The interquartile range and the standard deviation are higher for the Calculator paper.
- So scores on the Calculator paper are more spread out than those for the Non-calculator paper.

Tip: Don't forget to give your answer in the context of the question, so here you need to talk about scores on Calculator and Non-calculator papers.

Tip: You might be asked to comment on distributions after you've worked out some measures (e.g. mean or standard deviation).

Example 2

The box plots on the right show how the masses (in g) of the tomatoes in two harvests were distributed.

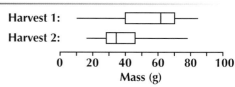

Compare the distributions of the two harvests.

Location:
- The median is more than 25 g higher for Harvest 1.
- So the tomatoes in Harvest 1 were generally heavier.

Tip: You may have to base your comparison on a **graph** or **diagram** instead of numbers.

Dispersion: • The interquartile range (IQR) and the range for Harvest 1 are higher than those for Harvest 2.

• So the masses of the tomatoes in Harvest 1 were more varied than the masses of the tomatoes in Harvest 2.

Tip: This question is to do with harvests of tomatoes, so you need to mention these in your answer.

Exercise 3.6

Q1 The box plots below show the prices of shoes (in £) from two different shops.

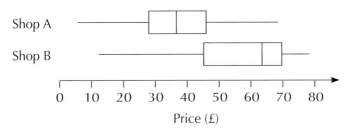

Use the box plots to compare the location and dispersion of the two shops' prices.

Q2 10 men and 10 women were asked how many hours of sleep they got on a typical night. The results are shown below.

Men: 6, 7, 9, 8, 8, 6, 7, 7, 10, 5

Women: 9, 9, 7, 8, 5, 11, 10, 8, 10, 8

Q2 Hint: You need to decide what measures of location and dispersion to find.

a) Compare the locations of the two data sets.

b) Compare the dispersion of the two data sets.

Q3 A travel agent is collecting data on two islands, A and B. She records the maximum daily temperature on 100 days. The cumulative frequency curves for her results are shown on the graph below.

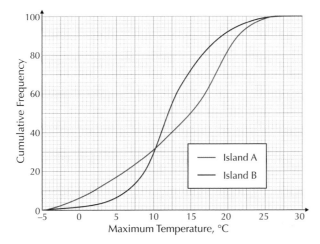

Compare the location and dispersion of the data for the two islands.

4. Correlation and Regression

Correlation measures how closely two variables are linked. On a scatter diagram, a line of best fit is drawn if two variables are linked. Finding the _best_ line of best fit is known as linear regression. This is useful for predicting how one variable will be affected by a change in the other.

Scatter diagrams and correlation

Sometimes variables are measured in **pairs** — perhaps because you want to investigate whether they're linked.

These pairs of variables might be things like:

- 'my age' and 'length of my feet',
- 'temperature' and 'number of accidents on a stretch of road'.

Data made up of pairs of values (x, y) is called **bivariate data**. You can plot bivariate data on a **scatter diagram** — where each variable is plotted along one of the axes. The pattern of points on a scatter diagram can tell you something about the data.

- For example, on this scatter diagram, the variables 'my age' and 'length of my feet' seem linked — you can tell because nearly all the points lie **close** to a **straight line**.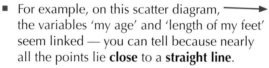

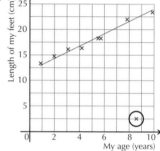

- As I got older, my feet got bigger and bigger (though I stopped measuring when I was 10 years old).

- The **line of best fit** on this scatter diagram lies **close** to **most** of the points.

- The circled point doesn't fit the pattern of the rest of the data at all — so the line of best fit doesn't need to pass close to it. A point like this could show a measurement error (like here), or just a 'freak' observation (an **outlier**).

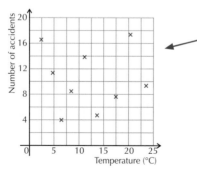

- It's a lot harder to see any connection between the variables 'temperature' and 'number of accidents' on this scatter diagram — the data seems scattered everywhere.

- You can't draw a line of best fit for this data — there isn't a line that lies close to **most** of the points. (It would be hard to draw a line lying close to more than about half the points.)

- You may also see scatter diagrams where it's clear that there is **more than one distinct section** within the population — the data will be in **separate clusters**.

- You may be able to tell from the **context** what the different clusters represent — for example, in this diagram, the longer tracks might all be in a particular style (e.g. classical).

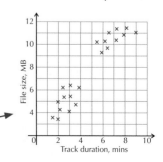

Correlation is all about whether points on a scatter diagram lie close to a **straight line**.

- Sometimes, as one variable gets bigger, the other one also gets bigger — in this case, the scatter diagram might look like this.

- Here, a line of best fit would have a **positive gradient**.

- The two variables are **positively correlated**.

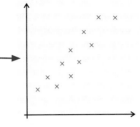

Tip: If the data points lie close to a straight line, the correlation is **strong**. If the data points are more scattered, there is **weak** correlation.

- But if one variable gets smaller as the other one gets bigger, then the scatter diagram would look like this.

- In this case, a line of best fit would have a **negative gradient**.

- The two variables are **negatively correlated**.

Tip: You can also say that there's **positive** or **negative correlation** between the variables.

- And if the two variables are **not** linked at all, you'd expect a **random scattering** of points.

- It's impossible to draw a line of best fit close to most of the points.

- The variables are **not correlated**.

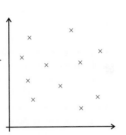

Tip: You can also say there's **no correlation** or **zero correlation** between the variables.

You have to be **careful** when writing about two variables that are **correlated** — changes in one variable might **not cause** changes in the other. They could be linked by a third factor, or it could just be coincidence.

For example, sales of barbecues and sales of ice cream might be positively correlated but higher sales of barbecues don't cause sales of ice cream to increase — they're both affected by another factor (temperature).

Tip: If the data has more than one cluster, you should consider the correlation of **each group separately**, as well as the overall correlation.

Exercise 4.1

(MODELLING)

Q1   The daily total rainfall (mm) and daily total sunshine (hours) on seven random days in Camborne in 1987 are shown in the table below.

Daily total rainfall (mm)	9.3	9.4	2.5	3.5	0.6	7	4.2
Daily total sunshine (hours)	0	11.4	9.1	2.5	5.1	5.9	8.8

a) Plot a scatter diagram to show this data.

b) Describe the type of correlation shown.

Q2   This table shows the average length and the average circumference of eggs for several species of bird, measured in cm.

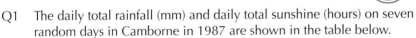

Length	5.9	2.1	3.4	5.1	8.9	6.6	7.2	4.5	6.8
Circumference	19.6	6.3	7.1	9.9	3.5	21	18.7	8.3	18.4

a) Plot a scatter diagram to show this data.

b) Describe any trends in the data.

c) One of the measurements was recorded incorrectly. Use your scatter diagram to determine which one.

Explanatory and response variables

When you draw a scatter diagram, you always have **two** variables. For example, this scatter diagram shows the load on a lorry, x (in tonnes), and the fuel efficiency, y (in km per litre).

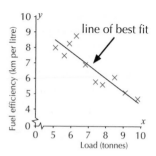

- The two variables are negatively correlated.
- In fact, all the points lie reasonably close to a straight line — the **line of best fit**.
- If you could find the equation of this line, then you could use it as a **model** to describe the relationship between x and y.

Linear regression is a method for finding the equation of a line of best fit on a scatter diagram. Or you can think of it as a method for **modelling** the relationship between two variables.

Before carrying out a linear regression, you first have to decide which variable is the **explanatory variable**, and which is the **response variable**.

- The **explanatory variable** (or **independent variable**) is the variable you can directly control, or the one that you think is **affecting** the other. In the above example, 'load' is the explanatory variable. The explanatory variable is always drawn along the **horizontal axis**.
- The **response variable** (or **dependent variable**) is the variable you think is **being affected**. In the above example, 'fuel efficiency' is the response variable. The response variable is always drawn up the **vertical axis**.

Tip: Latitude is an angle showing how far north or south of the equator a place lies.

The latitude of the North Pole is 90° north, while the latitude of the South Pole is 90° south.

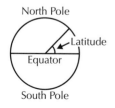

Examples

For each situation below, explain which quantity would be the explanatory variable, and which would be the response variable.

a) **A scientist is investigating the relationship between the amount of fertiliser applied to a tomato plant and the eventual yield.**

- The scientist can directly control the amount of fertiliser she gives each plant — so 'amount of fertiliser' is the explanatory variable.
- She then measures the effect this has on the plant's yield — so 'yield' is the response variable.

b) **A researcher is examining how a town's latitude and the number of days when the temperature rose above 10 °C are linked.**

- Although the researcher can't control the latitude of towns, it would be the difference in latitude that **leads to** a difference in temperature, and not the other way around.
- So the explanatory variable is 'town's latitude', and the response variable is 'number of days when the temperature rose above 10 °C'.

For each situation below, explain which quantity would be the explanatory variable, and which would be the response variable.

Q1 • the time spent practising the piano each week
    • the number of mistakes made in a test at the end of the week

Q2 • the age of a second-hand car
    • the value of a second-hand car

Q3 • the number of phone calls made in a town in a week
    • the population of a town

Q4 • the growth rate of a plant in an experiment
    • the amount of sunlight falling on a plant in an experiment

Regression lines

The **regression line** is essentially what we're going to call the 'line of best fit' from now on. The **regression line of y on x** is a straight line of the form:

$$y = a + bx$$

where a and b are constants. The '...**of y on x**' part means that x is the explanatory variable, and y is the response variable.
You don't need to know how to calculate a and b, but you should be able to interpret their values in context.

Tip: 'b' is the **gradient** of the regression line, and 'a' is its **intercept** on the y-axis.

Example 1

A company is collecting data on the fuel efficiency of a type of lorry. They compare the load on a lorry, x (in tonnes), with the fuel efficiency, y (in km per litre), and calculate the regression line of y on x to be: $y = 12.5 - 0.8x$

Interpret the values of a and b in this context.

- The value of **a** tells you that a load of 0 tonnes corresponds to a fuel efficiency of 12.5 km per litre — this is the fixed fuel efficiency of the lorry before you have even loaded anything on it.

- The value of **b** tells you that for every extra tonne carried, you'd expect the lorry's fuel efficiency to fall by 0.8 km per litre (since when x increases by 1, y falls by 0.8).

Tip: Make sure you give your explanations in the context of the question — so here you need to talk about lorries, fuel efficiency and loads.

Interpolation and extrapolation

You can use a regression line to predict values of your **response variable**. There are two forms of this — **interpolation** and **extrapolation**.

This scatter diagram shows the data from the previous example that was used to calculate the regression line — with the fuel efficiency of a lorry plotted against different loads.

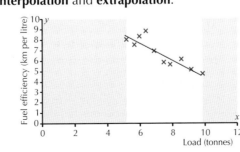

Tip: You can only use a regression line to predict a value of the response variable — **not** the explanatory variable.

In the data, the values of x are between 5.1 and 9.8.

- When you use values of x within this range (i.e. values of x in the yellow part of the graph) to predict corresponding values of y, this is called **interpolation**. It's okay to do this — the predicted value should be reliable.

- When you use values of x **outside** the range of your original data (i.e. values of x in the grey part of the graph) to predict corresponding values of y, this is called **extrapolation**. These predictions can be **unreliable** — so you need to be very **cautious** about it. In the example, you'd need to be very careful about using a value of x less than 5.1 or greater than 9.8.

- This is because you don't have any evidence that the relationship described by your regression line is true for values of x less than 5.1 or greater than 9.8 — if the relationship turns out **not to be valid** for these values of x, then your prediction could be wrong.

Example 2

The length of a spring (y, in cm) when loaded with different masses (m, in g) has the regression line of y on m: $y = 7.8 + 0.01043m$

a) **Estimate the length of the spring when loaded with a mass of:**
   (i) 370 g (ii) 670 g

- (i) $m = 370$, so $y = 7.8 + 0.01043 \times 370 =$ 11.7 cm (to 1 d.p.)

- (ii) $m = 670$, so $y = 7.8 + 0.01043 \times 670 =$ 14.8 cm (to 1 d.p.)

b) **The smallest value of m is 200 and the largest value of m is 500. Comment on the reliability of the estimates in part a).**

- $m = 370$ falls within the range of the original data for m, so this is an interpolation. This means the result should be fairly reliable.

- But $m = 670$ falls outside the range of the original data for m, so this is an extrapolation. This means the regression line may not be valid, and you need to treat this result with caution.

Exercise 4.3

Q1 The equation of the regression line of y on x is $y = 1.67 + 0.107x$.
   a) Which variable is the response variable?
   b) Find the predicted value of y corresponding to:
      (i) $x = 5$ (ii) $x = 20$

Q2 A volunteer counted the number of spots (s) on an area of skin after d days of acne treatment, where d had values 2, 6, 10, 14, 18 and 22.
   The equation of the regression line of s on d is $s = 58.8 - 2.47d$.
   a) Estimate the number of spots the volunteer had on day 7. Comment on the reliability of your answer.
   b) She forgot to count how many spots she had before starting to use the product. Estimate this number. Comment on your answer.
   c) The volunteer claims that the regression equation must be wrong, because it predicts that after 30 days she should have a negative number of spots. Comment on this claim.

Q1 Hint: For part a), use the fact that this is the regression line **of y on x** (and see page 265 if necessary).

1. Elementary Probability

Probability is a measure of how likely events are to happen. We're starting with a reminder of the basics, which you'll have seen before. But it's all important stuff as you'll be using it throughout the rest of the chapter.

The basics of probability

- In a **trial** (or experiment), the things that can happen are called **outcomes**. For example, if you roll a six-sided dice, the numbers 1-6 are the outcomes.

- **Events** are 'groups' of one or more outcomes. So a possible event for the dice roll is that 'you roll an odd number' (corresponding to the outcomes 1, 3 and 5). If any outcome corresponding to an event happens, then you can say that the event has also happened.

- When all the possible outcomes are **equally likely**, you can work out the **probability** of an event using this formula:

$$P(\text{event}) = \frac{\text{Number of outcomes where event happens}}{\text{Total number of possible outcomes}}$$

- Remember, the probability of any event has to be **between 0** (the event is impossible) **and 1** (the event is certain to happen).

Learning Objectives:

- Understand the meanings of the terms used in probability.
- Be able to calculate probabilities of events when all the outcomes are equally likely.
- Be able to identify sample spaces.

Tip: 'P(event)' is short for 'the probability of an event'.

Tip: Remember, you can write probabilities as fractions, decimals or percentages.

Examples

A bag contains 15 balls — 5 are red, 6 are blue and 4 are green. If one ball is selected from the bag at random, find the probability that:

a) **the ball is red**
   - The **event** is 'a red ball is selected'.
   - There are 5 red balls, so there are **5 outcomes** where the event happens and **15 possible outcomes** altogether.
   - So P(red ball) = $\frac{5}{15} = \frac{1}{3}$ ← It's usually best to simplify your answer as much as possible.

b) **the ball is blue**
   - The **event** is 'a blue ball is selected'.
   - There are 6 blue balls, so there are **6 outcomes** where the event happens and **15 possible outcomes** altogether.
   - So P(blue ball) = $\frac{6}{15} = \frac{2}{5}$

c) **the ball is red or green**
   - The **event** is 'a red ball or a green ball is selected'.
   - There are 5 red balls and 4 green balls, so there are **9 outcomes** where the event happens and **15 possible outcomes** altogether.
   - So P(red or green ball) = $\frac{9}{15} = \frac{3}{5}$

Tip: Always check that your probability is between 0 and 1.

The sample space

The **sample space** (called S) is the set of **all possible outcomes** of a trial. Drawing a **diagram** of the sample space can help you to count the outcomes you're interested in. Then it's an easy task to find probabilities using the formula on the previous page.

If a trial consists of two separate activities, then a good way to draw your sample space is as a grid.

Example 1

Tip: Because the dice is being rolled twice, the outcomes here are a **combination** of the score on the first roll and the score on the second roll.

Tip: When there are two completely separate parts to an experiment, like the two dice rolls here, the total number of outcomes equals the number of outcomes for one part × the number of outcomes for the other part.

A six-sided dice is rolled twice.

a) Draw a sample-space diagram to show all the possible outcomes.

- Draw a pair of axes, with the outcomes for the first roll on one axis and the outcomes for the second roll on the other axis.

- Mark the intersection of each pair of numbers to show every possible outcome for the two rolls combined.

  e.g. 1 then 1

6 × 6 = 36 outcomes altogether

b) Find the probability of rolling an odd number, followed by a 1.

- Circle the outcomes corresponding to the event 'odd number, then 1'.

- All of the outcomes are equally likely. There are **3** outcomes where the event happens and **36** outcomes in total.

So P(odd number, then 1) = $\frac{3}{36} = \frac{1}{12}$

Sometimes, the outcomes you're interested in aren't the numbers themselves, but are calculated from them...

Example 2

Tip: A sample-space diagram can also be drawn as a table — with the outcomes for one activity along the top and the outcomes for the other activity down the left-hand side. E.g:

Bag A

	+	1	3	3	4	5
Bag B	1	2	4	4	5	6
	2	3	5	5	6	7
	4	5	7	7	8	9
	4	5	7	7	8	9
	5	6	8	8	9	10

Two bags each contain five cards. Bag A contains cards numbered 1, 3, 3, 4 and 5, and bag B contains cards numbered 1, 2, 4, 4 and 5. A card is selected at random from each bag and the numbers on the two cards are added together to give a total score.

Use a sample-space diagram to find the probability that the total score is no more than 6.

- Start by drawing a sample-space diagram showing all the possible **total scores**.

- This time you need to show the total score for each pair of numbers at each intersection. e.g. 1 + 2 = 3

- Circle all the scores of 6 or less.

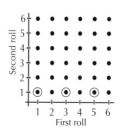

5 × 5 = 25 outcomes altogether

- So now you can use the probability formula. There are **12** outcomes where the event 'total score is no more than 6' happens and **25** outcomes altogether.

So P(total score is no more than 6) = $\frac{12}{25}$

Exercise 1.1

Q1 One card is selected at random from a standard pack of 52 playing cards. Find the probability of selecting each of the following:

a) the 7 of diamonds
b) the queen of spades
c) a 9 of any suit
d) a heart or a diamond

Q1 Hint: A pack of cards is split into 4 suits — hearts, diamonds, spades and clubs.

Q2 The following sample-space diagram represents a dice game where two dice are rolled and the product of the two scores is calculated:

×	1	2	3	4	5	6
1	1	2	3	4	5	6
2	2	4	6	8	10	12
3	3	6	9	12	15	18
4	4	8	12	16	20	24
5	5	10	15	20	25	30
6	6	12	18	24	30	36

a) Find the probability that the product is a prime number.
b) Find the probability that the product is less than 7.
c) Find the probability that the product is a multiple of 10.

Q3 A game involves picking a card at random from 10 cards, numbered 1 to 10, and tossing a coin.

a) Draw a sample-space diagram to show all the possible outcomes.
b) Find the probability that the card selected shows an even number and the coin shows 'tails'.

Q4 Martha rolls two fair six-sided dice and calculates a score by subtracting the smaller result from the larger.

a) Draw a sample-space diagram to show all the possible outcomes.
b) Find P(the score is zero).
c) Find P(the score is greater than 5).
d) What is the most likely score? And what is its probability?

Q5 Spinner 1 has five equal sections, labelled 2, 3, 5, 7 and 11, and spinner 2 has five equal sections, labelled 2, 4, 6, 8 and 10.

If each spinner is spun once, find the probability that the number on spinner 2 is greater than the number on spinner 1.

2. Solving Probability Problems

Venn diagrams and two-way tables are really useful for solving probability problems. Here you'll see how to use them to represent combinations of events, and how to use them to find probabilities.

Venn diagrams and two-way tables

Using Venn diagrams

A **Venn diagram** shows how a collection of **objects** is split up into different **groups**, where everything in a group has something in common.

- Here, for example, the objects are **outcomes** and the groups are **events**. So the collection of objects, represented by the **rectangle**, is the **sample space** (**S**). Inside the rectangle are two **circles** representing **two events**, **A** and **B**.

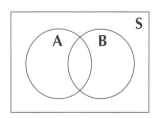

- The **circle A** represents all the outcomes corresponding to event A, and the **circle B** represents all the outcomes corresponding to event B.

- The diagram is usually labelled with the **number of outcomes** (or the **probabilities**) represented by each area.

- As **S** is the set of **all possible outcomes**, the **total probability** in S equals **1**.

- The area where the circles overlap represents all the outcomes corresponding to **both event A and event B** happening.

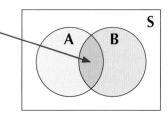

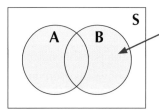

- The shaded area represents all the outcomes corresponding to **either event A or event B or both** happening.

- In probability questions, "**either event A or event B or both**" is often shortened to just "**A or B**".

- The shaded area represents all the outcomes corresponding to **event A not** happening.

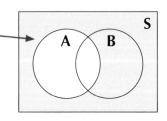

- Since an event A must either happen or not happen, and since P(S) = 1:

$$P(A) + P(\text{not } A) = 1 \implies P(\text{not } A) = 1 - P(A)$$

This can also be written as:

$$P(A) + P(A') = 1 \implies P(A') = 1 - P(A)$$

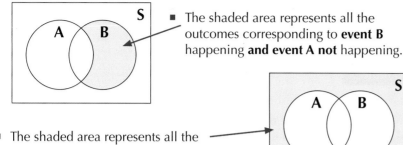

■ The shaded area represents all the outcomes corresponding to **event B** happening **and event A not** happening.

■ The shaded area represents all the outcomes corresponding to **event A not** happening **and event B not** happening.

Here's an example where the **objects** are **people**, and they're divided into groups based on whether they have **certain characteristics** in common.

Example 1

There are 30 pupils in a class. 14 of the pupils are girls and 11 of the pupils have brown hair. Of the pupils with brown hair, 6 are boys.

a) Show this information on a Venn diagram.

- OK, so first you need to identify the **groups**. Let **G** be the group of **girls** and **BH** be the group of **pupils** with **brown hair**.
- **Draw** a Venn diagram to represent the groups G and BH.
- Now you need to **label** it with the numbers of **pupils** in each part of the diagram.
- You're told that there are 6 boys with brown hair, which means there are **6 pupils** who **have brown hair and aren't girls**. Label the area that's **in BH** but **not in G** with 6 pupils.
- There are 11 pupils in total with brown hair, so there are **11 − 6 = 5 girls with brown hair**. So label the area that's in **both G and BH** with 5 pupils.
- There are 14 girls in total, so the number who **don't have brown hair** is **14 − 5 = 9**. Label the area that's **in G but not in BH** with 9 pupils.
- Finally, don't forget the pupils that **aren't in either group**. There are 30 pupils in total, so the number of **boys** who **don't have brown hair** = 30 − (9 + 5 + 6) = **10**. So label the area that's **not in G or BH** with **10** pupils.

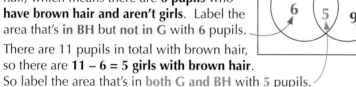

Tip: Each of the groups needs to be based on a characteristic that a person either has or doesn't have. Then if a person **has** that characteristic, they're included **inside** the circle. If they don't have the characteristic, they're outside the circle. E.g. all the girls are included in circle G, and all the boys ('not girls') are outside G.

b) A pupil is selected at random from the class.
Find the probability that the pupil is a girl who doesn't have brown hair.

Using the Venn diagram, there are **9** girls who don't have brown hair, out of the **30** pupils in the class.

So P(girl who doesn't have brown hair) = $\frac{9}{30}$ = $\frac{3}{10}$

Tip: All the outcomes are equally likely, so you can use the probability formula on page 267.

c) A girl is selected at random from the class.
Find the probability that she has brown hair.

Using the Venn diagram, there are **5** girls who have brown hair, out of the **14** girls in the class.

So P(the girl selected has brown hair) = $\frac{5}{14}$

You already know that the pupil is a girl, so you're only looking at the outcomes in circle G, not the whole class.

You also need to be able to draw and use Venn diagrams for **three groups** (or events). In the next example, instead of showing the 'number of objects' (or outcomes), the numbers show **proportions**, but the ideas are exactly the same.

Example 2

A survey was carried out to find out what pets people like.

The proportion who like dogs is 0.6, the proportion who like cats is 0.5, and the proportion who like gerbils is 0.4. The proportion who like dogs and cats is 0.4, the proportion who like cats and gerbils is 0.1, and the proportion who like gerbils and dogs is 0.2. Finally, the proportion who like all three kinds of animal is 0.1.

a) Draw a Venn diagram to represent this information.

- First, identify the **groups**. Let **C** be the group 'likes **cats**', **D** be the group 'likes **dogs**' and **G** be the group 'likes **gerbils**'.
- **Draw** a Venn diagram to represent the groups C, D and G.
- Now you need to **label** it — this time with the **proportions** for each area. It's best to **start in the middle** and work outwards...

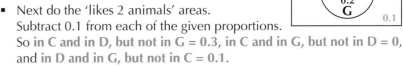

- The proportion who like all 3 animals is 0.1. Label the area that's **in C and D and G** with **0.1**.
- Next do the 'likes 2 animals' areas. Subtract 0.1 from each of the given proportions. So **in C and in D, but not in G = 0.3**, **in C and in G, but not in D = 0**, and **in D and in G, but not in C = 0.1**.
- Then complete each circle by making sure that the proportions add up to the proportion given in the question for each animal:
  in C, but not in D or G = 0.5 − (0.3 + 0.1 + 0) = 0.1,
  in D, but not in C or G = 0.6 − (0.3 + 0.1 + 0.1) = 0.1, and
  in G, but not in C or D = 0.4 − (0.1 + 0.1 + 0) = 0.2.
- Finally, subtract all the proportions from 1 to find the proportion who like none of these animals: **not in C or D or G = 1 − 0.9 = 0.1**.

One person who completed the survey is chosen at random.

b) Find the probability that this person likes dogs or cats (or both).

This is represented by the shaded area.
The **probability** of the person being in this area is **equal** to the **proportion** of people in the area. So you just need to add up the numbers.

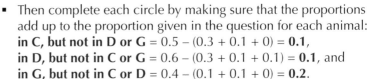

So P(likes dogs, cats or both)
= 0.1 + 0.3 + 0 + 0.1 + 0.1 + 0.1 = 0.7

c) Find the probability that this person likes gerbils, but not dogs.

This is represented by the shaded area.
So add up all the probabilities in this area.

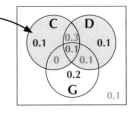

So P(likes gerbils, but not dogs)
= 0 + 0.2 = 0.2

Tip: Label the diagram with proportions this time, because that's the information you're given in the question.

Tip: If they like 3 animals, they'll also be in the 'likes 2 animals' bits. So subtracting this proportion gives the proportions of liking **just 2** of the animals.

Tip: When you select a person at random, the above proportions equal the probabilities of that person being in each area of the diagram.

Tip: You could also do part b) by subtracting the probabilities outside circles C and D from 1.

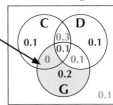

d) Find the probability that a dog-lover also likes cats.

- This is the proportion of dog-lovers who also like cats.
- People who like dogs **and** cats are represented by the shaded area, which forms a proportion of $0.3 + 0.1 = \mathbf{0.4}$ of the whole group of people.

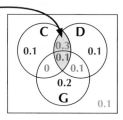

- But you're only interested in the '**likes dogs**' circle, not the whole group, so that means you need to **divide** by **0.6**.
- So P(dog-lover also likes cats) $= \dfrac{0.4}{0.6} = \dfrac{4}{6} = \dfrac{2}{3}$

Using two-way tables

Another sort of diagram you can use to represent probability problems is a **two-way table**.

- The idea is very similar to Venn diagrams — the **whole table** represents the **sample space** and the **cells** represent different **events** that can happen.

- You might be asked to **complete** a two-way table with **missing values** or use one to **find probabilities** of events.

Example 3

A shop sells balloons in three colours (red, blue and silver), and three designs (plain, stars and spots). The table shows the shop's sales of balloons for one day.

	Red	Blue	Silver	Total
Plain	11	21	13	45
Stars	43	29	48	120
Spots	45	20	20	85
Total	99	70	81	250

Each customer bought one balloon. Use the table to find the probability that a randomly-chosen customer:

a) bought a plain red balloon

- The number of plain red balloons sold is in the 'Plain' row and the 'Red' column — it's **11**. Or in probability terms, **11 outcomes** match the event 'customer bought a plain red balloon'.

- The total number of **possible outcomes** is the total number of **customers**. Since each customer bought one balloon, this is just the total number of balloons sold, which is given in the **bottom right-hand corner** of the table. So there are **250 outcomes** in total.

- Using the formula from p.267, P(bought plain red balloon) $= \dfrac{11}{250}$

b) bought a balloon with stars on it

- The **total sales** for each design are shown in the right-hand column.
- The total for the '**Stars**' row is **120**. In other words, **120 outcomes** match the **event** 'the customer bought a balloon with stars on it'.

- So using the formula, P(bought balloon with stars) $= \dfrac{120}{250} = \dfrac{12}{25}$

c) bought a balloon that was blue or had spots

- The number of outcomes you need here is the **total** number of **blue** balloons, plus the number of **red** and **silver** balloons with **spots**. So that's $70 + 45 + 20 = \mathbf{135}$ **outcomes**.

- So using the formula, P(bought a blue or spotty balloon) $= \dfrac{135}{250} = \dfrac{27}{50}$

Tip: The total number of possible outcomes is actually the total number of customers. But each customer bought one balloon, so this is just equal to the total number of balloons sold.

Tip: In part c), you could also find the number of outcomes that match the event by adding up the total number of balloons with spots, the number of blue plain balloons and the number of blue balloons with stars. You get the same answer: $85 + 21 + 29 = 135$.

In the next example, the two-way table shows **proportions** instead of the number of objects (you saw something similar with Venn diagrams on p.272).

Example 4

In any week, Carmelita goes to a maximum of two evening classes. She goes to a dance class, to a knitting class, to both classes, or to neither class.

The probability, P(D), that she attends the dance class is 0.6, the probability, P(K), that she attends the knitting class is 0.3, and the probability that she attends both classes is 0.15.

a) Draw a two-way table showing the probabilities of all possible outcomes.

Tip: It doesn't matter which event goes along the top and which goes down the side.

- If you decide to put D along the top and K down the side, you'll need columns for events D and D′ and rows for K and K′.

- Now fill in the **probabilities** you know.

  P(D) = 0.6 — that's the **total** for **column D.**

  P(K) = 0.3 — that's the **total** for **row K.**

  P(she attends both classes) = **0.15**, so that goes in the cell in **column D and row K.**

	D	D′	Total
K	0.15		0.30
K′			
Total	0.60		1.00

  And the **total** probability is **1**, so that goes in the bottom-right cell.

Tip: The Venn diagram for this situation looks like this:

D K
0.45 0.15 0.15
0.25

- Now you can use the totals to **fill in the gaps.**

  For example, 0.3 − 0.15 = 0.15

	D	D′	Total
K	0.15	0.15	0.30
K′	0.45	0.25	0.70
Total	0.60	0.40	1.00

b) Find the probability that in a given week:

i) Carmelita attends at least one evening class.

- Now you want to find the probability that Carmelita attends either the dance class **or** the knitting class, **or both** — in other words, **P(D or K).** This is made up of the probabilities in column D **or** row K, **or both.**

  So P(D or K) = 0.15 + 0.45 + 0.15 = 0.75

Tip: Or you could say that P(D or K) is the total of column D + the total of row K − the cell in column D and row K — see p.276 for an explanation why.

ii) She attends exactly one evening class.

- This time you want the probability that Carmelita attends the dance class but not the knitting class, **or** the knitting class but not the dance class — in other words **P[(D and K′) or (K and D′)].**

- P(D and K′) = 0.45 and P(K and D′) = 0.15.

  So P[(D and K′) or (K and D′)] = 0.45 + 0.15 = 0.6

Q1 Hint: You're given probabilities, rather than numbers of outcomes for each event, so label your diagram with probabilities.

Exercise 2.1

Q1 For events A and B, P(A) = 0.4, P(B) = 0.5 and P(A and B) = 0.15.
    a) Draw a Venn diagram to represent events A and B.
    b) What is P(neither A nor B)?

Q2   Rich only ever buys two brands of tea, 'BC Tops' and 'Cumbria Tea', and two brands of coffee, 'Nenco' and 'Yescafé'. On his weekly shopping trip, Rich buys either one brand of tea or no tea, and either one brand of coffee, or no coffee.

Q2 Hint: In a two-way table, the totals of the rows and the totals of the columns should each add up to the number in the bottom right-hand cell of the table.

a) Copy and complete the two-way table below, which shows the probabilities for each combination of tea and coffee Rich might buy in any one week.

	BC Tops	Cumbria	No tea	Total
Nenco	0.16	0.07		
Yescafé	0.11			0.18
No coffee		0.12	0.14	
Total	0.51		0.27	1

b) Find the probability that, on any given shopping trip:

(i)   Rich buys Cumbria Tea and Yescafé,

(ii)   Rich buys coffee,

(iii)   Rich buys tea but no coffee.

Q3   A sixth form college has 144 students.
46 of the students study maths, 38 study physics and 19 study both.

Q3 Hint: Draw the table and fill in the numbers given in the question — you should then be able to work out all the missing numbers.

a) Represent the information given above using a two-way table.

b) Find the probability that a randomly selected student from the college studies at least one of either maths or physics.

c) What is the probability that a randomly chosen maths student also studies physics?

Q4   Use the Venn diagram to find the following probabilities:

Q4 Hint: If two circles don't overlap, it means the events can't both happen.

a) P(L and M)

b) P(L and N)

c) P(N and not L)

d) P(neither L nor M nor N)

e) P(L or M)

f) P(not M)

Q5   Two hundred people were asked which of Spain, France and Germany they have visited. The results are shown in the diagram.

Find the probability that a randomly selected person has been to:

Q5b) Hint: The total number of people you're interested in here is just the number who have been to France.

a) none of the three countries

b) Germany, given that they have been to France

c) Spain, but not France

Q6   1000 football supporters were asked if they go to home league matches, away league matches, or cup matches. 560 go to home matches, 420 go to away matches, and 120 go to cup matches. 240 go to home and away matches, 80 go to home and cup matches, and 60 go to away and cup matches. 40 go to all 3 types of match.

Find the probability that a randomly selected supporter goes to:

a) exactly two types of match   b) at least one type of match

3. Laws of Probability

Learning Objectives:

- Be able to use the addition law to find probabilities.
- Be able to recognise mutually exclusive events.
- Be able to recognise independent events.
- Be able to use the product law for independent events.
- Be able to understand and use tree diagrams.

There are two main probability laws you need to know — the addition law and the product law for independent events. You'll see how to use these laws to find probabilities, and how to use them in real-life situations.

The addition law

For **two events**, A and B:

$$P(A \text{ or } B) = P(A) + P(B) - P(A \text{ and } B)$$

You can see why this is true, using Venn diagrams.

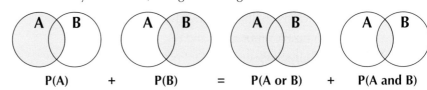

| P(A) | + | P(B) | = | P(A or B) | + | P(A and B) |

To get P(A or B) on its own, you need to subtract P(A and B) from P(A) + P(B).

The addition law is **really useful** for finding missing probabilities — as long as you know three of the values in the formula, you can **rearrange** the formula to find the remaining probability.

Tip: If you didn't subtract P(A and B) from P(A) + P(B), you'd be counting it twice — once in A and once in B.

Tip: You might also see the addition law called the 'sum law'.

Tip: Remember, A′ means "not A". Watch out for when you can use the formula P(A) = 1 − P(A′).

Example 1

For two events A and B, P(A or B) = 0.75, P(A) = 0.45 and P(B′) = 0.4.

a) Find P(A and B).

- To use the formula, you need to know P(A), P(B) and P(A or B). You're missing P(B), so start by finding that.
  P(B) = 1 − P(B′) = 1 − 0.4 = 0.6
- Rearrange the addition law formula to make P(A and B) the subject.
  P(A or B) = P(A) + P(B) − P(A and B)
  ⇒ P(A and B) = P(A) + P(B) − P(A or B)
- Substituting in the probabilities gives:
  P(A and B) = 0.45 + 0.6 − 0.75 = $\boxed{0.3}$

b) Find P(A′ and B′).

- **A′ and B′** is the **complement** of **A or B**.
- So P(A′ and B′) = 1 − P(A or B)
  = 1 − 0.75 = $\boxed{0.25}$

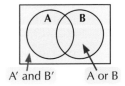

A′ and B′   A or B

c) Find P(A and B′).

- Event A is made up of **A and B** and **A and B′** — see Tip.
- So P(A and B′) = P(A) − P(A and B) = 0.45 − 0.3 = $\boxed{0.15}$

d) Find P(A′ or B).

- It's easiest to do this by drawing a Venn diagram.
- Use the probabilities you've worked out above.
- So P(A′ or B) = 0.3 + 0.25 + 0.3 = $\boxed{0.85}$

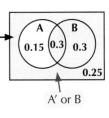

A′ or B

Tip:
A = A and B′ + A and B

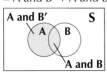

Example 2

On any given day, the probability that Jason eats an apple is 0.6, the probability that he eats a banana is 0.3, and the probability that he eats both an apple and a banana is 0.2.

a) Find the probability that he eats an apple or a banana (or both).

- Let **A** be the event 'eats an apple' and **B** be the event 'eats a banana'.
- You want to find **P(A or B)**, so use the addition law:
  P(A or B) = P(A) + P(B) − P(A and B) = 0.6 + 0.3 − 0.2 = 0.7
- So P(he eats an apple or a banana, or both) = $\boxed{0.7}$

b) Find the probability that he either doesn't eat an apple, or doesn't eat a banana.

- You want to find **P(A′ or B′)**.
  You can either do this using a Venn diagram, or you can use the addition law by replacing A with A′ and B with B′. Like this:
- P(A′ or B′) = P(A′) + P(B′) − P(A′ and B′)
  $\qquad\qquad$ = [1 − P(A)] + [1 − P(B)] − [1 − P(A or B)]
  $\qquad\qquad$ = (1 − 0.6) + (1 − 0.3) − (1 − 0.7)
  $\qquad\qquad$ = 0.4 + 0.7 − 0.3 = 0.8
- So P(he either doesn't eat an apple, or doesn't eat a banana) = $\boxed{0.8}$

Tip: A′ or B′ means everything that's not in both A and B, so you could work out:
P(A′ or B′)
= 1 − P(A and B)
= 1 − 0.2 = 0.8

Exercise 3.1

Q1 If P(A) = 0.3, P(B) = 0.5 and P(A and B) = 0.15, find:
   a) P(A′)   b) P(A or B)   c) P(A′ and B′)

Hint: Remember, you can always draw a Venn diagram to help you.

Q2 If P(A′) = 0.36, P(B) = 0.44 and P(A and B) = 0.27, find:
   a) P(B′)   b) P(A or B)   c) P(A and B′)   d) P(A or B′)

Q2d) Hint: You have all the information you need to use the addition law, replacing B with B′.

Q3 A car is selected at random from a car park. The probability of the car being blue is 0.25 and the probability of it being an estate is 0.15. The probability of the car being a blue estate is 0.08.
   a) What is the probability of the car not being blue?
   b) What is the probability of the car being blue or being an estate?
   c) What is the probability of the car being neither blue nor an estate?

Q4 If P(X or Y) = 0.77, P(X) = 0.43 and P(Y) = 0.56, find:
   a) P(Y′)   b) P(X and Y)
   c) P(X′ and Y′)   d) P(X′ or Y′)

Q5 If P(C′ or D) = 0.65, P(C) = 0.53 and P(D) = 0.44, find:
   a) P(C′ and D)   b) P(C′ and D′)
   c) P(C′ or D′)   d) P(C and D)

Q6   The probability that a student has read 'To Kill a Mockingbird' is 0.62.
      The probability that a student hasn't read 'Animal Farm' is 0.66.
      The probability that a student has read at least
      one of these two books is 0.79. Find:
      a) The probability that a student has read both the books.
      b) The probability that a student has read 'Animal Farm' but hasn't
          read 'To Kill a Mockingbird'.
      c) The probability that a student has read neither of the books.

Mutually exclusive events

Events can happen at the same time when they have one or more outcomes
in common. For example, the events 'I roll a 3' and 'I roll an odd number'
both happen if the outcome of my dice roll is a '3'. Events which have
no outcomes in common **can't happen** at the same time. These events
are called **mutually exclusive** (or just 'exclusive').

- If A and B are mutually exclusive events, then **P(A and B) = 0**.
- A Venn diagram would show the events as non-overlapping circles.

Tip: A Venn diagram for mutually exclusive events A and B might look like this:

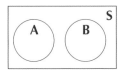

We defined the addition law on p.276 as P(A or B) = P(A) + P(B) – P(A and B).
When A and B are mutually exclusive, we can substitute P(A and B) = 0,
to give a slightly simpler version.

For two events, A and B, where A and B are **mutually exclusive**:

$$\boxed{\textbf{P(A or B) = P(A) + P(B)}}$$

And you can write a general form of this for n mutually exclusive events.
For mutually exclusive events A_1, A_2, ..., A_n:

$$\boxed{\textbf{P(A_1 or A_2 or ... or A_n) = P(A_1) + P(A_2) + ... + P(A_n)}}$$

Tip: With n mutually exclusive events, A_1, ..., A_n, none of the events can happen at the same time as **any** of the others.

In other words, **only one** out of A_1, ..., A_n can happen at a time.

Example 1

**A card is selected at random from a standard pack of 52 cards.
Find the probability that the card is either a picture card
(a Jack, Queen or King), or the 7, 8 or 9 of clubs.**

- Start by defining the two events. Let A be the event 'select a
  picture card' and B be the event 'select the 7, 8 or 9 of clubs'.
- You want to find the probability of A or B. The card **can't** be both
  a picture card **and** the 7, 8, or 9 of clubs, so A and B are mutually
  exclusive, which means that P(A or B) = P(A) + P(B).
- Using the formula for equally likely outcomes:

  $$P(A) = \frac{12}{52} \qquad \text{and} \qquad P(B) = \frac{3}{52}$$

  12 outcomes where event   3 outcomes where event
  happens out of a total of 52   happens out of a total of 52

- So P(A or B) = P(A) + P(B) = $\frac{12}{52} + \frac{3}{52} = \frac{15}{52}$

- This means P(card is either a picture card or the 7, 8 or 9 of clubs) = $\frac{15}{52}$

To show whether or not events A and B are mutually exclusive, you just need to show whether P(A and B) is zero or non-zero.

Example 2

a) **For two events, A and B, P(A) = 0.38, P(B) = 0.24 and P(A or B) = 0.6. Show whether or not events A and B are mutually exclusive.**

- Use the addition law to find P(A and B):
  P(A or B) = P(A) + P(B) − P(A and B)
  $\Rightarrow$ P(A and B) = P(A) + P(B) − P(A or B) = 0.38 + 0.24 − 0.6 = 0.02
- So P(A and B) ≠ 0, which means A and B are **not mutually exclusive**.

b) **For two events, A and B, P(A) = 0.75 and P(A and B′) = 0.75. Show whether or not events A and B are mutually exclusive.**

- This one looks a bit trickier, but you just need to think about the different areas that make up event A.
  P(A) = P(A and B) + P(A and B′)
  $\Rightarrow$ P(A and B) = P(A) − P(A and B′) = 0.75 − 0.75 = 0
- So P(A and B) = 0, which means that A and B **are mutually exclusive**.

Tip: You could also show that
P(A or B) ≠ P(A) + P(B)
— that's the same as showing that
P(A and B) ≠ 0.

Tip: Drawing a Venn diagram can be helpful to see areas.

Exercise 3.2

Q1   If X and Y are mutually exclusive events, with P(X) = 0.48 and P(Y) = 0.37, find:
    a)   P(X and Y)   b)   P(X or Y)   c)   P(X′ and Y′)

Q2   P(L) = 0.28, P(M) = 0.42 and P(N) = 0.33.
    If the pairs of events (L and M) and (L and N) are mutually exclusive, and P(M and N) = 0.16, find:
    a)   P(L or M)   b)   P(L or N)
    c)   P(M or N)   d)   P(L and M and N)
    e)   Draw and label a Venn diagram to show events L, M and N.

Q3   Kwame is planning his evening. The probabilities that he will go bowling, to the cinema or out for dinner are 0.17, 0.43 and 0.22 respectively. Given that he only has time to do one activity, find:
    a)   The probability that he either goes bowling or to the cinema.
    b)   The probability that he doesn't do any of the 3 activities.

Q4   For events A, B and C, P(A) = 0.28, P(B) = 0.66, P(C) = 0.49, P(A or B) = 0.86, P(A or C) = 0.77 and P(B or C) = 0.92.

    Find each of the probabilities below and say whether or not each pair of events is mutually exclusive.
    a)   P(A and B)   b)   P(A and C)   c)   P(B and C)

Q5   For events C and D, P(C′) = 0.6, P(D) = 0.25 and P(C and D′) = 0.4.
    a)   Show that C and D are mutually exclusive.
    b)   Find P(C or D)

Q6　A box contains 50 biscuits. Of the biscuits, 20 are chocolate-coated and the rest are plain. Half of all the biscuits are in wrappers. One biscuit is selected at random from the box.

If P is the event 'the biscuit is plain', and W is the event 'the biscuit is in a wrapper', show that events P and W are not mutually exclusive.

Independent events

If the probability of an event B happening **doesn't depend** on whether an event A has happened or not, events A and B are **independent**.

- For example, if a dice is rolled twice, the events A = 'first roll is a 4' and B = 'second roll is a 4', are independent, because the number rolled on the second roll doesn't depend on the number rolled on the first roll.

- Or, suppose a card is selected at random from a pack of cards, then replaced, then a second card is selected at random. The events A = 'first card is a 7' and B = 'second card is a 7', are independent because P(B) is unaffected by what was selected on the first pick.

Tip: If the first card **isn't** replaced, then A and B are not independent.
If A happens, $P(B) = \frac{3}{51}$, but if A doesn't happen, $P(B) = \frac{4}{51}$.

For two events, A and B, the **product law** for **independent events** is:

$$P(A \text{ and } B) = P(A)P(B)$$

Example 1

V and W are independent events, where P(V) = 0.2 and P(W) = 0.6.

a) Find P(V and W).

   P(V and W) = P(V)P(W) = 0.2 × 0.6 = 0.12

b) Find P(V or W).

   You know all the probabilities you need to use the **addition law**:
   P(V or W) = P(V) + P(W) − P(V and W) = 0.2 + 0.6 − 0.12 = 0.68

To show that events A and B are independent, you just need to show that P(A) × P(B) = P(A and B).

Example 2

A scientist is investigating the likelihood that a person will catch two infectious diseases, after being exposed to one and then the other. The probability of catching the first disease is 0.25, the probability of catching the second disease is 0.5, and the probability of catching both diseases is 0.2.

Show that the events 'catch first disease' and 'catch second disease' are not independent.

- Let A = 'catch first disease' and B = 'catch second disease'.
- Compare P(A) × P(B) with P(A and B).
- P(A) = 0.25, P(B) = 0.5 and P(A and B) = 0.2
  P(A) × P(B) = 0.25 × 0.5 = 0.125 ≠ 0.2

  So, since P(A) × P(B) ≠ P(A and B), the events 'catch first disease' and 'catch second disease' are not independent.

Example 3

For events A and B, P(A) = 0.4, P(A and B) = 0.1 and P(A′ and B) = 0.2. Say whether or not A and B are independent.

To check if A and B are independent, you need to work out whether or not P(A) × P(B) = P(A and B).

From the question, you know P(A) = 0.4 and P(A and B) = 0.1.

You need to find P(B): P(B) = P(A and B) + P(A′ and B) = 0.1 + 0.2 = 0.3

So P(A) × P(B) = 0.4 × 0.3 = 0.12 ≠ P(A and B) = 0.1,
so A and B are **not independent**.

Tip: It might be helpful to draw a Venn diagram to see how to work out P(B).

Exercise 3.3

Q1   If X and Y are independent events, with P(X) = 0.62 and P(Y) = 0.32, calculate P(X and Y).

Q2   P(A and B) = 0.45 and P(B′) = 0.25.
If A and B are independent events, what is P(A)?

Q3   X, Y and Z are independent events, with P(X) = 0.84, P(Y) = 0.68 and P(Z) = 0.48. Find the following probabilities:
a) P(X and Y)   b) P(Y′ and Z′)

Q3 Hint: If A and B are independent, then A′ and B′ are also independent.

Q4   Events M and N are independent, with P(M) = 0.4 and P(N) = 0.7. Calculate the following probabilities:
a) P(M and N)   b) P(M or N)   c) P(M and N′)

Q5   A card is picked at random from a standard pack of 52 cards.
The card is replaced and the pack is shuffled, before a second card is picked at random.
a) What is the probability that both cards picked are hearts?
b) Find the probability that the ace of hearts is chosen both times.

Q6   For events A, B and C: $P(A) = \frac{3}{11}$, $P(B) = \frac{1}{3}$, $P(C) = \frac{15}{28}$,
$P(A \text{ and } B) = \frac{1}{11}$, $P(A \text{ and } C) = \frac{2}{15}$ and $P(B \text{ and } C) = \frac{5}{28}$.
Show whether or not each of the pairs of events (A and B), (A and C) and (B and C) are independent.

Q7   Jess, Keisha and Lucy go shopping independently. The probabilities that they will buy a DVD are 0.66, 0.5 and 0.3 respectively.
a) What is the probability that all three of them buy a DVD?
b) What is the probability that at least two of them buy a DVD?

Q7 Hint: The product law for independent events applies for any number of events.

Tree diagrams

Tree diagrams show probabilities for **sequences** of two or more events.

Here's a tree diagram representing two **independent** trials. There are two possible results for the first trial — events A and not A, and there are two possible results for the second trial — events B and not B.

Tip: This tree diagram is for independent events A and B, where P(B) is the same whether A happens or not.

Tip: The 'and' probabilities are the probabilities of the different sequences of events.

Answers to questions are often found by adding the relevant 'and' probabilities.

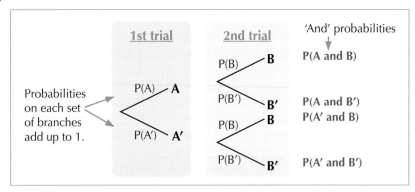

- Each '**chunk**' of the diagram represents one **trial**.
- Each **branch** of a 'chunk' is a **possible result** of the trial.
- To find the **probability** of a sequence of events, you **multiply along the branches** representing those events.
- The **total** of the 'and' probabilities is always **1**.

Example 1

A bag contains 10 balls, 6 of which are red and 4 of which are purple. One ball is selected from the bag at random, then replaced. A second ball is then selected at random.

a) Draw a tree diagram to show this information.

- There are **two trials** — '1st ball selection' and '2nd ball selection'.
- Each trial has **two possible results** — 'red' and 'purple'.
- The **probability** of selecting a **red** ball on each pick is **0.6** and the probability of selecting a **purple** ball on each pick is **0.4**.
- So you can draw a **tree diagram** like this:

Tip: Here, the selection is done '**with replacement**' — so the result of the second selection is independent of the result of the first.

Tip: You can answer questions like b) and c) without using a tree diagram, but often if you draw one, it helps to make things clearer.

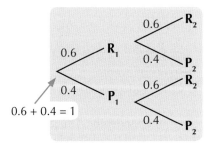

R_1 = 'first ball is red'
R_2 = 'second ball is red'
P_1 = 'first ball is purple'
P_2 = 'second ball is purple'

b) Find the probability that both balls are red.

Tip: This is the same as using the product rule for independent events R_1 and R_2.

- There is **1** 'path' along the branches that gives the result 'red and red'.
- Multiply along the branches R_1 and R_2 to give:
  $P(R_1 \text{ and } R_2) = 0.6 \times 0.6 = \boxed{0.36}$

c) Find the probability that one ball is red and the other is purple.

- There are **2 'paths'** along the branches that give the result 'red and purple' — (R_1 and P_2) or (P_1 and R_2).

- Multiply along these pairs of branches to give:

  $P(R_1 \text{ and } P_2) = 0.6 \times 0.4 = \mathbf{0.24}$, $P(P_1 \text{ and } R_2) = 0.4 \times 0.6 = \mathbf{0.24}$

- Now, you want to find the probability of (R_1 and P_2) **or** (P_1 and R_2), so you **add** these two probabilities together:

  $P(1 \text{ red and } 1 \text{ purple}) = P(R_1 \text{ and } P_2) + P(P_1 \text{ and } R_2)$
  $= 0.24 + 0.24 = \boxed{0.48}$

Tip: The end of each pair of branches represents a different sequence of events (e.g. R_1 and P_2). Only one of these sequences can happen, so they're mutually exclusive — that's why you can use the addition rule from p.278 here.

Tree diagrams for dependent events

Events are **dependent** if the probability of one event happening is **affected** by whether or not the other happens. For dependent events, the probabilities on the second set of branches **depend** on the result of the first set.

Example 2

A box of 6 biscuits contains 5 chocolate biscuits and 1 lemon biscuit. George takes out a biscuit at random and eats it. He then takes out another biscuit at random.

a) Draw a tree diagram to show this information.

- The **two trials** are '1st biscuit selection' and '2nd biscuit selection'. Let C_i = 'biscuit i is chocolate' and L_i = 'biscuit i is lemon', for $i = 1, 2$.

- The **probability** of selecting a **chocolate** biscuit on the first pick is $\frac{5}{6}$. The **probability** of selecting a **lemon** biscuit on the first pick is $\frac{1}{6}$.

- The probabilities for the **second** biscuit depend on the first pick:

  - If the first pick is **chocolate**, then: $P(C_2) = \frac{4}{5}$ and $P(L_2) = \frac{1}{5}$.

  - If the first pick is **lemon**, then there are no lemon biscuits left, so: $P(C_2) = \mathbf{1}$ and $P(L_2) = \mathbf{0}$.

- So you can draw a **tree diagram** like this:

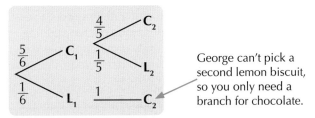

George can't pick a second lemon biscuit, so you only need a branch for chocolate.

Tip: Here, the selection is done '**without replacement**' — so the probabilities for the second selection depend on the result of the first.

Tip: If George took out a third biscuit, you'd get a third set of branches, looking like this:

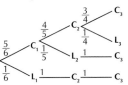

b) Find the probability that George takes out two chocolate biscuits.

- There is **1 'path'** along the branches that gives this result.
- Multiply along the branches C_1 and C_2 to give:

  $P(C_1 \text{ and } C_2) = \frac{5}{6} \times \frac{4}{5} = \frac{20}{30} = \frac{2}{3}$

- So P(George takes out two chocolate biscuits) = $\frac{2}{3}$

c) Find the probability that the second biscuit he takes is chocolate.

Tip: Another way to find P(2nd biscuit is choc) is to find P(2nd biscuit is lemon) and subtract this probability from 1. Some probabilities are easier to work out this way round.

- There are **2 'paths'** along the branches that give the result 'second biscuit is chocolate' — (C_1 and C_2) or (L_1 and C_2).
- You've already found P(C_1 and C_2), so find P(L_1 and C_2) in the same way:

$$P(L_1 \text{ and } C_2) = \frac{1}{6} \times 1 = \frac{1}{6}$$

- Now **add** the probabilities for the two 'paths' together:

$$P(\text{2nd biscuit is chocolate}) = P(C_1 \text{ and } C_2) + P(L_1 \text{ and } C_2) = \frac{2}{3} + \frac{1}{6} = \frac{5}{6}$$

Exercise 3.4

Q1 The probability that Jake will win two consecutive darts matches is shown on the tree diagram.

a) Explain whether the events 'wins 1st match' and 'wins 2nd match' are independent.

b) Find the probability that Jake will win:
   (i) both matches   (ii) at least one match

Q2 A game involves rolling a fair, six-sided dice and tossing a fair coin. A player wins if they roll a '6' and the coin shows 'tails'.

a) Complete the tree diagram by showing the probability on each branch.

b) Find the probability that a person wins the game.

Q3 The probability that a randomly selected Year 13 student has passed their driving test is 0.3. The probability that they intend to go to university is 0.75.

a) Assuming that 'passed driving test' and 'intends to go to university' are independent, draw a tree diagram to show this information.

b) Find the probability that a randomly selected student hasn't passed their driving test and does not intend to go to university.

Q4 A restaurant has found that if a diner orders a roast dinner, the probability that they order apple pie for pudding is 0.72. If they order a different main course, they order apple pie with probability 0.33. The probability that a diner orders a roast dinner is 0.56.

By drawing a tree diagram, find the probability that a randomly selected diner will order apple pie for pudding.

Q5 A game involves picking two balls at random from a bag containing 12 balls — 5 red, 4 yellow and 3 green — where the first ball isn't replaced. A player wins if they pick two balls of the same colour.

a) Draw a tree diagram to show the possible results of each pick.

b) Find the probability that a player wins the game.

c) The game changes so that the first ball is replaced before the second one is picked. Is a player more or less likely to win now?

1. Probability Distributions

Probability distributions show the probability of a discrete random variable taking certain values. They can be used to make predictions about the outcomes of random experiments.

Discrete random variables

First things first, you'll need to know what a discrete random variable is:

- A **variable** is just something that can take a variety of values — its value isn't fixed.

- A **random variable** is a variable that takes different values with different probabilities.

- A **discrete random variable** is a random variable which can take only a certain number of values.

A **discrete random variable** is usually represented by an **upper case** letter such as X. The **particular values** that X can take are represented by the **lower case** letter x.

These examples should help you to get used to the difference between x and X.

> Rolling a fair dice and recording the score:
>
> - X is the name of the random variable. Here it's '**score on dice**'.
>
> - x is a particular value that X can take. Here x could be **1, 2, 3, 4, 5** or **6**.

> Tossing a fair coin twice and counting the number of heads:
>
> - X is '**number of heads**'.
>
> - x could be **0, 1** or **2**.

Probability distributions and functions

A **probability distribution** is a **table** showing all the possible values a discrete random variable can take, plus the **probability** that it'll take each value.

Example 1

Draw the probability distribution table for X, where X is the score on a fair, six-sided dice.

X can take the values 1, 2, 3, 4, 5 and 6, each with probability $\frac{1}{6}$.

> List all the possible values that X can take here.

x	1	2	3	4	5	6
$P(X = x)$	$\frac{1}{6}$	$\frac{1}{6}$	$\frac{1}{6}$	$\frac{1}{6}$	$\frac{1}{6}$	$\frac{1}{6}$

> This notation means 'the probability that X takes the value x'.

> The probability of each number being rolled on a fair dice is $\frac{1}{6}$.

A **probability function** is a formula that generates the probability of X taking the value x, for every possible x. It is written **P($X = x$)** or sometimes just **p(x)**. A probability function is really just another way of representing the information in the probability distribution table.

Example 2

a) **A fair coin is tossed once and the number of tails, X, is counted. Write down the probability function of X.**

- To write down the probability function, you need to work out the **possible values**, x, that X can take and the **probability** of each value.

  The outcome can either be heads or tails, so X can either take the value **0** (if it lands on heads) or **1** (if it lands on tails).

  The probability of each outcome is $\frac{1}{2}$.

- Now you can write down the probability function:

  $$P(X = x) = \frac{1}{2} \quad x = 0, 1$$

  List the possible values of x after the 'formula'.

b) **A biased coin, for which the probability of heads is $\frac{3}{4}$ and tails is $\frac{1}{4}$, is tossed once and the number of tails, X, is counted. Write down the probability function of X.**

- Again, the outcome can either be heads or tails, so X can either be **0** or **1**. The probability of heads, $P(X = 0)$, is $\frac{3}{4}$ and the probability of tails, $P(X = 1)$, is $\frac{1}{4}$.

- This time, the probabilities are **different** for different values of x — so it's best to use two 'formulas', one for each x value. Write the probability function as a bracket like this:

  $$P(X = x) = \begin{cases} \frac{3}{4} & x = 0 \\ \frac{1}{4} & x = 1 \end{cases}$$

  Put each value of x next to the 'formula' which gives its probability.

There's an important rule about probabilities that you'll use in solving lots of discrete random variable problems:

> The **probabilities** of **all** the possible values that a discrete random variable can take **add up to 1**.

For a **discrete random variable** X:

$$\sum_{\text{all } x} P(X = x) = 1$$

We can check this works for the **fair coin** in **Example a)** above:

$$\sum_{\text{all } x} P(X = x) = \sum_{x = 0,1} P(X = x) = P(X = 0) + P(X = 1) = \frac{1}{2} + \frac{1}{2} = 1 \ \checkmark$$

The only values of x are 0 and 1.

The probability of each outcome is $\frac{1}{2}$.

You can use the fact that all the probabilities add up to 1 to solve problems where **probabilities** are **unknown** or contain unknown factors.

Example 3

The random variable X has probability function
$P(X = x) = kx$ $x = 1, 2, 3$. Find the value of k.

So X has three possible values ($x = 1$, 2 and 3), and the probability of each is kx (where you need to find the unknown k).

It's easier to understand if you write out the probability distribution:

x	1	2	3
$P(X = x)$	$k \times 1 = k$	$k \times 2 = 2k$	$k \times 3 = 3k$

Now just use the rule: $\sum_{\text{all } x} P(X = x) = 1$

Here, this means: $k + 2k + 3k = 6k = 1 \implies k = \dfrac{1}{6}$

Tip: It'll often help to write down the probability distribution table when solving problems like these — that way you won't miss out any values.

You may be asked to find the probability that X is **greater** or **less** than a value, or **lies between** two values. You just need to identify all the values that X can now take and then it's a simple case of **adding up** all their **probabilities**.

Example 4

The number of hot beverages drunk by GP Pits Tea staff each day is modelled by the discrete random variable X, which has the probability distribution:

x	0	1	2	3	4 or more
$P(X = x)$	0.1	0.2	0.3	0.2	a

Find: a) the value of a,   b) $P(2 \le X < 4)$,   c) the mode

a) Use $\sum_{\text{all } x} P(X = x) = 1$ again.

From the table: $0.1 + 0.2 + 0.3 + 0.2 + a = 1$

$$\implies 0.8 + a = 1 \implies a = 0.2$$

b) This is asking for the probability that
'X is greater than or equal to 2, but less than 4'.
In other words the probability that $X = 2$ or $X = 3$.

Just add up the probabilities:

$P(2 \le X < 4) = P(X = 2 \text{ or } 3)$ The events $X = 2$ and $X = 3$ are mutually exclusive so you can add the probabilities. See p.278.

$= P(X = 2) + P(X = 3)$

$= 0.3 + 0.2 = 0.5$

Tip: Careful with the inequality signs — you need to include $X = 2$ but not $X = 4$.

c) The **mode** is the most likely value — so it's the value with the highest probability. The highest probability in the table is 0.3 when $X = 2$, so the mode = 2 .

Tip: The mode of a **random variable** is the value you'd **expect** to occur most if you repeated the experiment lots of times — the most likely value.

When it's not clear what the probability distribution or function should be, it can be helpful to draw a **sample-space diagram** of all the **possible outcomes** and work it out from that. For more on sample-space diagrams, see page 268.

For more on sample-space diagrams, see page 268.

Example 5

An unbiased six-sided dice has faces marked 1, 1, 1, 2, 2, 3.
The dice is rolled twice.
Let X be the random variable 'sum of the two scores on the dice'.

a) Find the probability distribution of X.

- To find the probability distribution, you need to identify all the possible values, x, that X could take and the probability of each.

  The easiest way to do this is to draw a sample-space diagram showing the 36 possible outcomes of the dice rolls:

		Score on roll 1				
+	1	1	1	2	2	3
1	2	2	2	3	3	4
1	2	2	2	3	3	4
1	2	2	2	3	3	4
2	3	3	3	4	4	5
2	3	3	3	4	4	5
3	4	4	4	5	5	6

  (Score on roll 2 labels the left column)

- From the diagram you can see that there are only five values that X can take: $x = 2, 3, 4, 5, 6$.

- Since all 36 outcomes are equally likely, you can find the probability of each value by counting how many times it occurs in the diagram and dividing by 36.

Tip: See page 267 for the equally likely outcomes formula.

  9 out of the 36 outcomes give a score of 2.
  So $P(X = 2) = \frac{9}{36} = \frac{1}{4}$

  12 out of the 36 outcomes give a score of 3.
  So $P(X = 3) = \frac{12}{36} = \frac{1}{3}$

Tip: Don't forget to change the fractions into their simplest form.

  Similarly,
  $P(X = 4) = \frac{10}{36} = \frac{5}{18}$, $\quad P(X = 5) = \frac{4}{36} = \frac{1}{9}$, $\quad P(X = 6) = \frac{1}{36}$

- So the probability distribution is:

Tip: You should always check that all the probabilities in your table add up to 1 — if they don't, you've done something wrong.

x	2	3	4	5	6
$P(X = x)$	$\frac{1}{4}$	$\frac{1}{3}$	$\frac{5}{18}$	$\frac{1}{9}$	$\frac{1}{36}$

b) Find $P(X < 5)$.

- This is asking for the probability that X is strictly less than 5, in other words X takes values 2, 3 or 4. Just add the probabilities together.

  $P(X < 5) = P(X = 2) + P(X = 3) + P(X = 4) = \frac{1}{4} + \frac{1}{3} + \frac{5}{18} = \frac{31}{36}$

| **Example 6** |

A game involves rolling two fair dice. If the sum of the scores is greater than 10 then the player wins 50p. If the sum is between 8 and 10 (inclusive) then they win 20p. Otherwise they get nothing.

a) **If X is the random variable 'amount player wins', find the probability distribution of X.**

- There are three possible amounts of money to be won, so there are three possible values that X can take: 0, 20 and 50.

- For each x value, you need to find the probability of getting a sum of scores which results in that value of x.

$$P(X = 0) = P(\text{Sum of scores} < 8)$$

$$P(X = 20) = P(8 \leq \text{Sum of scores} \leq 10)$$

$$P(X = 50) = P(\text{Sum of scores} > 10)$$

- To find these probabilities, draw a sample-space diagram showing the 36 possible outcomes of the dice rolls.
  Mark on your diagram all the outcomes that give each value of x.

Score on dice 1

+	1	2	3	4	5	6
1	2	3	4	5	6	7
2	3	4	5	6	7	8
3	4	5	6	7	8	9
4	5	6	7	8	9	10
5	6	7	8	9	10	11
6	7	8	9	10	11	12

Score on dice 2

- 21 out of 36 outcomes give a sum of scores which is strictly less than 8, so $P(X = 0) = P(\text{Sum of scores} < 8) = \frac{21}{36} = \frac{7}{12}$

- 12 out of 36 outcomes give a sum of scores between 8 and 10 inclusive, so $P(X = 20) = P(8 \leq \text{Sum of scores} \leq 10) = \frac{12}{36} = \frac{1}{3}$

- 3 out of 36 outcomes give a sum of scores strictly greater than 10, so $P(X = 50) = P(\text{Sum of scores} > 10) = \frac{3}{36} = \frac{1}{12}$

- Using this information, draw the probability distribution:

x	0	20	50
$P(X = x)$	$\frac{7}{12}$	$\frac{1}{3}$	$\frac{1}{12}$

b) **The game costs 15p to play. Find the probability of making a profit.**

- A player will make a profit if they win more than 15p — so if they win 20p or 50p.

- So the probability of making a profit is
  $$P(X > 15) = P(X = 20) + P(X = 50) = \frac{1}{3} + \frac{1}{12} = \frac{5}{12}$$

The discrete uniform distribution

Sometimes you'll have a random variable where every value of X is **equally likely** — this is called a **uniform** distribution. For example, rolling a normal, unbiased dice gives you a **discrete uniform distribution**.

Example 7

A lottery involves a ball being picked at random from a box of 30 balls numbered from 11 to 40. The random variable X represents the number on the first ball to be picked. Write down the probability function of X, and find P$(X < 20)$.

- Each ball has a probability of $\frac{1}{30}$ of being picked first, so the probability function is:

$$P(X = x) = \frac{1}{30}, \quad x = 11, 12, ..., 40$$

- P$(X < 20)$ = P$(X = 19)$ + P$(X = 18)$ + ... + P$(X = 11)$

$$= \frac{1}{30} + \frac{1}{30} + ... + \frac{1}{30} = \frac{9}{30} = \frac{3}{10}$$

Exercise 1.1

Q1 For each of the following random experiments, identify:

    (i)   The discrete random variable, X.

    (ii) All possible values, x, that X can take.

  a) Tossing a fair coin 4 times and recording the number of tails.

  b) Rolling a fair four-sided dice (with sides numbered 1, 2, 3 and 4) twice, and recording the sum of the scores.

Q2 A fair six-sided dice is rolled. Write down the probability distribution for the following random variables:

  a) A = 'score rolled on the dice'.

  b) B = '1 if the score is even, 0 otherwise'.

  c) C = '5 times the score rolled on the dice'.

Q3 a) The number of items bought, X, in the 'less than five items' queue at a shop is modelled as a random variable with probability distribution:

x	1	2	3	4
P$(X = x)$	0.2	0.4	0.1	a

    (i) Find a (ii) Find P$(X \geq 2)$

  b) Tommy sells pieces of square turf. The size of turf (in m²), X, requested by each of his customers is modelled as a random variable with probability distribution:

x	1	4	9	16	25	36
P$(X = x)$	k	k	k	k	k	k

    (i) Find k (ii) Find P$(X \geq 5)$ (iii) Find P$(X \geq 10)$

    (iv) Find P$(3 \leq X \leq 15)$ (v) Find P$(X$ is divisible by three)

Q4 For each of the probability functions in a) to c) below:

    (i) Find k.   (ii) Write down the probability distribution of X.

a) $P(X = x) = kx^2$ $x = 1, 2, 3$

b) $P(X = x) = \dfrac{k}{x}$ $x = 1, 2, 3$

c) $P(X = x) = \begin{cases} kx & x = 1, 2, 3, 4 \\ k(8-x) & x = 5, 6, 7 \end{cases}$

Q4c) Hint: Remember that when a probability function is written in brackets, different values of x have probabilities given by different formulas.

Q5 An unbiased four-sided dice with possible scores 1, 2, 3 and 4 is rolled twice. X is the random variable 'product of the two scores on the dice'. Find $P(3 < X \le 10)$.

Q6 A random variable, X, has a discrete uniform distribution and can take consecutive integer values between 12 and 15 inclusive. Draw a table showing the distribution of X, and find $P(X \le 14)$.

Q7 In a raffle, the winning ticket is randomly picked from a box of 150 tickets, numbered from 1 to 150. The random variable Y represents the number on the winning ticket. Write down the probability function of Y and find $P(60 < Y \le 75)$.

The cumulative distribution function

The **cumulative distribution function**, written **F(x)**, gives the probability that X will be **less than or equal to** a particular value, x. It's like a **running total** of probabilities.

To find $F(x_0)$ for a given value x_0, you **add up** all of the probabilities of the values X can take which are less than or equal to x_0.

$$F(x_0) = P(X \le x_0) = \sum_{x \le x_0} P(X = x)$$

Tip: This is written in summation notation and is the sum of all the probabilities for which $x \le x_0$. You'll sometimes see this written as

$F(x_0) = \sum_{x \le x_0} p(x)$.

Remember that p(x) is just the same as writing $P(X = x)$.

Example 1

The discrete random variable H has probability distribution:

h	0.1	0.2	0.3	0.4
$P(H = h)$	$\dfrac{1}{4}$	$\dfrac{1}{4}$	$\dfrac{1}{3}$	$\dfrac{1}{6}$

Draw a table to show the cumulative distribution function F(h).

- There are 4 values of h, so you have to find the probability that H is less than or equal to each of them in turn.

- Start with the smallest value of h:

  $F(0.1) = P(H \le 0.1)$ — this is the same as $P(H = 0.1)$,

  since H can't be less than 0.1. So $F(0.1) = \dfrac{1}{4}$

  $F(0.2) = P(H \le 0.2)$ — this is the probability that $H = 0.1$ or $H = 0.2$.

  So, $F(0.2) = P(H = 0.1) + P(H = 0.2) = \dfrac{1}{4} + \dfrac{1}{4} = \dfrac{1}{2}$

Tip: This sounds trickier than it actually is — you only have to add up a few probabilities.

$F(0.3) = P(H \leq 0.3)$

$\quad = P(H = 0.1) + P(H = 0.2) + P(H = 0.3) = \frac{1}{4} + \frac{1}{4} + \frac{1}{3} = \boxed{\frac{5}{6}}$

$F(0.4) = P(H \leq 0.4)$

$\quad = P(H = 0.1) + P(H = 0.2) + P(H = 0.3) + P(H = 0.4)$

$\quad = \frac{1}{4} + \frac{1}{4} + \frac{1}{3} + \frac{1}{6} = \boxed{1}$

> This isn't a coincidence — $P(X \leq$ largest value of $x)$ is always 1 because it's the sum of all the possible probabilities, which you know is 1.

- Finally, put these values in a table, and you're done...

h	0.1	0.2	0.3	0.4
$F(h) = P(H \leq h)$	$\frac{1}{4}$	$\frac{1}{2}$	$\frac{5}{6}$	1

Sometimes you'll be asked to work backwards — you can work out the **probability function**, given the cumulative distribution function.

- The probability that X is **equal** to a certain x value is the same as the probability that X is less than or equal to that x value, but not less than or equal to the next lowest x value.

- To describe these x values, it can be useful to use the notation x_i. For example, if X can take the values $x = 2, 4, 6, 9$, then you can label these as $x_1 = 2$, $x_2 = 4$, $x_3 = 6$ and $x_4 = 9$.

- Using this notation, the probability that '$X = x_i$' is the same as the probability that 'X is **less than or equal** to x_i, but **NOT** less than or equal to x_{i-1}'.

- This clever trick can be written:

$$\boxed{P(X = x_i) = P(X \leq x_i) - P(X \leq x_{i-1}) = F(x_i) - F(x_{i-1})}$$

Example 2

The formula below gives the cumulative distribution function $F(x)$ for a discrete random variable X:

$$F(x) = kx, \text{ for } x = 1, 2, 3 \text{ and } 4$$

Find k, and the probability function for X.

Questions with an unknown quantity almost always want you to use the fact that all the probabilities must add up to 1.

- To find k, you know that X has to be 4 or less, so:

$$P(X \leq 4) = 1$$

> This is using the fact that all the probabilities must add up to 1.

Substitute 4 in for the 'x' in 'kx'.

$$F(4) = 1$$

$$\Rightarrow 4k = 1 \text{ so } k = \frac{1}{4}$$

Now you can use this to work out the probability function:

- First, work out the probabilities of X being **less than or equal** to 1, 2, 3 and 4. This is easy — just substitute $k = \frac{1}{4}$ into $F(x) = kx$ for each x value.

$$F(1) = P(X \le 1) = 1 \times k = \frac{1}{4}, \qquad F(2) = P(X \le 2) = 2 \times k = \frac{1}{2},$$

$$F(3) = P(X \le 3) = 3 \times k = \frac{3}{4}, \qquad F(4) = P(X \le 4) = 1$$

- But you need to find the probabilities of X being **equal** to 1, 2, 3 and 4. This is the clever bit, just use: $\boxed{P(X = x_i) = F(x_i) - F(x_{i-1})}$

Tip: In this example $x_1 = 1$, $x_2 = 2$, $x_3 = 3$ and $x_4 = 4$.

$$P(X = 4) = P(X \le 4) - P(X \le 3) = 1 - \frac{3}{4} = \frac{1}{4}$$

Think about it...
...if it's ≤ 4,
...but not ≤ 3,
...then it has to **be** 4.

$$P(X = 3) = P(X \le 3) - P(X \le 2) = \frac{3}{4} - \frac{1}{2} = \frac{1}{4}$$

$$P(X = 2) = P(X \le 2) - P(X \le 1) = \frac{1}{2} - \frac{1}{4} = \frac{1}{4}$$

$$P(X = 1) = P(X \le 1) = \frac{1}{4}$$

Because x doesn't take any values less than 1.

- Draw out the probability distribution using this information, so you can read off the probability function. The probability distribution of X is:

x	1	2	3	4
$P(X = x)$	$\frac{1}{4}$	$\frac{1}{4}$	$\frac{1}{4}$	$\frac{1}{4}$

So the probability function is: $P(X = x) = \frac{1}{4}$ for $x = 1, 2, 3, 4$

Exercise 1.2

Q1 Each of a)-d) shows the probability distribution for a discrete random variable, X. Draw up a table to show the cumulative distribution function $F(x)$ for each one.

a)

x	1	2	3	4	5
$p(x)$	0.1	0.2	0.3	0.2	0.2

b)

x	−2	−1	0	1	2
$p(x)$	$\frac{1}{5}$	$\frac{1}{5}$	$\frac{1}{5}$	$\frac{1}{5}$	$\frac{1}{5}$

c)

x	1	2	3	4
$p(x)$	0.3	0.2	0.3	0.2

d)

x	2	4	8	16	32	64
$p(x)$	$\frac{1}{2}$	$\frac{1}{4}$	$\frac{1}{8}$	$\frac{1}{16}$	$\frac{1}{32}$	$\frac{1}{32}$

Q2   Each of a)-b) shows the probability distribution for a discrete random variable, X. For each part, draw up a table showing the cumulative distribution function, $F(x)$, and use it to find the required probabilities.

a)

x	1	2	3	4
$p(x)$	0.3	0.1	0.45	0.15

Find (i) $P(X \le 3)$
      (ii) $P(1 < X \le 3)$

b)

x	-2	-1	0	1	2
$p(x)$	$\frac{1}{10}$	$\frac{2}{5}$	$\frac{1}{10}$	$\frac{1}{5}$	$\frac{1}{5}$

Find (i) $P(X \le 0)$
      (ii) $P(X > 0)$

Q3 Hint: This time you've been given the probability function instead of the probability distribution, but the method is just the same.

Q3   The discrete random variable X has probability function:

$$P(X = x) = \frac{1}{8}, \quad x = 1, 2, 3, 4, 5, 6, 7, 8$$

a) Draw up a table showing the cumulative distribution function, $F(x)$.
b) Find (i) $P(X \le 3)$ (ii) $P(3 < X \le 7)$

Q4   Each table shows the cumulative distribution function of a discrete random variable, X. Write down the probability distribution for X.

a)

x	1	2	3	4	5
$F(x)$	0.2	0.3	0.6	0.9	1

b)

x	-2	-1	0	1
$F(x)$	0.1	0.2	0.7	1

c)

x	2	4	8	16	32	64
$F(x)$	$\frac{1}{32}$	$\frac{1}{8}$	$\frac{1}{4}$	$\frac{1}{2}$	$\frac{3}{4}$	1

Q5   The discrete random variable X has the cumulative distribution function:

x	1	2	3	4
$F(x)$	0.3	a	0.8	1

Given that $P(X = 2) = P(X = 3)$,
draw a table showing the probability distribution of X.

Q6   For each cumulative distribution function, find the value of k, and give the probability distribution for the discrete random variable, X.

a) $F(x) = \dfrac{(x + k)^2}{25}, \quad x = 1, 2, 3$

b) $F(x) = \dfrac{(x + k)^3}{64}, \quad x = 1, 2, 3$

c) $F(x) = 2^{(x - k)}, \quad x = 1, 2, 3$

Q7a) Hint: You need to find $P(X \le x)$ — the probability that the largest score shown by the two dice is no more than x. This means that both rolls must score no more than x, so you're looking for the probability that two independent rolls each score no more than x.

Q7   The discrete random variable $X = $ 'the larger score showing when a pair of fair six-sided dice are rolled (or either score if they are the same)'.
a) Show that the cumulative distribution function, $F(x)$, is given by:

$$F(x) = \frac{x^2}{36}, \quad x = 1, 2, 3, 4, 5, 6$$

b) Hence, find the probability distribution for X.

2. Binomial Distributions

The binomial distribution is a discrete probability distribution, and so describes discrete random variables. But before getting started with probability, you need to revisit binomial coefficients — these were covered in Chapter 7.

Binomial coefficients

It's really important in probability to be able to **count** the possible **arrangements** of various objects. This is because **different** arrangements of outcomes can sometimes correspond to the **same** event — there's more detail about this on the next few pages.

It's slightly easier to get your head round some of these ideas if you think about things that are less 'abstract' than outcomes. So first of all, think about arranging n **different** objects on a shelf.

> n **different** objects can be arranged in $n!$ ('n factorial') different orders, where $n! = n \times (n-1) \times (n-2) \times ... \times 3 \times 2 \times 1$.

Example 1

a) In how many orders can 4 different ornaments be arranged on a shelf?

- Imagine placing the ornaments on the shelf one at a time.
  You have:
  4 choices for the first ornament ,
  3 choices for the second ornament ,
  2 choices for the third ornament ,
  and 1 choice for the last ornament .

Tip: The picture shows one possible order — 1st, 2nd, 3rd, 4th. The white areas are alternate choices for where the ornaments could be placed.

- So there are $4 \times 3 \times 2 \times 1 = 4! = \boxed{24}$ different orders.

b) In how many orders can 8 different objects be arranged?

- There are $8! = \boxed{40\ 320}$ different orders.

Keep thinking about arranging n objects on a shelf — but this time, imagine that x of those objects are the **same**.

> n objects, of which x are **identical**, can be arranged in $\dfrac{n!}{x!}$ orders.

Example 2

a) In how many different orders can 5 objects be arranged if 2 of those objects are identical?

- Imagine those 2 identical objects were actually different. Then there would be $5! = 120$ possible orders.

- But because those 2 objects are **identical**, you can **swap them round** without making a different arrangement. So there are really only $120 \div 2 = \boxed{60}$ different orders in which to arrange the objects.

Tip: 2 objects can be arranged in $2!\ (= 2)$ different orders.

Tip: This is
$$\frac{5!}{2!} = \frac{120}{2} = 60.$$

b) In how many different orders can 7 objects be arranged if 4 of those objects are identical?

- If all 7 objects were different, there would be 7! possible orders.

- But those 4 identical objects can be swapped around in 4! ways (since there are 4! different ways to arrange 4 objects).

- So there are $\frac{n!}{x!} = \frac{7!}{4!} = \frac{5040}{24} = \boxed{210}$ possible orders for the 7 objects.

Now imagine that you have n objects, but x of these are identical to each other, and the other $n - x$ are also identical to each other (so there are really only two different types of object — x of one type, and $n - x$ of the other).

> x objects of one type and $(n - x)$ objects of another type
> can be arranged in $\dfrac{n!}{x!(n-x)!}$ different orders.

You've seen $\dfrac{n!}{x!(n-x)!}$ before — it's a **binomial coefficient** (see page 112).

Example 3

In how many different orders can 8 identical blue books and 5 identical green books be arranged on a shelf?

- You have two different types of object — so the number of possible orders is given by a binomial coefficient.

- $n = 13$ and $x = 8$ (or 5), so there are $\binom{13}{8} = \frac{13!}{8!5!} = \boxed{1287}$ orders.

Counting 'numbers of arrangements' crops up in all sorts of places.

Example 4

a) How many ways are there to select 11 players from a squad of 16?

- This is basically a 'number of different arrangements' problem.

- Imagine the 16 players are lined up — then you could 'pick' or 'not pick' players by giving each of them a tick or a cross symbol.

- So just find the number of ways to order 11 ticks and 5 crosses — this is $\binom{16}{11} = \frac{16!}{11!5!} = \boxed{4368}$

b) How many ways are there to pick 6 lottery numbers from 59?

- Again, numbers are either 'picked' or 'unpicked', so there are $\binom{59}{6} = \frac{59!}{6!53!} = \boxed{45\,057\,474}$ possibilities.

Okay... it's time to get back to the subject of **probability**...

When there are only **two** possible outcomes, these outcomes are often **labelled** 'success' and 'failure'. This section is all about **success** and **failure**.

- For example, when you toss a coin, there are two possible outcomes — heads and tails. So 'success' could be heads, while 'failure' could be tails.

Tip: Or you could call tails 'success' and heads 'failure' — it doesn't matter which is which.

You're going to be working out the **probability** of getting x successes (in **any** order) when you try something n times in total (i.e. in n 'trials').

- For example, if you toss a coin 3 times, then you're going to find the probability of getting, say, 2 heads (so here, $n = 3$ and $x = 2$).

Tip: The 'in part' is explained on page 298.

But the probability of getting x successes in n trials depends **in part** on how many ways there are to **arrange** those x successes and $(n - x)$ failures.

- So to find the probability of getting 2 heads in 3 coin tosses, you'd need to find out how many ways there are to get 2 heads and 1 tail in any order.

- You could get:
    (i)   heads on 1st and 2nd tosses, tails on the 3rd
    (ii) heads on 1st and 3rd tosses, tails on the 2nd
    (iii) heads on 2nd and 3rd tosses, tails on the 1st

Tip: These 3 possible arrangements of heads and tails are given by the binomial coefficient $\binom{3}{2} = \frac{3!}{2!1!} = 3$.

These **different** arrangements of successes and failures are really important when you're finding the total probability of '2 heads and 1 tail'.

Tip: See the next page for finding probabilities.

Example 5

15 coins are tossed. How many ways are there to get:

a) 9 heads and 6 tails?

- This is $\binom{15}{9} = \frac{15!}{9!(15-9)!} = \frac{15!}{9! \times 6!} = \boxed{5005}$

b) 6 heads and 9 tails?

- This is $\binom{15}{6} = \frac{15!}{6!(15-6)!} = \frac{15!}{6! \times 9!} = \boxed{5005}$

Tip: You get the same answer for '9 heads and 6 tails' and '6 heads and 9 tails'.
This is why it doesn't matter whether you call heads 'success' or 'failure' — there are just as many ways to arrange '9 successes and 6 failures' as there are ways to arrange '6 successes and 9 failures'.
In fact, $\binom{n}{x} = \binom{n}{n-x}$ for any n and x.

Exercise 2.1

Q1 a) In how many ways can the letters of STARLING be arranged?
    b) In how many ways can the letters of STARLINGS be arranged?
    c) In how many ways can the letters of STARTER be arranged?

Q2 A school football squad consists of 20 players. How many different ways are there for the coach to choose 11 players out of 20?

Q3 Ten 'success or failure' trials are carried out.
    In how many different ways can the following be arranged:
    a) 3 successes and 7 failures?   b) 5 successes and 5 failures?

Q3, 4 Tip: A **trial** means a situation where there are different possible outcomes. So tossing a coin is a trial, because there are two different possible outcomes. Rolling a dice is also a trial, because there are six different possible outcomes.

Q4 Eleven 'success or failure' trials are carried out.
    In how many different ways can the results be arranged if there are:
    a) 4 successes?   b) 6 successes?   c) 8 successes?

The binomial distribution

I said on the previous page that the probability of getting x successes in n trials depended **in part** on the number of ways those x successes could be arranged.

But there's another factor as well — the **probability of success** in any of those trials. This example involves finding the probability of 3 successes in 4 trials.

Example 1

a) I roll a fair dice 4 times.
Find the probability of getting a five or a six on 3 of those rolls.

- First, note that each roll of the dice is **independent** of the others. That means you can **multiply** individual probabilities together.

- Now... '**success**' here means rolling a 5 or a 6.
  This has a probability of $\frac{2}{6}$, or $\frac{1}{3}$.
  So '**failure**' means rolling a 1, 2, 3 or 4 — with probability $1 - \frac{1}{3} = \frac{2}{3}$.

- There are $\binom{4}{3} = 4$ different possible orders that these 3 'successes' and 1 'failure' could happen in.

  So P(3 successes) = P(success) × P(success) × P(success) × P(failure)
  + P(success) × P(success) × P(failure) × P(success)
  + P(success) × P(failure) × P(success) × P(success)
  + P(failure) × P(success) × P(success) × P(success)

- Each line above contains the same probabilities — each line will equal $[\text{P(success)}]^3 \times \text{P(failure)} = \left(\frac{1}{3}\right)^3 \times \frac{2}{3}$.

- So if you add up all four lines, you find:
  P(3 successes) = 4 × $[\text{P(success)}]^3$ × P(failure)
  $$= 4 \times \left(\frac{1}{3}\right)^3 \times \frac{2}{3} = \frac{8}{81} = \boxed{0.0988 \text{ (to 3 s.f.)}}$$

b) I roll a fair dice 4 times.
Find the probability of getting a six on 3 of those rolls.

- This time, '**success**' means rolling a 6 — this has probability $\frac{1}{6}$.
  And '**failure**' means a 1, 2, 3, 4 or 5 — this has probability $1 - \frac{1}{6} = \frac{5}{6}$.

- You could go through the same process as in a) — you still have $n = 4$ and $x = 3$, so there are still 4 ways to arrange the 3 successes and 1 failure. The only difference would be the probabilities.

- So P(3 successes) = 4 × $[\text{P(success)}]^3$ × P(failure)
  $$= 4 \times \left(\frac{1}{6}\right)^3 \times \frac{5}{6} = \frac{4 \times 5}{6^4} = \frac{20}{1296} = \boxed{0.0154 \text{ (to 3 s.f.)}}$$

Tip: If the probability of an event (X) happening is p (i.e. P(X) = p), then the probability that X doesn't happen is $1 - p$ (i.e. P(X') = $1 - p$, where X' is the event "not X", i.e. X doesn't happen).

Tip: The 4 different arrangements shown are the $\binom{4}{3} = \frac{4!}{3! \times 1!} = 4$ ways to arrange 3 successes and 1 failure.

Tip: Remember... if events A and B are mutually exclusive, then P(A or B) = P(A) + P(B). If events A and B are independent, then P(A and B) = P(A) × P(B).

You could use exactly the same logic to work out the formula for the probability of x successes in n trials, for any values of x and n:

$$\text{P}(x \text{ successes in } n \text{ trials}) = \binom{n}{x} \times [\text{P(success)}]^x \times [\text{P(failure)}]^{n-x}$$

The formula on the previous page is the **probability function** for the **binomial distribution**. It tells you the probability that in a total of n separate trials, there will be x successes, for any value of x from 0 to n.

There are **5 conditions** that lead to a binomial distribution. If just one of these conditions is **not met**, then the logic you've just seen to get the formula won't hold, and you **won't** have a binomial distribution.

Tip: Remember... a **probability function** lets you work out the probability of a discrete random variable taking its possible values.

> A random variable X follows a **binomial distribution** as long as these 5 conditions are satisfied:
>
> 1) There is a **fixed** number (n) of trials.
>
> 2) Each trial involves either **'success'** or **'failure'**.
>
> 3) All the trials are **independent**.
>
> 4) The probability of 'success' (p) is the **same** in each trial.
>
> 5) The variable is the **total** number of **successes** in the n trials.
>
> In this case, $\mathbf{P(X = x) = \dbinom{n}{x} \times p^x \times (1 - p)^{n-x}}$ for $x = 0, 1, 2, ..., n,$
>
> and you can write $X \sim B(n, p)$.

Tip: Binomial random variables are **discrete**, since they only take values 0, 1, 2, ... , n.

Tip: n and p are the two **parameters** of the binomial distribution. (Or n is sometimes called the **'index'**.)

Tip: This formula is in the formula booklet — but you'll have to look in the A-level section to find it.

Example 2

Which of the random variables described below would follow a binomial distribution? For those that do, state the distribution's parameters.

a) **The number of red cards (R) drawn from a standard, shuffled 52-card pack in 10 picks, not replacing the cards each time.**
Not binomial, since the probability of 'success' changes each time (as the cards are not replaced).

b) **The number of red cards (R) drawn from a standard, shuffled 52-card pack in 10 picks, replacing the card each time.**
Binomial — there's a fixed number (10) of independent trials with two possible results ('red' or 'black/not red'), a constant probability of success (as the cards are replaced), and R is the number of red cards drawn. So $R \sim B(10, 0.5)$.

c) **The number of times (T) I have to toss a coin before I get heads.**
Not binomial, since the number of trials isn't fixed.

d) **The number of left-handed people (L) in a sample of 500 randomly chosen people if the proportion of left-handed people in the population of the United Kingdom is 0.13.**
Binomial — there's a fixed number (500) of independent trials with two possible results ('left-handed' or 'not left-handed'), a constant probability of success (0.13), and L is the number of left-handers. So $L \sim B(500, 0.13)$.

Sometimes you might need to make an **assumption** in order to justify using a binomial distribution. Any assumptions you need to make will be in order to satisfy the 5 conditions for a binomial distribution on the previous page.

Example 3

State any assumptions that would need to be made in order for N to be modelled by a binomial distribution, where N is the total number of defective widgets produced by a machine in a day, if it produces 5000 widgets every day.

- There's a fixed number (5000) of trials, and each trial has two possible results ('defective' or 'not defective'). N is the number of 'successes' over the 5000 trials.

- That leaves two conditions to satisfy. So you'd need to assume that the trials are **independent** (e.g. that one defective widget doesn't lead to another), and that the **probability** of a defective widget being produced is **always the same** (if the machine needed to 'warm up' every morning before it started working properly, then this might not be true).

Exercise 2.2

Q1 In each of the following situations, explain whether or not the random variable follows a binomial distribution. For those that follow a binomial distribution, state the parameters n and p.

     a) The number of spins (X) of a five-sided spinner (numbered 1-5) until a 3 is obtained.

     b) The number of defective light bulbs (X) in a batch of 2000 new bulbs, where 0.5% of light bulbs are randomly defective.

     c) The number of boys (Y) out of the next 10 children born in a town, assuming births are equally likely to produce a girl or a boy.

Q2 A circus performer successfully completes his circus act on 95% of occasions. He will perform his circus act on 15 occasions and X is the number of occasions on which he successfully completes the act.

     State the assumptions that would need to be made in order for X to be modelled by a binomial distribution.

Q3 Ahmed picks 10 cards from a standard, shuffled pack of 52 cards. If X is the number of picture cards (i.e. jacks, queens or kings), state the conditions under which X would follow a binomial distribution, giving the parameters of this distribution.

Q4 A sewing machine operator sews buttons onto jackets. The probability that a button sewed by this operator falls off a jacket before it leaves the factory is 0.001. On one particular day, the sewing machine operator sews 650 buttons, and X is the number of these buttons that fall off a jacket before it leaves the factory.

     Can X be modelled by a binomial distribution? State any assumptions you make and state the value of any parameters.

Using the binomial probability function

You've seen the conditions that give rise to a binomial probability distribution. And you've seen where the binomial probability function (below) comes from.

> For a random variable X, where $X \sim B(n, p)$:
>
> $$P(X = x) = \binom{n}{x} \times p^x \times (1 - p)^{n-x} \quad \text{for } x = 0, 1, 2, ..., n.$$

Tip: You might be able to do this on your calculator. If you can, be careful as some calculators have a probability function and a cumulative distribution function (see p.291) — you should be using the probability function for this type of question. Make sure you know how your own calculator works before the exam.

Now you need to make sure you know how to use it.

Example 1

If $X \sim B(12, 0.16)$, find:

a) $P(X = 0)$

Use the formula with $n = 12$, $p = 0.16$ and $x = 0$:

$$P(X = 0) = \binom{12}{0} \times 0.16^0 \times (1 - 0.16)^{12-0} = \frac{12!}{0!12!} \times 0.16^0 \times 0.84^{12}$$

$$= \boxed{0.123 \text{ (to 3 s.f.)}}$$

Tip: Remember... $a^0 = 1$ for any number a.

b) $P(X = 2)$

Use the formula with $n = 12$, $p = 0.16$ and $x = 2$:

$$P(X = 2) = \binom{12}{2} \times 0.16^2 \times (1 - 0.16)^{12-2} = \frac{12!}{2!10!} \times 0.16^2 \times 0.84^{10}$$

$$= \boxed{0.296 \text{ (to 3 s.f.)}}$$

Don't be put off if the question is asked in some kind of context.

Example 2

I spin the fair spinner on the right 7 times. Find the probability that I spin:

a) 2 fives

- For this part, call 'spin a five' a success, and 'spin anything other than a five' a failure.

- Then $P(\text{spin 2 fives}) = \binom{7}{2} \times \left(\frac{1}{5}\right)^2 \times \left(\frac{4}{5}\right)^5$

$$= \frac{7!}{2!5!} \times \frac{1}{25} \times \frac{1024}{3125} = \boxed{0.275 \text{ (to 3 s.f.)}}$$

Tip: There are 7 trials (n) and the probability of spinning a five (p) is $\frac{1}{5}$. So call the number of fives spun X, then:

$$X \sim B\left(7, \frac{1}{5}\right).$$

Now you can use the binomial probability function to calculate probabilities.

b) 3 fives

- Again, call 'spin a five' a success, and 'spin anything other than a five' a failure.

- Then $P(\text{spin 3 fives}) = \binom{7}{3} \times \left(\frac{1}{5}\right)^3 \times \left(\frac{4}{5}\right)^4$

$$= \frac{7!}{3!4!} \times \frac{1}{125} \times \frac{256}{625} = \boxed{0.115 \text{ (to 3 s.f.)}}$$

c) 4 numbers less than three

- This time, success means 'spin a one or a two', while failure is now 'spin a three, four or five'.
- So P(spin 4 numbers less than three) $= \binom{7}{4} \times \left(\frac{2}{5}\right)^4 \times \left(\frac{3}{5}\right)^3$

$$= \frac{7!}{4!3!} \times \frac{16}{625} \times \frac{27}{125} = \boxed{0.194 \text{ (to 3 s.f.)}}$$

Sometimes you might need to find several individual probabilities, and then add the results together.

Example 3

If $X \sim B(6, 0.32)$, find:

a) P($X \leq 2$)

- If $X \leq 2$, then X can be 0, 1 or 2.
- So use the formula to find P($X = 0$), P($X = 1$) and P($X = 2$), and then add the results together.
- This time, $n = 6$ and $p = 0.32$.

- $P(X = 0) = \binom{6}{0} \times 0.32^0 \times (1 - 0.32)^{6-0}$

$$= \frac{6!}{0!6!} \times 0.32^0 \times 0.68^6$$

$$= \mathbf{0.0988...}$$

- $P(X = 1) = \binom{6}{1} \times 0.32^1 \times (1 - 0.32)^{6-1}$

$$= \frac{6!}{1!5!} \times 0.32^1 \times 0.68^5$$

$$= \mathbf{0.2791...}$$

- $P(X = 2) = \binom{6}{2} \times 0.32^2 \times (1 - 0.32)^{6-2}$

$$= \frac{6!}{2!4!} \times 0.32^2 \times 0.68^4$$

$$= \mathbf{0.3284...}$$

- So P($X \leq 2$) = P($X = 0$) + P($X = 1$) + P($X = 2$)
$$= 0.0988... + 0.2791... + 0.3284... = \boxed{0.706 \text{ (to 3 s.f.)}}$$

b) P($2 \leq X < 4$)

- If $2 \leq X < 4$, then X can be 2 or 3.
- You've already found P($X = 2$), so you just need to find P($X = 3$) now.
- $P(X = 3) = \binom{6}{3} \times 0.32^3 \times (1 - 0.32)^{6-3}$

$$= \frac{6!}{3!3!} \times 0.32^3 \times 0.68^3$$

$$= \mathbf{0.2060...}$$

- So P($2 \leq X < 4$) = P($X = 2$) + P($X = 3$)
$$= 0.3284... + 0.2060... = \boxed{0.534 \text{ (to 3 s.f.)}}$$

Sometimes you're better off using a bit of cunning and coming at things from a different direction entirely.

Example 4

A drug with a success rate of 83% is tested on 8 people. X, the number of people the drug is successful on, can be modelled by the binomial distribution $X \sim B(8, 0.83)$. Find $P(X \leq 6)$: MODELLING

- You could use the method in the previous examples, and find $P(X \leq 6)$ by working out $P(X = 0) + P(X = 1) + ... + P(X = 6)$.

- But remember... $P(X \leq 6) = 1 - P(X > 6) = 1 - P(X = 7) - P(X = 8)$.

- So instead, use the formula to find $P(X = 7)$ and $P(X = 8)$, and then subtract them both from 1.

- So using $n = 8$ and $p = 0.83$.

- $P(X = 7) = \binom{8}{7} \times 0.83^7 \times (1 - 0.83)^{8-7}$

  $= \dfrac{8!}{7!1!} \times 0.83^7 \times 0.17^1$

  $= \mathbf{0.3690...}$

- $P(X = 8) = \binom{8}{8} \times 0.83^8 \times (1 - 0.83)^{8-8}$

  $= \dfrac{8!}{8!0!} \times 0.83^8 \times 0.17^0$

  $= \mathbf{0.2252...}$

- So $P(X \leq 6) = 1 - P(X = 7) - P(X = 8) = 1 - 0.3690... - 0.2252...$
  $= \boxed{0.406 \text{ (to 3 s.f.)}}$

Tip: Both methods give the same answer but being clever could save you time in the exam. Here you've reduced the number of probabilities you have to work out from seven to two.

Example 5

When I toss a grape in the air and try to catch it in my mouth, my probability of success is always 0.8. The number of grapes I catch in 10 throws is described by the discrete random variable X.

a) Explain why X can be modelled by a binomial distribution and give the values of any parameters.

- There's a fixed number (10) of independent trials with two possible results ('catch' and 'not catch'), a constant probability of success (0.8), and X is the total number of catches.

- Therefore X follows a binomial distribution, $\boxed{X \sim B(10, 0.8)}$

b) Find the probability of me catching at least 9 grapes in 10 throws.

- P(at least 9 catches) = P(9 catches) + P(10 catches)

  $= \left\{ \binom{10}{9} \times 0.8^9 \times 0.2^1 \right\} + \left\{ \binom{10}{10} \times 0.8^{10} \times 0.2^0 \right\}$

  $= 0.2684... + 0.1073... = \boxed{0.376 \text{ (to 3 s.f.)}}$

Q1 Find the probabilities below.
Give your answers to 3 significant figures.
a) For $X \sim B(10, 0.14)$:
(i) $P(X = 2)$ (ii) $P(X = 4)$ (iii) $P(X = 5)$

b) For $X \sim B(8, 0.27)$:
(i) $P(X = 3)$ (ii) $P(X = 5)$ (iii) $P(X = 7)$

Q2 Find the probabilities below.
Give your answers to 3 significant figures.
a) For $X \sim B(20, 0.16)$:
(i) $P(X < 2)$ (ii) $P(X \le 3)$ (iii) $P(1 < X \le 4)$

b) For $X \sim B(30, 0.88)$:
(i) $P(X > 28)$ (ii) $P(25 < X < 28)$ (iii) $P(X \ge 27)$

Q3 Find the probabilities below.
Give your answers to 3 significant figures.
a) For $X \sim B(5, \frac{1}{2})$:
(i) $P(X \le 4)$ (ii) $P(X > 1)$ (iii) $P(1 \le X \le 4)$

b) For $X \sim B(8, \frac{2}{3})$:
(i) $P(X < 7)$ (ii) $P(X \ge 2)$ (iii) $P(0 \le X \le 8)$

Q4 A fair, six-sided dice is rolled 5 times.
What is the probability of rolling exactly 2 sixes?

Q5 A multiple-choice test has three possible answers to each
question, only one of which is correct. A student guesses
the answer to each of the twelve questions at random.
The random variable X is the number of correct answers.
a) State the distribution of X and explain why this model is suitable.
b) Find the probability that the student gets
fewer than three questions correct.

Q6 5% of the items made using a particular production process
are defective. A quality control manager samples 15 items
at random. What is the probability that there are
between 1 and 3 defective items (inclusive)?

Q7 For each dart thrown by a darts player,
the probability that it scores 'treble-20' is 0.75.
a) The player throws 3 darts.
Find the probability that he gets a 'treble-20' with at least 2 darts.
b) He throws another 30 darts for a charity challenge. If he gets a
'treble-20' with at least 26 of the darts, he wins the charity a prize.
What is the probability that he wins the prize?

3. Using Binomial Tables

Adding lots of binomial probabilities together can be time-consuming if you don't have a calculator with probability functions. Fortunately, you can use binomial tables to help speed up your calculations.

Learning Objectives:

- Be able to use binomial tables to find probabilities.
- Be able to use binomial tables to find values for a random variable given a probability.

Using tables to find probabilities

Binomial tables show the sum of all the binomial probabilities less than or equal to a given number, for certain values of n and p.

Here's an example of a problem solved **without** binomial tables.

Example 1

I have an unfair coin. When I toss this coin, the probability of getting heads is 0.35. Find the probability that it will land on heads fewer than 3 times when I toss it 12 times in total.

- If the random variable X represents the number of heads I get in 12 tosses, then $X \sim B(12, 0.35)$. You need to find $P(X \leq 2)$.

- $P(X \leq 2) = P(X = 0) + P(X = 1) + P(X = 2)$

$$= \left\{ \binom{12}{0} \times 0.35^0 \times 0.65^{12} \right\} + \left\{ \binom{12}{1} \times 0.35^1 \times 0.65^{11} \right\}$$

$$+ \left\{ \binom{12}{2} \times 0.35^2 \times 0.65^{10} \right\}$$

$$= 0.005688... + 0.036753... + 0.108846...$$

$$= \boxed{0.1513 \text{ (to 4 s.f.)}}$$

But it's much quicker to use tables of the binomial **cumulative distribution function** (c.d.f.). These tables show $P(X \leq x)$, for $X \sim B(n, p)$.

So have another look at the problem in the previous example.
Here, $X \sim B(12, 0.35)$, and you need to find $P(X \leq 2)$.

- First find the table for the correct value of n. The table below is for $n = 12$.

- Then find the right value of p across the top of the table — here, $p = 0.35$.

Binomial Cumulative Distribution Function
Values show $P(X \leq x)$, where $X \sim B(n, p)$

②...then find p.

$p =$	0.05	0.10	0.15	0.20	0.25	0.30	0.35	0.40	0.45	0.50
$n = 12$, $x = 0$	0.5404	0.2824	0.1422	0.0687	0.0317	0.0138	0.0057	0.0022	0.0008	0.0002
1	0.8816	0.6590	0.4435	0.2749	0.1584	0.0850	0.0424	0.0196	0.0083	0.0032
2	0.9804	0.8891	0.7358	0.5583	0.3907	0.2528	0.1513	0.0834	0.0421	0.0193
3	0.9978	0.9744	0.9078	0.7946	0.6488	0.4925	0.3467	0.2253	0.1345	0.0730
4	0.9998	0.9957	0.9761	0.9274	0.8424	0.7237	0.5833	0.4382	0.3044	0.1938
5	1.0000	0.9995	0.9954	0.9806	0.9456	0.8822	0.7873	0.6652	0.5269	0.3872
6	1.0000	0.9999	0.9993	0.9961	0.9857	0.9614	0.9154	0.8418	0.7393	0.6128
7	1.0000	1.0000	0.9999	0.9994	0.9972	0.9905	0.9745	0.9427	0.8883	0.8062
8	1.0000	1.0000	1.0000	0.9999	0.9996	0.9983	0.9944	0.9847	0.9644	0.9270
9	1.0000	1.0000	1.0000	1.0000	1.0000	0.9998	0.9992	0.9972	0.9921	0.9807
10	1.0000	1.0000	1.0000	1.0000	1.0000	1.0000	0.9999	0.9997	0.9989	0.9968
11	1.0000	1.0000	1.0000	1.0000	1.0000	1.0000	1.0000	1.0000	0.9999	0.9998

① Find n...

- The numbers underneath your value of p then tell you $P(X \leq x)$ for all the different values of x down the left-hand side of the table. Here, you need $P(X \leq 2)$.

- So reading across, the table tells you $P(X \leq 2) = \textbf{0.1513}$.

Tip: The full set of binomial tables is on pages 378-382. These tables are the same ones that'll be in the formula booklet you'll get in your exam. Only tables for certain values of n and p are included (the biggest value included is $n = 50$, and p goes up in steps of 0.05).

Tip: If you can do this on your calculator, make sure you use the binomial cumulative distribution function instead of the binomial probability function (see p.301).

Example 2

I have an unfair coin. When I toss this coin, the probability of getting heads is 0.35. Find the probability that it will land on heads fewer than 6 times when I toss it 12 times in total.

- Since $n = 12$ again, you can use the table at the bottom of the previous page.

- And since $p = 0.35$, the probability you need will also be in the highlighted column.

- But this time, you need to find $P(X \leq 5)$, so find $x = 5$ down the left-hand side of the table, and then read across.

- This tells you that $P(X \leq 5) = $ 0.7873 .

For these next examples, the value of n is also 12, so you can still use the table on the previous page. The value of p is different, though — so you'll need to use a different column.

But be warned... in these examples, looking up the value in the table is just the start of the solution.

Example 3

I have a different unfair coin. When I toss this coin, the probability of getting heads is 0.4. Find the probability that it will land on heads more than 4 times when I toss it 12 times in total.

- This time, $p = 0.4$ — so find $p = 0.4$ along the top of the table, and look at the entries in that column.

- The tables only show $P(X \leq x)$, whereas you need to find $P(X > 4)$. But $P(X > 4) = 1 - P(X \leq 4)$ — so you can still use the information in the table to quickly find the answer.

- Find the entry for $x = 4$ — this tells you $P(X \leq 4) = \mathbf{0.4382}$.

- So $P(X > 4) = 1 - P(X \leq 4) = 1 - 0.4382 = $ 0.5618 .

With a bit of cunning, you can get binomial tables to tell you almost anything you want to know...

Example 4

The probability of getting heads when I toss my unfair coin is 0.4. When I toss this coin 12 times in total, find the probability that:

a) it will land on heads exactly 6 times.

- Again, $p = 0.4$ — so use the '$p = 0.4$' column in the table for $n = 12$.

- To find $P(X = 6)$, use the fact that $P(X \leq 6) = P(X \leq 5) + P(X = 6)$. This means $P(X = 6) = P(X \leq 6) - P(X \leq 5)$ — and you can find both $P(X \leq 6)$ and $P(X \leq 5)$ from the table.

- So $P(X = 6) = P(X \leq 6) - P(X \leq 5) = 0.8418 - 0.6652 = $ 0.1766 .

b) it will land on heads more than 3 times but fewer than 6 times.

- This time you need to find P(3 < X < 6).
  This is the same as P(3 < X ≤ 5).

- But P(X ≤ 5) = P(X ≤ 3) + P(3 < X ≤ 5).
  This means P(3 < X ≤ 5) = P(X ≤ 5) − P(X ≤ 3) — and you can find both P(X ≤ 5) and P(X ≤ 3) from the binomial tables.

- So P(3 < X < 6) = P(X ≤ 5) − P(X ≤ 3) = 0.6652 − 0.2253 = $\boxed{0.4399}$.

Tip: This time, call A the event 'X ≤ 3', and B the event '3 < X ≤ 5' — then A and B are mutually exclusive, with P(A or B)
= P(X ≤ 3 or 3 < X ≤ 5)
= P(X ≤ 5)

There's an easy way to remember which probability you need to subtract. For example, suppose you need to find P(a < X ≤ b).

- Use the table to find **P(X ≤ b)** — the probability that X is less than or equal to the largest value satisfying the inequality 'a < X ≤ b'...

- ...**and subtract P(X ≤ a)** to 'remove' the probability that X takes one of the smaller values not satisfying the inequality 'a < X ≤ b'.

Example 5

If X ~ B(12, 0.45), find:

a) P(5 < X ≤ 8)

- The largest value satisfying the inequality 5 < X ≤ 8 is X = 8.
  So you need to find P(X ≤ 8).

- Using the table for n = 12 and p = 0.45, P(X ≤ 8) = **0.9644**.

- You need to subtract the probability P(X ≤ 5), since X = 5 doesn't satisfy the inequality 5 < X ≤ 8, and neither does any value smaller than 5.

- From the table, P(X ≤ 5) = **0.5269**.

- So P(5 < X ≤ 8) = P(X ≤ 8) − P(X ≤ 5) = 0.9644 − 0.5269 = $\boxed{0.4375}$

Tip: n = 12 again — so you can either use the table on page 305, or refer to the tables on pages 378-382.

b) P(4 ≤ X < 10)

- The largest value satisfying the inequality 4 ≤ X < 10 is X = 9.
  So you need to find P(X ≤ 9).

- Using the table for n = 12 and p = 0.45, P(X ≤ 9) = **0.9921**.

- Now subtract the probability P(X ≤ 3), since X = 3 doesn't satisfy the inequality 4 ≤ X < 10, and neither does any value smaller than 3.

- From the table, P(X ≤ 3) = **0.1345**.

- So P(4 ≤ X < 10) = P(X ≤ 9) − P(X ≤ 3) = 0.9921 − 0.1345 = $\boxed{0.8576}$

Tip: The inequality 4 ≤ X < 10 can be written as 3 < X ≤ 9.

Using the tables is relatively straightforward as long as you can find the value of p you need. But the values of p only go as high as p = 0.5 — so if p > 0.5, you need to think about things slightly differently.

- Suppose X ~ B(12, 0.65), and you need to find P(X ≤ 5).

- This means you need to find the probability of 5 or fewer 'successes', when the probability of 'success' is p = 0.65.

- But you can switch things round and say you need to find the probability of 7 or more 'failures', where the probability of 'failure' is 1 − p = 0.35.

- It's easiest if you rewrite the problem using a new variable, Y, say. Y will represent the number of 'failures' in 12 trials, so $Y \sim B(12, 0.35)$.

- You can use tables to find $P(Y \geq 7) = 1 - P(Y < 7)$
$$= 1 - P(Y \leq 6) = 1 - 0.9154 = \mathbf{0.0846}$$

Tip: $n = 12$ again — so you can either use the table on page 305, or refer to the tables on pages 378-382.

- So the probability of 7 or more 'failures' is 0.0846 if the probability of each 'failure' is 0.35. This must equal the probability of 5 or fewer 'successes' if the probability of 'success' is 0.65.

- So if $X \sim B(12, 0.65)$, then $P(X \leq 5) = \mathbf{0.0846}$.

Tip: $h < X \leq k$ means that $X > h$ and $X \leq k$. So $Y < n - h$ and $Y \geq n - k$.
In other words:
$n - k \leq Y < n - h$.
Notice that, as well as having been subtracted from n, both k and h have 'swapped sides' in the inequality, and the $\leq$ and $<$ signs have moved with them.

> Where $X \sim B(n, p)$, but $p > 0.5$...
>
> First define $Y = n - X$, where $Y \sim B(n, 1 - p)$.
>
> Then, for constants k and h:
>
> - $P(X \leq k) = P(Y \geq n - k)$ and $P(X < k) = P(Y > n - k)$
>
> - $P(X \geq k) = P(Y \leq n - k)$ and $P(X > k) = P(Y < n - k)$
>
> - $P(h < X \leq k) = P(n - k \leq Y < n - h)$

Example 6

The probability of this spinner landing on blue is 0.7. The spinner is spun 12 times, and the random variable X represents the number of times the spinner lands on blue.

a) Find $P(X > 8)$.

- Since X represents the number of 'blues' in 12 spins, $X \sim B(12, 0.7)$.

Tip: Because $p = 0.7$ and the tables only go up to $p = 0.5$, you won't be able to use the tables directly — so create the random variable Y.

- Define a new random variable Y, where Y represents the number of 'reds' in 12 spins. Since the spinner can only land on either red or blue, $P(\text{red}) = 1 - P(\text{blue}) = 1 - 0.7 = 0.3$. This means $Y \sim B(12, 0.3)$.

- Then $P(X > 8) = P(Y < 4) = P(Y \leq 3) = \boxed{0.4925}$

b) Find $P(X \leq 4)$.

$P(X \leq 4) = P(Y \geq 8) = 1 - P(Y < 8) = 1 - P(Y \leq 7) = 1 - 0.9905 = \boxed{0.0095}$

c) Find $P(5 \leq X < 8)$.

$P(5 \leq X < 8) = P(4 < Y \leq 7) = P(Y \leq 7) - P(Y \leq 4)$
$$= 0.9905 - 0.7237 = \boxed{0.2668}$$

Exercise 3.1

Hint: The binomial tables start on page 378.

Q1 The random variable $X \sim B(10, 0.25)$.
Use the binomial table for $n = 10$ to find:
a) $P(X \leq 2)$ b) $P(X \leq 7)$ c) $P(X \leq 9)$
d) $P(X < 5)$ e) $P(X < 4)$ f) $P(X < 6)$

Q2 The random variable $X \sim B(15, 0.4)$.
Use the appropriate binomial table to find:
a) $P(X > 3)$ b) $P(X > 6)$ c) $P(X > 10)$
d) $P(X \geq 5)$ e) $P(X \geq 3)$ f) $P(X \geq 13)$

Q3 The random variable $X \sim B(20, 0.35)$.
Use the appropriate binomial table to find:

a) $P(X = 7)$ b) $P(X = 12)$ c) $P(2 < X \le 4)$
d) $P(10 < X \le 15)$ e) $P(7 \le X \le 10)$ f) $P(3 \le X < 11)$

Q4 The random variable $X \sim B(25, 0.8)$.
Use the appropriate binomial table to find:

a) $P(X \ge 17)$ b) $P(X \ge 20)$ c) $P(X > 14)$
d) $P(X = 21)$ e) $P(3 \le X < 14)$ f) $P(12 \le X < 18)$

Q5 The probability of having green eyes is known to be 0.18. In a class of thirty children, find the probability that fewer than ten children have green eyes.

Q5 Hint: 0.18 isn't in the binomial tables, so you'll have to use the binomial cumulative distribution function on your calculator.

Q6 In a production process it is known that approximately 5% of items are faulty. In a random sample of 25 objects, estimate the probability that fewer than 6 are faulty.

Using binomial tables 'backwards'

Sometimes, you'll need to use the tables 'the other way round'.

- So far you've been given a value for x, and you've had to find a probability such as $P(X \le x)$, $P(X > x)$, $P(X = x)$,... and so on.

- But you could be given a probability (c, say) and asked to find a value of x.

- These kinds of questions can get quite complicated.

Tip: You can also use the binomial cumulative distribution function on your calculator 'backwards' if the value of n or p isn't in the tables. Your calculator might allow you to produce a table of values for your n and p — otherwise you'll have to use trial and error to find the probability for different values of x.

Example 1

If $X \sim B(25, 0.2)$, find:

a) c if $P(X \le c) = 0.7800$

- Use the binomial table for $n = 25$, and the column for $p = 0.2$.

- Going down the column, you can see that $P(X \le 6) = 0.7800$, so $c = 6$.

b) d if $P(X \ge d) = 0.7660$

- If $P(X \ge d) = 0.7660$, then $P(X < d) = P(X \le d - 1)$
$$= 1 - 0.7660 = 0.2340.$$

- Using the table, you can see that $P(X \le 3) = 0.2340$.

- This means that $d - 1 = 3$, which gives $d = 4$.

Here are some slightly trickier examples.

Example 2

If $X \sim B(30, 0.4)$, find:

a) the maximum value a such that $P(X \le a) < 0.05$.

- Use the binomial table for $n = 30$, and the column for $p = 0.4$.

- You can see that $P(X \le 7) = 0.0435$ and $P(X \le 8) = 0.0940$.

- So the maximum value a such that $P(X \le a) < 0.05$ is $a = 7$.

---

b) the minimum value b such that $P(X > b) < 0.05$.

Tip: Remember...
$P(X \le b) = 1 - P(X > b)$.
So if $P(X > b) < 0.05$,
then $P(X \le b) > 0.95$.

- If $P(X > b) < 0.05$, then $P(X \le b) > 0.95$.
  So you need the smallest value of b with $P(X \le b) > 0.95$.

- Using the same binomial table as before, you can see that
  $P(X \le 15) = 0.9029$ and $P(X \le 16) = 0.9519$.

- So the minimum value of b with $P(X \le b) > 0.95$ is $b = 16$. This means that the minimum value of b with $P(X > b) < 0.05$ must also be $b = 16$.

This kind of question occurs in real-life situations.

Example 3

A teacher is writing a multiple-choice test, with 5 options for each of the 20 questions. She wants the probability of someone passing the test by guessing the answer to each question to be 10% or less. How high should the pass mark be to give a student guessing the answer to every question less than a 10% probability of passing the test?

Tip: The conditions for a binomial distribution are satisfied, since:
(i) there are a fixed number (20) of trials (i.e. each question is a trial),
(ii) the only possible outcomes of each trial are success or failure,
(iii) the trials are all independent — guessing the correct answer to one question has no effect on guessing the next answer correctly,
(iv) the probability of success in each trial is always 0.2,
(iv) X is the total number of successes in the 20 trials.

- Since each question has 5 possible answers, the probability of correctly guessing the answer to each question must be 0.2.

- There are 20 questions altogether, so if the random variable X is the overall score of a student who always guesses, then $X \sim B(20, 0.2)$.

- You need to find the minimum value m such that $P(X \ge m) < 0.1$, i.e. the minimum value m with $P(X < m) > 0.9$ or $P(X \le m - 1) > 0.9$.

- From tables, $P(X \le 5) = 0.8042$, but $P(X \le 6) = 0.9133$.

- So the probability of a student who always guesses getting more than 5 answers correct is $P(X > 5) = 1 - P(X \le 5) = 1 - 0.8042 = 0.1958$. But the probability of a student who always guesses getting more than 6 answers correct is $P(X > 6) = 1 - P(X \le 6) = 1 - 0.9133 = 0.0867$.

- So the pass mark should be set at 7 or more. Then the probability that a student who always guesses will pass the test is less than 10%.

Exercise 3.2

Hint: Use the binomial tables on p.378-382 to find your answers. With the wordy questions, read everything carefully and be very careful with the inequality signs.

Q1 The random variable $X \sim B(8, 0.35)$.
    Find the values of a, b, c and d such that:
    a) $P(X \le a) = 0.4278$ b) $P(X < b) = 0.9747$
    c) $P(X > c) = 0.8309$ d) $P(X \ge d) = 0.1061$

Q2 A teacher is writing a multiple-choice test, with 4 options for each of the 30 questions. He wants the probability of someone passing the test by guessing the answer to each question to be 10% or less.
    a) What is the lowest score that should be set as the pass mark?
    b) Another teacher says the probability of passing by guessing should be less than 1%. What should the minimum pass score be now?

Q3 In a fairground competition, a fair coin is tossed 20 times by a contestant. If the contestant scores x heads or more, they win a prize. If the random variable X represents the number of heads obtained, find the minimum number of heads that are needed to win if the probability of winning is to be kept below 0.05.

4. Modelling Real Problems

Exam questions often involve a 'realistic-sounding' situation.
It's not enough to know everything about the binomial distribution
— you have to know how to apply that knowledge in real life as well.

Learning Objective:

- Be able to apply knowledge of the binomial distribution to real-life situations.

Modelling real problems with B(*n*, *p*)

The first step with a real-world problem is to **model** it using a sensible probability distribution. If the situation satisfies all the conditions on p.299, then you'll need to use a **binomial distribution**.

When you've decided how to model the situation, you can 'do the maths'. Don't forget to include units in your answer where necessary.

You may then need to **interpret** your solution — saying what your answer means in the **context** of the question.

> **Tip:** You might need to make some **assumptions** before using a binomial distribution. If so, you should write down what those assumptions are (unless you've already been told in the question to assume that those things are true).

Example 1

A double-glazing salesman is handing out leaflets in a busy shopping centre. He knows that the probability of a passing person taking a leaflet is always 0.3. During a randomly chosen one-minute interval, 30 people passed him.

a) Suggest a suitable model to describe the number of people (*X*) who take a leaflet.

- During this one-minute interval:
  (i)   there's a **fixed number** (30) of trials,
  (ii) all the trials are **independent**,
  (iii) there are **two possible results** ('take a leaflet' and 'do not take a leaflet'),
  (iv) there's a **constant** probability of success (0.3),
  (v)   *X* is the **total number** of people taking leaflets.

  All the conditions for a binomial distribution are satisfied.

  So $X \sim B(30, 0.3)$

> **Tip:** You don't always need to write down the 5 conditions for a binomial distribution — but you should make sure they're satisfied. You **will** have to specify what values *n* and *p* take though.

b) What is the probability that more than 10 people take a leaflet?

- You know it's a binomial distribution, so you can get this probability from the binomial tables.

$$P(X > 10) = 1 - P(X \le 10)$$
$$= 1 - 0.7304$$
$$= 0.2696$$

Example 2

I am tossing a coin that I know is three times as likely to land on heads as it is on tails.

a) What is the probability that it lands on tails for the first time on the third toss?

- First you need to know the probabilities for heads and tails.

  P(heads) = 3 × P(tails).
  But P(heads) + P(tails) = 1.
  This means that P(heads) = 0.75 and P(tails) = 0.25.

> **Tip:** Careful... this doesn't need you to use one of the binomial formulas.

- If it lands on tails for the first time on the third toss, then the first two tosses must have been heads.

- Since all the tosses are independent, you know that:
  P(heads then heads then tails)
    = P(heads) × P(heads) × P(tails)

P(lands on tails for the first time on the third toss)
    = 0.75 × 0.75 × 0.25
    = 0.141 (to 3 s.f.)

b) What is the probability that in 10 tosses, it lands on heads at least 7 times?

- First define your random variable, and state how it is distributed.

If X represents the number of heads in 10 tosses, then $X \sim B(10, 0.75)$.

- $p = 0.75$ isn't in your tables, so define a new binomial random variable Y with probability of success $p = 0.25$.

The number of tails in 10 tosses can be described by the random variable $Y = 10 - X$, where $Y \sim B(10, 0.25)$.

- You need the probability of 'at least 7 heads' — this is the same as the probability of '3 or fewer tails'.

$P(X \geq 7) = P(Y \leq 3) = 0.7759$

Exercise 4.1

Q1 A hairdresser hands out leaflets. She knows there is always a probability of 0.25 that a passer-by will take a leaflet.
During a five-minute period, 50 people pass the hairdresser.

   a) Suggest a suitable model for X, the number of passers-by who take a leaflet in the five-minute period. Explain why this is a suitable model.

   b) What is the probability that more than 4 people take a leaflet?

   c) What is the probability that exactly 10 people take a leaflet?

Q2 Jasmine plants 15 randomly selected seeds in each of her plant trays. She knows that 35% of this type of plant grow with yellow flowers, while the remainder grow with white flowers. All her seeds grow successfully, and Jasmine counts how many plants in each tray grow with yellow flowers.

   a) Find the probability that a randomly selected tray has exactly 5 plants with yellow flowers.

   b) Find the probability that a randomly selected tray contains more plants with yellow flowers than plants with white flowers.

Q3 Simon tries to solve the crossword puzzle in his newspaper every day for 18 days. He either succeeds or fails to solve the puzzle.

   a) Simon believes that the number of successes, X, can be modelled by a random variable following a binomial distribution. State two conditions needed for this to be true.

   b) He believes that the situation has distribution $X \sim B(18, p)$, where p is the probability Simon successfully completes the crossword. If $P(X = 4) = P(X = 5)$, find p.

1. Hypothesis Tests

Hypothesis testing is all about using data from a sample to test whether a statement about a whole population is believable... or really unlikely.

Null and alternative hypotheses

Parameters are quantities that **describe** the characteristics of a **population** — e.g. the **mean** (μ), **variance** (σ^2), or a **proportion** (p). **Greek letters** such as μ and σ are often used for parameters.

A **hypothesis** (plural: **hypotheses**) is a claim or a statement that **might** be true, but which might **not** be.

- A **hypothesis test** is a method of testing a hypothesis about a population using **observed data** from a **sample**.

- You'll need **two** hypotheses for every hypothesis test — a **null** hypothesis and an **alternative** hypothesis.

Null hypothesis

- The **null hypothesis** is a statement about the **value** of a population parameter. The null hypothesis is always referred to as H_0.

- H_0 needs to give a **specific value** to the parameter, since all the calculations in your hypothesis test will be based on this value.

The example below (which I'll keep coming back to throughout the section) shows how you could use a hypothesis test to check whether a coin is 'fair' (i.e. whether it's equally likely to land on heads or tails).

> Aisha wants to test whether a coin is fair.
> She tosses it 100 times and then carries out a hypothesis test.
>
>
> - Testing whether a coin is fair is a test about the probability (p) that it lands on heads.
>
> - If the coin is **fair**, then the value of p will be 0.5. If the coin is **biased**, then the p-value could be **anything except 0.5**.
>
> - Aisha's null hypothesis needs to assume a **specific** p-value. So Aisha's null hypothesis is:
>
> $$H_0: p = 0.5$$

- Now then... the fact that Aisha is carrying out this test at all probably means that she has some doubts about whether the coin really is fair.

- But that's okay... you **don't** have to **believe** your null hypothesis — it's just an assumption you make for the purposes of carrying out the test.

- In fact, as you'll soon see, it's pretty common to choose a null hypothesis that you think is **false**.

Learning Objectives:

- Be able to formulate null and alternative hypotheses.

- Be able to decide when to use a one- or two-tailed test.

- Understand what is meant by significance levels.

- Understand what is meant by a test statistic, and be able to find a test statistic's sampling distribution.

- Be able to test an observed value of a test statistic for significance by calculating the p-value.

- Be able to find a critical region and identify the actual significance level of a test.

Tip: So if X is the number of heads, $X \sim B(100, 0.5)$.

Tip: Hypothesis testing is sometimes called significance testing.

Tip: Aisha's using p as the probability that the coin lands on heads, but you could equally use it as the probability the coin lands on tails.

Depending on your data, there are **two** possible results of a hypothesis test:

a) **"Fail to reject H₀"** — this means that your data provides **no evidence** to think that your null hypothesis is **untrue**.

b) **"Reject H₀"** — this means that your data provides evidence to think that your null hypothesis is **unlikely to be true**.

Tip: There's more about the possible outcomes of a hypothesis test on page 315.

If you need to reject H_0, you need an alternative hypothesis 'standing by'.

Two kinds of alternative hypothesis

Your **alternative hypothesis** is what you're going to conclude if you end up rejecting H_0 — i.e. what you're rejecting H_0 in favour of.

Tip: You **must** decide what your alternative hypothesis is before you collect any data.

The alternative hypothesis is always referred to as **H₁**.

There are **two kinds** of alternative hypothesis:

- A **one-tailed** alternative hypothesis.

    A one-tailed alternative hypothesis specifies whether the parameter you're investigating is **greater than** or **less than** the value you used in H_0. Using a one-tailed alternative hypothesis means you're carrying out a **one-tailed hypothesis test**.

Tip: You'll see more about one-tailed tests and two-tailed tests later.

- A **two-tailed** alternative hypothesis.

    A two-tailed alternative hypothesis **doesn't specify** whether the parameter you're investigating is greater than or less than the value you used in H_0 — all it says is that it's **not equal** to the value in H_0. Using a two-tailed alternative hypothesis means you're carrying out a **two-tailed hypothesis test**.

Aisha has a choice of alternative hypotheses, and she'll need to choose which to use **before** she starts collecting data.

- She could use a **one-tailed** alternative hypothesis — there are two possibilities:

    $H_1: p > 0.5$ — this would mean the coin is biased towards **heads**

    or $H_1: p < 0.5$ — this would mean the coin is biased towards **tails**

- She could use a **two-tailed** alternative hypothesis:

    $H_1: p \neq 0.5$ — this would mean the coin is **biased**, but it **doesn't** say whether it's biased in favour of heads or tails

Tip: Remember, p is the probability that the coin lands on heads.

Tip: Notice that H_1 does not give a specific value to the population parameter — it gives a range of values.

To decide which alternative hypothesis to use, you have to consider:

- **What you want to find out** about the parameter:
    For example, if you were investigating the proportion (q) of items produced in a factory that were faulty, then you might only want to test whether q has **increased** (testing whether it's decreased might not be as important).

- Any **suspicions** you might already have about the parameter's value:
    For example, if Aisha in the example above thought that the coin was actually biased towards heads, then she'd use $H_1: p > 0.5$.

Tip: So if Aisha's data means she can reject H_0, then she'll have gathered evidence to back up the suspicion she already has.

Possible conclusions after a hypothesis test

Okay... I'm going to assume now that you've written your null and alternative hypotheses, and **collected some data**. You need to know the two **possible conclusions** that you can come to after performing a hypothesis test.

Tip: The details of how you draw these conclusions are explained later — for now, just try to understand the logic of what's going on.

- Your **observed data** is **really unlikely** under the null hypothesis, H_0.

  - If your observed data is **really unlikely** when you assume that H_0 is true, then you might start to think 'Well, maybe H_0 isn't true after all.'

  - It could be that your observed data is actually much more **likely** to happen under your **alternative hypothesis**. Then you'd perhaps think H_1 is more likely to be true than H_0.

  - In this case, you would **reject H_0** in favour of H_1.

  - This **doesn't** mean that H_0 is **definitely false**. After all, as long as your observed data isn't impossible under H_0, then H_0 could still be true. All it means is that 'on the balance of probabilities', H_1 seems to be **more likely** to be true than H_0.

Tip: 'Under the null hypothesis' / 'under H_0' just means 'assuming that the null hypothesis is true'.

- The **observed data isn't** especially unlikely under the null hypothesis, H_0.

  - If your observed data could easily have come about under H_0, then you **can't reject H_0**.

  - In this case, you would '**fail to reject H_0**'.

  - However, this is **not** the same as saying that you have evidence that H_0 is **true** — all it means is that H_0 appears to be **believable**, and that you have **no evidence** that it's false.

  - But it's not really any better than having collected **no data** at all — you had **no evidence** to disbelieve the null hypothesis before you did your experiment... and you **still** don't. That's all this conclusion means.

Tip: How unlikely your results need to be before you reject H_0 is called the **significance level** — it's explained on page 318.

Tip: Remember, the choice is between **rejecting H_0** and **not rejecting H_0**. You **never** "accept H_0".

Because the conclusion of 'not rejecting H_0' is so **weak**, it's actually more meaningful when you can 'reject H_0' **in favour** of H_1.

This is why the alternative hypothesis H_1 is usually **more interesting** than the null hypothesis H_0.

- For example, with Aisha and her coin (pages 313-314), it was the **alternative** hypothesis that contained the claim that the coin was **biased**.

- It's also why H_0 often says something that you think is **false**. Your aim is to gather evidence to reject H_0 in favour of H_1 (and this is why H_1 might be what you actually **believe**).

- If Aisha **rejects H_0**:
  - She has **evidence** that H_0 is false (i.e. the coin is biased).
  - She **can't** be certain, but H_1 appears **more likely** to be true.

  (MODELLING)

- If Aisha **fails to reject H_0**:
  - She has **no** evidence that H_0 is false (i.e. that the coin is biased).
  - H_0 **could** be true, but she has no evidence to say so.
  - H_0 **could** also be false, but she has no evidence for that either.

Tip: A hypothesis test **can** provide evidence that H_1 is likely to be true, but it **can't** provide evidence that H_0 is likely to be true.

Example 1

A 4-sided spinner has sides labelled A–D. Adam thinks that
the spinner is biased towards side A. He wants to do a
hypothesis test to test this theory.

a) **Write down a suitable null hypothesis to test Adam's theory.**

The parameter Adam's interested in is the probability, p,
that the spinner will land on side A.

The null hypothesis must give a **specific value** to p, and it's the
statement that Adam is trying to get evidence to **reject**.

Adam thinks the spinner is biased. So his null hypothesis should be that
the spinner is **unbiased**, and that each side has a probability of 0.25 of
being spun. So: $H_0: p = 0.25$

Tip: The question will
usually give you a hint
about what H_1 should
be. Here it says Adam
suspects it is biased
towards side A, which
means he thinks p is
greater than 0.25.

b) **Write down a suitable alternative hypothesis.**

If the spinner is biased towards side A, then the probability, p,
of spinning A will be greater than 0.25. So:

$$H_1: p > 0.25$$

(This is the hypothesis that Adam actually believes.)

c) **State whether this test is one- or two-tailed.**

The alternative hypothesis specifies that p
is greater than 0.25, so the test is one-tailed.

Example 2

In a particular post office, the average probability over the course
of a day that a customer entering the post office has to queue for
more than 2 minutes is 0.6. The manager of the post office wants
to test whether the probability of having to queue for more than
2 minutes is different between the hours of 1 pm and 2 pm.

a) **Write down a suitable null hypothesis.**

The manager is interested in the population parameter p, the probability
of having to queue for more than 2 minutes between 1 pm and 2 pm.

The null hypothesis must give a **specific value** to p.
So: $$H_0: p = 0.6$$

Tip: The manager's null
hypothesis is that the
probability of having to
queue for more than
2 minutes between
1 pm and 2 pm is the
same as at other times.

b) **Write down a suitable alternative hypothesis.**
The manager wants to test for **any** difference
(rather than just an increase or just a decrease).
So: $$H_1: p \neq 0.6$$

c) **State whether this test is one- or two-tailed.**
The alternative hypothesis only specifies that p
is not equal to 0.6, so the test is two-tailed.

Q1 Over the last few years Jules has had a 90% success rate in germinating her geranium plants. This year she has bought an improved variety of seeds and hopes for even better results.

a) Which quantity is Jules investigating?

b) What value has this quantity taken over the last few years?

c) Write down a suitable null hypothesis.

d) Write down a suitable alternative hypothesis.

e) State whether this test is one- or two-tailed.

Q2 Each week, the probability that a cat catches a mouse is 0.7. The cat's owner has put a bell on its collar and wants to test if it now catches fewer mice.

a) State the quantity that the owner is investigating.

b) What value did this quantity take before?

c) Write down a suitable null hypothesis using parts a) and b).

d) Write down a suitable alternative hypothesis.

e) State whether this test is one- or two-tailed.

Q3 The school health team checks teenagers for the presence of an antibody before vaccinating them. Usually 35% of teenagers have the antibody present. The team is to visit a remote Scottish island where they think that the proportion of teenagers with the antibody may be different.

a) Write down the quantity that is being investigated.

b) Formulate the null and alternative hypotheses, H_0 and H_1.

c) State whether this test is one- or two-tailed.

Q4 The local council found that only 16% of residents were aware that grants were available to help pay to insulate their houses. The council ran a campaign to publicise the grants, and now want to test whether there is an increased awareness in the area.

Write down suitable null and alternative hypotheses involving the proportion of residents aware of the grants.

Q5 In a village shop, 3% of customers buy a jar of chilli chutney. The owner has changed the packaging of the chutney and wants to know if the proportion of customers buying a jar of chilli chutney has changed. Write down suitable null and alternative hypotheses.

Q6 It is claimed that the proportion of members of a particular gym who watch Australian soaps is 40%. Boyd wants to test his theory that the proportion is higher. Write down suitable null and alternative hypotheses.

Significance levels

- You've seen that you would reject H_0 if the data you collect is 'really unlikely' under H_0. But you need to decide exactly **how unlikely** your results will need to be before you decide to reject H_0.

- The **significance level** of a test shows how far you're prepared to believe that unlikely results are just down to **chance**, rather than because the assumption in H_0 is wrong.

> The **significance level** of a test (α) determines **how unlikely** your data needs to be under the null hypothesis (H_0) before you reject H_0.

Tip: If your results under H_0 have a probability lower than α, then you can say that your results are **significant**.

- For example, your significance level could be $\alpha = 0.05$ (or 5%). This would mean that you would **only** reject H_0 if your observed data fell into the **most extreme 5%** of possible outcomes.

Tip: Significance levels can be written as percentages or decimals.

- You'll usually be told what significance level to use, but the most common values are $\alpha = 0.1$ (or 10%), $\alpha = 0.05$ (or 5%) and $\alpha = 0.01$ (or 1%).

- The value of α also determines the strength of the evidence that the test has provided if you reject H_0 — the **lower** the value of α, the **stronger the evidence** you have that H_0 is false.
    - For example, if you use $\alpha = 0.05$ and your data lets you reject H_0, then you have evidence that H_0 is false.
    - But if you use $\alpha = 0.01$ and your data lets you reject H_0, then you have **stronger** evidence that H_0 is false.

- Also, the **lower** the value of α, the **lower** the probability of **incorrectly rejecting H_0** when it is in fact **true** — i.e. of getting extreme data due to chance rather than because H_0 was false.

- But although a **low** value of α sounds like a good thing, there's an important **disadvantage** to using a low significance level — you're **less likely to be able to reject H_0**. This means your experiment is more likely to end up 'failing to reject H_0' and concluding nothing.

Test statistics

Tip: A **statistic** is a quantity that is calculated from **known observations** — i.e. a sample.

To see if your results are **significant**, you need to find their probability under H_0. The way you do this is to '**summarise**' your data in something called a **test statistic**.

> A **test statistic** for a hypothesis test is a statistic calculated from **sample data**, which is used to **decide** whether or not to reject H_0.

Tip: If you need to remind yourself of the binomial distribution, see Chapter 16.

- The **probability distribution** of a statistic is called the **sampling distribution**. It gives all the possible values of the statistic, along with the corresponding probabilities. In this course, the sampling distribution of the test statistics you'll use will be a **binomial distribution** $B(n, p)$.

- Once you've found your test statistic (x), you then need to work out the p-value — this is the probability of a value **at least as extreme** as x using the parameter in your null hypothesis.

Tip: Don't mix up the p-value with the binomial probability p.

- If your p-value is less than the significance level α, you can reject H_0.

Deciding whether or not to reject H₀

1. Comparing the probability of the test statistic with α

Right... back to Aisha and her coin. Let's assume first that Aisha is carrying out a **one-tailed test** to check if the coin is biased **towards heads**.

- For this one-tailed test, Aisha's null and alternative hypotheses will be:

$$H_0: p = 0.5 \quad \text{and} \quad H_1: p > 0.5$$

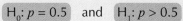

- Aisha's going to use a significance level of $\alpha = 0.05$.

- Aisha then throws the coin 30 times and records the number of heads.

- Her test statistic X is the **number of heads** she throws — so X follows a binomial distribution B(n, p). In fact, under H₀, $X \sim \text{B}(30, 0.5)$.

First suppose Aisha records **19 heads** — i.e. $X = 19$.

- The probability of a result **at least as extreme** as $X = 19$ is $P(X \geq 19)$.

- Under H₀, this is $1 - P(X < 19) = 1 - P(X \leq 18) = 1 - 0.8998 = 0.1002$

- This *p*-value of 0.1002 is **not less than** the significance level α, so she **cannot reject H₀** .

- Aisha has **no evidence** at the 5% level of significance that the coin is biased in favour of heads.

Suppose instead that Aisha records **20 heads** — i.e. $X = 20$.

- The probability of a result **at least as extreme** as $X = 20$ is $P(X \geq 20)$.

- Under H₀, this is $1 - P(X < 20) = 1 - P(X \leq 19) = 1 - 0.9506 = 0.0494$

- This *p*-value of 0.0494 is **less than** the significance value α, so she **can reject H₀** .

- Aisha has **evidence** at the 5% level of significance that the coin is biased in favour of heads.

Levels of significance can be shown on a graph of the **probability function** for your test statistic.

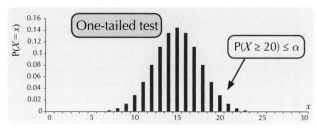

- The red bars form the 'one tail' of the test statistic's distribution where values of the test statistic would lead you to reject H₀ in favour of H₁.

- They're at the 'high' end of the distribution — because H₁ was of the form $H_1: p > 0.5$ (so high values of X are more likely under H₁ than under H₀).

- If Aisha had chosen her alternative hypothesis to be: $H_1: p < 0.5$, then the values that would lead her to reject H₀ would be at the 'low' end.

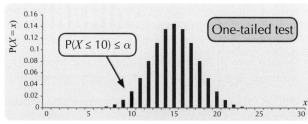

> **Tip:** Remember...
> n is the number of trials (here, $n = 30$).
> And p is the probability of success in each of those trials, which we're assuming to be 0.5 (because we're assuming that H₀ is true — see page 313).

> **Tip:** A result 'at least as extreme as 19' means '19 or more' here. See below for more details.

> **Tip:** In fact, any value for X of 20 or more would lead Aisha to reject H₀.

> **Tip:** Remember...
> under H₀, $X \sim \text{B}(30, 0.5)$.
> So for each value of x, the probability is worked out using
> $$P(X = x) = \binom{30}{x} 0.5^x 0.5^{30-x}$$

> **Tip:** If Aisha's alternative hypothesis had been $H_1: p < 0.5$, then she would reject H₀ for values of X of 10 or under. This is because for B(30, 0.5),
> $P(X \leq 10) = 0.0494 < \alpha$, but
> $P(X \leq 11) = 0.1002 > \alpha$.

Now assume that Aisha is carrying out a **two-tailed test** to check if the coin is biased towards **either heads or tails**.

There's one important difference from the one-tailed test.

- For this two-tailed test, Aisha's null and alternative hypotheses will be:
  $H_0: p = 0.5$ and $H_1: p \neq 0.5$
- Again, Aisha's going to use a significance level of $\alpha = 0.05$.
- Aisha then throws the coin 30 times and records the number of heads.
- Her test statistic X is the **number of heads** she throws — so X follows a binomial distribution B(n, p). In fact, under H_0, $X \sim B(30, 0.5)$.

So up to this point, things are pretty much identical to the one-tailed test.

But now think about which 'extreme' outcomes for the test statistic would favour H_1 over H_0.

- This time, extreme outcomes at **either** the 'high' end **or** the 'low' end of the distribution would favour your alternative hypothesis, $H_1: p \neq 0.5$.
- But the significance level is the **total** probability of the results that'd lead to you reject H_0. So for a two-tailed test, you have to **divide α by 2** and use **half** of the significance level ($\frac{\alpha}{2} = 0.025$) at each end of the distribution.

So suppose Aisha records **20 heads** — i.e. $X = 20$.
- The probability of a result **at least as extreme** as $X = 20$ is $P(X \geq 20)$.
- Under H_0, this is $1 - P(X < 20) = 1 - P(X \leq 19) = 1 - 0.9506 = 0.0494$.
- This p-value of 0.0494 is **not less than** 0.025, so she **cannot reject H_0**.
- Aisha has **no evidence** at the 5% level of significance that the coin is biased (in either direction).

Suppose instead that Aisha records **21 heads** — i.e. $X = 21$.
- The probability of a result **at least as extreme** as $X = 21$ is $P(X \geq 21)$.
- Under H_0, this is $1 - P(X < 21) = 1 - P(X \leq 20) = 1 - 0.9786 = 0.0214$
- This p-value of 0.0214 is **less than** 0.025, so she **can reject H_0**.
- Aisha has **evidence** at the 5% level of significance that the coin is biased (towards either heads or tails).

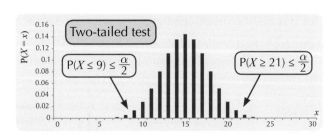

- Notice how in this two-tailed test, Aisha needs 21 heads to reject H_0, whereas in the one-tailed test, she only needed 20 heads.
- This is why you need to be careful when you choose your alternative hypothesis. Choosing the wrong H_1 can make it harder to reject H_0.

Tip: You **do** need to write down all these pieces of information for **every** hypothesis test you do.

Tip: Testing for significance is similar for one- and two-tailed tests. You just need to compare the p-value to a different number.

Tip: Always state the significance level of your evidence in your conclusion.

Tip: The values of X at the 'low' end that would lead Aisha to reject H_0 are those of 9 or under. For B(30, 0.5), $P(X \leq 9) = 0.0214$, which is less than $\frac{\alpha}{2}$, but $P(X \leq 10) = 0.0494$, which is greater than $\frac{\alpha}{2}$.

2. Finding the critical region

When Aisha was deciding whether to reject H_0 or not reject H_0:

1) she worked out her test statistic using her data,
2) then she calculated the probability (under H_0) of getting a value for the test statistic at least as extreme as the value she had found (the p-value).

Finding the **critical region** is another way of doing a hypothesis test.
You work out all the values of the test statistic that would lead you to reject H_0.

> The **critical region** (CR) is the **set** of all values of the **test statistic** that would cause you to **reject H_0**.

Tip: The critical region is just a set of values that X can take which fall far enough away from what's expected under the null hypothesis to allow you to reject it.

Using a critical region is like doing things the other way round, because:

1) you work out all the values that would make you reject H_0,
2) then you work out the value of your test statistic using your data, and check if it is in the critical region (and if it is, then reject H_0).

So if you find the **critical region** first, you can quickly say whether any observed value of the test statistic, X, is **significant**.

- As you've seen, **one-tailed tests** have a **single critical region**, containing either the highest or lowest values. Here are the graphs from pages 319 and 320 again — the values of x which are **red** would all cause you to reject H_0, so they are the values that make up the critical region.

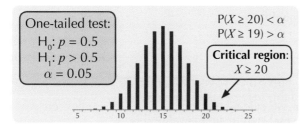

One-tailed test:
$H_0: p = 0.5$
$H_1: p > 0.5$
$\alpha = 0.05$

$P(X \geq 20) < \alpha$
$P(X \geq 19) > \alpha$

Critical region:
$X \geq 20$

Tip: When $X = 19$, Aisha couldn't reject H_0 (see page 319), so $X = 19$ is **not** in the critical region.

But $X = 20$ **is** in the critical region, since in this case Aisha **could** reject H_0.

$X = 20$ is called the **critical value** — it's the value on the 'edge' of the critical region.

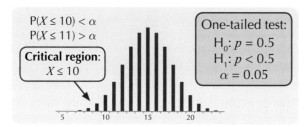

$P(X \leq 10) < \alpha$
$P(X \leq 11) > \alpha$

Critical region:
$X \leq 10$

One-tailed test:
$H_0: p = 0.5$
$H_1: p < 0.5$
$\alpha = 0.05$

Tip: For this test, $X = 10$ is the **critical value**.

- A **two-tailed test** has a **critical region** that's split into two 'tails' — one tail at each end of the distribution. Again, the **red** values of x make up the two parts of the critical region.

Tip: For the two-tailed test the **critical values** are $X = 9$ and $X = 21$.

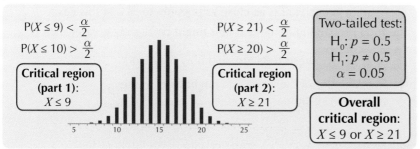

$P(X \leq 9) < \frac{\alpha}{2}$
$P(X \leq 10) > \frac{\alpha}{2}$

$P(X \geq 21) < \frac{\alpha}{2}$
$P(X \geq 20) > \frac{\alpha}{2}$

Critical region (part 1):
$X \leq 9$

Critical region (part 2):
$X \geq 21$

Two-tailed test:
$H_0: p = 0.5$
$H_1: p \neq 0.5$
$\alpha = 0.05$

Overall critical region:
$X \leq 9$ or $X \geq 21$

Tip: You might be asked to find the **acceptance region**. This is set of all values of the test statistic for which you have no evidence to reject H_0 — i.e. the blue bars on the diagrams.

Once you've calculated the critical region, you can easily find what's called the **actual significance level**.

- The **actual significance level** of the test is usually **slightly different** from the significance level you use to find the critical region in the first place.
- The **actual significance level** of a test is the **probability** of **rejecting H₀** when it is true. So the actual significance level is the probability of **incorrectly rejecting H₀**.
- You find the actual significance level by calculating the **probability** of X taking a value in the **critical region** (assuming H₀ is true).

Back to Aisha and her coin for the final time...

- Aisha's one-tailed test has a critical region of $X \geq 20$ (see page 321). She found this using a significance level $\alpha = 0.05$.
- But the **actual significance level** of this test is $P(X \geq 20) = \boxed{0.0494}$
- So the probability of Aisha rejecting H_0 when it is true is 0.0494.
- In other words, this means that there is a probability of 0.0494 of Aisha **incorrectly** rejecting H_0 — i.e. of the test producing this kind of **wrong result**.

The actual significance level of a **one-tailed test** will always be **less than or equal to** α.

- Similarly, Aisha's two-tailed test has a critical region of $X \geq 21$ or $X \leq 9$ (see page 321). She found this using a significance level $\alpha = 0.05$.
- But the **actual significance level** of this test is $P(X \geq 21) + P(X \leq 9) = 0.0214 + 0.0214 = \boxed{0.0428}$
- So the probability of Aisha rejecting H_0 when it's true this time is 0.0428.
- In other words, there is a probability of 0.0428 of Aisha **incorrectly** rejecting H_0 — i.e. of the test producing this kind of **wrong result**.

There are actually **two** different ways that you might be asked to find a critical region for a **two-tailed test**.

- You might be asked to find the critical region so that the probability in each tail is **no greater than** $\frac{\alpha}{2}$.
- Or you might be asked to find the critical region so that the probability in each tail is **as close as possible to** $\frac{\alpha}{2}$. In this case, the **total** probability in the two tails **might** be slightly **greater** than α.

So that's what hypothesis tests are, and how they work.

There are examples of the kinds you might meet in the exam in the next section.

Tip: The actual significance level is usually different from the original level of significance when the test statistic is a **discrete** random variable (as it is here).

This is because the value of $P(X \leq x)$ 'jumps' as the value of x changes, so it's usually impossible to find a critical region containing values with a probability of **exactly** α.

Tip: The acceptance region is $10 \leq X \leq 20$.

Tip: In a two-tailed test, you need to remember to find the probability of each end of the critical region and add them up.

2. Hypothesis Tests for a Binomial Distribution

In the previous section, a binomial example was used to demonstrate all the general theory of hypothesis testing. This section will go through lots more binomial examples, and there'll be loads of practice too. There's not much to actually learn here — it's just applying what you've already covered.

Setting up the test

In the last section, you saw that there were **two** different methods you could be asked to use in a hypothesis-test question — **testing for significance** and **finding a critical region**.

In both cases, you'll always **set up** the hypothesis to test in the same way. Follow this step-by-step method:

- Define the **population parameter** in **context**
  — for a binomial distribution it's always p, a **probability** of success, or **proportion** of a population.

- Write down the **null** hypothesis (H_0)
  — $H_0: p = a$ for some constant a.

- Write down the **alternative** hypothesis (H_1)
  — H_1 will either be $H_1: p < a$ or $H_1: p > a$ (one-tailed test)
  or $H_1: p \neq a$ (two-tailed test)

- State the **test statistic**, X
  — always just the number of '**successes**' in the sample.

- Write down the **sampling distribution** of the test statistic under H_0
  — $X \sim B(n, p)$ where n is the sample size.

- State the **significance level**, α
  — you'll usually be given this.

Example

Cleo wants to test whether a coin is more likely to land on heads than tails. She plans to flip it 15 times and record the results. Write down suitable null and alternative hypotheses. Define the test statistic, X, and give its sampling distribution under the null hypothesis.

- The population parameter p = probability of the coin landing on heads.

- The null hypothesis will be that the coin is unbiased, so $H_0: p = 0.5.$

- Cleo believes the coin is more likely to land on heads, so her alternative hypothesis is $H_1: p > 0.5.$

- The test statistic is X = the number of heads in the sample of 15 throws.

- The sampling distribution of X under H_0 is **binomial** with $p = 0.5$ and 15 trials so $X \sim B(15, 0.5).$

Tip: This test is about the **probability** of the coin landing on heads, so the test statistic will have a binomial distribution.

Tip: Remember...
to test for significance,
you need to find the
probability that the test
statistic is 'at least as
extreme' as your results.
See pages 318-322 for
the general theory on
testing for significance.

Testing for significance

If you're asked to test an observed value for significance, you need to work out the *p*-value using either the **binomial tables** or the **binomial cumulative distribution function** on your calculator (see p.305), and then compare it to α for a one-tailed test, or $\frac{\alpha}{2}$ if it's a two-tailed test.

- The binomial **tables** show the cumulative distribution function $P(X \leq x)$ — this lets you quickly find the probability of results '**at least as extreme**' as the observed value.

- The binomial **cumulative distribution function** on your calculator also gives $P(X \leq x)$ — use it when the tables don't include the probability you need.

The next three examples will guide you through one-tailed hypothesis tests — from forming the hypotheses to the final conclusion.

Example 1

A student believes that a five-sided spinner is biased towards landing on 5.
He spins the spinner 20 times and it lands on 5 ten times.
Using a 5% level of significance, test the hypothesis
that the spinner is biased towards landing on 5.

- Identify the **population parameter**:

    p = the probability of the spinner landing on 5

- Formulate the **null** and **alternative** hypotheses for p.
    The null hypothesis will be that the spinner is not biased, so $H_0: p = 0.2$
    The alternative hypothesis will be that the spinner is more
    likely to land on 5, so $H_1: p > 0.2$ ← What the student actually thinks.

- State the **test statistic** X — the number of 5s,
    and its **sampling distribution** under H_0.

    Let X = number of times the spinner lands on a **5** in the **sample**.
    Under H_0, $X \sim B(20, 0.2)$.

    number of trials   probability of a 5 under H_0

- State the **significance level** of the test. It's 5% here so $\alpha = 0.05$.

- Test for **significance** — your *p*-value is the probability of X being
    at least as extreme as the value you've observed, i.e. the probability of X
    being 10 or more, under the null hypothesis.

    Under the null hypothesis $p = 0.2$.

Tip: The full set of
binomial tables is given
on pages 378-382.
These tables are also
in the formula booklet
you'll get in your exam.

Using the binomial tables
$P(X \geq 10) = 1 - P(X < 10)$

$= 1 - P(X \leq 9)$

$= 1 - 0.9974$

$= 0.0026$

Binomial Cumulative Distribution Function
Values show P(X ≤ x), where X~B(n, p)

	p =	0.05	0.10	0.15	0.20
n = 20, x = 0		0.3585	0.1216	0.0388	0.0115
	...	...	...	...	...
8		1.0000	0.9999	0.9987	0.9900
9		1.0000	1.0000	0.9998	0.9974
10		1.0000	1.0000	1.0000	0.9994

Since $0.0026 < 0.05$, the result **is significant**.

- Write your **conclusion** — you will either reject the null hypothesis H_0 or have insufficient evidence to do so.

> There is evidence at the 5% level of significance to reject H_0 and to support the student's claim that the spinner is biased towards landing on 5.

Tip: Make sure you always state your conclusion. Just showing whether the result is significant is not enough.

Example 2

Pen-Gu Inc. sells stationery to 60% of the schools in the country. The manager of Pen-Gu Inc. claims that there has recently been a decrease in the number of schools buying their stationery. She rings 30 schools at random and finds that 16 buy Pen-Gu Inc. stationery. Test her claim using a 1% significance level.

- Identify the **population parameter**:

    p = the proportion of schools buying Pen-Gu Inc. stationery

- Formulate the **null** and **alternative** hypotheses for p.

    If the number of schools buying their stationery has not changed, then $H_0: p = 0.6$

    If the number of schools buying their stationery has decreased, then $H_1: p < 0.6$

- State the **test statistic** X, and its **sampling distribution** under H_0.

    Let X = number of **schools** in the sample who buy Pen-Gu Inc. stationery.
    Under H_0, $X \sim B(30, 0.6)$.

- State the **significance level** of the test. It's 1% here so $\alpha = 0.01$.

- Test for **significance** — your p-value is the probability of X being **at least as extreme** as the value you've observed, i.e. the probability of X being 16 or less, under the null hypothesis.

    The value of p under H_0 is greater than 0.5, so you need to do a bit of fiddling to be able to use the binomial tables.

    Let Y = number of schools in the sample who do **not** buy Pen-Gu Inc. stationery. Then $Y \sim B(30, 0.4)$.

Tip: When the null hypothesis is of the form $p = a$ and a is greater than 0.5, you'll need to manipulate the probabilities slightly to be able to use the tables. This method of using the tables was on pages 307-308.

Using the binomial tables:
$P(X \le 16) = P(Y \ge 14)$

$= 1 - P(Y < 14)$

$= 1 - P(Y \le 13)$

$= 1 - 0.7145$

$= 0.2855$

Binomial Cumulative Distribution Function		
Values show $P(X \le x)$, where $X \sim B(n, p)$		
$p =$ ...	0.35	0.40
$n = 30, x =$ ...	...	...
12 ...	0.7802	0.5785
13 ...	0.8737	0.7145
14 ...	0.9348	0.8246

Since $0.2855 > 0.01$, the result is **not significant**.

- Write your **conclusion**:

> There is insufficient evidence at the 1% level of significance to reject H_0 in favour of the manager's claim.

Tip: Always say:
'**there is sufficient evidence to reject H_0**'
or
'**there is insufficient evidence to reject H_0**'
Never talk about 'accepting H_0' or 'rejecting H_1'.

If you can't use the tables for your value of p, you have to use the **binomial probability function** or a **calculator** to work things out.

Example 3

The proportion of pupils at a school who support a particular football team is found to be 1 in 3. Nigel claims that there is less support for this team at his school. In a random sample of 20 pupils from Nigel's school, 3 support the team. Use a 10% level of significance to test Nigel's claim.

Tip: This is a test of the **proportion** of pupils who support a team, so the test statistic will have a binomial distribution.

- Let p = proportion of pupils who support the team at Nigel's school.

- Formulate the **hypotheses**: $H_0: p = \frac{1}{3}$ $H_1: p < \frac{1}{3}$

- Let X = number of sampled pupils supporting the team.
  Under H_0, $X \sim B(20, \frac{1}{3})$.

- The **significance level** is $\alpha = 0.1$.

- Now you need to find the probability under H_0 of getting a value less than or equal to 3. The tables don't have values for $p = \frac{1}{3}$, so you need to work out the probabilities individually and add them up:

  > Use the binomial probability function for each probability.

  $P(X \le 3) = P(X = 0) + P(X = 1) + P(X = 2) + P(X = 3)$

  $= \left(\frac{2}{3}\right)^{20} + 20\left(\frac{1}{3}\right)\left(\frac{2}{3}\right)^{19} + 190\left(\frac{1}{3}\right)^{2}\left(\frac{2}{3}\right)^{18} + 1140\left(\frac{1}{3}\right)^{3}\left(\frac{2}{3}\right)^{17}$

  $= 0.0604$

  $0.0604 < 0.1$, so the result is significant.

  There is sufficient evidence at the 10% level of significance to reject H_0 and to support Nigel's claim that there is less support for the team at his school.

Tip: Here you can use:
$P(X = x) = \binom{20}{x}\left(\frac{1}{3}\right)^{x}\left(\frac{2}{3}\right)^{20-x}$
or the binomial cumulative distribution function on your calculator.

With two-tailed tests, the only difference is the value that you compare the probability to in the test for significance.

Example 4

A wildlife photographer is taking photographs of a rare glass frog. He's established over a long period of time that the probability that he'll sight a glass frog during any day of searching is 0.05. He moves to another part of the rainforest believing that the probability will be different. During his first 6 days searching he spots the frog on 3 of the days. Use a 1% level of significance to test his claim.

- Let p = probability that the wildlife photographer will spot a glass frog in a day of searching.

- Formulate the **hypotheses**: $H_0: p = 0.05$ $H_1: p \ne 0.05$

- Let X = number of sampled days that he spots a frog.
  Under H_0, $X \sim B(6, 0.05)$.

- The **significance level** is $\alpha = 0.01$. So $\frac{\alpha}{2} = 0.005$.

- Test for **significance** — you're interested in the probability of X being **at least as extreme** as the value you've observed.

  Since the test is two-tailed, you need to work out **which** 'tail' you are working in — i.e. do you need to find the probability that X is less than, or more than, the observed value?

  Under H_0, the expected number of days on which a frog is seen is 0.3. 3 is greater than this expected value, so the p-value will be the probability of X being **3 or more**, under the null hypothesis.

  Using the binomial tables:

  $P(X \geq 3) = 1 - P(X < 3)$

  $\qquad\qquad = 1 - P(X \leq 2)$

  $\qquad\qquad = 1 - 0.9978$

  $\qquad\qquad = 0.0022$

  Binomial Cumulative Distribution Function
  Values show $P(X \leq x)$, where $X \sim B(n, p)$

	$p =$	0.05	0.10
$n = 6,$	$x = 0$	0.7351	0.5314
	1	0.9672	0.8857
	2	0.9978	0.9842

  Since $0.0022 \leq 0.005$, the result **is significant**.

- Write your **conclusion**:

  > There is sufficient evidence at the 1% level of significance to reject H_0 in favour of the wildlife photographer's claim that the probability of sighting a glass frog is different in another part of the rainforest.

Tip: The photographer believes he'll see a glass frog on 5% (= 0.05) of days when he looks. So in 6 days, he'd expect to see a glass frog on $0.05 \times 6 = 0.3$ days. For a binomial distribution in general: expected value = np.

Tip: If the observed value was less than the expected value under H_0, the p-value would be the probability that X was less than or equal to that value.

Exercise 2.1

MODELLING

Q1 Charlotte claims she can read Milly's mind. To test this claim Milly chooses a number from 1 to 5 and concentrates on it while Charlotte attempts to read her mind. Charlotte is right on 4 out of 10 occasions.

  a) Write down the population parameter and suitable null and alternative hypotheses.

  b) Define the test statistic and write down its sampling distribution under the null hypothesis.

  c) Are these results significant at a 5% level of significance?

Q1 Hint: Charlotte thinks she can do better than guessing a number between 1 and 5.

Q2 Last year 45% of students said that the chicken dinosaurs in the school canteen were good value. After this year's price increase Ellen says fewer people think they are good value. She asked 50 people and found only 16 said that chicken dinosaurs were good value. Test Ellen's claim at the 10% level.

Q3 In the past, 25% of John's violin pupils have gained distinctions in their exams. He's using a different examination board and wants to know if the percentage of distinctions will be significantly different. His first 12 exam candidates gained 6 distinctions. Test whether the percentage of distinctions is significantly different at the 1% level.

Q3 Hint: Remember the differences in the hypothesis test method when the test is two-tailed.

Q4 Jin is a keen birdwatcher. Over time he has found that 15% of the birds he sees are classified as 'rare'. He has bought a new type of birdseed and is not sure whether it will attract more or fewer rare birds. On the first day only 2 out of 40 of the birds were rare. Test whether the percentage of rare birds is significantly different at the 10% level.

Q5 10% of customers at a village newsagent's buy Pigeon Spotter Magazine. The owner has just opened a new shop in a different village and wants to know whether this proportion will be different in the new shop. One day 8 out of a random sample of 50 customers bought Pigeon Spotter Magazine. Is this significant at the 5% level?

Q6 Pete's Driving School advertises that 70% of its clients pass the driving test at their first attempt. Hati and three of her friends failed. Four other friends did pass first time. She complained that the advertisement was misleading and that the percentage was actually lower. Test whether there is evidence to support Hati's complaint at the 1% level.

Critical regions

- Remember that the critical region is just the **set of all values** which are **significant** under H_0. You use the binomial tables (or the binomial probability function) to find it.

- If the test is **one-tailed**, the critical region will be at only **one end** of the distribution. If the test is **two-tailed**, the critical region will be **split in two** with a bit at each end.

- For a two-tailed test, you could either be asked to make the probability of rejection in the tails **less than** $\frac{\alpha}{2}$, or **as close** to $\frac{\alpha}{2}$ as possible.

- The **actual significance level** is the probability (under H_0) that H_0 is rejected, which is found by calculating the **probability** that the observed value of the test statistic will fall in the critical region.

Example 1

A company manufactures kettles. Its records over the years show that 20% of its kettles will be faulty. Simon claims that the proportion of faulty kettles must be lower than this. He takes a sample of 30 kettles to test his claim.

a) **Find the critical region for a test of Simon's claim at the 5% level.**

- Let p = the probability that a kettle is faulty.

- Formulate the hypotheses:
$$H_0: p = 0.2 \qquad H_1: p < 0.2$$

- The test statistic is X = the number of faulty kettles in the sample, and under H_0 the sampling distribution is $X \sim B(30, 0.2)$.

- Use the binomial tables to find the two values of x for which $P(X \le x)$ is either side of the significance level 0.05.

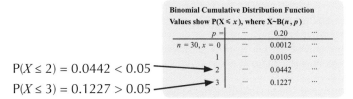

Binomial Cumulative Distribution Function
Values show $P(X \le x)$, where $X \sim B(n, p)$

$p =$	...	0.20	...
$n = 30, x = 0$	...	0.0012	...
1	...	0.0105	...
2	...	0.0442	...
3	...	0.1227	...

$P(X \le 2) = 0.0442 < 0.05$
$P(X \le 3) = 0.1227 > 0.05$

So the critical region is the set of values $X \le 2$.

Tip: If you're asked to do this for a probability that isn't in the binomial c.d.f. tables, you'll need to use the binomial probability function or a calculator.

b) **State the actual significance level.**

The actual significance level is the probability that H_0 will be rejected when it is true, which is $P(X \le 2) = $ 0.0442

Tip: The number $X = 2$ in this example is the critical value.

c) **Simon found that 1 kettle in his sample was faulty. Say whether this is significant evidence to reject H_0.**

1 lies in the critical region, so it is significant evidence to reject H_0 in favour of H_1.

Tip: Testing the hypothesis using the sample data is easy once you've found the critical region — just see if the observed value of the test statistic lies in the critical region.

Example 2

Records show that the proportion of trees in a wood that suffer from a particular leaf disease is 15%. Hasina thinks that recent weather conditions might have affected this proportion. She examines a random sample of 20 of the trees.

MODELLING

a) **Using a 10% level of significance, find the critical region for a two-tailed test of Hasina's theory. The probability of rejection in each tail should be as close to 0.05 as possible.**

- Let $p = $ proportion of trees with the leaf disease.

- Formulate the hypotheses: $H_0: p = 0.15$ $H_1: p \ne 0.15$

- Let $X = $ number of sampled trees with the disease. Under H_0, $X \sim B(20, 0.15)$.

- The significance level $\alpha = 0.1$.

- This is a two-tailed test, so you're interested in both ends of the sampling distribution.

  The **lower tail** is the set of 'low' values of X with a total probability as close to 0.05 as possible.

  The **upper tail** is the set of 'high' values of X with a total probability as close to 0.05 as possible.

- Using the binomial tables:

  Lower tail: $P(X \le 0) = 0.0388 < 0.05$
  $P(X \le 1) = 0.1756 > 0.05$

  Find the two values so that $P(X \le x)$ is either side of 0.05 and then see which is closer.

Tip: Be careful — this test is two-tailed, and it asks for the probability of rejection to be as close to $\frac{\alpha}{2}$ as possible.

<u>Upper tail</u>: You need to find X such that $P(X \geq x)$ is as close to 0.05 as possible.

$$P(X \geq 6) = 1 - P(X \leq 5) = 1 - 0.9327 = 0.0673 > 0.05$$
$$0.0673 - 0.05 = 0.0173$$

$$P(X \geq 7) = 1 - P(X \leq 6) = 1 - 0.9781 = 0.0219 < 0.05$$
$$0.05 - 0.0219 = 0.0281$$

You want the probability to be **as close as possible** to 0.05, so the lower tail is $X \leq 0$ and the upper tail is $X \geq 6$ because 0.0673 is closer to 0.05 than 0.0219 is.

So the critical region is $X = 0$ or $X \geq 6$.

b) **Find the actual significance level of a test based on your critical region from part a).**

The actual significance level is found by adding the probabilities (under H_0) of the test statistic falling in each part of the critical region.

$$P(X = 0) + P(X \geq 6) = 0.0388 + 0.0673$$
$$= 0.1061$$

You could also give this as 10.61%

c) **Hasina finds that 8 of the sampled trees have the leaf disease. Comment on this finding.**

The observed value of 8 is in the critical region. So there is evidence at the 10% level of significance to reject H_0 and to support Hasina's theory that there has been a change in the proportion of affected trees.

Exercise 2.2

Q1 A primary school hopes to increase the percentage of pupils reaching the top level in reading from its current value of 25% by limiting the time pupils spend playing games online. Twenty parents will be limiting their child's use of online games.

a) Using a 5% level, find the critical region for a one-tailed test of whether the proportion of pupils reaching the top reading level has increased.

b) State the actual significance level.

Q2 Miss Cackle wishes to decrease the percentage of pupils giving up her potion-making class after year 9 from its current level of 20%. Over the last 3 years she has tried a new teaching method in one of her classes of 30 pupils. Using a 10% significance level, find the critical region for a test of whether the number of pupils giving up potions after year 9 has decreased. State the actual significance level.

Q3 Politicians are testing for a difference in local councils' rubbish collection service between the North and the South. They've found that 40% of the northern councils provide a weekly service. They have randomly chosen 25 councils in the south of the country to investigate. Find the critical region for a test of whether the number of councils providing weekly collections is significantly different in the south at the 5% level. The probability of each tail should be as close to 2.5% as possible. Calculate the actual significance level.

Q3 Tip: The probability of each tail can be bigger than or smaller than 0.025.

Q4 A travel agent thinks that fewer people are booking their holidays early this year. In the past, 35% have booked their summer holiday by February 1st. She intends to ask 15 people on 2nd February whether they have booked their summer holiday.

a) Find the critical region for a test at the 5% level of whether fewer people are booking their holidays early this year.

b) State the actual significance level.

c) The travel agent finds that 3 of the people she asked had already booked their summer holiday.
Is this result significant at the 5% level?

Q5 A new drug is to be tested on 50 people to see if they report an improvement in their symptoms. In the past it has been found that with a placebo treatment, 15% of people report an improvement, so the new drug has to be significantly better than this. Find the critical region for a test at the 1% level of significance of whether the new drug is significantly better than a placebo. The probability of the tail should be less than 1%. State the actual significance level.

Q6 Tests conducted on five-year-old girls have found that 5% of them believe that they have magical powers. A group of 50 five-year-old boys are to be tested to see if the same proportion of boys believe that they have magical powers. Find the critical region for a test at the 10% level of whether the proportion of boys who believe they have magical powers is different from that of girls. The probability of each tail should be as close to 5% as possible.
Calculate the actual significance level.

Q6 Tip: For a two-tailed test, the actual significance level is the sum of the probabilities that the test statistic falls in each part of the critical region.

Q7 The British Furniture Company's top salesman has persuaded 60% of customers to take out a loyalty card. He has been on a motivational course and aims to improve even further. On his first day's work after the course he serves 12 customers.

a) Using a 5% level of significance, find the critical region for a test of whether the salesman has improved.

b) State the actual significance level.

c) He persuades 10 customers to take out a loyalty card.
Is this result significant at the 5% level?

1. Understanding Units

When answering Mechanics questions, you will be expected to give answers with units. They will be given with the quantities in the question, though you might have to derive the units of your answer from the ones you start with.

S.I. units

Learning Objectives:

- Understand and use base units in the S.I. system for length, time and mass.

- Be able to use derived units for quantities such as force and velocity.

The International System of Units (S.I.) was developed so that measurements could be consistent around the world. These units, which include the **metre**, the **kilogram** and the **second**, are set by certain scientific constants.

These units are referred to as **base units**, which means that they can be used to derive all other units of measurement.

Derived units

Tip: The base units are also mutually independent — this means that you can't derive one from the others.

Other units, such as **Newtons**, are called **derived** S.I. units because they are combinations of the base units. All quantities can be measured in units derived from the base S.I. units.

Example 1

Derive the S.I. units of velocity and acceleration.

- Velocity is defined as the change in displacement divided by the time taken. Displacement is measured in metres, and time in seconds, so velocity is measured in m ÷ s = ms^{-1} (or m/s)

- Similarly, acceleration is the change in velocity over time, so is measured in ms^{-1} ÷ s = ms^{-2}

Tip: You might also see non-S.I. derived units, such as miles per hour (mph) — the mile doesn't form part of the S.I. system as it's an imperial unit.

Example 2

Express the Newton in terms of S.I. base units.

- 1 Newton is the force that will cause a mass of 1 kg to accelerate at a rate of 1 ms^{-2}. The formula for the force exerted on an object is the mass of the object multiplied by its acceleration (see page 366).

- So in terms of base units, this is kg × ms^{-2} = $kgms^{-2}$

Exercise 1.1

Q1 Give the derived units of the following measurements using the S.I. base units kg, m and s:

    a) Volume = length × width × height

    b) Density = mass ÷ volume

    c) Momentum = mass × velocity

    d) Energy = force × distance

    e) Pressure = force ÷ area

2. Models in Mechanics

Mechanics is all about describing things that happen in the real world. However, things are normally simplified by modelling the situation as more basic than it actually is. You'll need to be able to explain the modelling assumptions you're making in each question, and there's usually plenty of them.

Learning Objectives:

- Be able to understand and use terminology used in mechanics.
- Be able to explain and evaluate assumptions made in modelling situations.

Modelling

Modelling is a **cycle** — having created a model you can improve it by making more (or fewer) assumptions.

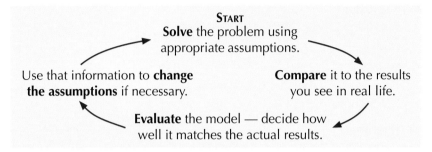

Keep going until you're satisfied with the model.

Mathematical models use lots of words that you already know, but which are used to mean something very precise.

- **Light** — the body has negligible mass.
- **Static** — the body is not moving.
- **Rough** — a body in contact with the surface will experience a frictional force which will act to oppose motion.
- **Smooth** — a body in contact with the surface will not experience a frictional force.
- **Rigid** — the body does not bend.
- **Thin** — the body has negligible thickness.
- **Inextensible** — the body can't be stretched.
- **Equilibrium** — there is no resultant force acting on the body.

Tip: These definitions refer to a '**body**' — this is just another way of saying 'an object'.

- **Particle** — a body whose mass acts at a point, so its dimensions don't matter.
- **Plane** — a flat surface.
- **Beam** or **Rod** — a long, thin, straight, rigid body.
- **Wire** — a thin, inextensible, rigid, light body.
- **String** — a thin body, usually modelled as being light and inextensible.
- **Peg** — a fixed support which a body can hang from or rest on.
- **Pulley** — a wheel, usually modelled as fixed and smooth, over which a string passes.

Tip: You won't be tested on these terms, but you need to be familiar with what they mean as they come up all the time.

Labelling forces

You have to know what **forces** are acting on a body when you're creating a mathematical model, so you need to understand what each **type** of force is.

- **Weight (W)**
  Due to the particle's mass, m, and the acceleration due to gravity, g: $W = mg$ — weight always acts **downwards**.

- The **Normal Reaction (R or N)**
  The reaction from a surface.
  Reaction is always at **90° to the surface**.

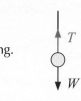

- **Tension (T)**
  Force in a **taut** rope, wire or string.

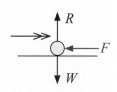

- **Friction (F)**
  A **resistance** force due to **roughness** between a body and surface.
  Always acts **against motion**, or likely motion.

- **Thrust or Compression**
  Force in a rod (e.g. the pole of an open umbrella).

Examples

Draw a diagram to model each of the following situations. In each case, state the assumptions you have made.

a) A brick is resting flat on a horizontal table.

Assumptions:
- The brick is a particle.
- There's no wind or other external forces involved.

b) An ice hockey player is accelerating across an ice rink.

Assumptions:
- The skater is a particle.
- There is no friction between the skates and the ice.
- There is no air resistance.
- The skater generates a constant forward force, S.

c) A golf ball is dropped from a tall building.

Assumptions:
- The ball is a particle.
- Air resistance can be ignored.
- There's no wind or other external forces involved.
- The effect of gravity (g) is constant.

d) A book is put flat on a table. One end of the table is slowly lifted and the angle to the horizontal is measured when the book starts to slide.

Assumptions:

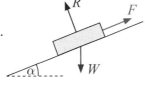

- The book is a particle.
- The book is rigid, so it doesn't bend or open.
- The surface of the table is rough, so there will be a frictional force acting between it and the book.
- There are no other external forces acting.

e) A sledge is steadily pulled along horizontal ground by a small child with a rope.

Assumptions:

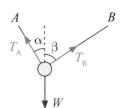

- The sledge is a particle.
- Friction is too big to be ignored (i.e. it's not ice).
- The rope is a light, inextensible string.
- The rope is horizontal (it's a small child).

> **Tip:** The weight of a rigid object can be assumed to act at a single point — the centre of mass of the object.

f) A ball is held by two strings, A and B, at angles α and β to the vertical.

Assumptions:

- The ball is a particle.
- The strings are light.
- The strings are inextensible.

Exercise 2.1

For each of the following questions, draw a diagram to model the situation and state any assumptions you have made.

Q1   An apple falls from a tree.

Q2   A shoe lace is threaded through a conker.
     The conker hangs vertically in equilibrium from the shoe lace.

Q3   A sledge is steadily pulled up an icy hill by a rope.

Q4   a) A wooden box is pushed across a polished marble floor.
     b) A crate is pulled across a carpeted floor by a horizontal rope.

Q5   A person pushes a small package along the road with a stick.
     The stick makes an angle of 20° with the horizontal.

Q6   a) A car is driven up a hill.   b) A car is driven down a hill.

Q7   A strongman pulls a lorry along a horizontal road
     by a rope parallel to the road.

> **Q6-7 Hint:** Both the car's engine and the strongman will generate a driving force D.

1. Motion Graphs

Learning Objectives:

- Be able to interpret displacement-time graphs to find a body's displacement and velocity.

- Be able to interpret velocity-time graphs to find a body's displacement, velocity and acceleration.

- Be able to draw displacement-time and velocity-time graphs.

Kinematics is the study of the motion of objects. Here, this means describing an object's displacement, velocity and acceleration.

Displacement-time and velocity-time graphs can both be used to represent an object's motion graphically.

Tip: Displacement, velocity and acceleration are all **vector** quantities— they have a magnitude and a direction (see p.214).

Displacement, velocity and acceleration

- **Displacement** is an object's **distance from a particular point** (often its starting point), measured in a straight line. It's not necessarily the same as the total distance travelled.

- **Velocity** is the **rate of change of displacement** with respect to **time**. It can be thought of as a measure of how **fast** an object is moving. It's different from **speed** because it takes into account the direction of movement. If distance is measured in metres (m) and time is measured in seconds (s), then velocity is measured in metres per second (ms^{-1}).

- **Acceleration** is the **rate of change** of an object's **velocity** with respect to **time** — i.e. how much an object is **speeding up** or **slowing down**. If velocity is measured in ms^{-1} and time is measured in s, then acceleration is measured in ms^{-2}.

Tip: A displacement-time graph is not the same as a distance-time graph. The height of a distance-time graph gives the **total distance** that a body has travelled up to that point. The gradient of a distance-time graph gives an object's **speed**, rather than its velocity (i.e. it says nothing about the direction in which the object is moving).

Displacement-time graphs

A **displacement-time (x-t) graph** shows how an object's **displacement** from a particular point changes over time. Displacement is plotted on the vertical axis, and time is plotted on the horizontal axis.

- The **height** of the graph gives the object's **displacement** at that time.

- The **gradient** of the graph at a particular point gives the object's **velocity** at that time — the **steeper** the line, the **greater** the velocity.

- A **negative gradient** shows that the object is moving in the **opposite direction** to when the gradient is positive.

- A horizontal line has a **zero gradient**, which means the object is **stationary**.

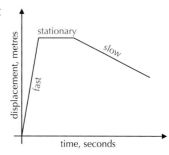

Example 1

A girl goes for a run along a straight path.
Her journey is detailed below:

- **She runs 1.5 km in 5 minutes, then rests for 2 minutes.**
- **She then jogs 0.5 km in 4 minutes, in the same direction as before.**
- **Finally, she runs 2.5 km back in the direction she came, passing her starting point along the way.**
- **She finishes 20 minutes after she first set off.**

Show her journey on a displacement-time graph.

Taking her initial direction as being positive,
draw the journey one stage at a time:

1. The graph should start at (0, 0) ($t = 0$ minutes, $x = 0$ km), then increase to a height of 1.5 km over 5 minutes.

2. In the next stage, the girl rests for 2 minutes, so this part of the graph will be a horizontal line.

3. The girl then jogs 0.5 km, from a displacement of 1.5 km to 2 km, over 4 minutes. She is travelling in the same direction as before, so the graph still has a positive gradient, but she is not travelling as fast, so the line is not as steep.

4. In the final stage, she travels in the opposite direction for 2.5 km, finishing at (20, –0.5) ($t = 20$ minutes, $x = -0.5$ km). In this stage, the graph has a negative gradient, as she is moving in the opposite direction to before.

> **Tip:** The 'straight path' bit tells you that all motion is in a straight line — so, given the distance travelled, you can work out the girl's displacement after each stage of the journey, measuring them from her starting point, $x = 0$.

> **Tip:** You should choose which direction you are going to take as being positive. Then any displacement in the opposite direction will be negative.

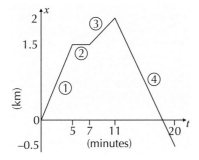

> **Tip:** The graph goes below the horizontal axis because the girl's final displacement is –0.5 km, i.e. she goes back through her starting point and finishes 0.5 km away in the opposite direction to her initial motion.

Example 2

A cyclist's journey is shown on this displacement-time graph. Given that the cyclist starts from rest and cycles in a straight line, describe the motion.

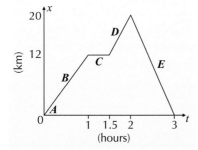

A: Starts from rest (when $t = 0$, $x = 0$).

B: Cycles 12 km in 1 hour.

Velocity $= \dfrac{12 \text{ km}}{1 \text{ hour}} = 12 \text{ kmh}^{-1}$

C: Rests for half an hour ($v = 0$).

D: Cycles 8 km (from 12 km to 20 km) in half an hour.

Velocity $= \dfrac{8 \text{ km}}{\frac{1}{2} \text{ hour}} = 16 \text{ kmh}^{-1}$

E: Returns to starting position, cycling 20 km in 1 hour.

Velocity $= -\dfrac{20 \text{ km}}{1 \text{ hour}} = -20 \text{ kmh}^{-1}$

Exercise 1.1

Q1 Hint: Make sure you get your signs right — remember that a negative gradient means a negative velocity.

Q1   The displacement-time graph shows the journey of a car travelling in a straight line. Calculate the velocity of the car during each stage of the journey.

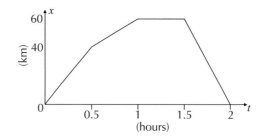

Q2   A coach travels in a straight line between three coach stops, *A*, *B* and *C*. Its journey is as follows:

- Leaves *A* at midday.

- Travels 30 km at a constant speed to *B* in one hour.

- Stops for 30 minutes.

- Leaves *B* and travels 60 km at a constant speed to point *C* in the same direction as before, moving at a constant speed of 40 kmh^{-1}.

- Stops for 30 minutes.

- Leaves *C* and returns to *A* at a constant speed, arriving at 18:00.

a) Draw a displacement-time graph to show the coach's journey. Plot the time of day on the horizontal axis, and the coach's displacement from *A* on the vertical axis.

Q2c) Hint: The average speed of an object is given by:

$\dfrac{\text{total distance travelled}}{\text{total time taken}}$

b) Find the velocity of the coach during the final stage of the journey.

c) Find the average speed of the coach over the whole journey.

Q3 A man leaves his house at 13:00. He walks in a straight line at a speed of 5 mph for one hour, then at a speed of 3 mph in the same direction for the next hour. He then rests for an hour. The man's wife leaves their house at 14:30 and travels at a constant speed to meet him at 15:30.

Draw a displacement-time graph to show the two journeys.

Q4 A man walks with velocity u ms^{-1} for 500 m, then with velocity $-2u$ ms^{-1} for 700 m. He then walks 600 m with velocity $1.5u$ ms^{-1}.
   a) Find the man's final displacement.
   b) Show his journey on a displacement-time graph.
   c) Find his total journey time. Give your answer in terms of u.
   d) Find his average speed in terms of u.

Q5 A car travels in a straight line with speed u ms^{-1} for t seconds, stops for 100 seconds, then returns back the way it came with speed $2u$ ms^{-1}.
   a) Draw a displacement-time graph to show the movement of the car.
   b) Find an expression in terms of u and t for the total distance travelled by the car.
   c) Find the average speed of the car (including its rest time). Give your answer in terms of u and t.

Velocity-time graphs

A **velocity-time (v-t) graph** shows how an object's **velocity** changes over time.

- The **height** of a velocity-time graph gives the object's **velocity** at that time, and its **gradient** gives its **acceleration**.

- A **negative gradient** can mean that the object is **decelerating** in the **positive direction**, or that it is **accelerating** in the **negative direction**.

- A **horizontal** line means the object is moving at a **constant velocity**.

- The **area** under the graph gives the object's **displacement**.

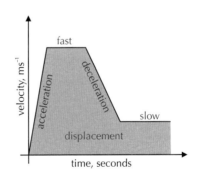

Tip: Remember that velocity is different from speed in that the **direction** of motion is important. So for velocity-time graph questions, you need to decide which direction is positive.

Example 1

A car starts from rest and reverses in a straight line with constant acceleration to a velocity of -5 ms^{-1} in 12 seconds.

Still reversing, it then decelerates to rest in 3 seconds and remains stationary for another 3 seconds.

The car then moves forward along the same straight line as before (but in the opposite direction), accelerating uniformly to a velocity of 8 ms^{-1} in 6 seconds. It maintains this speed for 6 seconds.

a) Show the car's movement on a velocity-time graph.

Draw the journey one stage at a time:

1. The graph should start at ($t = 0$ s, $v = 0$ ms^{-1}), then decrease to -5 ms^{-1} over 12 seconds.

2. In the next stage, the graph should return to ($v = 0$ ms^{-1}) in 3 seconds.

3. The car is then stationary, so the graph should remain at ($v = 0$ ms^{-1}) for 3 seconds.

4. In the next stage, the graph should increase to ($v = 8$ ms^{-1}) in 6 seconds.

5. Finally, the car travels at a constant velocity for 6 seconds — this is shown by a horizontal line.

Tip: If an object is moving with negative velocity, then the graph will go below the t axis.

Tip: To find the **total distance** travelled, you would add the magnitudes of the areas together:
$37.5 + 72 = 109.5$ m

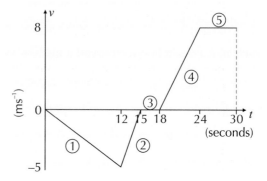

b) Use your graph to find the car's final displacement from its starting point.

- First find the area below the horizontal axis:
$$\text{Area} = \frac{1}{2} \times 15 \times -5$$
$$= -37.5 \text{ m}$$

- Then find the area above the horizontal axis. Using the formula for the area of a trapezium:
$$\text{Area} = \frac{1}{2}(6 + 12) \times 8$$
$$= 72 \text{ m}$$

- Now add these together to find the final displacement:
$$\text{Displacement} = -37.5 + 72$$
$$= \boxed{34.5 \text{ m}}$$

Exercise 1.2

Q1 The velocity-time graph below shows a bus journey.

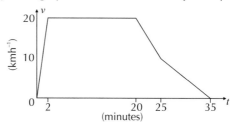

Describe the motion of the bus, given that it travels in a straight line.

Q2

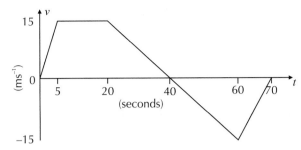

The velocity-time graph shows the motion of a particle travelling in a straight line. Find the particle's acceleration:

a) during the first 5 seconds of motion.

b) between 40 and 60 seconds.

c) during the final 10 seconds of motion.

Q3 A particle is travelling in a straight line. It passes point A with velocity 10 ms^{-1}. Immediately after passing A, it accelerates at 4 ms^{-2} for x metres up to a velocity of 50 ms^{-1}, then decelerates at 10 ms^{-2} for y metres to point B. It passes B with velocity 10 ms^{-1}. The particle takes T seconds to travel between A and B.

a) Show the particle's motion on a velocity-time graph.

b) Find the area under the graph in terms of T.

c) Calculate the values of x, y and T.

Q4 A train is travelling at a steady speed of 30 ms^{-1} along a straight track. As it passes a signal box, it begins to decelerate steadily, coming to rest at a station in 20 seconds. The train remains stationary for 20 seconds, then sets off back in the direction it came with an acceleration of 0.375 ms^{-2}. It reaches a speed of 15 ms^{-1} as it passes the signal box.

a) Draw a velocity-time graph to show the motion of the train. How long after leaving the station does the train reach the signal box?

b) Find the train's deceleration as it comes into the station.

c) Find the distance between the signal box and the station.

Q4 Hint: Make sure you decide which direction is positive — any velocities in the opposite direction will be negative. At these times, the graph will go below the horizontal axis.

Q5 A stone is held out over the edge of a cliff and thrown vertically upwards with a speed of 9.8 ms^{-1}. It decelerates until it becomes stationary at its highest point, 1 second after being thrown, then begins to fall back down. It lands in the sea below the cliff edge with speed 29.4 ms^{-1}, 4 seconds after it was thrown.

a) Draw a velocity-time graph to show the motion of the stone.

b) Use your graph to find:

(i) the distance the stone travels before it reaches its highest point,

(ii) the distance the stone travels from its highest point to the sea,

(iii) the height of the cliff above the sea.

Q5 Hint: Remember — displacement is not the same thing as distance travelled.

2. Constant Acceleration Equations

There are five constant acceleration equations — these are used to find out information about objects which are accelerating (or decelerating) uniformly. They're in the formula booklet, so you don't need to memorise them.

Learning Objectives:

- Know and recall the constant acceleration equations.
- Be able to derive the constant acceleration equations, both graphically and using calculus.
- Be able to use the equations to solve problems involving motion with constant acceleration.

Tip: The constant acceleration equations are often called '*suvat*' equations because of the five variables involved.

Constant acceleration equations

- The constant acceleration equations are:

$$v = u + at$$
$$s = ut + \frac{1}{2}at^2$$
$$s = \left(\frac{u+v}{2}\right)t$$
$$v^2 = u^2 + 2as$$
$$s = vt - \frac{1}{2}at^2$$

s = displacement in m
u = initial speed (or velocity) in ms^{-1}
v = final speed (or velocity) in ms^{-1}
a = acceleration in ms^{-2}
t = time that passes in s (seconds)

Remember — these equations only work if the acceleration is **constant**.

- You'll usually be given three variables — your job is to **choose the equation** that will help you find the missing fourth variable.

- In this book, all the motion you'll deal with will be in a **straight line**. You should choose which direction is **positive**, then any velocity, acceleration or displacement in the **opposite direction** will be **negative**.

- You can derive the *suvat* equations using motion graphs and a bit of algebra:

Consider a particle moving with constant acceleration a.
The particle will accelerate from an initial velocity u to a final velocity v.
As it accelerates, it will cover a distance s over time t.

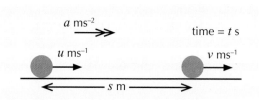

The velocity-time graph below shows the movement of the particle.

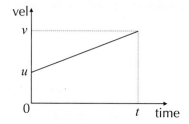

- The **acceleration** of the particle is given by the **gradient** of the graph:

$$a = \frac{v - u}{t}, \text{ or } v = u + at$$

- The **distance travelled** is given by the **area** under the graph:

  Area of A = ut

  Area of B = $\frac{1}{2}(v-u)t$

  So $s = ut + \frac{1}{2}(v-u)t$

  $\quad = ut + \frac{1}{2}vt - \frac{1}{2}ut$

  $\quad = \frac{1}{2}ut + \frac{1}{2}vt$

  $$s = \left(\frac{u+v}{2}\right)t$$

Tip: You could also find this area using the formula for the area of a trapezium: $s = \frac{1}{2}(u+v) \times t$

Now you can rearrange these two equations and make some substitutions to derive the remaining formulas.

- Substituting $v = u + at$ into $s = \left(\frac{u+v}{2}\right)t$ gives:

  $$s = \left(\frac{u+u+at}{2}\right)t = \left(u + \frac{1}{2}at\right)t$$

  $$\Rightarrow s = ut + \frac{1}{2}at^2$$

- Substituting $t = \left(\frac{v-u}{a}\right)$ into $s = \left(\frac{u+v}{2}\right)t$ gives:

  $$s = \left(\frac{u+v}{2}\right)\left(\frac{v-u}{a}\right)$$

  $$2as = (u+v)(v-u) = v^2 - u^2$$

  $$\Rightarrow v^2 = u^2 + 2as$$

- Substituting $u = v - at$ into $s = \left(\frac{u+v}{2}\right)t$ gives:

  $$s = \left(\frac{v-at+v}{2}\right)t = \left(v - \frac{1}{2}at\right)t$$

  $$\Rightarrow s = vt - \frac{1}{2}at^2$$

You can also derive these equations using calculus — you need to understand both methods.

- Acceleration is the **rate of change of velocity (v) with respect to time (t)**. This can be written as $a = \frac{dv}{dt}$.
- From the Fundamental Theorem of Calculus (see p.192), this means that $v = \int a\,dt$.
- Since a is constant, you can calculate this integral: $v = \int a\,dt = at + c$
- When $t = 0$, you get $v = a(0) + c \Rightarrow v = c$
- So c is just the velocity at time 0 — i.e. c is the initial velocity, u.
- This gives you the first of the *suvat* equations:

  $$v = u + at$$

- Similarly, velocity is the **rate of change of displacement with respect to time**, i.e. $v = \dfrac{ds}{dt} \Rightarrow s = \int v \, dt$.

- From before, you know that $v = u + at$:

$$s = \int u + at \, dt$$
$$= ut + \frac{1}{2}at^2 + C$$

- At $t = 0$, $s = 0 \Rightarrow u(0) + \frac{1}{2}a(0) + C = 0 \Rightarrow C = 0$

- This gives you the second *suvat* equation:

$$s = ut + \frac{1}{2}at^2$$

Tip: The place where the object begins at time $t = 0$ is the starting point where $s = 0$ as well.

Rearranging and substituting one of these equations into the other will give you the other *suvat* equations, as on the previous page. You can now use these results to solve all sorts of Mechanics problems.

Example 1

A jet ski travels in a straight line along a river. It passes under two bridges 200 m apart and is observed to be travelling at 5 ms⁻¹ under the first bridge and at 9 ms⁻¹ under the second bridge. Calculate its acceleration.

MODELLING

- List the variables:

$s = 200 \qquad u = 5 \qquad v = 9 \qquad a = a \leftarrow$ You have to work out a

- Choose the equation with s, u, v and a in it: $v^2 = u^2 + 2as$

- Substitute the values you're given: $9^2 = 5^2 + (2 \times a \times 200)$

$$81 = 25 + 400a$$
$$400a = 81 - 25 = 56$$
$$a = 56 \div 400 = \boxed{0.14 \text{ ms}^{-2}}$$

Tip: You're not told or asked for t, so don't bother writing it down.

Example 2

A particle accelerates from rest for 8 seconds at a rate of 12 ms⁻². The particle's motion is restricted to a straight path.

a) Find the velocity of the particle at the end of the 8 seconds.

- List the variables: You'll need to find s in part **b)**

$s = s \qquad u = 0 \qquad v = v \qquad a = 12 \qquad t = 8$

- Choose the equation with u, a, t and v in it: $v = u + at$

- Substitute the values you're given: $v = 0 + (12 \times 8) = \boxed{96 \text{ ms}^{-1}}$

Tip: If a particle 'starts from rest', then $u = 0$.

b) Find the distance travelled by the particle during this time.

- Choose the equation with u, a, t and s in it: $s = ut + \frac{1}{2}at^2$

- Substitute the values you're given: $s = (0 \times 8) + \frac{1}{2}(12 \times 8^2) = \boxed{384 \text{ m}}$

Tip: You could use a different equation as you now know v, but it's a good idea to use this one (just in case your answer for v is wrong).

Example 3

**A car decelerates at a rate of 16 kmh^{-2} for 6 minutes.
It travels 1.28 km along a straight road during this time.
Find the velocity of the car at the end of the 6 minutes.**

- List the variables:

$s = 1.28$ $v = v$ $a = -16$ $t = 6 \div 60 = 0.1$ *a is negative because the car is decelerating.*

- Choose the equation with *s*, *v*, *a* and *t* in it: $s = vt - \frac{1}{2}at^2$

- Substitute the values you're given: $1.28 = 0.1v - \frac{1}{2}(-16 \times 0.1^2)$

$$0.1v = 1.28 - \frac{1}{2}(0.16)$$

$$0.1v = 1.2$$

$$v = 12 \text{ kmh}^{-1}$$

Tip: Make sure you use consistent units throughout the question. Here, you should change the time from minutes to hours to match the units of acceleration.

Exercise 2.1

Q1 A car travels along a straight horizontal road. It accelerates uniformly from rest to a velocity of 12 ms^{-1} in 5 seconds.
  a) Find the car's acceleration.
  b) Find the total distance travelled by the car.

Hint: Remember — always write out the *suvat* variables.

Q2 A cyclist is travelling at 18 kmh^{-1}.
  He brakes steadily, coming to rest in 50 m.
  a) Calculate the cyclist's initial speed in ms^{-1} .
  b) Find the time it takes him to come to rest.
  c) Find his deceleration.

Q2 Hint: To convert from kmh^{-1} to ms^{-1}, multiply by 1000, then divide by 60^2.

Q3 A skier accelerates from 5 ms^{-1} to 25 ms^{-1} over a distance of 60 m.
  a) Find the skier's acceleration.
  b) What modelling assumptions have you made?

Q4 A car travels with uniform acceleration between three lamp posts, equally spaced at 18 m apart. It passes the second post 2 seconds after passing the first post, and passes the third post 1 second later.
  a) Find the car's acceleration.
  b) Calculate the car's velocity when it passes the first post.

Q4 Hint: Consider the motion between the first and second posts and the first and third posts separately to form a pair of simultaneous equations.

Q5 A bus is approaching a tunnel. At time $t = 0$ seconds, the driver begins slowing down steadily from a speed of U ms^{-1} until, at $t = 15$ s, he enters the tunnel, travelling at 20 ms^{-1}. The driver maintains this speed while he drives through the tunnel. After emerging from the tunnel at $t = 40$ s, he accelerates steadily, reaching a speed of U ms^{-1} at $t = 70$ s.
  a) Calculate the length of the tunnel.
  b) Given that the total distance travelled by the coach is 1580 m, find the value of U.

Q5 Hint: The motion you're interested in is between 15 and 40 seconds, so you can use $t = 40 - 15 = 25$ in your calculations.

Gravity

- An object moving through the air will experience an **acceleration** towards the centre of the earth due to **gravity**.

- Acceleration due to gravity is denoted by the letter g, where **$g = 9.8$ ms^{-2}**.

- Acceleration due to gravity always acts **vertically downwards**.

- For an object moving freely under gravity, you can use the *suvat* equations to find information such as the **speed of projection, time of flight, greatest height** and **landing speed**.

Tip: You might be given a different value of g in a particular question (e.g. $g = 10$ ms^{-2}). Use the one you're given, otherwise your answer might not match the examiner's.

Example 1

A pebble is dropped into an empty well 18 m deep and moves freely under gravity until it hits the bottom. Calculate the time it takes to reach the bottom.

- First, list the variables, taking downwards as positive:

  $s = 18 \qquad u = 0 \qquad a = 9.8 \qquad t = t$

- You need the equation with s, u, a and t in it: $\quad s = ut + \frac{1}{2}at^2$

- Substitute values: $\quad 18 = (0 \times t) + \left(\frac{1}{2} \times 9.8 \times t^2\right)$

  $$18 = 4.9t^2$$

  $$t^2 = \frac{18}{4.9} = 3.67...$$

  $$t = \sqrt{3.67...} = \boxed{1.92 \text{ s (3 s.f.)}}$$

Tip: Watch out for tricky questions like this — at first it looks like they've only given you one variable. You have to spot that the pebble was dropped (so $u = 0$) and that it's moving freely under gravity (so $a = g = 9.8$ ms^{-2}).

Example 2

A ball is projected vertically upwards at 3 ms^{-1} from a point 1.5 m above the ground.

a) How long does it take to reach its maximum height?

- First, list the variables, taking up as the positive direction:

  $u = 3$
  $v = 0$ ← When projected objects reach the top of their motion, they stop momentarily.
  $a = -9.8$ ← Because g always acts downwards and up was taken as positive, a is negative.
  $t = t$

- Use the equation with u, v, a and t in it: $\quad v = u + at$

- Substitute values: $\quad 0 = 3 + (-9.8 \times t)$

  $$0 = 3 - 9.8t$$

  $$t = \frac{3}{9.8} = \boxed{0.306 \text{ s (3 s.f.)}}$$

Tip: Make sure you decide which direction (upwards or downwards) you are going to take as being positive. This tells you whether each of your *suvat* variables is positive or negative.

b) What is the ball's speed when it hits the ground?

Think about the complete path of the ball.

The ball lands on the ground, 1.5 m below the point of projection.

So $s = -1.5$

Using $v^2 = u^2 + 2as$ where $v = v$, $u = 3$, $a = -9.8$, $s = -1.5$:

$$v^2 = u^2 + 2as = 3^2 + 2(-9.8 \times -1.5)$$
$$= 38.4$$

So speed $= \sqrt{38.4} = $ 6.20 ms^{-1} (to 3 s.f.)

Tip: Remember that s is **displacement** — the object's final position relative to its starting point, not its total distance travelled. Here, the ball lands below its initial point, and since upwards is positive, s is negative.

Tip: The question asks for its **speed**, so you can ignore the negative root.

Example 3

A particle is projected vertically upwards from ground level with a speed of u ms^{-1}. The particle takes 2.6 s to return to ground level.

a) Draw a velocity-time graph to show the particle's motion.

- The particle is projected with speed u, then decelerates due to gravity until it is momentarily at rest at its highest point.

- It then falls to the ground, accelerating due to gravity and reaching its initial speed u (but in the opposite direction to before) when it lands.

- There are two possible graphs, depending on which direction is taken as being positive.

- If upwards is taken as positive, then the particle's initial velocity is positive (u ms^{-1}), and its velocity on the way back down will be negative.

Tip: Remember that velocity takes into account the direction of motion, so can be positive or negative. Speed is all about the magnitude, so the direction doesn't matter.

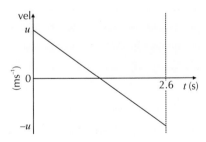

- If downwards is taken as positive, then the particle's initial velocity is negative ($-u$ ms^{-1}), and its velocity on the way back down will be positive.

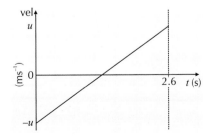

b) Find u, the particle's speed of projection.

Tip: The particle reaches its maximum height halfway through its flight time.

Think about the first half of the particle's motion, from ground level to its highest point. Taking upwards as positive:

$$u = u \qquad v = 0 \qquad a = -9.8 \qquad t = 2.6 \div 2 = 1.3$$

When it reaches its maximum height, the particle will stop momentarily.

Using $v = u + at$

$$0 = u - 9.8 \times 1.3$$

So $u = 9.8 \times 1.3 =$ 12.74 ms⁻¹

Example 4

A particle is fired vertically upwards from ground level with speed 49 ms⁻¹.

Assuming that air resistance can be ignored, find the amount of time that the particle is over 78.4 m above the ground.

- As the particle travels upwards, it will pass a height of 78.4 m.

- Once it has reached its highest point, it will start to fall, and will pass 78.4 m again, on the way back down.

Tip: It's assumed here that the particle will actually reach a height of 78.4 m — if it doesn't, then the quadratic will have **no real solutions**.

- Use a constant acceleration equation to form a quadratic to find the two moments in time that the particle is at 78.4 m.

- The difference between these two times will be the length of time the particle is above that height.

  - Taking up as the positive direction:

    $$s = 78.4 \qquad u = 49 \qquad a = -9.8 \qquad t = t$$

  - Using $s = ut + \frac{1}{2}at^2$

    $$78.4 = 49t - 4.9t^2$$

    $$\Rightarrow t^2 - 10t + 16 = 0$$

    $$(t - 2)(t - 8) = 0$$

    $$\Rightarrow t = 2, \ t = 8$$

  - So the particle is 78.4 m above the ground 2 seconds after being fired (on the way up), and 8 seconds after being fired (on the way back down).

  - This means that the particle is above 78.4 m for $8 - 2 =$ 6 seconds.

Example 5

A boot is thrown vertically upwards from a point x m above ground level. Its speed of projection is 4 ms⁻¹. The boot lands on the ground 2 seconds after being thrown.

a) Find the value of x.

- Taking up as the positive direction:

$$s = -x \qquad u = 4 \qquad a = -9.8 \qquad t = 2$$

- Using $s = ut + \frac{1}{2}at^2$

$$-x = (4 \times 2) + \frac{1}{2}(-9.8 \times 2^2)$$

$$-x = -11.6$$

So $x = \boxed{11.6 \text{ m}}$

Tip: $s = -x$ because the boot lands x m below its point of projection.

b) Find the speed and direction of the boot 0.8 seconds after it is thrown.

- Taking up as the positive direction:

$$u = 4 \qquad v = v \qquad a = -9.8 \qquad t = 0.8$$

- Using $v = u + at$

$$v = 4 + (-9.8 \times 0.8) = -3.84 \text{ ms}^{-1}$$

v is negative, so the boot is moving $\boxed{\text{downwards at 3.84 ms}^{-1}}$.

Tip: Notice that for all of these examples, the mass of the object is not part of the calculations. This is because the acceleration due to gravity does not depend on an object's mass.

Exercise 2.2

Q1 A pebble is dropped down a hole to see how deep it is. It reaches the bottom of the hole after 3 seconds. How deep is the hole?

Q1 Hint: The pebble is dropped, so $u = 0$.

Q2 A ball is dropped from a second floor window that is 5 metres from the ground.
  a) How long will it take to reach the ground?
  b) At what speed will it hit the ground?

Q3 An object is projected vertically upwards from ground level with a speed of 30 ms⁻¹.
  a) Find the maximum height reached by the object.
  b) Find the time it takes the object to reach the ground.
  c) Find the object's speed and direction 2 seconds after launch.

Q4 A particle is projected vertically upwards with a speed u ms^{-1} from a point d metres above the ground. After 3 seconds the particle hits the ground with a speed of 20 ms^{-1}.

a) Calculate the value of u.

b) Calculate the value of d.

Q5 Hint: Remember that the apple is not thrown from ground level.

Q5 An apple is thrown vertically upwards with speed 8 ms^{-1} from a height of 5 metres above the ground.

a) Calculate the apple's maximum height above the ground.

b) For how long is the apple 8 m or more above the ground?

Q6 A decorator is painting the frame of a fifth floor window and catapults a brush up to his mate exactly three floors above him. He catapults it vertically with a speed of 12 ms^{-1}, and it is at its maximum height when his mate catches it.

a) Find the distance between the decorator and his mate.

b) For how long is the brush in the air?

He later catapults a tub of putty vertically at the same speed but his mate fails to catch it. The floors of the building are equally spaced apart, and the decorator is positioned at the base of the fifth floor.

c) At what speed does it hit the ground?

Q7 The displacement-time graph below shows the motion of an object fired vertically upwards with speed 24.5 ms^{-1} over the edge of a cliff. The object travels in a vertical line and hits the ground below (at $x = 0$).

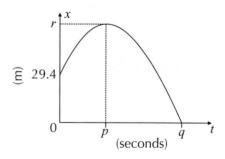

a) Find the value of p.

b) Find the value of q.

c) Find the value of r.

Q8 A projectile is fired from a point 50 m below ground level vertically upwards. It passes a target 100 m above ground level and 3 seconds later passes another target which is 220 m above ground level. Assume that air resistance can be ignored.

Q8 Hint: Work out part a) in two separate stages.

a) Find the speed of projection of the projectile.

b) Find the maximum height above the ground reached by the projectile.

c) Find the time taken by the projectile to reach the first target.

More complicated problems

Now you're nice and familiar with the constant acceleration equations, it's time to get your teeth into some trickier problems.

- Some questions will involve **motion graphs** — you may have to find areas and gradients as well as use the *suvat* equations.

- Some will involve **more than one** moving object. For these questions, *t* is often the same (or at least connected) because time ticks along for both objects at the same rate. The distance travelled might also be connected.

Example 1

A jogger and a cyclist are travelling along a straight path. Their movements are as follows:

- **The jogger runs with constant velocity.**

- **At the moment the jogger passes the cyclist, the cyclist accelerates from rest, reaching a velocity of 5 ms⁻¹ after 6 seconds, and then continues at this velocity.**

- **The cyclist overtakes the jogger after 15 seconds.**

a) **Taking the time that the cyclist begins to accelerate as $t = 0$ s, draw a speed-time graph to show their motion.**

- The graph of the jogger's motion will be a horizontal line, as the speed is constant. Call the jogger's speed V.

- The graph of the cyclist's motion will increase from ($t = 0$ s, $v = 0$ ms⁻¹) to ($t = 6$ s, $v = 5$ ms⁻¹), then will become horizontal.

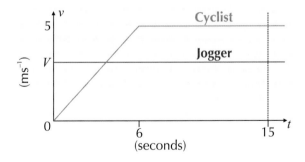

Tip: You know that the cyclist overtakes the jogger, so V must be less than 5 ms⁻¹.

b) **Find the speed of the jogger.**

- After 15 s the distances the jogger and cyclist have travelled are the same, so you can work out the area under the two graphs to get the distances:

  Jogger: Distance = area = $15V$

  Cyclist: Distance = area = $(6 \times 5) \div 2 + (9 \times 5) = 60$

  So $15V = 60$

  $\boxed{V = 4 \text{ ms}^{-1}}$

Tip: Find the area under the cyclist's graph by splitting it into a triangle and a rectangle, or just use the formula for the area of a trapezium.

Example 2

A bus is travelling along a straight road at V ms^{-1}. When it reaches point A it accelerates uniformly for 4 s, reaching a speed of 21 ms^{-1} as it passes point B. At point B, the driver brakes uniformly until the bus comes to a halt 7 s later. The magnitude of the deceleration is twice the magnitude of the previous acceleration.

(MODELLING)

a) **Draw a velocity-time graph to show the motion of the bus.**

- The graph will increase from ($t = 0$ s, $v = V$ ms^{-1}) to ($t = 4$ s, $v = 21$ ms^{-1}).

- It will then return to $v = 0$ ms^{-1} at time $t = 11$ s.

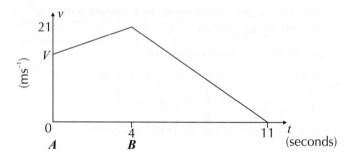

b) **Find the value of V.**

- Split the motion into two stages — 'between A and B', and 'after B'.

- First considering the stage 'after B', list the variables:

$$u = 21 \qquad v = 0 \qquad a = a \qquad t = 7$$

- To find the deceleration use $a = \dfrac{(v - u)}{t}$ ← Just $v = u + at$ rearranged.

$$a = \frac{(0 - 21)}{7} = -3 \text{ ms}^{-2}$$

> **Tip:** You can also use the graph to find the deceleration — it's the gradient of the line.

- The magnitude of the deceleration ('after B') is twice the magnitude of the acceleration ('between A and B'), so the acceleration is 1.5 ms^{-1}.

- Now considering the stage 'between A and B', list the variables:

$$u = V \qquad v = 21 \qquad a = 1.5 \qquad t = 4$$

- Find V using $u = v - at$

$$V = 21 - (1.5 \times 4)$$

So, $\boxed{V = 15 \text{ ms}^{-1}}$

c) **Find the distance travelled by the bus during the measured time.**

Find the area under the graph:

$$\text{Area} = (15 \times 4) + \frac{1}{2}(6 \times 4) + \frac{1}{2}(21 \times 7)$$

$$= \boxed{145.5 \text{ m}}$$

> **Tip:** There are various ways that you could split up this area — they all give the same answer.

Example 3

- **A car, A, travelling along a straight road at a constant 30 ms^{-1}, passes point R at time $t = 0$.**

- **Exactly 2 seconds later, a second car, B, passes point R with velocity 25 ms^{-1}, moving in the same direction as car A.**
- **Car B accelerates at a constant 2 ms^{-2}.**

Find the time when the two cars are level.

- Draw a diagram to help to picture what's going on:

- For each car, there are different *suvat* variables, so write separate lists and separate equations:

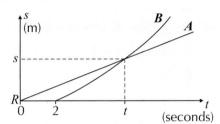

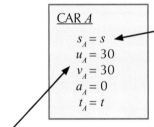

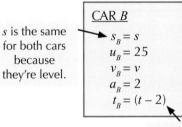

s is the same for both cars because they're level.

CAR A
$$s_A = s$$
$$u_A = 30$$
$$v_A = 30$$
$$a_A = 0$$
$$t_A = t$$

CAR B
$$s_B = s$$
$$u_B = 25$$
$$v_B = v$$
$$a_B = 2$$
$$t_B = (t - 2)$$

A is travelling at a constant speed.

B passes R 2 seconds after A passes point R.

- When the two cars are level they will have travelled the same distance, so choose an equation with s in it: $s = ut + \frac{1}{2}at^2$

  FOR CAR A: $s = 30t + \left(\frac{1}{2} \times 0 \times t^2\right)$

  $s = 30t$

  FOR CAR B: $s = 25(t - 2) + \left(\frac{1}{2} \times 2 \times (t - 2)^2\right)$

  $s = 25t - 50 + (t - 2)(t - 2)$

  $s = 25t - 50 + (t^2 - 4t + 4)$

  $s = t^2 + 21t - 46$

- Make the expressions for s equal to each other (because the cars have travelled the same distance):

  $$30t = t^2 + 21t - 46$$
  $$\Rightarrow \quad t^2 - 9t - 46 = 0$$

- Use the quadratic formula to solve for t:

  $t^2 - 9t - 46 = 0$

  $$t = \frac{-b \pm \sqrt{b^2 - 4ac}}{2a} = \frac{9 \pm \sqrt{9^2 - (4 \times 1 \times (-46))}}{2 \times 1}$$

  $$\Rightarrow \quad t = 12.639... \quad \text{or} \quad t = -3.639...$$

  Tip: You can ignore the negative value of t, as time is always positive.

- So the cars are level 12.6 seconds after car A passes R (correct to 3 s.f.).

Example 4

Particle A is projected vertically upwards with speed 34.3 ms⁻¹ from ground level. At the same time, particle B is dropped from a height of 686 m directly above the point that A is projected from. Assume that air resistance can be ignored.

Find the time that the two particles collide.

Tip: t is the same for both particles, as they set off at the same time.

- Write down the different *suvat* variables for each particle, taking upwards as the positive direction:

PARTICLE A	
$s_A = s_A$	$u_A = 34.3$
$v_A = v_A$	$a_A = -9.8$
$t_A = t$	

PARTICLE B	
$s_B = s_B$	$u_B = 0$
$v_B = v_B$	$a_B = -9.8$
$t_B = t$	

Tip: $a = -9.8$ for both particles because A is **decelerating** in the **positive** direction due to gravity, and B is **accelerating** in the **negative** direction due to gravity.

- To find the time that the particles collide, you need to know how far they have moved. Use $s = ut + \frac{1}{2}at^2$:

Tip: s_A is the displacement from the ground, and s_B is the displacement from the point B is dropped from.

$$\underline{\text{FOR PARTICLE } A:} \quad s_A = 34.3t + \left(\frac{1}{2} \times (-9.8) \times t^2\right)$$
$$\boldsymbol{s_A = 34.3t - 4.9t^2}$$

$$\underline{\text{FOR PARTICLE } B:} \quad s_B = 0 + \left(\frac{1}{2} \times (-9.8) \times t^2\right)$$
$$\boldsymbol{s_B = -4.9t^2}$$

- So, after t seconds, A is $(34.3t - 4.9t^2)$ m above the ground and B has moved $4.9t^2$ m downwards from a height of 686 m — i.e. B is $(686 - 4.9t^2)$ m above the ground.

Tip: They collide when they're the same distance above the ground.

- The particles collide when:
$$34.3t - 4.9t^2 = 686 - 4.9t^2$$

$$34.3t = 686$$

$$t = 686 \div 34.3 = 20$$

So the particles collide $\boxed{20 \text{ seconds}}$ after being released.

Exercise 2.3

Q1 At time $t = 0$, an object passes point W with speed 2 ms⁻¹.
It travels at this constant speed for 8 seconds, until it reaches point X.
Immediately after passing X, the object accelerates uniformly to point Y, 28 m away. The object's speed at Y is 6 ms⁻¹.
Immediately after passing Y, the object decelerates uniformly to V ms⁻¹ (where $V > 2$) in 5 seconds. The object travels a total distance of 67 m.

a) Find the time taken for the object to travel between X and Y.

b) Draw a velocity-time graph to show the motion of the object.

c) Find the value of V.

Q2 A van is travelling at a constant speed of 14 ms^{-1} along a straight road. At time $t = 0$, the van passes a motorbike, which then sets off from rest and travels along the same road in the same direction as the van. The motorbike accelerates uniformly to a speed of 18 ms^{-1} in 20 seconds, then maintains this speed.

a) Draw a velocity-time graph to show the motion of the two vehicles.

b) How long after setting off does the motorbike overtake the van?

Q3 Two remote-controlled cars, X and Y, lie on a straight line 30 m apart. At time $t = 0$, they are moving towards each other. X has initial speed 15 ms^{-1} and accelerates at a rate of 1 ms^{-2}. Y has initial speed 20 ms^{-1} and accelerates at a rate of 2 ms^{-2}.

a) Calculate the time taken for the cars to collide.

b) Calculate the speed of each car when they collide.

c) How far from the initial position of X do the two cars collide?

Q4 A particle travels between three points, P, Q and R. At time $t = 0$, the particle passes P with speed 15 ms^{-1}. Immediately after passing P, the particle accelerates uniformly at 3 ms^{-2} for 4 seconds, until it reaches Q with speed U ms^{-1}. It then travels at this constant speed in a straight line for 6 seconds to point R. Immediately after passing R, the particle decelerates uniformly for T seconds until it comes to rest.

a) Draw a velocity-time graph to show the particle's motion.

b) Find the value of U.

c) Given that the particle travels a total distance of 405 m, find how long after passing P the particle comes to rest.

d) Find the deceleration of the particle in coming to rest.

Q5 At time $t = 0$, a ball is rolled across a mat with speed 5 ms^{-1}. It decelerates at a rate of 0.5 ms^{-2} until it comes to rest. 3 seconds later, a second ball is rolled along a smooth floor, in a direction parallel to the first. This ball travels with a constant velocity of 4 ms^{-1}. The starting points of the two balls are side-by-side.

Q5 Hint: The second ball is rolled 3 seconds after the first ball, so if $t_1 = t$, then $t_2 = t - 3$.

a) How long after the first ball is rolled does the second ball pass the first ball?

b) Find the distance travelled by each ball before the second ball passes the first ball.

c) How far ahead of the first ball is the second ball 15 seconds after the first ball is rolled?

Q6 At time $t = 0$, particle A is dropped from a bridge 40 m above the ground. One second later, particle B is projected vertically upwards with speed 5 ms^{-1} from a point 10 m above the ground.

a) Find the distance travelled by A when B is at the highest point in its motion.

b) How long after A is dropped do the two particles become level?

c) How far from the ground are they at this time?

3. Non-Uniform Acceleration

Learning Objectives:

- Be able to find displacement, velocity and acceleration at a given time using an equation for displacement.
- Be able to find displacement, velocity and acceleration at a given time using an equation for velocity or acceleration and initial conditions.
- Be able to find points of maximum or minimum displacement and velocity by differentiating.

So far, this chapter has all been about situations where acceleration is constant. But when it isn't constant, the suvat equations won't work. You'll need a different method for solving these problems.

Displacement with non-uniform acceleration

When acceleration is constant, displacement, s, can be written as $s = ut + \frac{1}{2}at^2$ — i.e. it can be written as a quadratic in terms of t.

However, when acceleration **isn't** constant, displacement can be given by **any** function, not just a quadratic.

If you're given an equation for s in terms of t, then you can use differentiation to find the velocity and acceleration.

Remember that:

$$v = \frac{\mathrm{d}s}{\mathrm{d}t} \quad \text{and} \quad a = \frac{\mathrm{d}v}{\mathrm{d}t} = \frac{\mathrm{d}^2 s}{\mathrm{d}t^2}$$

Tip: Displacement might also be given by another letter, such as r, d or x — so you would have $v = \frac{\mathrm{d}r}{\mathrm{d}t}$, etc.

Tip: Check back on page 187 for more about calculus in mechanics.

Example 1

An object's displacement s (in metres) at time t (in seconds) is given by the equation:
$$s = t^3 - 3t^2 + 2t, \text{ where } t \geq 0$$

a) Find its displacement at time $t = 4$.

- Substitute $t = 4$ into the equation:
$$s = 4^3 - 3(4)^2 + 2(4)$$
$$= 64 - 48 + 8 = \boxed{24 \text{ m}}$$

b) Calculate the object's velocity at time $t = 1$.

- For this, you need to find the velocity function using $v = \frac{\mathrm{d}s}{\mathrm{d}t}$. Differentiating the equation gives:
$$v = \frac{\mathrm{d}s}{\mathrm{d}t} = 3t^2 - 6t + 2$$
- Now you can substitute $t = 1$:
$$v = 3(1)^2 - 6(1) + 2$$
$$= 3 - 6 + 2 = \boxed{-1 \text{ ms}^{-1}} \text{ (i.e. 1 ms}^{-1} \text{ in the negative direction)}$$

Example 2

An object has displacement s (in miles) at time t (in hours) given by the equation:
$$s = \frac{1}{9}t^4 - t^3 + 12t, \text{ where } t \geq 0$$

a) Calculate the object's initial velocity.

- First, differentiate to find the equation for velocity:
$$v = \frac{\mathrm{d}s}{\mathrm{d}t} = \frac{4}{9}t^3 - 3t^2 + 12$$
- The question asks for the initial velocity — i.e. when $t = 0$:
$$v = \frac{4}{9}(0)^3 - 3(0)^2 + 12 = 0 - 0 + 12 = \boxed{12 \text{ miles per hour}}$$

b) Find its acceleration at time $t = 3$.

- Now you need the object's acceleration: $a = \dfrac{dv}{dt}$ tells you that you need to differentiate the velocity equation:

$$v = \frac{4}{9}t^3 - 3t^2 + 12$$

$$a = \frac{4}{3}t^2 - 6t$$

- Substitute $t = 3$:

$$a = \frac{4}{3}(3)^2 - 6(3)$$

$$= 12 - 18 = -6 \text{ miles/hour}^2$$

Exercise 3.1

Q1 An object's displacement in metres at t seconds is given by the function: $s = 2t^3 - 4t^2 + 3$

  a) Calculate the object's displacement at time $t = 3$.

  b) Find the object's velocity equation.

  c) What is its velocity at time $t = 3$?

Q2 At time $t = 0$, a dog breaks its lead and runs along a straight path, 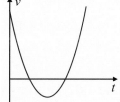 until it is caught again at $t = 4$. Its displacement in metres at time t seconds while it is running free is modelled by the equation:

$$s = \frac{1}{5}t^5 - 2t^4 + 7t^3 - 10t^2 + 5t$$

  a) Calculate the dog's initial velocity.

  b) What is the dog's acceleration at time $t = 2$?

Velocity and acceleration equations

Instead of being given the displacement function, sometimes you'll be told the object's acceleration or velocity. From this, you can then find an equation for its displacement.

Remember that: $\quad \boxed{s = \int v \, dt}\quad$ and $\quad\boxed{v = \int a \, dt}$

Initial conditions

You will always get a constant of integration, C, when finding the equation for displacement (or when finding velocity from acceleration). This is because different displacement equations can give you the same velocity equation:

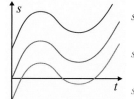

$$s = \frac{1}{3}t^3 - \frac{3}{2}t^2 + 2t + 3$$

$$s = \frac{1}{3}t^3 - \frac{3}{2}t^2 + 2t \longrightarrow v = t^2 - 3t + 2$$

$$s = \frac{1}{3}t^3 - \frac{3}{2}t^2 + 2t - \frac{3}{4}$$

Because of this, you'll often be given a **condition** so you can find C. Usually this will be the displacement (or velocity) at time $t = 0$, i.e. the initial displacement. However, some questions may make things harder by giving you conditions at a different time — always check that you're substituting the right value for t.

Example 1

An object's velocity is given by $v = t^2 - 3t + 2$.
Find its displacement as a function of t, given that:

a) the object is at $s = 0$ when $t = 0$.

Using $s = \int v \, dt$, integrate the velocity to find the displacement:

$$s = \int (t^2 - 3t + 2) \, dt$$
$$= \frac{1}{3}t^3 - \frac{3}{2}t^2 + 2t + C$$

You are told that when $t = 0$, $s = 0$, so substitute these values to find C:

$$0 = \frac{1}{3}(0)^3 - \frac{3}{2}(0)^2 + 2(0) + C$$
$$0 = C$$

So the displacement $s = \frac{1}{3}t^3 - \frac{3}{2}t^2 + 2t$

b) the object is at $s = 2.5$ when $t = 3$.

You already know that the displacement is given by:

$$s = \frac{1}{3}t^3 - \frac{3}{2}t^2 + 2t + C$$

Substitute in the conditions $t = 3$, $s = 2.5$:

$$2.5 = \frac{1}{3}(3)^3 - \frac{3}{2}(3)^2 + 2(3) + C$$
$$2.5 = 9 - 13.5 + 6 + C$$
$$C = 2.5 - 1.5 = 1$$

So the displacement is now given by $s = \frac{1}{3}t^3 - \frac{3}{2}t^2 + 2t + 1$

Example 2

The equation below gives the acceleration of
an object in kmh^{-2} at time t hours:

$$a = 20t^3 + 18t - 2$$

a) Given that its initial velocity is 1 kmh^{-1}, find the equation for its velocity
in terms of t.

- Begin by integrating the acceleration:

$$v = \int (20t^3 + 18t - 2) \, dt$$
$$= 20\left(\frac{t^4}{4}\right) + 18\left(\frac{t^2}{2}\right) - 2t + C$$
$$= 5t^4 + 9t^2 - 2t + C$$

- Given that $v = 1$ when $t = 0$:
$$1 = 0 + C \Rightarrow C = 1$$

- So the equation is $v = 5t^4 + 9t^2 - 2t + 1$

b) After 1 hour, the object's displacement was 4 km. Find its displacement after 2 hours.

- You need to integrate the equation again to get the displacement:
$$s = \int (5t^4 + 9t^2 - 2t + 1)\, dt$$
$$= t^5 + 3t^3 - t^2 + t + C$$

- The condition $s = 4$ when $t = 1$ will give you the value of C:
$$4 = 1^5 + 3(1)^3 - 1^2 + 1 + C \Rightarrow C = 0$$

- So substitute $t = 2$ into the equation:
$$s = t^5 + 3t^3 - t^2 + t$$
$$= 2^5 + 3(2)^3 - 2^2 + 2$$
$$= 32 + 24 - 4 + 2 = \boxed{54 \text{ km}}$$

Exercise 3.2

Q1 The velocity (in cms^{-1}) of a particle, t seconds after a chemical reaction, is found to be:
$$v = 1 + 6t + 6t^2 - 4t^3$$

a) Given that the particle starts at $s = 0$, give an equation for its displacement.

b) Find the displacement and velocity of the particle at $t = 2$.

Q2 A paper aeroplane is thrown from a height of 2 m. The plane's vertical velocity is 0 ms^{-1} at time $t = 1$ second. It experiences air resistance such that its vertical acceleration is given by the function: $a = -3t^2 + 6t - 4$. Find the formula for the plane's vertical displacement, measured in metres above the ground (upwards is the positive direction).

Maximum and minimum points

You can also find maximum and minimum points of these functions, just like on page 180. In this context, this means finding the maximum (or minimum) displacement or velocity that an object reaches. For example, you can find an object's maximum velocity by checking the points where $\dfrac{dv}{dt}$ (i.e. its acceleration) is zero.

Tip: Finding a maximum or a minimum point use the same method, although you'll probably see more questions asking for maximum points, particularly when an object starts or finishes at rest.

Example 1

A ball is rolled up a slope. Its displacement from the bottom, s m, at time t seconds after being released, is modelled by the function: $s = 8 + 2t - t^2, 0 \leq t < 4$

a) Explain the limits on t.

- The limits on t are that $t \geq 0$ and $t < 4$.

- When $t < 0$, the ball has yet to be released so its motion is not given by the same function.

- When $t = 4$, $s = 8 + 2(4) - 4^2$
$$= 8 + 8 - 16 = 0$$
That is, at time $t = 4$, the ball reaches the bottom of the slope, at which point you would expect its motion to change.

Tip: The best way to approach a question like this is to investigate what happens at the limits. A sketch of the graph might also help.

b) Find the maximum displacement reached by the ball.

- To help visualise the problem, sketch the graph of the function:

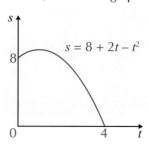

- You want the maximum displacement — i.e. the peak of the curve. This is the maximum of the function, which means that the gradient is zero. So you need to differentiate the displacement function (which will give you the velocity): $\dfrac{ds}{dt} = 2 - 2t$

- Setting the velocity equal to zero will tell you the time at which it reaches its maximum displacement: $0 = 2 - 2t$
$$2t = 2 \implies t = 1$$

- Now you just need to substitute this back into the original equation:
$$s = 8 + 2(1) - 1^2$$
$$= 8 + 2 - 1 = \boxed{9 \text{ m}}$$

Tip: The displacement reaches its maximum when the velocity is zero — once the velocity becomes negative, the object starts moving back towards $s = 0$.

Example 2

At time t (s), an object's displacement (cm) follows the function:
$$s = 10 - 8t + t^3 - \frac{1}{6}t^4$$

Find the time at which the object reaches its maximum velocity.

- First, find an equation for the object's velocity:
$$v = \frac{ds}{dt} = -8 + 3t^2 - \frac{2}{3}t^3$$

- You know that when the object reaches its maximum velocity, $\dfrac{dv}{dt} = 0$.
So find $\dfrac{dv}{dt}$ by differentiating and set it equal to 0:
$$\frac{dv}{dt} = 6t - 2t^2 = 0$$
$$2t(3 - t) = 0$$

- So there are two roots to investigate — when $t = 0$ and when $t = 3$.
Calculate $\dfrac{d^2v}{dt^2} = 6 - 4t$ and look for $\dfrac{d^2v}{dt^2} < 0$ to find the maximum point.

Tip: Here you're asked for the **time** that it's at its maximum velocity, not for the velocity itself. So make sure you give the right value as your answer.

$t = 0 \implies \dfrac{d^2v}{dt^2} = 6 - 4t$ $= 6 - 4(0)$ $= 6$ $6 > 0 \implies$ minimum at $t = 0$	$t = 3 \implies \dfrac{d^2v}{dt^2} = 6 - 4t$ $= 6 - 4(3)$ $= 6 - 12$ $= -6$ $-6 < 0 \implies$ maximum at $t = 3$

Tip: This is the method for checking stationary points that you've seen on page 180. You could check $t = 0$ and $t = 3$ in the equation for velocity to show that this gives you the right answer.

- So the object reaches its maximum velocity at $t = 3$ seconds.

Q1 The displacement of a yo-yo is measured as it extends out as far as the string allows and then retracts. The motion is modelled by the function:
$$s = 2t^4 - 8t^3 + 8t^2, \quad 0 \le t \le 2$$
where t is measured in seconds and s is measured in feet from the starting point.

a) What happens at the limits $t = 0$ and $t = 2$?

b) Find the length of the string (i.e. the maximum displacement of the yo-yo).

Q2 The velocity of a cat (in ms^{-1}) at time t (seconds) over a period of three seconds is approximated by the function:
$$v = t^3 - 6t^2 + 9t$$

a) Find the time at which the cat is travelling at the greatest velocity.

b) The cat's displacement at $t = 0$ is 5 metres. What is its displacement at $t = 2$ (assuming that its motion is in a straight line)?

Q3 Find the maximum displacement of the objects whose displacement functions are given below (where displacement, s, is measured in metres, and time, t, is measured in seconds):

a) $s = 2 + 3t - 2t^2$

b) $s = t^2 + t^3 - 1.25t^4$

c) $s = -3t^4 + 8t^3 - 6t^2 + 16$

> **Q3 Hint:** Remember that these all start from $t = 0$, so any stationary points where t is negative can be ignored.

Q4 Given that s is measured in metres and t in seconds, find the maximum (positive) velocity of an object whose displacement is given by:

a) $s = 15t + 6t^2 - t^3$

b) $s = \dfrac{-t^5}{20} + \dfrac{t^4}{4} - \dfrac{t^3}{3} + 11t$

> **Q3-4 Hint:** Remember that if a point has a second derivative of zero, it could be a maximum, minimum or a point of inflection, which means you'll have to test it anyway.

Q5 A computer is used to track the motion of a lizard, running back and forth along a track. The computer logs its position over a 7 second interval and computes that its displacement can be approximated by the following quartic function:
$$s = \frac{1}{6}t^4 - 2t^3 + 5t^2 + 2t \quad \text{for } 0 \le t \le 7$$
where s is measured in metres and t in seconds. Calculate the lizard's greatest speed (i.e. the velocity of greatest magnitude) over these 7 seconds.

> **Q5 Hint:** Since you're asked for the greatest speed, rather than velocity, you need to check all of the stationary points here, not just the maximums.

Q6 Find the maximum displacement, in metres, of an object whose acceleration is given by
$$a = (6t - 4) \text{ ms}^{-2},$$
with the conditions that $s = 0$ at both $t = 0$ and $t = 1$.

1. Forces

A force is an influence which can change the motion of a body (i.e. cause an acceleration). It can also be thought of as a 'push' or a 'pull' on an object. All forces are vectors, so the stuff you learnt about vectors in Chapter 12 should come in useful in this chapter.

Learning Objectives:

- Understand and use the fact that forces are vectors.

- Be able to find magnitudes and directions of forces.

Treating forces as vectors

You've done a fair amount of work with vectors already in Chapter 12, so hopefully this should be pretty straightforward.

- Forces are **vectors** — they have a **magnitude** (size) and a **direction** that they act in.

- The magnitude of a force is measured in **Newtons** (**N**). For a force F, you would write its magnitude as $|F|$

- A force's direction is an **angle** that is measured **anticlockwise** from the **horizontal** (unless a question says otherwise).

- A **component of a force** is the part of the force that acts in a **particular direction**.

Tip: A force acting on an object can cause that object's velocity to change (see p.366).

Tip: Remember, when writing by hand you should use underlining to show that something is a vector (e.g. $\underline{F}$) — it's a bit tricky to make your handwriting bold.

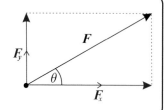

- F — force e.g. 17.5 N

- θ — direction e.g. 38°

- F_x — component of the force in the x-direction

- F_y — component in the y-direction

You can describe forces using the **unit vectors i** and **j**. The number in front of the **i** is the horizontal force component, and the number in front of the **j** is the vertical force component.

Tip: Unit vectors are a pair of perpendicular vectors, each of magnitude one unit. See page 211 for more information.

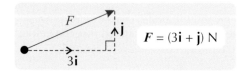

$F = (3\mathbf{i} + \mathbf{j})$ N

You can also represent a force with a column vector. The top number is the horizontal (**i**) component and the bottom is the vertical (**j**) component.

For example, $3\mathbf{i} + \mathbf{j}$ can be given as the vector $\begin{pmatrix} 3 \\ 1 \end{pmatrix}$.

For a force $F = x\mathbf{i} + y\mathbf{j}$, its magnitude is $|F| = \sqrt{x^2 + y^2}$

and the direction θ can be found by first finding the angle with the horizontal, which is given by $\tan^{-1}\left(\dfrac{y}{x}\right)$

Tip: $\tan^{-1}\left(\dfrac{y}{x}\right)$ will be the direction θ when $0 < \theta < 90°$. When θ is between 90° and 360°, you may need to add or subtract this angle to/from 180° or 360° — drawing a diagram will be very helpful.

Example

A force $F = 3\mathbf{i} - 2\mathbf{j}$ N acts on a particle P.
Find the magnitude and direction of the force.

- Draw a diagram of the force acting on the particle to get a clear idea of what's going on:

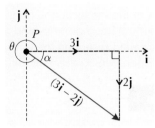

Tip: As a column vector, this force would be given by $\begin{pmatrix} 3 \\ -2 \end{pmatrix}$.

- The force and its $\mathbf{i}$ and $\mathbf{j}$ components form a right-angled triangle, so you can use Pythagoras' theorem to find the magnitude of the force:

$$\text{Magnitude of } F = \sqrt{3^2 + 2^2}$$
$$= \sqrt{13}$$
$$= \boxed{3.61 \text{ N (to 3 s.f.)}}$$

Tip: It's always a good idea to draw a diagram if you're not given one in the question.

- Use trigonometry to find the acute angle α:

$$\tan \alpha = \frac{2}{3}$$
$$\alpha = \tan^{-1}\left(\frac{2}{3}\right) = 33.690...$$
$$\theta = 360 - \alpha, \text{ so } \theta = \boxed{326° \text{ (to 3 s.f.)}}$$

Tip: You can see from the diagram that the direction is between 270° and 360°, so subtract α from 360° to get the answer in the correct range.

Exercise 1.1

Q1 Find the magnitude and direction of the following forces. Give your answers to 3 s.f. where appropriate:

a) $7\mathbf{i}$ N
b) $2\mathbf{i} + 2\mathbf{j}$ N
c) $3\mathbf{i} + 4\mathbf{j}$ N
d) $-3\mathbf{i} + 4\mathbf{j}$ N
e) $12\mathbf{i} - 5\mathbf{j}$ kN
f) $-\mathbf{i} - 4\mathbf{j}$ N

Q1 Hint: Estimate the direction before doing the calculation — drawing a diagram might help.

Q2 Find the magnitude and direction of each force below, giving your answers to 3 s.f. where appropriate:

a) $\begin{pmatrix} 3 \\ 1 \end{pmatrix}$ N
b) $\begin{pmatrix} -4 \\ -2 \end{pmatrix}$ N
c) $\begin{pmatrix} 12 \\ -3 \end{pmatrix}$ N
d) $\begin{pmatrix} -0.5 \\ 0.5 \end{pmatrix}$ kN
e) $\begin{pmatrix} 0 \\ -11 \end{pmatrix}$ N
f) $\begin{pmatrix} 15 \\ 25 \end{pmatrix}$ kN

Q3 Find the direction of the force $(\mathbf{i} + \sqrt{3}\,\mathbf{j})$ N.

Q4 The force $\begin{pmatrix} 56a \\ -42a \end{pmatrix}$ N (where a is a constant) has a magnitude of 35 N. Find the value of a.

Q5 The forces $\begin{pmatrix} 3 \\ 4 \end{pmatrix}$ N and $\begin{pmatrix} 4 \\ 3 \end{pmatrix}$ N act at the same point. Find the angle between these two forces.

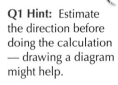

Resultant forces and equilibrium

The **resultant force** on an object is the **single** force that has the **same effect** as all the forces acting on the object combined.

To calculate the resultant force on an object, you need to **add the components** of the forces acting on the object in each direction (i.e. add all of the **i**-components and all of the **j**-components). This is often called **resolving** the forces in each direction. The total force in each direction will be the matching component of the resultant force.

Tip: Resistance forces always act in the opposite direction to the movement of an object (see page 334).

Example 1

An object is being pulled along a rough surface by a force of 12 N (acting parallel to the surface). It experiences a resistance force of 5 N directly opposing the motion. Draw a diagram showing the forces on the object, and calculate the resultant force on the object.

- The diagram looks like this:

- The pull force and the resistance force are acting in opposite directions.

- So the resultant force on the object is $12 - 5 = \boxed{7 \text{ N}}$ in the direction of the 12 N force.

Example 2

Two forces, given by the vectors 3i – j N and –2i + 4j N, act on an object. Calculate the resultant force on the object in both the i- and j-directions.

Resolve the forces in each direction:

    i: $3\mathbf{i} + (-2\mathbf{i}) = \boxed{\mathbf{i}}$

    j: $(-\mathbf{j}) + 4\mathbf{j} = \boxed{3\mathbf{j}}$

When the resultant force on an object is **zero** (usually when all the forces on the object **cancel** each other out), the object is in **equilibrium**.

Example 3

Four children are having a tug-of-war contest. The diagram below shows the forces acting on the rope.

Given that the rope is being held in equilibrium, find the force D.

- The rope is in equilibrium, so the resultant force is zero.

- Resolve forces horizontally (→):

$$-35 - 40 + 32 + D = 0 \implies \boxed{D = 43 \text{ N}}$$

Tip: When you're resolving, draw an arrow to show which direction you're taking as positive.

Example 4

A particle is suspended in equilibrium by three light, inextensible strings. The diagram shows all of the forces acting on the particle (in N).

Find the missing force $\begin{pmatrix} x \\ y \end{pmatrix}$.

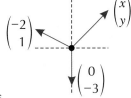

Tip: Check the definitions on page 333 if you're not sure what "light" or "inextensible" mean in this modelling context.

- The particle is in equilibrium, so both the horizontal and vertical components of the forces must add to zero.

- Resolving horizontally:
$$-2 + 0 + x = 0 \implies x = 2$$

- Resolving vertically:
$$1 - 3 + y = 0 \implies y = 2$$

- So the missing force is given by $\begin{pmatrix} 2 \\ 2 \end{pmatrix}$

Exercise 1.2

Q1   An object hangs in equilibrium on a string, as shown in the diagram.
Find the tension in the string, T.

Q2   Find the resultant of the two forces $8\mathbf{i} + 5\mathbf{j}$ N and $3\mathbf{i} - 2\mathbf{j}$ N.

Q3   A diver uses a diving jet to move around underwater. (MODELLING)
The forces on the diver and his jet are shown in the diagram below.

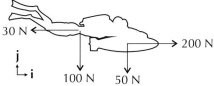

Find the resultant force, giving your answer in terms of $\mathbf{i}$ and $\mathbf{j}$.

Q4   An object is held in equilibrium by three forces:
$3\mathbf{i} + 2\mathbf{j}$ N, $x\mathbf{i} - 4\mathbf{j}$ N   and $-5\mathbf{i} + 2\mathbf{j}$ N
Find the value of the constant x.

Q5   As part of an experiment on magnetism, a magnetic stone (MODELLING) is held in place on a table, while some students hold two magnets on the table. The forces exerted on the stone by the magnets are given by $\mathbf{i}$ N and $-5\mathbf{i} - 2\mathbf{j}$ N respectively.

a) Draw a diagram showing the stone and the magnetic forces acting on it.

b) Find the resultant force acting on the stone.

Another two magnets are added, resulting in two new forces on the stone given by $4\mathbf{i} + \mathbf{j}$ N and $\mathbf{F}$ N respectively.

c) Given that the stone is now in equilibrium, find the force $\mathbf{F}$.

2. Newton's Laws of Motion

Learning Objectives:

- Know and understand Newton's three laws of motion.

- Be able to apply Newton's laws of motion to constant acceleration problems (where acceleration may be a vector).

- Be able to solve problems involving resistance forces when a particle is moving.

- Be able to solve simple problems involving two connected particles.

- Be able to solve problems involving a smooth peg or pulley and two moving connected particles.

In this section, you'll look at how the forces acting on a particle affect its motion, and whether or not they will cause the particle to accelerate.

Newton's laws of motion

- **Newton's first law:**

  > A body will stay at **rest** or maintain a **constant velocity** unless a **resultant force** acts on the body.

  - So if the forces acting on something are perfectly **balanced**, then it **won't accelerate**.

  - If it's stationary, it'll **stay stationary** and if it's moving in a straight line with constant speed, it'll carry on moving in the **same straight line** with the same **constant speed**.

- **Newton's second law:**

  > The **overall resultant force** (F_{net}) acting on a body is equal to the **mass** of the body multiplied by the body's **acceleration**.

  - So if the forces acting on a body **aren't** perfectly **balanced**, then the body will **accelerate** in the **direction** of the resultant force.

  - The magnitude of the acceleration will be proportional to the magnitude of F_{net}.

  - A body's mass, its acceleration and the resultant force acting on it are related by the following formula, sometimes called the **equation of motion**:

$$F_{net} = ma$$

  - A common use of this formula is calculating the **weight** of an object. An object's weight is a **force** caused by **gravity**. Gravity causes a **constant** acceleration of approximately 9.8 ms^{-2}, denoted g. Putting this into $F = ma$ gives the equation for weight (W):

$$W = mg$$

  - Remember that weight is a force and is measured in **Newtons**, while mass is measured in **kg**. 1 Newton is defined as the force needed to make a 1 kg mass accelerate at a rate of 1 ms^{-2}.

- **Newton's third law:**

  > For **two bodies**, A and B, **in contact** with each other, the force exerted by A on B is **equal in magnitude** but **opposite in direction** to the force exerted by B on A.

  - So for a particle sat on a horizontal surface, there is a force acting vertically **upwards** on the particle which has the **same magnitude** as the particle's **weight** (the weight acts vertically **downwards**).

  - This is called the **reaction force**, and is normally labelled R.

  - Newton's third law also applies to forces like tension, where an object and a connected rope pull on each other with equal force.

Tip: $F_{net} = ma$ is often written as $F = ma$, but the F always means resultant force.

Tip: The acceleration due to gravity g is usually treated as a constant value, although it would change if you left Earth. In fact, even on Earth it varies by a very small amount depending on where you are.

Tip: Newton's third law is often stated as: "Every action has an equal and opposite reaction".

Using Newton's laws

Newton's laws are a lot easier to understand once you start **using them**. If you're doing calculations, you'll probably use the second law ($F_{net} = ma$) more than the other two. You might also need to use the **constant acceleration equations** from Chapter 19.

Example 1

A particle of mass 12 kg is attached to the end of a light, vertical string. The particle is accelerating vertically downwards at a rate of 7 ms^{-2}.

a) Find W, the weight of the particle.

- Using the formula for weight:

$$W = mg$$
$$= 12 \times 9.8 = \boxed{117.6 \text{ N}}$$

Tip: Remember — unless a question tells you otherwise, take $g = 9.8$ ms^{-2}.

b) Find T, the tension in the string.

- Resolving vertically ($\downarrow$):

$$F_{net} = ma$$
$$117.6 - T = 12 \times 7$$
$$T = 117.6 - 84$$
$$= \boxed{33.6 \text{ N}}$$

Tip: You don't have to work out the resultant force separately before using $F = ma$. You can do the whole thing in one 'resolving' step.

c) Find the resultant force acting horizontally on the particle.

The particle is not accelerating horizontally, so from Newton's first law, there is no resultant force acting horizontally on the particle.

Example 2

A mass of 4 kg, initially at rest on a smooth horizontal plane, is acted on by a horizontal force of 5 N.

Find the magnitude of the acceleration of the mass and the normal reaction from the plane, R.

- Resolving forces horizontally ($\rightarrow$), $F_{net} = 5$
  So use Newton's second law to find the acceleration, a:

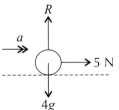

Tip: See page 334 for a reminder of the normal reaction force.

$$F_{net} = ma$$
$$5 = 4a \implies a = \boxed{1.25 \text{ ms}^{-2}}$$

- Resolving forces vertically ($\uparrow$), $F_{net} = R - 4g$
  There is no acceleration vertically, so using Newton's second law:

$$F_{net} = ma$$
$$R - 4g = 4 \times 0 \implies R = \boxed{39.2 \text{ N}}$$

Tip: It's pretty common for the normal reaction force to have the same magnitude as the weight of the object.

Example 3

A particle of weight 30 N is being accelerated across a rough horizontal plane by a force of 6 N acting parallel to the horizontal, as shown. The particle experiences a constant resistance force of 2.5 N. Given that the particle starts from rest, find its speed after 4 s.

> **Tip:** It always helps to draw a diagram showing the forces acting on a body and the direction of acceleration.

- First, since you're told the weight, you need to calculate the mass of the particle

$$W = mg \implies m = \frac{W}{g}$$

$$\implies m = \frac{30}{9.8} = 3.061... \text{ kg}$$

- Now resolve forces horizontally ($\rightarrow$), using Newton's second law to find the acceleration, a:

$$F_{net} = ma$$
$$6 - 2.5 = 3.061... \times a$$
$$\implies a = 3.5 \div 3.061... = 1.143... \text{ ms}^{-2}$$

> **Tip:** Take a look back at page 342 if you need a reminder of any of the constant acceleration equations.

- Use one of the constant acceleration equations to find the speed:

$$u = 0, \quad v = v, \quad a = 1.143..., \quad t = 4$$
$$v = u + at$$
$$= 0 + 1.143... \times 4$$
$$= 4.57 \text{ ms}^{-1} \text{ (to 3 s.f.)}$$

Example 4

A particle of mass m kg is acted upon by a force F of $(-8\mathbf{i} + 6\mathbf{j})$ N, resulting in an acceleration of magnitude 8 ms^{-2}.

a) Find the value of m.

- F_{net} = magnitude of $F = \sqrt{(-8)^2 + 6^2} = \sqrt{100} = 10$ N

- Now use Newton's second law to find m:

$$F_{net} = ma$$
$$10 = 8m$$
$$m = 1.25 \text{ kg}$$

b) The force on the particle changes to a force of $4\mathbf{i} + 7\mathbf{j}$. Find the new acceleration of the particle in vector form.

> **Tip:** Newton's second law still works when the force and acceleration are in vector form. Make sure it's clear in your working when you're using vectors by underlining the letters.

- You can use Newton's second law with vectors to get the acceleration:

$$\mathbf{F_{net}} = m\mathbf{a}$$
$$(4\mathbf{i} + 7\mathbf{j}) = 1.25\mathbf{a}$$
$$\mathbf{a} = (4 \div 1.25)\mathbf{i} + (7 \div 1.25)\mathbf{j}$$
$$= 3.2\mathbf{i} + 5.6\mathbf{j} \text{ N}$$

Q1   A particle with mass 15 kg is accelerating at 4 ms^{-2}.
Find the magnitude of the resultant force acting on the particle.

Q2   A block of mass 5 kg is acted on by a resultant force of 10 N. Find:
a) the acceleration of the block,
b) the speed of the block after 8 s (given that it starts from rest).

Q3   A particle of mass 18 kg is attached to the end of a light, vertical
string. Given that the particle is accelerating vertically upwards
at 0.4 ms^{-2}, find T, the tension in the string.

Q4   A model car, initially at rest on a horizontal plane, is acted on by a
resultant horizontal force of magnitude 18 N, causing it to accelerate
at 5 ms^{-2}. Find:
a) the mass of the model car,
b) the car's speed after 4 seconds,
c) the magnitude of the normal reaction from the plane.

Q5   A sack of flour of mass 55 kg is attached to the end of a light vertical
rope. The sack starts from rest and accelerates vertically upwards at a
constant rate so that after 4 seconds it is moving with speed 2.5 ms^{-1}.
a) Find the magnitude of the acceleration of the sack of flour.
b) Assuming that the sack experiences a non-gravitational
constant resistance to motion of magnitude 120 N,
find the tension in the rope.

Q6   A stone of mass 300 grams is dropped from the top of a mine shaft
and falls vertically down the shaft. It hits the bottom 12 seconds
after being released from rest. Assuming that the stone experiences a
constant resistance of 1.5 N, find the depth of the mine shaft.

> **Q6 Hint:** Use Newton's
> second law to find the
> acceleration of the stone
> first.

Q7   A particle of mass 10 kg is acted on by a force of $(8\mathbf{i} - 2\mathbf{j})$ N.
a) Find the acceleration of the particle in vector form.
b) Find the magnitude of the acceleration.
c) Assuming that the particle is initially at rest, find the speed of the
particle after 6 seconds have elapsed.

Q8   A particle of mass m kg is acted on by a force of $(8\mathbf{i} + 6\mathbf{j})$ N.
Given that the particle is initially at rest and accelerates
to a velocity of $(32\mathbf{i} + 24\mathbf{j})$ ms^{-1} in 2 seconds, find the value of m.

> **Q8-9 Hint:** Just like
> Newton's second
> law, you can use the
> equation $v = u + at$
> with vectors. Notice
> that t is a scalar.

Q9   Two constant forces are acting on a body of mass 2 kg.
10 seconds after starting to accelerate from rest, the velocity
of the body is given by $(30\mathbf{i} + 20\mathbf{j})$ ms^{-1}.
a) Calculate the resultant force acting on the body.
Give your answer in vector form.
b) If one of the forces is given by $(10\mathbf{i} - 3\mathbf{j})$ N,
what is the magnitude of the other force?

Connected particles

In situations where you have two (or more) particles **joined together**, you can still consider the motion of each **individually** and resolve the forces acting on each particle separately.

However, if the connection between the particles is **light**, **inextensible** and remains **taut**, and the particles are moving in the **same straight line**, they can also be considered to be moving as **one particle** with the **same acceleration**.

Example 1

A person of mass 70 kg is standing in a lift of mass 500 kg. The lift is attached to a vertical light, inextensible cable, as shown. By modelling the person as a particle, and given that the lift is accelerating vertically upwards at a rate of 0.6 ms⁻², find:

a) T, the tension in the cable,

- Resolving vertically (↑) for the whole system:

$$F_{net} = ma$$
$$T - 570g = 570 \times 0.6$$
$$T = (570 \times 0.6) + (570 \times 9.8)$$
$$= \boxed{5928 \text{ N}}$$

Tip: For part a), you can treat the whole system as one particle of mass (500 + 70) = 570 kg, because the whole system is accelerating together.

b) the magnitude of the force exerted by the person on the floor of the lift.

- You could resolve all of the forces on the lift, but it is easier to find the reaction force on the person from the lift (which has equal magnitude, by Newton's third law).

- Sketch a diagram showing the forces acting on the person:

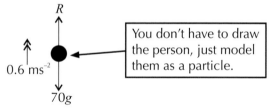

You don't have to draw the person, just model them as a particle.

Tip: In part b), you need to consider the lift and the person as separate objects.

- Resolving vertically (↑) for the person in the lift:

$$F_{net} = ma$$
$$R - 70g = 70 \times 0.6$$
$$R = 42 + 70g$$
$$= \boxed{728 \text{ N}}$$

Tension and thrust

When two objects are **connected** by a **light**, **taut** and **inextensible string**, the string exerts an equal **tension** force at both ends, usually (but not always) in **opposite directions**. For example, if the string passes over a **pulley**, then the tension forces will both act **towards the pulley** (see p.373).

Thrust (or **compression**) is the opposite effect, where a **rigid rod** pushes on two connected objects with equal force. For example, the legs of a **table** could be modelled as rigid rods, exerting a thrust force on both the **tabletop** and the **floor**.

Example 2

A **30-tonne locomotive engine is pulling a single 10-tonne carriage,** as shown. **They are accelerating at 0.3 ms⁻² due to the force** P **generated by the engine. The coupling between the engine and the carriage can be modelled as light and inextensible. It is assumed that there are no forces resisting the motion.**

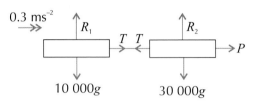

Tip: T is the tension in the coupling. It is experienced by both the engine and the carriage with equal magnitude but in opposite directions.

Tip: 1 tonne = 1000 kg.

a) **Find the magnitude of the driving force P.**

- Considering the engine and the carriage as a single particle, and resolving horizontally (→):

$$F_{net} = ma$$
$$P = 40\,000 \times 0.3$$
$$= \boxed{12\,000 \text{ N}}$$

> This is the combined mass of the engine and the carriage.

Tip: You don't need to know the value of the tension in part a) — you can just treat the whole system as one particle.

b) **Find the magnitude of the tension in the coupling.**

- Resolving horizontally (→), considering only the forces acting on the carriage:

$$F_{net} = ma$$
$$T = 10\,000 \times 0.3$$
$$= \boxed{3000 \text{ N}}$$

Tip: The coupling is modelled as being light and inextensible, so the tension will be constant throughout the coupling.

c) **When the engine and carriage are travelling at 15 ms⁻¹, the coupling breaks. Given that the driving force remains the same, find the distance travelled by the engine in the first 5 seconds after the coupling breaks.**

- Resolving horizontally (→), considering only the forces acting on the engine to find its new acceleration:

$$F_{net} = ma$$
$$P = 30\,000 \times a$$
$$a = 12\,000 \div 30\,000$$
$$= 0.4 \text{ ms}^{-2}$$

- Now use a constant acceleration equation to find the distance travelled: $s = s$ $u = 15$ $a = 0.4$ $t = 5$

$$s = ut + \frac{1}{2}at^2$$
$$s = (15 \times 5) + \left(\frac{1}{2} \times 0.4 \times 5^2\right)$$
$$= \boxed{80 \text{ m}}$$

Tip: In part b), you could consider only the forces acting on the engine instead, but there are fewer acting on the carriage, so the calculation is easier.

Q1 A lift of mass 2000 kg is carrying a load of weight 4000 N.

   a) Calculate the tension in the lift cable, given that the lift is accelerating vertically upwards at 0.2 ms⁻² and that the cable is light, inextensible and vertical.

   b) Find the reaction force between the floor of the lift and the load.

Q2 A lift is being tested for safety. The lift has a mass of 1000 kg and contains a load of mass 1400 kg. The lift is attached to a vertical light, inextensible cable.

   a) Calculate the tension in the cable given that the lift is accelerating vertically downwards at a rate of 1.5 ms⁻².

   b) Find the reaction force between the floor of the lift and the load.

   c) The lift is raised to a height of 30 m above the ground. The cable is cut and the lift falls freely from rest to the ground. Find the speed of the lift as it hits the ground.

Q3 Hint: Remember — thrust is the force in a rigid rod. In this question, thrust acts just like tension would, but in the opposite directions.

Q3 A tractor of mass 2 tonnes is pulling a trailer of mass 1.5 tonnes by means of a light, rigid coupling, as shown below. The tractor applies its brakes and both tractor and trailer decelerate at a rate of 0.3 ms⁻².

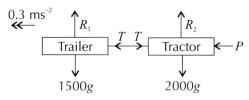

   a) Calculate the braking force, P, generated by the tractor.

Q3 Hint: Lots of assumptions have been made in this model — you only have to state one for part c). See Chapter 18 for more on modelling assumptions.

   b) Find the magnitude of T, the thrust in the coupling between the tractor and the trailer.

   c) State an assumption that has been made in this model of the motion of the tractor and trailer.

Q4 A car is towing a caravan along a level road. The car has mass 1200 kg and the caravan has mass 800 kg. Resistance forces of magnitude 600 N and 500 N act on the car and the caravan respectively. The acceleration of the car and caravan is 0.2 ms⁻².

   a) Calculate the driving force of the car.

Q4 Hint: In part a), add together the individual resistance forces to find the total resistance of the whole system.

   b) Find the tension in the tow bar.

   c) The car and caravan are travelling at a speed of 20 ms⁻¹ when the tow bar breaks. Given that the resistance forces remain constant, how long does the caravan take to come to rest?

Pegs and pulleys

Particles connected by a string which passes over a **peg** or **pulley** will move with the **same magnitude of acceleration** as each other (as long as the string is inextensible). However, the two connected particles **cannot** be treated as one because they will be moving in different directions.

If the peg or pulley is **smooth**, then the **magnitude** of the **tension** in the string connecting the particles will be the **same** either side of the peg or pulley.

Tip: You may see pegs and pulleys described as 'fixed' — this just means that the peg or pulley is held in place so that it won't move when the string passes over it.

Example 1

Masses of 3 kg and 5 kg are connected by a light, inextensible string and hang vertically either side of a smooth, fixed pulley. They are released from rest.

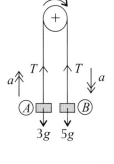

a) Find the magnitude of the acceleration of each mass.

- Resolving vertically ($\uparrow$) for A:

$$F_{net} = ma$$
$$T - 3g = 3a \quad \text{— call this equation } \textcircled{1}$$

- Resolving vertically ($\downarrow$) for B:

$$F_{net} = ma$$
$$5g - T = 5a$$
$$T = 5g - 5a \quad \text{— call this equation } \textcircled{2}$$

- Substitute equation $\textcircled{2}$ into equation $\textcircled{1}$:

$$(5g - 5a) - 3g = 3a$$
$$2 \times 9.8 = 8a$$
$$a = \boxed{2.45 \text{ ms}^{-2}}$$

b) Find the time it takes for each mass to move 40 cm.

Use one of the constant acceleration equations:

$$s = ut + \frac{1}{2}at^2$$
$$0.4 = (0 \times t) + \left(\frac{1}{2} \times 2.45 \times t^2\right)$$
$$0.4 = 1.225t^2$$
$$\text{So } t = \sqrt{\frac{0.4}{1.225}}$$
$$= \boxed{0.571 \text{ s (3 s.f.)}}$$

c) State any assumptions made in your model.

- A does not hit the pulley and B does not hit the ground.
- There's no air resistance.
- The string is 'light' so the tension is the same for both A and B, and it doesn't break.
- The string is inextensible so the acceleration is the same for both masses.
- The pulley is fixed and smooth.
- Acceleration due to gravity is constant ($g = 9.8 \text{ ms}^{-2}$).

Tip: Pulleys aren't usually completely smooth, but modelling them this way makes the calculations much easier.

Tip: When the particles are released from rest, the heavier particle will move downwards, and the lighter particle will move upwards.

Tip: The string is inextensible, so the acceleration of each particle will have the same magnitude, but opposite direction.

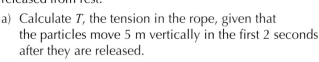

Example 2

A particle of mass 3 kg is placed on a smooth, horizontal table. A light, inextensible string connects it over a smooth, fixed peg to a particle of mass 5 kg which hangs vertically, as shown.

Find the tension in the string if the system is released from rest.

- Resolving horizontally ($\rightarrow$) for A:

$$F_{net} = ma$$
$$T = 3a \implies a = \frac{T}{3} \text{ — call this equation } \textcircled{1}$$

- Resolving vertically ($\downarrow$) for B:

$$F_{net} = ma$$
$$5g - T = 5a \text{ — call this equation } \textcircled{2}$$

- Substituting equation $\textcircled{1}$ into equation $\textcircled{2}$:

$$5g - T = 5 \times \frac{T}{3}$$

$$\text{So } \frac{8}{3}T = 5g \implies T = \boxed{18.4 \text{ N (3 s.f.)}}$$

Exercise 2.3

Q1 Two particles, A and B, of mass 3 kg and 2 kg respectively, are joined by a light inextensible string which passes over a fixed, smooth pulley. Initially, both particles are held at rest with particle A 60 cm higher than particle B. Both particles are then released from rest.

a) Draw a diagram showing the forces acting on the masses.

b) How long is it after the particles are released before they are level?

Q2 Particle A, mass 35 kg, and particle B, mass M kg ($M < 35$), are connected by a light, inextensible rope which passes over a fixed, smooth peg, as shown. Initially both particles are level and they are released from rest.

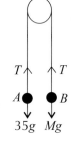

a) Calculate T, the tension in the rope, given that the particles move 5 m vertically in the first 2 seconds after they are released.

b) Find M.

Q3 Particles A and B, of mass 5 kg and 7 kg respectively, are connected by a light, inextensible string which passes over a fixed, smooth pulley. Particle A is resting on a smooth horizontal surface and particle B is hanging vertically. The system is released from rest.

a) Find the magnitude of the acceleration of the particles.

b) Find the tension in the string.

c) What assumptions have you made in your model?

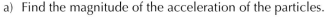

Q4   A bucket of stones with mass 50 kg is attached to one end of a
light inextensible rope, the other end of which is attached to a
counterweight of mass 10 kg. The rope passes over a smooth fixed
pulley. The bucket is raised from rest on the ground to a height of 12 m
in a time of 20 s by the addition of a constant force F acting vertically
downwards on the counterweight.

a) Draw a diagram to show the forces acting on this system.

b) Calculate the tension in the rope.

c) Find the magnitude of F.

When the bucket is 12 m above the ground, the stones are removed and
the force F stops acting on the counterweight.

d) Given that the bucket weighs 11 kg and the system is released from
rest, find the speed of the bucket as it hits the ground.

Q5   Two particles, A and B, of mass 15 kg and 12 kg
respectively, are attached to the ends of a light
inextensible string which passes over a fixed,
smooth pulley. The particles are held at rest so that
the string is taut and they are both 6 m above
the horizontal ground, as shown.

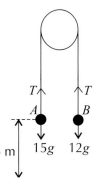

a) Find the acceleration of the particles
immediately after they are released from rest.

b) Find the magnitude of the force
which the string exerts on the pulley.

c) Particle A strikes the ground without rebounding.
Particle B then moves freely under gravity without striking the pulley.
Find the time between particle A hitting the ground and particle B
coming to rest for the first time.

Q5b) Hint: Consider
the parts of the string
either side of the
pulley separately and
remember that the
tension is constant
throughout the string.

Q5c) Hint: The string
is inextensible, so at the
instant that A hits the
ground, both A and B
will be travelling with
the same speed.

Q6

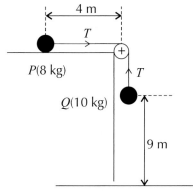

Two particles, P and Q, of mass 8 kg and 10 kg respectively, are
attached to the ends of a light, inextensible string which passes over a
fixed, smooth pulley. P is held at rest on a smooth horizontal surface,
4 m from the pulley, and Q hangs vertically, 9 m above the horizontal
ground, as shown.

The system is released from rest and P begins to accelerate towards
the pulley. At the instant P hits the pulley, the string breaks and Q then
moves freely under gravity until it hits the ground.

Find the time between the instant the particles are released from rest
and the instant when Q hits the ground.

Harder problems involving pegs and pulleys

These questions are just like those on the previous few pages, but they also include **resistance forces**. The method for answering them is exactly the same as for the problems on the previous pages: resolve the forces acting on **each particle** separately in the **direction of acceleration**.

Remember that as long as the string connecting the particles is **light** and **inextensible**, and the peg or pulley is **smooth**, the **tension** in the string will be **constant** and the two particles will have the same **magnitude** of **acceleration**.

Tip: Having well-drawn force diagrams is really important for these trickier problems.

Example

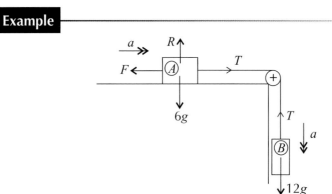

A block, A, of mass 6 kg, is placed on a rough horizontal table. A light inextensible string connects A to a second block, B, of mass 12 kg. The string passes over a fixed, smooth peg and B hangs vertically, as shown. The system is released from rest. Given that A experiences a fixed resistance force F of 30 N, find the tension in the string.

- Resolve horizontally for A ($\rightarrow$):

$$F_{net} = ma$$

$$T - F = 6a$$

$$a = \frac{1}{6}(T - 30) \text{ — call this equation } \textcircled{1}$$

- Resolve vertically for B ($\downarrow$):

$$F_{net} = ma$$

$$12g - T = 12a \text{ — call this equation } \textcircled{2}$$

- Substituting equation $\textcircled{1}$ into equation $\textcircled{2}$:

$$12g - T = 12 \times \frac{1}{6}(T - 30)$$

$$12g - T = 2T - 60$$

$$3T = 117.6 + 60 = 177.6$$

$$T = \boxed{59 \text{ N (to 2 s.f.)}}$$

Q1 Two particles A and B, of mass 6 kg and M kg respectively, are joined by a light, inextensible string which passes over a fixed, smooth pulley. The particles are held at rest with A on a rough, horizontal surface and B hanging vertically, as shown below.

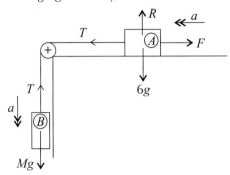

Given that A experiences a constant resistance force, F, of 10 N and that the tension in the string has magnitude 12 N, find:

a) the acceleration of A immediately after the particles are released,

b) the value of M.

Q2 A 4000 kg truck is lifting a 250 kg crate of building materials, using a light inextensible rope which passes over a fixed smooth pulley. Initially, the crate is at rest on the ground below the pulley and the rope is taut. The truck produces a driving force of D Newtons and is slowed by a constant resistance force F of 500 N.

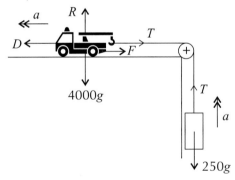

a) The crate reaches 3 ms^{-1} after 5 seconds.
Find the magnitude of the driving force, D.

b) When the crate reaches 3 ms^{-1}, the rope snaps.
Given that the driving force remains the same,
what is the truck's new acceleration?

Q2b) Hint: When the rope snaps, the tension force T will disappear.

c) After the rope snaps, the crate travels freely, experiencing no resistance forces. How much time elapses between the moment when the rope snaps, and when the crate hits the ground?

d) Give a possible improvement that could be made to this model.

Statistical Tables

The binomial cumulative distribution function
The values below show $P(X \le x)$, where $X \sim B(n, p)$.

	$p =$	0.05	0.10	0.15	0.20	0.25	0.30	0.35	0.40	0.45	0.50
$n = 5$ $x =$	0	0.7738	0.5905	0.4437	0.3277	0.2373	0.1681	0.1160	0.0778	0.0503	0.0313
	1	0.9774	0.9185	0.8352	0.7373	0.6328	0.5282	0.4284	0.3370	0.2562	0.1875
	2	0.9988	0.9914	0.9734	0.9421	0.8965	0.8369	0.7648	0.6826	0.5931	0.5000
	3	1.0000	0.9995	0.9978	0.9933	0.9844	0.9692	0.9460	0.9130	0.8688	0.8125
	4	1.0000	1.0000	0.9999	0.9997	0.9990	0.9976	0.9947	0.9898	0.9815	0.9688
$n = 6$ $x =$	0	0.7351	0.5314	0.3771	0.2621	0.1780	0.1176	0.0754	0.0467	0.0277	0.0156
	1	0.9672	0.8857	0.7765	0.6554	0.5339	0.4202	0.3191	0.2333	0.1636	0.1094
	2	0.9978	0.9842	0.9527	0.9011	0.8306	0.7443	0.6471	0.5443	0.4415	0.3438
	3	0.9999	0.9987	0.9941	0.9830	0.9624	0.9295	0.8826	0.8208	0.7447	0.6563
	4	1.0000	0.9999	0.9996	0.9984	0.9954	0.9891	0.9777	0.9590	0.9308	0.8906
	5	1.0000	1.0000	1.0000	0.9999	0.9998	0.9993	0.9982	0.9959	0.9917	0.9844
$n = 7$ $x =$	0	0.6983	0.4783	0.3206	0.2097	0.1335	0.0824	0.0490	0.0280	0.0152	0.0078
	1	0.9556	0.8503	0.7166	0.5767	0.4449	0.3294	0.2338	0.1586	0.1024	0.0625
	2	0.9962	0.9743	0.9262	0.8520	0.7564	0.6471	0.5323	0.4199	0.3164	0.2266
	3	0.9998	0.9973	0.9879	0.9667	0.9294	0.8740	0.8002	0.7102	0.6083	0.5000
	4	1.0000	0.9998	0.9988	0.9953	0.9871	0.9712	0.9444	0.9037	0.8471	0.7734
	5	1.0000	1.0000	0.9999	0.9996	0.9987	0.9962	0.9910	0.9812	0.9643	0.9375
	6	1.0000	1.0000	1.0000	1.0000	0.9999	0.9998	0.9994	0.9984	0.9963	0.9922
$n = 8$ $x =$	0	0.6634	0.4305	0.2725	0.1678	0.1001	0.0576	0.0319	0.0168	0.0084	0.0039
	1	0.9428	0.8131	0.6572	0.5033	0.3671	0.2553	0.1691	0.1064	0.0632	0.0352
	2	0.9942	0.9619	0.8948	0.7969	0.6785	0.5518	0.4278	0.3154	0.2201	0.1445
	3	0.9996	0.9950	0.9786	0.9437	0.8862	0.8059	0.7064	0.5941	0.4770	0.3633
	4	1.0000	0.9996	0.9971	0.9896	0.9727	0.9420	0.8939	0.8263	0.7396	0.6367
	5	1.0000	1.0000	0.9998	0.9988	0.9958	0.9887	0.9747	0.9502	0.9115	0.8555
	6	1.0000	1.0000	1.0000	0.9999	0.9996	0.9987	0.9964	0.9915	0.9819	0.9648
	7	1.0000	1.0000	1.0000	1.0000	1.0000	0.9999	0.9998	0.9993	0.9983	0.9961
$n = 9$ $x =$	0	0.6302	0.3874	0.2316	0.1342	0.0751	0.0404	0.0207	0.0101	0.0046	0.0020
	1	0.9288	0.7748	0.5995	0.4362	0.3003	0.1960	0.1211	0.0705	0.0385	0.0195
	2	0.9916	0.9470	0.8591	0.7382	0.6007	0.4628	0.3373	0.2318	0.1495	0.0898
	3	0.9994	0.9917	0.9661	0.9144	0.8343	0.7297	0.6089	0.4826	0.3614	0.2539
	4	1.0000	0.9991	0.9944	0.9804	0.9511	0.9012	0.8283	0.7334	0.6214	0.5000
	5	1.0000	0.9999	0.9994	0.9969	0.9900	0.9747	0.9464	0.9006	0.8342	0.7461
	6	1.0000	1.0000	1.0000	0.9997	0.9987	0.9957	0.9888	0.9750	0.9502	0.9102
	7	1.0000	1.0000	1.0000	1.0000	0.9999	0.9996	0.9986	0.9962	0.9909	0.9805
	8	1.0000	1.0000	1.0000	1.0000	1.0000	1.0000	0.9999	0.9997	0.9992	0.9980
$n = 10$ $x =$	0	0.5987	0.3487	0.1969	0.1074	0.0563	0.0282	0.0135	0.0060	0.0025	0.0010
	1	0.9139	0.7361	0.5443	0.3758	0.2440	0.1493	0.0860	0.0464	0.0233	0.0107
	2	0.9885	0.9298	0.8202	0.6778	0.5256	0.3828	0.2616	0.1673	0.0996	0.0547
	3	0.9990	0.9872	0.9500	0.8791	0.7759	0.6496	0.5138	0.3823	0.2660	0.1719
	4	0.9999	0.9984	0.9901	0.9672	0.9219	0.8497	0.7515	0.6331	0.5044	0.3770
	5	1.0000	0.9999	0.9986	0.9936	0.9803	0.9527	0.9051	0.8338	0.7384	0.6230
	6	1.0000	1.0000	0.9999	0.9991	0.9965	0.9894	0.9740	0.9452	0.8980	0.8281
	7	1.0000	1.0000	1.0000	0.9999	0.9996	0.9984	0.9952	0.9877	0.9726	0.9453
	8	1.0000	1.0000	1.0000	1.0000	1.0000	0.9999	0.9995	0.9983	0.9955	0.9893
	9	1.0000	1.0000	1.0000	1.0000	1.0000	1.0000	1.0000	0.9999	0.9997	0.9990

The binomial cumulative distribution function (continued)

p =	0.05	0.10	0.15	0.20	0.25	0.30	0.35	0.40	0.45	0.50
n = 12 x = 0	0.5404	0.2824	0.1422	0.0687	0.0317	0.0138	0.0057	0.0022	0.0008	0.0002
1	0.8816	0.6590	0.4435	0.2749	0.1584	0.0850	0.0424	0.0196	0.0083	0.0032
2	0.9804	0.8891	0.7358	0.5583	0.3907	0.2528	0.1513	0.0834	0.0421	0.0193
3	0.9978	0.9744	0.9078	0.7946	0.6488	0.4925	0.3467	0.2253	0.1345	0.0730
4	0.9998	0.9957	0.9761	0.9274	0.8424	0.7237	0.5833	0.4382	0.3044	0.1938
5	1.0000	0.9995	0.9954	0.9806	0.9456	0.8822	0.7873	0.6652	0.5269	0.3872
6	1.0000	0.9999	0.9993	0.9961	0.9857	0.9614	0.9154	0.8418	0.7393	0.6128
7	1.0000	1.0000	0.9999	0.9994	0.9972	0.9905	0.9745	0.9427	0.8883	0.8062
8	1.0000	1.0000	1.0000	0.9999	0.9996	0.9983	0.9944	0.9847	0.9644	0.9270
9	1.0000	1.0000	1.0000	1.0000	1.0000	0.9998	0.9992	0.9972	0.9921	0.9807
10	1.0000	1.0000	1.0000	1.0000	1.0000	1.0000	0.9999	0.9997	0.9989	0.9968
11	1.0000	1.0000	1.0000	1.0000	1.0000	1.0000	1.0000	1.0000	0.9999	0.9998
n = 15 x = 0	0.4633	0.2059	0.0874	0.0352	0.0134	0.0047	0.0016	0.0005	0.0001	0.0000
1	0.8290	0.5490	0.3186	0.1671	0.0802	0.0353	0.0142	0.0052	0.0017	0.0005
2	0.9638	0.8159	0.6042	0.3980	0.2361	0.1268	0.0617	0.0271	0.0107	0.0037
3	0.9945	0.9444	0.8227	0.6482	0.4613	0.2969	0.1727	0.0905	0.0424	0.0176
4	0.9994	0.9873	0.9383	0.8358	0.6865	0.5155	0.3519	0.2173	0.1204	0.0592
5	0.9999	0.9978	0.9832	0.9389	0.8516	0.7216	0.5643	0.4032	0.2608	0.1509
6	1.0000	0.9997	0.9964	0.9819	0.9434	0.8689	0.7548	0.6098	0.4522	0.3036
7	1.0000	1.0000	0.9994	0.9958	0.9827	0.9500	0.8868	0.7869	0.6535	0.5000
8	1.0000	1.0000	0.9999	0.9992	0.9958	0.9848	0.9578	0.9050	0.8182	0.6964
9	1.0000	1.0000	1.0000	0.9999	0.9992	0.9963	0.9876	0.9662	0.9231	0.8491
10	1.0000	1.0000	1.0000	1.0000	0.9999	0.9993	0.9972	0.9907	0.9745	0.9408
11	1.0000	1.0000	1.0000	1.0000	1.0000	0.9999	0.9995	0.9981	0.9937	0.9824
12	1.0000	1.0000	1.0000	1.0000	1.0000	1.0000	0.9999	0.9997	0.9989	0.9963
13	1.0000	1.0000	1.0000	1.0000	1.0000	1.0000	1.0000	1.0000	0.9999	0.9995
14	1.0000	1.0000	1.0000	1.0000	1.0000	1.0000	1.0000	1.0000	1.0000	1.0000
n = 20 x = 0	0.3585	0.1216	0.0388	0.0115	0.0032	0.0008	0.0002	0.0000	0.0000	0.0000
1	0.7358	0.3917	0.1756	0.0692	0.0243	0.0076	0.0021	0.0005	0.0001	0.0000
2	0.9245	0.6769	0.4049	0.2061	0.0913	0.0355	0.0121	0.0036	0.0009	0.0002
3	0.9841	0.8670	0.6477	0.4114	0.2252	0.1071	0.0444	0.0160	0.0049	0.0013
4	0.9974	0.9568	0.8298	0.6296	0.4148	0.2375	0.1182	0.0510	0.0189	0.0059
5	0.9997	0.9887	0.9327	0.8042	0.6172	0.4164	0.2454	0.1256	0.0553	0.0207
6	1.0000	0.9976	0.9781	0.9133	0.7858	0.6080	0.4166	0.2500	0.1299	0.0577
7	1.0000	0.9996	0.9941	0.9679	0.8982	0.7723	0.6010	0.4159	0.2520	0.1316
8	1.0000	0.9999	0.9987	0.9900	0.9591	0.8867	0.7624	0.5956	0.4143	0.2517
9	1.0000	1.0000	0.9998	0.9974	0.9861	0.9520	0.8782	0.7553	0.5914	0.4119
10	1.0000	1.0000	1.0000	0.9994	0.9961	0.9829	0.9468	0.8725	0.7507	0.5881
11	1.0000	1.0000	1.0000	0.9999	0.9991	0.9949	0.9804	0.9435	0.8692	0.7483
12	1.0000	1.0000	1.0000	1.0000	0.9998	0.9987	0.9940	0.9790	0.9420	0.8684
13	1.0000	1.0000	1.0000	1.0000	1.0000	0.9997	0.9985	0.9935	0.9786	0.9423
14	1.0000	1.0000	1.0000	1.0000	1.0000	1.0000	0.9997	0.9984	0.9936	0.9793
15	1.0000	1.0000	1.0000	1.0000	1.0000	1.0000	1.0000	0.9997	0.9985	0.9941
16	1.0000	1.0000	1.0000	1.0000	1.0000	1.0000	1.0000	1.0000	0.9997	0.9987
17	1.0000	1.0000	1.0000	1.0000	1.0000	1.0000	1.0000	1.0000	1.0000	0.9998
18	1.0000	1.0000	1.0000	1.0000	1.0000	1.0000	1.0000	1.0000	1.0000	1.0000

The binomial cumulative distribution function (continued)

		p =	0.05	0.10	0.15	0.20	0.25	0.30	0.35	0.40	0.45	0.50
n = 25	x =	0	0.2774	0.0718	0.0172	0.0038	0.0008	0.0001	0.0000	0.0000	0.0000	0.0000
		1	0.6424	0.2712	0.0931	0.0274	0.0070	0.0016	0.0003	0.0001	0.0000	0.0000
		2	0.8729	0.5371	0.2537	0.0982	0.0321	0.0090	0.0021	0.0004	0.0001	0.0000
		3	0.9659	0.7636	0.4711	0.2340	0.0962	0.0332	0.0097	0.0024	0.0005	0.0001
		4	0.9928	0.9020	0.6821	0.4207	0.2137	0.0905	0.0320	0.0095	0.0023	0.0005
		5	0.9988	0.9666	0.8385	0.6167	0.3783	0.1935	0.0826	0.0294	0.0086	0.0020
		6	0.9998	0.9905	0.9305	0.7800	0.5611	0.3407	0.1734	0.0736	0.0258	0.0073
		7	1.0000	0.9977	0.9745	0.8909	0.7265	0.5118	0.3061	0.1536	0.0639	0.0216
		8	1.0000	0.9995	0.9920	0.9532	0.8506	0.6769	0.4668	0.2735	0.1340	0.0539
		9	1.0000	0.9999	0.9979	0.9827	0.9287	0.8106	0.6303	0.4246	0.2424	0.1148
		10	1.0000	1.0000	0.9995	0.9944	0.9703	0.9022	0.7712	0.5858	0.3843	0.2122
		11	1.0000	1.0000	0.9999	0.9985	0.9893	0.9558	0.8746	0.7323	0.5426	0.3450
		12	1.0000	1.0000	1.0000	0.9996	0.9966	0.9825	0.9396	0.8462	0.6937	0.5000
		13	1.0000	1.0000	1.0000	0.9999	0.9991	0.9940	0.9745	0.9222	0.8173	0.6550
		14	1.0000	1.0000	1.0000	1.0000	0.9998	0.9982	0.9907	0.9656	0.9040	0.7878
		15	1.0000	1.0000	1.0000	1.0000	1.0000	0.9995	0.9971	0.9868	0.9560	0.8852
		16	1.0000	1.0000	1.0000	1.0000	1.0000	0.9999	0.9992	0.9957	0.9826	0.9461
		17	1.0000	1.0000	1.0000	1.0000	1.0000	1.0000	0.9998	0.9988	0.9942	0.9784
		18	1.0000	1.0000	1.0000	1.0000	1.0000	1.0000	1.0000	0.9997	0.9984	0.9927
		19	1.0000	1.0000	1.0000	1.0000	1.0000	1.0000	1.0000	0.9999	0.9996	0.9980
		20	1.0000	1.0000	1.0000	1.0000	1.0000	1.0000	1.0000	1.0000	0.9999	0.9995
		21	1.0000	1.0000	1.0000	1.0000	1.0000	1.0000	1.0000	1.0000	1.0000	0.9999
		22	1.0000	1.0000	1.0000	1.0000	1.0000	1.0000	1.0000	1.0000	1.0000	1.0000
n = 30	x =	0	0.2146	0.0424	0.0076	0.0012	0.0002	0.0000	0.0000	0.0000	0.0000	0.0000
		1	0.5535	0.1837	0.0480	0.0105	0.0020	0.0003	0.0000	0.0000	0.0000	0.0000
		2	0.8122	0.4114	0.1514	0.0442	0.0106	0.0021	0.0003	0.0000	0.0000	0.0000
		3	0.9392	0.6474	0.3217	0.1227	0.0374	0.0093	0.0019	0.0003	0.0000	0.0000
		4	0.9844	0.8245	0.5245	0.2552	0.0979	0.0302	0.0075	0.0015	0.0002	0.0000
		5	0.9967	0.9268	0.7106	0.4275	0.2026	0.0766	0.0233	0.0057	0.0011	0.0002
		6	0.9994	0.9742	0.8474	0.6070	0.3481	0.1595	0.0586	0.0172	0.0040	0.0007
		7	0.9999	0.9922	0.9302	0.7608	0.5143	0.2814	0.1238	0.0435	0.0121	0.0026
		8	1.0000	0.9980	0.9722	0.8713	0.6736	0.4315	0.2247	0.0940	0.0312	0.0081
		9	1.0000	0.9995	0.9903	0.9389	0.8034	0.5888	0.3575	0.1763	0.0694	0.0214
		10	1.0000	0.9999	0.9971	0.9744	0.8943	0.7304	0.5078	0.2915	0.1350	0.0494
		11	1.0000	1.0000	0.9992	0.9905	0.9493	0.8407	0.6548	0.4311	0.2327	0.1002
		12	1.0000	1.0000	0.9998	0.9969	0.9784	0.9155	0.7802	0.5785	0.3592	0.1808
		13	1.0000	1.0000	1.0000	0.9991	0.9918	0.9599	0.8737	0.7145	0.5025	0.2923
		14	1.0000	1.0000	1.0000	0.9998	0.9973	0.9831	0.9348	0.8246	0.6448	0.4278
		15	1.0000	1.0000	1.0000	0.9999	0.9992	0.9936	0.9699	0.9029	0.7691	0.5722
		16	1.0000	1.0000	1.0000	1.0000	0.9998	0.9979	0.9876	0.9519	0.8644	0.7077
		17	1.0000	1.0000	1.0000	1.0000	0.9999	0.9994	0.9955	0.9788	0.9286	0.8192
		18	1.0000	1.0000	1.0000	1.0000	1.0000	0.9998	0.9986	0.9917	0.9666	0.8998
		19	1.0000	1.0000	1.0000	1.0000	1.0000	1.0000	0.9996	0.9971	0.9862	0.9506
		20	1.0000	1.0000	1.0000	1.0000	1.0000	1.0000	0.9999	0.9991	0.9950	0.9786
		21	1.0000	1.0000	1.0000	1.0000	1.0000	1.0000	1.0000	0.9998	0.9984	0.9919
		22	1.0000	1.0000	1.0000	1.0000	1.0000	1.0000	1.0000	1.0000	0.9996	0.9974
		23	1.0000	1.0000	1.0000	1.0000	1.0000	1.0000	1.0000	1.0000	0.9999	0.9993
		24	1.0000	1.0000	1.0000	1.0000	1.0000	1.0000	1.0000	1.0000	1.0000	0.9998
		25	1.0000	1.0000	1.0000	1.0000	1.0000	1.0000	1.0000	1.0000	1.0000	1.0000

The binomial cumulative distribution function (continued)

	p =	0.05	0.10	0.15	0.20	0.25	0.30	0.35	0.40	0.45	0.50
n = 40 x =	0	0.1285	0.0148	0.0015	0.0001	0.0000	0.0000	0.0000	0.0000	0.0000	0.0000
	1	0.3991	0.0805	0.0121	0.0015	0.0001	0.0000	0.0000	0.0000	0.0000	0.0000
	2	0.6767	0.2228	0.0486	0.0079	0.0010	0.0001	0.0000	0.0000	0.0000	0.0000
	3	0.8619	0.4231	0.1302	0.0285	0.0047	0.0006	0.0001	0.0000	0.0000	0.0000
	4	0.9520	0.6290	0.2633	0.0759	0.0160	0.0026	0.0003	0.0000	0.0000	0.0000
	5	0.9861	0.7937	0.4325	0.1613	0.0433	0.0086	0.0013	0.0001	0.0000	0.0000
	6	0.9966	0.9005	0.6067	0.2859	0.0962	0.0238	0.0044	0.0006	0.0001	0.0000
	7	0.9993	0.9581	0.7559	0.4371	0.1820	0.0553	0.0124	0.0021	0.0002	0.0000
	8	0.9999	0.9845	0.8646	0.5931	0.2998	0.1110	0.0303	0.0061	0.0009	0.0001
	9	1.0000	0.9949	0.9328	0.7318	0.4395	0.1959	0.0644	0.0156	0.0027	0.0003
	10	1.0000	0.9985	0.9701	0.8392	0.5839	0.3087	0.1215	0.0352	0.0074	0.0011
	11	1.0000	0.9996	0.9880	0.9125	0.7151	0.4406	0.2053	0.0709	0.0179	0.0032
	12	1.0000	0.9999	0.9957	0.9568	0.8209	0.5772	0.3143	0.1285	0.0386	0.0083
	13	1.0000	1.0000	0.9986	0.9806	0.8968	0.7032	0.4408	0.2112	0.0751	0.0192
	14	1.0000	1.0000	0.9996	0.9921	0.9456	0.8074	0.5721	0.3174	0.1326	0.0403
	15	1.0000	1.0000	0.9999	0.9971	0.9738	0.8849	0.6946	0.4402	0.2142	0.0769
	16	1.0000	1.0000	1.0000	0.9990	0.9884	0.9367	0.7978	0.5681	0.3185	0.1341
	17	1.0000	1.0000	1.0000	0.9997	0.9953	0.9680	0.8761	0.6885	0.4391	0.2148
	18	1.0000	1.0000	1.0000	0.9999	0.9983	0.9852	0.9301	0.7911	0.5651	0.3179
	19	1.0000	1.0000	1.0000	1.0000	0.9994	0.9937	0.9637	0.8702	0.6844	0.4373
	20	1.0000	1.0000	1.0000	1.0000	0.9998	0.9976	0.9827	0.9256	0.7870	0.5627
	21	1.0000	1.0000	1.0000	1.0000	1.0000	0.9991	0.9925	0.9608	0.8669	0.6821
	22	1.0000	1.0000	1.0000	1.0000	1.0000	0.9997	0.9970	0.9811	0.9233	0.7852
	23	1.0000	1.0000	1.0000	1.0000	1.0000	0.9999	0.9989	0.9917	0.9595	0.8659
	24	1.0000	1.0000	1.0000	1.0000	1.0000	1.0000	0.9996	0.9966	0.9804	0.9231
	25	1.0000	1.0000	1.0000	1.0000	1.0000	1.0000	0.9999	0.9988	0.9914	0.9597
	26	1.0000	1.0000	1.0000	1.0000	1.0000	1.0000	1.0000	0.9996	0.9966	0.9808
	27	1.0000	1.0000	1.0000	1.0000	1.0000	1.0000	1.0000	0.9999	0.9988	0.9917
	28	1.0000	1.0000	1.0000	1.0000	1.0000	1.0000	1.0000	1.0000	0.9996	0.9968
	29	1.0000	1.0000	1.0000	1.0000	1.0000	1.0000	1.0000	1.0000	0.9999	0.9989
	30	1.0000	1.0000	1.0000	1.0000	1.0000	1.0000	1.0000	1.0000	1.0000	0.9997
	31	1.0000	1.0000	1.0000	1.0000	1.0000	1.0000	1.0000	1.0000	1.0000	0.9999
	32	1.0000	1.0000	1.0000	1.0000	1.0000	1.0000	1.0000	1.0000	1.0000	1.0000

The binomial cumulative distribution function (continued)

	$p =$	0.05	0.10	0.15	0.20	0.25	0.30	0.35	0.40	0.45	0.50
$n = 50$ $x =$	0	0.0769	0.0052	0.0003	0.0000	0.0000	0.0000	0.0000	0.0000	0.0000	0.0000
	1	0.2794	0.0338	0.0029	0.0002	0.0000	0.0000	0.0000	0.0000	0.0000	0.0000
	2	0.5405	0.1117	0.0142	0.0013	0.0001	0.0000	0.0000	0.0000	0.0000	0.0000
	3	0.7604	0.2503	0.0460	0.0057	0.0005	0.0000	0.0000	0.0000	0.0000	0.0000
	4	0.8964	0.4312	0.1121	0.0185	0.0021	0.0002	0.0000	0.0000	0.0000	0.0000
	5	0.9622	0.6161	0.2194	0.0480	0.0070	0.0007	0.0001	0.0000	0.0000	0.0000
	6	0.9882	0.7702	0.3613	0.1034	0.0194	0.0025	0.0002	0.0000	0.0000	0.0000
	7	0.9968	0.8779	0.5188	0.1904	0.0453	0.0073	0.0008	0.0001	0.0000	0.0000
	8	0.9992	0.9421	0.6681	0.3073	0.0916	0.0183	0.0025	0.0002	0.0000	0.0000
	9	0.9998	0.9755	0.7911	0.4437	0.1637	0.0402	0.0067	0.0008	0.0001	0.0000
	10	1.0000	0.9906	0.8801	0.5836	0.2622	0.0789	0.0160	0.0022	0.0002	0.0000
	11	1.0000	0.9968	0.9372	0.7107	0.3816	0.1390	0.0342	0.0057	0.0006	0.0000
	12	1.0000	0.9990	0.9699	0.8139	0.5110	0.2229	0.0661	0.0133	0.0018	0.0002
	13	1.0000	0.9997	0.9868	0.8894	0.6370	0.3279	0.1163	0.0280	0.0045	0.0005
	14	1.0000	0.9999	0.9947	0.9393	0.7481	0.4468	0.1878	0.0540	0.0104	0.0013
	15	1.0000	1.0000	0.9981	0.9692	0.8369	0.5692	0.2801	0.0955	0.0220	0.0033
	16	1.0000	1.0000	0.9993	0.9856	0.9017	0.6839	0.3889	0.1561	0.0427	0.0077
	17	1.0000	1.0000	0.9998	0.9937	0.9449	0.7822	0.5060	0.2369	0.0765	0.0164
	18	1.0000	1.0000	0.9999	0.9975	0.9713	0.8594	0.6216	0.3356	0.1273	0.0325
	19	1.0000	1.0000	1.0000	0.9991	0.9861	0.9152	0.7264	0.4465	0.1974	0.0595
	20	1.0000	1.0000	1.0000	0.9997	0.9937	0.9522	0.8139	0.5610	0.2862	0.1013
	21	1.0000	1.0000	1.0000	0.9999	0.9974	0.9749	0.8813	0.6701	0.3900	0.1611
	22	1.0000	1.0000	1.0000	1.0000	0.9990	0.9877	0.9290	0.7660	0.5019	0.2399
	23	1.0000	1.0000	1.0000	1.0000	0.9996	0.9944	0.9604	0.8438	0.6134	0.3359
	24	1.0000	1.0000	1.0000	1.0000	0.9999	0.9976	0.9793	0.9022	0.7160	0.4439
	25	1.0000	1.0000	1.0000	1.0000	1.0000	0.9991	0.9900	0.9427	0.8034	0.5561
	26	1.0000	1.0000	1.0000	1.0000	1.0000	0.9997	0.9955	0.9686	0.8721	0.6641
	27	1.0000	1.0000	1.0000	1.0000	1.0000	0.9999	0.9981	0.9840	0.9220	0.7601
	28	1.0000	1.0000	1.0000	1.0000	1.0000	1.0000	0.9993	0.9924	0.9556	0.8389
	29	1.0000	1.0000	1.0000	1.0000	1.0000	1.0000	0.9997	0.9966	0.9765	0.8987
	30	1.0000	1.0000	1.0000	1.0000	1.0000	1.0000	0.9999	0.9986	0.9884	0.9405
	31	1.0000	1.0000	1.0000	1.0000	1.0000	1.0000	1.0000	0.9995	0.9947	0.9675
	32	1.0000	1.0000	1.0000	1.0000	1.0000	1.0000	1.0000	0.9998	0.9978	0.9836
	33	1.0000	1.0000	1.0000	1.0000	1.0000	1.0000	1.0000	0.9999	0.9991	0.9923
	34	1.0000	1.0000	1.0000	1.0000	1.0000	1.0000	1.0000	1.0000	0.9997	0.9967
	35	1.0000	1.0000	1.0000	1.0000	1.0000	1.0000	1.0000	1.0000	0.9999	0.9987
	36	1.0000	1.0000	1.0000	1.0000	1.0000	1.0000	1.0000	1.0000	1.0000	0.9995
	37	1.0000	1.0000	1.0000	1.0000	1.0000	1.0000	1.0000	1.0000	1.0000	0.9998
	38	1.0000	1.0000	1.0000	1.0000	1.0000	1.0000	1.0000	1.0000	1.0000	1.0000

Answers

Chapter 2: Proof

1. Proof
Exercise 1.1 — Proof

Q1 **a)** Take two odd numbers $2l + 1$ and $2m + 1$
(where l and m are integers), then their sum is
$2l + 1 + 2m + 1 = 2l + 2m + 2 = 2(l + m + 1) =$ even.

b) Take two even numbers, $2j$ and $2k$ (where j and k
are integers), then their product is $2j \times 2k = 4jk$
$= 2(2jk) =$ even.

c) Take one even number, $2l$ and one odd number
$2m + 1$ (where l and m are integers), then their product
is $2l \times (2m + 1) = 4lm + 2l = 2(2lm + l) =$ even.

Q2 E.g. Let $p = 1 \Rightarrow \dfrac{1}{p^2} = \dfrac{1}{p}$, so the statement is not true.
You could have also taken p to be a negative number.

Q3 $(x + 5)^2 + 3(x - 1)^2 = x^2 + 10x + 25 + 3(x^2 - 2x + 1)$
$\qquad\qquad = x^2 + 10x + 25 + 3x^2 - 6x + 3$
$\qquad\qquad = 4x^2 + 4x + 28$
$\qquad\qquad = 4(x^2 + x + 7)$

This has a factor of 4 outside the brackets,
so it is always divisible by 4.

Q4 Proof by exhaustion:
Take three consecutive integers $(n - 1)$, n and $(n + 1)$.
Their product is $(n - 1)n(n + 1) = n(n^2 - 1) = n^3 - n$.
Consider the two cases — n even and n odd.
For n even, n^3 is even (as even $\times$ even = even) so $n^3 - n$ is
also even (as even – even = even). For n odd, n^3 is odd (as
odd $\times$ odd = odd) so $n^3 - n$ is even (as odd – odd
= even). So $n^3 - n$ is even when n is even and when n is
odd, and n must be either odd or even, so the product of
three consecutive integers is always even.
*Another approach to this proof is to take the product of three
consecutive integers n(n + 1)(n + 2) and consider n odd and
n even. If n is odd:
n(n + 1)(n + 2) = (odd × even) × odd = even × odd = even.
If n is even:
n(n + 1)(n + 2) = (even × odd) × even = even × even = even.*

Q5 The simplest way to disprove the statement is to find a
counter-example. Try some values of n and see if the
statement is true for them:
$n = 3 \Rightarrow n^2 - n - 1 = 3^2 - 3 - 1 = 5$ — prime
$n = 4 \Rightarrow n^2 - n - 1 = 4^2 - 4 - 1 = 11$ — prime
$n = 5 \Rightarrow n^2 - n - 1 = 5^2 - 5 - 1 = 19$ — prime
$n = 6 \Rightarrow n^2 - n - 1 = 6^2 - 6 - 1 = 29$ — prime
$n = 7 \Rightarrow n^2 - n - 1 = 7^2 - 7 - 1 = 41$ — prime
$n = 8 \Rightarrow n^2 - n - 1 = 8^2 - 8 - 1 = 55$ — not prime
$n^2 - n - 1$ is not prime when $n = 8$.
So the statement is false.
*Sometimes good old trial and error is the easiest way to find a
counter-example. Don't forget, if you've been told to disprove a
statement like this, then a counter-example must exist.*

Q6 Find a counter-example for which the statement isn't
true. Take $x = -1$ and $y = 2$. Then
$\sqrt{x^2 + y^2} = \sqrt{(-1)^2 + 2^2} = \sqrt{1 + 4} = \sqrt{5} = 2.236...$
and $x + y = -1 + 2 = 1$. $2.236... > 1$,
so the statement is not true.

Q7 Take any two rational numbers a and b. By the definition
of rational numbers we know that $a = \dfrac{p}{q}$ and $b = \dfrac{r}{s}$
where p, q, r and s are integers,
and q & s are non-zero.
So, the sum of a and b is $\dfrac{p}{q} + \dfrac{r}{s} = \dfrac{ps + rq}{qs}$.
ps and rq are the product of integers, so are also integers.
This means $ps + rq$ is also an integer. qs is the product of
non-zero integers, so must also be a non zero integer.
This shows that $a + b$ is the quotient of two integers, and
has a non-zero denominator, so by definition $a + b$ is
rational.

Q8 **a)** Proof by exhaustion:
Consider the two cases — n even and n odd.
Let n be even.
$n^2 - n = n(n - 1)$.
If n is even, $n - 1$ is odd so $n(n - 1)$ is even
(as even $\times$ odd = even). This means that
$n(n - 1) - 1$ is odd.
Let n be odd. If n is odd, $n - 1$ is even, so $n(n - 1)$ is
even (as odd $\times$ even = even). This means that
$n(n - 1) - 1$ is odd.
As any integer n has to be either odd or even,
$n^2 - n - 1$ is odd for any value of n.

b) As $n^2 - n - 1$ is odd, $n^2 - n - 2$ is even.
The product of even numbers is also even, so as
$(n^2 - n - 2)^3$ is the product of 3 even numbers,
it will always be even.

Chapter 3: Algebra

1. Algebraic Expressions
Exercise 1.1 — Expanding brackets

Q1 **a)** $5(x + 4) = 5x + (5 \times 4) = 5x + 20$

b) $a(4 - 2b) = 4a + (a \times -2b) = 4a - 2ab$

c) $-2(x^2 + y) = -2x^2 - 2y$

d) $6mn(m + 1) = 6mnm + 6mn = 6m^2n + 6mn$

e) $-4ht(t^2 - 2ht - 3h^3)$
$= -4ht \times t^2 + (-4ht \times -2ht) + (-4ht \times -3h^3)$
$= -4ht^3 + 8h^2t^2 + 12h^4t$

f) $7z^2(2 + z) = 14z^2 + 7z^2z = 14z^2 + 7z^3$

g) $4(x + 2) + 3(x - 5) = 4x + 8 + 3x - 15 = 7x - 7$

h) $p(3p^2 - 2q) + (q + 4p^3)$
$= (p \times 3p^2) + (p \times -2q) + q + 4p^3$
$= 3p^3 - 2pq + q + 4p^3 = 7p^3 - 2pq + q$

i) $7xy(x^2 + z^2) = (7xy \times x^2) + (7xy \times z^2) = 7x^3y + 7xyz^2$
Don't forget to simplify your answer if possible.

Q2 a) $(x + 5)(x - 3) = x^2 - 3x + 5x - 15 = x^2 + 2x - 15$

b) $(2z + 3)(3z - 2) = 6z^2 - 4z + 9z - 6 = 6z^2 + 5z - 6$

c) $(u + 8)^2 = (u + 8)(u + 8) = u^2 + 8u + 8u + 64$
$= u^2 + 16u + 64$

d) $(ab + cd)(ac + bd) = abac + abbd + cdac + cdbd$
$= a^2bc + ab^2d + ac^2d + bcd^2$

e) $(10 + f)(2f^2 - 3g) = 20f^2 - 30g + 2f^3 - 3fg$

f) $(7 + q)(7 - q) = 49 - 7q + 7q - q^2 = 49 - q^2$

g) $(2 - 3w)^2 = (2 - 3w)(2 - 3w) = 2^2 - 6w - 6w + 9w^2$
$= 4 - 12w + 9w^2$

h) $(4rs^2 + 3)^2 = (4rs^2 + 3)(4rs^2 + 3)$
$= 16r^2s^4 + 12rs^2 + 12rs^2 + 9$
$= 16r^2s^4 + 24rs^2 + 9$

i) $(5k^2l - 2kn)^2 = (5k^2l - 2kn)(5k^2l - 2kn)$
$= 25k^4l^2 - 10k^3nl - 10k^3nl + 4k^2n^2$
$= 25k^4l^2 - 20k^3ln + 4k^2n^2$

In parts c), g), h) and i), you could get straight to the answer by using $(a + b)^2 = a^2 + 2ab + b^2$.

Q3 a) $(l + 5)(l^2 + 2l + 3) = l(l^2 + 2l + 3) + 5(l^2 + 2l + 3)$
$= l^3 + 2l^2 + 3l + 5l^2 + 10l + 15$
$= l^3 + 7l^2 + 13l + 15$

b) $(2 + q)(3 - q + 4q^2) = 2(3 - q + 4q^2) + q(3 - q + 4q^2)$
$= 6 - 2q + 8q^2 + 3q - q^2 + 4q^3$
$= 6 + q + 7q^2 + 4q^3$

c) $(m + 1)(m + 2)(m - 4)$
$= (m^2 + 2m + m + 2)(m - 4)$
$= (m^2 + 3m + 2)(m - 4)$
$= m^2(m - 4) + 3m(m - 4) + 2(m - 4)$
$= m^3 - 4m^2 + 3m^2 - 12m + 2m - 8$
$= m^3 - m^2 - 10m - 8$

d) $(r + s)^3 = (r + s)(r + s)(r + s)$
$= (r^2 + rs + sr + s^2)(r + s)$
$= (r^2 + 2rs + s^2)(r + s)$
$= r^2(r + s) + 2rs(r + s) + s^2(r + s)$
$= r^3 + r^2s + 2r^2s + 2rs^2 + rs^2 + s^3$
$= r^3 + 3r^2s + 3rs^2 + s^3$

e) $(4 + x + y)(1 - x - y)$
$= 4(1 - x - y) + x(1 - x - y) + y(1 - x - y)$
$= 4 - 4x - 4y + x - x^2 - xy + y - xy - y^2$
$= 4 - 3x - 3y - 2xy - x^2 - y^2$

f) $(2c^2 - cd + d)(2d - c - 5c^2)$
$= 2c^2(2d - c - 5c^2) - cd(2d - c - 5c^2) + d(2d - c - 5c^2)$
$= 4c^2d - 2c^3 - 10c^4 - 2cd^2 + c^2d + 5c^3d$
$\qquad\qquad\qquad + 2d^2 - dc - 5c^2d$
$= -10c^4 - 2c^3 + 5c^3d - 2cd^2 - cd + 2d^2$

Q4 Carole's garden: $x \times x = x^2$ m^2
Mark's garden: $(x + 3)(2x + 1) = 2x^2 + x + 6x + 3$
$= 2x^2 + 7x + 3$ m^2

Difference: $2x^2 + 7x + 3 - x^2 = x^2 + 7x + 3$ m^2
For Mark's garden, use the information in the question to find the length of the sides. Then multiply the brackets and expand.

Exercise 1.2 — Factorising

Q1 a) $9k + 15l = (3 \times 3k) + (3 \times 5l) = 3(3k + 5l)$

b) $u^2 - uv = u(u - v)$

c) $10w + 15 = (5 \times 2w) + (5 \times 3) = 5(2w + 3)$

d) $2x^2y - 12xy^2 = (2xy \times x) - (2xy \times 6y) = 2xy(x - 6y)$

e) $f^2g^2 - fg = (fg \times fg) - (fg \times 1) = fg(fg - 1)$

f) $3u^2v^2 + 5u^4v^4 + 12u^2v$
$= (u^2v \times 3v) + (u^2v \times 5u^2v^3) + (u^2v \times 12)$
$= u^2v(3v + 5u^2v^3 + 12)$

g) $p^3 + 3pq^3 + 2p = (p \times p^2) + (p \times 3q^3) + (p \times 2)$
$= p(p^2 + 3q^3 + 2)$

h) $abcde - bcdef - cdefg$
$= (cde \times ab) - (cde \times bf) - (cde \times fg)$
$= cde(ab - bf - fg)$

i) $11xy^2 - 11x^2y - 11x^2y^2$
$= (11xy \times y) - (11xy \times x) - (11xy \times xy)$
$= 11xy(y - x - xy)$

j) $mnp^2 + 7m^2np^3 = (mnp^2 \times 1) + (mnp^2 \times 7mp)$
$= mnp^2(1 + 7mp)$

Q2 a) $x^2 - y^2 = (x + y)(x - y)$
This is just using the formula for the 'difference of two squares'.

b) $9a^2 - 4b^2 = (3a)^2 - (2b)^2 = (3a + 2b)(3a - 2b)$

c) $25x^2 - 49z^2 = (5x)^2 - (7z)^2 = (5x + 7z)(5x - 7z)$

d) $a^2c - 16b^2c = c(a^2 - 16b^2)$
$= c(a^2 - (4b)^2) = c(a + 4b)(a - 4b)$

e) $y^2 - 2 = y^2 - (\sqrt{2})^2 = (y + \sqrt{2})(y - \sqrt{2})$

f) $4x^2 - 3 = (2x)^2 - (\sqrt{3})^2 = (2x + \sqrt{3})(2x - \sqrt{3})$
Parts e) and f) use the fact that any number can be written as its square root squared.

Q3 a) $(4 - z)^2(2 - z) + p(2 - z) = (2 - z)[(4 - z)^2 + p]$

b) $(r - d)^3 + 5(r - d)^2 = (r - d)^2[(r - d) + 5]$
$= (r - d)^2(r - d + 5)$

c) $(b + c)^5(a + b) - (b + c)^5 = (b + c)^5[(a + b) - 1]$
$= (b + c)^5(a + b - 1)$

d) $l^2m(a - 2x) + rp^2(2x - a) = l^2m(a - 2x) + rp^2(-(a - 2x))$
$= l^2m(a - 2x) - rp^2(a - 2x)$
$= (a - 2x)(l^2m - rp^2)$
You might have factorised this slightly differently and ended up with $(2x - a)(rp^2 - l^2m)$ instead.

Q4 a) $(p + q)^2 + 2q(p + q) = (p + q)[(p + q) + 2q]$
$= (p + q)(p + 3q)$

b) $2(2x - y)^2 - 6x(2x - y) = 2(2x - y)[(2x - y) - 3x]$
$= -2(2x - y)(x + y)$

c) $(r + 6s)^2 - (r + 6s)(r - s) = (r + 6s)[(r + 6s) - (r - s)]$
$= (r + 6s)(7s) = 7s(r + 6s)$

d) $(l + w + h)^2 - l(l + w + h) = (l + w + h)[(l + w + h) - l]$
$= (l + w + h)(w + h)$

Q5 a) $(m + 5)(m^2 - 5m + 25)$
$= m(m^2 - 5m + 25) + 5(m^2 - 5m + 25)$
$= m^3 - 5m^2 + 25m + 5m^2 - 25m + 125 = m^3 + 125$

b) $(p - 2q)(p^2 + 2pq + 4q^2)$
$= p(p^2 + 2pq + 4q^2) - 2q(p^2 + 2pq + 4q^2)$
$= p^3 + 2p^2q + 4pq^2 - 2p^2q - 4pq^2 - 8q^3 = p^3 - 8q^3$
Parts a) and b) were likely to need the brackets expanding because the quadratic in the second bracket won't factorise.

c) $(u - v)(u + v) - (u + v)^2 = (u + v)[(u - v) - (u + v)]$
$= (u + v)(-2v) = -2v(u + v)$

d) $(c + d)^3 - c(c + d)^2 - d(c + d)^2 = (c + d)^2[(c + d) - c - d]$
$= (c + d)^2(0) = 0$

Exercise 1.3 — Algebraic fractions

Q1 a) The common denominator is 3×4:
$$\frac{x}{3} + \frac{x}{4} = \frac{4x}{12} + \frac{3x}{12} = \frac{7x}{12}$$

b) The common denominator is t^2:
$$\frac{2}{t} + \frac{13}{t^2} = \frac{2t}{t^2} + \frac{13}{t^2} = \frac{2t + 13}{t^2}$$

c) The common denominator is $2 \times p \times 5 \times q = 10pq$:
$$\frac{1}{2p} - \frac{1}{5q} = \frac{5q}{10pq} - \frac{2p}{10pq} = \frac{5q - 2p}{10pq}$$

d) The common denominator is $a \times b \times c$:
$$\frac{ab}{c} + \frac{bc}{a} + \frac{ca}{b} = \frac{abab}{abc} + \frac{bcbc}{abc} + \frac{caca}{abc}$$
$$= \frac{a^2 b^2 + b^2 c^2 + c^2 a^2}{abc}$$

e) The common denominator is mn:
$$\frac{2}{mn} - \frac{3m}{n} + \frac{n^2}{m} = \frac{2}{mn} - \frac{3m^2}{mn} + \frac{n^3}{mn}$$
$$= \frac{2 - 3m^2 + n^3}{mn}$$

f) The common denominator is $a^3 \times b^3 = a^3 b^3$:
$$\frac{2}{ab^3} - \frac{9}{a^3 b} = \frac{2a^2}{a^3 b^3} - \frac{9b^2}{a^3 b^3} = \frac{2a^2 - 9b^2}{a^3 b^3}$$

Q2 a) The common denominator is $(y - 1)(y - 2)$:
$$\frac{5}{y-1} + \frac{3}{y-2} = \frac{5(y-2)}{(y-1)(y-2)} + \frac{3(y-1)}{(y-1)(y-2)}$$
$$= \frac{5(y-2) + 3(y-1)}{(y-1)(y-2)}$$
$$= \frac{5y - 10 + 3y - 3}{(y-1)(y-2)}$$
$$= \frac{8y - 13}{(y-1)(y-2)}$$

b) The common denominator is $(r - 5)(r + 3)$:
$$\frac{7}{r-5} - \frac{4}{r+3} = \frac{7(r+3)}{(r-5)(r+3)} - \frac{4(r-5)}{(r-5)(r+3)}$$
$$= \frac{7(r+3) - 4(r-5)}{(r-5)(r+3)}$$
$$= \frac{7r + 21 - 4r + 20}{(r-5)(r+3)}$$
$$= \frac{3r + 41}{(r-5)(r+3)}$$

c) The common denominator is $p(p - 3)$:
$$\frac{8}{p} - \frac{1}{p-3} = \frac{8(p-3)}{p(p-3)} - \frac{p}{p(p-3)}$$
$$= \frac{8p - 24 - p}{p(p-3)} = \frac{7p - 24}{p(p-3)}$$

d) The common denominator is $2(w - 2)(w - 7)$:
$$\frac{w}{2(w-2)} + \frac{3w}{w-7} = \frac{w(w-7)}{2(w-2)(w-7)} + \frac{3w \times 2(w-2)}{2(w-2)(w-7)}$$
$$= \frac{w^2 - 7w}{2(w-2)(w-7)} + \frac{6w(w-2)}{2(w-2)(w-7)}$$
$$= \frac{w^2 - 7w + 6w(w-2)}{2(w-2)(w-7)}$$
$$= \frac{w^2 - 7w + 6w^2 - 12w}{2(w-2)(w-7)}$$
$$= \frac{7w^2 - 19w}{2(w-2)(w-7)} = \frac{w(7w-19)}{2(w-2)(w-7)}$$

e) The common denominator is $(z + 2)(z + 4)$:
$$\frac{z+1}{z+2} - \frac{z+3}{z+4} = \frac{(z+1)(z+4)}{(z+2)(z+4)} - \frac{(z+2)(z+3)}{(z+2)(z+4)}$$
$$= \frac{(z+1)(z+4) - (z+2)(z+3)}{(z+2)(z+4)}$$
$$= \frac{(z^2 + 5z + 4) - (z^2 + 5z + 6)}{(z+2)(z+4)}$$
$$= \frac{-2}{(z+2)(z+4)}$$

f) The common denominator is $(q + 1)(q - 2)$:
$$\frac{1}{q+1} + \frac{3}{q-2} = \frac{(q-2)}{(q+1)(q-2)} + \frac{3(q+1)}{(q+1)(q-2)}$$
$$= \frac{(q-2) + 3(q+1)}{(q+1)(q-2)}$$
$$= \frac{q - 2 + 3q + 3}{(q+1)(q-2)}$$
$$= \frac{4q + 1}{(q+1)(q-2)}$$

Q3 a) $\dfrac{2x + 10}{6} = \dfrac{2(x+5)}{6} = \dfrac{x+5}{3}$

b) $\dfrac{6a - 12b - 15c}{3} = \dfrac{3(2a - 4b - 5c)}{3} = 2a - 4b - 5c$

c) $\dfrac{np^2 - 2n^2 p}{np} = \dfrac{np(p - 2n)}{np} = p - 2n$

d) $\dfrac{4st + 6s^2 t + 9s^3 t}{2t} = \dfrac{st(4 + 6s + 9s^2)}{2t} = \dfrac{s(4 + 6s + 9s^2)}{2}$

e) $\dfrac{10yz^3 - 40y^3 z^3 + 60y^2 z^3}{10z^2} = \dfrac{10yz^3(1 - 4y^2 + 6y)}{10z^2}$
$$= yz(1 - 4y^2 + 6y)$$

f) $\dfrac{12cd - 6c^2 d + 3c^3 d^2}{12c^2 de} = \dfrac{3cd(4 - 2c + c^2 d)}{12c^2 de}$
$$= \dfrac{4 - 2c + c^2 d}{4ce}$$

2. Laws of Indices
Exercise 2.1 — Laws of indices

Q1 a) $10 \times 10^4 = 10^{1+4} = 10^5$

b) $y^{-1} \times y^{-2} \times y^7 = y^{-1-2+7} = y^4$

c) $5^{\frac{1}{2}} \times 5^3 \times 5^{-\frac{3}{2}} = 5^{\frac{1}{2} + 3 - \frac{3}{2}} = 5^2$

d) $6^5 \div 6^2 = 6^{5-2} = 6^3$

e) $3^4 \div 3^{-1} = 3^{4 - (-1)} = 3^{4+1} = 3^5$

f) $\dfrac{6^{11}}{6} = 6^{11-1} = 6^{10}$

g) $\dfrac{r^2}{r^6} = r^{2-6} = r^{-4}$

h) $(3^2)^3 = 3^{2 \times 3} = 3^6$

i) $(k^{-2})^5 = k^{(-2) \times 5} = k^{-10}$

j) $(z^4)^{\frac{1}{8}} = z^{4 \times (-\frac{1}{8})} = z^{-\frac{4}{8}} = z^{\frac{1}{2}}$

k) $(8^{-6})^{-\frac{1}{2}} = 8^{-6 \times -\frac{1}{2}} = 8^{\frac{6}{2}} = 8^3$

l) $\dfrac{p^5 q^4}{p^4 q} = (p^{5-4})(q^{4-1}) = p^1 q^3 = pq^3$

m) $\dfrac{c^{-1} d^{-2}}{c^2 d^4} = c^{-1-2} d^{-2-4} = c^{-3} d^{-6} = \dfrac{1}{c^3 d^6}$

n) $(ab^2)^2 = (a)^2(b^2)^2 = a^2 b^{2 \times 2} = a^2 b^4$

o) $\dfrac{12yz^{-\frac{1}{2}}}{4yz^{\frac{1}{2}}} = \left(\dfrac{12}{4}\right)(y^{1-1})(z^{-\frac{1}{2}-\frac{1}{2}}) = 3y^0 z^{-1} = \dfrac{3}{z}$

Q2 a) $4^{\frac{1}{2}} \times 4^{\frac{3}{2}} = 4^{\frac{1}{2}+\frac{3}{2}} = 4^2 = 16$

b) $\dfrac{2^3 \times 2}{2^5} = \dfrac{2^{3+1}}{2^5} = \dfrac{2^4}{2^5} = 2^{4-5} = 2^{-1} = \dfrac{1}{2}$

c) $\dfrac{7^5 \times 7^3}{7^6} = \dfrac{7^{5+3}}{7^6} = \dfrac{7^8}{7^6} = 7^{8-6} = 7^2 = 49$

d) $(3^2)^5 \div (3^3)^3 = 3^{2 \times 5} \div 3^{3 \times 3}$
$\qquad = 3^{10} \div 3^9 = 3^{10-9} = 3^1 = 3$

e) $\left(4^{-\frac{1}{2}}\right)^2 \times \left(4^{-3}\right)^{-\frac{1}{3}} = 4^{-\frac{1}{2} \times 2} \times 4^{(-3)\times\left(-\frac{1}{3}\right)}$
$\qquad = 4^{-1} \times 4^1 = 4^{-1+1} = 4^0 = 1$

f) $\dfrac{\left(2^{\frac{1}{2}}\right)^6 \times \left(2^{-2}\right)^{-2}}{\left(2^{-1}\right)^{-1}} = \dfrac{2^{\frac{1}{2} \times 6} \times 2^{(-2)\times(-2)}}{2^{(-1)\times(-1)}} = \dfrac{2^3 \times 2^4}{2^1} = \dfrac{2^{3+4}}{2^1}$
$\qquad = \dfrac{2^7}{2^1} = 2^6 = 64$

g) $1^0 = 1$ **h)** $\left(\dfrac{4}{5}\right)^0 = 1$ **i)** $(-5.726324)^0 = 1$

Q3 a) $\dfrac{1}{p} = p^{-1}$ **b)** $\sqrt{q} = q^{\frac{1}{2}}$

c) $\sqrt{r^3} = (r^3)^{\frac{1}{2}} = r^{3 \times \frac{1}{2}} = r^{\frac{3}{2}}$ **d)** $\sqrt[4]{s^5} = (s^5)^{\frac{1}{4}} = s^{5 \times \frac{1}{4}} = s^{\frac{5}{4}}$

e) $\dfrac{1}{\sqrt[3]{t}} = \dfrac{1}{\left(t^{\frac{1}{3}}\right)} = t^{-\frac{1}{3}}$

Q4 a) $9^{\frac{1}{2}} = \sqrt{9} = 3$ **b)** $8^{\frac{1}{3}} = \sqrt[3]{8} = 2$

c) $4^{\frac{3}{2}} = 4^{\frac{1}{2} \times 3} = \left(4^{\frac{1}{2}}\right)^3 = \left(\sqrt{4}\right)^3 = (2)^3 = 8$

d) $27^{-\frac{1}{3}} = \dfrac{1}{27^{\frac{1}{3}}} = \dfrac{1}{\sqrt[3]{27}} = \dfrac{1}{3}$

e) $16^{-\frac{3}{4}} = \dfrac{1}{16^{\frac{3}{4}}} = \dfrac{1}{\left(16^{\frac{1}{4}}\right)^3} = \dfrac{1}{\left(\sqrt[4]{16}\right)^3} = \dfrac{1}{(2)^3} = \dfrac{1}{8}$

Q5 a) $p^{\frac{1}{2}} = \left(\dfrac{1}{16}q^2\right)^{\frac{1}{2}} = \left(\dfrac{1}{16}\right)^{\frac{1}{2}}(q^2)^{\frac{1}{2}}$
$\qquad = \sqrt{\dfrac{1}{16}}\, q^{2 \times \frac{1}{2}} = \dfrac{1}{\sqrt{16}}q = \dfrac{1}{4}q$

b) $2p^{-1} = 2\left(\dfrac{1}{16}q^2\right)^{-1} = 2\left(\dfrac{1}{16}\right)^{-1}(q^2)^{-1}$
$\qquad = 2 \times 16 \times q^{2 \times -1} = 32q^{-2} = \dfrac{32}{q^2}$

c) $p^{\frac{1}{2}} \div 2p^{-1} = \dfrac{1}{4}q \div \left(\dfrac{32}{q^2}\right) = \dfrac{1}{4}q \times \dfrac{q^2}{32}$
$\qquad = \dfrac{q^3}{128} = \dfrac{1}{128}q^3$

Substitute the answers from a) and b) into the division and use the rule for dividing by fractions. You could also simplify the expression to $\frac{1}{2}p^{\frac{3}{2}}$ first.

Q6 a) Write the RHS as 4 to the power 'something':
$\sqrt[3]{16} = (16)^{\frac{1}{3}} = (4^2)^{\frac{1}{3}} = 4^{2 \times \frac{1}{3}} = 4^{\frac{2}{3}}$, so $x = \dfrac{2}{3}$.

b) Write the RHS as 9 to the power 'something':
$\dfrac{1}{3} = \dfrac{1}{\sqrt{9}} = \dfrac{1}{9^{\frac{1}{2}}} = 9^{-\frac{1}{2}}$, so $x = -\dfrac{1}{2}$.

c) Write the LHS as 5 to the power 'something':
$\sqrt{5} \times 5^x = 5^{\frac{1}{2}} \times 5^x = 5^{x+\frac{1}{2}}$
Write the RHS as 5 to the power 'something':
$\dfrac{1}{25} = \dfrac{1}{5^2} = 5^{-2}$
Then equate the two 'something's:
$x + \dfrac{1}{2} = -2$. So $x = -2 - \dfrac{1}{2} = -\dfrac{5}{2}$.

You could have used the laws in a different order for parts a), b) and c) to get the same answers. In part c) you could simplify both sides first to make the question easier.

3. Surds

Exercise 3.1 — The laws of surds

Q1 a) $\sqrt{8} = \sqrt{4 \times 2} = \sqrt{4}\sqrt{2} = 2\sqrt{2}$

b) $\sqrt{24} = \sqrt{4 \times 6} = \sqrt{4}\sqrt{6} = 2\sqrt{6}$

c) $\sqrt{50} = \sqrt{25 \times 2} = \sqrt{25}\sqrt{2} = 5\sqrt{2}$

d) $\sqrt{63} = \sqrt{9 \times 7} = \sqrt{9}\sqrt{7} = 3\sqrt{7}$

e) $\sqrt{72} = \sqrt{36 \times 2} = \sqrt{36}\sqrt{2} = 6\sqrt{2}$

f) $\sqrt{\dfrac{5}{4}} = \dfrac{\sqrt{5}}{\sqrt{4}} = \dfrac{\sqrt{5}}{2}$

g) $\sqrt{\dfrac{7}{100}} = \dfrac{\sqrt{7}}{\sqrt{100}} = \dfrac{\sqrt{7}}{10}$

h) $\sqrt{\dfrac{11}{9}} = \dfrac{\sqrt{11}}{\sqrt{9}} = \dfrac{\sqrt{11}}{3}$

Q2 a) $2\sqrt{3} \times 4\sqrt{3} = 2 \times 4 \times \sqrt{3} \times \sqrt{3}$
$\qquad = 8\sqrt{3}\sqrt{3} = 8 \times 3 = 24$

b) $\sqrt{5} \times 3\sqrt{5} = 3\sqrt{5}\sqrt{5} = 3 \times 5 = 15$

c) $\left(\sqrt{7}\right)^2 = \sqrt{7}\sqrt{7} = 7$

d) $2\sqrt{2} \times 3\sqrt{5} = 2 \times 3 \times \sqrt{2} \times \sqrt{5} = 6\sqrt{2}\sqrt{5} = 6\sqrt{10}$

e) $\left(2\sqrt{11}\right)^2 = (2\sqrt{11})(2\sqrt{11}) = 4\sqrt{11}\sqrt{11} = 4 \times 11 = 44$

f) $5\sqrt{8} \times 2\sqrt{2} = 5\sqrt{4 \times 2} \times 2\sqrt{2}$
$\qquad = 5 \times 2\sqrt{2} \times 2\sqrt{2}$
$\qquad = 5 \times 4 \times \sqrt{2} \times \sqrt{2} = 20 \times 2 = 40$

g) $4\sqrt{3} \times 2\sqrt{27} = 4 \times 2 \times \sqrt{3}\sqrt{27}$
$\qquad = 8\sqrt{3 \times 27} = 8\sqrt{81} = 8 \times 9 = 72$

h) $2\sqrt{6} \times 5\sqrt{24} = 2 \times 5 \times \sqrt{6} \times \sqrt{24}$
$\qquad = 10\sqrt{6 \times 24} = 10\sqrt{144}$
$\qquad = 10 \times 12 = 120$

i) $\dfrac{\sqrt{10}}{6} \times \dfrac{12}{\sqrt{5}} = \dfrac{12\sqrt{10}}{6\sqrt{5}} = \dfrac{12}{6} \times \dfrac{\sqrt{10}}{\sqrt{5}} = 2 \times \sqrt{\dfrac{10}{5}} = 2\sqrt{2}$

j) $\dfrac{\sqrt{12}}{3} \times \dfrac{2}{\sqrt{27}} = \dfrac{2\sqrt{12}}{3\sqrt{27}} = \dfrac{2}{3} \times \dfrac{\sqrt{12}}{\sqrt{27}}$
$\qquad = \dfrac{2}{3} \times \dfrac{\sqrt{4 \times 3}}{\sqrt{9 \times 3}} = \dfrac{2}{3} \times \dfrac{\sqrt{4}\sqrt{3}}{\sqrt{9}\sqrt{3}}$
$\qquad = \dfrac{2}{3} \times \dfrac{2\sqrt{3}}{3\sqrt{3}} = \dfrac{2}{3} \times \dfrac{2}{3} = \dfrac{4}{9}$

Q3 a) $\sqrt{20} + \sqrt{5} = \sqrt{4 \times 5} + \sqrt{5} = \sqrt{4}\sqrt{5} + \sqrt{5}$
$\qquad = 2\sqrt{5} + \sqrt{5} = 3\sqrt{5}$

b) $\sqrt{32} - \sqrt{8} = \sqrt{16 \times 2} - \sqrt{4 \times 2}$
$\qquad = \sqrt{16}\sqrt{2} - \sqrt{4}\sqrt{2} = 4\sqrt{2} - 2\sqrt{2} = 2\sqrt{2}$

c) $\sqrt{27} + 4\sqrt{3} = \sqrt{9 \times 3} + 4\sqrt{3} = \sqrt{9}\sqrt{3} + 4\sqrt{3}$
$\qquad = 3\sqrt{3} + 4\sqrt{3} = 7\sqrt{3}$

d) $2\sqrt{8} - 3\sqrt{2} = 2\sqrt{4 \times 2} - 3\sqrt{2}$
$\qquad = 2\sqrt{4}\sqrt{2} - 3\sqrt{2} = 4\sqrt{2} - 3\sqrt{2} = \sqrt{2}$

e) $3\sqrt{10} + \sqrt{250} = 3\sqrt{10} + \sqrt{25 \times 10}$
$\qquad = 3\sqrt{10} + \sqrt{25}\sqrt{10}$
$\qquad = 3\sqrt{10} + 5\sqrt{10} = 8\sqrt{10}$

f) $4\sqrt{27} + 2\sqrt{48} + 5\sqrt{108}$
$\qquad = 4\sqrt{9 \times 3} + 2\sqrt{16 \times 3} + 5\sqrt{36 \times 3}$
$\qquad = 4\sqrt{9}\sqrt{3} + 2\sqrt{16}\sqrt{3} + 5\sqrt{36}\sqrt{3}$
$\qquad = 12\sqrt{3} + 8\sqrt{3} + 30\sqrt{3} = 50\sqrt{3}$

Q4 a) $(1+\sqrt{2})(2+\sqrt{2}) = 2+\sqrt{2}+2\sqrt{2}+\sqrt{2}\sqrt{2}$
$$= 2+3\sqrt{2}+2 = 4+3\sqrt{2}$$

b) $(3+4\sqrt{3})(2-\sqrt{3}) = 6-3\sqrt{3}+8\sqrt{3}-4\sqrt{3}\sqrt{3}$
$$= 6+5\sqrt{3}-12 = 5\sqrt{3}-6$$

c) By the difference of two squares rule:
$$(\sqrt{11}+2)(\sqrt{11}-2) = (\sqrt{11})^2-2^2 = 11-4 = 7$$

d) By the difference of two squares rule:
$$(9-2\sqrt{5})(9+2\sqrt{5}) = 9^2-(2\sqrt{5})^2 = 81-20 = 61$$

e) $(\sqrt{3}+2)^2 = (\sqrt{3}+2)(\sqrt{3}+2)$
$$= \sqrt{3}\sqrt{3}+2\sqrt{3}+2\sqrt{3}+4$$
$$= 3+4\sqrt{3}+4 = 7+4\sqrt{3}$$

f) $(3\sqrt{5}-4)^2 = (3\sqrt{5}-4)(3\sqrt{5}-4)$
$$= (3\sqrt{5})^2-12\sqrt{5}-12\sqrt{5}+16$$
$$= 45-24\sqrt{5}+16$$
$$= 61-24\sqrt{5}$$

You could have used the rule $(a+b)^2 = a^2 + 2ab + b^2$ for parts e and f.

Q5 You may want to draw the triangle:

Using Pythagoras:
$$(\sqrt{2})^2 + (BC)^2 = (5\sqrt{2})^2$$
$$2 + (BC)^2 = 50$$
$$\Rightarrow (BC)^2 = 48$$
$$\Rightarrow BC = \sqrt{48} = \sqrt{16\times3} = 4\sqrt{3} \text{ cm}$$

Exercise 3.2 — Rationalising the denominator

Q1 a) $\dfrac{6}{\sqrt{3}} = \dfrac{6\sqrt{3}}{\sqrt{3}\sqrt{3}} = \dfrac{6\sqrt{3}}{3} = 2\sqrt{3}$

b) $\dfrac{21}{\sqrt{7}} = \dfrac{21\sqrt{7}}{\sqrt{7}\sqrt{7}} = \dfrac{21\sqrt{7}}{7} = 3\sqrt{7}$

c) $\dfrac{30}{\sqrt{5}} = \dfrac{30\sqrt{5}}{\sqrt{5}\sqrt{5}} = \dfrac{30\sqrt{5}}{5} = 6\sqrt{5}$

d) $\sqrt{45}+\dfrac{15}{\sqrt{5}} = \sqrt{45}+\dfrac{15\sqrt{5}}{\sqrt{5}\sqrt{5}} = \sqrt{45}+\dfrac{15\sqrt{5}}{5}$
$$= \sqrt{9\times5}+3\sqrt{5}$$
$$= \sqrt{9}\sqrt{5}+3\sqrt{5}$$
$$= 3\sqrt{5}+3\sqrt{5} = 6\sqrt{5}$$

e) $\dfrac{\sqrt{54}}{3}-\dfrac{12}{\sqrt{6}} = \dfrac{\sqrt{9\times6}}{3}-\dfrac{12\sqrt{6}}{\sqrt{6}\sqrt{6}}$
$$= \dfrac{\sqrt{9}\sqrt{6}}{3}-\dfrac{12\sqrt{6}}{6}$$
$$= \dfrac{3\sqrt{6}}{3}-\dfrac{12\sqrt{6}}{6} = \sqrt{6}-2\sqrt{6} = -\sqrt{6}$$

f) $\dfrac{\sqrt{300}}{5}+\dfrac{30}{\sqrt{12}} = \dfrac{\sqrt{100\times3}}{5}+\dfrac{30\sqrt{12}}{\sqrt{12}\sqrt{12}}$
$$= \dfrac{\sqrt{100}\sqrt{3}}{5}+\dfrac{30\sqrt{4\times3}}{12}$$
$$= \dfrac{10\sqrt{3}}{5}+\dfrac{30\sqrt{4}\sqrt{3}}{12}$$
$$= 2\sqrt{3}+\dfrac{60\sqrt{3}}{12} = 2\sqrt{3}+5\sqrt{3} = 7\sqrt{3}$$

Q2 a) $\dfrac{4}{1+\sqrt{3}} = \dfrac{4(1-\sqrt{3})}{(1+\sqrt{3})(1-\sqrt{3})}$
$$= \dfrac{4-4\sqrt{3}}{1-3} = \dfrac{4-4\sqrt{3}}{-2} = -2+2\sqrt{3}$$

The denominator was simplified by using the difference of two squares rule. It will be used in almost every question in the rest of this exercise, so watch out for it and make sure you understand what's going on.

b) $\dfrac{8}{-1+\sqrt{5}} = \dfrac{8(-1-\sqrt{5})}{(-1+\sqrt{5})(-1-\sqrt{5})}$
$$= \dfrac{-8-8\sqrt{5}}{1-5} = \dfrac{-8-8\sqrt{5}}{-4} = 2+2\sqrt{5}$$

c) $\dfrac{18}{\sqrt{10}-4} = \dfrac{18(\sqrt{10}+4)}{(\sqrt{10}-4)(\sqrt{10}+4)} = \dfrac{18\sqrt{10}+72}{10-16}$
$$= \dfrac{18\sqrt{10}+72}{-6} = -12-3\sqrt{10}$$

Q3 a) $\dfrac{\sqrt{2}+1}{\sqrt{2}-1} = \dfrac{(\sqrt{2}+1)(\sqrt{2}+1)}{(\sqrt{2}-1)(\sqrt{2}+1)}$
$$= \dfrac{2+\sqrt{2}+\sqrt{2}+1}{2-1} = \dfrac{2\sqrt{2}+3}{1} = 3+2\sqrt{2}$$

b) $\dfrac{\sqrt{5}+3}{\sqrt{5}-2} = \dfrac{(\sqrt{5}+3)(\sqrt{5}+2)}{(\sqrt{5}-2)(\sqrt{5}+2)}$
$$= \dfrac{5+2\sqrt{5}+3\sqrt{5}+6}{5-4} = \dfrac{11+5\sqrt{5}}{1} = 11+5\sqrt{5}$$

c) $\dfrac{3-\sqrt{3}}{4+\sqrt{3}} = \dfrac{(3-\sqrt{3})(4-\sqrt{3})}{(4+\sqrt{3})(4-\sqrt{3})} = \dfrac{12-3\sqrt{3}-4\sqrt{3}+3}{16-3}$
$$= \dfrac{15-7\sqrt{3}}{13} = \dfrac{15}{13}-\dfrac{7}{13}\sqrt{3}$$

d) $\dfrac{3\sqrt{5}-1}{2\sqrt{5}-3} = \dfrac{(3\sqrt{5}-1)(2\sqrt{5}+3)}{(2\sqrt{5}-3)(2\sqrt{5}+3)}$
$$= \dfrac{(2\sqrt{5})(3\sqrt{5})+9\sqrt{5}-2\sqrt{5}-3}{(2\sqrt{5})^2-9}$$
$$= \dfrac{27+7\sqrt{5}}{(2\sqrt{5})^2-9} = \dfrac{27+7\sqrt{5}}{11} = \dfrac{27}{11}+\dfrac{7}{11}\sqrt{5}$$

e) $\dfrac{\sqrt{2}+\sqrt{3}}{3\sqrt{2}-\sqrt{3}} = \dfrac{(\sqrt{2}+\sqrt{3})(3\sqrt{2}+\sqrt{3})}{(3\sqrt{2}-\sqrt{3})(3\sqrt{2}+\sqrt{3})}$
$$= \dfrac{3\sqrt{2}\sqrt{2}+\sqrt{2}\sqrt{3}+3\sqrt{3}\sqrt{2}+3}{(3\sqrt{2})^2-(\sqrt{3})^2}$$
$$= \dfrac{6+\sqrt{6}+3\sqrt{6}+3}{18-3}$$
$$= \dfrac{9+4\sqrt{6}}{15} = \dfrac{9}{15}+\dfrac{4}{15}\sqrt{6}$$
$$= \dfrac{3}{5}+\dfrac{4}{15}\sqrt{6}$$

f) $\dfrac{2\sqrt{7}-\sqrt{5}}{\sqrt{7}+2\sqrt{5}} = \dfrac{(2\sqrt{7}-\sqrt{5})(\sqrt{7}-2\sqrt{5})}{(\sqrt{7}+2\sqrt{5})(\sqrt{7}-2\sqrt{5})}$
$$= \dfrac{2\sqrt{7}\sqrt{7}-4\sqrt{7}\sqrt{5}-\sqrt{5}\sqrt{7}+10}{7-(2\sqrt{5})^2}$$
$$= \dfrac{14-4\sqrt{35}-\sqrt{35}+10}{7-20}$$
$$= \dfrac{24-5\sqrt{35}}{-13} = -\dfrac{24}{13}+\dfrac{5}{13}\sqrt{35}$$

Q4 a) $\dfrac{4}{\sqrt{7}-\sqrt{3}} = \dfrac{4(\sqrt{7}+\sqrt{3})}{(\sqrt{7}-\sqrt{3})(\sqrt{7}+\sqrt{3})}$
$$= \dfrac{4(\sqrt{7}+\sqrt{3})}{7-3} = \dfrac{4(\sqrt{7}+\sqrt{3})}{4} = \sqrt{7}+\sqrt{3}$$

b) $\dfrac{24}{\sqrt{11}-\sqrt{17}} = \dfrac{24(\sqrt{11}+\sqrt{17})}{(\sqrt{11}-\sqrt{17})(\sqrt{11}+\sqrt{17})}$

$\qquad = \dfrac{24(\sqrt{11}+\sqrt{17})}{11-17} = \dfrac{24(\sqrt{11}+\sqrt{17})}{-6}$

$\qquad = -4(\sqrt{11}+\sqrt{17})$

c) $\dfrac{2}{\sqrt{13}+\sqrt{5}} = \dfrac{2(\sqrt{13}-\sqrt{5})}{(\sqrt{13}+\sqrt{5})(\sqrt{13}-\sqrt{5})}$

$\qquad = \dfrac{2(\sqrt{13}-\sqrt{5})}{13-5} = \dfrac{2(\sqrt{13}-\sqrt{5})}{8}$

$\qquad = \dfrac{1}{4}(\sqrt{13}-\sqrt{5})$

Q5 $8 = (\sqrt{5}-1)x \Rightarrow x = \dfrac{8}{(\sqrt{5}-1)} = \dfrac{8(\sqrt{5}+1)}{(\sqrt{5}-1)(\sqrt{5}+1)}$

$\qquad = \dfrac{8\sqrt{5}+8}{5-1} = \dfrac{8\sqrt{5}+8}{4} = 2 + 2\sqrt{5}$

Q6 $5 + \sqrt{7} = (3-\sqrt{7})y$

$\qquad \Rightarrow y = \dfrac{5+\sqrt{7}}{3-\sqrt{7}} = \dfrac{(5+\sqrt{7})(3+\sqrt{7})}{(3-\sqrt{7})(3+\sqrt{7})}$

$\qquad = \dfrac{15+5\sqrt{7}+3\sqrt{7}+7}{9-7} = \dfrac{22+8\sqrt{7}}{2} = 11 + 4\sqrt{7}$

Q7 The area of a rectangle is given by area (A) = length (*l*) × width (*w*) so:

$(2+\sqrt{2}) = l \times (3\sqrt{2}-4)$

$\Rightarrow l = \dfrac{(2+\sqrt{2})}{(3\sqrt{2}-4)} = \dfrac{(2+\sqrt{2})(3\sqrt{2}+4)}{(3\sqrt{2}-4)(3\sqrt{2}+4)}$

$\qquad = \dfrac{6\sqrt{2}+8+6+4\sqrt{2}}{(3\sqrt{2})^2-16}$

$\qquad = \dfrac{14+10\sqrt{2}}{18-16} = \dfrac{14+10\sqrt{2}}{2} = (7+5\sqrt{2}) \text{ cm}$

Don't forget the units here.

Chapter 4: Quadratics and Cubics

1. Quadratic Equations

Exercise 1.1 — Factorising a quadratic

Q1 a) $x^2 - 6x + 5 = (x-5)(x-1)$

b) $x^2 - 3x - 18 = (x-6)(x+3)$

c) $x^2 + 22x + 121 = (x+11)(x+11) = (x+11)^2$

d) $x^2 - 12x = x(x-12)$
  Note that if every term contains an x, you can just take a factor of x out of the bracket.

e) $y^2 - 13y + 42 = (y-6)(y-7)$

f) $x^2 + 51x + 144 = (x+48)(x+3)$

g) $x^2 - 121 = (x+11)(x-11)$
  If there is no 'b' term, see if the expression is a 'difference of two squares' (chances are it will be).

h) $x^2 - 35x + 66 = (x-2)(x-33)$

Q2 a) $x^2 - 2x - 8 = 0$
  $(x-4)(x+2) = 0$
  $\Rightarrow x - 4 = 0$ or $x + 2 = 0 \Rightarrow x = 4$ or $x = -2$

b) $2x^2 + 2x - 40 = 0$
  $2(x^2 + x - 20) = 0$
  This is an example of a question where you can simplify the equation before factorising. You can divide through by 2.
  $x^2 + x - 20 = 0$
  $(x+5)(x-4) = 0$
  $\Rightarrow x + 5 = 0$ or $x - 4 = 0 \Rightarrow x = -5$ or $x = 4$

c) $p^2 + 21p + 38 = 0$
  $(p+19)(p+2) = 0$
  $\Rightarrow p + 19 = 0$ or $p + 2 = 0 \Rightarrow p = -19$ or $p = -2$

d) $x^2 - 15x + 54 = 0$
  $(x-9)(x-6) = 0$
  $\Rightarrow x - 9 = 0$ or $x - 6 = 0 \Rightarrow x = 9$ or $x = 6$

e) $x^2 + 18x = -65$
  $x^2 + 18x + 65 = 0$
  $(x+5)(x+13) = 0$
  $\Rightarrow x + 5 = 0$ or $x + 13 = 0 \Rightarrow x = -5$ or $x = -13$

f) $x^2 - x = 42$
  $x^2 - x - 42 = 0$
  $(x-7)(x+6) = 0$
  $\Rightarrow x - 7 = 0$ or $x + 6 = 0 \Rightarrow x = 7$ or $x = -6$

g) $x^2 + 1100x + 100\,000 = 0$
  $(x+100)(x+1000) = 0$
  $\Rightarrow x + 100 = 0$ or $x + 1000 = 0$
  $\Rightarrow x = -100$ or $x = -1000$

h) $3x^2 - 3x - 6 = 0$
  $3(x^2 - x - 2) = 0$
  $x^2 - x - 2 = 0$
  $(x-2)(x+1) = 0$
  $\Rightarrow x - 2 = 0$ or $x + 1 = 0 \Rightarrow x = 2$ or $x = -1$

Q3 a) $4x^2 - 4x - 3 = (2x+1)(2x-3)$

b) $2x^2 + 23x + 11 = (2x+1)(x+11)$

c) $7x^2 - 19x - 6 = (7x+2)(x-3)$

d) $-x^2 - 5x + 36 = (-x+4)(x+9)$

e) $2x^2 - 2 = 2(x^2-1) = 2(x+1)(x-1)$

f) $3x^2 - 3 = 3(x^2-1) = 3(x+1)(x-1)$

Q4 a) $-5x^2 - 22x + 15 = 0$
  $5x^2 + 22x - 15 = 0$
  $(5x-3)(x+5) = 0$
  $\Rightarrow 5x - 3 = 0$ or $x + 5 = 0 \Rightarrow x = \dfrac{3}{5}$ or $x = -5$
  If you want to get rid of the minus sign in front of the x^2 just multiply through by −1 — the right hand side will remain 0 and the left hand side will change signs.

b) $32x^2 + 60x + 13 = 0$
  $(4x+1)(8x+13) = 0$
  $\Rightarrow 4x + 1 = 0$ or $8x + 13 = 0 \Rightarrow x = -\dfrac{1}{4}$ or $x = -\dfrac{13}{8}$

c) $5a^2 + 12a = 9$
  $5a^2 + 12a - 9 = 0$
  $(5a-3)(a+3) = 0$
  $\Rightarrow 5a - 3 = 0$ or $a + 3 = 0 \Rightarrow a = \dfrac{3}{5}$ or $a = -3$

d) $8x^2 + 22x + 15 = 0$
  $(4x+5)(2x+3) = 0$
  $\Rightarrow 4x + 5 = 0$ or $2x + 3 = 0 \Rightarrow x = -\dfrac{5}{4}$ or $x = -\dfrac{3}{2}$

Q5 $(x-1)(x-2) = 37 - x$
$x^2 - 3x + 2 = 37 - x$
$x^2 - 2x - 35 = 0$
$(x-7)(x+5) = 0$
$\Rightarrow x - 7 = 0$ or $x + 5 = 0 \Rightarrow x = 7$ or $x = -5$

Q6 The function f(x) meets the x-axis when f(x) = 0
so set the expression for f(x) equal to 0.
$-x^2 + 7x + 30 = 0$
$x^2 - 7x - 30 = 0$
$(x-10)(x+3) = 0$
$\Rightarrow x - 10 = 0$ or $x + 3 = 0 \Rightarrow x = 10$ or $x = -3$
So the graph of f(x) meets the x-axis when
$x = 10$ and $x = -3$.

Q7 Here, you have to set T equal to 0 and solve the
quadratic equation to find the values of h:
$0 = -2h^2 + 13h - 20$
$0 = 2h^2 - 13h + 20$
$0 = (2h - 5)(h - 4)$
$\Rightarrow 0 = 2h - 5$ or $0 = h - 4 \Rightarrow h = \dfrac{5}{2} = 2.5$ or $h = 4$

So the temperature is 0 °C after 2.5 hours
and again after 4 hours.

Q8 *This question looks harder because it has y's in it as well as x's*
— just treat the y as a constant. You'll need two numbers which
multiply to give 8y² and add or subtract to give 6y.

4y and 2y multiply to 8y² and add to give 6y
so these are the numbers you need.
$x^2 + 6xy + 8y^2 = (x + 4y)(x + 2y)$

Exercise 1.2 — The quadratic formula

Q1 **a)** $x^2 - 4x = -2$
$x^2 - 4x + 2 = 0$
$a = 1, b = -4, c = 2$
$x = \dfrac{-b \pm \sqrt{b^2 - 4ac}}{2a} = \dfrac{-(-4) \pm \sqrt{(-4)^2 - 4 \times 1 \times 2}}{2 \times 1}$
$= \dfrac{4 \pm \sqrt{16 - 8}}{2} = \dfrac{4 \pm \sqrt{8}}{2} = \dfrac{4 \pm 2\sqrt{2}}{2} = 2 \pm \sqrt{2}$

b) $x^2 - 2x - 44 = 0$
$a = 1, b = -2, c = -44$
$x = \dfrac{-b \pm \sqrt{b^2 - 4ac}}{2a} = \dfrac{-(-2) \pm \sqrt{(-2)^2 - 4 \times 1 \times (-44)}}{2 \times 1}$
$= \dfrac{2 \pm \sqrt{4 + (4 \times 1 \times 44)}}{2} = \dfrac{2 \pm \sqrt{180}}{2} = \dfrac{2 \pm \sqrt{36 \times 5}}{2}$
$= \dfrac{2 \pm 6\sqrt{5}}{2} = 1 \pm 3\sqrt{5}$

c) $x^2 - 14x + 42 = 0$
$a = 1, b = -14, c = 42$
$x = \dfrac{-b \pm \sqrt{b^2 - 4ac}}{2a} = \dfrac{-(-14) \pm \sqrt{(-14)^2 - 4 \times 1 \times 42}}{2 \times 1}$
$= \dfrac{14 \pm \sqrt{196 - 168}}{2} = \dfrac{14 \pm \sqrt{28}}{2} = \dfrac{14 \pm \sqrt{4 \times 7}}{2}$
$= \dfrac{14 \pm 2\sqrt{7}}{2} = 7 \pm \sqrt{7}$

d) $4x^2 + 4x - 1 = 0$
$a = 4, b = 4, c = -1$
$x = \dfrac{-b \pm \sqrt{b^2 - 4ac}}{2a} = \dfrac{-4 \pm \sqrt{(4)^2 - 4 \times 4 \times (-1)}}{2 \times 4}$
$= \dfrac{-4 \pm \sqrt{16 + 16}}{8} = \dfrac{-4 \pm \sqrt{32}}{8} = \dfrac{-4 \pm \sqrt{16 \times 2}}{8}$
$= \dfrac{-4 \pm 4\sqrt{2}}{8} = -\dfrac{1}{2} \pm \dfrac{1}{2}\sqrt{2}$

e) $x^2 - \dfrac{5}{6}x + \dfrac{1}{6} = 0$
$6x^2 - 5x + 1 = 0$
$a = 6, b = -5, c = 1$
$x = \dfrac{-b \pm \sqrt{b^2 - 4ac}}{2a} = \dfrac{-(-5) \pm \sqrt{(-5)^2 - 4 \times 6 \times 1}}{2 \times 6}$
$= \dfrac{5 \pm \sqrt{25 - 24}}{12} = \dfrac{5 \pm 1}{12} = \dfrac{1}{2}$ or $\dfrac{1}{3}$

Removing the fractions right at the start here saves you
lots of fraction headaches in the working. This one wasn't
actually too hard to factorise — you'd get (3x − 1)(2x − 1).

f) $x^2 - x - \dfrac{35}{2} = 0$
$a = 1, b = -1, c = -\dfrac{35}{2}$
$x = \dfrac{-b \pm \sqrt{b^2 - 4ac}}{2a}$
$= \dfrac{-(-1) \pm \sqrt{(-1)^2 - 4 \times 1 \times \left(-\dfrac{35}{2}\right)}}{2 \times 1}$
$= \dfrac{1 \pm \sqrt{1 + \left(4 \times 1 \times \dfrac{35}{2}\right)}}{2}$
$= \dfrac{1 \pm \sqrt{1 + 70}}{2} = \dfrac{1 \pm \sqrt{71}}{2} = \dfrac{1}{2} \pm \dfrac{1}{2}\sqrt{71}$

Q2 **a)** $(x - 2 + \sqrt{5})(x - 2 - \sqrt{5})$
$= x(x - 2 - \sqrt{5}) - 2(x - 2 - \sqrt{5}) + \sqrt{5}(x - 2 - \sqrt{5})$
$= x^2 - 2x - \sqrt{5}x - 2x + 4 + 2\sqrt{5} + \sqrt{5}x - 2\sqrt{5} - 5$
$= x^2 - 4x - 1$
Use the method for multiplying out long brackets
from Chapter 3.

b) $x^2 - 4x - 1 = 0$
$a = 1, b = -4, c = -1$
$x = \dfrac{-b \pm \sqrt{b^2 - 4ac}}{2a} = \dfrac{-(-4) \pm \sqrt{(-4)^2 - 4 \times 1 \times (-1)}}{2 \times 1}$
$= \dfrac{4 \pm \sqrt{16 + 4}}{2} = \dfrac{4 \pm \sqrt{20}}{2} = \dfrac{4 \pm 2\sqrt{5}}{2} = 2 \pm \sqrt{5}$

c) The roots produced by the quadratic formula in part
b) are the same as the numbers subtracted from x in
the expression from a) — this is because it's just the
factorised version of the same quadratic. If you put
the factorised version equal to zero and solved the
equation, you'd get the same roots.

Q3 $x^2 + 8x + 13 = 0$
$a = 1, b = 8, c = 13$
$x = \dfrac{-b \pm \sqrt{b^2 - 4ac}}{2a} = \dfrac{-8 \pm \sqrt{8^2 - 4 \times 1 \times 13}}{2 \times 1}$
$= \dfrac{-8 \pm \sqrt{64 - 52}}{2} = \dfrac{-8 \pm \sqrt{12}}{2}$
$= \dfrac{-8 \pm 2\sqrt{3}}{2} = -4 \pm \sqrt{3}$
So A = − 4 and B = 3.

Q4 a) $x^2 + x + \dfrac{1}{4} = 0$

$a = 1,\ b = 1,\ c = \dfrac{1}{4}$

$x = \dfrac{-b \pm \sqrt{b^2 - 4ac}}{2a} = \dfrac{-1 \pm \sqrt{1^2 - 4 \times 1 \times \frac{1}{4}}}{2 \times 1}$

$= \dfrac{-1 \pm \sqrt{1-1}}{2} = \dfrac{-1 \pm 0}{2} = -\dfrac{1}{2}$

Multiplying the first equation by 4 gives $4x^2 + 4x + 1 = 0$.
This factorises to $(2x + 1)^2 = 0$, giving the same answer.

b) $25x^2 - 30x + 7 = 0$

$a = 25,\ b = -30,\ c = 7$

$x = \dfrac{-b \pm \sqrt{b^2 - 4ac}}{2a} = \dfrac{-(-30) \pm \sqrt{(-30)^2 - 4 \times 25 \times 7}}{2 \times 25}$

$= \dfrac{30 \pm \sqrt{900 - 700}}{2 \times 25} = \dfrac{30 \pm \sqrt{200}}{50}$

$= \dfrac{30 \pm 10\sqrt{2}}{50} = \dfrac{30}{50} \pm \dfrac{10}{50}\sqrt{2} = \dfrac{3}{5} \pm \dfrac{1}{5}\sqrt{2}$

c) $60x - 5 = -100x^2 - 3$

$100x^2 + 60x - 2 = 0$

$a = 100,\ b = 60,\ c = -2$

$x = \dfrac{-b \pm \sqrt{b^2 - 4ac}}{2a} = \dfrac{-60 \pm \sqrt{60^2 - 4 \times 100 \times (-2)}}{2 \times 100}$

$= \dfrac{-60 \pm \sqrt{3600 + 800}}{200} = \dfrac{-60 \pm \sqrt{4400}}{200}$

$= \dfrac{-60 \pm \sqrt{44 \times 100}}{200} = \dfrac{-60 \pm \sqrt{4 \times 11 \times 100}}{200}$

$= \dfrac{-60 \pm \sqrt{4}\sqrt{100}\sqrt{11}}{200} = \dfrac{-60 \pm 20\sqrt{11}}{200}$

$= -\dfrac{3}{10} \pm \dfrac{1}{10}\sqrt{11}$

d) $2x(x - 4) = 7 - 3x$

$2x^2 - 8x = 7 - 3x$

$2x^2 - 5x - 7 = 0$

$a = 2,\ b = -5,\ c = -7$

$x = \dfrac{-b \pm \sqrt{b^2 - 4ac}}{2a} = \dfrac{-(-5) \pm \sqrt{(-5)^2 - 4 \times 2 \times (-7)}}{2 \times 2}$

$= \dfrac{5 \pm \sqrt{25 + 56}}{4} = \dfrac{5 \pm \sqrt{81}}{4} = \dfrac{5 \pm 9}{4}$

$= \dfrac{5 + 9}{4}$ or $\dfrac{5 - 9}{4} = \dfrac{14}{4}$ or $\dfrac{-4}{4}$

$= \dfrac{7}{2}$ or -1

This factorises to $(2x - 7)(x + 1) = 0$

Exercise 1.3 — Completing the square

Q1 a) Take the square root of both sides to get:

$x + 4 = \pm\sqrt{25} \Rightarrow x = -4 \pm \sqrt{25} = -4 \pm 5$

So $x = 1$ or -9

b) Take the square root of both sides to get:

$5x - 3 = \pm\sqrt{21} \Rightarrow 5x = 3 \pm \sqrt{21} \Rightarrow x = \dfrac{3}{5} \pm \dfrac{\sqrt{21}}{5}$

Q2 a) $x^2 + 6x + 8 = (x + 3)^2 - 9 + 8 = (x + 3)^2 - 1$

b) $x^2 + 8x - 10 = (x + 4)^2 - 16 - 10 = (x + 4)^2 - 26$

c) $x^2 - 3x - 10 = \left(x - \dfrac{3}{2}\right)^2 - \dfrac{9}{4} - 10$

$= \left(x - \dfrac{3}{2}\right)^2 - \dfrac{9}{4} - \dfrac{40}{4} = \left(x - \dfrac{3}{2}\right)^2 - \dfrac{49}{4}$

d) $x^2 - 20x + 15 = (x - 10)^2 - 100 + 15$

$= (x - 10)^2 - 85$

e) $x^2 - 2mx + n = (x - m)^2 - m^2 + n$

$= (x - m)^2 + (-m^2 + n)$

f) $3x^2 - 12x + 7 = 3(x - 2)^2 - 12 + 7 = 3(x - 2)^2 - 5$

Q3 a) First complete the square of the expression:

$x^2 - 6x - 16 = (x - 3)^2 - 9 - 16 = (x - 3)^2 - 25$

Now set the completed square equal to zero:

$(x - 3)^2 - 25 = 0 \Rightarrow (x - 3)^2 = 25$

$\Rightarrow x - 3 = \pm\sqrt{25} \Rightarrow x = 3 \pm \sqrt{25} = 3 \pm 5$

$\Rightarrow x = 8$ or -2

b) Write the equation in standard quadratic form:

$p^2 - 10p = 200 \Rightarrow p^2 - 10p - 200 = 0$

Then complete the square of the expression:

$p^2 - 10p - 200 = (p - 5)^2 - 25 - 200$

$= (p - 5)^2 - 225$

Now set the completed square equal to zero:

$(p - 5)^2 - 225 = 0 \Rightarrow (p - 5)^2 = 225$

$\Rightarrow p - 5 = \pm\sqrt{225} \Rightarrow p = 5 \pm \sqrt{225} = 5 \pm 15$

$\Rightarrow p = 20$ or -10

c) First complete the square of the expression:

$x^2 + 2x + k = (x + 1)^2 - 1 + k = (x + 1)^2 + (k - 1)$

Now set the completed square equal to zero:

$(x + 1)^2 + (k - 1) = 0 \Rightarrow (x + 1)^2 = 1 - k$

$\Rightarrow x + 1 = \pm\sqrt{1 - k} \Rightarrow x = -1 \pm \sqrt{1 - k}$

d) Write the equation in standard quadratic form:

$9x^2 + 18x = 16 \Rightarrow 9x^2 + 18x - 16 = 0$

Then complete the square of the expression:

$9x^2 + 18x - 16 = 9(x + 1)^2 - 9 - 16$

$= 9(x + 1)^2 - 25$

Now set the completed square equal to zero:

$9(x + 1)^2 - 25 = 0 \Rightarrow 9(x + 1)^2 = 25$

$\Rightarrow (x + 1)^2 = \dfrac{25}{9} \Rightarrow x + 1 = \pm\sqrt{\dfrac{25}{9}}$

$\Rightarrow x = -1 \pm \sqrt{\dfrac{25}{9}} \Rightarrow x = -1 \pm \dfrac{5}{3}$

So $x = \dfrac{2}{3}$ or $-\dfrac{8}{3}$

e) First complete the square of the expression:

$x^2 + 4x - 8 = (x + 2)^2 - 4 - 8 = (x + 2)^2 - 12$

Now set the completed square equal to zero:

$(x + 2)^2 - 12 = 0 \Rightarrow (x + 2)^2 = 12$

$\Rightarrow x + 2 = \pm\sqrt{12} \Rightarrow x = \pm\sqrt{12} - 2$

So $x = -2 \pm 2\sqrt{3}$

f) First complete the square of the expression:

$2x^2 - 12x + 9 = 2(x - 3)^2 - 18 + 9$

$= 2(x - 3)^2 - 9$

Now set the completed square equal to zero:

$2(x - 3)^2 - 9 = 0 \Rightarrow 2(x - 3)^2 = 9$

$\Rightarrow (x - 3)^2 = \dfrac{9}{2} \Rightarrow x - 3 = \pm\sqrt{\dfrac{9}{2}}$

$\Rightarrow x = 3 \pm \sqrt{\dfrac{9}{2}} \Rightarrow x = 3 \pm \dfrac{3}{\sqrt{2}} = 3 \pm \dfrac{3\sqrt{2}}{2}$

Here you should rationalise the denominator by multiplying the top and bottom of the fraction by $\sqrt{2}$.

g) First divide through by 2:

$x^2 - 6x - 27 = (x - 3)^2 - 9 - 27 = (x - 3)^2 - 36$

Now set the completed square equal to zero:

$(x - 3)^2 - 36 = 0 \Rightarrow (x - 3)^2 = 36$

$\Rightarrow x - 3 = \pm 6 \Rightarrow x = 3 \pm 6$

So $x = 9$ or -3

h) First complete the square of the expression:

$$5x^2 - 3x + \frac{2}{5} = 5\left(x - \frac{3}{10}\right)^2 - \frac{9}{20} + \frac{2}{5}$$

$$= 5\left(x - \frac{3}{10}\right)^2 + \frac{-9 + 8}{20}$$

$$= 5\left(x - \frac{3}{10}\right)^2 - \frac{1}{20}$$

Now set the completed square equal to zero:

$$5\left(x - \frac{3}{10}\right)^2 - \frac{1}{20} = 0 \Rightarrow 5\left(x - \frac{3}{10}\right)^2 = \frac{1}{20}$$

$$\Rightarrow \left(x - \frac{3}{10}\right)^2 = \frac{1}{100} \Rightarrow x - \frac{3}{10} = \pm\sqrt{\frac{1}{100}}$$

$$\Rightarrow x - \frac{3}{10} = \pm\frac{1}{10} \Rightarrow x = \frac{3}{10} \pm \frac{1}{10}$$

So $x = \frac{2}{5}$ or $\frac{1}{5}$

Q4 Complete the square of the expression:
$3x^2 - 12x + 14 = 3(x - 2)^2 - 12 + 14 = 3(x - 2)^2 + 2$
Since $(x - 2)^2 \geq 0$ for all x, $3(x - 2)^2 + 2 \geq 2$
So $3x^2 - 12x + 14 > 0$ for all x, as required.

Q5 First complete the square of the expression:

$$ax^2 + bx + c = a\left(x^2 + \frac{b}{a}x + \frac{c}{a}\right)$$

$$= a\left(x + \frac{b}{2a}\right)^2 - \frac{b^2}{4a} + c$$

Now set the completed square equal to zero and rearrange to find the roots:

$$a\left(x + \frac{b}{2a}\right)^2 - \frac{b^2}{4a} + c = 0 \Rightarrow \left(x + \frac{b}{2a}\right)^2 = \frac{b^2}{4a^2} - \frac{c}{a}$$

$$\Rightarrow \left(x + \frac{b}{2a}\right)^2 = \frac{b^2 - 4ac}{4a^2} \Rightarrow x + \frac{b}{2a} = \pm\sqrt{\frac{b^2 - 4ac}{4a^2}}$$

$$\Rightarrow x = -\frac{b}{2a} \pm \frac{\sqrt{b^2 - 4ac}}{2a} \Rightarrow x = \frac{-b \pm \sqrt{b^2 - 4ac}}{2a}$$

This last question was quite tricky, but if you got there you should have noticed something quite special — you've just proved the quadratic formula... wow.

Exercise 1.4 — Quadratics involving functions of x

Q1 a) $u = x^{\frac{1}{2}} (= \sqrt{x})$

b) $e^x(e^x - 6) = 8 \Rightarrow e^{2x} - 6e^x - 8 = 0$
$\Rightarrow (e^x)^2 - 6(e^x) - 8 = 0$. So $u = e^x$

c) $5^x + 5^{2x} = 4 \Rightarrow 5^{2x} + 5^x - 4 = 0 \Rightarrow (5^x)^2 + (5^x) - 4 = 0$
So $u = 5^x$

d) $2\cos^2 x + 3 = 5\cos x \Rightarrow 2\cos^2 x - 5\cos x + 3 = 0$
$\Rightarrow 2(\cos x)^2 - 5(\cos x) + 3 = 0$. So $u = \cos x$

Q2 a) $x^2 + 6x + 7 = (x + 3)^2 - 9 + 7 = (x + 3)^2 - 2$
This is just completing the square.

b) Let $u = (2x + 1)$
So $(2x + 1)^2 + 6(2x + 1) + 7$ becomes
$u^2 + 6u + 7$, which can be written as $(u + 3)^2 - 2$.
$(u + 3)^2 - 2 = 0 \Rightarrow (u + 3)^2 = 2 \Rightarrow u + 3 = \pm\sqrt{2}$
$\Rightarrow u = -3 \pm\sqrt{2}$
Now replace u with $(2x + 1)$:
$(2x + 1) = -3 \pm\sqrt{2} \Rightarrow 2x = -4 \pm\sqrt{2}$
So $x = -2 \pm \frac{\sqrt{2}}{2}$

Q3 Let $u = x^2$
So $x^4 - 17x^2 + 16 = 0$ becomes $u^2 - 17u + 16 = 0$
$(u - 1)(u - 16) = 0 \Rightarrow u = 1$ or $u = 16$
This means $x^2 = 1$ or $x^2 = 16$, so $x = \pm 1$ or $x = \pm 4$
So the four solutions are $x = 1$, $x = -1$, $x = 4$ and $x = -4$

Q4 Let $u = \frac{1}{5x + 2}$

So $\frac{3}{(5x + 2)^2} + \frac{1}{5x + 2} = 10$ becomes $3u^2 + u - 10 = 0$

$(3u - 5)(u + 2) = 0 \Rightarrow u = \frac{5}{3}$ or $u = -2$

This means $\frac{1}{5x + 2} = \frac{5}{3} \Rightarrow 3 = 5(5x + 2)$

$\Rightarrow 3 = 25x + 10 \Rightarrow 25x = -7 \Rightarrow x = -\frac{7}{25}$

or $\frac{1}{5x + 2} = -2 \Rightarrow 1 = -2(5x + 2) \Rightarrow 1 = -10x - 4$

$\Rightarrow 10x = -5 \Rightarrow x = -\frac{1}{2}$

2. Quadratic Functions and Roots

Exercise 2.1 — The roots of a quadratic function

Q1 a) 2 real roots.   **b)** 1 real root.
c) no real roots.   **d)** 2 real roots.

Q2 Completing the square:
$f(x) = x^2 + 6x + 10 = (x + 3)^2 - 9 + 10 = (x + 3)^2 + 1$
The smallest the $(x + 3)^2$ bit can be is 0, and 1 is positive which means that $f(x)$ is always positive and the smallest it can be is 1. So $f(x)$ has no real roots.
$q = 3$, so the graph has a line of symmetry at $x = -3$.

Q3 Comparing $f(x) = -\left(x + \frac{7}{2}\right)^2 + \frac{25}{4}$ to $p(x + q)^2 + r$ gives
$p = -1$, $r = \frac{25}{4}$
These have different signs, so $f(x)$ has two real roots.
Alternatively, $-\left(x + \frac{7}{2}\right)^2 + \frac{25}{4} = 0 \Rightarrow \left(x + \frac{7}{2}\right)^2 = \frac{25}{4}$.
This can be solved by taking the square root
(since the RHS is positive) — so it has real roots.

Exercise 2.2 — Using the discriminant

Q1 a) $a = 1$, $b = 8$, $c = 15$.
So $b^2 - 4ac = 8^2 - 4 \times 1 \times 15 = 64 - 60 = 4$.
Discriminant > 0 so the equation has 2 real roots.

b) $a = 1$, $b = 2\sqrt{3}$, $c = 3$.
So $b^2 - 4ac = (2\sqrt{3})^2 - 4 \times 1 \times 3 = 12 - 12 = 0$.
Discriminant $= 0$ so the equation has 1 real root.

c) Write in standard form:
$(2x + 1)(5x - 3) = 10x^2 - x - 3$
so $a = 10$, $b = -1$ and $c = -3$.
$b^2 - 4ac = (-1)^2 - 4 \times 10 \times -3 = 1 + 120 = 121$
Discriminant > 0 so the equation has 2 real roots.

d) $a = -3$, $b = -\frac{11}{5}$, $c = -\frac{2}{5}$.
So $b^2 - 4ac = \left(-\frac{11}{5}\right)^2 - 4 \times (-3) \times \left(-\frac{2}{5}\right)$
$= \frac{121}{25} - \frac{24}{5} = \frac{121}{25} - \frac{120}{25} = \frac{1}{25}$
Discriminant > 0 so the equation has 2 real roots.

e) $a = 9$, $b = 20$, $c = 0$.
So $b^2 - 4ac = 20^2 - 4 \times 9 \times 0 = 400 - 0 = 400$.
Discriminant > 0 so the equation has 2 real roots.

f) $a = \frac{19}{16}$, $b = 0$, $c = -4$.
So $b^2 - 4ac = 0^2 - 4 \times \frac{19}{16} \times (-4) = 0 + 19 = 19$.
Discriminant > 0 so the equation has 2 real roots.

Q2 Find the discriminant of the equation by first writing it in standard form: $15x^2 + bx = 2 \Rightarrow 15x^2 + bx - 2 = 0$
$a = 15$, $b = b$, $c = -2$.
So $b^2 - 4ac = b^2 - 4 \times 15 \times (-2) = b^2 + 120$.
Now you know that the discriminant is 169 so let
$b^2 + 120 = 169 \Rightarrow b^2 = 49 \Rightarrow b = \pm 7$.

Q3 First find the discriminant: $a = a$, $b = 7$, $c = \frac{1}{4}$.
So $b^2 - 4ac = 7^2 - 4 \times a \times \frac{1}{4} = 49 - a$.
The equation has one real root which means its discriminant must be 0. So $49 - a = 0 \Rightarrow a = 49$.

Q4 a) $a = 13$, $b = 8$, $c = 2$
so $b^2 - 4ac = 8^2 - 4 \times 13 \times 2 = 64 - 104 = -40$.
The discriminant is negative so the equation has no real roots.

b) $a = \frac{1}{3}$, $b = \frac{5}{2}$, $c = 3$
so $b^2 - 4ac = \left(\frac{5}{2}\right)^2 - 4 \times \frac{1}{3} \times 3 = \frac{25}{4} - 4$
$= \frac{25}{4} - \frac{16}{4} = \frac{9}{4}$
The discriminant is positive so the equation has two real roots.

Q5 $a = 1$, $b = -12$, $c = 27 + p$.
So $b^2 - 4ac = (-12)^2 - 4 \times 1 \times (27 + p)$
$= 144 - (108 + 4p) = 36 - 4p$

If the equation has two distinct real roots, the discriminant must be positive so $36 - 4p > 0$
$\Rightarrow 36 > 4p \Rightarrow p < 9$.

Q6 $a = 10$, $b = -10$, $c = \frac{q}{2}$.
So $b^2 - 4ac = (-10)^2 - 4 \times 10 \times \frac{q}{2} = 100 - 20q$
If the equation has two distinct real roots, the discriminant must be positive so $100 - 20q > 0$
$\Rightarrow 100 > 20q \Rightarrow q < 5$

Q7 $a = 2$, $b = 10p + 1$, $c = 5$
So $b^2 - 4ac = (10p + 1)^2 - 4 \times 2 \times 5$
$= (100p^2 + 20p + 1) - 40 = 100p^2 + 20p - 39$

If the equation has no real roots, the discriminant must be negative so $100p^2 + 20p - 39 < 0$
$\Rightarrow 100p^2 + 20p < 39 \Rightarrow 20p(5p + 1) < 39$
$\Rightarrow p(5p + 1) < \frac{39}{20}$

Q8 First find the discriminant of the equation.
$a = -2$, $b = -2$, $c = k$.
So $b^2 - 4ac = (-2)^2 - 4 \times (-2) \times k = 4 + 8k$.

a) If the equation has two distinct real roots, the discriminant must be positive so $4 + 8k > 0$
$\Rightarrow 8k > -4 \Rightarrow k > -\frac{1}{2}$

b) If the equation has one real root, the discriminant must be zero so $4 + 8k = 0 \Rightarrow k = -\frac{1}{2}$

c) If the equation has no real roots, the discriminant must be negative so $4 + 8k < 0 \Rightarrow k < -\frac{1}{2}$.

Q9 a) First work out the discriminant:
$a = 1$, $b = k + 5$, $c = \frac{k^2}{4}$
So $b^2 - 4ac = (k + 5)^2 - 4 \times 1 \times \frac{k^2}{4}$
$= (k^2 + 10k + 25) - k^2 = 10k + 25$
The equation has no real roots so the discriminant is negative so $10k + 25 < 0$.

b) To find the range of values of k, solve the inequality in part a).
$10k + 25 < 0 \Rightarrow 10k < -25 \Rightarrow k < -\frac{25}{10} = -\frac{5}{2}$
So $k < -\frac{5}{2}$

Q10 a) $a = k - \frac{6}{5}$, $b = \sqrt{k}$, $c = \frac{5}{4}$
$b^2 - 4ac = \left(\sqrt{k}\right)^2 - 4 \times \left(k - \frac{6}{5}\right) \times \frac{5}{4}$
$= k - 5\left(k - \frac{6}{5}\right)$
$= k - 5k + 6 = -4k + 6$

b) (i) For one real root, discriminant = 0:
$-4k + 6 = 0 \Rightarrow k = \frac{6}{4} = \frac{3}{2}$

(ii) For no real roots, discriminant is negative:
$-4k + 6 < 0$ so $k > \frac{3}{2}$

(iii) For two real roots, discriminant is positive:
$-4k + 6 > 0$ so $k < \frac{3}{2}$

3. Quadratic Graphs

Exercise 3.1 — Sketching a quadratic graph

Q1 a) & b)

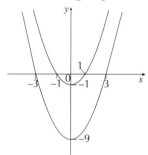

Q2 a) $f(x) = x^2 - 10x + 9 = (x - 9)(x - 1)$

b) & c)

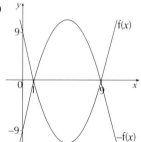

Q3 a) $y = -x^2 + 2x + 1$

(i) The x^2 coefficient is -1 so it is n-shaped.

(ii) Letting $x = 0$, $y = 1$ is the y-intercept.

(iii) Calculate the discriminant to work out the number of roots: $a = -1$, $b = 2$, $c = 1$.
$b^2 - 4ac = 2^2 - 4 \times (-1) \times 1 = 4 + 4 = 8$
The discriminant is positive so there are 2 distinct real roots.

(iv) To find the x-intercepts — find the roots:
$y = -x^2 + 2x + 1 = -(x - 1)^2 + 2$ by completing the square. Setting this equal to zero:
$-(x - 1)^2 + 2 = 0$ so $(x - 1)^2 = 2$
so $x - 1 = \pm\sqrt{2} \Rightarrow x = 1 \pm \sqrt{2}$

(v) The vertex is a maximum since the graph's n-shaped. The maximum can be found by looking at the completed square $y = -(x - 1)^2 + 2$. The highest value $-(x - 1)^2$ can take is 0, so the maximum is at $y = 2$ and $x = 1$ (to make the bracket 0).

(vi)

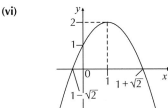

b) $y = x^2 - 7x + 15$

  (i) The x^2 coefficient is 1 so the graph's u-shaped.

  (ii) Letting $x = 0$, $y = 15$ is the y-intercept.

  (iii) Calculate the discriminant to work out the number of roots: $a = 1$, $b = -7$, $c = 15$.
$b^2 - 4ac = (-7)^2 - 4 \times 1 \times 15 = 49 - 60 = -11$
The discriminant is negative so there are no real roots.

  (iv) There are no real roots so the graph does not intersect the x-axis.

  (v) The vertex is a minimum since the graph's u-shaped. The minimum can be found by completing the square.
$y = x^2 - 7x + 15 = \left(x - \dfrac{7}{2}\right)^2 + \dfrac{11}{4}$
The lowest value $\left(x - \dfrac{7}{2}\right)^2$ can take is zero — so the minimum is at $y = \dfrac{11}{4}$ and so $x = \dfrac{7}{2}$ (to make the bracket 0).

  (vi)

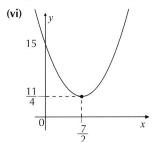

c) $y = 2x^2 + 4x - 9$

  (i) The x^2 coefficient is 2 so it is u-shaped.

  (ii) Letting $x = 0$, $y = -9$ is the y-intercept.

  (iii) Calculate the discriminant to work out the number of roots: $a = 2$, $b = 4$, $c = -9$.
$b^2 - 4ac = 4^2 - 4 \times 2 \times (-9) = 16 + 72 = 88$
The discriminant is positive so there are 2 distinct real roots.

  (iv) To find the x-intercepts, find the roots:
$2x^2 + 4x - 9 = 0$
Completing the square gives:
$2(x + 1)^2 - 2 - 9 = 0$
$2(x + 1)^2 - 11 = 0$
Solving: $(x + 1)^2 = \dfrac{11}{2} \Rightarrow x = -1 \pm \sqrt{\dfrac{11}{2}}$

  (v) The vertex is a minimum since the graph is u-shaped. The minimum occurs when the square is 0, so it's $(-1, -11)$

(vi)

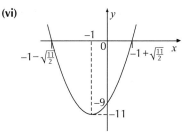

Q4 **a)** The minimum point is shown on the graph as $(-4, 2)$. The coordinates of the vertex of the function $f(x) = p(x + q)^2 + r$ are $(-q, r)$. In this case $p = 1$ and from the minimum on the graph you can see $-q = -4$, so $q = 4$ and $r = 2$.
So you can write the function $f(x) = (x + 4)^2 + 2$.

b) $g(x) = (x + 4)^2$ is in the form $p(x + q)^2 + r$ with $p = 1$ so the graph is u-shaped and the minimum is at $(-q, r) = (-4, 0)$.

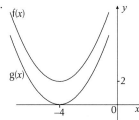

c) $f(x)$ does not have any real roots as its graph does not touch the x-axis. $g(x)$ has one real root as its graph touches the x-axis once (at $x = -4$).

Q5 **a)** $x^2 - 6x + 5 = (x - 3)^2 - 9 + 5 = (x - 3)^2 - 4$

b) $x^2 - 6x + 5 = 0 \Rightarrow (x - 3)^2 - 4 = 0 \Rightarrow (x - 3)^2 = 4$
$\Rightarrow x - 3 = \pm\sqrt{4} \Rightarrow x = 3 \pm \sqrt{4} = 3 \pm 2 = 5$ or 1

c) The graph is u-shaped. The function has roots $x = 1$ and 5 so these are the x-intercepts. Putting $x = 0$ into the original equation gives $y = 5$, so this is the y-intercept. Completing the square gives the minimum as $(3, -4)$.
Putting all this together gives the following graph:

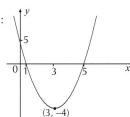

Q6 **a)** $f(x) = x^2 - 2x + 1 = (x - 1)^2$ so the function has one repeated root at $x = 1$. Letting $x = 0$ gives $f(x) = 1$ so the y-intercept is at 1. The graph is u-shaped.

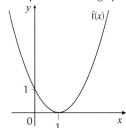

b) $f(x) = x^2 + x - 1 = \left(x + \frac{1}{2}\right)^2 - \frac{5}{4}$ and solving $f(x) = 0$

gives $x = -\frac{1}{2} \pm \frac{\sqrt{5}}{2}$ as the x-intercepts. Letting $x = 0$
we get $f(x) = -1$ so this is the y-intercept. The graph
is u-shaped.

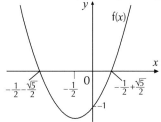

c) $f(x) = x^2 - 8x + 18 = (x - 4)^2 + 2$. Solving $f(x) = 0$
gives $x = 4 \pm \sqrt{-2}$ so there are no x-intercepts as you
cannot take the square root of -2.
*You could have worked out the discriminant to see that there
were no real roots to save you trying to solve the equation.*

Letting $x = 0$ gives $f(x) = 18$. The graph is u-shaped
but it could be one of two graphs which are u-shaped
with a y-intercept of 18. To find out which, work out
the vertex. It has a minimum as it is u-shaped and
from completing the square, the minimum is at $(4, 2)$.

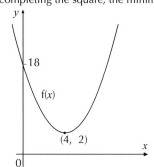

d) $f(x) = -x^2 + 3$ so setting $f(x) = 0$ gives $x = \pm\sqrt{3}$ as the
x-intercepts. Letting $x = 0$ gives $f(x) = 3$ so 3 is the
y-intercept. The graph is n-shaped.

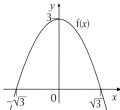

Q7 a) The roots of the quadratic function are the values of x
where the graph crosses the x-axis. So the roots are
$x = -2$ and $x = 1$.

b) One root of the equation is $x = -2$ which means
$x + 2$ will be a factor. The other root $x = 1$ means
that $x - 1$ will be a factor. So the quadratic function
should be of the form $y = a(x + 2)(x - 1)$ for some
value of a. But you know the equation has the form
$y = -x^2 + px + q$. So a should be -1 to produce the
term $-x^2$. So $y = -(x + 2)(x - 1)$ which gives
$y = -x^2 - x + 2$, so $p = -1$ and $q = 2$.
*The trickiest part of this question is realising you might also
need a number factor, a, to form the factorised quadratic.
Without it, you'd have got the wrong answer of $x^2 + x - 2$.*

Q8 a) Setting $t = 0$ gives the h-intercept at $h = 4$.
Setting $h = 0$ gives $0.25t^2 - 2.5t + 4 = 0$, so
$t^2 - 10t + 16 = 0 \Rightarrow (t - 2)(t - 8) = 0$
so the t-intercepts are at $t = 2$ or $t = 8$.
Setting $t = 10$ gives $h = 25 - 25 + 4 = 4$.
So the graph is u-shaped and looks like this:

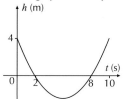

b) (i) The height of the raised platform is where the
roller coaster sets off from (i.e. at $t = 0$).
From part a), this is 4 m.

(ii) The lowest point of the roller coaster is the value
of h at the minimum point of the graph. Using
the symmetry of the graph, this point occurs
halfway between $t = 2$ and $t = 8$ (i.e. at $t = 5$).
When $t = 5$, $h = 0.25(5)^2 - 2.5(5) + 4 = -2.25$ m.

(iii) The roller coaster is underground when $h < 0$.
From the graph, you can see that this is between
$t = 2$ and $t = 8$, so it is underground for
$8 - 2 = 6$ seconds.

4. Factorising Cubics
Exercise 4.1 — Factorising a cubic (when x is a factor)

Q1 a) $x(x^2 + 5x + 6) = x(x + 2)(x + 3)$
b) $x(x^2 + 6x - 7) = x(x + 7)(x - 1)$
c) $x(x^2 - 18x + 81) = x(x - 9)(x - 9) = x(x - 9)^2$
d) $x(x^2 + 7x + 10) = x(x + 5)(x + 2)$
e) $-x(x^2 - 4x + 3) = -x(x - 3)(x - 1)$
f) $x(2x^2 + 15x + 25) = x(2x + 5)(x + 5)$
g) $x(x^2 - 49) = x(x + 7)(x - 7)$
h) $x\left(x^2 - \frac{9}{4}\right) = x\left(x + \frac{3}{2}\right)\left(x - \frac{3}{2}\right)$

Q2 a) $-x^3 + 2x^2 + 24x = 0$
$\Rightarrow -x(x^2 - 2x - 24) = 0$
$\Rightarrow -x(x - 6)(x + 4) = 0$
So either $-x = 0$, $x - 6 = 0$ or $x + 4 = 0$.
So the roots are $x = 0$, $x = 6$ and $x = -4$.

b) $x^3 - \frac{7}{9}x^2 + \frac{10}{81}x = 0$
$\Rightarrow x\left(x^2 - \frac{7}{9}x + \frac{10}{81}\right) = 0$
$\Rightarrow x\left(x - \frac{5}{9}\right)\left(x - \frac{2}{9}\right) = 0$
So either $x = 0$, $x - \frac{5}{9} = 0$ or $x - \frac{2}{9} = 0$.
So the roots are $x = 0$, $x = \frac{5}{9}$ and $x = \frac{2}{9}$.

c) $2x^3 + 9x^2 + 4x = 0$
$\Rightarrow x(2x^2 + 9x + 4) = 0$
$\Rightarrow x(2x + 1)(x + 4) = 0$
So either $x = 0$, $2x + 1 = 0$ or $x + 4 = 0$.
So the roots are $x = 0$, $x = -\frac{1}{2}$ or $x = -4$.

d) $3x^3 - 3x^2 + 4x = 0 \Rightarrow x(3x^2 - 3x + 4) = 0$

This quadratic won't factorise — so use the quadratic formula: $a = 3$, $b = -3$, $c = 4$

$$x = \frac{-b \pm \sqrt{b^2 - 4ac}}{2a} = \frac{3 \pm \sqrt{(-3)^2 - 4 \times 3 \times 4}}{2 \times 3}$$

$$= \frac{3 \pm \sqrt{9 - 48}}{6} = \frac{3 \pm \sqrt{-39}}{6}$$

These aren't possible solutions since you can't take the square root of a negative number, so the only real solution is $x = 0$.

e) $x^2(4x + 3) = x \Rightarrow 4x^3 + 3x^2 = x$
$\Rightarrow 4x^3 + 3x^2 - x = 0$
$\Rightarrow x(4x^2 + 3x - 1) = 0$
$\Rightarrow x(4x - 1)(x + 1) = 0$

So either $x = 0$, $4x - 1 = 0$ or $x + 1 = 0$.

So the roots are $x = 0$, $x = \frac{1}{4}$ or $x = -1$.

f) $2x^3 + 8x^2 = -3x \Rightarrow 2x^3 + 8x^2 + 3x = 0$
$\Rightarrow x(2x^2 + 8x + 3) = 0$

So one root is $x = 0$, but the quadratic won't factorise so use the quadratic formula.

Now $a = 2$, $b = 8$ and $c = 3$.

$$x = \frac{-b \pm \sqrt{b^2 - 4ac}}{2a} = \frac{-8 \pm \sqrt{8^2 - 4 \times 2 \times 3}}{2 \times 2}$$

$$= \frac{-8 \pm \sqrt{40}}{4} = -2 \pm \frac{1}{2}\sqrt{10}$$

So the roots are $x = 0$ and $x = -2 \pm \frac{1}{2}\sqrt{10}$.

Exercise 4.2 — The Remainder Theorem

Q1 a) $a = 1$, $f(1) = 2(1)^3 - 3(1)^2 - 39(1) + 20 = -20$

b) $a = -1$, $f(-1) = (-1)^3 - 3(-1)^2 + 2(-1) = -6$

c) $a = -1$, $f(-1) = 6(-1)^3 + (-1)^2 - 5(-1) - 2 = -2$

d) $a = -3$, $f(-3) = (-3)^3 + 2(-3)^2 - 7(-3) - 2 = 10$

e) $a = 2$ and $b = -1$
$f\left(-\frac{1}{2}\right) = 4\left(-\frac{1}{2}\right)^3 - 6\left(-\frac{1}{2}\right)^2 - 12\left(-\frac{1}{2}\right) - 6 = -2$

f) $a = 2$ and $b = 1$
$f\left(\frac{1}{2}\right) = \left(\frac{1}{2}\right)^3 - 3\left(\frac{1}{2}\right)^2 - 6\left(\frac{1}{2}\right) + 8 = \frac{35}{8}$ or $4\frac{3}{8}$

Q2 a) You need to find $f(-2)$. This is
$(-2)^4 - 3(-2)^3 + 7(-2)^2 - 12(-2) + 14$
$= 16 + 24 + 28 + 24 + 14 = 106$.

b) You need to find $f\left(\frac{-4}{2}\right) = f(-2)$.
You found this in part a), so remainder = 106.
You might also have noticed that $2x + 4$ is a multiple of $x + 2$ (from part a), so the remainder must be the same.

c) You need to find $f(3)$. This is
$(3)^4 - 3(3)^3 + 7(3)^2 - 12(3) + 14$
$= 81 - 81 + 63 - 36 + 14 = 41$.

d) You need to find $f\left(\frac{6}{2}\right) = f(3)$.
You found this in part c), so remainder = 41.
You might also have noticed that $2x - 6$ is a multiple of $x - 3$, so the remainder must be the same.

Q3 $f(-3) = -16$,
$f(-3) = (-3)^3 + c(-3)^2 + 17(-3) - 10$
$= -27 + 9c - 51 - 10 = -88 + 9c$
$\Rightarrow -88 + 9c = -16$
$9c = 72$
$c = 8$
So $f(x) = x^3 + 8x^2 + 17x - 10$

Q4 $a = -2$, $f(-2) = (-2)^3 + p(-2)^2 - 10(-2) - 19 = 5$
$4p - 7 = 5$
$4p = 12 \Rightarrow p = 3$
So $f(x) = x^3 + 3x^2 - 10x - 19$

Q5 $a = -2$, $f(-2) = (-2)^3 - d(-2)^2 + d(-2) + 1 = -25$
$-6d - 7 = -25$
$-6d = -18 \Rightarrow d = 3$
So $f(x) = x^3 - 3x^2 + 3x + 1$

Q6 $a = -1$, $f(-1) = (-1)^3 - 2(-1)^2 + 7(-1) + k = -8$
$-10 + k = -8$
$k = 2$
So $f(x) = x^3 - 2x^2 + 7x + 2$

Q7 $a = 2$, $f(2) = (2)^4 + 5(2)^3 + 2p + 156 = 2p + 212$
$a = -1$, $f(-1) = (-1)^4 + 5(-1)^3 - p + 156 = 152 - p$
$\Rightarrow 2p + 212 = 152 - p$
$3p = -60$
$p = -20$
So $f(x) = x^4 + 5x^3 - 20x + 156$

Exercise 4.3 — The Factor Theorem

Q1 a) $a = 1$, find $f(a)$ and show the result is 0:
$f(1) = (1)^3 - (1)^2 - 3(1) + 3 = 1 - 1 - 3 + 3 = 0$
So by the Factor Theorem, $(x - 1)$ is a factor.
The question asked you to use the Factor Theorem, but you could also show it was a factor by adding the coefficients (1, –1, –3, 3) to get 0. (If the coefficients in a polynomial add up to 0, then (x – 1) is a factor.)

b) $a = -1$, find $f(a)$ and show the result is 0:
$f(-1) = (-1)^3 + 2(-1)^2 + 3(-1) + 2$
$= -1 + 2 - 3 + 2 = 0$
So by the Factor Theorem, $(x + 1)$ is a factor.

c) $a = -2$, find $f(a)$ and show the result is 0:
$f(-2) = (-2)^3 + 3(-2)^2 - 10(-2) - 24$
$= -8 + 12 + 20 - 24 = 0$
So by the Factor Theorem, $(x + 2)$ is a factor.

Q2 a) Substitute $x = \frac{1}{2}$ and show the result is 0:
$$f\left(\frac{1}{2}\right) = 2\left(\frac{1}{2}\right)^3 - \left(\frac{1}{2}\right)^2 - 8\left(\frac{1}{2}\right) + 4$$
$$= \frac{2}{8} - \frac{1}{4} - 4 + 4 = 0$$
So by the Factor Theorem, $(2x - 1)$ is a factor.

b) Substitute $x = \frac{2}{3}$ and show the result is 0:
$$f\left(\frac{2}{3}\right) = 3\left(\frac{2}{3}\right)^3 - 5\left(\frac{2}{3}\right)^2 - 16\left(\frac{2}{3}\right) + 12$$
$$= \frac{8}{9} - \frac{20}{9} - \frac{32}{3} + 12$$
$$= \frac{8}{9} - \frac{20}{9} - \frac{96}{9} + 12 = 0$$
So by the Factor Theorem, $(3x - 2)$ is a factor.

Q3 a) $f(3) = (3)^3 - 2(3)^2 - 5(3) + 6 = 27 - 18 - 15 + 6 = 0$
So by the Factor Theorem, $(x - 3)$ is a factor.

b) $1 - 2 - 5 + 6 = 0$
The coefficients add up to 0, so by the Factor Theorem, $(x - 1)$ is a factor.

Q4 a) $f(-4) = 3(-4)^3 - 5(-4)^2 - 58(-4) + 40$
$= -192 - 80 + 232 + 40 = 0$
So by the Factor Theorem, $(x + 4)$ is a factor.

b) $f\left(\frac{2}{3}\right) = 3\left(\frac{2}{3}\right)^3 - 5\left(\frac{2}{3}\right)^2 - 58\left(\frac{2}{3}\right) + 40$
$= \frac{8}{9} - \frac{20}{9} - \frac{116}{3} + 40 = -\frac{120}{3} + 40 = 0$
So by the Factor Theorem, $(3x - 2)$ is a factor.

Q5 $(x - 3)$ is a factor of $f(x) = qx^3 - 4x^2 - 7qx + 12$,
so $f(3) = 0$. Using the Factor Theorem in reverse:
$f(3) = q(3)^3 - 4(3)^2 - 7q(3) + 12$
$= 27q - 36 - 21q + 12 = 6q - 24$
$\Rightarrow 6q - 24 = 0$
$\quad\quad 6q = 24$
$\quad\quad\quad q = 4$
So $f(x) = 4x^3 - 4x^2 - 28x + 12$

Q6 $(x - 1)$ and $(x - 2)$ are factors, so using the Factor Theorem in reverse, $f(1) = 0$ and $f(2) = 0$.
$f(1) = (1)^3 + c(1)^2 + d(1) - 2 = 1 + c + d - 2 = 0$
$c + d = 1$ (equation 1)
$f(2) = (2)^3 + c(2)^2 + d(2) - 2 = 8 + 4c + 2d - 2 = 0$
$4c + 2d = -6$ (equation 2)
Rearrange (1) to get $d = 1 - c$, and sub into (2):
$\Rightarrow 4c + 2(1 - c) = -6$
$\quad 4c + 2 - 2c = -6$
$\quad\quad 2c = -8$
$\quad\quad\;\; c = -4$

Sub c into rearranged (1):
$d = 1 - c = 1 + 4 = 5$
So $f(x) = x^3 - 4x^2 + 5x - 2$

Exercise 4.4 — Factorising a cubic (when x isn't a factor)

Q1 a) x is a common factor, so you get:
$x(x^2 - 3x + 2) = x(x - 1)(x - 2)$

b) Adding the coefficients gives you -6, so $(x - 1)$ is not a factor. Using trial and error, $f(2) = 0$, so $(x - 2)$ is a factor. Factorise to get:
$(x - 2)(2x^2 + 7x + 3) = (x - 2)(x + 3)(2x + 1)$

c) Add the coefficients $(1 - 3 + 3 - 1)$ to get 0, so $(x - 1)$ is a factor. Factorise to get:
$(x - 1)(x^2 - 2x + 1) = (x - 1)^3$

d) Adding the coefficients gives you 2, so $(x - 1)$ is not a factor. Using trial and error, $f(2) = 0$, so $(x - 2)$ is a factor. Factorise to get:
$(x - 2)(x^2 - x - 2) = (x - 2)(x - 2)(x + 1)$

e) Adding the coefficients gives you 0, so $(x - 1)$ is a factor. Factorise to get:
$(x - 1)(x^2 - 2x - 35) = (x - 1)(x + 5)(x - 7)$

f) Adding the coefficients gives you 21, so $(x - 1)$ is not a factor. Using trial and error, $f(2) = 0$, so $(x - 2)$ is a factor. Factorise to get:
$(x - 2)(x^2 + 2x - 24) = (x - 2)(x - 4)(x + 6)$

Q2 a) Adding the coefficients gives you -3, so $(x - 1)$ is not a factor. Using trial and error, $f(-2) = 0$, so $(x + 2)$ is a factor. Factorise to get:
$(x + 2)(x^2 + 2x - 4)$
You're asked for the product of a linear factor and a quadratic factor, so you don't need to try to factorise the quadratic.

b) There is one solution at $x = -2$.
The quadratic doesn't factorise, so use the quadratic formula: $a = 1$, $b = 2$, $c = -4$
$$x = \frac{-b \pm \sqrt{b^2 - 4ac}}{2a} = \frac{-2 \pm \sqrt{2^2 - 4 \times 1 \times (-4)}}{2 \times 1}$$
$$= \frac{-2 \pm \sqrt{4 + 16}}{2} = \frac{-2 \pm \sqrt{20}}{2} = -1 \pm \sqrt{5}$$
So the solutions are $x = -2$, $x = -1 + \sqrt{5}$ and $x = -1 - \sqrt{5}$.

Q3 Add the coefficients $(1 - 1 - 3 + 3)$ to get 0, so $(x - 1)$ is a factor. Factorise to get:
$(x - 1)(x^2 - 3)$. So the roots are $x = 1$ and $x = \pm\sqrt{3}$.

Q4 $(3x - 1)(2x^2 + 13x + 6) = (3x - 1)(2x + 1)(x + 6)$

Q5 a) $(x - 5)$ is a factor, so $f(5) = 0$
$f(5) = (5)^3 - p(5)^2 + 17(5) - 10$
$= 125 - 25p + 85 - 10 = 200 - 25p$
$\Rightarrow 200 - 25p = 0$
$\quad\quad 200 = 25p$
$\quad\quad\quad p = 8$

b) $(x - 5)(x^2 - 3x + 2) = (x - 5)(x - 1)(x - 2)$

c) So the roots are $x = 5$, 1 and 2.

Q6 a) Adding the coefficients gives you 0, so $(x - 1)$ is a factor. Factorise to get:
$(x - 1)(3x^2 + 5x - 2) = (x - 1)(3x - 1)(x + 2)$

b) Adding the coefficients gives you 0, so $(x - 1)$ is a factor. Factorise to get:
$(x - 1)(5x^2 - 8x - 4) = (x - 1)(5x + 2)(x - 2)$

Q7 If $x = 2$ is a root, $f(2) = 0$:
$f(2) = 2(2)^3 - 2^2 - 2(2) - 8 = 16 - 4 - 4 - 8 = 0$
So $x = 2$ is a root, and $(x - 2)$ is a factor. Now factorise:
$(x - 2)(2x^2 + 3x + 4) = 0$.
The discriminant of the quadratic factor is $b^2 - 4ac$, which is $3^2 - 4 \times 2 \times 4 = 9 - 32 = -23$.
The discriminant is negative so the quadratic has no real roots. Hence the only real root of the cubic is $x = 2$.
You could have put the values of a, b and c into the quadratic formula here — you'd end up with a negative number inside the square root, which would mean the quadratic has no real roots.

Exercise 4.5 — Algebraic division

Q1 a)
$$x - 3 \overline{\smash{)}\begin{array}{l} x^2 + x - 12 \\ \overline{x^3 - 2x^2 - 15x + 36} \end{array}}$$
$-\underline{(x^3 - 3x^2)}$
$\quad\quad\quad x^2 - 15x$
$\quad\quad -\underline{(x^2 - 3x)}$
$\quad\quad\quad\quad\quad -12x + 36$
$\quad\quad\quad -\underline{(-12x + 36)}$
$\quad\quad\quad\quad\quad\quad\quad\quad 0$

Factorise the quadratic: $x^2 + x - 12 = (x - 3)(x + 4)$
So $x^3 - 2x^2 - 15x + 36 = (x - 3)(x - 3)(x + 4)$
$= (x - 3)^2(x + 4)$

b)

$$x + 2 \overline{)\, x^3 - x^2 - 11x - 10 \,} \quad \frac{x^2 - 3x - 5}{}$$

$$\underline{-(x^3 + 2x^2)}$$
$$-3x^2 - 11x$$
$$\underline{-(-3x^2 - 6x)}$$
$$-5x - 10$$
$$\underline{-(-5x - 10)}$$
$$0$$

The quadratic doesn't factorise,
so the full factorisation is:
$x^3 - x^2 - 11x - 10 = (x + 2)(x^2 - 3x - 5)$

c)

$$x - 2 \overline{)\, 2x^3 + 11x^2 - 23x - 14 \,} \quad \frac{2x^2 + 15x + 7}{}$$

$$\underline{-(2x^3 - 4x^2)}$$
$$15x^2 - 23x$$
$$\underline{-(15x^2 - 30x)}$$
$$7x - 14$$
$$\underline{-(7x - 14)}$$
$$0$$

Factorise the quadratic:
$2x^2 + 15x + 7 = (2x + 1)(x + 7)$
So $2x^3 + 11x^2 - 23x - 14 = (x - 2)(2x + 1)(x + 7)$

Q2 Add the coefficients $(1 - 5 + 4)$ to get 0, so $(x - 1)$
is a factor. Now factorise using long division:

$$x - 1 \overline{)\, x^3 + 0x^2 - 5x + 4 \,} \quad \frac{x^2 + x - 4}{}$$

$$\underline{-(x^3 - x^2)}$$
$$x^2 - 5x$$
$$\underline{-(x^2 - x)}$$
$$-4x + 4$$
$$\underline{-(-4x + 4)}$$
$$0$$

Finally, write the cubic as the product of a linear factor
and a quadratic factor: $(x^3 - 5x + 4) = (x - 1)(x^2 + x - 4)$

Q3

$$x - 2 \overline{)\, x^3 + 2x^2 - 7x - 2 \,} \quad \frac{x^2 + 4x + 1}{}$$

$$\underline{-(x^3 - 2x^2)}$$
$$4x^2 - 7x$$
$$\underline{-(4x^2 - 8x)}$$
$$x - 2$$
$$\underline{-(x - 2)}$$
$$0$$

So $f(x) = (x - 2)(x^2 + 4x + 1)$.

Q4 If $f(-2) = 0$ then $(x + 2)$ is a factor. Now factorise using
long division:

$$x + 2 \overline{)\, x^3 + 0x^2 - 7x - 6 \,} \quad \frac{x^2 - 2x - 3}{}$$

$$\underline{-(x^3 + 2x^2)}$$
$$-2x^2 - 7x$$
$$\underline{-(-2x^2 - 4x)}$$
$$-3x - 6$$
$$\underline{-(-3x - 6)}$$
$$0$$

Then factorise the quadratic:
$x^2 - 2x - 3 = (x - 3)(x + 1)$
So $f(x) = (x + 2)(x - 3)(x + 1)$
So the solutions to $f(x) = 0$ are $x = -2$, $x = 3$ and $x = -1$.

Chapter 5: Inequalities and Simultaneous Equations

1. Inequalities

Exercise 1.1 — Linear inequalities

Q1 **a)** $2x - 1 < x + 4 \Rightarrow x < 5$

b) $4 - 3x \geq 10 - 5x \Rightarrow 2x \geq 6 \Rightarrow x \geq 3$

c) $5x + 7 > 3x + 1 \Rightarrow 2x > -6 \Rightarrow x > -3$

d) $3 - 2x \leq 5x - 4 \Rightarrow -7x \leq -7 \Rightarrow x \geq 1$

e) $9 - x \geq 7x + 5 \Rightarrow -8x \geq -4 \Rightarrow x \leq \frac{1}{2}$

Q2 **a)** $2(x + 3) > 3(x + 2)$
$\Rightarrow 2x + 6 > 3x + 6 \Rightarrow -x > 0 \Rightarrow x < 0$
In set notation, this is $\{x : x < 0\}$

b) $5(1 + 3x) \leq 7 \Rightarrow 5 + 15x \leq 7 \Rightarrow 15x \leq 2 \Rightarrow x \leq \frac{2}{15}$
In set notation, this is $\left\{x : x \leq \frac{2}{15}\right\}$

Q3 **a)** $\frac{6 - 5x}{2} < \frac{4 - 8x}{3} \Rightarrow 3(6 - 5x) < 2(4 - 8x)$
$\Rightarrow 18 - 15x < 8 - 16x \Rightarrow x < -10$

b) $\frac{3x - 1}{4} \geq 2x \Rightarrow 3x - 1 \geq 8x \Rightarrow x \leq -\frac{1}{5}$

c) $\frac{x - 2}{2} - \frac{2x + 3}{3} < 7$
$\Rightarrow 3(x - 2) - 2(2x + 3) < 42$
$\Rightarrow 3x - 6 - 4x - 6 < 42 \Rightarrow -x < 54 \Rightarrow x > -54$

Q4 **a)** $-5 < 2x - 3 < 15 \Rightarrow -2 < 2x < 18 \Rightarrow -1 < x < 9$
In set notation, this is either $\{x : -1 < x < 9\}$
or $\{x : x > -1\} \cap \{x : x < 9\}$

b) $-5 \leq 4 - 3x < 19$
$\Rightarrow -9 \leq -3x < 15 \Rightarrow 3 \geq x > -5 \Rightarrow -5 < x \leq 3$
In set notation, this is either $\{x : -5 < x \leq 3\}$
or $\{x : x > -5\} \cap \{x : x \leq 3\}$

Q5 **a)** $2x \geq 3 - x \Rightarrow 3x \geq 3 \Rightarrow x \geq 1$

b) $5x - 1 < 3x + 5 \Rightarrow 2x < 6 \Rightarrow x < 3$

c) $2x + 1 \geq 3x + 2 \Rightarrow -x \geq 1 \Rightarrow x \leq -1$

d) $3(x - 3) \leq 5(x - 1) \Rightarrow 3x - 9 \leq 5x - 5$
$\Rightarrow -2x \leq 4 \Rightarrow x \geq -2$

e) $9 - x \leq 3 - 4x \Rightarrow 3x \leq -6 \Rightarrow x \leq -2$

f) $\dfrac{2(x-3)}{3} + 1 < \dfrac{2x-1}{2}$

$\Rightarrow 4(x-3) + 6 < 3(2x-1)$

$\Rightarrow 4x - 12 + 6 < 6x - 3 \Rightarrow -2x < 3 \Rightarrow x > -\dfrac{3}{2}$

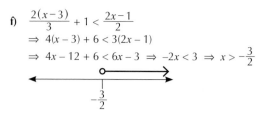

Q6 a) $7 \leq 3x - 2 < 16 \Rightarrow 9 \leq 3x < 18 \Rightarrow 3 \leq x < 6$

b)

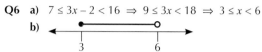

Q7 $4 - 2x < 10 \Rightarrow -2x < 6 \Rightarrow x > -3$

$3x - 1 < x + 7 \Rightarrow 2x < 8 \Rightarrow x < 4$

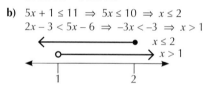

The answer will be the intersection of these solutions, i.e. $\{x : x < 4\} \cap \{x : x > -3\}$

The solutions overlap between -3 and 4, so this is the same as $\{x : -3 < x < 4\}$

Q8 a) $2x \geq 3x - 5 \Rightarrow -x \geq -5 \Rightarrow x \leq 5$

$3x - 2 \geq x - 6 \Rightarrow 2x \geq -4 \Rightarrow x \geq -2$

Solution: $-2 \leq x \leq 5$

b) $5x + 1 \leq 11 \Rightarrow 5x \leq 10 \Rightarrow x \leq 2$

$2x - 3 < 5x - 6 \Rightarrow -3x < -3 \Rightarrow x > 1$

Solution: $1 < x \leq 2$

c) $2x - 1 \leq 3x - 5 \Rightarrow -x \leq -4 \Rightarrow x \geq 4$

$5x - 6 > x + 22 \Rightarrow 4x > 28 \Rightarrow x > 7$

Solution: $x > 7$

Only these values satisfy both of the inequalities.

d) $3x + 5 < x + 1 \Rightarrow 2x < -4 \Rightarrow x < -2$

$6x - 1 \geq 3x + 5 \Rightarrow 3x \geq 6 \Rightarrow x \geq 2$

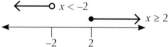

There is no solution that satisfies both inequalities.
The solutions don't overlap on the number line.

Exercise 1.2 — Quadratic inequalities

Q1 a) $-3 < x < 1$

b) $x < 0$ or $x > 4$

c) $2x^2 \geq 5 - 9x \Rightarrow 2x^2 + 9x - 5 \geq 0$

$\Rightarrow x \leq -5$ or $x \geq \dfrac{1}{2}$

d) $x < 1 - \sqrt{6}$ or $x > 1 + \sqrt{6}$

Q2 a) Solve the equation $x^2 = 4$ to find the x-intercepts:

$x^2 = 4 \Rightarrow x^2 - 4 = 0 \Rightarrow (x-2)(x+2) = 0$

$x = -2$ or $x = 2$

Solution: $x^2 \leq 4 \Rightarrow x^2 - 4 \leq 0 \Rightarrow -2 \leq x \leq 2$

In set notation, this is either $\{x : -2 \leq x \leq 2\}$ or $\{x : x \geq -2\} \cap \{x : x \leq 2\}$

b) $13x = 3x^2 + 4 \Rightarrow -3x^2 + 13x - 4 = 0$

$\Rightarrow 3x^2 - 13x + 4 = 0 \Rightarrow (3x - 1)(x - 4) = 0$

$\Rightarrow x = \dfrac{1}{3}$ or $x = 4$

Solution: $13x < 3x^2 + 4 \Rightarrow -3x^2 + 13x - 4 < 0$

$\Rightarrow x < \dfrac{1}{3}$ or $x > 4$

In set notation, this is $\left\{x : x < \dfrac{1}{3}\right\} \cup \{x : x > 4\}$

c) $x^2 + 4 = 6x \Rightarrow x^2 - 6x + 4 = 0$

$\Rightarrow x = \dfrac{6 \pm \sqrt{36-16}}{2} = \dfrac{6 \pm \sqrt{20}}{2} = \dfrac{6 \pm 2\sqrt{5}}{2}$

$\Rightarrow x = 3 \pm \sqrt{5}$

Solution: $x^2 + 4 < 6x \Rightarrow x^2 - 6x + 4 < 0$

$\Rightarrow 3 - \sqrt{5} < x < 3 + \sqrt{5}$

In set notation, this is either $\{x : 3 - \sqrt{5} < x < 3 + \sqrt{5}\}$ or $\{x : x > 3 - \sqrt{5}\} \cap \{x : x < 3 + \sqrt{5}\}$

Q3 a) $x^2 + 5x - 6 = 0 \Rightarrow (x + 6)(x - 1) = 0$

$\Rightarrow x = -6$ or $x = 1$

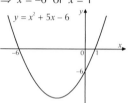

$x^2 + 5x - 6 \geq 0 \Rightarrow x \leq -6$ or $x \geq 1$

b) $x^2 - 3x + 2 = 0 \Rightarrow (x - 1)(x - 2) = 0$

$\Rightarrow x = 1$ or $x = 2$

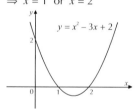

$x^2 - 3x + 2 < 0 \Rightarrow 1 < x < 2$

c) $6 - 5x = 6x^2 \Rightarrow -6x^2 - 5x + 6 = 0$

$\Rightarrow 6x^2 + 5x - 6 = 0 \Rightarrow (3x - 2)(2x + 3) = 0$

$\Rightarrow x = \dfrac{2}{3}$ or $x = -\dfrac{3}{2}$

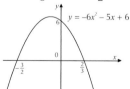

$6 - 5x > 6x^2 \Rightarrow -6x^2 - 5x + 6 > 0 \Rightarrow -\dfrac{3}{2} < x < \dfrac{2}{3}$

You could have rearranged the inequality into $6x^2 + 5x - 6 < 0$ and sketched the corresponding graph. You'd get the same final answer, but the graph would be the other way up.

d) $x^2 - 5x + 24 = 5x + 3 \Rightarrow x^2 - 10x + 21 = 0$
$\Rightarrow (x - 3)(x - 7) = 0 \Rightarrow x = 3$ or $x = 7$

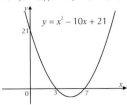

$x^2 - 5x + 24 \leq 5x + 3 \Rightarrow x^2 - 10x + 21 \leq 0$
$\Rightarrow 3 \leq x \leq 7$

e) $36 - 4x^2 = 0 \Rightarrow 9 - x^2 = 0$
$\Rightarrow (3 - x)(3 + x) = 0 \Rightarrow x = \pm 3$

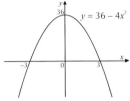

$36 - 4x^2 \leq 0 \Rightarrow x \leq -3$ or $x \geq 3$

f) $x^2 - 6x + 3 = 0 \Rightarrow x = \dfrac{6 \pm \sqrt{36 - 12}}{2}$
$\Rightarrow x = \dfrac{6 \pm \sqrt{24}}{2} = \dfrac{6 \pm 2\sqrt{6}}{2} = 3 \pm \sqrt{6}$

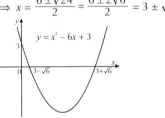

$x^2 - 6x + 3 > 0 \Rightarrow x < 3 - \sqrt{6}$ or $x > 3 + \sqrt{6}$

g) $x^2 - x + 3 = 0 \Rightarrow x = \dfrac{1 \pm \sqrt{1 - 12}}{2}$
$\Rightarrow$ no roots ($\sqrt{-11}$ is not real)
so the graph doesn't cross the x-axis.

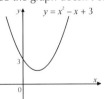

$x^2 - x + 3 > 0 \Rightarrow x$ can take any real value

h) $6 = 5x^2 + 13x \Rightarrow -5x^2 - 13x + 6 = 0$
$\Rightarrow 5x^2 + 13x - 6 = 0 \Rightarrow (5x - 2)(x + 3) = 0$
$\Rightarrow x = \dfrac{2}{5}$ or $x = -3$

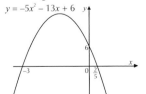

$6 \geq 5x^2 + 13x$
$\Rightarrow -5x^2 - 13x + 6 \geq 0$
$\Rightarrow -3 \leq x \leq \dfrac{2}{5}$

Again, you might have rearranged the inequality differently and ended up with the graph the other way up.

Q4 a) $\dfrac{1}{x} > 5 \Rightarrow x > 5x^2 \Rightarrow 5x^2 - x < 0 \Rightarrow x(5x - 1) < 0$
$\Rightarrow 0 < x < \dfrac{1}{5}$, or in set notation, $\{x : 0 < x < \dfrac{1}{5}\}$

b) $7 > \dfrac{3}{x} \Rightarrow 7x^2 > 3x \Rightarrow 7x^2 - 3x > 0$
$\Rightarrow x(7x - 3) > 0 \Rightarrow x < 0$ or $x > \dfrac{3}{7}$,
or in set notation, $\{x : x < 0\} \cup \{x : x > \dfrac{3}{7}\}$

Q5 The area of the office will be $(x - 9)(x - 6)$ m², so use this to form an inequality for the necessary floor space:
$(x - 9)(x - 6) \geq 28 \Rightarrow x^2 - 15x + 54 \geq 28$
$\Rightarrow x^2 - 15x + 26 \geq 0$
Find the x-intercepts of the graph:
$x^2 - 15x + 26 = 0 \Rightarrow (x - 2)(x - 13) = 0$
$\Rightarrow x = 2$ and $x = 13$

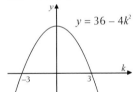

$x^2 - 15x + 26 \geq 0 \Rightarrow x \leq 2$ or $x \geq 13$
But $x \leq 2$ would mean that the sides of the office would have negative lengths, so the only possible values of x are $x \geq 13$ metres.

Q6 a) $kx^2 - 6x + k = 0 \Rightarrow a = k, b = -6, c = k$
$b^2 - 4ac = (-6)^2 - (4 \times k \times k) = 36 - 4k^2$
The original equation has two distinct real solutions, so the discriminant must be > 0. So $36 - 4k^2 > 0$.
Factorise the quadratic: $36 - 4k^2 = 4(3 + k)(3 - k)$
So the graph is n-shaped and crosses the k-axis at $k = 3$ and $k = -3$.

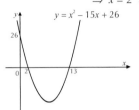

Solution: $-3 < k < 3$

b) $x^2 - kx + k = 0 \Rightarrow a = 1, b = -k, c = k$
$b^2 - 4ac = (-k)^2 - (4 \times 1 \times k) = k^2 - 4k$
The original equation has no real solutions, so the discriminant must be < 0. So $k^2 - 4k < 0$
Factorise the quadratic: $k^2 - 4k = k(k - 4)$
So the graph is u-shaped and crosses the k-axis at $k = 0$ and $k = 4$.

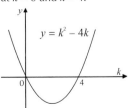

Solution: $\{k : 0 < k < 4\}$
or $\{k : k > 0\} \cap \{k : k < 4\}$

Q7 $4(3 - x) \geq 13 - 5x \Rightarrow 12 - 4x \geq 13 - 5x \Rightarrow x \geq 1$
$7x + 6 \geq 3x^2 \Rightarrow -3x^2 + 7x + 6 \geq 0$
$-3x^2 + 7x + 6 = 0 \Rightarrow 3x^2 - 7x - 6 = 0$
$\Rightarrow (3x + 2)(x - 3) = 0$
$\Rightarrow x = -\dfrac{2}{3}$ or $x = 3$

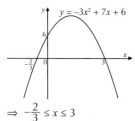

$\Rightarrow -\dfrac{2}{3} \le x \le 3$

So, for both inequalities:

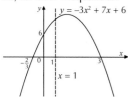

Solution that satisfies both inequalities: $1 \le x \le 3$

Your graphs might be the other way up if you rearranged the inequality differently at the start.

Exercise 1.3 — Graphing inequalities

Q1 **a)** Write as equations and rearrange:
$y = -x + 5$ (dotted), $y = -2x + 4$ (solid),
$y = -\dfrac{1}{2}x + 3$ (dotted)

Try (0, 0) in each inequality:
$x + y < 5 \Rightarrow 0 < 5$ — this is true so shade this side.
$2x + y \ge 4 \Rightarrow 0 \ge 4$ — this is false
so shade the other side.
$x + 2y > 6 \Rightarrow 0 > 6$ — this is false
so shade the other side.

So the final region is:

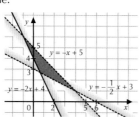

b) Write as equations and rearrange:
$x = 4$ (solid), $y = 7$ (solid), $y = -x + 4$ (dotted)

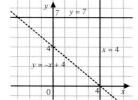

Try (0, 0) in each inequality:
$x \le 4 \Rightarrow 0 \le 4$ — this is true so shade this side.
$y \le 7 \Rightarrow 0 \le 7$ — this is true so shade this side.
$x + y > 4 \Rightarrow 0 > 4$ — this is false
so shade the other side.

So the final region is:

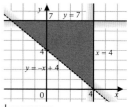

c) Write as equations and rearrange:
$y = x^2$ (dotted), $y = x + 3$ (solid)

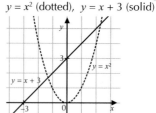

You can't use (0, 0) as it lies on one of the lines,
so try (0, 1) in each inequality:
$y > x^2 \Rightarrow 1 > 0$ — this is true so shade this side.
$x - y \ge -3 \Rightarrow -1 \ge -3$ — this is true
so shade this side.

So the final region is:

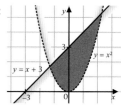

d) Write as equations and rearrange:
$y = x^2 + 2$ (solid), $y = 2x^2 - 2$ (dotted)

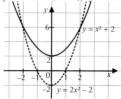

Try (0, 0) in each inequality:
$y - 2 \le x^2 \Rightarrow -2 \le 0$ — this is true so shade this side.
$2x^2 - y < 2 \Rightarrow 0 < 2$ — this is true so shade this side.

So the final region is:

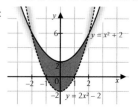

Q2 *A*: Write as equations and rearrange:
$y = 6 - \dfrac{1}{2}x$, $y = \dfrac{3}{2}x + 2$, $y = 2$

Then plot these lines (all solid):

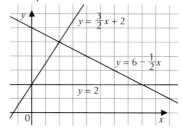

Try (0, 0) in each inequality:
$x + 2y \le 12 \Rightarrow 0 \le 12$ — this is true
so shade the other side.
$2y - 3x \le 4 \Rightarrow 0 \le 4$ — this is true
so shade the other side.
$y \ge 2 \Rightarrow 0 \ge 2$ — this is false so shade this side.

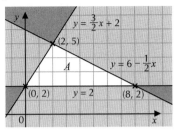

B: Write as equations and rearrange:
$x = 3, \ y = 2x - 9, \ y = 5 - \frac{1}{3}x$
Then plot these lines (all solid):

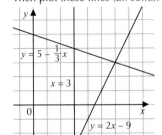

Try (0, 0) in each inequality:
$x \ge 3 \Rightarrow 0 \ge 3$
This is false so shade this side.
$2x \le y + 9 \Rightarrow 0 \le 9$
This is true so shade the other side.
$x + 3y \le 15 \Rightarrow 0 \le 15$
This is true so shade the other side.

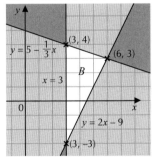

The coordinates of the vertices of triangles A and B can be read off the graphs. In order to decide which region is larger, calculate the area of each triangle.
You can also find the vertices by equating the lines to find their points of intersection.

A has base $8 - 0 = 8$ and height $5 - 2 = 3$
$\Rightarrow$ Area $A = \frac{1}{2} \times 8 \times 3 = 12$
B has base $4 - (-3) = 7$ and height $6 - 3 = 3$
$\Rightarrow$ Area $B = \frac{1}{2} \times 7 \times 3 = 10.5$
So region A is larger.

Q3 a) $3x + y \le 42$

b) Write as equations and rearrange:
$y = 12 - \frac{1}{2}x, \ y = 42 - 3x$
Plotting the graphs and testing the point (1, 1) in each inequality gives the region labelled R:

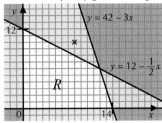

c) Checking the point (8, 10) on the graph (marked in b)) shows that it isn't in the possible region.
Test $x = 8$ and $y = 10$ in both inequalities:
Flour: $x + 2y = 8 + 20 = 28 > 24$
Eggs: $3x + y = 24 + 10 = 34 \le 42$
So the bakery has enough eggs, but not enough flour to meet the order.

2. Simultaneous Equations

Exercise 2.1 — Simultaneous equations — both linear

Q1 a) ① $2x - 3y = 3$
② $x + 3y = 6$
①+② $3x = 9 \Rightarrow x = 3$
$x = 3$ in ② $3 + 3y = 6 \Rightarrow 3y = 3 \Rightarrow y = 1$
So the solution is $x = 3, y = 1$

b) ① $3x + 2y = 7$
② $7x - y = -12$
②×2 $14x - 2y = -24$ ③
①+③ $17x = -17 \Rightarrow x = -1$
$x = -1$ in ① $-3 + 2y = 7 \Rightarrow 2y = 10 \Rightarrow y = 5$
So the solution is $x = -1, y = 5$

c) ① $4x + 3y = -4$
② $6x - 4y = 11$
①×3 $12x + 9y = -12$ ③
②×2 $12x - 8y = 22$ ④
③−④ $17y = -34 \Rightarrow y = -2$
$y = -2$ in ② $6x + 8 = 11 \Rightarrow 6x = 3 \Rightarrow x = \frac{1}{2}$
So the solution is $x = \frac{1}{2}, y = -2$

d) ① $7x - 6y = 4$
② $11x + 9y = -6$
①×3 $21x - 18y = 12$ ③
②×2 $22x + 18y = -12$ ④
③+④ $43x = 0 \Rightarrow x = 0$
$x = 0$ in ② $0 + 9y = -6 \Rightarrow y = -\frac{6}{9} = -\frac{2}{3}$
So the solution is $x = 0, y = -\frac{2}{3}$

e) Rearrange ① $6x + 2y = 8$
     Rearrange ② $4x + 3y = -3$
     ① × 2 $12x + 4y = 16$ ③
     ② × 3 $12x + 9y = -9$ ④
     ③ − ④ $-5y = 25 \Rightarrow y = -5$
     $y = -5$ in ② $4x - 15 = -3 \Rightarrow 4x = 12 \Rightarrow x = 3$
     So the solution is $x = 3$, $y = -5$

f) Rearrange ① $2x + 18y = 21$
     Rearrange ② $-3x - 14y = 14$
     ① × 3 $6x + 54y = 63$ ③
     ② × 2 $-6x - 28y = 28$ ④
     ③ + ④ $26y = 91 \Rightarrow y = \frac{7}{2}$
     $y = \frac{7}{2}$ in ① $2x + 63 = 21 \Rightarrow 2x = -42$
                             $\Rightarrow x = -21$
     So the solution is $x = -21$, $y = \frac{7}{2}$

g) ① $2x + 16y = 10$
     Rearrange ② $3x + 64y = 5$
     ① × 4 $8x + 64y = 40$ ③
     ② − ③ $-5x = -35 \Rightarrow x = 7$
     $x = 7$ in ① $14 + 16y = 10 \Rightarrow 16y = -4$
                             $\Rightarrow y = -\frac{1}{4}$
     So the solution is $x = 7$, $y = -\frac{1}{4}$

Q2 a) ① $y = 2x - 3$
     ② $y = \frac{1}{2}x + 3$
     ② × 4 $4y = 2x + 12$ ③
     ① − ③ $-3y = -15 \Rightarrow y = 5$
     $y = 5$ in ① $5 = 2x - 3 \Rightarrow 8 = 2x \Rightarrow x = 4$
     So they intersect at $(4, 5)$

b) ① $y = -\frac{2}{3}x + 7$
     ② $y = \frac{1}{2}x + \frac{21}{2}$
     ① × 3 $3y = -2x + 21$ ③
     ② × 4 $4y = 2x + 42$ ④
     ③ + ④ $7y = 63 \Rightarrow y = 9$
     $y = 9$ in ① $9 = -\frac{2}{3}x + 7$
                    $2 = -\frac{2}{3}x \Rightarrow x = -3$
     So they intersect at $(-3, 9)$

c) Rearrange ① $x + 2y = -5$
     Rearrange ② $3x - 5y = 7$
     ① × 3 $3x + 6y = -15$ ③
     ② − ③ $-11y = 22 \Rightarrow y = -2$
     $y = -2$ in ① $x - 4 = -5 \Rightarrow x = -1$
     So they intersect at $(-1, -2)$

d) ① $2x - 3y = 7$
     ② $5x - \frac{15}{2}y = 9$
     ① × 5 $10x - 15y = 35$ ③
     ② × 2 $10x - 15y = 18$ ④
     ③ − ④ $0 = 17$
     This is not possible — so these lines do not intersect.
     The lines are actually parallel.

e) Rearrange ① $8x + 3y = 10$
     Rearrange ② $6x + 9y = 3$
     ① × 3 $24x + 9y = 30$ ③
     ② − ③ $-18x = -27 \Rightarrow x = \frac{3}{2}$
     $x = \frac{3}{2}$ in ② $9 + 9y = 3$
                     $9y = -6 \Rightarrow y = -\frac{2}{3}$
     So they intersect at $\left(\frac{3}{2}, -\frac{2}{3}\right)$

f) ① $7x - 5y = 15$
     Rearrange ② $2x - 3y = 9$
     ① × 2 $14x - 10y = 30$ ③
     ② × 7 $14x - 21y = 63$ ④
     ③ − ④ $11y = -33 \Rightarrow y = -3$
     $y = -3$ in ② $2x + 9 = 9 \Rightarrow 2x = 0 \Rightarrow x = 0$
     So they intersect at $(0, -3)$

Q3 There will be a signpost at the point of intersection of each pair of straight lines:

A and B: ① $5x + 2y = -11$
          Rearrange ② $2x - y = 1$
          ② × 2 $4x - 2y = 2$ ③
          ① + ③ $9x = -9 \Rightarrow x = -1$
          $x = -1$ in ② $-2 - y = 1 \Rightarrow y = -3$
          So they intersect at $(-1, -3)$

B and C: Rearrange ① $2x - y = 1$
          Rearrange ② $-x + 5y = 13$
          ② × 2 $-2x + 10y = 26$ ③
          ① + ③ $9y = 27 \Rightarrow y = 3$
          $y = 3$ in ① $2x - 3 = 1 \Rightarrow 2x = 4$
                        $\Rightarrow x = 2$
          So they intersect at $(2, 3)$

A and C: ① $5x + 2y = -11$
          Rearrange ② $-x + 5y = 13$
          ② × 5 $-5x + 25y = 65$ ③
          ① + ③ $27y = 54 \Rightarrow y = 2$
          $y = 2$ in ② $-x + 10 = 13$
                      $\Rightarrow -x = 3 \Rightarrow x = -3$
          So they intersect at $(-3, 2)$

So the three signposts are at $(-1, -3)$, $(2, 3)$ and $(-3, 2)$.

Exercise 2.2 — Simultaneous equations — if one is not linear

Q1 a) ① $y = 4x + 3$
     ② $2y - 3x = 1$
     Sub ① in ② $2(4x + 3) - 3x = 1$
                   $8x + 6 - 3x = 1$
                          $5x = -5 \Rightarrow x = -1$
     $x = -1$ in ① $y = 4 \times -1 + 3 = -1$
     So the solution is $x = -1$, $y = -1$

b) ① $\qquad 5x + 2y = 16$

Rearrange ② $\quad x = 2y - 4$

Sub ② in ① $\quad 5(2y - 4) + 2y = 16$
$$12y - 20 = 16$$
$$12y = 36 \Rightarrow y = 3$$

$y = 3$ in ② $\quad x = 2 \times 3 - 4 = 2$

So the solution is $x = 2$, $y = 3$

Q2 a) ① $\quad y = 2x + 5$

② $\quad y = x^2 - x + 1$

Sub ① in ② $\quad 2x + 5 = x^2 - x + 1$
$$x^2 - 3x - 4 = 0$$
$$(x - 4)(x + 1) = 0 \Rightarrow x = 4 \text{ or } x = -1$$

From ①, when $x = 4$, $\quad y = 8 + 5 = 13$, and
when $x = -1$, $\quad y = -2 + 5 = 3$

So $x = 4$, $y = 13$ or $x = -1$, $y = 3$

b) ① $\quad y = 2x^2 - 3$

② $\quad y = 3x + 2$

Sub ② in ① $\quad 3x + 2 = 2x^2 - 3$
$$2x^2 - 3x - 5 = 0$$
$$(2x - 5)(x + 1) = 0 \Rightarrow x = \frac{5}{2} \text{ or } x = -1$$

From ②, when $x = \frac{5}{2}$, $\quad y = \frac{15}{2} + 2 = \frac{19}{2}$, and
when $x = -1$, $\quad y = -3 + 2 = -1$

So $x = \frac{5}{2}$, $y = \frac{19}{2}$ or $x = -1$, $y = -1$

c) ① $\qquad 2x^2 - xy = 6$

Rearrange ② $\quad y = 3x - 7$

Sub ② in ① $\quad 2x^2 - x(3x - 7) = 6$
$$2x^2 - 3x^2 + 7x - 6 = 0$$
$$-x^2 + 7x - 6 = 0$$
$$x^2 - 7x + 6 = 0$$
$$(x - 6)(x - 1) = 0$$
$$\Rightarrow x = 6 \text{ or } x = 1$$

From ②, when $x = 6$, $\quad y = 18 - 7 = 11$, and
when $x = 1$, $\quad y = 3 - 7 = -4$

So $x = 6$, $y = 11$ or $x = 1$, $y = -4$

d) ① $\qquad xy = 6$

Rearrange ② $\quad 2y + 4 = x$

Sub ② in ① $\quad y(2y + 4) = 6$
$$2y^2 + 4y - 6 = 0$$
$$y^2 + 2y - 3 = 0$$
$$(y + 3)(y - 1) = 0$$
$$\Rightarrow y = -3 \text{ or } y = 1$$

From ②, when $y = -3$, $\quad x = -6 + 4 = -2$, and
when $y = 1$, $\quad x = 2 + 4 = 6$

So $x = -2$, $y = -3$ or $x = 6$, $y = 1$

e) ① $\quad y = x^2 - 2x - 3$

Rearrange ② $\quad y = -x - 8$

Sub ② in ① $\quad -x - 8 = x^2 - 2x - 3$
$$x^2 - x + 5 = 0$$

Check discriminant: $b^2 - 4ac = 1 - 20 = -19$,
which is negative so there are no real roots.

So there are no solutions for the simultaneous equations.

f) ① $\quad y = 2x^2 - 3x + 5$

Rearrange ② $\quad 5x - 3 = y$

Sub ② in ① $\quad 5x - 3 = 2x^2 - 3x + 5$
$$2x^2 - 8x + 8 = 0$$
$$x^2 - 4x + 4 = 0$$
$$(x - 2)^2 = 0 \Rightarrow x = 2$$

From ②, when $x = 2$, $y = 10 - 3 = 7$

So $x = 2$, $y = 7$

There is only one solution here, so the straight line is a tangent to the curve.

g) ① $\qquad 2x^2 + 3y^2 + 18x = 347$

Rearrange ② $\quad y = -4x + 7$

Sub ② in ① $\quad 2x^2 + 3(-4x + 7)^2 + 18x = 347$
$$2x^2 + 3(16x^2 - 56x + 49) + 18x - 347 = 0$$
$$2x^2 + 48x^2 - 168x + 147 + 18x - 347 = 0$$
$$50x^2 - 150x - 200 = 0$$
$$x^2 - 3x - 4 = 0$$
$$(x + 1)(x - 4) = 0 \Rightarrow x = -1 \text{ or } x = 4$$

From ②, when $x = -1$, $\quad y = 4 + 7 = 11$, and
when $x = 4$, $\quad y = -16 + 7 = -9$

So $x = -1$, $y = 11$ or $x = 4$, $y = -9$

Q3 a) ① $\quad y = \frac{1}{2}x^2 + 4x - 8$

② $\quad y = 4 + \frac{3}{2}x$

Sub ② in ① $\quad 4 + \frac{3}{2}x = \frac{1}{2}x^2 + 4x - 8$
$$8 + 3x = x^2 + 8x - 16$$
$$0 = x^2 + 5x - 24$$
$$(x + 8)(x - 3) = 0 \Rightarrow x = -8 \text{ or } x = 3$$

From ②, when $x = -8$, $\quad y = 4 - 12 = -8$, and
when $x = 3$, $\quad y = 4 + \frac{9}{2} = \frac{17}{2}$

So they intersect at $(-8, -8)$ and $\left(3, \frac{17}{2}\right)$

b) ① $\qquad y = 2x^2 + x - 6$

Rearrange ② $\quad y = 5x + 10$

Sub ② in ① $\quad 2x^2 + x - 6 = 5x + 10$
$$2x^2 - 4x - 16 = 0$$
$$x^2 - 2x - 8 = 0$$
$$(x - 4)(x + 2) = 0 \Rightarrow x = 4 \text{ or } x = -2$$

From ②, when $x = 4$, $\quad y = 20 + 10 = 30$, and
when $x = -2$, $\quad y = -10 + 10 = 0$

So they intersect at $(4, 30)$ and $(-2, 0)$

c) ① $\qquad x^2 + y^2 = 50$

Rearrange ② $\quad x = -2y + 5$

Sub ② in ① $\quad (-2y + 5)^2 + y^2 = 50$
$$4y^2 - 20y + 25 + y^2 - 50 = 0$$
$$5y^2 - 20y - 25 = 0$$
$$y^2 - 4y - 5 = 0$$
$$(y - 5)(y + 1) = 0 \Rightarrow y = 5 \text{ or } y = -1$$

From ②, when $y = 5$, $\quad x = -10 + 5 = -5$, and
when $y = -1$, $\quad x = 2 + 5 = 7$

So they intersect at $(-5, 5)$ and $(7, -1)$

d) ① $\qquad 2x^2 - y + 3x + 1 = 0$

Rearrange ② $\quad y = x + 5$

Sub ② in ① $\quad 2x^2 - (x + 5) + 3x + 1 = 0$
$$2x^2 + 2x - 4 = 0$$
$$x^2 + x - 2 = 0$$
$$(x + 2)(x - 1) = 0 \Rightarrow x = -2 \text{ or } x = 1$$

From ②, when $x = -2$, $\quad y = -2 + 5 = 3$, and
when $x = 1$, $\quad y = 1 + 5 = 6$

So they intersect at $(-2, 3)$ and $(1, 6)$

Q4 a) ① $x^2 + y^2 = 10$

Rearrange ② $x = 3y - 10$

Sub ② in ① $(3y - 10)^2 + y^2 = 10$

$9y^2 - 60y + 100 + y^2 - 10 = 0$

$10y^2 - 60y + 90 = 0$

$y^2 - 6y + 9 = 0$

$(y - 3)^2 = 0 \Rightarrow y = 3$

From ②, when $y = 3$, $x = 9 - 10 = -1$

So $x = -1$, $y = 3$.

b) $x^2 + y^2 = 10$ is a circle and $x - 3y + 10 = 0$ is a straight line. Part a) tells us that they intersect at a single point, so the line must actually be a tangent to the circle.

Q5 a) ① $y = x^2 + 6x - 7$

② $y = 2x - 3$

Sub ② in ① $2x - 3 = x^2 + 6x - 7$

$x^2 + 4x - 4 = 0$

So $b^2 - 4ac = 16 + 16 = 32 > 0$

So they will intersect at two points.

b) ① $3x^2 + 4y^2 + 6x = 9$

Rearrange ② $x = 3 - 2y$

Sub ② in ① $3(3 - 2y)^2 + 4y^2 + 6(3 - 2y) = 9$

$27 - 36y + 12y^2 + 4y^2 + 18 - 12y - 9 = 0$

$16y^2 - 48y + 36 = 0$

$4y^2 - 12y + 9 = 0$

Now $b^2 - 4ac = 144 - 144 = 0$

So they will intersect only once —

② is a tangent to the curve ①.

You could have rearranged differently to get an equation in terms of x — you would still get a discriminant of O.

c) ① $xy + 2x - y = 8$

Rearrange ② $x = 1 - y$

Sub ② in ① $(1 - y)y + 2(1 - y) - y = 8$

$y - y^2 + 2 - 2y - y = 8$

$-y^2 - 2y - 6 = 0$

$y^2 + 2y + 6 = 0$

So $b^2 - 4ac = 4 - 24 = -20 < 0$

So the graphs will not intersect.

Chapter 6: Coordinate Geometry, Graphs and Circles

1. The Equation of a Straight Line

Exercise 1.1 — $y - y_1 = m(x - x_1)$ and $y = mx + c$

Q1 a) gradient = -4, y-intercept = $(0, 11)$

b) gradient = -1, y-intercept = $(0, 4)$

c) gradient = 1.7, y-intercept = $(0, -2.3)$

Q2 a) $y = -3x + 2$

b) $y = 5x - 3$

c) $y = \frac{1}{2}x + 6$

d) $y = 0.8x + 1.2$

Q3 a) $c = 8$

$(x_1, y_1) = (-4, 0)$, $(x_2, y_2) = (0, 8)$

$m = \frac{8 - 0}{0 - (-4)} = \frac{8}{4} = 2$

$\Rightarrow y = 2x + 8$

b) $c = -5$

$(x_1, y_1) = (-2, 11)$, $(x_2, y_2) = (0, -5)$

$m = \frac{-5 - 11}{0 - (-2)} = \frac{-16}{2} = -8$

$\Rightarrow y = -8x - 5$

Q4 a) $(x_1, y_1) = (4, 1)$, $(x_2, y_2) = (0, -3)$

$m = \frac{-3 - 1}{0 - 4} = \frac{-4}{-4} = 1$

(i) $y - 1 = 1(x - 4)$

$\Rightarrow y - 1 = x - 4$

(ii) $y = x - 3$

b) $(x_1, y_1) = (12, -3)$, $(x_2, y_2) = (14, 1)$

$m = \frac{1 - (-3)}{14 - 12} = \frac{4}{2} = 2$

(i) $y - (-3) = 2(x - 12)$

$\Rightarrow y + 3 = 2(x - 12)$

(ii) $y = 2x - 27$

c) $(x_1, y_1) = (5, 7)$, $(x_2, y_2) = (-2, 5)$

$m = \frac{5 - 7}{-2 - 5} = \frac{-2}{-7} = \frac{2}{7}$

(i) $y - 7 = \frac{2}{7}(x - 5)$

(ii) $y = \frac{2}{7}x + \frac{39}{7}$

d) $(x_1, y_1) = (-3, 6)$, $(x_2, y_2) = (4, -2)$

$m = \frac{-2 - 6}{4 - (-3)} = -\frac{8}{7}$

(i) $y - 6 = -\frac{8}{7}(x - (-3))$

$\Rightarrow y - 6 = -\frac{8}{7}(x + 3)$

(ii) $y = -\frac{8}{7}x + \frac{18}{7}$

Q5 $y = mx + c$

$\Rightarrow -3 = \frac{1}{4} \times (-4) + c$

$\Rightarrow -3 = -1 + c \Rightarrow c = -2$

$\Rightarrow y = \frac{1}{4}x - 2$

Q6 Find the equation of the line first.

$m = 3$, find c using the point $(2, -7)$ on the line:

$y = mx + c$

$\Rightarrow -7 = 3 \times 2 + c$

$\Rightarrow -7 = 6 + c \Rightarrow c = -13 \Rightarrow y = 3x - 13$

The points a), c) and e) lie on the line.

Sub in the x value from each point — if the resulting value for y matches the value of y in the original point, then the point lies on that line.

Q7 a) The gradient (m) is given as 32. To find c, substitute in the conditions $t = 0$ and $d = 0$:

$d = 32t + c$

$0 = 32(0) + c$

$c = 0$

So the equation is $d = 32t$.

b) Solve the equation where $d = 9.6$:

$9.6 = 32t$

$t = 9.6 \div 32 = 0.3$ hours

$0.3 \times 60 = 18$ minutes

c) Some possible answers include:
- It is unrealistic that the car would travel at exactly the same speed for any length of time — it would probably vary slightly, which would make the model less accurate.
- In practice, external factors would probably affect the speed of the car during its journey, such as bends in the road, or other vehicles.
- The car wouldn't start at 32 km/h — it would take time for it to reach this speed.

Exercise 1.2 — $ax + by + c = 0$

Q1 a) $5x - y + 2 = 0$

b) $3y = -\frac{1}{2}x + 3$
$\Rightarrow \frac{1}{2}x + 3y - 3 = 0 \Rightarrow x + 6y - 6 = 0$

c) $2(x - 1) = 4y - 1$
$\Rightarrow 2x - 2 = 4y - 1 \Rightarrow 2x - 4y - 1 = 0$

d) $7x - 2y - 9 = 0$

e) $\frac{1}{2}(4x + 3) = 3(y - 2)$
$\Rightarrow 2x + \frac{3}{2} = 3y - 6$
$\Rightarrow 2x - 3y + \frac{15}{2} = 0 \Rightarrow 4x - 6y + 15 = 0$

f) $3(y - 4) = 4(x - 3)$
$\Rightarrow 3y - 12 = 4x - 12 \Rightarrow 4x - 3y = 0$

Q2 a) $6x - 2y + 3 = 0$
$\Rightarrow 2y = 6x + 3 \Rightarrow y = 3x + \frac{3}{2}$
$m = 3$, y-intercept $= \left(0, \frac{3}{2}\right)$

b) $-9x + 3y - 12 = 0$
$\Rightarrow 3y = 9x + 12 \Rightarrow y = 3x + 4$
$m = 3$, y-intercept $= (0, 4)$

c) $-x - 4y - 2 = 0$
$\Rightarrow -4y = x + 2 \Rightarrow y = -\frac{1}{4}x - \frac{1}{2}$
$m = -\frac{1}{4}$, y-intercept $= \left(0, -\frac{1}{2}\right)$

d) $7x + 8y + 11 = 0$
$\Rightarrow 8y = -7x - 11 \Rightarrow y = -\frac{7}{8}x - \frac{11}{8}$
$m = -\frac{7}{8}$, y-intercept $= \left(0, -\frac{11}{8}\right)$

Q3 a) $(x_1, y_1) = (5, 2)$, $(x_2, y_2) = (3, 4)$
$m = \frac{4 - 2}{3 - 5} = \frac{2}{-2} = -1$
$y - y_1 = m(x - x_1)$
$\Rightarrow y - 2 = -1(x - 5) \Rightarrow y - 2 = -x + 5$
$\Rightarrow x + y - 7 = 0$

b) $(x_1, y_1) = (9, -1)$, $(x_2, y_2) = (7, 2)$
$m = \frac{2 - (-1)}{7 - 9} = -\frac{3}{2}$
$y - y_1 = m(x - x_1)$
$\Rightarrow y - (-1) = -\frac{3}{2}(x - 9) \Rightarrow y + 1 = -\frac{3}{2}x + \frac{27}{2}$
$\Rightarrow \frac{3}{2}x + y - \frac{25}{2} = 0 \Rightarrow 3x + 2y - 25 = 0$

c) $(x_1, y_1) = (-6, 1)$, $(x_2, y_2) = (4, 0)$
$m = \frac{0 - 1}{4 - (-6)} = -\frac{1}{10}$
$y - y_1 = m(x - x_1)$
$\Rightarrow y - 1 = -\frac{1}{10}(x - (-6)) \Rightarrow y - 1 = -\frac{1}{10}x - \frac{6}{10}$
$\Rightarrow \frac{1}{10}x + y - \frac{4}{10} = 0 \Rightarrow x + 10y - 4 = 0$

d) $(x_1, y_1) = (-12, 3)$, $(x_2, y_2) = (5, 7)$
$m = \frac{7 - 3}{5 - (-12)} = \frac{4}{17}$
$y - y_1 = m(x - x_1)$
$\Rightarrow y - 3 = \frac{4}{17}(x - (-12))$
$\Rightarrow y - 3 = \frac{4}{17}x + \frac{48}{17} \Rightarrow -\frac{4}{17}x + y - \frac{99}{17} = 0$
$\Rightarrow -4x + 17y - 99 = 0 \Rightarrow 4x - 17y + 99 = 0$

Q4 a) $(x_1, y_1) = (0, -5)$, $(x_2, y_2) = (-5, 0)$
$m = \frac{0 - (-5)}{-5 - 0} = -1$
$y - y_1 = m(x - x_1)$
$\Rightarrow y - (-5) = -1(x - 0)$
$\Rightarrow y + 5 = -x \Rightarrow x + y + 5 = 0$

b) $(x_1, y_1) = (0, -2)$, $(x_2, y_2) = (3, 0)$
$m = \frac{0 - (-2)}{3 - 0} = \frac{2}{3}$
$y - y_1 = m(x - x_1)$
$\Rightarrow y - (-2) = \frac{2}{3}(x - 0) \Rightarrow y + 2 = \frac{2}{3}x$
$\Rightarrow -\frac{2}{3}x + y + 2 = 0 \Rightarrow 2x - 3y - 6 = 0$

Q5 a) $3x + 4y = 18 \Rightarrow 3x + 4y - 18 = 0$

b)
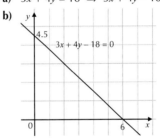

c) $x + 2y = 8 \Rightarrow x + 2y - 8 = 0$

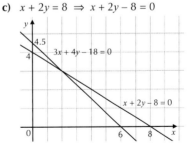

d) Read off the point of intersection from the graph: $x = 2$, $y = 3$ — that is, the cost of a small cup is £2 and the cost of a large cup is £3.

2. Parallel and Perpendicular Lines

Exercise 2.1 — Parallel lines

Q1 a), c) and e) are parallel.
Rearrange each equation so it's in the form $y = mx + c$ and then compare gradients. If a line is parallel to $y = -3x + c$, then it'll have a gradient of -3.

Q2 a) $y = 4x + c$
Sub in $x = 3$ and $y = 2$
$\Rightarrow 2 = 4 \times 3 + c \Rightarrow -10 = c$
So $y = 4x - 10 \Rightarrow 4x - y - 10 = 0$

b) First rearrange the given equation:
$4x - 2y - 1 = 0$
$-2y = -4x + 1$
$y = 2x - \frac{1}{2}$
So the equation of the line you want is:
$y = 2x + c$
Sub in $x = -4$, $y = -5 \Rightarrow -5 = 2(-4) + c \Rightarrow c = 3$
So $y = 2x + 3 \Rightarrow 2x - y + 3 = 0$

Q3 a) no   **b)** yes   **c)** yes

Q4 a) Find the gradient of the other line first:
Rearrange $2x - 4y + 3 = 0$
$\Rightarrow 4y = 2x + 3 \Rightarrow y = \frac{1}{2}x + \frac{3}{4}$
So gradient, $m = \frac{1}{2}$
$y = \frac{1}{2}x + c$
Sub in $x = 4$ and $y = 3$
$\Rightarrow 3 = \frac{1}{2} \times 4 + c \Rightarrow c = 1$
$y = \frac{1}{2}x + 1$

b) Rearrange $y = \frac{1}{2}x + 1$
$\Rightarrow \frac{1}{2}x - y + 1 = 0 \Rightarrow x - 2y + 2 = 0$

Exercise 2.2 — Perpendicular lines

Q1 a) $m = -1 \div 2 = -\frac{1}{2} \Rightarrow y = -\frac{1}{2}x + c$
Sub in $(-2, 5)$
$\Rightarrow 5 = \left(-\frac{1}{2}\right) \times (-2) + c \Rightarrow c = 5 - 1 = 4$
$\Rightarrow y = -\frac{1}{2}x + 4$

b) Rearrange $x - 5y - 30 = 0 \Rightarrow y = \frac{1}{5}x - 6$
$m = -1 \div \frac{1}{5} = -5 \Rightarrow y = -5x + c$
Sub in $(5, 2)$
$\Rightarrow 2 = -5 \times 5 + c \Rightarrow c = 2 + 25 = 27$
$\Rightarrow y = -5x + 27$

Q2 a) $m = -1 \div \frac{1}{4} = -4$
$\Rightarrow y = -4x + c$
Sub in $(-1, 2)$
$\Rightarrow 2 = (-4) \times (-1) + c \Rightarrow c = 2 - 4 = -2$
$\Rightarrow y = -4x - 2 \Rightarrow 4x + y + 2 = 0$

b) Rearrange to get $y = -\frac{2}{3}x + \frac{1}{3}$
$m = -1 \div -\frac{2}{3} = \frac{3}{2} \Rightarrow y = \frac{3}{2}x + c$
Sub in $(-3, -1)$
$\Rightarrow -1 = \frac{3}{2} \times (-3) + c \Rightarrow c = -1 + \frac{9}{2} = \frac{7}{2}$
$\Rightarrow y = \frac{3}{2}x + \frac{7}{2} \Rightarrow 2y = 3x + 7$
$\Rightarrow 3x - 2y + 7 = 0$

c) Rearrange to get $y = \frac{1}{2}x + \frac{1}{10}$
$m = -1 \div \frac{1}{2} = -2 \Rightarrow y = -2x + c$
Sub in $(6, -5)$
$\Rightarrow -5 = -2 \times 6 + c \Rightarrow c = -5 + 12 = 7$
$\Rightarrow y = -2x + 7 \Rightarrow 2x + y - 7 = 0$

d) $m = -1 \div \frac{3}{2} = -\frac{2}{3} \Rightarrow y = -\frac{2}{3}x + c$
Sub in $(2, 1)$
$\Rightarrow 1 = -\frac{2}{3} \times 2 + c \Rightarrow c = 1 + \frac{4}{3} = \frac{7}{3}$
$\Rightarrow y = -\frac{2}{3}x + \frac{7}{3} \Rightarrow 3y = -2x + 7$
$\Rightarrow 2x + 3y - 7 = 0$

Q3 a) Rearrange $3x + 4y - 1 = 0 \Rightarrow y = -\frac{3}{4}x + \frac{1}{4}$
Multiply the gradients of both lines: $\frac{4}{3} \times -\frac{3}{4} = -1$
So the lines are perpendicular.
Remember, if you multiply the gradients of two perpendicular lines you get −1.

b) Rearrange $3x + 2y - 3 = 0 \Rightarrow y = -\frac{3}{2}x + \frac{3}{2}$
Multiply the gradients of both lines: $\frac{3}{2} \times -\frac{3}{2} = -\frac{9}{4}$
So the lines are not perpendicular.

c) Rearrange $4x - y + 3 = 0 \Rightarrow y = 4x + 3$
Rearrange $2x + 8y + 1 = 0 \Rightarrow y = -\frac{1}{4}x - \frac{1}{8}$
Multiply the gradients of both lines: $4 \times -\frac{1}{4} = -1$
So the lines are perpendicular.

Q4 a) AB: $m = \frac{3 - 2}{4 - 0} = \frac{1}{4} \Rightarrow y = \frac{1}{4}x + c$
Sub in $(0, 2) \Rightarrow 2 = 0 + c \Rightarrow c = 2 \Rightarrow y = \frac{1}{4}x + 2$

BC: $m = \frac{-1 - 3}{5 - 4} = -4 \Rightarrow y = -4x + c$
Sub in $(4, 3) \Rightarrow 3 = -4 \times 4 + c \Rightarrow c = 19$
$\Rightarrow y = -4x + 19$

AC: $m = \frac{-1 - 2}{5 - 0} = -\frac{3}{5} \Rightarrow y = -\frac{3}{5}x + c$
Sub in $(0, 2) \Rightarrow 2 = 0 + c \Rightarrow c = 2 \Rightarrow y = -\frac{3}{5}x + 2$

b) The triangle is right-angled, as AB is perpendicular to BC:
$m_{AB} \times m_{BC} = \frac{1}{4} \times -4 = -1$

Q5 $3x - 2y = 6$
Rearrange into $y = mx + c$: $-2y = -3x + 6 \Rightarrow y = \frac{3}{2}x - 3$
So the line we want will have gradient $m = -1 \div \frac{3}{2} = -\frac{2}{3}$
Now sub in (a, b) to find c: $y = -\frac{2}{3}x + c$
$$b = -\frac{2}{3}a + c$$
$$c = b + \frac{2}{3}a$$
So the equation of line A is $y = -\frac{2}{3}x + \frac{2}{3}a + b$
You could also have given the line in the form $2x + 3y - 2a - 3b = 0$ as the question didn't tell you which form to use.

Q6 The gradient of the line AB is $\frac{2 - 4}{5 - 1} = -\frac{1}{2}$.
So the gradient of the perpendicular bisector is:
$m = -1 \div -\frac{1}{2} = 2$
The bisector will pass through the midpoint of the line — this will be at $\left(\frac{1 + 5}{2}, \frac{4 + 2}{2}\right) = (3, 3)$.

So the bisector has gradient 2 and passes through the point (3, 3).
$$y = 2x + c$$
$$\Rightarrow 3 = 2(3) + c$$
$$\Rightarrow c = 3 - 6 = -3$$
So the equation of the perpendicular bisector is $y = 2x - 3$.

3. Proportion

Exercise 3.1 — Direct proportion

Q1 **a)** $y \propto x \Rightarrow y = kx$
When $x = 8$, $24 = 8k \Rightarrow k = \frac{24}{8} = 3 \Rightarrow y = 3x$
So when $x = 5$, $a = 3 \times 5 = 15$

b) $y \propto x \Rightarrow y = kx$
When $x = 26$, $13 = 26k \Rightarrow k = \frac{13}{26} = \frac{1}{2} \Rightarrow y = \frac{1}{2}x$
So when $x = 14$, $a = \frac{1}{2} \times 14 = 7$

c) $y \propto x \Rightarrow y = kx$
When $x = 7$, $28 = 7k \Rightarrow k = \frac{28}{7} = 4 \Rightarrow y = 4x$
So when $y = 96$, $96 = 4a \Rightarrow a = \frac{96}{4} = 24$

d) $y \propto x \Rightarrow y = kx$
When $x = 6$, $21 = 6k \Rightarrow k = \frac{21}{6} = \frac{7}{2} \Rightarrow y = \frac{7}{2}x$
So when $x = 3$, $a = \frac{7}{2} \times 3 = \frac{21}{2} = 10.5$

e) Form two equations: $36 = ka$ and $a = 9k \Rightarrow k = \frac{a}{9}$
Substitute $k = \frac{a}{9}$ into $36 = ka$:
$$36 = \left(\frac{a}{9}\right)a = \frac{a^2}{9}$$
$$a^2 = 36 \times 9 = 324$$
$\Rightarrow a = \sqrt{324} = 18$ (you can ignore the negative root since you are told that $a > 0$)

Q2 If $y \propto x$ and $y \propto z$, then we can write
$y = k_1x$ and $y = k_2z$, where k_1 and k_2 are constants.
Equating y's: $k_1x = k_2z \Rightarrow x = \frac{k_2}{k_1}z$
$\frac{k_2}{k_1}$ must be a constant, since k_1 and k_2 are both constants.
So $x \propto z$ with constant of proportionality $\frac{k_2}{k_1}$.

Q3 **a)** The +2 means that the equation cannot be written in the form $y = kx$ (the graph also does not pass through the origin), so y is not directly proportional to x.

b) The equation can be written as $y = (a - b)x$, where the constant of proportionality is equal to $(a - b)$, so y is directly proportional to x.

c) Simplifying the equation gives $y = x - 2$, which cannot be written as $y = kx$, so y is not directly proportional to x.

d) Expanding the brackets gives:
$$y = x^2 + 6x + 9 - (x^2 - 6x + 9)$$
$$\Rightarrow y = x^2 + 6x + 9 - x^2 + 6x - 9$$
$$\Rightarrow y = 12x, \text{ so they are in direct proportion.}$$

Q4 $F \propto m$ and $F = 15$ when $m = 12$.
So $F = km$
$15 = 12k$
$\Rightarrow k = \frac{15}{12} = 1.25$
So when $m = 18$, $F = 1.25 \times 18 = 22.5$ N

4. Curve Sketching

Exercise 4.1 — Cubic and quartic functions

Q1 **a)** $y = -1.5x^4$ will be n-shaped and below the x-axis since the power is even and the coefficient is negative, so it must be graph D.

b) $y = 0.5x^3$ has an odd power and a positive coefficient so it will have a bottom-left to top-right curve. It must be graph B.

c) $y = 2x^6$ has an even power and a positive coefficient so it'll be u-shaped and above the x-axis. It must be graph A.

d) $y = -3x^3$ has an odd power of x and a negative coefficient so it must have a top-left to bottom-right curve. It must be graph C.

Q2 **a)**

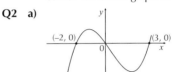

b)

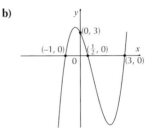

c)

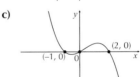

Your graphs don't need to look exactly like these — you don't need to get the size of the 'dips' right, as long as you've got the rough shape and the intercepts with the x-axis.

Q3 **a)**

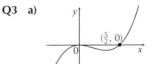

There's a repeated root at x = 0 because of the x^2 factor.

b)

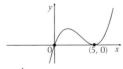

c)

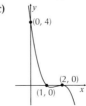

Remember — putting in values for x near the key points can really help understand the shape of the graphs. E.g. for part c), pop in x = 1.5 and 2.5 to check that both give negative values for y.

Q4 a)

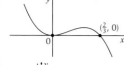

b)

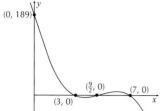

c)

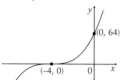

Q5 a) First take out a factor of x:
$x^3 - 7x^2 + 12x = x(x^2 - 7x + 12)$
Then factorise the quadratic:
$x^2 - 7x + 12 = (x - 3)(x - 4)$
So $x^3 - 7x^2 + 12x = x(x - 3)(x - 4)$.

b)

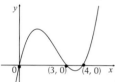

Q6 a) $x^3 - 16x = x(x^2 - 16) = x(x + 4)(x - 4)$
Using this information we can sketch the graph:

b) $2x^3 - 12x^2 + 18x = 2x(x^2 - 6x + 9)$
$= 2x(x - 3)^2$
Using this information we can sketch the graph:

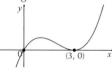

Q7 a)

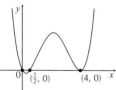

Watch out for the repeated root — the $(x - 4)$ bracket is squared so it only touches the axis at $x = 4$.

b)

Here there are two double roots, so the graph never crosses the x-axis. Since the coefficient of x^4 is negative, the graph is below the x-axis.

Q8 a) $y = x^2(x^2 - 9x + 14) = x^2(x - 2)(x - 7)$

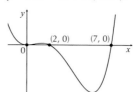

coefficient of x^4 is positive, double root at $x = 0$, roots at $x = 2$ and $x = 7$

b) $y = (x + 1)(2 - 3x)(4x^2 - 9)$
$= (x + 1)(2 - 3x)(2x + 3)(2x - 3)$

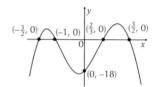

coefficient of x^4 is negative, y-intercept is at $(0, -18)$, roots at $x = -\frac{3}{2}, -1, \frac{2}{3}, \frac{3}{2}$

c) $y = (x - 5)(2x^3 + 5x^2 - 3x)$
$= (x - 5)[x(2x^2 + 5x - 3)] = x(x - 5)(2x - 1)(x + 3)$

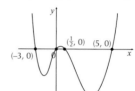

coefficient of x^4 is positive, roots at $-3, 0, \frac{1}{2}, 5$

Exercise 4.2 — Reciprocal functions and negative powers

Q1 a) $y = x^{-2} = \dfrac{1}{x^2}$.
$n = 2$ is and even so you'll get a graph with two bits next to each other. $k = 1$ is positive so the graph will all be above the axis so it must be graph D.

b) $y = -3x^{-3} = -\dfrac{3}{x^3}$.
$n = 3$ is odd so you'll get a graph with two bits opposite each other. $k = -3$ is negative so the graph will be in the top-left and bottom-right quadrants so it must be graph A.

c) $y = -\dfrac{3}{x^4}$.
$n = 4$ is even so you'll get a graph with two bits next to each other. $k = -3$ so the graph will all be below the x-axis so it must be graph B.

d) $y = 2x^{-5} = \dfrac{2}{x^5}$.
$n = 5$ is odd so you'll get a graph with two bits opposite each other. $k = 2$ is positive so the graph will be in the bottom-left and top-right quadrants so it must be graph C.

Q2 a)

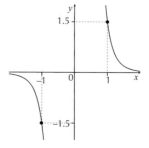

b)

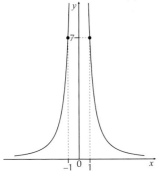

c)

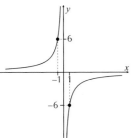

d)

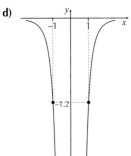

Q3 a) $y = -x^3 - 2x^2 = -x^2(x + 2)$

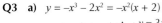
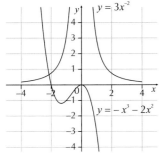

b) The number of real roots of the equation $3x^{-2} = -x^3 - 2x^2$ is just the number of times the two graphs cross. This equation therefore has 1 real root.

Q4 a)

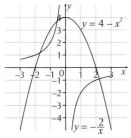

b) The solutions are at the points of intersection on the graph in part a). The actual solutions are $x = -0.54$, -1.68 and 2.21 (to 2 d.p.). Acceptable solutions are: between -0.4 and -0.7, between -1.6 and -1.8 and between 2.1 and 2.3.

5. Graph Transformations
Exercise 5.1 — Translations

Q1 a)

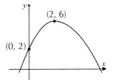

b)

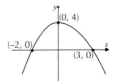

Q2 a) The asymptotes are at $x = 0$ and $y = 0$.

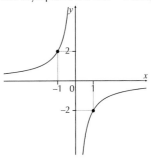

b) The asymptotes are at $x = -3$ and $y = 0$.

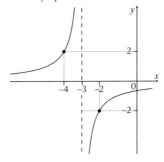

c) The asymptotes are at $x = 0$ and $y = 3$.

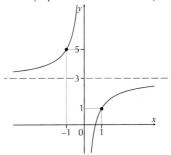

Q3 If $x^2(x - 4) = f(x)$, then $(x - 2)^2(x - 6) = f(x - 2)$. So the translation is 2 units right, i.e. by the vector $\begin{pmatrix} 2 \\ 0 \end{pmatrix}$.

Q4 If $x^3 + 3x + 7 = f(x)$, then $x^3 + 3x + 2 = f(x) - 5$.
So the translation is 5 units down, i.e. by the vector $\begin{pmatrix} 0 \\ -5 \end{pmatrix}$.

Q5 If $f(x) = x^2 - 3x + 7$, then the translation is
$f(x + 1) = (x + 1)^2 - 3(x + 1) + 7$
$= x^2 + 2x + 1 - 3x - 3 + 7 = x^2 - x + 5.$

Q6 a) and b)

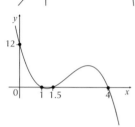

Q7 a)

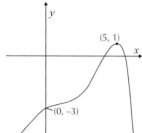

b) If $f(x) = (x - 1)(2x - 3)(4 - x)$, then the translation is:
$f(x - 2) = ((x - 2) - 1)(2(x - 2) - 3)(4 - (x - 2))$
$= (x - 3)(2x - 4 - 3)(4 - x + 2)$
$= (x - 3)(2x - 7)(6 - x)$

c)

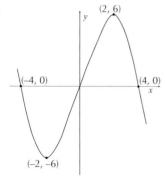

Exercise 5.2 — Stretches and reflections

Q1 a)

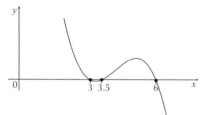

b)

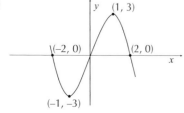

c)

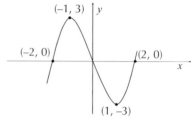

d)

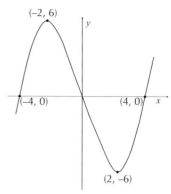

Q2 The graph has been squashed to half its width, so it's a horizontal stretch of scale factor $\frac{1}{2}$, so it must be b).

Q3 The graph has been reflected in the x-axis and stretched vertically by a factor of 3 so it must be b).

Q4 a) $f(x) = x^3 - x = x(x^2 - 1) = x(x + 1)(x - 1)$

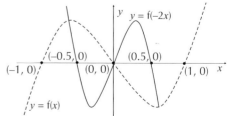

b)

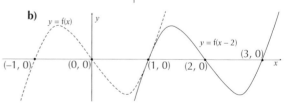

c)

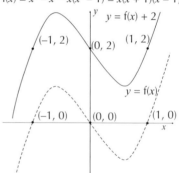

d)

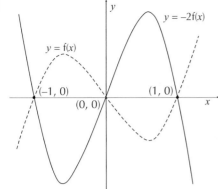

$y = -2f(x)$
$y = f(x)$
$(-1, 0)$
$(0, 0)$
$(1, 0)$

Q5 $3x^3 + 6x + 12 = 3(x^3 + 2x + 4)$ so the whole function has been multiplied by 3. This means the transformation is a stretch vertically by a scale factor of 3.

Q6 $4x^2 - 2x + 4 = (-2x)^2 + (-2x) + 4$ so x has been replaced with $-2x$. The transformation is therefore a reflection in the y-axis followed by a horizontal stretch by a scale factor of $\frac{1}{2}$ (i.e. a squash).

Q7 **a)** $f(x) = x^2 - 6x - 7 = (x - 3)^2 - 16$,
so the minimum point is at $(3, -16)$.
Solving $(x - 3)^2 - 16 = 0$ gives $x = -1$ or 7.
So the graph is:

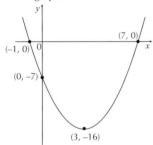

$(7, 0)$
$(-1, 0)$
$(0, -7)$
$(3, -16)$

b) $y = -2f(x) = -2(x^2 - 6x - 7)$

c)

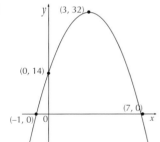

$(3, 32)$
$(0, 14)$
$(7, 0)$
$(-1, 0)$

6. Circles

Exercise 6.1 — The equation of a circle

Q1 $x^2 + y^2 = 25$

Q2 $x^2 + y^2 = 49$

Q3 **a)** $a = 2, b = 5, r = 3$
$(x - 2)^2 + (y - 5)^2 = 9$

b) $a = -3, b = 2, r = 5$
$(x + 3)^2 + (y - 2)^2 = 25$

c) $a = -2, b = -3, r = 7$
$(x + 2)^2 + (y + 3)^2 = 49$

d) $a = 3, b = 0, r = 4$
$(x - 3)^2 + y^2 = 16$

Q4 **a)** $a = 1, b = 5, r = \sqrt{4}$
So the centre is (1, 5) and the radius is 2.

b) $a = 3, b = 5, r = \sqrt{64}$
So the centre is (3, 5) and the radius is 8.

c) $a = 3, b = -2, r = \sqrt{25}$
So the centre is (3, -2) and the radius is 5.

Q5 $a = 5, b = 3, r = 8$
$(x - 5)^2 + (y - 3)^2 = 64$

Q6 $a = 3, b = 1, r = \sqrt{31}$
$(x - 3)^2 + (y - 1)^2 = 31$

Q7 **a)** $a = 6, b = 4$, so the centre is (6, 4)

b) Radius $= \sqrt{20} = \sqrt{4 \times 5} = 2\sqrt{5}$

Q8 $a = -3, b = -2, r = \sqrt{5}$
$(x + 3)^2 + (y + 2)^2 = 5$

Exercise 6.2 — Rearranging circle equations

Q1 **a)** Complete the square for the x's and y's:
$x^2 + y^2 + 2x - 6y - 6 = 0$
$x^2 + 2x + y^2 - 6y - 6 = 0$
$(x + 1)^2 - 1 + (y - 3)^2 - 9 - 6 = 0$
$(x + 1)^2 + (y - 3)^2 = 16$
Radius = 4, centre is (-1, 3).

b) Complete the square for the x's and y's:
$x^2 + y^2 - 2y - 4 = 0$
$x^2 + (y - 1)^2 - 1 - 4 = 0$
$x^2 + (y - 1)^2 = 5$
Radius = $\sqrt{5}$, centre is (0, 1)

c) Complete the square for the x's and y's:
$x^2 + y^2 - 6x - 4y = 12$
$x^2 - 6x + y^2 - 4y = 12$
$(x - 3)^2 - 9 + (y - 2)^2 - 4 = 12$
$(x - 3)^2 + (y - 2)^2 = 25$
Radius = 5, centre is (3, 2)

d) Complete the square for the x's and y's:
$x^2 + y^2 - 10x + 6y + 13 = 0$
$x^2 - 10x + y^2 + 6y + 13 = 0$
$(x - 5)^2 - 25 + (y + 3)^2 - 9 + 13 = 0$
$(x - 5)^2 + (y + 3)^2 = 21$
Radius = $\sqrt{21}$, centre is (5, -3)

Q2 **a)** Complete the square for the x's and y's:
$x^2 + y^2 + 2x - 4y - 3 = 0$
$x^2 + 2x + y^2 - 4y - 3 = 0$
$(x + 1)^2 - 1 + (y - 2)^2 - 4 - 3 = 0$
$(x + 1)^2 + (y - 2)^2 = 8$
Centre is (-1, 2).

b) Radius $= \sqrt{8} = \sqrt{2 \times 4} = 2\sqrt{2}$

Q3 **a)** Complete the square for the x's and y's:
$x^2 + y^2 - 3x + 1 = 0$
$x^2 - 3x + y^2 + 1 = 0$
$\left(x - \frac{3}{2}\right)^2 - \frac{9}{4} + y^2 + 1 = 0$
$\left(x - \frac{3}{2}\right)^2 + y^2 = \frac{5}{4}$
Centre is $\left(\frac{3}{2}, 0\right)$

b) Radius $= \sqrt{\frac{5}{4}} = \frac{\sqrt{5}}{2}$

Exercise 6.3 — Using circle properties

Q1 a) Centre is (3, 1)

b) Gradient of radius $= \dfrac{1-4}{3-4} = \dfrac{-3}{-1} = 3$

c) Gradient of the tangent is $-\dfrac{1}{3}$,

use $y - y_1 = m(x - x_1)$ to find equation of tangent:

$y - 4 = -\dfrac{1}{3}(x - 4)$

$3y - 12 = -x + 4$

$x + 3y = 16$

You're asked for the equation in a particular form, so don't forget to rearrange it.

Q2 Centre of the circle is (−1, 2)

Gradient of radius $= \dfrac{2-(-1)}{-1-(-3)} = \dfrac{3}{2}$

Gradient of the tangent $= -\dfrac{2}{3}$

Use $y - y_1 = m(x - x_1)$ to find equation of tangent:

$y - (-1) = -\dfrac{2}{3}(x - (-3))$

$3y + 3 = -2(x + 3)$

$3y + 3 = -2x - 6$

$2x + 3y + 9 = 0$

Q3 Rearrange $x^2 + y^2 + 2x - 7 = 0$ and complete the square for the x terms to get:

$(x + 1)^2 + y^2 = 8$

Centre of the circle is (−1, 0)

Gradient of radius $= \dfrac{0-2}{-1-(-3)} = \dfrac{-2}{2} = -1$

Gradient of the tangent $= 1$

Use $y - y_1 = m(x - x_1)$ to find equation of tangent:

$y - 2 = 1(x - (-3))$

$y - 2 = x + 3$

$y = x + 5$

Q4 Rearrange $x^2 + y^2 + 2x + 4y = 5$ and complete the square for the x and y terms to get:

$(x + 1)^2 + (y + 2)^2 = 10$

Centre of the circle is (−1, −2)

Gradient of the radius $= \dfrac{-2-(-5)}{-1-0} = \dfrac{3}{-1} = -3$

Gradient of the tangent $= \dfrac{1}{3}$

Use $y - y_1 = m(x - x_1)$ to find equation of tangent:

$y - (-5) = \dfrac{1}{3}(x - 0)$

$3y + 15 = x$

$x - 3y = 15$

Q5 The line from the centre of the circle to A has gradient:

$\dfrac{1-4}{n-(-2)} = -\dfrac{3}{n+2}$

Since the tangent at A is perpendicular to this line,

$m_1 \times m_2 = -1$

$-\dfrac{3}{n+2} \times \dfrac{5}{3} = -1$

$-\dfrac{5}{n+2} = -1$

$-5 = -1(n + 2)$

$n + 2 = 5 \Rightarrow n = 3$

You could also find the equation of this radius in the form $y = mx + c$, then substitute in the point (n, 1) to find n.

Q6 a) The line l is perpendicular to the chord AB. So find the gradient of AB:

Gradient of AB $= \dfrac{1-7}{-1-(-3)} = -\dfrac{6}{2} = -3$

So the gradient of l is $\dfrac{1}{3}$.

Then sub the gradient of l and point M (−1, 1) into $y - y_1 = m(x - x_1)$ to find the equation:

$y - 1 = \dfrac{1}{3}(x - (-1))$

$3y - 3 = x + 1$

$x - 3y + 4 = 0$

b) The centre is (2, 2), so $a = 2$ and $b = 2$ in the equation $(x - a)^2 + (y - b)^2 = r^2$.

The radius is the length CA, which can be found using Pythagoras:

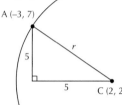

$r^2 = CA^2 = (-3 - 2)^2 + (7 - 2)^2 = (-5)^2 + 5^2 = 50$

So the equation of the circle is:

$(x - 2)^2 + (y - 2)^2 = 50$

Q7 a) If AC is the diameter, the angle ABC will be 90°. So find out if AB and BC are perpendicular.

Gradient of AB $= \dfrac{14-12}{4-(-2)} = \dfrac{2}{6} = \dfrac{1}{3}$

Gradient of BC $= \dfrac{2-14}{8-4} = \dfrac{-12}{4} = -3$

For perpendicular lines: $m_1 \times m_2 = -1$

$\dfrac{1}{3} \times -3 = -1$

As AB and BC are perpendicular, the angle ABC must be 90° and so AC must be the diameter of the circle.

b) Since AC is a diameter, the centre of the circle must be the midpoint of A and C.

$\left(\dfrac{(-2)+8}{2}, \dfrac{12+2}{2} \right) = \left(\dfrac{6}{2}, \dfrac{14}{2} \right) = (3, 7)$

The radius is the distance from the centre to a point on the circle, so choose a point and use Pythagoras' theorem (here using C).

$(8 - 3)^2 + (2 - 7)^2 = r^2$

$r^2 = 5^2 + 5^2 = 50$

So the equation of the circle is:

$(x - 3)^2 + (y - 7)^2 = 50$

Q8 Find the perpendicular bisectors of two of the line segments AB, BC and CA.

AB: midpoint $= \left(\dfrac{2+6}{2}, \dfrac{11+5}{2} \right) = \left(\dfrac{8}{2}, \dfrac{16}{2} \right) = (4, 8)$

gradient $= \dfrac{5-11}{6-2} = \dfrac{-6}{4} = -\dfrac{3}{2}$

So the perpendicular bisector passes through (4, 8) and has a gradient of $\left(-1 \div -\dfrac{3}{2} \right) = \dfrac{2}{3}$.

$y - y_1 = m(x - x_1)$

$y - 8 = \dfrac{2}{3}(x - 4)$

$y = \dfrac{2}{3}x - \dfrac{8}{3} + 8 \Rightarrow y = \dfrac{2}{3}x + \dfrac{16}{3}$

BC: midpoint = $\left(\frac{6+(-9)}{2}, \frac{5+0}{2}\right) = \left(-\frac{3}{2}, \frac{5}{2}\right)$

gradient = $\frac{0-5}{(-9)-6} = \frac{-5}{-15} = \frac{1}{3}$

So the perpendicular bisector passes through $\left(-\frac{3}{2}, \frac{5}{2}\right)$ and has a gradient of $\left(-1 \div \frac{1}{3}\right) = -3$.

$y - y_1 = m(x - x_1)$

$y - \frac{5}{2} = (-3)\left(x - \left(-\frac{3}{2}\right)\right)$

$y = -3x - \frac{9}{2} + \frac{5}{2} \Rightarrow y = -3x - 2$

Now find the centre of the circle, which is the point where these lines intersect:

$\frac{2}{3}x + \frac{16}{3} = -3x - 2$

$2x + 16 = -9x - 6$

$11x = -22 \Rightarrow x = -2$

Substitute $x = -2$ into $y = -3x - 2$

$y = -3(-2) - 2 = 6 - 2 = 4$

So the circle has its centre at (–2, 4).

You could also have used the perpendicular bisector of CA here to find the centre of the circle — it has equation $y = 2 - x$.

The radius is the distance from the centre to one of the points — here we use B:

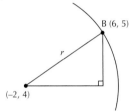

Use Pythagoras' theorem to find r^2:

$(6 - (-2))^2 + (5 - 4)^2 = r^2$

$8^2 + 1^2 = r^2$

$r^2 = 64 + 1 = 65$

So the equation of the circle is:

$(x + 2)^2 + (y - 4)^2 = 65$

Chapter 7: The Binomial Expansion

1. Binomial Expansions

Exercise 1.1 — Binomial expansions — $(1 + x)^n$

Q1 Pascal's triangle is

$$
\begin{array}{ccccccccc}
& & & & 1 & & & & \\
& & & 1 & & 1 & & & \\
& & 1 & & 2 & & 1 & & \\
& 1 & & 3 & & 3 & & 1 & \\
1 & & 4 & & 6 & & 4 & & 1
\end{array}
$$

The expansion of $(1 + x)^4$ takes its coefficients of each term, in ascending powers of x, from the 5th row:

$(1 + x)^4 = 1 + 4x + 6x^2 + 4x^3 + x^4$

Q2 a) $^6C_2 = 15$

b) $\binom{12}{5} = {}^{12}C_5 = 792$

c) $\frac{30!}{4!26!} = {}^{30}C_4 = 27\ 405$

d) $^8C_8 = 1$

Q3 a) $\frac{9!}{4!5!} = \frac{9 \times 8 \times 7 \times 6 \times 5 \times 4 \times 3 \times 2 \times 1}{(4 \times 3 \times 2 \times 1)(5 \times 4 \times 3 \times 2 \times 1)}$

$= \frac{9 \times 8 \times 7 \times 6}{4 \times 3 \times 2 \times 1} = 3 \times 7 \times 6 = 126$

b) $^{10}C_3 = \frac{10!}{3!(10-3)!} = \frac{10 \times 9 \times 8}{3 \times 2 \times 1}$

$= 10 \times 3 \times 4 = 120$

c) $\frac{15!}{11!4!} = \frac{15 \times 14 \times 13 \times 12}{4 \times 3 \times 2 \times 1} = 15 \times 7 \times 13 = 1365$

d) $\binom{8}{6} = \frac{8!}{6!(8-6)!} = \frac{8 \times 7}{2 \times 1} = 4 \times 7 = 28$

Q4 $(1 + x)^{10} = 1 + {}^{10}C_1 x + {}^{10}C_2 x^2 + {}^{10}C_3 x^3 + \dots$

You can work out the coefficients ^nC_r using a calculator, or using the method below. Using the notation $\binom{n}{r}$ instead of ^nC_r for the coefficients is fine too.

$^nC_r = \frac{n!}{r!\,(n-r)!}$

$^{10}C_1 = \frac{10!}{1!(10-1)!} = \frac{10 \times 9 \times 8 \times \dots 1}{1 \times 9 \times 8 \times \dots 1} = 10$

$^{10}C_2 = \frac{10!}{2!(10-2)!} = \frac{10 \times 9 \times 8 \times \dots 1}{2 \times 1 \times 8 \times 7 \times \dots 1}$

$= \frac{10 \times 9}{2} = 45$

$^{10}C_3 = \frac{10!}{3!(10-3)!} = \frac{10 \times 9 \times 8 \times 7 \times \dots 1}{3 \times 2 \times 1 \times 7 \times \dots 1}$

$= \frac{10 \times 9 \times 8}{3 \times 2}$

$= 10 \times 3 \times 4 = 120$

$(1 + x)^{10} = 1 + 10x + 45x^2 + 120x^3 + \dots$

For the rest of this exercise you can use one of the methods shown in question 1 or 4 to find the coefficients ^nC_r, or you can use a calculator.

Q5 $(1 + x)^6 = 1 + {}^6C_1 x + {}^6C_2 x^2 + {}^6C_3 x^3 + {}^6C_4 x^4 + {}^6C_5 x^5 + {}^6C_6 x^6$

$= 1 + 6x + 15x^2 + 20x^3 + 15x^4 + 6x^5 + x^6$

Q6 $(1 + x)^7 = 1 + {}^7C_1 x + {}^7C_2 x^2 + {}^7C_3 x^3 + \dots$

$= 1 + 7x + 21x^2 + 35x^3 + \dots$

Exercise 1.2 — Binomial expansions — $(1 + ax)^n$

Q1 a) $(1 - x)^6 = 1 + {}^6C_1(-x) + {}^6C_2(-x)^2 + {}^6C_3(-x)^3$
$\qquad + {}^6C_4(-x)^4 + {}^6C_5(-x)^5 + {}^6C_6(-x)^6$

$= 1 - 6x + 15x^2 - 20x^3 + 15x^4 - 6x^5 + x^6$

For part a) you could use the formula for the expansion of $(1 - x)^n$: $(1 - x)^n = 1 - {}^nC_1 x + {}^nC_2 x^2 - {}^nC_3 x^3 + \dots$

b) $(1 + x)^9 = 1 + {}^9C_1 x + {}^9C_2 x^2 + {}^9C_3 x^3 + {}^9C_4 x^4 + {}^9C_5 x^5 + \dots$

$(1 - x)^9 = 1 - {}^9C_1 x + {}^9C_2 x^2 - {}^9C_3 x^3 + {}^9C_4 x^4 - {}^9C_5 x^5 + \dots$

So: $(1 + x)^9 - (1 - x)^9 = 2({}^9C_1 x + {}^9C_3 x^3 + {}^9C_5 x^5 + \dots)$

The even powers cancel out, so only the terms with odd powers appear (and they're doubled because one term comes from each expansion).

$= 2(9x + 84x^3 + 126x^5 + 36x^7 + x^9)$

$= 18x + 168x^3 + 252x^5 + 72x^7 + 2x^9$

c) $(1 - 2x)^5 = 1 + {}^5C_1(-2x) + {}^5C_2(-2x)^2 + {}^5C_3(-2x)^3$
$\qquad + {}^5C_4(-2x)^4 + {}^5C_5(-2x)^5$

$= 1 + 5(-2x) + 10(4x^2) + 10(-8x^3) + 5(16x^4) + 1(-32x^5)$

$= 1 - 10x + 40x^2 - 80x^3 + 80x^4 - 32x^5$

Q2 The first 3 terms will include 1 and the terms in x and x^2 so expand each bracket up to and including the term in x^2:

$(1 + x)^3(1 - x)^4$
$= (1 + 3x + 3x^2 + ...)(1 - 4x + 6x^2 - ...)$
$= 1 - 4x + 6x^2 + ... + 3x - 12x^2$
$\qquad\qquad + ... + 3x^2 + (higher\ power\ terms)$
$= 1 - x - 3x^2 + ...$

Q3 The expansion of $(1 + x)^5(1 + y)^7$ is the expansions of $(1 + x)^5$ and $(1 + y)^7$ multiplied together. We need the x^3 term from $(1 + x)^5$ and the y^2 term from $(1 + y)^7$. Multiplying the coefficients gives the x^3y^2 coefficient:

x^3 coefficient: $\dfrac{5!}{3!(5-3)!} = \dfrac{5 \times 4}{2 \times 1} = 10$

y^2 coefficient: $\dfrac{7!}{2!(7-2)!} = \dfrac{7 \times 6}{2 \times 1} = 21$

x^3y^2 coefficient: $10 \times 21 = 210$

Q4 $(1 + kx)^8 = 1 + {}^8C_1 kx + {}^8C_2(kx)^2 + {}^8C_3(kx)^3 + ...$
$\qquad = 1 + 8kx + 28k^2x^2 + 56k^3x^3 + ...$

Q5 We need the coefficient of x^2 to equal 135:
${}^6C_2(-kx)^2 = 15k^2x^2$
So $15k^2 = 135$
$\quad k^2 = 9$
$\quad k = 3$
The question says k is positive so ignore the negative root.

Q6 $(1 - 3x)^6 = 1 + {}^6C_1(-3x) + {}^6C_2(-3x)^2 + {}^6C_3(-3x)^3 + ...$
$\qquad = 1 - 18x + 135x^2 - 540x^3 + ...$

$(1 + x)(1 - 3x)^6 = (1 + x)(1 - 18x + ...)$
$\qquad\qquad = 1 - 18x + ... + x - 18x^2 + ...$
$\qquad\qquad \approx 1 - 17x$
You're told you can ignore x^2 and higher terms.

Q7 a) $\left(1 + \dfrac{x}{2}\right)^{12} = 1 + {}^{12}C_1\left(\dfrac{x}{2}\right) + {}^{12}C_2\left(\dfrac{x}{2}\right)^2$
$\qquad\qquad + {}^{12}C_3\left(\dfrac{x}{2}\right)^3 + {}^{12}C_4\left(\dfrac{x}{2}\right)^4 + ...$
$\qquad = 1 + 6x + \dfrac{33}{2}x^2 + \dfrac{55}{2}x^3 + \dfrac{495}{16}x^4 + ...$

b) $1 + \left(\dfrac{x}{2}\right) = 1.005$ when $x = 0.01$.
Substitute this value into the expansion:
$1.005^{12} \approx 1 + 6(0.01) + \dfrac{33}{2}(0.01)^2$
$\qquad\qquad + \dfrac{55}{2}(0.01)^3 + \dfrac{495}{16}(0.01)^4$
$1.005^{12} \approx 1.061677809 = 1.0616778$ to 7 d.p.

Exercise 1.3 — Binomial expansions — $(a + b)^n$

Q1 Using the formula for the expansion of $(a + b)^n$:
$(a + b)^n = a^n + \dbinom{n}{1}a^{n-1}b + \dbinom{n}{2}a^{n-2}b^2 + ... + b^n$

In this case $a = 3$ and $b = x$:
$(3 + x)^6 = 3^6 + {}^6C_1 3^5x + {}^6C_2 3^4x^2 + {}^6C_3 3^3x^3 + ...$
$\qquad = 729 + 6(243x) + 15(81x^2) + 20(27x^3) + ...$
$\qquad = 729 + 1458x + 1215x^2 + 540x^3 + ...$

Q2 In this case $a = 2$ and $b = x$:
$(2 + x)^4 = 2^4 + {}^4C_1 2^3x + {}^4C_2 2^2x^2 + {}^4C_3 2x^3 + {}^4C_4 x^4$
$\qquad = 16 + 4(8x) + 6(4x^2) + 4(2x^3) + x^4$
$\qquad = 16 + 32x + 24x^2 + 8x^3 + x^4$

Q3 a) The term in x^5 is ${}^8C_5(\lambda x)^5 = 56\lambda^5 x^5$
Therefore $56\lambda^5 = 57\,344$
$\qquad \Rightarrow \lambda^5 = 1024 \Rightarrow \lambda = \sqrt[5]{1024} = 4$

b) $(1 + 4x)^8 = 1 + {}^8C_1(4x) + {}^8C_2(4x)^2 + ...$
$\qquad\qquad = 1 + 32x + 448x^2 + ...$

Q4 a) $(2 + x)^8$
$= 2^8 + {}^8C_1 2^7x + {}^8C_2 2^6x^2 + {}^8C_3 2^5x^3 + {}^8C_4 2^4x^4 + ...$
$= 256 + 1024x + 1792x^2 + 1792x^3 + 1120x^4 + ...$

b) $2 + x = 2.01$ when $x = 0.01$
Hence: $2.01^8 = 256 + 1024(0.01) + 1792(0.01)^2$
$\qquad\qquad + 1792(0.01)^3 + 1120(0.01)^4 + ...$
$\qquad\qquad \approx 266.4210032$
An approximation to 2.01^8 is: 266.42100
(to 5 d.p.)

Q5 $(3 + 5x)^7 = 3^7 + {}^7C_1 3^6(5x) + {}^7C_2 3^5(5x)^2 + {}^7C_3 3^4(5x)^3 + ...$
$\qquad = 2187 + 25\,515x + 127\,575x^2 + 354\,375x^3 + ...$

Q6 Expand the first five terms of $(3 + 2x)^6$ and multiply by $(1 + x)$:
$(3 + 2x)^6$
$= 3^6 + {}^6C_1 3^5(2x) + {}^6C_2 3^4(2x)^2 + {}^6C_3 3^3(2x)^3 + {}^6C_4 3^2(2x)^4 + ...$
$= 729 + 2916x + 4860x^2 + 4320x^3 + 2160x^4 + ...$
$(1 + x)(3 + 2x)^6 = (3 + 2x)^6 + x(3 + 2x)^6$
$= (729 + 2916x + 4860x^2 + 4320x^3 + 2160x^4 + ...)$
$\qquad + (729x + 2916x^2 + 4860x^3 + 4320x^4 + 2160x^5 + ...)$
$= 729 + 3645x + 7776x^2 + 9180x^3 + 6480x^4 + ...$
(The term in x^5 is the 6th term.)

Q7 a) Expansion of $(1 + x)^n = 1 + nx + \dfrac{n(n-1)}{2}x^2 + ...$

So: $\dfrac{n(n-1)}{2} = 231$
$\qquad n(n-1) = 462$
$\qquad n^2 - n - 462 = 0$
$\qquad (n + 21)(n - 22) = 0$
$\qquad\quad n = -21$ or $n = 22$

Hence $n = 22$ since $n > 0$.
This factorisation was a bit tricky, but you know that 462 is the product of two consecutive numbers. So to give you an idea of the factors, try square rooting 462. $\sqrt{462} = 21.49...$ so the roots are 21 and 22.

b) Coefficient of term in x^3 is:
$\dfrac{22!}{3!(22-3)!} = \dfrac{22 \times 21 \times 20}{3 \times 2 \times 1} = 1540$
So the term in x^3 is: $1540x^3$

Q8 The coefficient of x^2 is ${}^8C_2 a^6 3^2$
The coefficient of x^5 is ${}^8C_5 a^3 3^5$

Therefore: $28 \times a^6 \times 3^2 = \dfrac{32}{27} \times 56 \times a^3 \times 3^5$

$\qquad \Rightarrow 28a^3 = \dfrac{32}{27} \times 56 \times 3^3$

$\qquad \Rightarrow a^3 = \dfrac{32 \times 56 \times 27}{27 \times 28} = 64$

$\qquad \Rightarrow a = \sqrt[3]{64} = 4$.

Q9 Expand each bracket up to the term in x^3:
$(1 + 2x)^5 = 1 + 5(2x) + 10(2x)^2 + 10(2x)^3 + ...$
$\qquad = 1 + 10x + 40x^2 + 80x^3 + ...$
$(3 - x)^4 = 3^4 + 4(3)^3(-x) + 6(3)^2(-x)^2 + 4(3)(-x)^3 + ...$
$\qquad = 81 - 108x + 54x^2 - 12x^3 + ...$
Multiply the terms that will give a result in x^3:
$(1 \times -12x^3) + (10x \times 54x^2) + (40x^2 \times -108x)$
$\qquad\qquad + (80x^3 \times 81) = 2688x^3$
So the coefficient of x^3 is 2688.

Q10 a) The coefficient of x^3 is: $\dfrac{n!}{3!(n-3)!} = \dfrac{n(n-1)(n-2)}{3 \times 2 \times 1}$

The coefficient of x^2 is: $\dfrac{n!}{2!(n-2)!} = \dfrac{n(n-1)}{2}$

The coefficient of x^3 is three times the coefficient of x^2, so:
$\dfrac{n(n-1)(n-2)}{3 \times 2 \times 1} = 3 \times \dfrac{n(n-1)}{2} \Rightarrow \dfrac{n-2}{3} = 3 \Rightarrow n = 11$

b) $(1 + x)^{11} = 1 + 11x + 55x^2 + ...$
The coefficient of x^2 is $a \times$ (coefficient of x),
so $55 = 11a \Rightarrow a = 5$.

Q11 $(2 + \mu x)^8 = 2^8 + {}^8C_1 2^7(\mu x) + {}^8C_2 2^6(\mu x)^2 + ...$
$= 256 + (8 \times 128)(\mu x) + (28 \times 64)(\mu x)^2 + ...$
$= 256 + 1024\mu x + 1792\mu^2 x^2 + ...$

The coefficient of x^2 is:
$87\,808 = 1792\mu^2 \Rightarrow \mu^2 = 49 \Rightarrow \mu = 7$ or -7.

Chapter 8 — Trigonometry

1. The Sine and Cosine Rules

Exercise 1.1 — The sine and cosine rules

Q1 The angle measured anticlockwise from the positive x-axis is $41° + 90° = 131°$.
P is on the unit circle, so the coordinates are $(\cos 131°, \sin 131°) = (-0.656, 0.755)$ (3 s.f.)

Q2 $a^2 = b^2 + c^2 - 2bc \cos A$
$QR^2 = 9^2 + 10^2 - (2 \times 9 \times 10 \times \cos 42°) = 47.2...$
$QR = 6.87$ cm (3 s.f.)

Q3 Using the sine rule: $\dfrac{a}{\sin A} = \dfrac{b}{\sin B}$
$\Rightarrow TW = \dfrac{FW \times \sin F}{\sin T} = \dfrac{15 \times \sin 39°}{\sin 82°} = 9.53$ cm (3 s.f.)

Q4 Using the cosine rule: $a^2 = b^2 + c^2 - 2bc \cos A$
$\Rightarrow \cos A = \dfrac{b^2 + c^2 - a^2}{2bc}$
$\Rightarrow D = \cos^{-1}\left(\dfrac{6^2 + 9^2 - 8^2}{2 \times 6 \times 9}\right) = 60.6°$ (3 s.f.)

Q5 Using the cosine rule: $a^2 = b^2 + c^2 - 2bc \cos A$
$\Rightarrow (JK)^2 = 24^2 + 29^2 - (2 \times 24 \times 29 \times \cos 62°)$
$\Rightarrow JK = \sqrt{763.4...} = 27.6$ cm (3 s.f.)

Q6 The diagram below models the information given, which is then simplified. You want to find W:

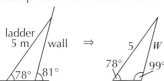

Using the sine rule:
$\dfrac{W}{\sin 78°} = \dfrac{5}{\sin 99°} \Rightarrow W = \dfrac{5 \sin 78°}{\sin 99°} = 4.95$ m (3 s.f.)

Q7 Angle $Q = 180° - 38° - 43° = 99°$
Using the sine rule:
$\dfrac{PQ}{\sin 43°} = \dfrac{48}{\sin 99°} \Rightarrow PQ = \dfrac{48 \sin 43°}{\sin 99°} = 33.1$ m (3 s.f.)

Q8 The smallest angle is between the two biggest sides, so angle F is the smallest angle.
To be safe you could just work out all 3 angles and then see which is smallest.

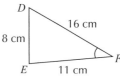

Using the cosine rule: $a^2 = b^2 + c^2 - 2bc \cos A$
$\Rightarrow \cos F = \dfrac{11^2 + 16^2 - 8^2}{2 \times 11 \times 16}$
$\Rightarrow F = \cos^{-1}\left(\dfrac{11^2 + 16^2 - 8^2}{2 \times 11 \times 16}\right) = 27.2°$ (3 s.f.)

Q9 Find the lengths XY, YZ and ZX.
$XY = \sqrt{(5 - -2)^2 + (8 - 2)^2} = \sqrt{85}$
$YZ = \sqrt{(5 - 3)^2 + (8 - -2)^2} = \sqrt{104}$
$ZX = \sqrt{(-2 - 3)^2 + (2 - -2)^2} = \sqrt{41}$
Using the cosine rule: $\cos A = \dfrac{b^2 + c^2 - a^2}{2bc}$.

So angle $XYZ = \cos^{-1}\left(\dfrac{104 + 85 - 41}{2 \times \sqrt{104} \times \sqrt{85}}\right) = 38.1°$ (3 s.f.)

It might help to draw a sketch here to make sure you're using the sides in the correct place in the cosine rule.

Q10 Area $= \dfrac{1}{2} ab \sin C = \dfrac{1}{2} \times 12 \times 10.5 \times \sin 53°$
$= 50.3$ cm^2 (3 s.f.)

Q11 Start by finding any angle (M here).
Using the cosine rule: $a^2 = b^2 + c^2 - 2bc \cos A$
$\Rightarrow \cos M = \dfrac{5^2 + 7^2 - 4.2^2}{2 \times 5 \times 7}$
$\Rightarrow M = \cos^{-1}\left(\dfrac{5^2 + 7^2 - 4.2^2}{2 \times 5 \times 7}\right) = 36.3...°$
Now you can find the area.

Area $= \dfrac{1}{2} ab \sin C = \dfrac{1}{2} \times 5 \times 7 \times \sin 36.3...°$
$= 10.38$ cm^2 (2 d.p.)
You could have found any angle to start off then used the corresponding sides.

Q12 Start by sketching the triangle:

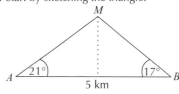

a) Angle $M = 180° - 21° - 17° = 142°$.
Using the sine rule:
$\dfrac{a}{\sin A} = \dfrac{m}{\sin M} \Rightarrow a = \dfrac{5 \times \sin 21°}{\sin 142°} = 2.91043...$
$= 2.91$ km (3 s.f.)
Here a is the distance BM and m is the distance AB.

b) To find the height, draw a line through the triangle from M at a right angle to AB (the dotted line shown in the diagram above).

Height $= \sin 17° \times 2.91043... = 0.85092...$ km
$= 851$ m (to the nearest m).
The final step just uses SOHCAHTOA — height is the opposite side and 2.91043... is the hypotenuse.

Q13 a)

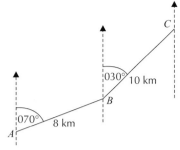

b) The angle anticlockwise from the vertical at B to A is $180° - 70° = 110°$ (parallel lines), so the angle ABC is $110° + 30° = 140°$. Now you can use the cosine rule to find the distance AC:

$a^2 = b^2 + c^2 - 2bc \cos A$

$\Rightarrow AC = \sqrt{(BC)^2 + (AB)^2 - 2(BC)(AB)\cos B}$

$\Rightarrow AC = \sqrt{100 + 64 - 160\cos 140°}$

$\quad\quad = 16.928... = 16.9$ km (3 s.f.)

c) Start by finding the angle ACB using the cosine rule:

$a^2 = b^2 + c^2 - 2bc \cos A$

$\Rightarrow \cos ACB = \dfrac{10^2 + 16.928...^2 - 8^2}{2 \times 10 \times 16.928...}$

$\Rightarrow ACB = \cos^{-1}\left(\dfrac{10^2 + 16.928...^2 - 8^2}{2 \times 10 \times 16.928...}\right)$

$\quad\quad = 17.68°$ (2 d.p.)

The bearing required is therefore
$180° + 17.68° + 30°$ (parallel lines) $= 228°$ (3 s.f.).

You could also have found angle ACB using the sine rule.

Q14 Using the cosine rule: $a^2 = b^2 + c^2 - 2bc \cos A$

$\Rightarrow AC = \sqrt{9^2 + 11^2 - (2 \times 9 \times 11 \times \cos 148°)}$

$\quad\quad = 19.233... = 19.2$ m (3 s.f.)

Find the area of each triangle individually.
For the top triangle:

Area $= \dfrac{1}{2}\, ab \sin C$

$\quad\quad = \dfrac{1}{2} \times 9 \times 11 \times \sin 148° = 26.231...\text{m}^2$

For the bottom triangle:

Area $= \dfrac{1}{2}\, ab \sin C$

$\quad\quad = \dfrac{1}{2} \times 8 \times 19.233... \times \sin 79° = 75.519...$ m^2

So the area of the quadrilateral is
$26.231... + 75.519... = 101.750... = 102$ m^2 (3 s.f.).

2. Trig Identities
Exercise 2.1 — Trig identities

Q1 Use $\tan \theta \equiv \dfrac{\sin \theta}{\cos \theta}$:

$\dfrac{\sin \theta}{\tan \theta} - \cos \theta \equiv \dfrac{\sin \theta}{\left(\dfrac{\sin \theta}{\cos \theta}\right)} - \cos \theta \equiv \cos \theta - \cos \theta \equiv 0$

Q2 Use $\sin^2 \theta + \cos^2 \theta \equiv 1$:
$\cos^2 \theta \equiv 1 - \sin^2 \theta \equiv (1 - \sin \theta)(1 + \sin \theta)$

Q3 Use $\sin^2 x + \cos^2 x \equiv 1$:
$\cos^2 x \equiv 1 - \sin^2 x$

$\Rightarrow \cos x = \sqrt{1 - \sin^2 x} = \sqrt{1 - \left(\dfrac{1}{2}\right)^2} = \sqrt{\dfrac{3}{4}} = \dfrac{\sqrt{3}}{2}$

You could have used your knowledge of common angles for this.

Q4 Use $\sin^2 x + \cos^2 x \equiv 1$:
$4\sin^2 x - 3\cos x + 1 \equiv 4(1 - \cos^2 x) - 3\cos x + 1$
$\equiv 4 - 4\cos^2 x - 3\cos x + 1$
$\equiv 5 - 3\cos x - 4\cos^2 x$

Q5 $\cos^2 x \equiv 1 - \sin^2 x$, $\tan x \equiv \dfrac{\sin x}{\cos x}$

$\Rightarrow \tan x \equiv \dfrac{\sqrt{\sin^2 x}}{\sqrt{1 - \sin^2 x}} \equiv \dfrac{\dfrac{\sqrt{3}}{2}}{\dfrac{1}{2}} = \sqrt{3}$

Q6 Use $\tan x \equiv \dfrac{\sin x}{\cos x}$ and $\sin^2 x + \cos^2 x \equiv 1$:

$(\tan x + 1)(\tan x - 1) \equiv \tan^2 x - 1 \equiv \dfrac{\sin^2 x}{\cos^2 x} - 1$

$\equiv \dfrac{1 - \cos^2 x}{\cos^2 x} - 1 \equiv \dfrac{1}{\cos^2 x} - \dfrac{\cos^2 x}{\cos^2 x} - 1 \equiv \dfrac{1}{\cos^2 x} - 2$

Q7 Here the student has divided both sides by $\sin \theta$. But $\sin \theta$ could equal 0, so you shouldn't divide by it. Instead the student should have rearranged:

$\cos \theta \sin \theta = \dfrac{1}{2}\sin \theta \Rightarrow \cos \theta \sin \theta - \dfrac{1}{2}\sin \theta = 0$

$\Rightarrow \sin \theta (\cos \theta - \dfrac{1}{2}) = 0$.

So there's a solution when $\cos \theta = \dfrac{1}{2} \Rightarrow \theta = 60°$,

as the student found. But there's also a solution when $\sin \theta = 0 \Rightarrow \theta = 0°$. This was not found because the student had cancelled the sin terms.

Q8 Use $\sin^2 x + \cos^2 x \equiv 1$ and $\tan x \equiv \dfrac{\sin x}{\cos x}$:

$\tan x + \dfrac{1}{\tan x} \equiv \dfrac{\sin x}{\cos x} + \dfrac{\cos x}{\sin x}$

$\equiv \dfrac{\sin^2 x + \cos^2 x}{\sin x \cos x} \equiv \dfrac{1}{\sin x \cos x}$

Q9 Use $\sin^2 x + \cos^2 x \equiv 1$:
$4 + \sin x - 6\cos^2 x \equiv 4 + \sin x - 6(1 - \sin^2 x)$
$\equiv -2 + \sin x + 6\sin^2 x \equiv (2\sin x - 1)(3\sin x + 2)$
If you're struggling to factorise, let $y = \sin x$, then it becomes $-2 + y + 6y^2$.

Q10 Use $\sin^2 x + \cos^2 x \equiv 1$:
$\sin^2 x \cos^2 y - \cos^2 x \sin^2 y$
$\equiv (1 - \cos^2 x)\cos^2 y - \cos^2 x(1 - \cos^2 y)$
$\equiv \cos^2 y - \cos^2 x \cos^2 y - \cos^2 x + \cos^2 x \cos^2 y$
$\equiv \cos^2 y - \cos^2 x$

Q11 Look at the right-angled triangle below:

Here, $\sin \theta = \dfrac{O}{H}$ and $\cos \theta = \dfrac{A}{H}$.

Substitute these fractions into $\sin^2 \theta + \cos^2 \theta = 1$:

$\left(\dfrac{O}{H}\right)^2 + \left(\dfrac{A}{H}\right)^2 = 1 \Rightarrow \dfrac{O^2}{H^2} + \dfrac{A^2}{H^2} = 1$

$\Rightarrow O^2 + A^2 = H^2$ — this is Pythagoras' theorem.

3. Trig Functions
Exercise 3.1 — Graphs of trig functions

Q1

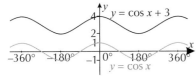

Q2 $y = \cos(x + 90°)$

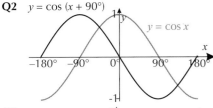

Q3

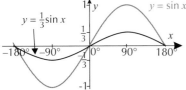

Q4

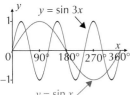

Q5

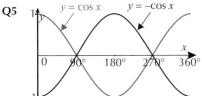

Q6 a)

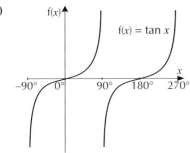

b)

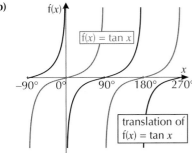

translation of
$f(x) = \tan x$

c) $f(x) = \tan(x + 90°)$
Because the graph of tan x repeats every 180°, the transformation could also be $f(x) = \tan(x − 90°)$.

Q7 a)

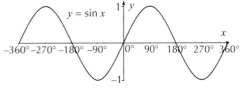

b)

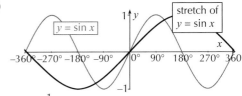

stretch of
$y = \sin x$

c) $y = \sin \frac{1}{2}x$.

Q8 a) The graph has been translated to the left by 90°.

b) $y = \sin(x + 90°)$.
You might have noticed that this graph is exactly the same as the graph of y = cos x.

Q9 a) The graph is stretched vertically by a factor of 2.

b) $y = 2\cos x$.

4. Solving Trig Equations
Exercise 4.1 — Sketching a graph

Q1 a) Find the first solution using a calculator:
$\sin x = 0.75 \Rightarrow x = 48.6°$ (1 d.p.).
Then sketch a graph:

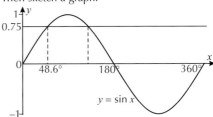

You can see from the graph that there are 2 solutions in the given interval. Using the symmetry of the graph, if one solution is at 48.6°, the other will be at $180° − 48.6° = 131.4°$ (1 d.p.).

b) Find the first solution: $\cos x = 0.31 \Rightarrow x = 71.9°$ (1 d.p.). Then sketch a graph:

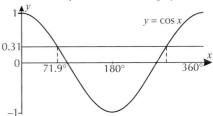

Using the symmetry of the graph to find the second solution: if one solution is at 71.9°, the other will be at $360° − 71.9° = 288.1°$ (1 d.p.).

c) Find the first solution: $\tan x = -1.5 \Rightarrow x = -56.3°$ (1 d.p.). This is outside the given interval, so add on 180° to find the first solution: $-56.3° + 180° = 123.7°$ (1 d.p.).

Then sketch a graph:

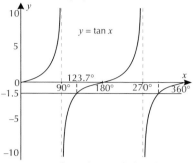

You can see from the graph that the next solution will be at 180° + 123.7° = 303.7° (1 d.p.) as tan x repeats every 180°.

d) Find the first solution: $\sin x = -0.42 \Rightarrow x = -24.8°$ (1 d.p.). This is outside the given interval, so add on 360° to find one solution: $-24.8° + 360°$ = 335.2° (1 d.p.). Then sketch a graph:

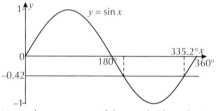

Using the symmetry of the graph, the solution you know is 360° − 335.2° = 24.8° away from 360°, so the other solution will be 24.8° away from 180°, i.e. at 180° + 24.8° = 204.8° (1 d.p.).

e) Find the first solution: $\cos x = -0.56 \Rightarrow x = 124.1°$ (1 d.p.). Then sketch a graph:

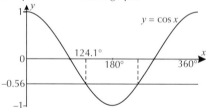

Using the symmetry of the graph to find the second solution: if one solution is at 124.1°, the other will be at 360° − 124.1° = 235.9° (1 d.p.).

f) Find the first solution: $\tan x = -0.67 \Rightarrow x = -33.8°$ (1 d.p.). This is outside the given interval, so add on 180° to find the first solution: $-33.8° + 180°$ = 146.2° (1 d.p.). Then sketch a graph:

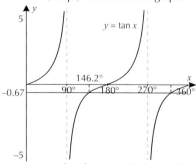

You can see that the next solution will be at 180° + 146.2° = 326.2° (1 d.p.) as tan x repeats every 180°.

Q2 a) Using your knowledge of common angles, the first solution is at $x = 45°$. Then sketch a graph:

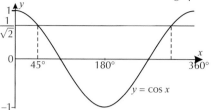

Using the symmetry of the graph, the second solution is at 360° − 45° = 315°.

b) Using common angles, the first solution is at $x = 60°$. Then sketch a graph:

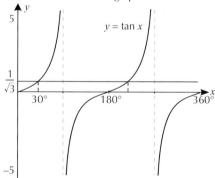

By the symmetry of the graph, the second solution is at 180° + 60° = 240°.

c) Using common angles, the first solution is at $x = 30°$. Then sketch a graph:

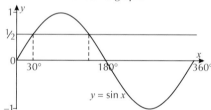

By the symmetry of the graph, the second solution is at 180° − 30° = 150°.

d) Using common angles, the first solution is at $x = 30°$. Then sketch a graph:

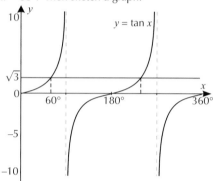

By the symmetry of the graph, the second solution is at 180° + 30° = 210°.

e) Using common angles, the first solution is at $x = 45°$. Then sketch a graph:

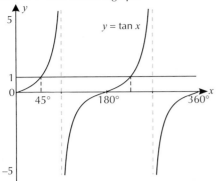

By the symmetry of the graph, the second solution is at $180° + 45° = 225°$.

f) Using your knowledge of common angles, the first solution is at $x = 30°$. Then sketch a graph:

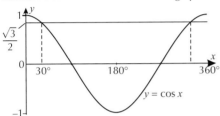

Using the symmetry of the graph, the second solution is at $360° - 30° = 330°$.

Q3 You're told that there is a solution at $143.1°$, and from the graph you can see that there is another solution in the given interval. The first solution is $180° - 143.1° = 36.9°$ away from $180°$, so the other solution will be at $180° + 36.9° = 216.9°$ (1 d.p.).
You could also have worked this one out by doing $360° - 143.1°$.

Q4 Use a calculator to find the first solution: $\tan x = 2.5 \Rightarrow x = 68.2°$ (1 d.p.). Then sketch a graph — this time the interval is bigger, so you'll need more repetitions of the tan shape:

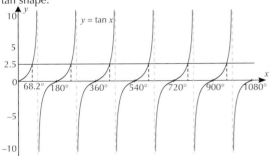

You can see from the graph that there are 6 solutions in the given interval — so just keep adding lots of $180°$ onto the first solution: $x = 68.2°, 248.2°, 428.2°, 608.2°, 788.2°, 968.2°$ (all to 1 d.p.).
You don't have to draw out the whole graph if you don't want — just sketch the first part to find the first solution, then keep adding on lots of $180°$ until the solutions are bigger than $1080°$.

Q5 Find the first solution: $\sin x = 0.81 \Rightarrow x = 54.1°$ (3 s.f.). Then sketch a graph for the interval $-360° \leq x \leq 360°$:

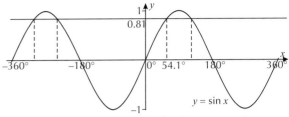

You can see from the graph that there are 4 solutions. Using the symmetry of the graph, there's another solution at $180° - 54.1° = 126°$ (3 s.f.). To find the other 2 solutions, subtract $360°$ from the values you've just found: $54.1° - 360° = -306°$ (3 s.f.) and $126° - 360° = -234°$ (3 s.f.).

Exercise 4.2 — Using a CAST diagram

Q1 0.45 is positive, so look at the quadrants where $\sin x$ is positive:

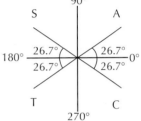

The second quadrant is the other one, so the only other solution is $180° - 26.7° = 153.3°$.

Q2 a) Use a calculator to find the first solution: $\cos x = 0.8 \Rightarrow x = 36.9°$ (1 d.p.). 0.8 is positive, so look at the other quadrants where cos is positive:

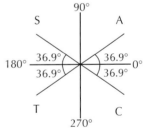

Cos is positive in the 4th quadrant, so the other solution is at $360° - 36.9° = 323.1°$ (1 d.p.).

b) Use a calculator to find the first solution: $\tan x = 2.7 \Rightarrow x = 69.7°$ (1 d.p.). 2.7 is positive, so look at the other quadrants where tan is positive:

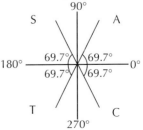

Tan is positive in the 3rd quadrant, so the other solution is at $180° + 69.7° = 249.7°$ (1 d.p.).

c) Use a calculator to find the first solution:
$\sin x = -0.15 \Rightarrow x = -8.6°$ (1 d.p.). -0.15 is negative, so look at the quadrants where sin is negative:

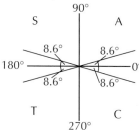

Sin is negative in the 3rd and 4th quadrants, so the solutions are at $180° + 8.6° = 188.6°$ and $360° - 8.6° = 351.4°$ (both to 1 d.p.).

d) Use a calculator to find the first solution:
$\tan x = 0.3 \Rightarrow x = 16.7°$ (1 d.p.). 0.3 is positive, so look at the other quadrants where tan is positive:

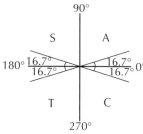

Tan is positive in the 3rd quadrant, so the other solution is at $180° + 16.7° = 196.7°$ (1 d.p.).

e) Use a calculator to find the first solution:
$\tan x = -0.6 \Rightarrow x = -31.0°$ (1 d.p.). -0.6 is negative, so look at the quadrants where tan is negative:

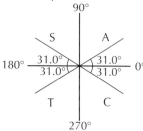

Tan is negative in the 2nd and 4th quadrants. So the solutions are at $180° - 31.0° = 149.0°$ and $360° - 31.0° = 329.0°$ (both to 1 d.p.).

f) Use a calculator to find the first solution:
$\sin x = -0.29 \Rightarrow x = -16.9°$ (1 d.p.).
-0.29 is negative, so look at the quadrants where sin is negative:

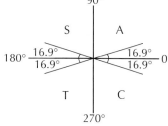

Sin is negative in the 3rd and 4th quadrants, so the solutions are at $180° + 16.9° = 196.9°$ and $360° - 16.9° = 343.1°$ (both to 1 d.p.).

g) Rearranging $4 \sin x - 1 = 0$ to make $\sin x$ the subject gives $\sin x = 0.25$. Use a calculator to find the first solution: $\sin x = 0.25 \Rightarrow x = 14.5°$ (1 d.p.). 0.25 is positive, so look at the other quadrants where sin is positive:

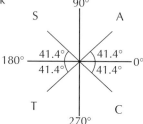

Sin is positive in the 2nd quadrant, so the other solution is at $180° - 14.5° = 165.5°$ (1 d.p.).

h) Rearranging $4 \cos x - 3 = 0$ to make $\cos x$ the subject gives $\cos x = 0.75$. Use a calculator to find the first solution: $\cos x = 0.75 \Rightarrow x = 41.4°$ (1 d.p.). 0.75 is positive, so look at the other quadrants where cos is positive:

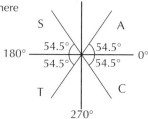

Cos is positive in the 4th quadrant, so the other solution is at $360° - 41.4° = 318.6°$ (1 d.p.).

i) Rearranging $5 \tan x + 7 = 0$ to make $\tan x$ the subject gives $\tan x = -1.4$. Use a calculator to find the first solution: $\tan x = -1.4 \Rightarrow x = -54.5°$ (1 d.p.). -1.4 is negative, so look at the quadrants where tan is negative:

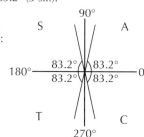

Tan is negative in the 2nd and 4th quadrants, so the solutions are at $180° - 54.5° = 125.5°$ and $360° - 54.5° = 305.5°$ (both to 1 d.p.).

Q3 Use a calculator to find the first solution:
$\tan x = -8.4 \Rightarrow x = -83.2°$ (3 s.f.).
-8.4 is negative, so look at the quadrants where tan is negative:

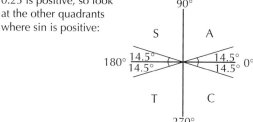

Tan is negative in the 2nd and 4th quadrants, so the solutions are at $180° - 83.2° = 96.8°$ and $360° - 83.2° = 277°$ (both to 3 s.f.).

Q4 The first solution is $x = 48.6°$ (1 d.p.).

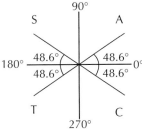

Using a CAST diagram, the solutions of sin x are also positive in the second quadrant. So the next solution is $180° - 48.6° = 131.4°$ (1 d.p.). To find the other solutions in the given interval, add on $360°$ to the solutions already found: $48.6° + 360° = 408.6°$ (1 d.p.) and $131.4° + 360° = 491.4°$ (1 d.p.).

Q5 The first solution is $x = 71.9°$ (1 d.p.).

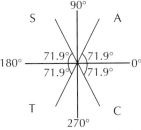

Using a CAST diagram, the solutions of cos x are also positive in the 4th quadrant. So the next solution is $360° - 71.9° = 288.1°$, but this is outside the given interval for x. To find the other solutions in the given interval, subtract $360°$ from the solutions already found: $71.9° - 360° = -288.1°$ (outside interval) and $288.1° - 360° = -71.9°$. So the solutions to 1 d.p. are $x = 71.9°$ and $-71.9°$.
You could have found the negative solutions more directly by reading the CAST diagram in the negative (i.e. clockwise) direction. Reading clockwise from O°, the angle in the 4th quadrant is −71.9°.

Q6 The first solution is $x = 55.1°$ (3 s.f.).

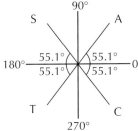

Using a CAST diagram, the solutions of sin x are also positive in the second quadrant. So the next solution is $180° - 55.1° = 125°$ (3 s.f.). To find the other solutions in the given interval, add on $360°$ to the solutions already found: $55.1° + 360° = 415°$ (3 s.f.) and $125° + 360° = 485°$ (3 s.f.).

Exercise 4.3 — Changing the interval

For all the questions in this exercise, you can either sketch a graph or use a CAST diagram.

Q1 sin $2x = 0.6$, so look for solutions in the interval $0° \leq 2x \leq 720°$. The first solution is $2x = 36.87°$ (2 d.p.). Using a CAST diagram, sin is also positive in the 2nd quadrant, so there's another solution at $2x = 180° - 36.87° = 143.13°$ (2 d.p.). The sin graph repeats every $360°$, so add $360°$ onto the answers already found: $2x = 396.87°, 503.13°$ (2 d.p.). These are solutions for $2x$, so divide them all by 2: $x = 18.4°, 71.6°, 198.4°, 251.6°$ (1 d.p.).

Q2 tan $4x = 4.6$, so look for solutions in the interval $0° \leq 4x \leq 1440°$. The first solution is $4x = 77.74°$ (2 d.p.). From the pattern of the graph, there will be another solution at $4x = 77.74° + 180° = 257.74°$ (2 d.p.). Then just keep adding on $180°$ to find the rest of the solutions within the interval: $4x = 437.74°, 617.74°, 797.74°, 977.74°, 1157.74°, 1337.74°$ (2 d.p.). These are solutions for $4x$, so divide them all by 4: $x = 19.4°, 64.4°, 109.4°, 154.4°, 199.4°, 244.4°, 289.4°, 334.4°$ (1 d.p.).

Q3 cos $3x = -0.24$, so look for solutions in the interval $0° \leq 3x \leq 1080°$. The first solution is $3x = 103.89°$ (2 d.p.). Using the symmetry of the graph, there's another solution at $3x = 360° - 103.89° = 256.11°$ (2 d.p.). To find the other solutions within the interval, add on multiples of $360°$: $3x = 463.89°, 616.11°, 823.89°, 976.11°$ (2 d.p.). These are solutions for $3x$, so divide them all by 3: $x = 34.6°, 85.4°, 154.6°, 205.4°, 274.6°, 325.4°$ (1 d.p.).

Q4 cos $2x = 0.72$, so look for solutions in the interval $0° \leq 2x \leq 720°$. The first solution is $2x = 43.95°$ (2 d.p.). Looking at the symmetry of the graph of cos x, the other solutions are $360° - 43.95° = 316.05°$, $360° + 43.95° = 403.95°$ and $720° - 43.95° = 676.05°$ (all to 2 d.p.). These are solutions for $2x$, so divide them all by 2: $x = 22.0°, 158.0°, 202.0°, 338.0°$ (1 d.p.)

Q5 First, rearrange: $\frac{1}{2}$ sin $3x - 0.61 = -0.75$
$\Rightarrow \frac{1}{2}$ sin $3x = -0.14 \Rightarrow$ sin $3x = -0.28$,
so look for solutions in the interval $0° \leq 3x \leq 1080°$. The first solution is $3x = -16.26°$ (2 d.p.). This is outside the interval, but putting $16.26°$ into a CAST diagram and looking at the quadrants where sin is negative gives $3x = 180° + 16.26° = 196.26°$ and $3x = 360° - 16.26° = 343.74°$ (2 d.p.). Add on multiples of $360°$ to find the other solutions in the interval: $3x = 556.26°, 703.74°, 916.26°, 1063.74°$ (2 d.p.). These are solutions for $3x$, so divide them all by 3: $x = 65.4°, 114.6°, 185.4°, 234.6°, 305.4°, 354.6°$ (1 d.p.).

Q6 tan $\frac{x}{2} = 2.1$, so look for solutions in the interval $0° \leq \frac{x}{2} \leq 180°$. The first solution is $\frac{x}{2} = 64.54°$ (2 d.p.). This is the only solution in the interval, as tan doesn't repeat any values between $0°$ and $180°$ (looking at its graph). Multiply by 2 to get the value of x: $x = 129.1°$ (1 d.p.).

Q7 $\cos(x - 27°) = 0.64$, so look for solutions in the interval $-27° \leq x - 27° \leq 333°$. The first solution is $x - 27° = 50.2°$ (1 d.p.). Using the symmetry of the graph, there's another solution at $x - 27° = 360° - 50.2° = 309.8°$ (1 d.p.). So the solutions are $x = 77.2°$ and $336.8°$ (1 d.p.).

Q8 $\tan(x - 140°) = -0.76$, so look for solutions in the interval $-140° \leq x - 140° \leq 220°$. The first solution is $x - 140° = -37.2°$ (1 d.p.). The tan graph repeats every $180°$, so there's another solution at $x - 140° = -37.2° + 180° = 142.8°$ (1 d.p.) (if you add on another $180°$, the answer is outside the interval). So the solutions are $x = 102.8°$ and $282.8°$ (1 d.p.).

Q9 $\sin(x + 36°) = 0.45$, so look for solutions in the interval $36° \leq x + 36° \leq 396°$. The first solution is $x + 36° = 26.7°$ (1 d.p.). This is outside the interval, so add on $360°$ to find a solution in the interval: $x + 36° = 26.7° + 360° = 386.7°$ (1 d.p.). Using a CAST diagram, the other quadrant where sin is positive is the 2nd quadrant, so there's another solution at $x + 36° = 180° - 26.7° = 153.3°$. So the solutions are $x = 117.3°$ and $350.7°$ (1 d.p.).

Q10 $\tan(x + 73°) = 1.84$, so look for solutions in the interval $73° \leq x + 73° \leq 433°$. The first solution is $x + 73° = 61.5°$ (1 d.p.). This is out of the interval, but use this and the pattern of the graph of tan x to find the other solutions. tan x repeats every $180°$, so the next two solutions are $x + 73° = 241.5°$ and $x + 73° = 421.5°$ (1 d.p.). So the two solutions are $x = 168.5°$ and $348.5°$ (1 d.p.).

Q11 $\sin(x - 45°) = -0.25$, so look for solutions in the interval $-225° \leq x - 45° \leq 315°$.
The first solution is $x - 45° = -14.48°$ (2 d.p.).
Using a CAST diagram, the other solutions are at $x - 45° = 180° + 14.48° = 194.48°$ and $x - 45° = -180° + 14.48° = -165.52°$.
So adding $45°$ to each solution gives $x = -120.5°$, $30.5°$ and $239.5°$ (1 d.p.).
There's no solution at $360° - 14.48°$ because it's outside the interval.

Q12 $\cos(x + 22.5°) = 0.13$, so look for solutions in the interval $22.5° \leq x + 22.5° \leq 382.5°$.
The first solution is $x + 22.5° = 82.53°$ (2 d.p.).
Using the symmetry of the graph, there's another solution at $x + 22.5° = 360° - 82.53° = 277.47°$.
So subtracting $22.5°$ from each solution gives $x = 60.0°$ and $255.0°$ (1 d.p.).

Exercise 4.4 — Using trig identities to solve equations

For all the questions in this exercise, you can either sketch a graph or use a CAST diagram.

Q1 a) This equation has already been factorised.
Either $\tan x - 5 = 0$ or $3 \sin x - 1 = 0$.
$\tan x - 5 = 0 \Rightarrow \tan x = 5$
$\Rightarrow x = 78.7°$ (1 d.p.)
This is the first solution. tan repeats itself every $180°$, so the other solution is $258.7°$ (1 d.p.).
$3 \sin x = 1 \Rightarrow \sin x = \frac{1}{3} \Rightarrow x = 19.5°$ (1 d.p.)
Using the symmetry of the graph, the other solution is $180° - 19.5° = 160.5°$ (1 d.p.).

b) $5 \sin x \tan x - 4 \tan x = 0$
$\tan x(5 \sin x - 4) = 0$
So $\tan x = 0$ or $5 \sin x - 4 = 0$.
$\tan x = 0 \Rightarrow x = 0°$, $180°$ and $360°$
(from the graph of tan x).
$5 \sin x - 4 = 0 \Rightarrow \sin x = \frac{4}{5}$
$\Rightarrow x = 53.1°$ (1 d.p.)
Using the symmetry of the graph, the other solution is $180° - 53.1° = 126.9°$ (1 d.p.).

c) $\tan^2 x = 9 \Rightarrow \tan x = 3$ or -3.
$\tan x = 3 \Rightarrow x = 71.6°$ (1 d.p.)
Using the repetition of the tan graph, the other solution is $180° + 71.6° = 251.6°$ (1 d.p.).
$\tan x = -3 \Rightarrow x = -71.6°$ (1 d.p.)
This is outside the interval. Keep adding $180°$ until you've found all the solutions within the interval:
$-71.6° + 180° = 108.4°$ (1 d.p.) and $108.4° + 180° = 288.4°$ (1 d.p.).

d) $4 \cos^2 x = 3 \cos x$
$4 \cos^2 x - 3 \cos x = 0$
$\cos x(4 \cos x - 3) = 0$
So $\cos x = 0$ or $4 \cos x - 3 = 0$
$\cos x = 0 \Rightarrow x = 90°$
Using the cos graph, the other solution is $270°$.
$4\cos x - 3 = 0 \Rightarrow \cos x = \frac{3}{4}$
$\Rightarrow x = 41.4°$ (1 d.p.)
Using the symmetry of the graph, the other solution is $360° - 41.4° = 318.6°$ (1 d.p.).

e) $3 \sin x = 5 \cos x \Rightarrow \tan x = \frac{5}{3}$. The first solution is $x = 59.0°$ (1 d.p.). tan x repeats every $180°$, so the other solution is $239.0°$ (1 d.p.).

f) $5 \tan^2 x - 2 \tan x = 0 \Rightarrow \tan x(5 \tan x - 2) = 0$.
So either $\tan x = 0$ or $\tan x = 0.4$. If $\tan x = 0$ then the solutions are $x = 0°$, $180°$ and $360°$.
If $\tan x = 0.4$, the first solution is $21.8°$ (1 d.p.).
The graph of tan x repeats every $180°$, so another solution is $x = 201.8°$ (1 d.p.).

g) $6 \cos^2 x - \cos x - 2 = 0$
$\Rightarrow (3 \cos x - 2)(2 \cos x + 1) = 0$
So either $\cos x = \frac{2}{3}$ or $\cos x = -0.5$. If $\cos x = \frac{2}{3}$, the first solution is $48.2°$ (1 d.p.). Looking at the symmetry of the graph of cos x, the other solution is $x = 360° - 48.2° = 311.8°$ (1 d.p.).
If $\cos x = -0.5$, the first solution is $120°$. Looking at the symmetry of the graph of cos x, the other solution is $360° - 120° = 240°$.

h) $7 \sin x + 3 \cos x = 0 \Rightarrow 7 \sin x = -3 \cos x$
$\Rightarrow \tan x = -\frac{3}{7} \Rightarrow x = -23.2°$ (1 d.p.)
This is outside the required interval. Using a CAST diagram, tan is negative in the 2nd and 4th quadrants, so the solutions are $x = 180° - 23.2° = 156.8°$ (1 d.p.) and $x = 360° - 23.2° = 336.8°$ (1 d.p.).

Q2 a) $\tan x = \sin x \cos x \Rightarrow \dfrac{\sin x}{\cos x} - \sin x \cos x = 0$
$\Rightarrow \sin x - \sin x \cos^2 x = 0$
$\Rightarrow \sin x (1 - \cos^2 x) = 0$
$\Rightarrow \sin x (\sin^2 x) = 0 \Rightarrow \sin^3 x = 0$
So $\sin x = 0$. The solutions are $x = 0°$, $180°$ and $360°$.

b) $5\cos^2 x - 9\sin x = 3 \Rightarrow 5(1 - \sin^2 x) - 9\sin x = 3$
$$\Rightarrow 5\sin^2 x + 9\sin x - 2 = 0$$
$$\Rightarrow (5\sin x - 1)(\sin x + 2) = 0$$
So either $\sin x = 0.2$ or $\sin x = -2$. $\sin x$ can't be -2, so only $\sin x = 0.2$ will give solutions.
The first solution is $x = 11.54°$ (2 d.p.).
The interval covers three intervals of 360°, so there will be 6 solutions. Looking at the symmetry of the sin graph and adding or subtracting 360°, the other solutions are
$x = -348.5°, -191.5°, 11.5°, 168.5°, 371.5°$ and $528.5°$ (1 d.p.).
If you'd used a CAST diagram here, you'd find 11.5° and 168.5° first, then add or subtract 360°.

c) $2\sin^2 x + \sin x - 1 = 0$
$(2\sin x - 1)(\sin x + 1) = 0$
So $2\sin x - 1 = 0$ or $\sin x + 1 = 0$.
$2\sin x - 1 = 0 \Rightarrow \sin x = \frac{1}{2}$
$\Rightarrow x = 30°$. Using the symmetry of the graph, another solution is $180° - 30° = 150°$.
To find the other solutions in the required interval, subtract 360° from each of these:
$30° - 360° = -330°$, and $150° - 360° = -210°$.
$\sin x + 1 = 0 \Rightarrow \sin x = -1$
From the graph, the solutions to this are
$x = -90°$ and $x = 270°$.

Q3 a) $4\sin^2 x = 3 - 3\cos x$
$4(1 - \cos^2 x) = 3 - 3\cos x$
$4 - 4\cos^2 x = 3 - 3\cos x$
$\Rightarrow 4\cos^2 x - 3\cos x - 1 = 0$, as required.

b) Solve the equation from a).
$4\cos^2 x - 3\cos x - 1 = 0$
$(4\cos x + 1)(\cos x - 1) = 0$
So $4\cos x + 1 = 0$ or $\cos x - 1 = 0$
$4\cos x + 1 = 0 \Rightarrow \cos x = -\frac{1}{4}$
$\Rightarrow x = 104.5°$ (1 d.p.)
Using the symmetry of the graph, the other solution is $360° - 104.5° = 255.5°$ (1 d.p.)
$\cos x - 1 = 0 \Rightarrow \cos x = 1$
Using the cos graph, the solutions are
$x = 0$ and $x = 360°$.

Q4 $9\sin^2 2x + 3\cos 2x = 7 \Rightarrow 9(1 - \cos^2 2x) + 3\cos 2x = 7$
$$\Rightarrow 9 - 9\cos^2 2x + 3\cos 2x = 7$$
$$\Rightarrow 9\cos^2 2x - 3\cos 2x - 2 = 0$$
$$\Rightarrow (3\cos 2x + 1)(3\cos 2x - 2) = 0$$
So either $\cos 2x = -\frac{1}{3}$ or $\cos 2x = \frac{2}{3}$. For $\cos 2x = -\frac{1}{3}$ look for solutions in the interval $0° \leq 2x \leq 720°$.
The first solution is $2x = 109.47°$ (2 d.p.). Looking at the symmetry of the graph of $\cos x$, the other solutions are $2x = 250.53°, 469.47°$ and $610.53°$ (2 d.p.).
Dividing by 2 gives the solutions: $x = 54.7°, 125.3°, 234.7°$ and $305.3°$ (1 d.p.).
For $\cos 2x = \frac{2}{3}$, again look for solutions in the interval $0° \leq 2x \leq 720°$. The first solution is $2x = 48.19°$ (2 d.p.). Looking at the symmetry of the graph of $\cos x$, the other solutions are $2x = 311.81°, 408.19°, 671.81°$ (2 d.p.). Dividing by 2 gives the solutions:
$x = 24.1°, 155.9°, 204.1°$ and $335.9°$ (1 d.p.).

Q5 $\dfrac{\cos x}{\tan x} + \sin x = 3 \Rightarrow \dfrac{\cos x}{\left(\dfrac{\sin x}{\cos x}\right)} + \sin x = 3$

$$\Rightarrow \frac{\cos^2 x}{\sin x} + \sin x = 3 \Rightarrow \cos^2 x + \sin^2 x = 3\sin x$$
$$\Rightarrow 1 = 3\sin x \Rightarrow \sin x = \frac{1}{3}$$
The first solution is $x = 19.5°$ (1 d.p.). Looking at the symmetry of the graph of $\sin x$, the other solutions are $x = -340.5°, -199.5°$ and $160.5°$ (1 d.p.).

Chapter 9: Exponentials and Logarithms

1. Exponentials

Exercise 1.1 — Exponentials

Q1 a) – c)

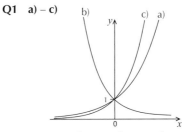

Q2 a) $3e^{3x} = h(x)$ **b)** $3^x = f(x)$ **c)** $3e^{-x} = g(x)$

Q3 a) $y = e^{3x}$, so the gradient at any value of x is $3e^{3x}$.
At $x = 0$, gradient $= 3e^{3 \times 0} = 3e^0 = 3 \times 1 = 3$
At $x = 1$, gradient $= 3e^{3 \times 1} = 3e^3$
The question asks for exact answers, so leave them in terms of e.

b) $y = 5e^{0.5x}$, so the gradient at any value of x is $2.5e^{0.5x}$.
At $x = -2$, gradient $= 2.5e^{0.5 \times -2} = 2.5e^{-1} = \dfrac{2.5}{e}$
At $x = 2$, gradient $= 2.5e^{0.5 \times 2} = 2.5e^1 = 2.5e$

c) $x = 2.5e^{6t}$, so the gradient at any value of t is $15e^{6t}$.
At $t = \dfrac{1}{3}$, gradient $= 15e^{6 \times \frac{1}{3}} = 15e^2$
At $t = 5$, gradient $= 15e^{6 \times 5} = 15e^{30}$

Q4 "The gradient of the curve of f(t) is always 0.4 times the value of f(t)" — this tells you that the gradient is directly proportional to the curve, i.e. it's the exponential function where $f(t) = Ae^{kt}$ for constants A and k.
You also know that the gradient of an exponential is kAe^{kt} — so $k = 0.4 \Rightarrow f(t) = Ae^{0.4t}$.
"When first counted, there were 7 rabbits" — this tells you that at $t = 0$, $f(t) = 7$
$\Rightarrow 7 = Ae^{0.4 \times 0} = Ae^0 = A$. So $f(t) = 7e^{0.4t}$.
An estimate for the number of rabbits after 5 years is:
$f(5) = 7 \times e^{0.4 \times 5} = 7 \times e^2 \approx 52$ rabbits.

2. Logs

Exercise 2.1 — Logs

Q1 a) $\log_2 8 = 3$ **b)** $\log_5 625 = 4$
c) $\log_{49} 7 = \dfrac{1}{2}$ **d)** $\log_8 4 = \dfrac{2}{3}$
e) $\log_{10} \dfrac{1}{100} = -2$ **f)** $\log_2 0.125 = -3$
g) $\log_4 9 = x$ **h)** $\log_x 40 = 3$
i) $\log_8 x = 11$

Q2 a) $a = e^6$ **b)** $t = 5^{0.2}$ **c)** $m = 4^1 = 4$

d) $p = e^{13}$ **e)** $k = 10^5 = 100\,000$ **f)** $a = x^m$

Q3 a) 3 **b)** –2 **c)** 0.477 (3 d.p.)

d) 0.693 (3 d.p.) **e)** 0 **f)** 1.792 (3 d.p.)

Use the 'log' or 'ln' button on your calculator to work these out.

Q4 a) $a = \log_2 4 \Rightarrow 2^a = 4 = 2^2 \Rightarrow a = 2$

b) $b = \log_3 27 \Rightarrow 3^b = 27 = 3^3 \Rightarrow b = 3$

c) $c = \log_5 0.2 \Rightarrow 5^c = 0.2 = \frac{1}{5} = 5^{-1} \Rightarrow c = -1$

Q5 a) $x^2 = 49 \Rightarrow x = 7$

b) $x^3 = 8 \Rightarrow x = 2$

c) $x^5 = 100\,000 \Rightarrow x = 10$

d) $x^{\frac{1}{2}} = 3 \Rightarrow x = 3^2 \Rightarrow x = 9$

e) $x^{\frac{1}{3}} = 7 \Rightarrow x = 7^3 \Rightarrow x = 343$

f) $x^{\frac{1}{5}} = 2 \Rightarrow x = 2^5 \Rightarrow x = 32$

Q6 a) (i) $e^x = 5 \Rightarrow \ln e^x = \ln 5 \Rightarrow x = \ln 5$

(ii) $\ln 5 = 1.61$ (3 s.f.)

b) (i) $\ln x = 8 \Rightarrow e^{\ln x} = e^8 \Rightarrow x = e^8$

(ii) $e^8 = 2980$ (3 s.f.)

c) (i) $e^{3t} = 11 \Rightarrow \ln e^{3t} = \ln 11 \Rightarrow 3t = \ln 11$

$\Rightarrow t = \dfrac{\ln 11}{3}$

(ii) $\dfrac{\ln 11}{3} = 0.799$ (3 s.f.)

Q7 a) $a^2 = x$ and $a^4 = y$, so $y = x^2$.

b) $a^3 = x$ and $(2a)^3 = y \Rightarrow 8a^3 = y$, so $y = 8x$.

c) $e^5 = x$ and $e^{20} = y$, $(e^5)^4 = y$, so $y = x^4$

3. Solving Equations

Exercise 3.1 — Laws of logs

Q1 a) $\log_a 2 + \log_a 5 = \log_a (2 \times 5) = \log_a 10$

b) $\ln 8 + \ln 7 = \ln (8 \times 7) = \ln 56$

c) $\log_b 8 - \log_b 4 = \log_b (8 \div 4) = \log_b 2$

d) $\log_m 15 - \log_m 5 = \log_m (15 \div 5) = \log_m 3$

e) $3 \log_a 4 = \log_a (4^3) = \log_a 64$

f) $2 \ln 7 = \ln (7^2) = \ln 49$

g) $\frac{1}{2} \log_b 16 = \log_b (16^{\frac{1}{2}}) = \log_b 4$

h) $\frac{2}{3} \log_a 125 = \log_a (125^{\frac{2}{3}}) = \log_a 25$

i) $\frac{1}{5} \ln 4^5 = \ln ((4^5)^{\frac{1}{5}}) = \ln (4^{5 \times \frac{1}{5}}) = \ln 4^1 = \ln 4$

Q2 a) $2 \log_a 5 + \log_a 4 = \log_a (5^2) + \log_a 4$
$= \log_a (25 \times 4) = \log_a 100$

b) $3 \log_m 2 - \log_m 4 = \log_m (2^3) - \log_m 4$
$= \log_m (8 \div 4) = \log_m 2$

c) $3 \ln 4 - 2 \ln 8 = \ln (4^3) - \ln (8^2)$
$= \ln (64 \div 64) = \ln 1 = 0$

d) $\frac{2}{3} \ln 216 - 2 \ln 3 = \ln (216^{\frac{2}{3}}) - \ln (3^2)$
$= \ln (36 \div 9) = \ln 4$

e) $1 + \log_a 6 = \log_a a + \log_a 6 = \log_a 6a$

f) $2 - \log_b 5 = 2 \log_b b - \log_b 5 = \log_b b^2 - \log_b 5$
$= \log_b \left(\dfrac{b^2}{5}\right)$

Q3 a) $\log_a 6 = \log_a (2 \times 3) = \log_a 2 + \log_a 3 = x + y$

b) $\log_a 16 = \log_a 2^4 = 4 \log_a 2 = 4x$

c) $\log_a 60 = \log_a (2 \times 2 \times 3 \times 5)$
$= \log_a 2^2 + \log_a 3 + \log_a 5 = 2x + y + z$

Q4 a) $\log_b b^3 = 3 \log_b b = 3$

b) $\log_a \sqrt{a} = \log_a a^{\frac{1}{2}} = \frac{1}{2} \log_a a = \frac{1}{2}$

c) $\ln 4e - 2 \ln 2 = \ln 4 + \ln e - \ln 2^2$
$= \ln 4 + 1 - \ln 4 = 1$

d) $\ln 9 + \ln \frac{e}{3} - \ln 3 = \ln 3^2 + \ln e - \ln 3 - \ln 3$
$= 2 \ln 3 + \ln e - 2 \ln 3 = \ln e = 1$

Q5 a) $\log_2 4^x = x \log_2 4 = x \log_2 2^2 = 2x \log_2 2 = 2x$

b) $\dfrac{\ln 54 - \ln 6}{\ln 3} = \dfrac{\ln (54 \div 6)}{\ln 3} = \dfrac{\ln 9}{\ln 3} = \dfrac{\ln 3^2}{\ln 3} = \dfrac{2 \ln 3}{\ln 3} = 2$

Q6 $4 + \log_c \dfrac{1}{c^2} + \log_c \sqrt{c} = 4 + \log_c c^{-2} + \log_c c^{\frac{1}{2}}$
$= 4 - 2 \log_c c + \frac{1}{2} \log_c c = 4 - 2 + \frac{1}{2} = 2\frac{1}{2}$

Exercise 3.2 — Changing the base of a log

Q1 a) $\dfrac{\log_{10} 2}{\log_{10} 9}$ **b)** $\dfrac{\log_{10} 8}{\log_{10} 4}$ **c)** $\dfrac{\log_{10} 16}{\log_{10} 17}$

Q2 a) 0.613 (3 s.f.) **b)** 0.315 (3 s.f.)

c) 2.33 (3 s.f.) **d)** 0.861 (3 s.f.)

If your calculator can't do logs of any base, you'll need to use the change of base formula.

Q3 a) $\log_{11} 19$

b) $\log_7 2$

c) $\log_3 4 \times \log_4 5 = \dfrac{\log_{10} 4}{\log_{10} 3} \times \dfrac{\log_{10} 5}{\log_{10} 4} = \dfrac{\log_{10} 5}{\log_{10} 3} = \log_3 5$

This question uses the 'change of base' formula in reverse.

Exercise 3.3 — Solving equations

Q1 a) Take logs of both sides:
$\log 2^x = \log 3 \Rightarrow x \log 2 = \log 3$
$\Rightarrow x = \dfrac{\log 3}{\log 2} = 1.584... = 1.58$ (3 s.f.)

b) $7^x = 2 \Rightarrow \log 7^x = \log 2 \Rightarrow x \log 7 = \log 2$
$\Rightarrow x = \dfrac{\log 2}{\log 7} = 0.3562... = 0.356$ (3 s.f.)

c) $1.8^x = 0.4 \Rightarrow \log 1.8^x = \log 0.4$
$\Rightarrow x \log 1.8 = \log 0.4$
$\Rightarrow x = \dfrac{\log 0.4}{\log 1.8} = -1.558... = -1.56$ (3 s.f.)

Notice this solution is negative, because log 0.4 is negative.

d) $0.7^x = 3 \Rightarrow \log 0.7^x = \log 3 \Rightarrow x \log 0.7 = \log 3$
$\Rightarrow x = \dfrac{\log 3}{\log 0.7} = -3.080... = -3.08$ (3 s.f.)

e) $2^{3x-1} = 5 \Rightarrow \log 2^{3x-1} = \log 5 \Rightarrow (3x-1)\log 2 = \log 5$
$\Rightarrow 3x \log 2 = \log 5 + \log 2 = \log (5 \times 2)$
$\Rightarrow x = \dfrac{\log 10}{3 \log 2} = 1.11$ (3 s.f.)

f) $0.4^{5x-4} = 2 \Rightarrow \log 0.4^{5x-4} = \log 2$
$\Rightarrow (5x - 4)\log 0.4 = \log 2$
$\Rightarrow 5x \log 0.4 = \log 2 + 4 \log 0.4$
$\Rightarrow x = \dfrac{\log 2 + 4 \log 0.4}{5 \log 0.4} = 0.649$ (3 s.f.)

Q2 a) $2^{4x} = 3^{100} \Rightarrow \log_2 2^{4x} = \log_2 3^{100}$
$\Rightarrow 4x \log_2 2 = 100 \log_2 3 \Rightarrow 4x = 100 \log_2 3$
$\Rightarrow x = 25 \log_2 3$

b) $11^{6x} = 10^{90} \Rightarrow \log_{11} 11^{6x} = \log_{11} 10^{90}$
$\Rightarrow 6x \log_{11} 11 = 90 \log_{11} 10 \Rightarrow 6x = 90 \log_{11} 10$
$\Rightarrow x = 15 \log_{11} 10$

c) $6^{50-x} = 2^{50} \Rightarrow \log_6 6^{50-x} = \log_6 2^{50}$
$\Rightarrow (50 - x) \log_6 6 = 50 \log_6 2 \Rightarrow 50 - x = 50 \log_6 2$
$\Rightarrow x = 50 - 50 \log_6 2 = 50(1 - \log_6 2)$
$= 50(\log_6 6 - \log_6 2) = 50 \log_6 3$

Q3 a) Take exponentials of both sides using base 10 (since the logarithm is base 10):
$10^{\log 5x} = 10^3 \Rightarrow 5x = 1000 \Rightarrow x = 200$

b) Take exponentials of both sides (using base 2):
$\Rightarrow 2^{\log_2 (x+3)} = 2^4 \Rightarrow x + 3 = 16 \Rightarrow x = 13$

c) Take exponentials of both sides (using base 3):
$\Rightarrow 3^{\log_3 (5-2x)} = 3^{2.5} \Rightarrow 5 - 2x = 3^{2.5}$
$\Rightarrow x = \dfrac{5 - 3^{2.5}}{2} = -5.294... = -5.29$ (3 s.f.)

Q4 a) $4^{x+1} = 3^{2x} \Rightarrow \log 4^{x+1} = \log 3^{2x}$
$\Rightarrow (x + 1) \log 4 = 2x \log 3$

Multiply out the brackets:
$\Rightarrow x \log 4 + \log 4 = 2x \log 3$

Collect x-terms on one side:
$\Rightarrow \log 4 = 2x \log 3 - x \log 4 = x (2 \log 3 - \log 4)$
$\Rightarrow x = \dfrac{\log 4}{2 \log 3 - \log 4} = 1.709... = 1.71$ (3 s.f.)

b) $2^{5-x} = 4^{x+3} \Rightarrow \log 2^{5-x} = \log 4^{x+3}$
$\Rightarrow (5 - x) \log 2 = (x + 3) \log 4$

But $\log 4 = \log 2^2 = 2 \log 2$
$\Rightarrow (5 - x) \log 2 = 2(x + 3) \log 2$
$\Rightarrow 5 - x = 2(x + 3)$
$\Rightarrow -1 = 3x \Rightarrow x = -\dfrac{1}{3}$

c) $3^{2x-1} = 6^{3-x} \Rightarrow \log 3^{2x-1} = \log 6^{3-x}$
$\Rightarrow (2x - 1) \log 3 = (3 - x) \log 6$
$\Rightarrow 2x \log 3 - \log 3 = 3 \log 6 - x \log 6$
$\Rightarrow 2x \log 3 + x \log 6 = 3 \log 6 + \log 3$
$\Rightarrow x (2 \log 3 + \log 6) = 3 \log 6 + \log 3$
$\Rightarrow x = \dfrac{3 \log 6 + \log 3}{2 \log 3 + \log 6} = 1.622... = 1.62$ (3 s.f.)

Q5 a) $\log_6 x = 1 - \log_6 (x + 1)$
$\Rightarrow \log_6 x + \log_6 (x + 1) = 1 \Rightarrow \log_6 x(x + 1) = 1$
Take exponentials of base 6 of both sides to get:
$\Rightarrow x(x + 1) = 6^1 \Rightarrow x^2 + x - 6 = 0$
$\Rightarrow (x + 3)(x - 2) = 0 \Rightarrow x = 2$
$x = -3$ is not a solution because logarithms of negative numbers don't exist.

b) $\log_2 (2x + 1) = 3 + 2 \log_2 x$
$\Rightarrow \log_2 (2x + 1) = 3 + \log_2 x^2$
$\Rightarrow \log_2 (2x + 1) - \log_2 x^2 = 3 \Rightarrow \log_2 \dfrac{2x + 1}{x^2} = 3$
Take exponentials of base 2 of both sides to get:
$\Rightarrow \dfrac{2x + 1}{x^2} = 2^3 \Rightarrow 2x + 1 = 8x^2$
$\Rightarrow 8x^2 - 2x - 1 = 0 \Rightarrow (4x + 1)(2x - 1) = 0$
So $x = \dfrac{1}{2}$

Q6 a) $5e^{3t} = 11 \Rightarrow e^{3t} = \dfrac{11}{5} \Rightarrow \ln e^{3t} = \ln\left(\dfrac{11}{5}\right)$
$\Rightarrow 3t = \ln\left(\dfrac{11}{5}\right) \Rightarrow t = \dfrac{1}{3} \ln\left(\dfrac{11}{5}\right)$

b) $e^{(0.5x + 3)} = 9 \Rightarrow \ln e^{(0.5x + 3)} = \ln 9 \Rightarrow 0.5x + 3 = \ln 9$
$\Rightarrow 0.5x = \ln 9 - 3 \Rightarrow x = 2 (\ln 9 - 3)$

c) $10 - 3e^{(1-2x)} = 8 \Rightarrow 3e^{(1-2x)} = 2 \Rightarrow e^{(1-2x)} = \dfrac{2}{3}$
$\Rightarrow \ln e^{(1-2x)} = \ln \dfrac{2}{3} \Rightarrow 1 - 2x = \ln \dfrac{2}{3}$
$\Rightarrow 2x = 1 - \ln \dfrac{2}{3} \Rightarrow x = \dfrac{1}{2}\left(1 - \ln \dfrac{2}{3}\right)$

d) $3 \ln (2x) = 7 \Rightarrow \ln (2x) = \dfrac{7}{3}$
$\Rightarrow e^{\ln (2x)} = e^{\frac{7}{3}} \Rightarrow 2x = e^{\frac{7}{3}} \Rightarrow x = \dfrac{1}{2} e^{\frac{7}{3}}$

e) $\ln (5t - 3) = 4 \Rightarrow e^{\ln (5t-3)} = e^4 \Rightarrow 5t - 3 = e^4$
$\Rightarrow t = \dfrac{1}{5} (e^4 + 3)$

f) $6 - \ln (0.5x) = 3 \Rightarrow \ln (0.5x) = 3 \Rightarrow e^{\ln (0.5x)} = e^3$
$\Rightarrow 0.5x = e^3 \Rightarrow x = 2e^3$

Q7 a) $e^{3x} = 27 \Rightarrow \ln (e^{3x}) = \ln 27 \Rightarrow 3x = \ln 27 = \ln (3^3)$
$\Rightarrow 3x = 3 \ln 3 \Rightarrow x = \ln 3$.

If you're asked to give your answer in the form ln a where a is a number, try and write the number inside the logarithm as a power of a and use the third log law to get it in the form you want.

b) $e^{(6x-1)} = \dfrac{1}{3} \Rightarrow \ln e^{(6x-1)} = \ln\left(\dfrac{1}{3}\right) \Rightarrow 6x - 1 = \ln (3^{-1})$
$\Rightarrow 6x = 1 - \ln 3 \Rightarrow x = \dfrac{1}{6} (1 - \ln 3)$

c) $\dfrac{1}{3} e^{(1-x)} - 3 = 0 \Rightarrow e^{(1-x)} = 9 \Rightarrow \ln e^{(1-x)} = \ln 9$
$\Rightarrow 1 - x = \ln 9 \Rightarrow x = 1 - \ln (3^2) \Rightarrow x = 1 - 2 \ln 3$

Q8 a) $\ln 5 + \ln x = 7 \Rightarrow \ln (5x) = 7 \Rightarrow e^{\ln (5x)} = e^7 \Rightarrow 5x = e^7$
$\Rightarrow x = \dfrac{e^7}{5}$

b) $\ln (2x) + \ln (3x) = 15 \Rightarrow \ln (2x \times 3x) = 15$
$\Rightarrow \ln (6x^2) = 15 \Rightarrow e^{\ln 6x^2} = e^{15} \Rightarrow 6x^2 = e^{15}$
$\Rightarrow x = \sqrt{\dfrac{1}{6} e^{15}} = \dfrac{1}{\sqrt{6}} e^{\frac{15}{2}}$

c) $\ln (x^2 - 4) - \ln (2x) = 0 \Rightarrow \ln\left(\dfrac{x^2 - 4}{2x}\right) = 0$
$\Rightarrow \dfrac{x^2 - 4}{2x} = e^0 = 1 \Rightarrow x^2 - 4 = 2x$
$\Rightarrow x^2 - 2x - 4 = 0 \Rightarrow x = \dfrac{2 \pm \sqrt{20}}{2} = 1 \pm \sqrt{5}$
But $x > 0$ otherwise $\ln 2x$ would be undefined, so $x = 1 + \sqrt{5}$.
You might have spotted that ln (x² − 4) − ln (2x) = 0
⇒ ln (x² − 4) = ln (2x) ⇒ x² − 4 = 2x, then solved the resulting quadratic to find the answer.

d) $3 \ln (x^2) + 5 \ln x = 2 \Rightarrow 6 \ln x + 5 \ln x = 2$
$\Rightarrow 11 \ln x = 2 \Rightarrow \ln x = \dfrac{2}{11} \Rightarrow x = e^{\frac{2}{11}}$

Q9 $9^{x-2} = 3^y \Rightarrow (3^2)^{x-2} = 3^y \Rightarrow 3^{(2(x-2))} = 3^y$ so $2(x - 2) = y$
$\log_3 2x = 1 + \log_3 y \Rightarrow \log_3 2x - \log_3 y = 1$
$\Rightarrow \log_3 \dfrac{2x}{y} = 1 \Rightarrow \dfrac{2x}{y} = 3^1 \Rightarrow 2x = 3y$
Solve $2(x - 2) = y$ and $2x = 3y$ simultaneously:
$2x = 3y$ so put this into $2(x - 2) = y$
$\Rightarrow 3y - 4 = y \Rightarrow 2y = 4 \Rightarrow y = 2$ and $x = 3$

Q10 a) Let $y = 2^x$, then $2^{2x} - 5(2^x) + 4 = 0$ is equivalent to the quadratic equation $y^2 - 5y + 4 = 0$
$\Rightarrow (y - 1)(y - 4) = 0$, so $y = 1$ or $y = 4$
So $2^x = 4$ or $2^x = 1 \Rightarrow x = 2$ or $x = 0$.
The y² in the quadratic equation comes from 2²ˣ = (2ˣ)².

b) Let $y = 4^x$, then $4^{2x} - 17(4^x) + 16 = 0$ is equivalent to the quadratic equation $y^2 - 17y + 16 = 0$
$\Rightarrow (y - 1)(y - 16) = 0$, so $y = 1$ or $y = 16$
So $4^x = 1$ or $4^x = 16 \Rightarrow x = 0$ or $x = 2$.

c) Let $y = 3^x$, then $3^{2x+2} = 3^{2x} \times 3^2 = y^2 \times 9 = 9y^2$.
So $3^{2x+2} - 82(3^x) + 9 = 0$ is equivalent to the quadratic equation $9y^2 - 82y + 9 = 0$.
$\Rightarrow (9y - 1)(y - 9) = 0$, so $y = \frac{1}{9}$ or $y = 9$.
So $3^x = \frac{1}{9}$ or $3^x = 9 \Rightarrow x = -2$ or $x = 2$.

d) Let $y = 2^x$, then $2^{2x+3} = 2^{2x} \times 2^3 = y^2 \times 8 = 8y^2$.
So $2^{2x+3} - 9(2^x) + 1 = 0$ is equivalent to the quadratic equation $8y^2 - 9y + 1 = 0$.
$\Rightarrow (8y - 1)(y - 1) = 0$, so $y = \frac{1}{8}$ or $y = 1$.
So $2^x = \frac{1}{8}$ or $2^x = 1 \Rightarrow x = -3$ or $x = 0$.

e) Substitute $y = e^{2x} \Rightarrow y^2 + 4y + 5 = 0$.
Using the quadratic formula:
$$x = \frac{-4 \pm \sqrt{4^2 - (4 \times 5 \times 1)}}{2}$$
$$= \frac{-4 \pm \sqrt{16 - 20}}{2} = \frac{-4 \pm \sqrt{-4}}{2}$$
There are no real solutions since there is a negative square root.
The question says "where possible", which implies that there might not be any real solutions.

f) Substitute $y = e^x \Rightarrow 3y^2 + 10y + 3 = 0$
$\Rightarrow (3y + 1)(y + 3) = 0 \Rightarrow e^x = -\frac{1}{3}$ or $e^x = -3$,
both of which are impossible since $e^x > 0$.
There are no solutions.

4. Modelling Exponential Growth and Decay

Exercise 4.1 — Modelling exponential growth and decay

Q1 When $t = 10$, $A = \frac{A_0}{2}$ so $\frac{A_0}{2} = A_0 e^{-10k} \Rightarrow \frac{1}{2} = e^{-10k}$
$\Rightarrow k = -\frac{1}{10} \ln\left(\frac{1}{2}\right) = 0.0693... = 0.0693$ (3 s.f.)

a) You want to find t when $A = \frac{A_0}{4}$,
so $\frac{A_0}{4} = A_0 e^{(-0.0693... \times t)} \Rightarrow \frac{1}{4} = e^{(-0.0693... \times t)}$
$\Rightarrow t = -\frac{1}{0.0693...} \ln\left(\frac{1}{4}\right) = 20.0$ years (3 s.f.).
So after 20 years the substance will be reduced to a quarter of its original activity.
Note that a much easier way to do this would be to think of it as 'half and half again'. The substance will be a quarter of its activity after two half lives which is $2 \times 10 = 20$ years.

b) When $t = 5$, $A = 200$, so $200 = A_0 e^{(-0.0693... \times 5)}$,
so $A_0 = 200 e^{(0.0693... \times 5)} = 283$ Bq (3 s.f.).

c) If $t = 15$, then $A = 283 \times e^{(-0.0693... \times 15)} = 100$ Bq (3 s.f.)

Q2 a) If $t = 0$, $T = 225 - 207e^0 = 18$ °C.

b) Let $t = 5$, then $T = 225 - 207 e^{-\frac{5}{8}} = 114$ °C. (3 s.f.).

c) Let $T = 190$ °C. Then $190 = 225 - 207 e^{-\frac{t}{8}}$
$\Rightarrow e^{-\frac{t}{8}} = \frac{190 - 225}{-207} = \frac{35}{207} \Rightarrow -\frac{t}{8} = \ln\left(\frac{35}{207}\right)$
$\Rightarrow t = -8 \ln\left(\frac{35}{207}\right) = 14.2$ min (to 3 s.f.).
So the oven reaches 190 °C just after 12:14.

d)

e) As $t \to \infty$, $e^{-\frac{t}{8}} \to 0$, so $T \to 225 - 0 = 225$.
So in the model, the asymptote at $T = 225$ acts as a "cap" — even if left on forever, the oven temperature would never rise above 225 °C.

Q3 a) When $t = 0$, $F = 4$, so $F_0 = 4$.
When $t = 6$, $F = 10$ so $10 = 4e^{6g}$ so
$g = \frac{1}{6} \ln\left(\frac{10}{4}\right) = 0.1527... = 0.153$ (3 s.f.).

b) Let $t = 12$, then $F = 4e^{(12 \times 0.1527...)} = 25$.
So after 12 hours the fungus will be 25 mm².

c) Let $F = 15$. Then $15 = 4e^{(0.1527... \times t)}$
$\Rightarrow e^{(0.1527... \times t)} = \frac{15}{4}$
$\Rightarrow t = \frac{1}{0.1527...} \ln\left(\frac{15}{4}\right) = 8.66$ (3 s.f.).
The fungus will take 8.66 hours (or 8 hours 39 minutes) to grow to 15 mm².

d) E.g. there's no restriction, so according to the model the fungus could grow infinitely large.

Q4 When $t = 0$, $N = 3$. So $3 = Ae^0 \Rightarrow A = 3$.

a) Let $t = 0.5$ (hours). Then $N = 3e^{-t} = 3e^{-0.5} = 1.82$ mg/l.

b) Let $N = 0.1$. Then $0.1 = 3e^{-t}$ so
$t = -\ln\left(\frac{0.1}{3}\right) = 3.40$ hours (3 s.f.).

c)

d) The gradient is $-3e^{-t}$.
The gradient of the curve Ae^{kt} is kAe^{kt}. Here, $k = -1$ and $A = 3$.

Q5 a) The negative coefficient means that as t gets larger, V gets smaller — this is exponential decay. The car will lose value over time.

b) When $t = 0$, $V = 1500 + 9000e^0 = £10\,500$.

c) Let $t = 5$, then $V = 1500 + 9000 e^{-\frac{5}{3}} = £3200$ (3 s.f.).

d) Let $V = 2500$, then $2500 = 1500 + 9000 e^{-\frac{t}{3}}$
$\Rightarrow 1000 = 9000 e^{-\frac{t}{3}} \Rightarrow \frac{1}{9} = e^{-\frac{t}{3}}$
$\Rightarrow t = -3\ln\left(\frac{1}{9}\right) = 6.59$ (3 s.f.). The car will have a value less than £2500 after 7 whole years.
Note: After 6 years the car will still have a value above £2500 so the answer is 7 and not 6.

e)
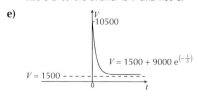

Q6 a) When $t = 0$, $H = 20\,e^{b \times 0} = 20$. So 20 represents the initial burnt area of forest, in hectares.

b) $b = \ln 1.8 = 0.5877... = 0.588$ (3 s.f.)

c) Let $t = 3$ then $H = 20e^{(0.5877... \times 3)} = 117$ hectares (3 s.f.).

d) If $H = 500$, $500 = 20e^{(0.5877... \times t)} \Rightarrow 25 = e^{(0.5877... \times t)}$
$\Rightarrow \ln 25 = 0.5877... \times t$
$\Rightarrow t = \dfrac{1}{0.5877...}\ln 25 = 5.48$ hours (3 s.f.)

e) At $t = k$, $H = H_k = 20e^{(\ln 1.8)k}$
At $t = k + 1$, $H = H_{k+1} = 20e^{(\ln 1.8)(k+1)}$
$= 20e^{(\ln 1.8)k + \ln 1.8} = 20e^{(\ln 1.8)k}e^{\ln 1.8} = H_k \times 1.8$
Every hour the burnt area is multiplied by 1.8.
This represents a percentage increase of 80%.

f) E.g. if the fire burnt unchecked, then according to the model $H \to \infty$ as $t \to \infty$, i.e. the area of burnt forest would be infinitely large. This is clearly unrealistic, as the forest will have a finite area.

5. Using Logarithmic Graphs

Exercise 5.1 — Logarithmic graphs in linear form

Q1 l is a straight line of the form $y = mx + c$, where $y = \log V$, $x = t$, gradient $m = -\dfrac{1}{40}$ and intercept $c = 4$, so:
$\log V = 4 - \dfrac{1}{40}t$. When the machine is 20 years old, $t = 20$, so $\log V = 4 - \dfrac{1}{40} \times 20 = 4 - \dfrac{1}{2} = \dfrac{7}{2}$.
So $V = 10^{\frac{7}{2}} = £3162.2776...$
$= £3200$ (to the nearest £100)

Q2 a) (i)

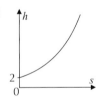

(ii)

log₃ h graph

(iii) E.g. the second graph is more useful for calculations — it's easier to calculate the gradient of a straight line than it is a curve.

b) E.g. as $s \to \infty$, $h \to \infty$. This implies that the tank is capable of holding an infinite amount of water, which is obviously unrealistic.
A tank reaches its maximum capacity, H, at time S. So adjust the model to say that for $s \geq S$, $h = H$.

Q3 The graph is of the form $p = at^b$
$\Rightarrow \log p = \log a + b\log t$. To find the straight-line form you need to find logs of both t and p (each to 3 d.p.):

log t	0	0.477	0.602	0.778	0.954
log p	0.301	1.146	1.342	1.643	1.944

You can now plot $\log p$ against $\log t$:

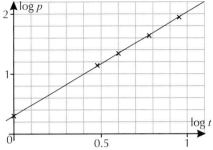

When $\log t = 0$, $\log a = 0.301 = \log 2 \Rightarrow a = 2$
b is the gradient of the graph, so take 2 points
— e.g. $(0, 0.301)$ and $(0.602, 1.342)$. The gradient is
$\dfrac{1.342 - 0.301}{0.602 - 0} = \dfrac{1.041}{0.602} = 1.72... = 1.7$ (1 d.p.)
So the graph can be approximated using the equation $p = 2t^{1.7}$

Q4 $x = kb^t$, so $\log x = \log k + t \log b$. So to make a linear graph, you need to find $\log x$ (3 d.p.) for each value of x:

t	5	50	100	200	300
x	80.449	32.411	11.803	1.565	0.207
$\log x$	1.906	1.511	1.072	0.195	−0.684

You can now plot $\log x$ against t:

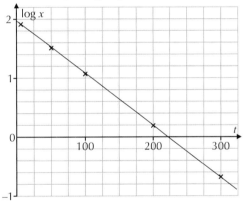

The line of best fit meets the vertical axis at around 1.95 — i.e. when $t = 0$, $\log x = 1.95 \Rightarrow x = 89.12... \approx 89$ Bq.
The line of best fit may vary slightly, so your reading might be a bit different. It should be between 1.92 and 2, so accept any answer between 83 Bq and 100 Bq.

Q5 Area = length × width. The area is always 120 m², so $lw = 120$. Take logs: $\log lw = \log 120$
$\Rightarrow \log l + \log w = \log 120 \Rightarrow \log l = \log 120 - \log w$
This can be plotted on a graph of $\log w$ against $\log l$:

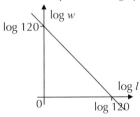

Chapter 10: Differentiation

1. The Gradient of a Curve

Exercise 1.1 — Differentiating from first principles

Q1 *The gradient of the straight line joining points (x_1, y_1) and (x_2, y_2) is given by $\frac{y_2 - y_1}{x_2 - x_1}$.*

   a) **(i)** When $x = 1$, $y = 1$ and when $x = 2$, $y = 8$ so the gradient is $\frac{8-1}{2-1} = \frac{7}{1} = 7$.

   (ii) When $x = 1$, $y = 1$ and when $x = 1.5$, $y = 3.375$ so the gradient is $\frac{3.375-1}{1.5-1} = \frac{2.375}{0.5} = 4.75$.

   (iii) When $x = 1$, $y = 1$ and when $x = 1.1$, $y = 1.331$ so the gradient is $\frac{1.331-1}{1.1-1} = \frac{0.331}{0.1} = 3.31$.

   b) The gradients of the straight lines in part a) move closer to 3 as the value of x moves closer to 1.

Q2 a) $\frac{dy}{dx} = \lim_{h \to 0} \left[\frac{(x+h)-x}{(x+h)-x} \right] = \lim_{h \to 0}[1] = 1$

   b) $f'(x) = \lim_{h \to 0} \left[\frac{(x+h)^3 - x^3}{(x+h)-x} \right]$

   $= \lim_{h \to 0} \left[\frac{x^3 + 3x^2h + 3xh^2 + h^3 - x^3}{(x+h)-x} \right]$

   $= \lim_{h \to 0} \left[\frac{3x^2h + 3xh^2 + h^3}{h} \right]$

   $= \lim_{h \to 0} [3x^2 + 3xh + h^2] = 3x^2$

   c) $f'(x) = \lim_{h \to 0} \left[\frac{2(x+h)-2x}{(x+h)-x} \right] = \lim_{h \to 0} \left[\frac{2x+2h-2x}{h} \right]$

   $= \lim_{h \to 0} \left[\frac{2h}{h} \right] = \lim_{h \to 0}[2] = 2$

Q3 a) $\frac{dy}{dx} = \lim_{h \to 0} \left[\frac{5(x+h)^2 + 1 - (5x^2 + 1)}{(x+h)-x} \right]$

   $= \lim_{h \to 0} \left[\frac{5(x^2 + 2xh + h^2) + 1 - (5x^2 + 1)}{(x+h)-x} \right]$

   $= \lim_{h \to 0} \left[\frac{5x^2 + 10xh + 5h^2 + 1 - 5x^2 - 1}{(x+h)-x} \right]$

   $= \lim_{h \to 0} \left[\frac{10xh + 5h^2}{h} \right] = \lim_{h \to 0}[10x + 5h] = 10x$

   b) $\frac{dy}{dx} = \lim_{h \to 0} \left[\frac{(x+h)-(x+h)^2 - (x - x^2)}{(x+h)-x} \right]$

   $= \lim_{h \to 0} \left[\frac{(x+h)-(x^2 + 2xh + h^2) - (x - x^2)}{(x+h)-x} \right]$

   $= \lim_{h \to 0} \left[\frac{x+h-x^2 - 2xh - h^2 - x + x^2}{(x+h)-x} \right]$

   $= \lim_{h \to 0} \left[\frac{h - 2xh - h^2}{h} \right] = \lim_{h \to 0}[1 - 2x - h] = 1 - 2x$

   c) $\frac{dy}{dx} = \lim_{h \to 0} \left[\frac{2(x+h)^3 + 3(x+h) - (2x^3 + 3x)}{(x+h)-x} \right]$

   $= \lim_{h \to 0} \left[\frac{2(x^3 + 3x^2h + 3xh^2 + h^3) + 3(x+h) - (2x^3 + 3x)}{(x+h)-x} \right]$

   $= \lim_{h \to 0} \left[\frac{2x^3 + 6x^2h + 6xh^2 + 2h^3 + 3x + 3h - 2x^3 - 3x}{(x+h)-x} \right]$

   $= \lim_{h \to 0} \left[\frac{6x^2h + 6xh^2 + 2h^3 + 3h}{h} \right]$

   $= \lim_{h \to 0} [6x^2 + 6xh + 2h^2 + 3] = 6x^2 + 3$

2. Differentiating $y = f(x)$

Exercise 2.1 — Differentiating x^n

Q1 a) $\frac{dy}{dx} = 6x^5$ **b)** $\frac{dy}{dx} = 3x^2$

   c) $\frac{dy}{dx} = -2x^{-3} = -\frac{2}{x^3}$ **d)** $\frac{dy}{dx} = 6x$

   e) $\frac{dy}{dx} = 7$ **f)** $\frac{dy}{dx} = 0$

   g) $\frac{dy}{dx} = \frac{3}{2}x^{-\frac{1}{2}} = \frac{3}{2\sqrt{x}}$ **h)** $\frac{dy}{dx} = -2x^{-2} = -\frac{2}{x^2}$

Q2 a) $f'(x) = 5x^4$ **b)** $f'(x) = 7x^6$

   c) $f'(x) = -4x^{-5} = -\frac{4}{x^5}$ **d)** $f'(x) = 12x^2$

   e) $f'(x) = 4x^{-\frac{1}{2}} = \frac{4}{\sqrt{x}}$ **f)** $f'(x) = x^{-\frac{2}{3}} = \frac{1}{\sqrt[3]{x^2}}$

   g) $f'(x) = 0$ **h)** $f'(x) = -8x^{-3} = -\frac{8}{x^3}$

Q3 a) $\frac{dy}{dx} = 4x \Rightarrow$ At $x = 4$, $\frac{dy}{dx} = 16$

   b) $\frac{dy}{dx} = -x^{-2} = -\frac{1}{x^2} \Rightarrow$ At $x = 2$, $\frac{dy}{dx} = -\frac{1}{4}$

   c) $\frac{dy}{dx} = -20x^4 \Rightarrow$ At $x = 1$, $\frac{dy}{dx} = -20$

   d) $f'(x) = x^{-\frac{1}{2}} = \frac{1}{\sqrt{x}} \Rightarrow f'(9) = \frac{1}{3}$

   e) $f'(x) = 4x^3 \Rightarrow f'(-2) = -32$

   f) $f(x) = -250 \Rightarrow -250 = -2x^3 \Rightarrow 125 = x^3 \Rightarrow x = 5$
   $f'(x) = -6x^2 \Rightarrow f'(5) = -150$

Exercise 2.2 — Differentiating functions

Q1 a) $\frac{dy}{dx} = 12x^2 - 2x$

   b) $\frac{dy}{dx} = 1 + (-x^{-2}) = 1 - \frac{1}{x^2}$

   c) $\frac{dy}{dx} = 6x + \frac{1}{2}x^{-\frac{1}{2}} = 6x + \frac{1}{2\sqrt{x}}$

   d) $f'(x) = -10x^4 + 4 - (-2x^{-3}) = -10x^4 + 4 + \frac{2}{x^3}$

   e) $f'(x) = \frac{3}{2}x^{\frac{1}{2}} - 1 = \frac{3}{2}\sqrt{x} - 1$

   f) $f'(x) = 5 - 2(-3x^{-4}) + \frac{1}{3}x^{-\frac{2}{3}} = 5 + \frac{6}{x^4} + \frac{1}{3\sqrt[3]{x^2}}$

Q2 a) $\frac{d}{dx}(x(x^6 - 1)) = \frac{d}{dx}(x^7 - x) = 7x^6 - 1$

   b) $\frac{d}{dx}((x-3)(x+4)) = \frac{d}{dx}(x^2 - 3x + 4x - 12)$

   $= \frac{d}{dx}(x^2 + x - 12) = 2x + 1$

   c) $\frac{d}{dx}(x(x-1)(x-2)) = \frac{d}{dx}(x(x^2 - x - 2x + 2))$

   $= \frac{d}{dx}(x(x^2 - 3x + 2))$

   $= \frac{d}{dx}(x^3 - 3x^2 + 2x)$

   $= 3x^2 - 3(2x) + 2 = 3x^2 - 6x + 2$

   d) $\frac{d}{dx}((x-3)(x+4)(x-1)) = \frac{d}{dx}((x-3)(x^2 + 3x - 4))$

   $= \frac{d}{dx}(x^3 + 3x^2 - 4x - 3x^2 - 9x + 12)$

   $= \frac{d}{dx}(x^3 - 13x + 12) = 3x^2 - 13$

e) $\dfrac{d}{dx}(x^2(x-4)(3-x^3)) = \dfrac{d}{dx}(x^2(3x-x^4-12+4x^3))$

$= \dfrac{d}{dx}(3x^3-x^6-12x^2+4x^5) = 9x^2-6x^5-24x+20x^4$

f) $\dfrac{d}{dx}((x-3)^2(x^2-2)) = \dfrac{d}{dx}((x^2-3x-3x+9)(x^2-2))$

$= \dfrac{d}{dx}((x^2-6x+9)(x^2-2))$

$= \dfrac{d}{dx}((x^4-6x^3+9x^2)+(-2x^2+12x-18))$

$= \dfrac{d}{dx}(x^4-6x^3+7x^2+12x-18)$

$= 4x^3-18x^2+14x+12$

Q3 **a)** $\dfrac{dy}{dx} = 4x^3-2x$. At $x=3$, $\dfrac{dy}{dx} = 102$.

b) $\dfrac{dy}{dx} = 10x^4+(-x^{-2}) = 10x^4-\dfrac{1}{x^2}$

At $x=-2$, $\dfrac{dy}{dx} = 159.75$

c) $y = x(x-1)(x-2) = x(x^2-3x+2) = x^3-3x^2+2x$

$\dfrac{dy}{dx} = 3x^2-6x+2$. At $x=-3$, $\dfrac{dy}{dx} = 47$.

d) $y = 5(x^2-1)(3-x) = 5(-x^3+3x^2+x-3)$

$= -5x^3+15x^2+5x-15$

$\dfrac{dy}{dx} = -15x^2+30x+5$. At $x=0$, $\dfrac{dy}{dx} = 5$.

e) $y = \sqrt{x}(x-1) = x^{\frac{1}{2}}(x-1) = x^{\frac{3}{2}}-x^{\frac{1}{2}}$

$\dfrac{dy}{dx} = \dfrac{3}{2}x^{\frac{1}{2}}-\dfrac{1}{2}x^{-\frac{1}{2}} = \dfrac{3}{2}\sqrt{x}-\dfrac{1}{2\sqrt{x}}$.

At $x=4$, $\dfrac{dy}{dx} = 2.75$

f) $f(x) = x^3(x^2-5) = x^5-5x^3$

$f'(x) = 5x^4-15x^2$. $f'(-1) = -10$

g) $f(x) = \dfrac{1}{x^2}(x^3-x) = x-x^{-1}$

$f'(x) = 1+x^{-2} = 1+\dfrac{1}{x^2}$. $f'(5) = \dfrac{26}{25}$.

h) $f(x) = \dfrac{3x^3+18x^2+24x}{x+4}$

$= \dfrac{3x(x+4)(x+2)}{x+4} = 3x(x+2) = 3x^2+6x$

$f'(x) = 6x+6$. $f'(-2) = -6$.

Q4 **a)**

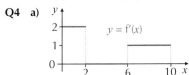

Work out the gradient for each bit of the line. You should get $f'(x) = 2$ for $0 \le x \le 2$ and $f'(x) = 1$ for $6 \le x \le 10$.

b)

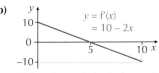

Differentiate and sketch the graph of the gradient function.

Q5 **a)** $f(x) = (x+3)(x+4) = x^2+7x+12$

$f'(x) = 2x+7$

b) $f(x) = \dfrac{x^3-3x^2+2x}{x-1} = \dfrac{x(x-1)(x-2)}{x-1} = x^2-2x$

$f'(x) = 2x-2$

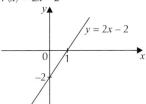

c) $f'(x) = 4x^3-12x^2+8x = 4x(x^2-3x+2)$

$= 4x(x-1)(x-2)$

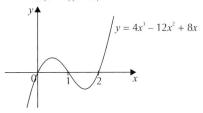

d) $f(x) = (x-1)^2(x+5) = (x^2-2x+1)(x+5)$

$= x^3+5x^2-2x^2-10x+x+5$

$= x^3+3x^2-9x+5$

$f'(x) = 3x^2+6x-9 = 3(x^2+2x-3) = 3(x-1)(x+3)$

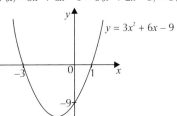

Q6 **a)** $\dfrac{dy}{dx} = 2x-2$. If $2x-2=0 \Rightarrow 2x=2 \Rightarrow x=1$.

So $y = (1)^2-2(1) = -1$. Coordinates are $(1, -1)$.

b) $\dfrac{dy}{dx} = 6x+4$. If $6x+4=0 \Rightarrow 6x=-4$

$\Rightarrow x = -\dfrac{4}{6} = -\dfrac{2}{3}$

So $y = 3(-\dfrac{2}{3})^2+4(-\dfrac{2}{3}) = -\dfrac{4}{3}$.

Coordinates are $(-\dfrac{2}{3}, -\dfrac{4}{3})$.

c) $\dfrac{dy}{dx} = 10x-3$. If $10x-3=0 \Rightarrow 10x=3$

$\Rightarrow x = \dfrac{3}{10} \Rightarrow y = 5(\dfrac{3}{10})^2-3(\dfrac{3}{10}) = -\dfrac{9}{20}$

Coordinates are $(\dfrac{3}{10}, -\dfrac{9}{20})$.

d) $\dfrac{dy}{dx} = 9-9x^2$. If $9-9x^2=0 \Rightarrow 9=9x^2 \Rightarrow 1=x^2$

$\Rightarrow x = 1$ or -1

$\Rightarrow y = 9(1)-3(1)^3 = 6$ or $y = 9(-1)-3(-1)^3 = -6$.

Coordinates of points are $(1, 6)$ and $(-1, -6)$.

e) $\dfrac{dy}{dx} = 6x^2-2x$. If $6x^2-2x=0 \Rightarrow 2x(3x-1)=0$

$\Rightarrow 2x=0$ or $3x-1=0 \Rightarrow x=0$ or $x=\dfrac{1}{3}$

So $y = 2(0)^3-(0)^2 = 0$ or $y = 2(\dfrac{1}{3})^3-(\dfrac{1}{3})^2 = -\dfrac{1}{27}$.

So points are $(0, 0)$ and $(\dfrac{1}{3}, -\dfrac{1}{27})$.

f) $\frac{dy}{dx} = 6x^2 + 6x - 12$. If $6x^2 + 6x - 12 = 0$
$\Rightarrow 6(x^2 + x - 2) = 0 \Rightarrow x^2 + x - 2 = 0$
$\Rightarrow (x + 2)(x - 1) = 0 \Rightarrow x = -2$ or $x = 1$.
So $y = 2(-2)^3 + 3(-2)^2 - 12(-2) = 20$ or
$y = 2(1)^3 + 3(1)^2 - 12(1) = -7$.
So the points are $(-2, 20)$ and $(1, -7)$.

Q7 a) $y = \frac{x^2 - 3x - 4}{x + 1} = \frac{(x - 4)(x + 1)}{x + 1} = x - 4 \Rightarrow \frac{dy}{dx} = 1$

b) $f(x) = \frac{x^4 - 9}{x^2 + 3} = \frac{(x^2 + 3)(x^2 - 3)}{x^2 + 3} = x^2 - 3 \Rightarrow f'(x) = 2x$

c) $f(x) = \frac{x^5 - 16x^3}{x + 4} = \frac{x^3(x + 4)(x - 4)}{x + 4} = x^3(x - 4)$
$= x^4 - 4x^3 \Rightarrow f'(x) = 4x^3 - 12x^2$

d) $y = \frac{1}{x}(x - 3)(x - 4) = \frac{1}{x}(x^2 - 3x - 4x + 12)$
$= \frac{1}{x}(x^2 - 7x + 12) = x - 7 + \frac{12}{x} = x - 7 + 12x^{-1}$
$\Rightarrow \frac{dy}{dx} = 1 - 12x^{-2} = 1 - \frac{12}{x^2}$

e) $y = \sqrt{x}(x^3 - \sqrt{x}) = x^{\frac{1}{2}}(x^3 - x^{\frac{1}{2}}) = x^{\frac{7}{2}} - x$
$\Rightarrow \frac{dy}{dx} = \frac{7}{2}x^{\frac{5}{2}} - 1 = \frac{7}{2}\sqrt{x^5} - 1$

f) $f(x) = \frac{3 - \sqrt{x}}{\sqrt{x}} = \frac{3 - x^{\frac{1}{2}}}{x^{\frac{1}{2}}} = x^{-\frac{1}{2}}(3 - x^{\frac{1}{2}})$
$= 3x^{-\frac{1}{2}} - x^0 = 3x^{-\frac{1}{2}} - 1$
$f'(x) = 3(-\frac{1}{2}x^{-\frac{3}{2}}) = -\frac{3}{2}x^{-\frac{3}{2}} = -\frac{3}{2\sqrt{x^3}}$

g) $f(x) = \frac{x + 5\sqrt{x}}{\sqrt{x}} = \frac{x + 5x^{\frac{1}{2}}}{x^{\frac{1}{2}}} = x^{-\frac{1}{2}}(x + 5x^{\frac{1}{2}})$
$= x^{\frac{1}{2}} + 5x^0 = x^{\frac{1}{2}} + 5$
$f'(x) = \frac{1}{2}x^{-\frac{1}{2}} = \frac{1}{2\sqrt{x}}$

h) Factorising the numerator:
$f(x) = \frac{x - 3\sqrt{x} + 2}{\sqrt{x} - 1} = \frac{(\sqrt{x} - 2)(\sqrt{x} - 1)}{\sqrt{x} - 1}$
$= \sqrt{x} - 2 = x^{\frac{1}{2}} - 2$
$f'(x) = \frac{1}{2}x^{-\frac{1}{2}} = \frac{1}{2\sqrt{x}}$

Exercise 2.3 — Finding tangents and normals

Q1 a) $\frac{dy}{dx} = 9 - 4x$. At $(1, 7)$, $\frac{dy}{dx} = 5$
$\Rightarrow$ tangent has a gradient of 5 and has an equation of the form $y = 5x + c$.
Using the point $(1, 7)$, $7 = 5 + c$
$\Rightarrow c = 2$. So the tangent's equation is $y = 5x + 2$.

b) $\frac{dy}{dx} = 3x^2 - 2$. At $(2, 7)$, $\frac{dy}{dx} = 10$
$\Rightarrow$ tangent has a gradient of 10 and has an equation of the form $y = 10x + c$.
Using the point $(2, 7)$, $7 = 20 + c \Rightarrow c = -13$.
So the tangent's equation is $y = 10x - 13$.

c) $y = (x + 2)(2x - 3) = 2x^2 + x - 6$
$\frac{dy}{dx} = 4x + 1$. At $(2, 4)$, $\frac{dy}{dx} = 9$
$\Rightarrow$ tangent has a gradient of 9 and has an equation of the form $y = 9x + c$.
Using the point $(2, 4)$, $4 = 18 + c \Rightarrow c = -14$.
So the tangent's equation is $y = 9x - 14$.

d) $y = x(x - 1)^2 = x(x^2 - 2x + 1) = x^3 - 2x^2 + x$
$\frac{dy}{dx} = 3x^2 - 4x + 1$. At $(-1, -4)$, $\frac{dy}{dx} = 8$
$\Rightarrow$ tangent has a gradient of 8 and has an equation of the form $y = 8x + c$.
Using the point $(-1, -4)$, $-4 = -8 + c \Rightarrow c = 4$.
So the tangent's equation is $y = 8x + 4$.

e) $y = x^2(x + 3) - 10 = x^3 + 3x^2 - 10$
$\frac{dy}{dx} = 3x^2 + 6x$. At $(2, 10)$, $\frac{dy}{dx} = 24$
$\Rightarrow$ tangent has a gradient of 24 and has an equation of the form $y = 24x + c$.
Using the point $(2, 10)$, $10 = 48 + c \Rightarrow c = -38$.
So the tangent's equation is $y = 24x - 38$.

f) $y = x(2x^2 - 2x - 12) = 2x^3 - 2x^2 - 12x$
$\frac{dy}{dx} = 6x^2 - 4x - 12$. At $(-1, 8)$, $\frac{dy}{dx} = -2$
$\Rightarrow$ tangent has a gradient of -2 and has an equation of the form $y = -2x + c$.
Using the point $(-1, 8)$, $8 = 2 + c \Rightarrow c = 6$.
So the tangent's equation is $y = -2x + 6$.

Q2 a) $y = x^{-1} + x + 3$
$\frac{dy}{dx} = -x^{-2} + 1$. At $(2, 5\frac{1}{2})$, $\frac{dy}{dx} = \frac{3}{4}$
$\Rightarrow$ tangent has a gradient of $\frac{3}{4}$ and has an equation of the form $y = \frac{3}{4}x + c$.
Using the point $(2, 5\frac{1}{2})$, $5\frac{1}{2} = 1\frac{1}{2} + c \Rightarrow c = 4$.
So the tangent's equation is $y = \frac{3}{4}x + 4$
$\Rightarrow 4y = 3x + 16 \Rightarrow 3x - 4y + 16 = 0$

b) $y = 4x^2 - 3x^{\frac{1}{2}}$
$\frac{dy}{dx} = 8x - 3(\frac{1}{2}x^{-\frac{1}{2}}) = 8x - \frac{3}{2}x^{-\frac{1}{2}}$. At $(1, 1)$, $\frac{dy}{dx} = 6\frac{1}{2}$
$\Rightarrow$ tangent has a gradient of $6\frac{1}{2}$ and has an equation of the form $y = 6\frac{1}{2}x + c$.
Using the point $(1, 1)$, $1 = 6\frac{1}{2} + c \Rightarrow c = -5\frac{1}{2}$.
So the tangent's equation is $y = 6\frac{1}{2}x - 5\frac{1}{2}$
$\Rightarrow 2y = 13x - 11 \Rightarrow 13x - 2y - 11 = 0$.

c) $y = 3x^{-1} + 2x^{\frac{1}{2}}$
$\frac{dy}{dx} = 3(-x^{-2}) + 2(\frac{1}{2}x^{-\frac{1}{2}}) = -3x^{-2} + x^{-\frac{1}{2}}$
At $(4, 4\frac{3}{4})$, $\frac{dy}{dx} = \frac{5}{16}$
$\Rightarrow$ tangent has a gradient of $\frac{5}{16}$ and has an equation of the form $y = \frac{5}{16}x + c$.
Using the point $(4, 4\frac{3}{4})$, $4\frac{3}{4} = \frac{5}{4} + c \Rightarrow c = 3\frac{1}{2}$.
So the tangent's equation is $y = \frac{5}{16}x + 3\frac{1}{2}$
$\Rightarrow 16y = 5x + 56 \Rightarrow 5x - 16y + 56 = 0$.

d) $y = x^{-1} + 4x^{-2}$
$\frac{dy}{dx} = -x^{-2} + 4(-2x^{-3}) = -x^{-2} - 8x^{-3}$
At $(2, 1\frac{1}{2})$, $\frac{dy}{dx} = -\frac{5}{4}$
$\Rightarrow$ tangent has a gradient of $-\frac{5}{4}$ and has an equation of the form $y = -\frac{5}{4}x + c$.

Using the point $(2, 1\frac{1}{2})$, $1\frac{1}{2} = -\frac{5}{2} + c \Rightarrow c = 4$.

So the tangent's equation is $y = -\frac{5}{4}x + 4$

$\Rightarrow 4y = -5x + 16 \Rightarrow 5x + 4y - 16 = 0$.

e) $y = \frac{1}{3}x^2 - 4x^{\frac{1}{2}} - \frac{1}{3}$

$\frac{dy}{dx} = \frac{1}{3}(2x) - 4(\frac{1}{2}x^{-\frac{1}{2}}) = \frac{2}{3}x - 2x^{-\frac{1}{2}}$.

At $(4, -3)$, $\frac{dy}{dx} = \frac{5}{3}$

$\Rightarrow$ tangent has a gradient of $\frac{5}{3}$ and has an equation of the form $y = \frac{5}{3}x + c$.

Using the point $(4, -3)$, $-3 = \frac{20}{3} + c \Rightarrow c = -\frac{29}{3}$.

So the tangent's equation is $y = \frac{5}{3}x - \frac{29}{3}$

$\Rightarrow 3y = 5x - 29 \Rightarrow 5x - 3y - 29 = 0$.

f) $y = x - 2x^{-1} + 3x^{-2}$

$\frac{dy}{dx} = 1 + 2x^{-2} - 6x^{-3}$. At $(-3, -2)$, $\frac{dy}{dx} = \frac{13}{9}$

$\Rightarrow$ tangent has a gradient of $\frac{13}{9}$ and has an equation of the form $y = \frac{13}{9}x + c$.

Using the point $(-3, -2)$, $-2 = -\frac{13}{3} + c \Rightarrow c = \frac{7}{3}$.

So the tangent's equation is $y = \frac{13}{9}x + \frac{7}{3}$

$\Rightarrow 9y = 13x + 21 \Rightarrow 13x - 9y + 21 = 0$.

Q3 a) $\frac{dy}{dx} = 6x - 4$. At $(2, 6)$, $\frac{dy}{dx} = 8$.

So the normal has a gradient of $-\frac{1}{8}$ and an equation of the form $y = -\frac{1}{8}x + c$.

Don't forget — the gradient of the normal to a curve at a point is $\frac{-1}{\text{Gradient of the curve}}$.

Using the point $(2, 6)$, $6 = -\frac{1}{4} + c \Rightarrow c = 6\frac{1}{4}$

So the normal's equation is $y = -\frac{1}{8}x + 6\frac{1}{4}$

$\Rightarrow 8y = -x + 50 \Rightarrow x + 8y - 50 = 0$.

b) $y = x^3 + 4x^2 - 5x$

$\frac{dy}{dx} = 3x^2 + 8x - 5$. At $(-1, 8)$, $\frac{dy}{dx} = -10$.

So the normal has a gradient of $\frac{1}{10}$ and an equation of the form $y = \frac{1}{10}x + c$.

Using the point $(-1, 8)$, $8 = -\frac{1}{10} + c \Rightarrow c = \frac{81}{10}$

So the normal's equation is $y = \frac{1}{10}x + \frac{81}{10}$

$\Rightarrow 10y = x + 81 \Rightarrow x - 10y + 81 = 0$.

c) $y = x(x^2 - 3x + 2) = x^3 - 3x^2 + 2x$

$\frac{dy}{dx} = 3x^2 - 6x + 2$. At $(3, 6)$, $\frac{dy}{dx} = 11$.

So the normal has a gradient of $-\frac{1}{11}$ and an equation of the form $y = -\frac{1}{11}x + c$.

Using the point $(3, 6)$, $6 = -\frac{3}{11} + c \Rightarrow c = \frac{69}{11}$.

So the normal's equation is $y = -\frac{1}{11}x + \frac{69}{11}$

$\Rightarrow 11y = -x + 69 \Rightarrow x + 11y - 69 = 0$.

d) $y = x(x^2 + x - 12) - 10 = x^3 + x^2 - 12x - 10$

$\frac{dy}{dx} = 3x^2 + 2x - 12$. At $(-2, 10)$, $\frac{dy}{dx} = -4$.

So the normal has a gradient of $\frac{1}{4}$ and an equation of the form $y = \frac{1}{4}x + c$.

Using the point $(-2, 10)$, $10 = -\frac{1}{2} + c \Rightarrow c = \frac{21}{2}$.

So the normal's equation is $y = \frac{1}{4}x + \frac{21}{2}$

$\Rightarrow 4y = x + 42 \Rightarrow x - 4y + 42 = 0$.

e) $y = \frac{(x + 2)(x^2 - 7x)}{x + 2} = x^2 - 7x$

$\frac{dy}{dx} = 2x - 7$. At $(5, -10)$, $\frac{dy}{dx} = 3$.

So the normal has a gradient of $-\frac{1}{3}$ and an equation of the form $y = -\frac{1}{3}x + c$.

Using the point $(5, -10)$, $-10 = -\frac{5}{3} + c \Rightarrow c = -\frac{25}{3}$

So the normal's equation is $y = -\frac{1}{3}x - \frac{25}{3}$

$\Rightarrow 3y = -x - 25 \Rightarrow x + 3y + 25 = 0$.

Q4 a) $y = \frac{2x^5 - 2x^4}{3x^3} = \frac{2}{3}x^2 - \frac{2}{3}x$

Remember — if the denominator is a single term, split the equation up into separate terms.

$\frac{dy}{dx} = \frac{2}{3}(2x) - \frac{2}{3} = \frac{4}{3}x - \frac{2}{3}$

At $(-2, 4)$, $\frac{dy}{dx} = -\frac{10}{3}$.

So the normal has a gradient of $\frac{3}{10}$ and an equation of the form $y = \frac{3}{10}x + c$.

Using the point $(-2, 4)$, $4 = -\frac{6}{10} + c \Rightarrow c = \frac{23}{5}$.

So the normal's equation is $y = \frac{3}{10}x + \frac{23}{5}$

$\Rightarrow 10y = 3x + 46 \Rightarrow 3x - 10y + 46 = 0$.

b) $y = \frac{5x^2 - 2x + 3}{x^2} = 5 - \frac{2}{x} + \frac{3}{x^2}$

$\frac{dy}{dx} = -2(-x^{-2}) + 3(-2x^{-3}) = \frac{2}{x^2} - \frac{6}{x^3}$

At $(2, 4\frac{3}{4})$, $\frac{dy}{dx} = -\frac{1}{4}$.

So the normal has a gradient of 4 and an equation of the form $y = 4x + c$.

Using the point $(2, 4\frac{3}{4})$, $4\frac{3}{4} = 8 + c \Rightarrow c = -\frac{13}{4}$.

So the normal's equation is

$y = 4x - \frac{13}{4} \Rightarrow 4y = 16x - 13 \Rightarrow 16x - 4y - 13 = 0$.

c) $y = 3xx^{-\frac{1}{2}} - x^2x^{-\frac{1}{2}} = 3x^{\frac{1}{2}} - x^{\frac{3}{2}}$

$\frac{dy}{dx} = 3(\frac{1}{2}x^{-\frac{1}{2}}) - \frac{3}{2}x^{\frac{1}{2}} = \frac{3}{2\sqrt{x}} - \frac{3}{2}\sqrt{x}$

At $(4, -2)$, $\frac{dy}{dx} = -\frac{9}{4}$.

So the normal has a gradient of $\frac{4}{9}$ and an equation of the form $y = \frac{4}{9}x + c$.

Using the point $(4, -2)$, $-2 = \frac{16}{9} + c \Rightarrow c = -\frac{34}{9}$.

So the normal's equation is

$y = \frac{4}{9}x - \frac{34}{9} \Rightarrow 9y = 4x - 34 \Rightarrow 4x - 9y - 34 = 0$.

d) $y = \frac{1}{x} - \frac{3}{x^2} - \frac{4}{x^3} + \frac{7}{4} = x^{-1} - 3x^{-2} - 4x^{-3} + \frac{7}{4}$

$\frac{dy}{dx} = -x^{-2} - 3(-2x^{-3}) - 4(-3x^{-4}) = -x^{-2} + 6x^{-3} + 12x^{-4}$

At $(-2, 1)$, $\frac{dy}{dx} = -\frac{1}{4}$.

So the normal has a gradient of 4 and an equation of the form $y = 4x + c$.

Using the point $(-2, 1)$, $1 = -8 + c \Rightarrow c = 9$.

So the normal's equation is $y = 4x + 9$.

e) $y = \dfrac{x^3 - 5x^2 - 4x}{x^{\frac{3}{2}}} = x^{\frac{3}{2}} - 5x^{\frac{1}{2}} - 4x^{-\frac{1}{2}}$

$\dfrac{dy}{dx} = \dfrac{3}{2}x^{\frac{1}{2}} - 5(\dfrac{1}{2}x^{-\frac{1}{2}}) - 4(-\dfrac{1}{2}x^{-\frac{3}{2}})$

$= \dfrac{3}{2}\sqrt{x} - \dfrac{5}{2\sqrt{x}} + \dfrac{2}{x\sqrt{x}}$

At $(4, -4)$, $\dfrac{dy}{dx} = 2$.

So the normal has a gradient of $-\dfrac{1}{2}$ and an equation of the form $y = -\dfrac{1}{2}x + c$.

Using the point $(4, -4)$, $-4 = -2 + c \Rightarrow c = -2$.

So the equation of the normal is $y = -\dfrac{1}{2}x - 2$
$\Rightarrow 2y = -x - 4 \Rightarrow x + 2y + 4 = 0$.

Q5 a) $f'(x) = 3x^2 - 6x$. If $f'(x) = 9$, $3x^2 - 6x = 9$
$\Rightarrow 3x^2 - 6x - 9 = 0 \Rightarrow x^2 - 2x - 3 = 0$
$\Rightarrow (x - 3)(x + 1) = 0 \Rightarrow x = 3$ or $x = -1$.
So $x = 3$ since $x > 0$. So $y = f(3) = 3^3 - 3(3)^2 + 3 = 3$.
The coordinates are $(3, 3)$.

b) The gradient of the tangent at $(3, 3)$ is 9 from part a).
So the equation is of the form $y = 9x + c$. You know the tangent goes through $(3, 3)$ so use this point:
$3 = 27 + c \Rightarrow c = -24$.
So the equation is $y = 9x - 24$.

c) The gradient of the normal is $-\dfrac{1}{9}$ so the equation has the form $y = -\dfrac{1}{9}x + c$. Again, use the point $(3, 3)$, so
$3 = -\dfrac{1}{3} + c \Rightarrow c = \dfrac{10}{3}$.
So the equation is $y = -\dfrac{1}{9}x + \dfrac{10}{3}$
$\Rightarrow 9y = -x + 30 \Rightarrow x + 9y - 30 = 0$.

Q6 a) Putting $x = -2$ into the equation gives:
$y = \dfrac{x^3 + x^2 + x + 5}{x^2}$

$= \dfrac{(-2)^3 + (-2)^2 + (-2) + 5}{(-2)^2}$

$= \dfrac{-8 + 4 - 2 + 5}{4} = -\dfrac{1}{4}$

so $(2, -\dfrac{1}{4})$ is a point on the curve.

b) $y = \dfrac{x^3 + x^2 + x + 5}{x^2} = x + 1 + \dfrac{1}{x} + \dfrac{5}{x^2}$

$\dfrac{dy}{dx} = 1 + 0 + (-x^{-2}) + 5(-2x^{-3}) = 1 - \dfrac{1}{x^2} - \dfrac{10}{x^3}$

At $(-2, -\dfrac{1}{4})$, $\dfrac{dy}{dx} = 2$. So the gradient of the tangent at this point is 2 and it has equation $y = 2x + c$.

Using the point $(-2, -\dfrac{1}{4})$, $-\dfrac{1}{4} = -4 + c \Rightarrow c = \dfrac{15}{4}$.

So the equation of the tangent is $y = 2x + \dfrac{15}{4}$
$\Rightarrow 4y = 8x + 15 \Rightarrow 8x - 4y + 15 = 0$.

c) The gradient of the normal at $(-2, -\dfrac{1}{4})$ is $-\dfrac{1}{2}$ and so it has equation $y = -\dfrac{1}{2}x + c$. Using the point $(-2, -\dfrac{1}{4})$,
$-\dfrac{1}{4} = 1 + c \Rightarrow c = -\dfrac{5}{4}$. So the equation of the normal is $y = -\dfrac{1}{2}x - \dfrac{5}{4} \Rightarrow 4y = -2x - 5 \Rightarrow 2x + 4y + 5 = 0$.

3. Using Differentiation
Exercise 3.1 — Finding second order derivatives

Q1 a) $\dfrac{dy}{dx} = 3x^2$ and $\dfrac{d^2y}{dx^2} = 6x$.

b) $\dfrac{dy}{dx} = 5x^4$ and $\dfrac{d^2y}{dx^2} = 20x^3$.

c) $\dfrac{dy}{dx} = 4x^3$ and $\dfrac{d^2y}{dx^2} = 12x^2$.

d) $\dfrac{dy}{dx} = 1$ and $\dfrac{d^2y}{dx^2} = 0$.

e) $y = x^{-1}$, so $\dfrac{dy}{dx} = -x^{-2} = -\dfrac{1}{x^2}$ and $\dfrac{d^2y}{dx^2} = 2x^{-3} = \dfrac{2}{x^3}$.

f) $y = x^{\frac{1}{2}}$, so $\dfrac{dy}{dx} = \dfrac{1}{2}x^{-\frac{1}{2}} = \dfrac{1}{2\sqrt{x}}$

and $\dfrac{d^2y}{dx^2} = -\dfrac{1}{4}x^{-\frac{3}{2}} = -\dfrac{1}{4(\sqrt{x})^3}$.

g) $y = x^{-2}$, so $\dfrac{dy}{dx} = -2x^{-3} = -\dfrac{2}{x^3}$ and $\dfrac{d^2y}{dx^2} = 6x^{-4} = \dfrac{6}{x^4}$.

h) $y = x\sqrt{x} = x^1 x^{\frac{1}{2}} = x^{1+\frac{1}{2}} = x^{\frac{3}{2}}$,

so $\dfrac{dy}{dx} = \dfrac{3}{2}x^{\frac{1}{2}} = \dfrac{3}{2}\sqrt{x}$ and $\dfrac{d^2y}{dx^2} = \dfrac{3}{4}x^{-\frac{1}{2}} = \dfrac{3}{4\sqrt{x}}$.

Q2 a) $f(x) = x(4x^2 - x) = 4x^3 - x^2$
$f'(x) = 12x^2 - 2x$
$f''(x) = 24x - 2$

b) $f(x) = (x^2 - 3)(x - 4) = x^3 - 4x^2 - 3x + 12$
$f'(x) = 3x^2 - 8x - 3$
$f''(x) = 6x - 8$

c) $f(x) = \dfrac{4x^5 + 12x^3 - 40x}{4(x^2 + 5)} = \dfrac{4x(x^4 + 3x^2 - 10)}{4(x^2 + 5)}$

$= \dfrac{4x(x^2 + 5)(x^2 - 2)}{4(x^2 + 5)} = x(x^2 - 2) = x^3 - 2x$

$f'(x) = 3x^2 - 2$
$f''(x) = 6x$

d) $f(x) = 3x^{\frac{1}{2}} + xx^{\frac{1}{2}} = 3x^{\frac{1}{2}} + x^{\frac{3}{2}}$

$f'(x) = \dfrac{3}{2}x^{-\frac{1}{2}} + \dfrac{3}{2}x^{\frac{1}{2}} = \dfrac{3}{2\sqrt{x}} + \dfrac{3}{2}\sqrt{x}$

$f''(x) = \dfrac{3}{2}(-\dfrac{1}{2}x^{-\frac{3}{2}}) + \dfrac{3}{2}(\dfrac{1}{2}x^{-\frac{1}{2}}) = -\dfrac{3}{4}x^{-\frac{3}{2}} + \dfrac{3}{4}x^{-\frac{1}{2}}$

$= -\dfrac{3}{4(\sqrt{x})^3} + \dfrac{3}{4\sqrt{x}}$ $\left(= -\dfrac{3}{4x\sqrt{x}} + \dfrac{3}{4\sqrt{x}}\right)$

e) $f(x) = \dfrac{1}{x}(3x^4 - 2x^3) = 3x^3 - 2x^2$
$f'(x) = 9x^2 - 4x$
$f''(x) = 18x - 4$

f) $f(x) = \dfrac{x^2 - xx^{\frac{1}{2}} + 7x}{x^{\frac{1}{2}}} = x^2 x^{-\frac{1}{2}} - xx^{\frac{1}{2}}x^{-\frac{1}{2}} + 7xx^{-\frac{1}{2}}$

$= x^{\frac{3}{2}} - x + 7x^{\frac{1}{2}}$

$f'(x) = \dfrac{3}{2}x^{\frac{1}{2}} - 1 + 7(\dfrac{1}{2}x^{-\frac{1}{2}}) = \dfrac{3}{2}\sqrt{x} - 1 + \dfrac{7}{2\sqrt{x}}$

$f''(x) = \dfrac{3}{2}(\dfrac{1}{2}x^{-\frac{1}{2}}) + \dfrac{7}{2}(-\dfrac{1}{2}x^{-\frac{3}{2}}) = \dfrac{3}{4\sqrt{x}} - \dfrac{7}{4(\sqrt{x})^3}$

Q3 a) $f'(x) = 3x^2 - 2x$, so $f''(x) = 6x - 2$.
$f''(3) = 16$.

b) $y = xx^{\frac{1}{2}} - x^{-1} = x^{\frac{3}{2}} - x^{-1}$ so $\dfrac{dy}{dx} = \dfrac{3}{2}x^{\frac{1}{2}} + x^{-2}$

so $\dfrac{d^2y}{dx^2} = \dfrac{3}{2}(\dfrac{1}{2}x^{-\frac{1}{2}}) - 2x^{-3} = \dfrac{3}{4\sqrt{x}} - \dfrac{2}{x^3}$

so at $x = 4$, $\dfrac{d^2y}{dx^2} = \dfrac{11}{32}$.

c) $f(x) = x^2(x^3 - 4x^2 - 5x) = x^5 - 4x^4 - 5x^3$
so $f'(x) = 5x^4 - 16x^3 - 15x^2$
and $f''(x) = 20x^3 - 48x^2 - 30x$.
$f''(-1) = -38$.

d) $y = \dfrac{x^3(x+6)(x-2)}{(x+6)} = x^3(x-2) = x^4 - 2x^3$
so $\dfrac{dy}{dx} = 4x^3 - 6x^2$, $\dfrac{d^2y}{dx^2} = 12x^2 - 12x$.
At $x = 5$, $\dfrac{d^2y}{dx^2} = 240$.

e) $f(x) = \dfrac{9x^2 + 3x}{3\sqrt{x}} = 3x^{\frac{3}{2}} + x^{\frac{1}{2}}$ so
$f'(x) = 3(\frac{3}{2}x^{\frac{1}{2}}) + \frac{1}{2}x^{-\frac{1}{2}} = \frac{9}{2}\sqrt{x} + \frac{1}{2\sqrt{x}}$ and so
$f''(x) = \frac{9}{2}(\frac{1}{2}x^{-\frac{1}{2}}) + \frac{1}{2}(-\frac{1}{2}x^{-\frac{3}{2}}) = \frac{9}{4\sqrt{x}} - \frac{1}{4(\sqrt{x})^3}$
$f''(1) = 2$.

f) $y = (x^{-2} + x^{-1})(5 - x)$
$= 5x^{-2} - x^{-2}x + 5x^{-1} - xx^{-1}$
$= 5x^{-2} - x^{-1} + 5x^{-1} - 1 = 5x^{-2} + 4x^{-1} - 1$
$\dfrac{dy}{dx} = 5(-2x^{-3}) + 4(-x^{-2}) = -10x^{-3} - 4x^{-2}$
so $\dfrac{d^2y}{dx^2} = 30x^{-4} + 8x^{-3} = \dfrac{30}{x^4} + \dfrac{8}{x^3}$.
At $x = -3$, $\dfrac{d^2y}{dx^2} = \dfrac{2}{27}$.

Exercise 3.2 — Stationary points

Q1 a) The graph has 2 stationary points — a minimum and a point of inflection.

b) The graph has 3 stationary points — a maximum, a minimum and a point of inflection.

Q2 a) $\dfrac{dy}{dx} = 2x + 3$. When $\dfrac{dy}{dx} = 0$, $2x + 3 = 0 \Rightarrow x = -\dfrac{3}{2}$

b) $y = (3 - x)(4 + 2x) = 12 + 2x - 2x^2$
$\dfrac{dy}{dx} = 2 - 4x$. When $\dfrac{dy}{dx} = 0$, $2 - 4x = 0 \Rightarrow x = \dfrac{1}{2}$

Q3 a) $\dfrac{dy}{dx} = 4x - 5$. When $\dfrac{dy}{dx} = 0$, $4x - 5 = 0 \Rightarrow x = \dfrac{5}{4}$
When $x = \dfrac{5}{4}$, $y = 2(\dfrac{5}{4})^2 - 5(\dfrac{5}{4}) + 2 = -\dfrac{9}{8}$
So the coordinates are $(\dfrac{5}{4}, -\dfrac{9}{8})$.

b) $\dfrac{dy}{dx} = -2x + 3$. When $\dfrac{dy}{dx} = 0$, $-2x + 3 = 0$
$\Rightarrow x = \dfrac{3}{2}$. When $x = \dfrac{3}{2}$, $y = -(\dfrac{3}{2})^2 + 3(\dfrac{3}{2}) - 4 = -\dfrac{7}{4}$.
So the coordinates are $(\dfrac{3}{2}, -\dfrac{7}{4})$.

c) $\dfrac{dy}{dx} = -6 - 6x$. When $\dfrac{dy}{dx} = 0$, $-6 - 6x = 0 \Rightarrow x = -1$
When $x = -1$, $y = 7 - 6(-1) - 3(-1)^2 = 10$.
So the coordinates are $(-1, 10)$.

d) $y = (x - 1)(2x + 3) = 2x^2 + x - 3$
$\dfrac{dy}{dx} = 4x + 1$. When $\dfrac{dy}{dx} = 0$, $4x + 1 = 0 \Rightarrow x = -\dfrac{1}{4}$
When $x = -\dfrac{1}{4}$, $y = (-\dfrac{1}{4} - 1)(2(-\dfrac{1}{4}) + 3) = -\dfrac{25}{8}$.
So the coordinates are $(-\dfrac{1}{4}, -\dfrac{25}{8})$.

Q4 a) $\dfrac{dy}{dx} = 3x^2 - 3$. When $\dfrac{dy}{dx} = 0$, $3x^2 - 3 = 0 \Rightarrow x = \pm 1$.
When $x = 1$, $y = 1^3 - 3(1) + 2 = 0$.
When $x = -1$, $y = (-1)^3 - 3(-1) + 2 = 4$.
So the coordinates are $(1, 0)$ and $(-1, 4)$.

b) $\dfrac{dy}{dx} = 12x^2$. When $\dfrac{dy}{dx} = 0$, $12x^2 = 0 \Rightarrow x = 0$
When $x = 0$, $y = 4(0)^3 + 5 = 5$.
So the coordinates are $(0, 5)$.

Q5 $f'(x) = 5x^4 + 3$. When $f'(x) = 0$, $5x^4 + 3 = 0 \Rightarrow x^4 = -\dfrac{3}{5}$.
Finding a solution would involve finding the fourth root of a negative number. But $x^4 = (x^2)^2$, so x^4 is always positive and so there are no stationary points.

Q6 a) $\dfrac{dy}{dx} = 3x^2 - 14x - 5$

b) When $\dfrac{dy}{dx} = 0$, $3x^2 - 14x - 5 = 0$
$\Rightarrow (3x + 1)(x - 5) = 0$, so $x = -\dfrac{1}{3}$ and $x = 5$.
When $x = -\dfrac{1}{3}$, $y = (-\dfrac{1}{3})^3 - 7(-\dfrac{1}{3})^2 - 5(-\dfrac{1}{3}) + 2 = \dfrac{77}{27}$.
When $x = 5$, $y = 5^3 - 7(5)^2 - 5(5) + 2 = -73$.
So the coordinates are $(-\dfrac{1}{3}, \dfrac{77}{27})$ and $(5, -73)$.

Q7 For stationary points to occur, $f'(x)$ must equal zero, so $f'(x) = 3x^2 + k = 0 \Rightarrow -\dfrac{k}{3} = x^2$. For this equation to have a solution, k can't be positive (or it would be taking the square root of a negative number), so $k \leq 0$. Therefore, if the graph has no stationary points, $k > 0$.

Exercise 3.3 — Maximum and minimum points

Q1 a) negative **b)** positive **c)** negative
d) negative **e)** positive

Q2 a) $\dfrac{dy}{dx} = 3x^2 - 12$ $\dfrac{d^2y}{dx^2} = 6x$
At $(2, -12)$, $\dfrac{d^2y}{dx^2} = 6 \times 2 = 12 > 0$,
so $(2, -12)$ is a minimum.

b) $\dfrac{dy}{dx} = 8x^3 - 48x^2$ $\dfrac{d^2y}{dx^2} = 24x^2 - 96x$
At $(6, 36)$, $\dfrac{d^2y}{dx^2} = 24 \times 6^2 - 96 \times 6 = 288 > 0$,
so $(6, 36)$ is a minimum.

c) $\dfrac{dy}{dx} = 20x^4 + 60x^3$ $\dfrac{d^2y}{dx^2} = 80x^3 + 180x^2$
At $(-3, -7)$, $\dfrac{d^2y}{dx^2} = 80 \times (-3)^3 + 180 \times (-3)^2$
$= -540 < 0$, so $(-3, -7)$ is a maximum.

d) $\dfrac{dy}{dx} = 5x^4 - 20x^3 + 10x - 40$
$\dfrac{d^2y}{dx^2} = 20x^3 - 60x^2 + 10$
At $(4, 64)$, $\dfrac{d^2y}{dx^2} = 20 \times 4^3 - 60 \times 4^2 + 10 = 330 > 0$,
so $(4, 64)$ is a minimum.

Q3 a) $(1, 3)$
All the clues are in the question — the derivative when $x = 1$ is zero so you know it's a stationary point, and the y-value when $x = 1$ is 3.

b) The second derivative at $x = 1$ is positive, so it's a minimum.

Q4 a) $\dfrac{dy}{dx} = -2x$. When $\dfrac{dy}{dx} = 0$, $x = 0$. When $x = 0$,
$y = 5 - 0 = 5$. So the coordinates are $(0, 5)$.
$\dfrac{d^2y}{dx^2} = -2$, so it's a maximum turning point.

b) $\frac{dy}{dx} = 6x^2 - 6$. When $\frac{dy}{dx} = 0$, $6x^2 = 6 \Rightarrow x = \pm 1$

When $x = 1$, $y = 2 - 6 + 2 = -2$. When $x = -1$,
$y = -2 + 6 + 2 = 6$. So the coordinates are $(1, -2)$
and $(-1, 6)$. $\frac{d^2y}{dx^2} = 12x$.

At $(1, -2)$, $\frac{d^2y}{dx^2} = 12$, so it's a minimum.

At $(-1, 6)$, $\frac{d^2y}{dx^2} = -12$ so it's a maximum.

c) $\frac{dy}{dx} = 3x^2 - 6x - 24$. When $\frac{dy}{dx} = 0$, $x^2 - 2x - 8 = 0$

$\Rightarrow (x - 4)(x + 2) = 0 \Rightarrow x = 4$ and -2.
When $x = 4$, $y = 64 - 48 - 96 + 15 = -65$.
When $x = -2$, $y = -8 - 12 + 48 + 15 = 43$.
So the coordinates are $(4, -65)$ and $(-2, 43)$.

$\frac{d^2y}{dx^2} = 6x - 6$. At $(4, -65)$, $\frac{d^2y}{dx^2} = 24 - 6 = 18$,
so it's a minimum.

At $(-2, 43)$, $\frac{d^2y}{dx^2} = -12 - 6 = -18$, so it's a maximum.

d) $\frac{dy}{dx} = 4x^3 + 12x^2 + 8x$.

When $\frac{dy}{dx} = 0$, $x^3 + 3x^2 + 2x = 0$
$\Rightarrow x(x + 2)(x + 1) = 0$, so $x = 0$, -1 and -2.
When $x = 0$, $y = 0 + 0 + 0 - 10 = -10$.
When $x = -1$, $y = 1 - 4 + 4 - 10 = -9$.
When $x = -2$, $y = 16 - 32 + 16 - 10 = -10$.
So the stationary points are $(0, -10)$, $(-1, -9)$
and $(-2, -10)$.

$\frac{d^2y}{dx^2} = 12x^2 + 24x + 8$. At $(0, -10)$,

$\frac{d^2y}{dx^2} = 0 + 0 + 8 = 8$, so it's a minimum.

At $(-1, -9)$, $\frac{d^2y}{dx^2} = 12 - 24 + 8 = -4$,
so it's a maximum.

At $(-2, -10)$, $\frac{d^2y}{dx^2} = 48 - 48 + 8 = 8$,
so it's a minimum.

Q5 a) $f'(x) = 24x^2 + 32x + 8$.

When $f'(x) = 0$, $3x^2 + 4x + 1 = 0$
$\Rightarrow (3x + 1)(x + 1) = 0$, so $x = -1$ and $-\frac{1}{3}$.
When $x = -1$, $f(x) = -8 + 16 - 8 + 1 = 1$.

When $x = -\frac{1}{3}$, $f(x) = -\frac{8}{27} + \frac{16}{9} - \frac{8}{3} + 1 = -\frac{5}{27}$.

So the coordinates are $(-1, 1)$ and $(-\frac{1}{3}, -\frac{5}{27})$.

$f''(x) = 48x + 32$. At $(-1, 1)$ $f''(x) = -48 + 32 = -16$,
so it's a maximum.

At $(-\frac{1}{3}, -\frac{5}{27})$, $f''(x) = -\frac{48}{3} + 32 = 16$,
so it's a minimum.

b) $f(x) = \frac{27}{x^3} + x = 27x^{-3} + x \Rightarrow f'(x) = -81x^{-4} + 1$.

When $f'(x) = 0$, $x^4 = 81 \Rightarrow x = \pm 3$.

When $x = 3$, $f(x) = \frac{27}{27} + 3 = 4$.

When $x = -3$, $f(x) = -\frac{27}{27} - 3 = -4$.

So the coordinates are $(3, 4)$ and $(-3, -4)$.

$f''(x) = 324x^{-5}$. At $(3, 4)$ $f''(x) = \frac{4}{3}$,
so it's a minimum.

At $(-3, -4)$ $f''(x) = -\frac{4}{3}$, so it's a maximum.

Q6 a) $f'(x) = 3x^2 - 6x$. $f''(x) = 6x - 6$.

b) When $f'(x) = 0$, $3x^2 - 6x = 0 \Rightarrow x(x - 2) = 0$,
so $x = 0$ and $x = 2$. When $x = 0$, $f(x) = 0 - 0 + 4 = 4$.
When $x = 2$, $f(x) = 8 - 12 + 4 = 0$.
So the coordinates are $(0, 4)$ and $(2, 0)$.
At $(0, 4)$ $f''(x) = 0 - 6 = -6$, so it's a maximum.
At $(2, 0)$ $f''(x) = 12 - 6 = 6$, so it's a minimum.

Q7 a) $y = x^2 + \frac{2000}{x} = x^2 + 2000x^{-1} \Rightarrow \frac{dy}{dx} = 2x - \frac{2000}{x^2}$

When $\frac{dy}{dx} = 0$, $2x = \frac{2000}{x^2} \Rightarrow x^3 = 1000 \Rightarrow x = 10$

b) $\frac{d^2y}{dx^2} = 2 + \frac{4000}{x^3}$. When $x = 10$,

$\frac{d^2y}{dx^2} = 2 + 4 = 6$, so it's a minimum.

Q8 $f(x) = x^3 + ax^2 + bx + c \Rightarrow f'(x) = 3x^2 + 2ax + b$.
$\Rightarrow f''(x) = 6x + 2a$. At the point $(3, 10)$:
$10 = 3^3 + a(3^2) + b(3) + c \Rightarrow 10 = 27 + 9a + 3b + c$
As $(3, 10)$ is a stationary point, $0 = 3(3^2) + 2a(3) + b$
$\Rightarrow 0 = 27 + 6a + b$. We know that $f''(3) = 0$,
so $0 = 6(3) + 2a \Rightarrow 0 = 18 + 2a \Rightarrow a = -9$.
Then $0 = 27 + 6a + b = 27 + 6(-9) + b \Rightarrow b = 27$
And $10 = 27 + 9a + 3b + c = 27 + 9(-9) + 3(27) + c$
$\Rightarrow c = -17$. So $f(x) = x^3 - 9x^2 + 27x - 17$.

Q9 a) $\frac{dy}{dx} = 4x^3 + 3kx^2 + 2x$.

Stationary points occur when $\frac{dy}{dx} = 0$,
so $4x^3 + 3kx^2 + 2x = 0 \Rightarrow x(4x^2 + 3kx + 2) = 0$
so $x = 0$ or $4x^2 + 3kx + 2 = 0$.
As you know the only stationary point occurs at
$x = 0$, the part in brackets can't have any solutions.
This gives you information about the discriminant of
the quadratic equation:
$b^2 - 4ac < 0 \Rightarrow 9k^2 < 32 \Rightarrow k^2 < \frac{32}{9}$.

b) When $x = 0$, $y = 0 + 0 + 0 + 17 = 17$, so the
coordinates are $(0, 17)$.
$\frac{d^2y}{dx^2} = 12x^2 + 6kx + 2$. When $x = 0$, $\frac{d^2y}{dx^2} = 2$,
so it's a minimum.

Exercise 3.4 — Increasing and decreasing functions

Q1 a) $\frac{dy}{dx} = 2x + 7$. If the function is increasing, $\frac{dy}{dx} > 0$
$\Rightarrow 2x > -7 \Rightarrow x > -\frac{7}{2}$.

b) $\frac{dy}{dx} = 10x + 3$. If the function is increasing,
$\frac{dy}{dx} > 0 \Rightarrow 10x > -3 \Rightarrow x > -\frac{3}{10}$.

c) $\frac{dy}{dx} = -18x$. If the function is increasing, $\frac{dy}{dx} > 0$
$\Rightarrow -18x > 0 \Rightarrow x < 0$.
*Be careful with the direction of the inequality sign if you're
dividing by a negative number.*

Q2 a) $f'(x) = -3 - 4x$. If the function is decreasing,
$f'(x) < 0 \Rightarrow -4x < 3 \Rightarrow x > -\frac{3}{4}$.

b) $f(x) = (6 - 3x)(6 + 3x) = 36 - 9x^2 \Rightarrow f'(x) = -18x$.
If the function is decreasing, $f'(x) < 0$
$\Rightarrow -18x < 0 \Rightarrow x > 0$.

c) $f(x) = (1 - 2x)(7 - 3x) = 7 - 17x + 6x^2$
$f'(x) = -17 + 12x$. If the function is decreasing,
$f'(x) < 0 \Rightarrow 12x < 17 \Rightarrow x < \frac{17}{12}$.

Q3 a) $\frac{dy}{dx} = 3x^2 - 12x - 15$. If the function is increasing,
$\frac{dy}{dx} > 0 \Rightarrow 3x^2 - 12x - 15 > 0$
$\Rightarrow x^2 - 4x - 5 > 0 \Rightarrow (x - 5)(x + 1) > 0$
For this expression to be > 0, both brackets must be positive or both brackets must be negative.
So either $x > 5$ and $x > -1$ or $x < 5$ and $x < -1$. So the function is increasing when $x < -1$ and when $x > 5$.

b) $\frac{dy}{dx} = 3x^2 + 12x + 12$.
If the function is increasing, $\frac{dy}{dx} > 0$
$\Rightarrow 3x^2 + 12x + 12 > 0 \Rightarrow x^2 + 4x + 4 > 0$
$\Rightarrow (x + 2)(x + 2) > 0 \Rightarrow (x + 2)^2 > 0$
So x can be any real value except $x = -2$, which means that the function is increasing for all values of x except $x = -2$.
Remember that you can use a different method, e.g. sketching the quadratic, to solve the inequality if you prefer.

Q4 a) $f'(x) = 3x^2 - 6x - 9$. If the function is decreasing,
$f'(x) < 0 \Rightarrow 3x^2 - 6x - 9 < 0 \Rightarrow x^2 - 2x - 3 < 0$
$\Rightarrow (x - 3)(x + 1) < 0$. For the expression to be < 0, one bracket must be positive and one negative.
So either $x < 3$ and $x > -1$ or $x > 3$ and $x < -1$.
The second situation is impossible, so $-1 < x < 3$.

b) $f'(x) = 3x^2 - 8x + 4$. If the function is decreasing,
$f'(x) < 0 \Rightarrow 3x^2 - 8x + 4 < 0 \Rightarrow (3x - 2)(x - 2) < 0$.
For the expression to be < 0, either $x < \frac{2}{3}$ and $x > 2$ or $x > \frac{2}{3}$ and $x < 2$. The first situation is impossible, so $\frac{2}{3} < x < 2$.

Q5 $f'(x) = 3x^2 + 1$. x^2 can't be negative ($x^2 \geq 0$), so $f'(x)$ must always be positive and so $f(x)$ is an increasing function for all real values of x.

Q6 $f'(x) = -3 - 3x^2$. x^2 can't be negative ($x^2 \geq 0$), so $f'(x)$ is always ≤ -3 (so negative), so $f(x)$ is a decreasing function.

Q7 a) $\frac{dy}{dx} = 8x^3 + 1$. If the function is decreasing,
$\frac{dy}{dx} < 0 \Rightarrow 8x^3 + 1 < 0 \Rightarrow x^3 < -\frac{1}{8} \Rightarrow x < -\frac{1}{2}$

b) $\frac{dy}{dx} = 4x^3 - 6x^2 - 10x$. If the function is decreasing, $\frac{dy}{dx} < 0 \Rightarrow 4x^3 - 6x^2 - 10x < 0$
$\Rightarrow x(2x - 5)(x + 1) < 0$. For this to be true, there are 4 possibilities — all are less than zero, or one is less than zero and the other two are not:
Either $x < 0$ and $x < \frac{5}{2}$ and $x < -1$, so $x < -1$
Remember, if x must be smaller than 0, $\frac{5}{2}$ and −1, you can just dismiss the two higher numbers and simplify it to x being smaller than −1.
Or $x < 0$ and $x > \frac{5}{2}$ and $x > -1$ (impossible)
Or $x > 0$ and $x < \frac{5}{2}$ and $x > -1$, so $0 < x < \frac{5}{2}$
Or $x > 0$ and $x > \frac{5}{2}$ and $x < -1$ (impossible)
This gives the ranges $x < -1$ and $0 < x < \frac{5}{2}$.

Q8 a) $y = x^2 + \sqrt{x} = x^2 + x^{\frac{1}{2}} \Rightarrow \frac{dy}{dx} = 2x + \frac{1}{2\sqrt{x}}$
$\frac{dy}{dx} > 0$ for all $x > 0$, so the function is increasing for all $x > 0$.

b) $y = 4x^2 + \frac{1}{x} = 4x^2 + x^{-1} \Rightarrow \frac{dy}{dx} = 8x - \frac{1}{x^2}$
The function is increasing when $\frac{dy}{dx} > 0$
$\Rightarrow 8x - \frac{1}{x^2} > 0 \Rightarrow x^3 > \frac{1}{8} \Rightarrow x > \frac{1}{2}$

Q9 If the function is decreasing, $\frac{dy}{dx} < 0$ for all x.
$\frac{dy}{dx} = -3 - 5ax^4 \Rightarrow -3 - 5ax^4 < 0 \Rightarrow ax^4 > -\frac{3}{5}$.
The right-hand side is negative, so as $x^4 \geq 0$, a must also be positive to make the LHS > RHS for all x. So $a > 0$.

Q10 If the function is increasing, $\frac{dy}{dx}$ will always be greater than 0. $\frac{dy}{dx} = kx^{k-1} + 1 \Rightarrow kx^{k-1} + 1 > 0$.
When $k = 1$, $x^0 + 1 > 0$ — true for all x
When $k = 2$, $2x^1 + 1 > 0$ — not true for all x
When $k = 3$, $3x^2 + 1 > 0$ — true for all x
When $k = 4$, $4x^3 + 1 > 0$ — not true for all x, etc.
So k must be an odd number greater than zero.

Exercise 3.5 — Curve sketching

Q1 a) When $x = 0$, $y = 0^3 - 2(0)^2 = 0$, so the curve crosses the axes at $(0, 0)$. When $y = 0$,
$x^3 - 2x^2 = 0 \Rightarrow x^2(x - 2) = 0 \Rightarrow x = 0$ and $x = 2$.
So the curve also crosses the axes at $(2, 0)$.
You already knew it crossed the x-axis at x = 0, so you can ignore that one.

b) $\frac{dy}{dx} = 3x^2 - 4x$. When $\frac{dy}{dx} = 0$, $3x^2 - 4x = 0$
$\Rightarrow x(3x - 4) = 0 \Rightarrow x = 0$ and $x = \frac{4}{3}$. When $x = \frac{4}{3}$,
$y = (\frac{4}{3})^3 - 2(\frac{4}{3})^2 = -\frac{32}{27}$.
So the coordinates are $(0, 0)$ and $(\frac{4}{3}, -\frac{32}{27})$.

c) $\frac{d^2y}{dx^2} = 6x - 4$. At $x = 0$, $\frac{d^2y}{dx^2} = -4$, so it's a maximum.
At $x = \frac{4}{3}$, $\frac{d^2y}{dx^2} = 4$, so it's a minimum.

d) A positive cubic goes from bottom left to top right:

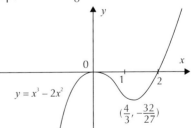

$y = x^3 - 2x^2$

$(\frac{4}{3}, -\frac{32}{27})$

Q2 a) $x^3 + x^2 = 0 \Rightarrow x^2(x + 1) = 0 \Rightarrow x = 0$ or $x = -1$.

b) $f'(x) = 3x^2 + 2x$. When $f'(x) = 0$, $3x^2 + 2x = 0$
$\Rightarrow x(3x + 2) = 0 \Rightarrow x = 0$ and $x = -\frac{2}{3}$.
When $x = 0$, $y = 0$. When $x = -\frac{2}{3}$, $y = \frac{4}{27}$,
so the stationary points are at $(0, 0)$ and $(-\frac{2}{3}, \frac{4}{27})$.
$f''(x) = 6x + 2$. At $(0, 0)$, $f''(x) = 2$, so it's a minimum.
At $(-\frac{2}{3}, \frac{4}{27})$, $f''(x) = -2$, so it's a maximum.

c)

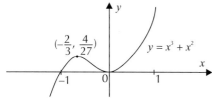

It's a positive cubic, so it goes from bottom left to top right.

Q3 a) $f'(x) = 4x^3 - 3x^2$, $f''(x) = 12x^2 - 6x$.

b) $f(x)$ is increasing for $f'(x) > 0 \Rightarrow 4x^3 - 3x^2 > 0$
$\Rightarrow x^2(4x - 3) > 0$, so either:

$x^2 > 0$ and $x > \frac{3}{4}$ $(\Rightarrow x > \frac{3}{4})$, or

$x^2 < 0$ and $x < \frac{3}{4}$ (x^2 can't be less
than 0, so this situation is impossible)

So it's increasing when $x > \frac{3}{4}$.

$f(x)$ is decreasing for $f'(x) < 0 \Rightarrow 4x^3 - 3x^2 < 0$
$\Rightarrow x^2(4x - 3) < 0$, so either:

$x^2 < 0$ and $x > \frac{3}{4}$ (x^2 can't be less
than 0, so this situation is impossible), or

$x^2 > 0$ and $x < \frac{3}{4}$

So it's decreasing when $x < \frac{3}{4}$, $x \neq 0$.

c) When $x = 0$, $f(x) = 0$. When $f(x) = 0$, $x^4 - x^3 = 0$
$\Rightarrow x^3(x - 1) = 0$, so $x = 0$ or $x = 1$. So the curve
crosses the axes at $(0, 0)$ and $(1, 0)$.

Stationary points occur when $f'(x) = 0$.
$f'(x) = 4x^3 - 3x^2 = 0 \Rightarrow x^2(4x - 3) = 0$, so $x = 0$
or $x = \frac{3}{4}$. When $x = 0$, $y = 0$ and
when $x = \frac{3}{4}$, $y = -\frac{27}{256} = -0.11$ (2 d.p.).

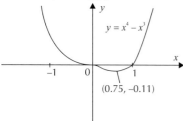

$f''(0) = 0$ so we cannot say whether the point $(0, 0)$ is a
maximum or a minimum — but the function is decreasing
for $x < 0.75$ so $(0, 0)$ must be a point of inflection.

Q4 a) When $x = 0$, $y = 0$. When $y = 0$, $3x^3 + 3x^2 = 0$
$\Rightarrow 3x^2(x + 1) = 0$, so $x = 0$ and -1.
When $\frac{dy}{dx} = 0$, $9x^2 + 6x = 0 \Rightarrow 3x(3x + 2) = 0$
so $x = 0$ and $x = -\frac{2}{3}$. When $x = -\frac{2}{3}$, $y = \frac{4}{9}$.
$\frac{d^2y}{dx^2} = 18x + 6$. When $x = 0$, $\frac{d^2y}{dx^2} = 6$,
so it's a minimum. When $x = -\frac{2}{3}$, $\frac{d^2y}{dx^2} = -6$,
so it's a maximum. It's a positive cubic, so it'll go
from bottom left to top right.

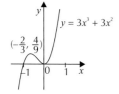

b) When $x = 0$, $y = 0$. When $y = 0$, $-x^3 + 9x = 0$
$\Rightarrow x(9 - x^2) = 0$, so $x = 0$ and $x = \pm 3$.
When $\frac{dy}{dx} = 0$, $-3x^2 + 9 = 0 \Rightarrow x = \pm\sqrt{3}$.
When $x = \sqrt{3}$, $y = 6\sqrt{3}$ and when $x = -\sqrt{3}$, $y = -6\sqrt{3}$
$\frac{d^2y}{dx^2} = -6x$.
When $x = \sqrt{3}$, $\frac{d^2y}{dx^2} = -6\sqrt{3}$, so it's a maximum.

When $x = -\sqrt{3}$, $\frac{d^2y}{dx^2} = 6\sqrt{3}$, so it's a minimum.

It's a negative cubic, so it'll go
from top left to bottom right.

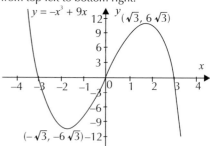

c) When $x = 0$, $y = 0$. When $y = 0$, $x^4 - x^2 = 0$
$\Rightarrow x^2(x^2 - 1) = 0$, so $x = 0$ and ± 1.
When $\frac{dy}{dx} = 0$, $4x^3 - 2x = 0 \Rightarrow x(2x^2 - 1) = 0$.
So $x = 0$ and $\pm\frac{1}{\sqrt{2}}$.

When $x = \frac{1}{\sqrt{2}}$, $y = -\frac{1}{4}$ and when $x = -\frac{1}{\sqrt{2}}$, $y = -\frac{1}{4}$.
$\frac{d^2y}{dx^2} = 12x^2 - 2$.

When $x = 0$, $\frac{d^2y}{dx^2} = -2$, so it's a maximum.

When $x = \frac{1}{\sqrt{2}}$, $\frac{d^2y}{dx^2} = 4$, so it's a minimum.

When $x = -\frac{1}{\sqrt{2}}$, $\frac{d^2y}{dx^2} = 4$, so it's a minimum.

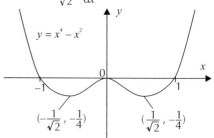

d) When $x = 0$, $y = 0$. When $y = 0$, $x^4 + x^2 = 0$
$\Rightarrow x^2(x^2 + 1) = 0$, so $x = 0$ ($x^2 = -1$ has no solutions).
When $\frac{dy}{dx} = 0$, $4x^3 + 2x = 0$
$\Rightarrow x(2x^2 + 1) = 0$, so $x = 0$.
$\frac{d^2y}{dx^2} = 12x^2 + 2$.

When $x = 0$, $\frac{d^2y}{dx^2} = 2$, so it's a minimum.

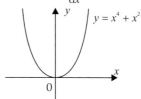

Q5 When $x = 0$, $y = 1$.
When $y = 0$, $(x + 1)(x - 1)^2 = 0$, so $x = 1$ and -1.
When $\dfrac{dy}{dx} = 0$, $3x^2 - 2x - 1 = 0 \Rightarrow (3x + 1)(x - 1) = 0$
so $x = 1$ and $-\dfrac{1}{3}$.
When $x = 1$, $y = 0$ and when $x = -\dfrac{1}{3}$, $y = \dfrac{32}{27}$.
$\dfrac{d^2y}{dx^2} = 6x - 2$.
When $x = 1$, $\dfrac{d^2y}{dx^2} = 4$, so it's a minimum.
When $x = -\dfrac{1}{3}$, $\dfrac{d^2y}{dx^2} = -4$, so it's a maximum.
It's a positive cubic, so it'll go
from bottom left to top right.

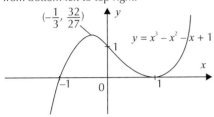

Q6 **a)** When $x = 2$, $x^3 - 4x = 8 - 8 = 0$.
When $x = -2$, $x^3 - 4x = -8 - (-8) = 0$
When $x = 0$, $x^3 - 4x = 0 - 0 = 0$.

b) $\dfrac{dy}{dx} = 3x^2 - 4$, $\dfrac{d^2y}{dx^2} = 6x$.
When $\dfrac{dy}{dx} = 0$, $3x^2 - 4 = 0 \Rightarrow x = \pm\dfrac{2\sqrt{3}}{3}$
$= \pm 1.2$ (to 1 d.p.)
When $x = \dfrac{2\sqrt{3}}{3}$, $y = -3.1$ (1 d.p.)
and when $x = -\dfrac{2\sqrt{3}}{3}$, $y = 3.1$ (1 d.p.).
So the coordinates of the stationary points to 1 d.p.
are $(1.2, -3.1)$ and $(-1.2, 3.1)$.
At $(\dfrac{2\sqrt{3}}{3}, -3.1)$, $\dfrac{d^2y}{dx^2} = 6 \times \dfrac{2\sqrt{3}}{3} = 4\sqrt{3}$,
so it's a minimum.
At $(-, 3.1)$, $\dfrac{d^2y}{dx^2} = 6 \times -\dfrac{2\sqrt{3}}{3} = -4\sqrt{3}$,
so it's a maximum.

c)

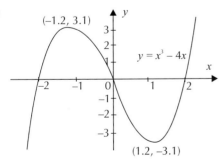

Q7 **a)** $f'(x) = 1 - \dfrac{1}{x^2}$. When $f'(x) = 0$, $1 - \dfrac{1}{x^2} = 0$
$\Rightarrow x^2 = 1 \Rightarrow x = \pm 1$. So the graph of $f(x) = x + \dfrac{1}{x}$ has
stationary points at $x = 1$ and $x = -1$.

b) When $x = 1$, $y = 1 + 1 = 2$, and when $x = -1$,
$y = -1 - 1 = -2$. So the coordinates are $(1, 2)$
and $(-1, -2)$.
$f''(x) = \dfrac{2}{x^3}$. At $(1, 2)$, $f''(x) = 2$, so it's a minimum.
At $(-1, -2)$, $f''(x) = -2$, so it's a maximum.

c) $f(x) = x + \dfrac{1}{x}$.
As x tends to 0 from below (x is negative),
$f(x)$ tends to $-\infty$.
As $x \to 0$ from above (x is positive), $f(x) \to \infty$.

d) As x tends to ∞, $f(x)$ tends to x
i.e. the graph tends towards the line $y = x$.
As x tends to $-\infty$, $f(x)$ tends to x
i.e. the graph tends towards the line $y = x$.

e)

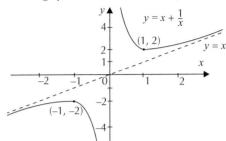

Q8 **a)** $\dfrac{dy}{dx} = 4x^3 - \dfrac{4}{\sqrt{x^3}}$. When $x = 1$, $\dfrac{dy}{dx} = 4 - 4 = 0$.

b) When $x = 1$, $y = 9$
As $x \to 0$, $y \to \infty$ and as $x \to \infty$, $y \to x^4$.
When $y = 0$, $x^4 + \dfrac{8}{\sqrt{x}} = 0 \Rightarrow \sqrt{x^9} = -8$. This has
no solutions, so the curve doesn't cross the x-axis.
$\dfrac{d^2y}{dx^2} = 12x^2 + \dfrac{6}{\sqrt{x^5}}$. When $x = 1$, $\dfrac{d^2y}{dx^2} = 18$,
so it's a minimum.

4. Real-Life Problems

Exercise 4.1 — Speed and acceleration problems

Q1 **a)** $\dfrac{dx}{dt} = 6t - 7$

b) **(i)** $t = 2 \Rightarrow \dfrac{dx}{dt} = 12 - 7 = 5$ ms^{-1}

   (ii) $t = 5 \Rightarrow \dfrac{dx}{dt} = 30 - 7 = 23$ ms^{-1}

c) If $\dfrac{dx}{dt} = 17 \Rightarrow 6t - 7 = 17 \Rightarrow 6t = 24 \Rightarrow t = 4$ s.

d) $\dfrac{d^2x}{dt^2} = 6$ ms^{-2}
Although you were asked for $\dfrac{d^2x}{dt^2}$ as a function of t,
it happens to be constant in this example.

Q2 **a)** $\dfrac{dx}{dt} = 6t^2 - 8t$

b) If $\dfrac{dx}{dt} = 30$ then $6t^2 - 8t = 30 \Rightarrow 6t^2 - 8t - 30 = 0$
$\Rightarrow 3t^2 - 4t - 15 = 0 \Rightarrow (3t + 5)(t - 3) = 0$
$\Rightarrow t = 3$ or $t = -\dfrac{5}{3}$. But $t > 0$ so $t = 3$.
If $t = 3$, $x = 2t^3 - 4t^2 = 18$.
So $t = 3$ s and $x = 18$ m.

c) $\dfrac{d^2x}{dt^2} = 12t - 8$.

d) $t = 5 \Rightarrow \dfrac{d^2x}{dt^2} = 52$ ms^{-2}

e) If $\dfrac{d^2x}{dt^2} = 16 \Rightarrow 12t - 8 = 16 \Rightarrow 12t = 24 \Rightarrow t = 2$.

$\dfrac{dx}{dt} = 6t^2 - 8t = 8$ ms^{-1}.

Exercise 4.2 — Length, area and volume problems

Q1 Total length of fence for a rectangular area of length x m and width y m $= 2x + 2y$.

Total area $= 100 = xy \Rightarrow y = \dfrac{100}{x}$

Sub this into equation for length: $f(x) = 2x + \dfrac{200}{x}$

You want to minimise the length, so find $f'(x)$:

$f'(x) = 2 - \dfrac{200}{x^2}$. When $f'(x) = 0$, $2 - \dfrac{200}{x^2} = 0$

$\Rightarrow x^2 = 100 \Rightarrow x = 10$ (length can't be negative).

Check to see if this gives a minimum value by differentiating again:

$f''(x) = \dfrac{400}{x^3} \Rightarrow f''(10) = 0.4$, so it's a minimum.

Now find the value of y when $x = 10$:

$100 = xy \Rightarrow y = 10$.

Finally, length $= 2x + 2y = 20 + 20 = 40$ m.

Q2 $\dfrac{dh}{dt} = 30 - 9.8t$. When $\dfrac{dh}{dt} = 0$, $30 - 9.8t = 0$

$\Rightarrow t = 3.061... = 3.06$ (3 s.f.).

Check this gives a maximum value:

$\dfrac{d^2h}{dt^2} = -9.8$, so it's a maximum. So the maximum value of $h = 30(3.061...) - 4.9(3.061...)^2 = 45.9$ m (3 s.f.).

Q3 Let the length of fence parallel to the wall be x and the lengths perpendicular to the wall be y.

We want to maximise area, i.e $A = xy$.

Total length of fence $= 66 = x + 2y \Rightarrow y = \dfrac{66 - x}{2}$

So we want to maximise $A = x\left(\dfrac{66 - x}{2}\right) = 33x - \dfrac{x^2}{2}$.

$\dfrac{dA}{dx} = 33 - x$, so when $\dfrac{dA}{dx} = 0$, $x = 33$.

Check that this gives a maximum value by differentiating again: $\dfrac{d^2A}{dx^2} = -1$, so it's a maximum.

When $x = 33$, $y = \dfrac{66 - 33}{2} = 16.5$.

Area $= 33 \times 16.5 = 544.5$ m^2.

If you'd labelled the sides the other way round, your working would be different but you'd still get the same answer.

Q4 a) Surface area = area of top and bottom plus area of curved face $= \pi r^2 + \pi r^2 + (2\pi r \times h) = 2\pi r^2 + 2\pi rh$.

To match the question, find an expression for h by thinking about the volume of the tin:

Volume = area of base $\times$ height $= \pi r^2 h = 500$

$\Rightarrow h = \dfrac{500}{\pi r^2}$. So surface area $= 2\pi r^2 + 2\pi r\dfrac{500}{\pi r^2}$

$= 2\pi r^2 + \dfrac{1000}{r}$.

b) $\dfrac{dA}{dr} = 4\pi r - \dfrac{1000}{r^2}$. When $\dfrac{dA}{dr} = 0$,

$4\pi r - \dfrac{1000}{r^2} = 0 \Rightarrow r = \sqrt[3]{\dfrac{250}{\pi}} = 4.30$ cm (3 s.f.).

Check that this gives a minimum value:

$\dfrac{d^2A}{dr^2} = 4\pi + \dfrac{2000}{r^3}$.

When $r = 4.30$, $\dfrac{d^2A}{dr^2} = 37.7$, so it's a minimum.

You don't really need to work out $\dfrac{d^2A}{dr^2}$ when $r = 4.30$ — you can tell it's positive straight away.

c) Surface area $= 2\pi r^2 + \dfrac{1000}{r} = 349$ cm^2 (3 s.f.).

Q5 a) Volume of the box = length $\times$ width $\times$ height

$= (40 - 2x) \times (40 - 2x) \times x = 4x^3 - 160x^2 + 1600x$

b) $\dfrac{dV}{dx} = 12x^2 - 320x + 1600$. When $\dfrac{dV}{dx} = 0$,

$12x^2 - 320x + 1600 = 0 \Rightarrow 3x^2 - 80x + 400 = 0$

$\Rightarrow (3x - 20)(x - 20) = 0 \Rightarrow x = 20$ or $x = \dfrac{20}{3}$.

Differentiate again to find which of these is a maximum: $\dfrac{d^2V}{dx^2} = 24x - 320$. When $x = 20$,

$\dfrac{d^2V}{dx^2} = 160$, and when $x = \dfrac{20}{3}$, $\dfrac{d^2V}{dx^2} = -160$,

so V is a maximum when $x = \dfrac{20}{3}$.

Note that if $x = 20$, the volume of the box $V = 0$, so this can't be the maximum of V — it's always worth checking that answers are sensible in the context of the question.

So the maximum volume is:

$4\left(\dfrac{20}{3}\right)^3 - 160\left(\dfrac{20}{3}\right)^2 + 1600\left(\dfrac{20}{3}\right) = 4740$ cm^3 (3 s.f.).

Q6 a) The prism is made up of 5 shapes:

2 triangles with base x and height x (area $= \dfrac{1}{2}x^2$),

2 rectangles with width x and length l (area $= xl$) and 1 rectangle with width h and length l (area $= hl$).

So the total surface area is given by:

$A = x^2 + 2xl + hl$. To get rid of the l, find an expression for l by looking at the volume:

$300 = \dfrac{1}{2}x^2l \Rightarrow l = \dfrac{600}{x^2}$

To get rid of the h, form an expression for it in terms of x. It's the hypotenuse of a right-angled triangle, so $h^2 = x^2 + x^2 \Rightarrow h = \sqrt{2x^2} = \sqrt{2}x$.

Now put these into the original formula for A:

$A = x^2 + 2x\left(\dfrac{600}{x^2}\right) + \sqrt{2}x\left(\dfrac{600}{x^2}\right) = x^2 + \dfrac{600(2 + \sqrt{2})}{x}$

b) $\dfrac{dA}{dx} = 2x - \dfrac{600(2 + \sqrt{2})}{x^2}$. When $\dfrac{dA}{dx} = 0$,

$2x - \dfrac{600(2 + \sqrt{2})}{x^2} = 0 \Rightarrow x^3 = 300(2 + \sqrt{2})$

$\Rightarrow x = \sqrt[3]{600 + 300\sqrt{2}}$

Check that this gives a minimum value:

$\dfrac{d^2A}{dx^2} = 2 + \dfrac{1200(2 + \sqrt{2})}{x^3}$.

When $x = \sqrt[3]{600 + 300\sqrt{2}}$, $\dfrac{d^2A}{dx^2} = 6$, so it's a minimum.

You don't really need to work out $\dfrac{d^2A}{dt^2}$ when $x = \sqrt[3]{600 + 300\sqrt{2}}$ — you can see it's positive.

Chapter 11: Integration

1. Indefinite Integration

Exercise 1.1 — Integrating x^n

Q1 a) $y = \displaystyle\int \dfrac{dy}{dx} \, dx = \int x^7 \, dx = \dfrac{x^8}{8} + C$

b) $y = \displaystyle\int \dfrac{dy}{dx} \, dx = \int 2x^3 \, dx = 2\int x^3 \, dx$

$= 2\left(\dfrac{x^4}{4}\right) + C = \dfrac{x^4}{2} + C$

c) $y = \int \dfrac{dy}{dx}\,dx = \int 8x\,dx = 8\int x\,dx$

$\quad = 8\left(\dfrac{x^2}{2}\right) + C = 4x^2 + C$

d) $y = \int \dfrac{dy}{dx}\,dx = \int -5x^4\,dx = -5\int x^4\,dx$

$\quad = -5\left(\dfrac{x^5}{5}\right) + C = -x^5 + C$

e) $y = \int \dfrac{dy}{dx}\,dx = \int x^{-3}\,dx = \dfrac{x^{-2}}{-2} + C = -\dfrac{1}{2x^2} + C$

f) $y = \int \dfrac{dy}{dx}\,dx = \int 4x^{-4}\,dx = 4\int x^{-4}\,dx$

$\quad = 4\left(\dfrac{x^{-3}}{-3}\right) + C = \dfrac{4x^{-3}}{-3} + C = -\dfrac{4}{3x^3} + C$

g) $y = \int \dfrac{dy}{dx}\,dx = \int -6x^{-5}\,dx = -6\int x^{-5}\,dx$

$\quad = -6\left(\dfrac{x^{-4}}{-4}\right) + C = \dfrac{3x^{-4}}{2} + C = \dfrac{3}{2x^4} + C$

h) $y = \int \dfrac{dy}{dx}\,dx = \int -12\,dx = \dfrac{-12x}{1} + C = -12x + C$

i) $y = \int \dfrac{dy}{dx}\,dx = \int x^{\frac{1}{2}}\,dx = \dfrac{x^{\frac{3}{2}}}{\left(\frac{3}{2}\right)} + C = \dfrac{2x^{\frac{3}{2}}}{3} + C$

Don't forget that dividing by a fraction is the same as multiplying by the flipped fraction.

j) $y = \int \dfrac{dy}{dx}\,dx = \int x^{\frac{1}{3}}\,dx = \dfrac{x^{\frac{4}{3}}}{\left(\frac{4}{3}\right)} + C = \dfrac{3x^{\frac{4}{3}}}{4} + C$

Q2 a) $\int x^{\frac{2}{3}}\,dx = \dfrac{x^{\frac{5}{3}}}{\left(\frac{5}{3}\right)} + C = \dfrac{3x^{\frac{5}{3}}}{5} + C$

b) $\int 7x^{\frac{4}{3}}\,dx = 7\int x^{\frac{4}{3}}\,dx = 7\left(\dfrac{x^{\frac{7}{3}}}{\left(\frac{7}{3}\right)}\right) + C = 3x^{\frac{7}{3}} + C$

c) $\int x^{-\frac{1}{2}}\,dx = \dfrac{x^{\frac{1}{2}}}{\left(\frac{1}{2}\right)} + C = 2x^{\frac{1}{2}} + C$

d) $\int 2x^{-\frac{1}{3}}\,dx = 2\int x^{-\frac{1}{3}}\,dx = 2\dfrac{x^{\frac{2}{3}}}{\left(\frac{2}{3}\right)} + C = 3x^{\frac{2}{3}} + C$

e) $\int 14x^{0.4}\,dx = 14\int x^{0.4}\,dx = 14\left(\dfrac{x^{1.4}}{1.4}\right) + C$

$\quad = 10x^{1.4} + C$

f) $\int -1.2x^{-0.6}\,dx = -1.2\int x^{-0.6}\,dx$

$\quad = -1.2\left(\dfrac{x^{0.4}}{0.4}\right) + C = -3x^{0.4} + C$

g) $\int -2x^{-\frac{5}{4}}\,dx = -2\int x^{-\frac{5}{4}}\,dx = -2\dfrac{x^{-\frac{1}{4}}}{\left(-\frac{1}{4}\right)} + C$

$\quad = 8x^{-\frac{1}{4}} + C$

h) $\int -\dfrac{3}{2}x^{-\frac{1}{2}}\,dx = -\dfrac{3}{2}\int x^{-\frac{1}{2}}\,dx = -\dfrac{3}{2}\left(\dfrac{x^{\frac{1}{2}}}{\left(\frac{1}{2}\right)}\right) + C$

$\quad = -3x^{\frac{1}{2}} + C$

i) $\int -\dfrac{4}{3}x^{-\frac{4}{3}}\,dx = -\dfrac{4}{3}\int x^{-\frac{4}{3}}\,dx = -\dfrac{4}{3}\left(\dfrac{x^{-\frac{1}{3}}}{\left(-\frac{1}{3}\right)}\right) + C$

$\quad = 4x^{-\frac{1}{3}} + C$

Exercise 1.2 — Integrating functions

Q1 a) $f(x) = \int f'(x)\,dx = \int (5x + 3x^{-4})\,dx$

$\quad = 5\int x\,dx + 3\int x^{-4}\,dx$

$\quad = 5\left(\dfrac{x^2}{2}\right) + 3\left(\dfrac{x^{-3}}{-3}\right) + C = \dfrac{5x^2}{2} - x^{-3} + C$

b) $f(x) = \int f'(x)\,dx = \int 4x(x^2 - 1)\,dx$

$\quad = \int (4x^3 - 4x)\,dx = 4\int x^3\,dx - 4\int x\,dx$

$\quad = 4\left(\dfrac{x^4}{4}\right) - 4\left(\dfrac{x^2}{2}\right) + C = x^4 - 2x^2 + C$

c) $f(x) = \int f'(x)\,dx = \int (x - 3)^2\,dx$

$\quad = \int (x^2 - 6x + 9)\,dx$

$\quad = \int x^2\,dx - 6\int x\,dx + 9\int 1\,dx$

$\quad = \dfrac{x^3}{3} - 6\left(\dfrac{x^2}{2}\right) + 9\left(\dfrac{x^1}{1}\right) + C = \dfrac{x^3}{3} - 3x^2 + 9x + C$

d) $f(x) = \int f'(x)\,dx = \int x\left(6x + \dfrac{4}{x^4}\right)\,dx$

$\quad = \int \left(6x^2 + \dfrac{4}{x^3}\right)\,dx = \int (6x^2 + 4x^{-3})\,dx$

$\quad = 6\int x^2\,dx + 4\int x^{-3}\,dx$

$\quad = 6\left(\dfrac{x^3}{3}\right) + 4\left(\dfrac{x^{-2}}{-2}\right) + C$

$\quad = 2x^3 - 2x^{-2} + C = 2x^3 - \dfrac{2}{x^2} + C$

e) $f(x) = \int f'(x)\,dx = \int \left(x + \dfrac{2}{x}\right)^2\,dx$

$\quad = \int \left(x^2 + 4 + \dfrac{4}{x^2}\right)\,dx = \int (x^2 + 4 + 4x^{-2})\,dx$

$\quad = \int x^2\,dx + 4\int 1\,dx + 4\int x^{-2}\,dx$

$\quad = \dfrac{x^3}{3} + 4\left(\dfrac{x^1}{1}\right) + 4\left(\dfrac{x^{-1}}{-1}\right) + C = \dfrac{x^3}{3} + 4x - \dfrac{4}{x} + C$

f) $f(x) = \int f'(x)\,dx = \int x\left(3x^{\frac{1}{2}} - \dfrac{2}{x^{\frac{4}{3}}}\right)\,dx$

$\quad = \int \left(3x^{\frac{3}{2}} - \dfrac{2}{x^{\frac{1}{3}}}\right)\,dx = \int (3x^{\frac{3}{2}} - 2x^{-\frac{1}{3}})\,dx$

$\quad = 3\int x^{\frac{3}{2}}\,dx - 2\int x^{-\frac{1}{3}}\,dx$

$\quad = 3\left(\dfrac{x^{\frac{5}{2}}}{\left(\frac{5}{2}\right)}\right) - 2\dfrac{x^{\frac{2}{3}}}{\left(\frac{2}{3}\right)} + C = \dfrac{6}{5}x^{\frac{5}{2}} - 3x^{\frac{2}{3}} + C$

g) $f(x) = \int f'(x)\,dx = \int \left(6\sqrt{x} - \dfrac{1}{x^2}\right)\,dx$

$\quad = 6\int x^{\frac{1}{2}}\,dx - \int x^{-2}\,dx$

$\quad = 6\left(\dfrac{x^{\frac{3}{2}}}{\left(\frac{3}{2}\right)}\right) - \dfrac{x^{-1}}{-1} + C$

$\quad = \dfrac{12}{3}x^{\frac{3}{2}} + \dfrac{1}{x} + C = 4x^{\frac{3}{2}} + \dfrac{1}{x} + C$

$\quad = 4x\sqrt{x} + \dfrac{1}{x} + C$

h) $f(x) = \int f'(x)\,dx = \int \left(\dfrac{2}{\sqrt{x}} - 7x^2\sqrt{x}\right)\,dx$

$\quad = \int (2x^{-\frac{1}{2}} - 7x^2 x^{\frac{1}{2}})\,dx = \int (2x^{-\frac{1}{2}} - 7x^{\frac{5}{2}})\,dx$

$\quad = 2\int x^{-\frac{1}{2}}\,dx - 7\int x^{\frac{5}{2}}\,dx$

$\quad = 2\left(\dfrac{x^{\frac{1}{2}}}{\left(\frac{1}{2}\right)}\right) - 7\dfrac{x^{\frac{7}{2}}}{\left(\frac{7}{2}\right)} + C$

$\quad = 4x^{\frac{1}{2}} - 2x^{\frac{7}{2}} + C = 4\sqrt{x} - 2(\sqrt{x})^7 + C$

i) $f(x) = \int f'(x)\,dx = \int \left(5(\sqrt{x})^3 - \dfrac{3x}{\sqrt{x}}\right)\,dx$

$\quad = \int (5(x^{\frac{1}{2}})^3 - 3xx^{-\frac{1}{2}})\,dx$

$\quad = \int (5x^{\frac{3}{2}} - 3x^{\frac{1}{2}})\,dx$

$\quad = 5\int x^{\frac{3}{2}}\,dx - 3\int x^{\frac{1}{2}}\,dx$

$\quad = 5\left(\dfrac{x^{\frac{5}{2}}}{\left(\frac{5}{2}\right)}\right) - 3\left(\dfrac{x^{\frac{3}{2}}}{\left(\frac{3}{2}\right)}\right) + C$

$\quad = 2x^{\frac{5}{2}} - 2x^{\frac{3}{2}} + C = 2(\sqrt{x})^5 - 2(\sqrt{x})^3 + C$

Q2 a) $\int (0.55x^{0.1} - 3x^{-1.5}x)\,dx = \int (0.55x^{0.1} - 3x^{-0.5})\,dx$

$$= 0.55\int x^{0.1}\,dx - 3\int x^{-0.5}\,dx$$

$$= 0.55\left(\frac{x^{1.1}}{1.1}\right) - 3\left(\frac{x^{0.5}}{0.5}\right) + C$$

$$= 0.5x^{1.1} - 6x^{0.5} + C$$

b) $\int \left(8x^3 - \frac{2}{\sqrt{x}} + \frac{5}{x^2}\right)dx = \int (8x^3 - 2x^{-\frac{1}{2}} + 5x^{-2})\,dx$

$$= 8\int x^3\,dx - 2\int x^{-\frac{1}{2}}\,dx + 5\int x^{-2}\,dx$$

$$= 8\left(\frac{x^4}{4}\right) - 2\left(\frac{x^{\frac{1}{2}}}{\left(\frac{1}{2}\right)}\right) + 5\left(\frac{x^{-1}}{-1}\right) + C$$

$$= 2x^4 - 4x^{\frac{1}{2}} - 5x^{-1} + C = 2x^4 - 4\sqrt{x} - \frac{5}{x} + C$$

c) $\int \left((\sqrt{x})^5 + \frac{1}{2\sqrt{x}}\right)dx = \int \left((x^{\frac{1}{2}})^5 + \frac{1}{2}x^{-\frac{1}{2}}\right)dx$

$$= \int x^{\frac{5}{2}}\,dx + \frac{1}{2}\int x^{-\frac{1}{2}}\,dx$$

$$= \left(\frac{x^{\frac{7}{2}}}{\left(\frac{7}{2}\right)}\right) + \frac{1}{2}\left(\frac{x^{\frac{1}{2}}}{\left(\frac{1}{2}\right)}\right) + C$$

$$= \frac{2x^{\frac{7}{2}}}{7} + x^{\frac{1}{2}} + C = \frac{2}{7}(\sqrt{x})^7 + \sqrt{x} + C$$

d) $\int \left(\sqrt{x}\left(7x^2 - 1 - \frac{2}{x}\right)\right)dx$

$$= \int \left(x^{\frac{1}{2}}(7x^2 - 1 - 2x^{-1})\right)dx$$

$$= \int \left(7x^{\frac{5}{2}} - x^{\frac{1}{2}} - 2x^{-\frac{1}{2}}\right)dx$$

$$= 7\int x^{\frac{5}{2}}\,dx - \int x^{\frac{1}{2}}\,dx - 2\int x^{-\frac{1}{2}}\,dx$$

$$= 7\left(\frac{x^{\frac{7}{2}}}{\left(\frac{7}{2}\right)}\right) - \left(\frac{x^{\frac{3}{2}}}{\left(\frac{3}{2}\right)}\right) - 2\left(\frac{x^{\frac{1}{2}}}{\left(\frac{1}{2}\right)}\right) + C$$

$$= 2x^{\frac{7}{2}} - \frac{2}{3}x^{\frac{3}{2}} - 4x^{\frac{1}{2}} + C$$

$$= 2(\sqrt{x})^7 - \frac{2}{3}(\sqrt{x})^3 - 4\sqrt{x} + C$$

e) $\int (3x - 5\sqrt{x})^2\,dx = \int (9x^2 - 30x\sqrt{x} + 25x)\,dx$

$$= \int (9x^2 - 30x^{\frac{3}{2}} + 25x)\,dx$$

$$= 9\int x^2\,dx - 30\int x^{\frac{3}{2}}\,dx + 25\int x\,dx$$

$$= 9\left(\frac{x^3}{3}\right) - 30\left(\frac{2}{5}x^{\frac{5}{2}}\right) + 25\left(\frac{1}{2}x^2\right) + C$$

$$= 3x^3 - 12(\sqrt{x})^5 + \frac{25}{2}x^2 + C$$

f) $\int \left(\frac{2x^3 - \sqrt{x}}{x}\right)dx = \int \left(\frac{2x^3}{x} - \frac{\sqrt{x}}{x}\right)dx$

$$= \int (2x^2 - x^{-\frac{1}{2}})\,dx$$

$$= 2\int x^2\,dx - \int x^{-\frac{1}{2}}\,dx$$

$$= 2\left(\frac{x^3}{3}\right) - \left(\frac{x^{\frac{1}{2}}}{\left(\frac{1}{2}\right)}\right) + C = \frac{2}{3}x^3 - 2\sqrt{x} + C$$

g) $\int \left(\frac{(5x-3)^2}{\sqrt{x}}\right)dx = \int \left(\frac{(25x^2 - 30x + 9)}{\sqrt{x}}\right)dx$

$$= \int \left(\frac{25x^2}{\sqrt{x}} - \frac{30x}{\sqrt{x}} + \frac{9}{\sqrt{x}}\right)dx$$

$$= \int (25x^{\frac{3}{2}} - 30x^{\frac{1}{2}} + 9x^{-\frac{1}{2}})\,dx$$

$$= 25\int x^{\frac{3}{2}}\,dx - 30\int x^{\frac{1}{2}}\,dx + 9\int x^{-\frac{1}{2}}\,dx$$

$$= 25\left(\frac{x^{\frac{5}{2}}}{\left(\frac{5}{2}\right)}\right) - 30\left(\frac{x^{\frac{3}{2}}}{\left(\frac{3}{2}\right)}\right) + 9\left(\frac{x^{\frac{1}{2}}}{\left(\frac{1}{2}\right)}\right) + C$$

$$= 10x^{\frac{5}{2}} - 20x^{\frac{3}{2}} + 18x^{\frac{1}{2}} + C$$

$$= 10(\sqrt{x})^5 - 20(\sqrt{x})^3 + 18\sqrt{x} + C$$

h) $\int (x^{\frac{1}{2}} + 1)(x^{-\frac{1}{2}} - 3)\,dx = \int (1 - 3x^{\frac{1}{2}} + x^{-\frac{1}{2}} - 3)\,dx$

$$= \int (x^{-\frac{1}{2}} - 3x^{\frac{1}{2}} - 2)\,dx$$

$$= \int x^{-\frac{1}{2}}\,dx - 3\int x^{\frac{1}{2}}\,dx - 2\int 1\,dx$$

$$= \left(\frac{x^{\frac{1}{2}}}{\left(\frac{1}{2}\right)}\right) - 3\left(\frac{x^{\frac{3}{2}}}{\left(\frac{3}{2}\right)}\right) - 2\left(\frac{x^1}{1}\right) + C$$

$$= 2x^{\frac{1}{2}} - 2x^{\frac{3}{2}} - 2x + C$$

Q3 $y = \int \frac{dy}{dx}\,dx = \int \left(1.5x^2 - \frac{4}{x^3}\right)dx$

$$= \int (1.5x^2 - 4x^{-3})\,dx = 1.5\int x^2\,dx - 4\int x^{-3}\,dx$$

$$= 1.5\left(\frac{x^3}{3}\right) - 4\left(\frac{x^{-2}}{-2}\right) + C = \frac{x^3}{2} + \frac{2}{x^2} + C$$

Q4 $f(x) = \int f'(x)\,dx = \int \left(\frac{4}{3(x^{\frac{1}{3}})^4} + 5x^{\frac{3}{2}}\right)dx$

$$= \int \left(\frac{4}{3x^{\frac{4}{3}}} + 5x^{\frac{3}{2}}\right)dx = \int \left(\frac{4}{3}x^{-\frac{4}{3}} + 5x^{\frac{3}{2}}\right)dx$$

$$= \frac{4}{3}\int x^{-\frac{4}{3}}\,dx + 5\int x^{\frac{3}{2}}\,dx$$

$$= \frac{4}{3}\left(\frac{x^{-\frac{1}{3}}}{\left(-\frac{1}{3}\right)}\right) + 5\frac{x^{\frac{5}{2}}}{\left(\frac{5}{2}\right)} + C$$

$$= -4x^{-\frac{1}{3}} + 2x^{\frac{5}{2}} + C \left(= -\frac{4}{\sqrt[3]{x}} + 2(\sqrt{x})^5 + C\right)$$

Q5 a) $\int \left(\frac{(\sqrt{x}+3)(\sqrt{x}-1)}{\sqrt{x}}\right)dx = \int \left(\frac{x + 2\sqrt{x} - 3}{\sqrt{x}}\right)dx$

$$= \int \left(\frac{x}{\sqrt{x}} + \frac{2\sqrt{x}}{\sqrt{x}} - \frac{3}{\sqrt{x}}\right)dx$$

$$= \int (x^{\frac{1}{2}} + 2 - 3x^{-\frac{1}{2}})\,dx$$

$$= \int x^{\frac{1}{2}}\,dx + 2\int 1\,dx - 3\int x^{-\frac{1}{2}}\,dx$$

$$= \left(\frac{x^{\frac{3}{2}}}{\left(\frac{3}{2}\right)}\right) + 2\left(\frac{x^1}{1}\right) - 3\left(\frac{x^{\frac{1}{2}}}{\left(\frac{1}{2}\right)}\right) + C$$

$$= \frac{2}{3}x^{\frac{3}{2}} + 2x - 6x^{\frac{1}{2}} + C$$

$$= \frac{2}{3}(\sqrt{x})^3 + 2x - 6\sqrt{x} + C$$

b) $\int \left(\sqrt{x}\left(\sqrt{x} - \frac{1}{\sqrt{x}}\right)^2\right)dx = \int \left(\sqrt{x}\left(x - 2 + \frac{1}{x}\right)\right)dx$

$$= \int \left(x\sqrt{x} - 2\sqrt{x} + \frac{\sqrt{x}}{x}\right)dx$$

$$= \int (x^{\frac{3}{2}} - 2x^{\frac{1}{2}} + x^{-\frac{1}{2}})\,dx$$

$$= \int x^{\frac{3}{2}}\,dx - 2\int x^{\frac{1}{2}}\,dx + \int x^{-\frac{1}{2}}\,dx$$

$$= \left(\frac{x^{\frac{5}{2}}}{\left(\frac{5}{2}\right)}\right) - 2\left(\frac{x^{\frac{3}{2}}}{\left(\frac{3}{2}\right)}\right) + \left(\frac{x^{\frac{1}{2}}}{\left(\frac{1}{2}\right)}\right) + C$$

$$= \frac{2}{5}x^{\frac{5}{2}} - \frac{4}{3}x^{\frac{3}{2}} + 2x^{\frac{1}{2}} + C$$

$$= \frac{2}{5}(\sqrt{x})^5 - \frac{4}{3}(\sqrt{x})^3 + 2\sqrt{x} + C$$

Exercise 1.3 — Integrating to find equations of curves

Q1 a) $f(x) = \int f'(x)\,dx = \int 4x^3\,dx = 4\int x^3\,dx$

$$= 4\left(\frac{x^4}{4}\right) + C = x^4 + C$$

At the point $(0, 5)$, $x = 0$ and $f(x) = y = 5$,
so $5 = 0^4 + C$. So $C = 5$ and $f(x) = x^4 + 5$.

b) $f(x) = \int f'(x)\,dx = \int (3x^2 - 4x + 3)\,dx$

$\quad = 3\int x^2\,dx - 4\int x\,dx + 3\int 1\,dx$

$\quad = 3\left(\dfrac{x^3}{3}\right) - 4\left(\dfrac{x^2}{2}\right) + 3\left(\dfrac{x^1}{1}\right) + C = x^3 - 2x^2 + 3x + C$

At the point $(1, -3)$ $x = 1$ and $f(x) = y = -3$,
so $-3 = 1^3 - 2(1^2) + 3(1) + C = 2 + C$.
So $C = -5$ and $f(x) = x^3 - 2x^2 + 3x - 5$.

c) $f(x) = \int f'(x)\,dx = \int 6x(x + 2)\,dx$

$\quad = \int (6x^2 + 12x)\,dx$

$\quad = 6\int x^2\,dx + 12\int x\,dx$

$\quad = 6\left(\dfrac{x^3}{3}\right) + 12\left(\dfrac{x^2}{2}\right) + C = 2x^3 + 6x^2 + C$

At the point $(-1, 1)$ $x = -1$ and $f(x) = y = 1$,
so $1 = 2(-1)^3 + 6(-1)^2 + C = 4 + C$.
So $C = -3$ and $f(x) = 2x^3 + 6x^2 - 3$.

d) $f(x) = \int f'(x)\,dx = \int \left(\dfrac{5}{x^2} + 2x\right)dx$

$\quad = \int (5x^{-2} + 2x)\,dx$

$\quad = 5\int x^{-2}\,dx + 2\int x\,dx$

$\quad = 5\left(\dfrac{x^{-1}}{-1}\right) + 2\left(\dfrac{x^2}{2}\right) + C = -\dfrac{5}{x} + x^2 + C$

At the point $(5, 4)$ $x = 5$ and $f(x) = y = 4$,
so $4 = -\dfrac{5}{5} + 5^2 + C = 24 + C$.

So $C = -20$ and $f(x) = -\dfrac{5}{x} + x^2 - 20$.

e) $f(x) = \int f'(x)\,dx = \int 3x^2(x - 4)\,dx$

$\quad = \int (3x^3 - 12x^2)\,dx$

$\quad = 3\int x^3\,dx - 12\int x^2\,dx$

$\quad = 3\left(\dfrac{x^4}{4}\right) - 12\left(\dfrac{x^3}{3}\right) + C = \dfrac{3}{4}x^4 - 4x^3 + C$

At the point $(2, -10)$ $x = 2$ and $f(x) = y = -10$,
so $-10 = \dfrac{3}{4}(2^4) - 4(2^3) + C = -20 + C$.
So $C = 10$ and $f(x) = \dfrac{3}{4}x^4 - 4x^3 + 10$.

f) $f(x) = \int f'(x)\,dx = \int (3x + 1)(x - 1)\,dx$

$\quad = \int (3x^2 - 2x - 1)\,dx$

$\quad = 3\int x^2\,dx - 2\int x\,dx - \int 1\,dx$

$\quad = 3\left(\dfrac{x^3}{3}\right) - 2\left(\dfrac{x^2}{2}\right) - \left(\dfrac{x^1}{1}\right) + C = x^3 - x^2 - x + C$

At the point $(3, -3)$ $x = 3$ and $f(x) = y = -3$,
so $-3 = 3^3 - 3^2 - 3 + C = 15 + C$.
So $C = -18$ and $f(x) = x^3 - x^2 - x - 18$.

g) $f(x) = \int f'(x)\,dx = \int x\left(x + \dfrac{3}{x^3}\right)dx$

$\quad = \int \left(x^2 + \dfrac{3}{x^2}\right)dx = \int x^2\,dx + 3\int x^{-2}\,dx$

$\quad = \dfrac{x^3}{3} + 3\left(\dfrac{x^{-1}}{-1}\right) + C = \dfrac{x^3}{3} - \dfrac{3}{x} + C$

At the point $(-3, 5)$ $x = -3$ and $f(x) = y = 5$,
so $5 = \dfrac{(-3)^3}{3} - \dfrac{3}{-3} + C = -8 + C$.

So $C = 13$ and $f(x) = \dfrac{x^3}{3} - \dfrac{3}{x} + 13$.

h) $f(x) = \int f'(x)\,dx = \int \dfrac{9x^3 + 2x^{-2}}{x}\,dx$

$\quad = \int \left(\dfrac{9x^3}{x} + \dfrac{2x^{-2}}{x}\right)dx = \int (9x^2 + 2x^{-3})\,dx$

$\quad = 9\int x^2\,dx + 2\int x^{-3}\,dx$

$\quad = 9\left(\dfrac{x^3}{3}\right) + 2\left(\dfrac{x^{-2}}{-2}\right) + C = 3x^3 - \dfrac{1}{x^2} + C$

At the point $(-1, 2)$ $x = -1$ and $f(x) = y = 2$,
so $2 = 3(-1)^3 - \dfrac{1}{(-1)^2} + C = -4 + C$.

So $C = 6$ and $f(x) = 3x^3 - \dfrac{1}{x^2} + 6$.

Q2 $y = f(x) = \int f'(x)\,dx = \int \left(\dfrac{3}{\sqrt{x}} + 2x\right)dx$

$\quad = \int (3x^{-\frac{1}{2}} + 2x)\,dx = 3\int x^{-\frac{1}{2}}\,dx + 2\int x\,dx$

$\quad = 3\left(\dfrac{x^{\frac{1}{2}}}{\left(\frac{1}{2}\right)}\right) + 2\left(\dfrac{x^2}{2}\right) + C = 6x^{\frac{1}{2}} + x^2 + C = 6\sqrt{x} + x^2 + C$

At the point $(4, 9)$ $x = 4$ and $y = 9$,
so $9 = 6\sqrt{4} + 4^2 + C = 28 + C$.
So $C = -19$ and $y = 6\sqrt{x} + x^2 - 19$.

Q3 $y = \int \dfrac{dy}{dx}\,dx = \int \left(3\sqrt{x} + \dfrac{1}{x^2}\right)dx = \int (3x^{\frac{1}{2}} + x^{-2})\,dx$

$\quad = 3\int x^{\frac{1}{2}}\,dx + \int x^{-2}\,dx = 3\left(\dfrac{x^{\frac{3}{2}}}{\left(\frac{3}{2}\right)}\right) + \left(\dfrac{x^{-1}}{-1}\right) + C$

$\quad = 2x^{\frac{3}{2}} - \dfrac{1}{x} + C = 2(\sqrt{x})^3 - \dfrac{1}{x} + C$

At the point $(1, 7)$ $x = 1$ and $y = 7$, so
$7 = 2((\sqrt{1})^3) - \dfrac{1}{1} + C = 1 + C$.
So $C = 6$ and $y = 2(\sqrt{x})^3 - \dfrac{1}{x} + 6$.

Q4 $y = \int \dfrac{dy}{dt}\,dt = \int (\sqrt{t} - 3)^2\,dt = \int (t - 6\sqrt{t} + 9)\,dt$

$\quad = \int t\,dt - 6\int t^{\frac{1}{2}}\,dt + 9\int 1\,dt$

$\quad = \dfrac{t^2}{2} - 6\left(\dfrac{t^{\frac{3}{2}}}{\left(\frac{3}{2}\right)}\right) + 9\left(\dfrac{t^1}{1}\right) + C$

$\quad = \dfrac{t^2}{2} - 4t^{\frac{3}{2}} + 9t + C = \dfrac{t^2}{2} - 4(\sqrt{t})^3 + 9t + C$

When $t = 4$, $y = 9$ so
$9 = \dfrac{4^2}{2} - 4(\sqrt{4})^3 + 9(4) + C = 12 + C$.
So $C = -3$ and $y = \dfrac{t^2}{2} - 4(\sqrt{t})^3 + 9t - 3$.

Q5 $f(x) = \int f'(x)\,dx = \int (\sqrt{x}(5x - 1))\,dx$

$\quad = \int (5x\sqrt{x} - \sqrt{x})\,dx = \int (5x^{\frac{3}{2}} - x^{\frac{1}{2}})\,dx$

$\quad = 5\int x^{\frac{3}{2}}\,dx - \int x^{\frac{1}{2}}\,dx = 5\left(\dfrac{x^{\frac{5}{2}}}{\left(\frac{5}{2}\right)}\right) - \left(\dfrac{x^{\frac{3}{2}}}{\left(\frac{3}{2}\right)}\right) + C$

$\quad = 2x^{\frac{5}{2}} - \dfrac{2}{3}x^{\frac{3}{2}} + C = 2(\sqrt{x})^5 - \dfrac{2}{3}(\sqrt{x})^3 + C$

When $x = 1$, $f(x) = y = \dfrac{1}{3}$ so

$\dfrac{1}{3} = 2(\sqrt{1})^5 - \dfrac{2}{3}(\sqrt{1})^3 + C = \dfrac{4}{3} + C$.
So $C = -1$ and $f(x) = 2(\sqrt{x})^5 - \dfrac{2}{3}(\sqrt{x})^3 - 1$.

Q6 $y = f(x) = \int f'(x)\,dx = \int \left(x^2 + \frac{2}{x^{\frac{3}{2}}}\right)dx$

$= \int \left(x^2 + 2x^{-\frac{3}{2}}\right)dx = \int x^2\,dx + 2\int x^{-\frac{3}{2}}\,dx$

$= \frac{x^3}{3} + 2\left(\frac{x^{-\frac{1}{2}}}{\left(-\frac{1}{2}\right)}\right) + C = \frac{x^3}{3} - \frac{4}{\sqrt{x}} + C$

When $x = 1$, $y = -\frac{5}{3}$ so

$-\frac{5}{3} = \frac{1^3}{3} - \frac{4}{\sqrt{1}} + C = -\frac{11}{3} + C$.

So $C = 2$ and $y = \frac{x^3}{3} - \frac{4}{\sqrt{x}} + 2$.

Q7 $y = \int \frac{dy}{dx}\,dx = \int \left(\frac{x-6}{x^3} + 2\right)dx$

$= \int \left(\frac{x}{x^3} - \frac{6}{x^3} + 2\right)dx = \int (x^{-2} - 6x^{-3} + 2)\,dx$

$= \int x^{-2}\,dx - 6\int x^{-3}\,dx + 2\int 1\,dx$

$= \left(\frac{x^{-1}}{-1}\right) - 6\left(\frac{x^{-2}}{-2}\right) + 2\left(\frac{x^1}{1}\right) + C = -\frac{1}{x} + \frac{3}{x^2} + 2x + C$

When $x = 3$, $y = -1$ so

$-1 = -\frac{1}{3} + \frac{3}{3^2} + 2(3) + C = 6 + C$.

So $C = -7$ and $y = -\frac{1}{x} + \frac{3}{x^2} + 2x - 7$.

2. Definite Integration
Exercise 2.1 — Evaluating definite integrals

Q1 a) $\int_{-2}^{0}(4x^3 + 2x)\,dx = \left[x^4 + x^2\right]_{-2}^{0}$

$= (0^4 + 0^2) - ((-2)^4 + (-2)^2)$

$= -(16 + 4) = -20$

b) $\int_{-2}^{5}(x^3 + x)\,dx = \left[\frac{x^4}{4} + \frac{x^2}{2}\right]_{-2}^{5}$

$= \left(\frac{5^4}{4} + \frac{5^2}{2}\right) - \left(\frac{(-2)^4}{4} + \frac{(-2)^2}{2}\right)$

$= \frac{625}{4} + \frac{25}{2} - \frac{16}{4} - \frac{4}{2} = \frac{651}{4}$

c) $\int_{-5}^{-2}(x+1)^2\,dx = \int_{-5}^{-2}(x^2 + 2x + 1)\,dx$

$= \left[\frac{x^3}{3} + x^2 + x\right]_{-5}^{-2}$

$= \left(\frac{(-2)^3}{3} + (-2)^2 + (-2)\right) - \left(\frac{(-5)^3}{3} + (-5)^2 + (-5)\right)$

$= \left(\frac{-8}{3} + 4 - 2\right) - \left(\frac{-125}{3} + 25 - 5\right) = 21$

d) $\int_{3}^{4}(6x^{-4} + x^{-2})\,dx = \left[\frac{6x^{-3}}{-3} + \frac{x^{-1}}{-1}\right]_{3}^{4}$

$= \left[-\frac{2}{x^3} - \frac{1}{x}\right]_{3}^{4} = \left(-\frac{2}{4^3} - \frac{1}{4}\right) - \left(-\frac{2}{3^3} - \frac{1}{3}\right)$

$= -\frac{2}{64} - \frac{1}{4} + \frac{2}{27} + \frac{1}{3} = \frac{109}{864}$

e) $\int_{1}^{2}\left(x^2 + \frac{1}{x^2}\right)dx = \int_{1}^{2}(x^2 + x^{-2})\,dx = \left[\frac{x^3}{3} + \frac{x^{-1}}{-1}\right]_{1}^{2}$

$= \left[\frac{x^3}{3} - \frac{1}{x}\right]_{1}^{2} = \left(\frac{2^3}{3} - \frac{1}{2}\right) - \left(\frac{1^3}{3} - \frac{1}{1}\right)$

$= \frac{8}{3} - \frac{1}{2} - \frac{1}{3} + 1 = \frac{17}{6}$

f) $\int_{1}^{4}(3x^{-4} + \sqrt{x})\,dx = \int_{1}^{4}(3x^{-4} + x^{\frac{1}{2}})\,dx$

$= \left[\frac{3x^{-3}}{-3} + \frac{x^{\frac{3}{2}}}{\left(\frac{3}{2}\right)}\right]_{1}^{4} = \left[-\frac{1}{x^3} + \frac{2}{3}(\sqrt{x})^3\right]_{1}^{4}$

$= \left(-\frac{1}{4^3} + \frac{2}{3}(\sqrt{4})^3\right) - \left(-\frac{1}{1^3} + \frac{2}{3}(\sqrt{1})^3\right)$

$= \left(-\frac{1}{64} + \frac{2}{3} \times 2^3\right) - \left(-1 + \frac{2}{3}\right) = \frac{1085}{192}$

g) $\int_{0}^{1}(2x + 3)(x + 2)\,dx = \int_{0}^{1}(2x^2 + 7x + 6)\,dx$

$= \left[\frac{2x^3}{3} + \frac{7x^2}{2} + 6x\right]_{0}^{1}$

$= \left(\frac{2 \times 1^3}{3} + \frac{7 \times 1^2}{2} + (6 \times 1)\right)$

$\quad - \left(\frac{2 \times 0^3}{3} + \frac{7 \times 0^2}{2} + (6 \times 0)\right)$

$= \left(\frac{2}{3} + \frac{7}{2} + 6\right) - 0 = \frac{61}{6}$

h) $\int_{1}^{4}\frac{x^2 + 2}{\sqrt{x}}\,dx = \int_{1}^{4}(x^{\frac{3}{2}} + 2x^{-\frac{1}{2}})\,dx$

$= \left[\frac{x^{\frac{5}{2}}}{\left(\frac{5}{2}\right)} + 2\frac{x^{\frac{1}{2}}}{\left(\frac{1}{2}\right)}\right]_{1}^{4} = \left[\frac{2}{5}(\sqrt{x})^5 + 4\sqrt{x}\right]_{1}^{4}$

$= \left(\frac{2}{5}(\sqrt{4})^5 + 4\sqrt{4}\right) - \left(\frac{2}{5}(\sqrt{1})^5 + 4\sqrt{1}\right)$

$= \left(\frac{2}{5} \times 2^5 + 8\right) - \left(\frac{2}{5} + 4\right)$

$= \frac{64}{5} + 8 - \frac{2}{5} - 4 = \frac{82}{5}$

i) $\int_{4}^{9}\left(\frac{1}{x} + \sqrt{x}\right)^2 dx = \int_{4}^{9}\left(\frac{1}{x^2} + 2\frac{\sqrt{x}}{x} + x\right)dx$

$= \int_{4}^{9}(x^{-2} + 2x^{-\frac{1}{2}} + x)\,dx$

$= \left[\frac{x^{-1}}{-1} + \frac{2x^{\frac{1}{2}}}{\left(\frac{1}{2}\right)} + \frac{x^2}{2}\right]_{4}^{9}$

$= \left[-\frac{1}{x} + 4\sqrt{x} + \frac{x^2}{2}\right]_{4}^{9}$

$= \left(-\frac{1}{9} + 4\sqrt{9} + \frac{9^2}{2}\right) - \left(-\frac{1}{4} + 4\sqrt{4} + \frac{4^2}{2}\right)$

$= -\frac{1}{9} + 12 + \frac{81}{2} + \frac{1}{4} - 8 - 8 = \frac{1319}{36}$

Q2 $\int_{0}^{a}x^3\,dx = \left[\frac{x^4}{4}\right]_{0}^{a} = \left(\frac{a^4}{4}\right) - \left(\frac{0^4}{4}\right) = \frac{a^4}{4}$

So $\frac{a^4}{4} = 64 \Rightarrow a^4 = 64 \times 4 = 256 \Rightarrow a = 4$

a can't be −4 since the question tells you that a > 0.

Q3 a) The area is all above the x-axis so just integrate:

$\int_{0}^{4}(x + \sqrt{x})\,dx = \int_{0}^{4}(x + x^{\frac{1}{2}})\,dx$

$= \left[\frac{x^2}{2} + \frac{x^{\frac{3}{2}}}{\left(\frac{3}{2}\right)}\right]_{0}^{4} = \left[\frac{1}{2}x^2 + \frac{2}{3}(\sqrt{x})^3\right]_{0}^{4}$

$= \left(\frac{1}{2}4^2 + \frac{2}{3}(\sqrt{4})^3\right) - \left(\frac{1}{2}0^2 + \frac{2}{3}(\sqrt{0})^3\right)$

$= \left(\frac{16}{2} + \frac{2}{3} \times 2^3\right) - 0 = \frac{40}{3}$

b) The limits aren't shown on the graph, but they are just the roots of the equation $0 = 4 - x^2$.

Set $y = 0$:

$4 - x^2 = 0 \Rightarrow x^2 = 4 \Rightarrow x = 2$ or -2.

So the limits of integration are -2 and 2:

$$\int_{-2}^{2} (4 - x^2)\, dx = \left[4x - \frac{x^3}{3}\right]_{-2}^{2}$$

$$= \left((4 \times 2) - \frac{2^3}{3}\right) - \left((4 \times (-2)) - \frac{(-2)^3}{3}\right)$$

$$= \left(8 - \frac{8}{3}\right) - \left(-8 - \frac{-8}{3}\right)$$

$$= 8 - \frac{8}{3} + 8 - \frac{8}{3} = \frac{32}{3}$$

c) This area lies above and below the x-axis so you'll have to integrate the bits above and below the axis separately.

First you need to find the points where the curve crosses the axis: $y = x(x - 1)(x - 3)$ is already factorised, so it's easy.

If $x(x - 1)(x - 3) = 0$ then either $x = 0$, $x = 1$ or $x = 3$. So these are the three points where the curve crosses the axis.

The area above the x-axis is between 0 and 1 so integrate:

$$\int_{0}^{1} x(x - 1)(x - 3)\, dx = \int_{0}^{1} (x^3 - 4x^2 + 3x)\, dx$$

$$= \left[\frac{x^4}{4} - \frac{4x^3}{3} + \frac{3x^2}{2}\right]_{0}^{1}$$

$$= \left(\frac{1^4}{4} - \frac{4 \times 1^3}{3} + \frac{3 \times 1^2}{2}\right) - \left(\frac{0^4}{4} - \frac{4 \times 0^3}{3} + \frac{3 \times 0^2}{2}\right)$$

$$= \frac{1}{4} - \frac{4}{3} + \frac{3}{2} - 0 = \frac{5}{12}$$

The area below the x-axis is between 1 and 3, so integrate:

$$\int_{1}^{3} x(x - 1)(x - 3)\, dx = \int_{1}^{3} (x^3 - 4x^2 + 3x)\, dx$$

$$= \left[\frac{x^4}{4} - \frac{4x^3}{3} + \frac{3x^2}{2}\right]_{1}^{3}$$

$$= \left(\frac{3^4}{4} - \frac{4 \times 3^3}{3} + \frac{3 \times 3^2}{2}\right) - \left(\frac{1}{4} - \frac{4}{3} + \frac{3}{2}\right)$$

$$= \left(\frac{81}{4} - \frac{108}{3} + \frac{27}{2}\right) - \frac{5}{12} = -\frac{8}{3}$$

Areas cannot be negative so the area of the bit below the x-axis is $\frac{8}{3}$.

So the total area is $\frac{5}{12} + \frac{8}{3} = \frac{37}{12}$.

Q4 The graph of $y = (x - 1)(3x + 9)$ crosses the x-axis at $x = 1$ and $x = -3$, so between $x = -2$ and $x = 2$, the graph crosses the axes at $x = 1$ which means the area lies both above and below the x-axis.

It might help to sketch a graph, but you don't really need to know which area is positive and which is negative — doing the integration will tell you which is which. Just integrate between $x = -2$ and $x = 1$ and then between $x = 1$ and $x = 2$.

Work out the area between $x = -2$ and $x = 1$:

$$\int_{-2}^{1} (x - 1)(3x + 9)\, dx = \int_{-2}^{1} (3x^2 + 6x - 9)\, dx$$

$$= [x^3 + 3x^2 - 9x]_{-2}^{1}$$

$$= ((1)^3 + 3(1)^2 - 9(1)) - ((-2)^3 + 3(-2)^2 - 9(-2))$$

$$= -5 - 22 = -27$$

So the area below the x-axis is 27.

Now work out the area between $x = 1$ and $x = 2$.

$$\int_{1}^{2} (x - 1)(3x + 9)\, dx = [x^3 + 3x^2 - 9x]_{1}^{2}$$

$$= ((2)^3 + 3(2)^2 - 9(2)) - ((1)^3 + 3(1)^2 - 9(1)) = 2 - (-5) = 7$$

So the area above the x-axis is 7.

Therefore the total area is $27 + 7 = 34$.

Q5 $y = \dfrac{20}{x^5}$ is positive between $x = 1$ and $x = 2$ so integrate:

$$\int_{1}^{2} \frac{20}{x^5}\, dx = \int_{1}^{2} 20x^{-5}\, dx = \left[\frac{20x^{-4}}{-4}\right]_{1}^{2} = \left[-\frac{5}{x^4}\right]_{1}^{2}$$

$$= \left(-\frac{5}{2^4}\right) - \left(-\frac{5}{1^4}\right) = -\frac{5}{16} + 5 = \frac{75}{16}$$

So the area is $\frac{75}{16}$.

Q6 In order to find this area, you need to split it into two sections and find the area of each section separately:

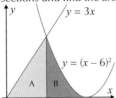

First, find the places where the graphs meet the x-axis.

$y = 3x$ crosses the x-axis at $x = 0$

$y = (x - 6)^2$ touches the x-axis at $x = 6$

The point of intersection is where the two lines meet, i.e. where $3x = (x - 6)^2$. So solve this to find x:

$$3x = (x - 6)^2 = x^2 - 12x + 36$$

$$x^2 - 15x + 36 = 0$$

$$(x - 12)(x - 3) = 0$$

So $x = 3$ or $x = 12$, and since you're looking for the intersection between $x = 0$ and $x = 6$, you want the solution $x = 3$.

Now the graph looks like this:

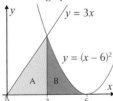

Now find the areas of the two sections.

Area A is a triangle with base length 3.

For the height, substitute $x = 3$ into the equation of the line: $y = 3 \times 3 = 9$

So the area of the triangle is $\frac{1}{2} \times 3 \times 9 = \frac{27}{2}$

$$\text{Area B} = \int_{3}^{6} (x - 6)^2\, dx = \int_{3}^{6} (x^2 - 12x + 36)\, dx$$

$$= \left[\frac{1}{3}x^3 - 6x^2 + 36x\right]_{3}^{6}$$

$$= (72 - 216 + 216) - (9 - 54 + 108) = 72 - 63 = 9$$

So the total area is $\frac{27}{2} + 9 = \frac{45}{2}$.

Q7 a) First, evaluate the integral, treating A as a constant.

$$\int_{2}^{3} (1 - 2Ax)\, dx = [x - Ax^2]_{2}^{3} = (3 - 9A) - (2 - 4A)$$

$$= 1 - 5A$$

From the question, you know that this is equal to $6A^2$, so set up and solve the quadratic.

$$1 - 5A = 6A^2$$

$$6A^2 + 5A - 1 = 0$$

$$(6A - 1)(A + 1) = 0, \text{ so } A = \frac{1}{6} \text{ or } A = -1$$

b) Again, integrate the function with constant A:

$$\int_{-2}^{2}\left(\frac{21}{8}x^2 + \frac{A}{x^2}\right)dx = \int_{-2}^{2}\left(\frac{21}{8}x^2 + Ax^{-2}\right)dx$$

$$= \left[\frac{21}{8} \times \frac{1}{3}x^3 - Ax^{-1}\right]_{-2}^{2}$$

$$= \left[\frac{7}{8}x^3 - \frac{A}{x}\right]_{-2}^{2}$$

$$= \left(\frac{7}{8}(8) - \frac{A}{2}\right) - \left(\frac{7}{8}(-8) - \frac{A}{-2}\right)$$

$$= \left(7 - \frac{A}{2}\right) - \left((-7) + \frac{A}{2}\right) = 14 - A$$

Set this equal to $3A^2$ from the question to form a quadratic in A.

$14 - A = 3A^2$

$3A^2 + A - 14 = 0$

$(3A + 7)(A - 2) = 0$,

so $A = -\frac{7}{3}$ or $A = 2$

Q8 a) $\int_{1}^{3}(10t - t^2)\,dt = \left[5t^2 - \frac{1}{3}t^3\right]_{1}^{3}$

$$= (45 - 9) - \left(5 - \frac{1}{3}\right) = \frac{94}{3} \text{ m (or } 31\frac{1}{3}\text{ m)}$$

b) First work out at what times the object's velocity is 0:

$10t - t^2 = 0$

$t(10 - t) = 0$

So $t = 0$ or $t = 10$

This means the object starts at time $t = 0$ and comes to rest at $t = 10$. To find the total distance travelled, integrate between these limits:

$$\int_{0}^{10}(10t - t^2)\,dt = \left[5t^2 - \frac{1}{3}t^3\right]_{0}^{10}$$

$$= \left(500 - \frac{1000}{3}\right) - 0$$

$$= \frac{500}{3} \text{ m (or } 166\frac{2}{3}\text{ m)}$$

Chapter 12: Vectors

1. Vectors

Exercise 1.1 — Introducing vectors

Q1 a) vector   **b)** scalar   **c)** vector

Q2 a)   **b)**

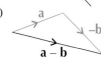

c)   **d)**

Q3 a) $\overrightarrow{AC}$ **b)** $\overrightarrow{BA}$ **c)** $\overrightarrow{DB}$

Q4 a) $\overrightarrow{XY} = -\mathbf{q}$

b) $\overrightarrow{YZ} = \overrightarrow{YX} + \overrightarrow{XZ} = \mathbf{q} + \mathbf{p}$

c) $\overrightarrow{ZY} = \overrightarrow{ZX} + \overrightarrow{XY} = -\mathbf{p} - \mathbf{q}$
or $\overrightarrow{ZY} = -\overrightarrow{YZ} = -\mathbf{q} - \mathbf{p}$

Q5 $4\mathbf{b} + 8\mathbf{a} = 4(2\mathbf{a} + \mathbf{b}) = -4(-\mathbf{b} - 2\mathbf{a})$,
so $4\mathbf{b} + 8\mathbf{a}$, $2\mathbf{a} + \mathbf{b}$ and $-\mathbf{b} - 2\mathbf{a}$ are parallel.

$2\mathbf{p} + \mathbf{q} = 2(\frac{1}{2}\mathbf{q} + \mathbf{p})$, so $2\mathbf{p} + \mathbf{q}$ and $\frac{1}{2}\mathbf{q} + \mathbf{p}$ are parallel.

$10\mathbf{a} - 5\mathbf{b} = 5(2\mathbf{a} - \mathbf{b})$,
so $10\mathbf{a} - 5\mathbf{b}$ and $2\mathbf{a} - \mathbf{b}$ are parallel.

Q6 a) $\overrightarrow{DF} = \frac{2}{3}\overrightarrow{DC}$. $\overrightarrow{DC}$ is parallel to $\overrightarrow{AB}$ and the same length because ABCD is a rectangle,
so $\overrightarrow{DC} = \overrightarrow{AB} = \mathbf{b}$. So $\overrightarrow{DF} = \frac{2}{3}\mathbf{b}$.

b) $\overrightarrow{BE} = \overrightarrow{BA} + \overrightarrow{AE} = -\overrightarrow{AB} + \frac{1}{2}\overrightarrow{AD} = -\mathbf{b} + \frac{1}{2}\mathbf{d}$

c) $\overrightarrow{EF} = \overrightarrow{ED} + \overrightarrow{DF} = \frac{1}{2}\overrightarrow{AD} + \overrightarrow{DF} = \frac{1}{2}\mathbf{d} + \frac{2}{3}\mathbf{b}$

Q7 $\overrightarrow{AB} = \overrightarrow{OB} - \overrightarrow{OA} = \mathbf{b} - \mathbf{a}$

$\overrightarrow{BC} = \overrightarrow{OC} - \overrightarrow{OB} = (5\mathbf{a} - 4\mathbf{b}) - \mathbf{b} = 5(\mathbf{a} - \mathbf{b})$

So $\overrightarrow{BC} = -5\overrightarrow{AB}$, so A, B & C lie on the same straight line — i.e. they are collinear.

Q8 $\overrightarrow{JL} = \overrightarrow{JD} + \overrightarrow{DL}$

J is the midpoint of ED, so $\overrightarrow{JD} = \frac{1}{2}\overrightarrow{ED} = \frac{1}{2}\mathbf{d}$.

And L is the midpoint of DF, so $\overrightarrow{DL} = \frac{1}{2}\overrightarrow{DF}$.

$\overrightarrow{DF} = \overrightarrow{DE} + \overrightarrow{EF} = -\mathbf{d} + \mathbf{f} \Rightarrow \overrightarrow{DL} = \frac{1}{2}(\mathbf{f} - \mathbf{d})$

So, $\overrightarrow{JL} = \frac{1}{2}\mathbf{d} + \frac{1}{2}(\mathbf{f} - \mathbf{d}) = \frac{1}{2}\mathbf{f}$.

Exercise 1.2 — Position vectors

Q1 Position vector for Jack's house: $\begin{pmatrix} 2 \\ 3 \end{pmatrix}$

Position vector for Jack's school: $\begin{pmatrix} 4 \\ -5 \end{pmatrix}$

Q2 a) C $(-1, 2)$, D $(4, -3)$

b) $\overrightarrow{CD} = \overrightarrow{OD} - \overrightarrow{OC} = (4\mathbf{i} - 3\mathbf{j}) - (-\mathbf{i} + 2\mathbf{j}) = 5\mathbf{i} - 5\mathbf{j}$
$\overrightarrow{DC} = -\overrightarrow{CD} = -(5\mathbf{i} - 5\mathbf{j}) = -5\mathbf{i} + 5\mathbf{j}$

c) Distance $= \sqrt{(4 - (-1))^2 + ((-3) - 2)^2} = \sqrt{25 + 25} = 5\sqrt{2}$

Q3 a) $\overrightarrow{PM} = \overrightarrow{MQ}$ because M is the midpoint of PQ.
This is because the lines are the same length and point in the same direction.

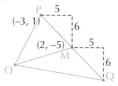

$\overrightarrow{MQ} = \overrightarrow{PM} = \overrightarrow{OM} - \overrightarrow{OP} = 2\mathbf{i} - 5\mathbf{j} - (-3\mathbf{i} + \mathbf{j}) = 5\mathbf{i} - 6\mathbf{j}$
So $\overrightarrow{OQ} = \overrightarrow{OM} + \overrightarrow{MQ} = 2\mathbf{i} - 5\mathbf{j} + (5\mathbf{i} - 6\mathbf{j}) = 7\mathbf{i} - 11\mathbf{j}$

b) Length $= \sqrt{10^2 + 12^2} = \sqrt{244} = 2\sqrt{61}$

Q4 $\overrightarrow{OA} = \begin{pmatrix} 2 \\ 4 \end{pmatrix}$, $\overrightarrow{OB} = \begin{pmatrix} 0 \\ 1 \end{pmatrix}$, $\overrightarrow{OC} = \begin{pmatrix} -1 \\ 3 \end{pmatrix}$

You could use unit form instead of column vectors to answer this question if you prefer.

$\overrightarrow{AB} = \overrightarrow{OB} - \overrightarrow{OA} = \begin{pmatrix} 0 \\ 1 \end{pmatrix} - \begin{pmatrix} 2 \\ 4 \end{pmatrix} = \begin{pmatrix} -2 \\ -3 \end{pmatrix}$

$\overrightarrow{BC} = \overrightarrow{OC} - \overrightarrow{OB} = \begin{pmatrix} -1 \\ 3 \end{pmatrix} - \begin{pmatrix} 0 \\ 1 \end{pmatrix} = \begin{pmatrix} -1 \\ 2 \end{pmatrix}$

$\overrightarrow{CA} = \overrightarrow{OA} - \overrightarrow{OC} = \begin{pmatrix} 2 \\ 4 \end{pmatrix} - \begin{pmatrix} -1 \\ 3 \end{pmatrix} = \begin{pmatrix} 3 \\ 1 \end{pmatrix}$

Q5 a) $\overrightarrow{OD} = \begin{pmatrix} -7 \\ -2 \end{pmatrix}$, $\overrightarrow{OE} = \begin{pmatrix} -3 \\ -1 \end{pmatrix}$, $\overrightarrow{OF} = \begin{pmatrix} -1 \\ 5 \end{pmatrix}$, $\overrightarrow{OG} = \begin{pmatrix} -3 \\ 10 \end{pmatrix}$

$$\overrightarrow{DE} = \overrightarrow{OE} - \overrightarrow{OD} = \begin{pmatrix} -3 \\ -1 \end{pmatrix} - \begin{pmatrix} -7 \\ -2 \end{pmatrix} = \begin{pmatrix} 4 \\ 1 \end{pmatrix}$$

$$\overrightarrow{EF} = \overrightarrow{OF} - \overrightarrow{OE} = \begin{pmatrix} -1 \\ 5 \end{pmatrix} - \begin{pmatrix} -3 \\ -1 \end{pmatrix} = \begin{pmatrix} 2 \\ 6 \end{pmatrix}$$

$$\overrightarrow{FG} = \overrightarrow{OG} - \overrightarrow{OF} = \begin{pmatrix} -3 \\ 10 \end{pmatrix} - \begin{pmatrix} -1 \\ 5 \end{pmatrix} = \begin{pmatrix} -2 \\ 5 \end{pmatrix}$$

$$\overrightarrow{GD} = \overrightarrow{OD} - \overrightarrow{OG} = \begin{pmatrix} -7 \\ -2 \end{pmatrix} - \begin{pmatrix} -3 \\ 10 \end{pmatrix} = \begin{pmatrix} -4 \\ -12 \end{pmatrix}$$

b) The vacuum cleaner could have travelled along vector $\overrightarrow{DE} + \overrightarrow{EF} = \overrightarrow{DF} = \begin{pmatrix} 4 \\ 1 \end{pmatrix} + \begin{pmatrix} 2 \\ 6 \end{pmatrix} = \begin{pmatrix} 6 \\ 7 \end{pmatrix}$

2. Calculating with Vectors
Exercise 2.1 — Calculating with vectors

Q1 a) (i) $\sqrt{6^2 + 8^2} = \sqrt{36 + 64} = \sqrt{100} = 10$

(ii) $\theta = \tan^{-1} \dfrac{8}{6} = 53.13°$
Both components are positive, so direction = 53.13°

b) (i) $\sqrt{12^2 + (-5)^2} = 13$

(ii) $\theta = \tan^{-1} \dfrac{-5}{12} = -22.62°$
The horizontal component is positive and the vertical component is negative, so direction = 360° − 22.62° = 337.38°

c) (i) $\sqrt{2^2 + 4^2} = \sqrt{20} = 2\sqrt{5}$

(ii) $\theta = \tan^{-1} \dfrac{4}{2} = 63.43°$
Both components are positive, so direction = 63.43°

d) (i) $\sqrt{(-3)^2 + (-1)^2} = \sqrt{10}$

(ii) $\theta = \tan^{-1} \dfrac{-1}{-3} = 18.43°$
Both components are negative, so direction = 180° + 18.43° = 198.43°

e) (i) $\sqrt{(24)^2 + (-7)^2} = 25$

(ii) $\theta = \tan^{-1} \dfrac{-7}{24} = -16.26°$
The horizontal component is positive and the vertical component is negative, so direction = 360° − 16.26° = 343.74°

f) (i) $\sqrt{(-\sqrt{13})^2 + 6^2} = \sqrt{13 + 36} = \sqrt{49} = 7$

(ii) $\theta = \tan^{-1} \dfrac{6}{-\sqrt{13}} = 59.00°$
The horizontal component is negative and the vertical component is positive, so direction = 180° − 59.00° = 121.00°

g) (i) $\sqrt{3^2 + (\sqrt{7})^2} = 4$

(ii) $\theta = \tan^{-1} \dfrac{\sqrt{7}}{3} = 41.41°$
Both components are positive so direction = 41.41°

h) (i) $\sqrt{0^2 + (-7)^2} = 7$

(ii) The horizontal component is 0 and the vertical component is negative, so direction = 270.00°

Q2 $|\overrightarrow{OS}| = \sqrt{10^2 + 5^2} = \sqrt{100 + 25} = \sqrt{125} = 5\sqrt{5}$

Q3 a) $\mathbf{a} + \mathbf{b} = (2\mathbf{i} + \mathbf{j}) + (2\mathbf{i} - 4\mathbf{j}) = 4\mathbf{i} - 3\mathbf{j}$
The magnitude of the resultant is $\sqrt{4^2 + (-3)^2} = 5$

b) $\mathbf{u} + \mathbf{v} = 4\mathbf{i} - 4\mathbf{j}$, $|4\mathbf{i} - 4\mathbf{j}| = \sqrt{4^2 + (-4)^2} = \sqrt{32} = 4\sqrt{2}$

c) $\mathbf{f} + \mathbf{g} = \begin{pmatrix} 24 \\ -10 \end{pmatrix}$, $\left| \begin{pmatrix} 24 \\ -10 \end{pmatrix} \right| = \sqrt{24^2 + (-10)^2} = 26$

d) $\mathbf{d} + \mathbf{e} = \begin{pmatrix} 3 \\ -6 \end{pmatrix}$, $\left| \begin{pmatrix} 3 \\ -6 \end{pmatrix} \right| = \sqrt{3^2 + (-6)^2} = \sqrt{45} = 3\sqrt{5}$

Q4 $\overrightarrow{WY}$ is horizontal, so you can make a right-angled triangle:

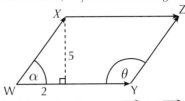

So, find the angle α between $\overrightarrow{WX}$ and $\overrightarrow{WY}$,
$\tan \alpha = \dfrac{5}{2} \Rightarrow \alpha = \tan^{-1} \dfrac{5}{2}$
$\overrightarrow{WX}$ and $\overrightarrow{YZ}$ are parallel, so $\theta = 180° - \alpha$
$$= 180° - \tan^{-1} \dfrac{5}{2}$$
$$= 111.8° \text{ (1 d.p.)}$$
You could also find θ by using the cosine rule with the lengths of $\overrightarrow{WY}$, $\overrightarrow{YZ}$ and $\overrightarrow{WZ}$ — you should get the same answer.

Q5 $\overrightarrow{AC} = \overrightarrow{AB} + \overrightarrow{BC} = 3\mathbf{i} - 2\mathbf{j} + \mathbf{i} + 5\mathbf{j} = 4\mathbf{i} + 3\mathbf{j}$
$|\overrightarrow{AC}| = \sqrt{4^2 + 3^2} = 5$
So unit vector $= \dfrac{4}{5}\mathbf{i} + \dfrac{3}{5}\mathbf{j}$

Q6 $\overrightarrow{BA} = (2\mathbf{i} - \mathbf{j}) - (7\mathbf{i} - 13\mathbf{j}) = -5\mathbf{i} + 12\mathbf{j}$,
$|\overrightarrow{BA}| = \sqrt{(-5)^2 + 12^2} = \sqrt{169} = 13$
So unit vector $= -\dfrac{5}{13}\mathbf{i} + \dfrac{12}{13}\mathbf{j}$

Q7 $|\mathbf{d}| = \sqrt{8^2 + (-6)^2} = \sqrt{100} = 10$
The magnitude of $\mathbf{c}$ is seven times the magnitude of $\mathbf{d}$, so $\mathbf{c} = 7\mathbf{d} = 7(8\mathbf{i} - 6\mathbf{j}) = 56\mathbf{i} - 42\mathbf{j}$

Q8 $|\mathbf{a}| = \sqrt{3^2 + 3^2} = \sqrt{18}$,
$|\mathbf{b}| = \sqrt{(-2)^2 + 5^2} = \sqrt{29}$
To be able to use the cosine rule to find θ, you also need to know the magnitude of the resultant vector
$\mathbf{a} - \mathbf{b} = \begin{pmatrix} 5 \\ -2 \end{pmatrix}$. $|\mathbf{a} - \mathbf{b}| = \sqrt{5^2 + (-2)^2} = \sqrt{29}$

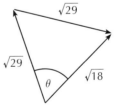

So, $\cos \theta = \dfrac{(\sqrt{29})^2 + (\sqrt{18})^2 - (\sqrt{29})^2}{2 \times \sqrt{29} \times \sqrt{18}} = \dfrac{18}{2 \times \sqrt{29} \times 3\sqrt{2}}$
$$= \dfrac{3}{\sqrt{29} \times \sqrt{2}} = \dfrac{3}{\sqrt{58}}$$
$$\Rightarrow \theta = \cos^{-1} \left(\dfrac{3}{\sqrt{58}} \right) = 66.80° \text{ (2 d.p.)}.$$

3. Modelling with Vectors
Exercise 3.1 — Modelling with vectors

Q1 $|\mathbf{a}| = \sqrt{1^2 + 2^2} = \sqrt{5}$ ms⁻²

Q2 From the diagram you can see that
$$\overrightarrow{AB} = \begin{pmatrix} 10 \\ 0 \end{pmatrix}, \overrightarrow{BC} = \begin{pmatrix} -3 \\ 6 \end{pmatrix}, \overrightarrow{CD} = \begin{pmatrix} -7 \\ 2 \end{pmatrix}.$$

Now, calling the start point of the path S and the end point T, you get

$$\mathbf{p} = \overrightarrow{ST} = \overrightarrow{SB} + \overrightarrow{BC} + \overrightarrow{CT} = \frac{3}{10}\overrightarrow{AB} + \overrightarrow{BC} + \frac{1}{2}\overrightarrow{CD}$$

$$= \frac{3}{10}\begin{pmatrix}10\\0\end{pmatrix} + \begin{pmatrix}-3\\6\end{pmatrix} + \frac{1}{2}\begin{pmatrix}-7\\2\end{pmatrix} = \begin{pmatrix}3\\0\end{pmatrix} + \begin{pmatrix}-3\\6\end{pmatrix} + \begin{pmatrix}-3.5\\1\end{pmatrix}$$

$$= \begin{pmatrix}-3.5\\7\end{pmatrix}. \text{ So, } x = -3.5 \text{ and } y = 7.$$

Q3 $|\mathbf{v_1}| = \sqrt{3^2 + (-2)^2} = \sqrt{13}$, $|\mathbf{v_2}| = \sqrt{1^2 + 3^2} = \sqrt{10}$.

To be able to use the cosine rule, you also need to know the length of the resultant of these two vectors,

$$\mathbf{v_1} + \mathbf{v_2} = \begin{pmatrix}4\\1\end{pmatrix}, \text{ so } |\mathbf{v_1} + \mathbf{v_2}| = \sqrt{4^2 + 1^2} = \sqrt{17}$$

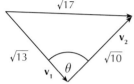

Using the cosine rule:

$$\cos\theta = \frac{(\sqrt{13})^2 + (\sqrt{10})^2 - (\sqrt{17})^2}{2 \times \sqrt{13} \times \sqrt{10}} = \frac{13 + 10 - 17}{2\sqrt{130}} = \frac{3}{\sqrt{130}}$$

$$\Rightarrow \theta = \cos^{-1}\left(\frac{3}{\sqrt{130}}\right) = 74.74° \text{ (2 d.p.)}$$

Q4 $\overrightarrow{EF}$ is parallel to $\overrightarrow{GH}$, as $-2(-\mathbf{i} - \frac{3}{2}\mathbf{j}) = 2\mathbf{i} + 3\mathbf{j}$.
$\overrightarrow{HE}$ has two negative components, while $\overrightarrow{FG}$ has one positive and one negative, so they cannot be parallel. So this quadrilateral has one and only one pair of parallel sides. This means it must be a trapezium.

Q5 a)

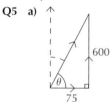

The two vectors form a right-angled triangle.
So, $\tan\theta = \frac{600}{75} = 8 \Rightarrow \theta = \tan^{-1} 8$.
So the aircraft's actual bearing is $90° - \tan^{-1} 8 = 007°$

b) The speed is the magnitude of the resultant vector.
Using Pythagoras, speed $= \sqrt{600^2 + 75^2} = \sqrt{365\,625}$
$= 604.67$ km/hr (to 2 d.p.)

Q6 $\overrightarrow{PW} = \overrightarrow{PQ} + \overrightarrow{QW}$.
Because W divides QR in the ratio $a:b$, we get that:
$$\overrightarrow{QW} = \frac{a}{a+b}\overrightarrow{QR}$$
$\overrightarrow{QR} = \overrightarrow{QP} + \overrightarrow{PR} = (-\mathbf{s}) + \mathbf{t} = \mathbf{t} - \mathbf{s}$, so $\overrightarrow{QW} = \frac{a}{a+b}(\mathbf{t} - \mathbf{s})$
We also know that $\overrightarrow{PQ} = \mathbf{s}$, so if we substitute these back into the formula for $\overrightarrow{PW}$ we get:
$$\overrightarrow{PW} = \mathbf{s} + \frac{a}{a+b}(\mathbf{t} - \mathbf{s}) = \left(1 - \frac{a}{a+b}\right)\mathbf{s} + \frac{a}{a+b}\mathbf{t}.$$
The question tells us that $\overrightarrow{PW} = \frac{5}{9}\mathbf{s} + \frac{4}{9}\mathbf{t}$
$$\Rightarrow \frac{5}{9}\mathbf{s} + \frac{4}{9}\mathbf{t} = \left(1 - \frac{a}{a+b}\right)\mathbf{s} + \frac{a}{a+b}\mathbf{t}.$$
By equating the coefficients of $\mathbf{t}$ this gives you
$$\frac{4}{9} = \frac{a}{a+b} \Rightarrow a = 4 \text{ and } b = 5$$
Equating the coefficients just means setting the numbers in front of the same variable equal to one another.

Chapter 13: Statistical Sampling

1. Populations and Samples

Exercise 1.1 — Sampling

Q1 a) Finite   **b)** Infinite
Although there are technically a finite number of people in Australia, counting them precisely would be impossible.
c) Infinite   **d)** Finite   **e)** Finite   **f)** Infinite

Q2 a) The population is all the members of the book club.

b) A census should be used because all members of the book club should be consulted about the new book. Since it is a local book club, there should be few enough members to ask everyone.

Q3 a) The population is the 1200 students at the school.

b) One reason for using a sample is that it would be time-consuming and difficult to test every student in the school. Another reason is that it would be difficult to process the large amount of data.

Q4 a) A census would be more sensible. The results will be more accurate and there are only 8 people in the population, so it wouldn't take long to find out the required information for each person.

b) A sample survey should be done. Testing all 500 toys would take too long, but more importantly it would destroy all the toys.

c) A sample survey is the only option. The population is all the possible dice rolls — there are an infinite number of dice rolls, so you can only examine a sample of them.

Q5 a) The 108 dogs admitted to the sanctuary between 2015 and 2016.

b) Give each dog a 3-digit number between 001 and 108. Calculate the regular interval: $108 \div 12 = 9$
Use a random-number generator to choose a starting point from 1 to 9. Keep adding 9 to the starting point and add all these dogs to the sample.
e.g. if the starting point is 8, then the sample will be
008, 017, 026, 035, 044, 053,
062, 071, 080, 089, 098, 107

Q6 Give each house a 3-digit number between 001 and 173 corresponding to its house number. Using a random-number table, choose a starting point on the table and move along it 3 digits at a time. For each 3 digits, see if it is a 3-digit number between 001 and 173. If it is, include the house with that number. Choose the first 40 distinct numbers between 001 and 173 that you come across in the table. Survey the 40 houses which match the numbers you have chosen.

Q7 The sample is not random. For example: The ages of her mother's friends might not be representative of the entire population, or there might be a bias towards either men or women. Pooja's mother might have a group of friends who all have similar opinions on ethically-sourced products — this would introduce bias. Similarly, Pooja's mother might have very strong opinions on ethically-sourced products and give the questionnaires to people that she knows share her views.

Q8 Simple random sampling means the sample will not be affected by sampling bias.

Q9 a) Quota sample. The sample is non-random, so it could be biased. For example: the interviewer is not told which ages to sample, so they might ask younger people, whose tea-drinking habits might be different from those of older people.

b) Systematic sample. There could be a pattern making the sample biased. For example: every 100th ticket number could correspond to a seat with a bad view — every 100th seat could be at the end of a row, which could have a worse view than seats in the middle.

c) Convenience sample. The sample isn't representative of the population. For example: many people work between the hours of 9 am and 5 pm on a Monday — these people are excluded from the sample.

Q10 Total population = 45 + 33 + 15 + 57 = 150

Under 20: $\frac{45}{150} \times 10 = 3$ 20 to 40: $\frac{33}{150} \times 10 = 2.2 \approx 2$

41 to 60: $\frac{15}{150} \times 10 = 1$ Over 60: $\frac{57}{150} \times 10 = 3.8 \approx 4$

Answers have been rounded to the nearest whole number because you can't have decimal amounts of people.

Chapter 14: Data Presentation and Interpretation

1. Representing Data

Exercise 1.1 — Data basics

Q1 a) Make, Colour

b) Mileage, Number of doors, Cost of service

Q2 a) Number of medals won last season, Shoe size

b) Height, Mass

Q3 a) There are no 'gaps' between possible heights.

b)

Height, h (cm)	No. of members	Lower class b'dary (cm)	Upper class b'dary (cm)	Class width (cm)	Class mid-point (cm)
$140 \le h < 150$	3	140	150	10	145
$150 \le h < 160$	9	150	160	10	155
$160 \le h < 170$	17	160	170	10	165
$170 \le h < 180$	12	170	180	10	175
$180 \le h < 190$	5	180	190	10	185
$190 \le h < 200$	1	190	200	10	195

c) Plot the mid-point of the classes on the x-axis and the frequencies on the y-axis.

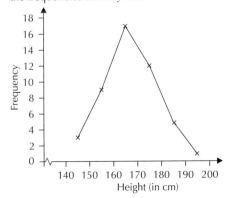

Exercise 1.2 — Histograms

Q1 First add columns to the table to show class boundaries, the class widths and the frequency densities.

Humidity, h (%)	Lower class boundary	Upper class boundary	Class width	Freq.	F.D.
$60 < h \le 80$	60	80	20	2	0.1
$80 < h \le 90$	80	90	10	9	0.9
$90 < h \le 95$	90	95	5	5	1
$95 < h \le 100$	95	100	5	4	0.8

Then you can draw the histogram:

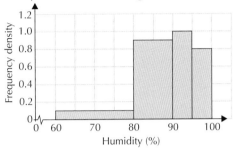

Q2 a) First you need to work out how many people are represented by each square unit on the graph — use the information that the bar for 30-45 seconds represents 54 contestants.

Bar for 30-45 seconds:
Width = 45 – 30 = 15 and height = 1.8
So area = 15 × 1.8 = 27
— this represents 54 contestants.
So each square unit represents 54 ÷ 27 = 2 people.
Or 'frequency = 2 × area'.

Bar for 10-30 seconds:
Width = 30 – 10 = 20 and height = 0.3
So area = 20 × 0.3 = 6
— this represents 6 × 2 = 12 contestants
So 12 auditions lasted less than 30 seconds.

b) Now you need to add on the frequencies represented by the other bars as well.
Area of '45-55' bar = 10 × 2.6 = 26,
which represents 26 × 2 = 52 contestants.
Area of '55-60' bar = 5 × 3.0 = 15,
which represents 15 × 2 = 30 contestants.
Area of '60-75' bar = 15 × 1.0 = 15,
which represents 15 × 2 = 30 contestants.
Area of '75-90' bar = 15 × 0.4 = 6,
which represents 6 × 2 = 12 contestants.
Total number of contestants who auditioned:
12 + 54 + 52 + 30 + 30 + 12 = 190

Q3 a) The area of the bar is 1.5 × 9 = 13.5 cm². This represents 12 butterflies. So each butterfly is represented by an area of 13.5 ÷ 12 = 1.125 cm².

b) 22.5 ÷ 1.125 = 20, so the frequency was 20.

c) The class 54-58 mm has lower class boundary 53.5 and upper class boundary 58.5. So the class width is 58.5 – 53.5 = 5. The first bar, representing a class of width 3, was 1.5 cm wide. So the bar representing the class 54-58 mm must be <u>2.5 cm wide</u>.
And because it needs to represent a frequency of 14, its area must be 14 × 1.125 = 15.75 cm².
This means it must be 15.75 ÷ 2.5 = <u>6.3 cm high</u>.

2. Location: Mean, Median & Mode

Exercise 2.1 — The mean

Q1 The sum of all 12 prices is £13.92.
So the mean price is £13.92 ÷ 12 = £1.16

Q2 99.8 ÷ 20 = 4.99 hours

Q3

Number of goals, x	0	1	2	3	4	Total
Frequency, f	5	7	4	3	1	20
fx	0	7	8	9	4	28

So the mean is 28 ÷ 20 = 1.4 goals

Q4 Old total of ages = 15 × 47.4 = 711 years
New total of ages = 711 + 17 = 728 years
So new mean = 728 ÷ 16 = 45.5 years
Or you could have used the formula with n_1 = 15, $\bar{x}_1$ = 47.4,
n_2 = 1 and $\bar{x}_2$ = 17 to get the same answer.

Exercise 2.2 — The mode and the median

Q1 **a)** First put the amounts in order:
£19, £45, £67, £77, £84, £98, £101, £108, £110,
£123, £140, £185, £187, £194, £216, £250, £500
There are 17 amounts in total. Since 17 ÷ 2 = 8.5 is
not a whole number, round this up to 9 to find the
position of the median.
So the median = £110.

b) All the values occur just once.

Q2 **a)** 80% and 95%

b) First put the values in order:
80%, 80%, 82%, 84%, 86%, 88%,
89%, 91%, 93%, 95%, 95%, 97%
There are 12 values in total. Since 12 ÷ 2 = 6 is a
whole number, the median is halfway between the
6th and 7th values in the ordered list.
So the median = (88% + 89%) ÷ 2 = 88.5%.

Q3 **a)** 5

b) There are 176 ratings in total.
176 ÷ 2 = 88, so the median is midway between the
88th and 89th values.
Add a column to the table to show cumulative
frequencies:

Rating	Number of customers	Cumulative frequency
1	7	7
2	5	12
3	25	37
4	67	104
5	72	176

From the cumulative frequencies, the 88th and 89th
values are both 4, so the median = 4.

Exercise 2.3 — Averages of grouped data

Q1 **a)**

Time (t, mins)	Frequency, f	Mid-point, x	fx
$3 \le t < 4$	7	3.5	24.5
$4 \le t < 5$	14	4.5	63
$5 \le t < 6$	24	5.5	132
$6 \le t < 8$	10	7	70
$8 \le t < 10$	5	9	45

b) $\sum f$ = 60, $\sum fx$ = 334.5
So estimate of mean = 334.5 ÷ 60
= 5.6 mins (to 1 d.p.).

Q2 **a)** 0-2 letters
All the classes are the same width, so use the frequency to
find the modal class (instead of the frequency density).

b) Add some extra columns to the table:

Number of letters	Number of houses, f	Mid-point, x	fx
0-2	20	1	20
3-5	16	4	64
6-8	7	7	49
9-11	5	10	50
12-14	2	13	26

$\sum f$ = 50, $\sum fx$ = 209
So estimate of mean = 209 ÷ 50 = 4.18 letters

c) Since $\sum f \div 2$ = 50 ÷ 2 = 25, the median is halfway
between the values in this position (25) and the next
position (26) in the ordered list.
So the median must be in the class 3-5.

Q3 Add a cumulative frequency column to the table:

Temperature (t, °C)	Frequency	Cumulative frequency
$10 \le t < 13$	1	1
$13 \le t < 16$	12	13
$16 \le t < 19$	9	22
$19 \le t < 22$	5	27
$22 \le t < 25$	3	30

So $\frac{n}{2} = \frac{30}{2}$ = 15, meaning the median must lie in the
class '$16 \le t < 19$'. Now you need to sketch that class.

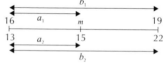

Finally, solve $\frac{a_1}{b_1} = \frac{a_2}{b_2}$. This gives:

$$\frac{m-16}{19-16} = \frac{15-13}{22-13} \Rightarrow \frac{m-16}{3} = \frac{2}{9}$$

$$\Rightarrow m = 3 \times \frac{2}{9} + 16 = 16.7 \text{ °C (to 1 d.p.)}$$

Q4 **a)** Estimated mean = 16 740 ÷ 60 = 279 minutes

b) Add a cumulative frequency column to the table:

Time (t, mins)	Frequency, f	Cumulative frequency
$180 \le t < 240$	8	8
$240 \le t < 270$	19	27
$270 \le t < 300$	21	48
$300 \le t < 360$	9	57
$360 \le t < 480$	3	60

So $\frac{n}{2}$ = 30, meaning the median must lie in the
class '$270 \le t < 300$'. Now sketch that class.

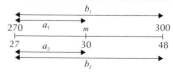

Finally, solve $\frac{a_1}{b_1} = \frac{a_2}{b_2}$. This gives:

$$\frac{m-270}{300-270} = \frac{30-27}{48-27} \Rightarrow \frac{m-270}{30} = \frac{3}{21}$$

$$\Rightarrow m = 30 \times \frac{3}{21} + 270 = 274.3 \text{ mins (to 1 d.p.).}$$

Exercise 2.4 — Comparing measures of location

Q1 a) Median — most employees will earn relatively low salaries but a few may earn much higher salaries, so the mean could be heavily affected by a few high salaries.

b) Mean — the data should be reasonably symmetrical so the mean would be a good measure of location. The median would be good as well (for a symmetric data set, it should be roughly equal to the mean).

c) Mode — make of car is qualitative data so the mode is the only average that can be found.

d) Mean — the data should be reasonably symmetrical so the mean would be a good measure of location. The median would be good as well (for a symmetric data set, it should be roughly equal to the mean).

e) Median — most employees will perhaps travel fairly short distances to work but a few employees may live much further away. The median would not be affected by these few high values.
The mode is unlikely to be suitable in b), d) and e) (and possibly a) as well) because all the values may be different.

Q2 There is a very extreme value of 8 that would affect the mean quite heavily.

3. Dispersion

Exercise 3.1 — Range, interquartile range and interpercentile range

Q1 a) Highest value = 88 846 miles
Lowest value = 3032 miles
So range = 88 846 – 3032 = 85 814 miles

b) (i) There are 8 values, and the ordered list is
3032, 4222, 7521, 7926, 30 778, 31 763, 74 898, 88 846
Since $\frac{n}{4} = 2$, the lower quartile (Q_1) is halfway between the values in this position (2) and the next position (3) in the ordered list.
So $Q_1 = (4222 + 7521) \div 2 = 5871.5$ miles.

(ii) Since $\frac{3n}{4} = 6$, the upper quartile (Q_3) is halfway between the values in this position (6) and the next position (7) in the ordered list.
So $Q_3 = (31 763 + 74 898) \div 2 = 53 330.5$ miles.

(iii) IQR = $Q_3 - Q_1 = 53 330.5 - 5871.5$
$= 47 459$ miles

Q2 a) and b)
In town at 8:45 am:
The ordered list of 18 values is:
13, 14, 14, 15, 15, 15, 15, 15, 16, 16, 16, 16, 16, 17, 17, 18, 18, 18
So the range = 18 – 13 = 5 mph
Since $\frac{n}{4} = 4.5$, the lower quartile (Q_1) is in position 5 in the ordered list. So $Q_1 = 15$ mph.

Since $\frac{3n}{4} = 13.5$, the upper quartile (Q_3) is in position 14 in the ordered list. So $Q_3 = 17$ mph. This means IQR = $Q_3 - Q_1 = 17 - 15 = 2$ mph.
In town at 10:45 am:
The ordered list of 18 values is:
25, 29, 29, 29, 30, 30, 31, 31, 31, 32, 33, 34, 34, 35, 36, 36, 38, 39
So the range = 39 – 25 = 14 mph
The lower quartile (Q_1) is in position 5 in the ordered list. So $Q_1 = 30$ mph.
The upper quartile (Q_3) is in position 14 in the ordered list. So $Q_3 = 35$ mph.
This means IQR = $Q_3 - Q_1 = 35 - 30 = 5$ mph.
On the motorway at 1 pm:
The ordered list of 18 values is:
67, 69, 69, 71, 71, 73, 73, 74, 74, 75, 75, 76, 76, 76, 78, 78, 88, 95
So the range = 95 – 67 = 28 mph
The lower quartile (Q_1) is in position 5 in the ordered list. So $Q_1 = 71$ mph.
The upper quartile (Q_3) is in position 14 in the ordered list. So $Q_3 = 76$ mph.
This means IQR = $Q_3 - Q_1 = 76 - 71 = 5$ mph.

Q3 a) Add a cumulative frequency column to the table:

Maximum temperature (t)	Frequency	Cumulative frequency
$10 \leq t < 15$	19	19
$15 \leq t < 20$	66	85
$20 \leq t < 25$	49	134
$25 \leq t < 30$	16	150

So $\frac{n}{4} = 150 \div 4 = 37.5$, meaning the lower quartile (Q_1) must lie in the class '$15 \leq t < 20$'.

Now you need to sketch that class.

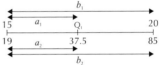

Finally, solve $\frac{a_1}{b_1} = \frac{a_2}{b_2}$. This gives:

$$\frac{Q_1 - 15}{20 - 15} = \frac{37.5 - 19}{85 - 19} \Rightarrow \frac{Q_1 - 15}{5} = \frac{18.5}{66}$$

$$\Rightarrow Q_1 = 5 \times \frac{18.5}{66} + 15 = 16.4 \text{ °C (to 1 d.p.).}$$

b) $\frac{3n}{4} = 150 \div 4 \times 3 = 112.5$, meaning the upper quartile (Q_3) must lie in the class '$20 \leq t < 25$'.
Now you need to sketch that class.

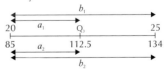

Finally, solve $\frac{a_1}{b_1} = \frac{a_2}{b_2}$. This gives:

$$\frac{Q_3 - 20}{25 - 20} = \frac{112.5 - 85}{134 - 85} \Rightarrow \frac{Q_3 - 20}{5} = \frac{27.5}{49}$$

$$\Rightarrow Q_3 = 5 \times \frac{27.5}{49} + 20 = 22.8 \text{ °C (1 d.p.).}$$

c) So IQR = $Q_3 - Q_1 = 22.8 - 16.4$
$= 6.4$ °C (to 1 d.p.).

d) $\frac{10}{100} \times n = \frac{10}{100} \times 150 = 15$, meaning the 10th percentile (P_{10}) must lie in the class '$10 \le t < 15$'. Now you need to sketch that class.

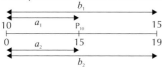

Finally, solve $\frac{a_1}{b_1} = \frac{a_2}{b_2}$. This gives:

$\frac{P_{10}-10}{15-10} = \frac{15-0}{19-0} \Rightarrow \frac{P_{10}-10}{5} = \frac{15}{19}$

$\Rightarrow P_{10} = 5 \times \frac{15}{19} + 10 = 13.9$ °C (1 d.p.).

e) $\frac{90}{100} \times n = \frac{90}{100} \times 150 = 135$, meaning the 90th percentile (P_{90}) must lie in the class '$25 \le t < 30$'. Now you need to sketch that class.

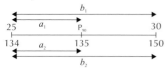

Finally, solve $\frac{a_1}{b_1} = \frac{a_2}{b_2}$. This gives:

$\frac{P_{90}-25}{30-25} = \frac{135-134}{150-134} \Rightarrow \frac{P_{90}-25}{5} = \frac{1}{16}$

$\Rightarrow P_{90} = 5 \times \frac{1}{16} + 25 = 25.3$ °C (1 d.p.)

f) So 10% to 90% interpercentile range
$= P_{90} - P_{10} = 25.3 - 13.9 = 11.4$ °C (to 1 d.p.).

Q4 a) Add a cumulative frequency column to the table:

Length (l)	Number of beetles	Cumulative frequency
0-5	82	82
6-10	28	110
11-15	44	154
16-30	30	184
31-50	16	200

$\frac{20}{100} \times n = \frac{20}{100} \times 200 = 40$, meaning that P_{20} must lie in the class '0-5'.
Now you need to sketch that class.

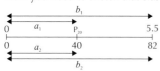

Finally, solve $\frac{a_1}{b_1} = \frac{a_2}{b_2}$.

This gives: $\frac{P_{20}-0}{5.5-0} = \frac{40-0}{82-0} \Rightarrow \frac{P_{20}}{5.5} = \frac{40}{82}$

$\Rightarrow P_{20} = 5.5 \times \frac{40}{82} = 2.7$ mm (to 1 d.p.).

$\frac{80}{100} \times n = \frac{80}{100} \times 200 = 160$, meaning that P_{80} must lie in the class '16-30'.
Now you need to sketch that class.

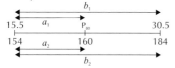

Finally, solve $\frac{a_1}{b_1} = \frac{a_2}{b_2}$. This gives:

$\frac{P_{80}-15.5}{30.5-15.5} = \frac{160-154}{184-154} \Rightarrow \frac{P_{80}-15.5}{15} = \frac{6}{30}$

$\Rightarrow P_{80} = 15 \times \frac{6}{30} + 15.5 = 18.5$ mm

So the 20% to 80% interpercentile range
$= P_{80} - P_{20} = 18.5 - 2.7 = 15.8$ mm (to 1 d.p.).

b) $\frac{5}{100} \times n = \frac{5}{100} \times 200 = 10$, meaning that P_5 must lie in the class '0-5'. Now sketch that class.

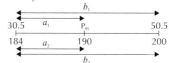

Finally, solve $\frac{a_1}{b_1} = \frac{a_2}{b_2}$.

This gives: $\frac{P_5-0}{5.5-0} = \frac{10-0}{82-0} \Rightarrow \frac{P_5}{5.5} = \frac{10}{82}$

$\Rightarrow P_5 = 5.5 \times \frac{10}{82} = 0.7$ mm (to 1 d.p.).

$\frac{95}{100} \times n = \frac{95}{100} \times 200 = 190$, meaning that P_{95} must lie in the class '31-50'.
Now you need to sketch that class.

Finally, solve $\frac{a_1}{b_1} = \frac{a_2}{b_2}$. This gives:

$\frac{P_{95}-30.5}{50.5-30.5} = \frac{190-184}{200-184} \Rightarrow \frac{P_{95}-30.5}{20} = \frac{6}{16}$

$\Rightarrow P_{95} = 20 \times \frac{6}{16} + 30.5 = 38$ mm

So the 5% to 95% interpercentile range
$= P_{95} - P_5 = 38 - 0.7 = 37.3$ mm (to 1 d.p.).
You use the lower and upper class boundaries when you sketch the classes because of how the data is grouped.

Exercise 3.2 — Cumulative frequency diagrams

Q1 Add a cumulative frequency column to the table.

Distance walked, d (km)	No. of walkers	Cumulative freq.
$0 < d \le 2$	1	1
$2 < d \le 4$	10	11
$4 < d \le 6$	7	18
$6 < d \le 8$	2	20

Then you can plot the cumulative frequency diagram.

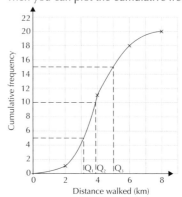

So median = $Q_2 \approx 3.9$ km and
interquartile range = $Q_3 - Q_1 \approx 5 - 3.2 = 1.8$ km.

Q2 a) Approximately 5 boys weigh less than 55 kg.

b) Approximately 17 boys weigh less than 73 kg.
So 24 – 17 = 7 boys weigh more than 73 kg.

c) The data is grouped so you don't know the actual values.

Q3 a) 84 people

b) Median earnings = £67

c) Approximately16 people earned less than £46 and approximately 70 people earned less than £84.
70 – 16 = 54, so approximately 54 people earned between £46 and £84.

Exercise 3.3 — Outliers and box plots

Q1 $IQR = Q_3 - Q_1 = 31 - 19 = 12$
Lower fence $= Q_1 - (1.5 \times IQR) = 19 - (1.5 \times 12) = 1$
Upper fence $= Q_3 + (1.5 \times IQR) = 31 + (1.5 \times 12) = 49$

The value 4 is inside the lower fence, so 4 is not an outlier. The value 52 is outside the upper fence, so 52 is an outlier.

Q2 a) $IQR = Q_3 - Q_1 = 37 - 16 = 21$

b) Lower fence $= Q_1 - (1.5 \times IQR)$
$= 16 - (1.5 \times 21) = -15.5$
Upper fence $= Q_3 + (1.5 \times IQR)$
$= 37 + (1.5 \times 21) = 68.5$

Since the minimum value and the maximum value both fall inside the fences, there are no outliers in this data set.

c)
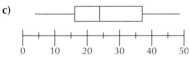

Q3 a) Put the values in order:
74, 82, 85, 86, 88, 90, 90, 90, 91, 92, 92, 95, 95, 96, 97, 97, 97, 98, 98, 99, 99, 99, 99, 99, 99, 99, 99, 99, 99, 99, 99, 100, 100, 100, 100, 100, 100, 100, 100

There are 41 data values altogether, i.e. $n = 41$.
Since $41 \div 2 = 20.5$ is not a whole number, round this up to 21 to find the position of the median.
So the median = 99% humidity.

Since $41 \div 4 = 10.25$ is not a whole number, round this up to 11 to find the position of the lower quartile. So the lower quartile (Q_1) = 92% humidity.

Since $3 \times 41 \div 4 = 30.75$ is not a whole number, round this up to 31 to find the position of the upper quartile. So the upper quartile (Q_3) = 99% humidity.

$IQR = Q_3 - Q_1 = 99 - 92 = 7\%$ humidity

b) The lower fence is
$Q_1 - (1.5 \times IQR) = 92 - (1.5 \times 7) = 81.5\%$

The upper fence is
$Q_3 + (1.5 \times IQR) = 99 + (1.5 \times 7) = 109.5\%$
This is greater than 100% which is impossible, so there are no outliers outside the upper fence.

The value 74 is outside the lower fence, so that is the only outlier.

c)
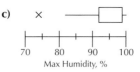

$Q_2 = Q_3 = 99$, so the median and upper quartile are both represented by the right-hand edge of the box.

Q4 a) There are 18 data values for Pigham.
Since $18 \div 2 = 9$, the median is halfway between the 9th and 10th data values (which are both 35). So the median = 35.

Since $18 \div 4 = 4.5$, the lower quartile (Q_1) is the 5th data value. So $Q_1 = 23$.

Since $3 \times 18 \div 4 = 13.5$, the upper quartile ($Q_3$) is the 14th data value. So $Q_3 = 46$.

The interquartile range $= Q_3 - Q_1 = 46 - 23 = 23$

The lower fence is
$Q_1 - (1.5 \times IQR) = 23 - (1.5 \times 23) = -11.5$
This is less than 0, which is an impossible number of items of junk mail, so there are no outliers outside the lower fence.

The upper fence is
$Q_3 + (1.5 \times IQR) = 46 + (1.5 \times 23) = 80.5$

None of the values fall outside the fences, so there are no outliers.

b)
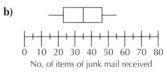

c) There are 18 data values for Goossea, so the median is halfway between the 9th and 10th data values. So the median = 27.5.

The lower quartile (Q_1) is the 5th data value. So the lower quartile = 15.

The upper quartile (Q_3) is the 14th data value. So the upper quartile = 35.

The interquartile range $= Q_3 - Q_1 = 35 - 15 = 20$.

The lower fence is
$Q_1 - (1.5 \times IQR) = 15 - (1.5 \times 20) = -15$
This means there are no 'low outliers'.

The upper fence is
$Q_3 + (1.5 \times IQR) = 35 + (1.5 \times 20) = 65$

This means that the value of 75 is an outlier (but the next highest value, 50, is not an outlier).

So the box plot looks like this:
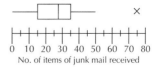

Exercise 3.4 — Variance and standard deviation

Q1 a) $\overline{x} = \dfrac{756 + 755 + 764 + 778 + 754 + 759}{6}$

$= \dfrac{4566}{6} = 761$

b) $\sum x^2 = 756^2 + 755^2 + 764^2 + 778^2 + 754^2 + 759^2$
$= 3\,475\,138$

c) variance $= \dfrac{\sum x^2}{n} - \overline{x}^2 = \dfrac{3\,475\,138}{6} - 761^2$

$\qquad\qquad = 68.666... = 68.7$ (to 3 s.f.)

d) standard deviation $= \sqrt{\text{variance}} = \sqrt{68.666...}$

$\qquad\qquad\qquad\qquad\qquad = 8.29$ (to 3 s.f.)

e) There are no outliers or extreme values to affect the standard deviation in a way that would make it unrepresentative of the rest of the data set.

Q2 a) Start by adding an extra row to the table for fx.

x	1	2	3	4
frequency, f	7	8	4	1
fx	7	16	12	4

Then $\overline{x} = \dfrac{\sum fx}{\sum f} = \dfrac{39}{20} = 1.95$

b) Now add two more rows to the table.

x	1	2	3	4
frequency, f	7	8	4	1
fx	7	16	12	4
x^2	1	4	9	16
fx^2	7	32	36	16

So $\sum fx^2 = 7 + 32 + 36 + 16 = 91$

c) variance $= \dfrac{\sum fx^2}{\sum f} - \overline{x}^2 = \dfrac{91}{20} - 1.95^2 = 0.7475$

d) standard deviation $= \sqrt{\text{variance}} = \sqrt{0.7475}$

$\qquad\qquad\qquad\qquad\qquad = 0.865$ (to 3 s.f.).

Q3 a) $\overline{x} = \dfrac{\sum x}{n} = \dfrac{290.7}{100} = 2.907$ mm

$\text{variance} = \dfrac{\sum x^2}{n} - \overline{x}^2 = \dfrac{6150.83}{100} - 2.907^2$

$\qquad\qquad = 53.05765...$ mm²

standard deviation $= \sqrt{\text{variance}} = \sqrt{53.05765...}$

$\qquad\qquad\qquad\qquad\qquad = 7.284068... = 7.28$ mm (3 s.f.)

b) Outliers are more than 3 standard deviations away from the mean.

$2.907 + 3 \times 7.284068... = 24.8$ (3 s.f.)

The x-value $35.5 > 24.8$ so it is an outlier.

You only need to consider $\overline{x} + 3$ standard deviations because the x-value 35.5 is greater than $\overline{x}$.

Q4 a) Add some more columns to the table showing the class mid-points (x), as well as fx, x^2 and fx^2.

Yield, w (kg)	f	Mid-point, x	fx	x^2	fx^2
$50 \le w < 60$	23	55	1265	3025	69575
$60 \le w < 70$	12	65	780	4225	50700
$70 \le w < 80$	15	75	1125	5625	84375
$80 \le w < 90$	6	85	510	7225	43350
$90 \le w < 100$	2	95	190	9025	18050

So $\sum f = 58$, $\sum fx = 3870$, $\sum fx^2 = 266050$. Then:

$\text{variance} = \dfrac{\sum fx^2}{\sum f} - \left(\dfrac{\sum fx}{\sum f}\right)^2 = \dfrac{266050}{58} - \left(\dfrac{3870}{58}\right)^2$

$\qquad = 134.95838... = 135$kg² (to 3 s.f.)

b) Standard deviation $= \sqrt{134.95838...}$

$\qquad\qquad\qquad\qquad = 11.6$ kg (to 3 s.f.)

c) Because the data is grouped.

Q5 a) Work out the total duration of all the 23 eruptions that Su has timed. This is $\sum x = n\overline{x} = 23 \times 3.42 = 78.66$ minutes. Work out the total duration of all the 37 eruptions that Ellen has timed. This is $\sum y = n\overline{y} = 37 \times 3.92 = 145.04$ minutes So the total duration of the last 60 eruptions is:

$\sum x + \sum y = 78.66 + 145.04 = 223.7$ minutes

So the mean duration of the last 60 eruptions is:

$\dfrac{223.7}{60} = 3.72833 = 3.73$ minutes (to 3 s.f.)

b) Work out the sum of squares of the durations of all the 23 eruptions that Su has timed. The s.d. is 1.07, so the variance is 1.07² — use this in the formula for variance.

$\text{variance} = \dfrac{\sum x^2}{n} - \overline{x}^2 \Rightarrow 1.07^2 = \dfrac{\sum x^2}{23} - 3.42^2$

So $\sum x^2 = 23 \times (1.07^2 + 3.42^2) = 295.3499$

Do the same for the 37 eruptions that Ellen has timed. The s.d. is 0.97, so the variance is 0.97² — use this in the formula for variance.

$\text{variance} = \dfrac{\sum y^2}{n} - \overline{y}^2 \Rightarrow 0.97^2 = \dfrac{\sum y^2}{37} - 3.92^2$

So $\sum y^2 = 37 \times (0.97^2 + 3.92^2) = 603.3701$

Now you can work out the total sum of squares (for all 60 eruptions):

$\sum x^2 + \sum y^2 = 295.3499 + 603.3701 = 898.72$

So the variance for all 60 eruptions is:

$\text{variance} = \dfrac{898.72}{60} - \left(\dfrac{223.7}{60}\right)^2$

$\qquad\qquad = 1.0781... = 1.08$ min² (to 3 sig. fig.)

When finding the variance of the 60 durations you use the mean from part a) written as a fraction (or the full decimal) so your answer is as accurate as possible.

c) This means the standard deviation of the durations is $\sqrt{1.0781...} = 1.0383... = 1.04$ min (to 3 s.f.)

Exercise 3.5 — Coding

Q1 Since $y = \dfrac{x - 20\,000}{15}$, $\overline{y} = \dfrac{\overline{x} - 20\,000}{15}$.

This means $\overline{x} = 15 \times 12.4 + 20000 = 20186$.

s.d. of $x = 15 \times$ s.d. of $y = 15 \times 1.34 = 20.1$

Q2 a) All the values are of the form '0.6_', and so if you subtract 0.6 from all the values, and then multiply what's left by 100, you'll end up with coded data values between 1 and 10.

So code the data values using $y = 100(x - 0.6)$, where x is an original data value and y is the corresponding coded value.

This gives y-values of: 1, 7, 3, 3, 6, 5, 4, 8, 4, 2

b) $\overline{y} = \dfrac{1 + 7 + 3 + 3 + 6 + 5 + 4 + 8 + 4 + 2}{10} = \dfrac{43}{10} = 4.3$

Find the sum of squares of the coded values, $\sum y^2$. This is $\sum y^2 = 229$.

So variance $= \dfrac{\sum y^2}{n} - \overline{y}^2 = \dfrac{229}{10} - 4.3^2 = 4.41$

This gives a standard deviation of $\sqrt{4.41} = 2.1$

Since $y = 100(x - 0.6)$, $\overline{y} = 100(\overline{x} - 0.6)$

This means: $\overline{x} = \dfrac{\overline{y}}{100} + 0.6 = \dfrac{4.3}{100} + 0.6 = 0.643$ cm

Since $y = 100(x - 0.6)$,
s.d. of $y = 100 \times$ s.d. of x
So s.d. of $x =$ s.d. of $y \div 100 = 2.1 \div 100 = 0.021$ cm

Q3 Make a new table showing the class mid-points (x) and their corresponding coded values (y), as well as fy, y^2 and fy^2.

Weight (nearest g)	100-104	105-109	110-114	115-119
Frequency, f	2	6	3	1
Class mid-point, x	102	107	112	117
Coded value, y	0	5	10	15
fy	0	30	30	15
y^2	0	25	100	225
fy^2	0	150	300	225

Then $\overline{y} = \dfrac{\sum fy}{\sum f} = \dfrac{75}{12} = 6.25$

variance of $y = \dfrac{\sum fy^2}{\sum f} - \overline{y}^2 = \dfrac{675}{12} - 6.25^2 = 17.1875$

This means standard deviation of $y = \sqrt{17.1875}$
$= 4.15$ (to 3 s.f.).

Now you can convert these back to values for x.
Since $y = x - 102$: $\overline{x} = \overline{y} + 102 = 6.25 + 102 = 108.25$ g
s.d. of $x =$ s.d. of $y = 4.15$ g (to 3 s.f.)

Q4 Using the coding $y = x + 2$.
Then $\sum y = 7$ and $\sum y^2 = 80$.

So $\overline{y} = \dfrac{\sum y}{n} = \dfrac{7}{20} = 0.35$

And the variance of y is:
$\dfrac{\sum y^2}{n} - \overline{y}^2 = \dfrac{80}{20} - 0.35^2 = 3.8775$

So standard deviation for $y = \sqrt{3.8775} = 1.97$ (to 3 s.f.)

So $\overline{x} = \overline{y} - 2 = 0.35 - 2 = -1.65$.
And standard deviation of x
$=$ standard deviation of $y = 1.97$ (to 3 s.f.)

Exercise 3.6 — Comparing distributions

Q1 The median is higher for Shop B. This shows that the prices in Shop B are generally higher. The median in Shop A is approximately £37 while the median in Shop B is approximately £63, so the difference between the average prices is around £26.

Although the ranges in the two shops are quite similar, the interquartile range (IQR) for Shop B is higher than that for Shop A. This shows that the prices of shoes in Shop B are more varied than the prices in Shop A.

Q2 **a)** <u>For the men:</u> mean $= \dfrac{\sum x}{n} = \dfrac{73}{10} = 7.3$ hours
There are 10 values, so the median is halfway between the 5th and 6th values in the ordered list. So the median is 7 hours.
Don't forget to sort the list before trying to find the median — it's an easy mistake to make.

<u>For the women:</u> mean $= \dfrac{\sum x}{n} = \dfrac{85}{10} = 8.5$ hours
Again, there are 10 values, so the median is halfway between the 5th and 6th values. So the median is 8.5 hours.

The mean and median are both higher for the women, so they get between 1 and 1.5 hours more sleep per night, on average, than the men.

b) <u>For the men:</u> s.d. $= \sqrt{\dfrac{\sum x^2}{n} - \overline{x}^2} = \sqrt{\dfrac{553}{10} - 7.3^2}$
$= 1.42$ hours (to 3 s.f.)

<u>For the women:</u> s.d. $= \sqrt{\dfrac{\sum x^2}{n} - \overline{x}^2} = \sqrt{\dfrac{749}{10} - 8.5^2}$
$= 1.63$ hours (to 3 s.f.)
The standard deviation is slightly higher for the women, so the number of hours of sleep for the women varies slightly more from the mean than it does for the men.

Q3 Read the quartiles off the graphs:
Island A: $Q_1 \approx 8$ °C, $Q_2 \approx 15$ °C, $Q_3 \approx 19$ °C
$\Rightarrow$ IQR ≈ 11 °C
Island B: $Q_1 \approx 9.5$ °C, $Q_2 \approx 12$ °C, $Q_3 \approx 15.5$ °C
$\Rightarrow$ IQR ≈ 6 °C

Island A has a higher median temperature, suggesting that the temperatures on island A are generally hotter than island B.

The data for island A has a larger interquartile range than that of island B — the data for island B is grouped more closely about the median, while the data for island A is more spread out. This suggests that the temperatures on island A tend to vary more than those on island B.

4. Correlation and Regression
Exercise 4.1 — Scatter diagrams and correlation

Q1 **a)**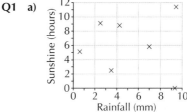

b) No correlation

Q2 **a)**

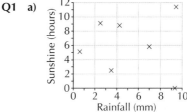

b) The data shows overall positive correlation, but there are two clusters of data.
One shows some positive correlation, while the other does not look correlated at all.

c) The circumference of 3.5 cm
<u>or</u> the length of 8.9 cm.

Exercise 4.2 — Explanatory and response variables

Q1 **Explanatory variable**: the time spent practising the piano each week
Response variable: the number of mistakes made in a test at the end of the week

It is the amount of practice that would determine the performance in the test, not the other way around.

Q2 **Explanatory variable**: the age of a second-hand car
Response variable: the value of a second-hand car
It is the age of the car that would affect its value, not the other way around.

Q3 **Explanatory variable**: the population of a town
Response variable: the number of phone calls made in a town in a week
It is the population that would affect the number of calls, not the other way around.

Q4 **Explanatory variable**: the amount of sunlight falling on a plant in an experiment
Response variable: the growth rate of a plant in an experiment
It is the amount of sunlight that would affect the growth rate, not the other way around.
(Or you could say that the amount of sunlight can be directly controlled, as this is an experiment.)

Exercise 4.3 — Regression lines

Q1 **a)** y is the response variable (since this is the regression line of y on x).
b) **(i)** $1.67 + 0.107 \times 5 = 2.205$
(ii) $1.67 + 0.107 \times 20 = 3.81$

Q2 **a)** $58.8 - 2.47 \times 7 = 41.51$ — so the volunteer would be predicted to have approximately 42 spots. This is interpolation (since 7 is between 2 and 22, which are the values of x between which data was collected). This estimate should be reliable.
b) $58.8 - 2.47 \times 0 = 58.8$ — so the volunteer would be predicted to have approximately 59 spots. This is extrapolation (since 0 is less than 2, which was the smallest value of d for which data was collected). This estimate may not be reliable.
c) Using the formula for $d = 30$ is extrapolation, since 30 is greater than 22, the largest value of d for which data was collected. The model isn't valid for $d = 30$, since you can't have a negative number of spots. But this doesn't mean that the regression equation is wrong.

Chapter 15: Probability

1. Elementary Probability

Exercise 1.1 — The sample space

Q1 **a)** There is 1 outcome corresponding to the 7 of diamonds, and 52 outcomes in total.
So P(7 of diamonds) $= \frac{1}{52}$

b) There is 1 outcome corresponding to the queen of spades, and 52 outcomes in total.
So P(queen of spades) $= \frac{1}{52}$
c) There are 4 outcomes corresponding to a '9', and 52 outcomes in total.
So P(9 of any suit) $= \frac{4}{52} = \frac{1}{13}$
d) There are 26 outcomes corresponding to a heart or a diamond, and 52 outcomes in total.
So P(heart or diamond) $= \frac{26}{52} = \frac{1}{2}$

Q2 **a)** 6 of the 36 outcomes are prime numbers.
So P(product is a prime number) $= \frac{6}{36} = \frac{1}{6}$
b) 14 of the 36 outcomes are less than 7.
So P(product is less than 7) $= \frac{14}{36} = \frac{7}{18}$
c) 6 of the 36 outcomes are multiples of 10.
So P(product is a multiple of 10) $= \frac{6}{36} = \frac{1}{6}$

Q3 **a)** E.g.

	1	2	3	4	5	6	7	8	9	10
T	•	•	•	•	•	•	•	•	•	•
H	•	•	•	•	•	•	•	•	•	•

b) There are 5 ways of getting an even number and 'tails', and 20 outcomes altogether.
So P(even number and tails) $= \frac{5}{20} = \frac{1}{4}$

Q4 **a)** E.g.

–	1	2	3	4	5	6
1	0	1	2	3	4	5
2	1	0	1	2	3	4
3	2	1	0	1	2	3
4	3	2	1	0	1	2
5	4	3	2	1	0	1
6	5	4	3	2	1	0

b) 6 of the 36 outcomes are zero.
So P(score is zero) $= \frac{6}{36} = \frac{1}{6}$
c) None of the outcomes are greater than 5.
So P(score is greater than 5) $= 0$
d) The most likely score is the one corresponding to the most outcomes — so it's 1.
10 of the 36 outcomes give a score of 1, so:
P(1) $= \frac{10}{36} = \frac{5}{18}$

Q5 Start by drawing a sample-space diagram to show all the possible outcomes for the two spins combined. Then circle the ones that correspond to the event 'number on spinner 2 is greater than number on spinner 1'.
E.g.

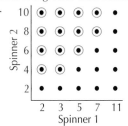

There are 13 outcomes that correspond to the event 'number on spinner 2 is greater than number on spinner 1', and 25 outcomes altogether.
So P(spinner 2 > spinner 1) $= \frac{13}{25}$

2. Solving Probability Problems

Exercise 2.1 — Venn diagrams and two-way tables

Q1 a) Label the diagram by starting in the middle with the probability for A and B. Then subtract this probability from P(A) and P(B). And remember to find P(neither A nor B) by subtracting the other probabilities from 1. So:

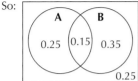

b) P(neither A nor B) = 0.25

Q2 a) Use the totals to fill in the gaps:
No coffee/BC Tops = 0.51 − 0.16 − 0.11 = 0.24
'No coffee' total = 0.24 + 0.12 + 0.14 = 0.50
'Nenco' total = 1 − 0.18 − 0.50 = 0.32
Nenco/No tea = 0.32 − 0.16 − 0.07 = 0.09
'Cumbria' total = 1 − 0.51 − 0.27 = 0.22
Yescafé/No tea = 0.27 − 0.09 − 0.14 = 0.04
Yescafé/Cumbria = 0.22 − 0.07 − 0.12 = 0.03

	BC Tops	Cumbria	No tea	Total
Nenco	0.16	0.07	**0.09**	**0.32**
Yescafé	0.11	**0.03**	**0.04**	0.18
No coffee	**0.24**	0.12	0.14	**0.50**
Total	0.51	**0.22**	0.27	1

b) (i) P(Cumbria and Yescafé) = 0.03

(ii) P(Coffee) = 1 − P(No coffee) = 1 − 0.50 = 0.50
You could also find this by adding up the totals for the two brands of coffee: P(Coffee) = P(Nenco) + P(Yescafé) = 0.32 + 0.18 = 0.50

(iii) P(tea but no coffee) = P(BC Tops and no coffee) + P(Cumbria and no coffee) = 0.24 + 0.12 = 0.36
Another way to find this is P(No coffee) − P(No coffee and no tea) = 0.50 − 0.14 = 0.36

Q3 a) Let M be 'studies maths' and P be 'studies physics'. The total number of students is 144, so that goes in the bottom right-hand corner. You can also fill in the totals for the P row and the M column — these are the total number of students studying each subject. You also know the number that study both:

	M	not M	Total
P	19		38
not P			
Total	46		144

Now you can work out all the missing values:

	M	not M	Total
P	19	38 − 19 = **19**	38
not P	46 − 19 = **27**	98 − 19 = **79**	144 − 38 = **106**
Total	46	144 − 46 = **98**	144

b) M or P has 19 + 27 + 19 = 65 outcomes.
So P(M or P) = $\frac{65}{144}$

c) So you're only interested in the 46 students who study maths. 19 students study maths and physics, so P(maths student also studies physics) = $\frac{19}{46}$.

Q4 a) P(L and M) = 0.1

b) P(L and N) = 0

c) P(N and not L) = 0.25
Since N doesn't overlap with L, N and not L is just N.

d) P(neither L nor M nor N)
= 1 − (0.25 + 0.1 + 0.15 + 0.25) = 0.25

e) P(L or M) = 0.25 + 0.1 + 0.15 = 0.5

f) P(not M) = 0.25 + 0.25 + 0.25 = 0.75
Don't forget to include P(neither L nor M nor N). You could also find P(not M) by doing 1 − P(M) = 1 − (0.1 + 0.15).

Q5 a) Number of outcomes not in S or F or G
= 200 − (17 + 18 + 49 + 28 + 11 + 34 + 6) = 37
So P(not in S or F or G) = $\frac{37}{200}$

b) You're only interested in those people who have been to France — 49 + 28 + 34 + 11 = 122 people. The number of people who have been to France **and** Germany = 28 + 34 = 62.
So P(G, given F) = $\frac{62}{122} = \frac{31}{61}$

c) Number of outcomes in S and not F = 17 + 18 = 35.
So P(S and not F) = $\frac{35}{200} = \frac{7}{40}$

Q6 a) Start by drawing a Venn diagram to represent the information. If H = 'goes to home league matches', A = 'goes to away league matches' and C = 'goes to cup matches', then:

The people who go to exactly 2 types of match are those in (H and A and not C), (H and C and not A), and (A and C and not H).
That's 200 + 40 + 20 = 260 people.
So P(2 types of match) = $\frac{260}{1000} = \frac{13}{50}$

b) P(at least 1 type of match) = 1 − P(no matches)
= 1 − $\frac{240}{1000} = \frac{760}{1000} = \frac{19}{25}$

3. Laws of Probability

Exercise 3.1 — The addition law

Q1 a) P(A′) = 1 − P(A) = 1 − 0.3 = 0.7

b) P(A or B) = P(A) + P(B) − P(A and B)
= 0.3 + 0.5 − 0.15 = 0.65

c) P(A′ and B′) = 1 − P(A or B) = 1 − 0.65 = 0.35
Remember, A′ and B′ is the complement of A or B.

Q2 a) P(B′) = 1 − P(B) = 1 − 0.44 = 0.56

b) P(A or B) = P(A) + P(B) − P(A and B)
= (1 − 0.36) + 0.44 − 0.27 = 0.81

c) P(A and B′) = P(A) − P(A and B) = 0.64 − 0.27 = 0.37

d) P(A or B′) = P(A) + P(B′) − P(A and B′)
= 0.64 + 0.56 − 0.37 = 0.83

Q3 Let B = 'car is blue' and E = 'car is an estate'.

a) P(B′) = 1 − P(B) = 1 − 0.25 = 0.75

b) P(B or E) = P(B) + P(E) − P(B and E)
= 0.25 + 0.15 − 0.08 = 0.32

c) $P(B'$ and $E') = 1 - P(B$ or $E) = 1 - 0.32 = 0.68$

Q4 a) $P(Y') = 1 - P(Y) = 1 - 0.56 = 0.44$

b) $P(X$ and $Y) = P(X) + P(Y) - P(X$ or $Y)$
$= 0.43 + 0.56 - 0.77 = 0.22$

c) $P(X'$ and $Y') = 1 - P(X$ or $Y) = 1 - 0.77 = 0.23$

d) $P(X'$ or $Y') = 1 - P(X$ and $Y) = 1 - 0.22 = 0.78$

Q5 a) $P(C'$ and $D) = P(C') + P(D) - P(C'$ or $D)$
$= (1 - 0.53) + 0.44 - 0.65 = 0.26$

b) $P(C'$ and $D') = P(C') - P(C'$ and $D)$
$= 0.47 - 0.26 = 0.21$
*Just as C = **C and D + C and D'**,*
*C' = **C' and D + C' and D'**.*

c) $P(C'$ or $D') = P(C') + P(D') - P(C'$ and $D')$
$= 0.47 + 0.56 - 0.21 = 0.82$

d) $P(C$ and $D) = P(C) + P(D) - P(C$ or $D)$
$= P(C) + P(D) - [1 - P(C'$ and $D')]$
$= 0.53 + 0.44 - (1 - 0.21) = 0.18$

Q6 Let M = 'has read To Kill a Mockingbird'
and A = 'has read Animal Farm'.
Then $P(M) = 0.62$, $P(A') = 0.66$, and $P(M$ or $A) = 0.79$.

a) $P(M$ and $A) = P(M) + P(A) - P(M$ or $A)$
$= 0.62 + (1 - 0.66) - 0.79 = 0.17$

b) $P(M'$ and $A) = P(A) - P(M$ and $A)$
$= 0.34 - 0.17 = 0.17$

c) $P(M'$ and $A') = 1 - P(M$ or $A) = 1 - 0.79 = 0.21$

Exercise 3.2 — Mutually exclusive events

Q1 a) $P(X$ and $Y) = 0$

b) $P(X$ or $Y) = P(X) + P(Y) = 0.48 + 0.37 = 0.85$

c) $P(X'$ and $Y') = 1 - P(X$ or $Y) = 1 - 0.85 = 0.15$

Q2 a) $P(L$ or $M) = P(L) + P(M) = 0.28 + 0.42 = 0.7$

b) $P(L$ or $N) = P(L) + P(N) = 0.28 + 0.33 = 0.61$

c) $P(M$ or $N) = P(M) + P(N) - P(M$ and $N)$
$= 0.42 + 0.33 - 0.16 = 0.59$

d) $P(L$ and M and $N) = 0$

e) Draw 3 circles to represent events L, M and N, making sure that mutually exclusive events don't overlap. As usual, start the labelling with the middle of the overlapping circles and work outwards.

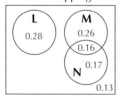

Q3 a) Let B = 'goes bowling', C = 'goes to the cinema', and D = 'goes out for dinner'. All 3 events are mutually exclusive, so:
$P(B$ or $C) = P(B) + P(C) = 0.17 + 0.43 = 0.6$

b) P(doesn't do B, C or D)
$= P(B'$ and C' and $D')$
Since either none of B, C and D happen, or at least one of B, C and D happen, "B' and C' and D'" and "B or C or D" are complementary events. So:
$P(B'$ and C' and $D') = 1 - P(B$ or C or $D)$
$= 1 - [P(B) + P(C) + P(D)]$
$= 1 - (0.17 + 0.43 + 0.22) = 1 - 0.82 = 0.18$

Q4 a) $P(A$ and $B) = P(A) + P(B) - P(A$ or $B)$
$= 0.28 + 0.66 - 0.86 = 0.08$
$P(A$ and $B) \neq 0$, so A and B aren't mutually exclusive.

b) $P(A$ and $C) = P(A) + P(C) - P(A$ or $C)$
$= 0.28 + 0.49 - 0.77 = 0$
$P(A$ and $C) = 0$, so A and C are mutually exclusive.

c) $P(B$ and $C) = P(B) + P(C) - P(B$ or $C)$
$= 0.66 + 0.49 - 0.92 = 0.23$
$P(B$ and $C) \neq 0$, so B and C aren't mutually exclusive.

Q5 a) You need to show that $P(C$ and $D) = 0$.
$P(C) = 1 - 0.6 = 0.4$
$P(C$ and $D) = P(C) - P(C$ and $D') = 0.4 - 0.4 = 0$,
so C and D are mutually exclusive.

b) $P(C$ or $D) = P(C) + P(D) = 0.4 + 0.25 = 0.65$

Q6 Out of the total of 50 biscuits, 30 are plain, and 20 are chocolate-coated. Half of the biscuits are in wrappers, so 25 biscuits are in wrappers. Since there are more biscuits in wrappers than there are chocolate-coated ones, there must be some biscuits (at least 5) which are plain and in wrappers. So events P and W can happen at the same time (i.e. $P(P$ and $W) \neq 0$), which means they are not mutually exclusive.

Exercise 3.3 — Independent events

Q1 $P(X$ and $Y) = P(X)P(Y) = 0.62 \times 0.32 = 0.1984$

Q2 $P(A)P(B) = P(A$ and $B)$, so:
$P(A) = P(A$ and $B) \div P(B) = 0.45 \div (1 - 0.25) = 0.6$

Q3 a) $P(X$ and $Y) = P(X)P(Y) = 0.84 \times 0.68 = 0.5712$

b) $P(Y'$ and $Z') = P(Y')P(Z')$
$= (1 - 0.68)(1 - 0.48) = 0.32 \times 0.52 = 0.1664$

Q4 a) $P(M$ and $N) = P(M)P(N) = 0.4 \times 0.7 = 0.28$

b) $P(M$ or $N) = P(M) + P(N) - P(M$ and $N)$
$= 0.4 + 0.7 - 0.28 = 0.82$

c) $P(M$ and $N') = P(M)P(N') = 0.4 \times 0.3 = 0.12$

Q5 a) Let A = '1st card is hearts' and B = '2nd card is hearts'. Since the first card is replaced before the second is picked, A and B are independent events. So $P(A$ and $B) = P(A) \times P(B)$.
There are 13 hearts out of the 52 cards, so $P(A)$ and $P(B)$ both equal $\frac{13}{52} = \frac{1}{4}$.
So $P(A$ and $B) = \frac{1}{4} \times \frac{1}{4} = \frac{1}{16}$.

b) Let A = '1st card is ace of hearts' and B = '2nd card is ace of hearts'. The first card is replaced before the second is picked, so A and B are independent events.
So, $P(A$ and $B) = P(A) \times P(B)$
There is 1 'ace of hearts' out of the 52 cards, so $P(A)$ and $P(B)$ both equal $\frac{1}{52}$.
So $P(A$ and $B) = \frac{1}{52} \times \frac{1}{52} = \frac{1}{2704}$.

Q6 <u>A and B</u>: $P(A) \times P(B) = \frac{3}{11} \times \frac{1}{3} = \frac{3}{33} = \frac{1}{11}$
$P(A) \times P(B) = \frac{1}{11} = P(A$ and $B)$,
so A and B are independent.

<u>A and C</u>: $P(A) \times P(C) = \frac{3}{11} \times \frac{15}{28} = \frac{45}{308}$
$P(A) \times P(C) = \frac{45}{308} \neq \frac{2}{15} = P(A$ and $C)$,
so A and C are not independent.

<u>B and C</u>: $P(B) \times P(C) = \frac{1}{3} \times \frac{15}{28} = \frac{15}{84} = \frac{5}{28}$

$P(B) \times P(C) = \frac{5}{28} = P(B \text{ and } C)$,

so B and C are independent.

Q7 Let J = 'Jess buys a DVD', K = 'Keisha buys a DVD' and L = 'Lucy buys a DVD'.

a) The probability that all 3 buy a DVD is P(J and K and L). Since the 3 events are independent, you can multiply their probabilities together to get:
$P(J) \times P(K) \times P(L) = 0.66 \times 0.5 \times 0.3 = 0.099$

b) The probability that at least 2 of them buy a DVD will be the probability that one of the following happens: J and K and L, or J and K and L', or J and K' and L, or J' and K and L.
Since these events are mutually exclusive, you can add their probabilities together to give:
$0.099 + (0.66 \times 0.5 \times 0.7) + (0.66 \times 0.5 \times 0.3) + (0.34 \times 0.5 \times 0.3)$
$= 0.099 + 0.231 + 0.099 + 0.051 = 0.48$

Exercise 3.4 — Tree diagrams

Q1 **a)** The events are not independent because the probability that Jake wins his 2nd match depends on whether or not he won his 1st match.

b) **(i)** P(Win then Win) = $0.6 \times 0.75 = 0.45$

(ii) P(Wins at least 1) = P(Win then Win) + P(Win then Lose) + P(Lose then Win)
$= 0.45 + (0.6 \times 0.25) + (0.4 \times 0.35) = 0.74$
Or you could find 1 – P(Lose then Lose).

Q2 **a)**

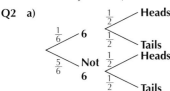

b) P(wins) = P(6 and Tails) = $\frac{1}{6} \times \frac{1}{2} = \frac{1}{12}$

Q3 **a)** Let D = 'passed driving test' and U = 'intend to go to university'.

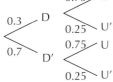

Because the events are independent, you could also draw this tree diagram with the 'U' branches first, then the 'D' branches.

b) P(D' and U') = $0.7 \times 0.25 = 0.175$

Q4 Let R = 'orders roast dinner' and let A = 'orders apple pie for pudding'. Then you can draw the following tree diagram:

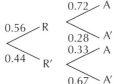

So P(A) = P(R and A) + P(R' and A)
$= (0.56 \times 0.72) + (0.44 \times 0.33) = 0.5484$

Q5 **a)** Let R_i = 'ball i is red', Y_i = 'ball i is yellow' and G_i = 'ball i is green', for i = 1 and 2. Since the first ball isn't replaced, the second pick depends on the first pick and you get the following tree diagram:

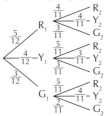

b) P(wins) = P(R_1 and R_2) + P(Y_1 and Y_2) + P(G_1 and G_2)
$= \left(\frac{5}{12} \times \frac{4}{11}\right) + \left(\frac{4}{12} \times \frac{3}{11}\right) + \left(\frac{3}{12} \times \frac{2}{11}\right)$
$= \frac{20}{132} + \frac{12}{132} + \frac{6}{132} = \frac{38}{132} = \frac{19}{66}$

c) If the first ball is replaced, the probability of winning becomes: $\left(\frac{5}{12} \times \frac{5}{12}\right) + \left(\frac{4}{12} \times \frac{4}{12}\right) + \left(\frac{3}{12} \times \frac{3}{12}\right)$
$= \frac{25}{144} + \frac{16}{144} + \frac{9}{144} = \frac{50}{144} = \frac{25}{72}$
Since $\frac{25}{72} > \frac{19}{66}$, a player is more likely to win now that the game has been changed.
You could also answer this question by explaining that when a ball of one colour is selected, then replaced, the proportion of balls of that colour left for the second pick is higher than if it isn't replaced. So the probability of picking the colour again is higher.

Chapter 16: Statistical Distributions

1. Probability Distributions

Exercise 1.1 — Probability distributions and functions

Q1 **a)** **(i)** The discrete random variable X is 'number of tails'.
(ii) x could be 0, 1, 2, 3 or 4.

b) **(i)** The discrete random variable X is 'sum of the two dice scores'.
(ii) x could be 2, 3, 4, 5, 6, 7 or 8.

Q2 **a)**

a	1	2	3	4	5	6
$P(A = a)$	$\frac{1}{6}$	$\frac{1}{6}$	$\frac{1}{6}$	$\frac{1}{6}$	$\frac{1}{6}$	$\frac{1}{6}$

b) The probability of the score being even is $\frac{3}{6} = \frac{1}{2}$ and the probability of 'otherwise' (the score being odd) is the same. The probability distribution is:

b	0	1
$P(B = b)$	$\frac{1}{2}$	$\frac{1}{2}$

c) C can take 6 values, c = 5, 10, 15, 20, 25, 30 (each score × 5) and each one will have probability $\frac{1}{6}$. The probability distribution is:

c	5	10	15	20	25	30
$P(C = c)$	$\frac{1}{6}$	$\frac{1}{6}$	$\frac{1}{6}$	$\frac{1}{6}$	$\frac{1}{6}$	$\frac{1}{6}$

Q3 **a)** **(i)** $\sum_{\text{all } x} P(X = x) = 0.2 + 0.4 + 0.1 + a = 1$
So, $a = 1 - 0.2 - 0.4 - 0.1 = 0.3$

(ii) $P(X \geq 2) = P(X = 2) + P(X = 3) + P(X = 4)$
$= 0.4 + 0.1 + 0.3 = 0.8$

b) (i) $\sum_{\text{all } x} P(X = x) = 6k = 1$. So, $k = \frac{1}{6}$.

(ii) $P(X \geq 5)$
$= P(X = 9) + P(X = 16) + P(X = 25) + P(X = 36)$
$= 4k = \frac{4}{6} = \frac{2}{3}$.

(iii) $P(X \geq 10) = P(X = 16) + P(X = 25) + P(X = 36)$
$= 3k = \frac{3}{6} = \frac{1}{2}$.

(iv) $P(3 \leq X \leq 15) = P(X = 4) + P(X = 9) = 2k = \frac{2}{6} = \frac{1}{3}$

(v) $P(X$ is divisible by 3$) = P(X = 9$ or $36)$
$= P(X = 9) + P(X = 36) = 2k = \frac{2}{6} = \frac{1}{3}$

Q4 a) (i) $\sum_{\text{all } x} P(X = x) = k + 4k + 9k = 14k = 1$
So $k = \frac{1}{14}$.

(ii)

x	1	2	3
$P(X = x)$	$\frac{1}{14}$	$\frac{2}{7}$	$\frac{9}{14}$

b) (i) $\sum_{\text{all } x} P(X = x) = k + \frac{k}{2} + \frac{k}{3} = \frac{11k}{6} = 1$
So $k = \frac{6}{11}$.

(ii)

x	1	2	3
$P(X = x)$	$\frac{6}{11}$	$\frac{3}{11}$	$\frac{2}{11}$

c) (i) $\sum_{\text{all } x} P(X = x) = k + 2k + 3k + 4k + 3k + 2k + k = 1$
$16k = 1$, so $k = \frac{1}{16}$.

(ii)

x	1	2	3	4	5	6	7
$P(X = x)$	$\frac{1}{16}$	$\frac{1}{8}$	$\frac{3}{16}$	$\frac{1}{4}$	$\frac{3}{16}$	$\frac{1}{8}$	$\frac{1}{16}$

Q5 Draw a sample-space diagram to show all the possible outcomes:

Score on dice 1

×	1	2	3	4
1	1	2	3	4
2	2	4	6	8
3	3	6	9	12
4	4	8	12	16

(Score on dice 2)

So the possible values that X can take are
1, 2, 3, 4, 6, 8, 9, 12 and 16.
To find the probability of X taking each value, count the number of outcomes that give the value and divide by the total number, 16.
So the probability distribution looks like this:

x	1	2	3	4	6	8	9	12	16
$P(X = x)$	$\frac{1}{16}$	$\frac{1}{8}$	$\frac{1}{8}$	$\frac{3}{16}$	$\frac{1}{8}$	$\frac{1}{8}$	$\frac{1}{16}$	$\frac{1}{8}$	$\frac{1}{16}$

$P(3 < X \leq 10) = P(X = 4) + P(X = 6) + P(X = 8) + P(X = 9)$
$= \frac{3}{16} + \frac{1}{8} + \frac{1}{8} + \frac{1}{16} = \frac{1}{2}$

Q6

x	12	13	14	15
$P(X = x)$	$\frac{1}{4}$	$\frac{1}{4}$	$\frac{1}{4}$	$\frac{1}{4}$

$P(X \leq 14) = P(X = 14) + P(X = 13) + P(X = 12)$
$= \frac{1}{4} + \frac{1}{4} + \frac{1}{4} = \frac{3}{4}$

Q7 $P(Y = y) = \frac{1}{150}$, $y = 1, 2, ..., 150$
$P(60 < Y \leq 75) = P(Y = 61) + P(Y = 62) + ... + P(Y = 75)$
$= \frac{1}{150} + \frac{1}{150} + ... + \frac{1}{150} = \frac{15}{150} = \frac{1}{10}$

Exercise 1.2 — The cumulative distribution function

Q1 a) Add up the probabilities to work out the values of F(x):
F(1) = $P(X \leq 1) = P(X = 1) = 0.1$
F(2) = $P(X \leq 2) = P(X = 2) + P(X = 1)$
$= 0.2 + 0.1 = 0.3$
F(3) = $P(X \leq 3) = P(X = 3) + P(X = 2) + P(X = 1)$
$= 0.3 + 0.2 + 0.1 = 0.6$
F(4) = $P(X \leq 4)$
$= P(X = 4) + P(X = 3) + P(X = 2) + P(X = 1)$
$= 0.2 + 0.3 + 0.2 + 0.1 = 0.8$
F(5) = $P(X \leq 5)$
$= P(X = 5) + P(X = 4) + P(X = 3)$
$+ P(X = 2) + P(X = 1)$
$= 0.2 + 0.2 + 0.3 + 0.2 + 0.1 = 1$
Using all this information, the cumulative distribution function is:

x	1	2	3	4	5
F(x)	0.1	0.3	0.6	0.8	1

b) Add up the probabilities to work out the values of F(x):

F(−2) = $P(X \leq -2) = P(X = -2) = \frac{1}{5}$
F(−1) = $P(X \leq -1) = P(X = -1) + P(X = -2)$
$= \frac{1}{5} + \frac{1}{5} = \frac{2}{5}$
F(0) = $P(X \leq 0) = P(X = 0) + P(X = -1) + P(X = -2)$
$= \frac{1}{5} + \frac{1}{5} + \frac{1}{5} = \frac{3}{5}$
F(1) = $P(X \leq 1)$
$= P(X = 1) + P(X = 0) + P(X = -1) + P(X = -2)$
$= \frac{1}{5} + \frac{1}{5} + \frac{1}{5} + \frac{1}{5} = \frac{4}{5}$
F(2) = $P(X \leq 2)$
$= P(X = 2) + P(X = 1) + P(X = 0)$
$+ P(X = -1) + P(X = -2)$
$= \frac{1}{5} + \frac{1}{5} + \frac{1}{5} + \frac{1}{5} + \frac{1}{5} = 1$
Using all this information, the cumulative distribution function is:

x	−2	−1	0	1	2
F(x)	$\frac{1}{5}$	$\frac{2}{5}$	$\frac{3}{5}$	$\frac{4}{5}$	1

c) Add up the probabilities to work out the values of F(x):
F(1) = $P(X \leq 1) = P(X = 1) = 0.3$
F(2) = $P(X \leq 2) = P(X = 2) + P(X = 1) = 0.2 + 0.3 = 0.5$
F(3) = $P(X \leq 3) = P(X = 3) + P(X = 2) + P(X = 1)$
$= 0.3 + 0.2 + 0.3 = 0.8$
F(4) = $P(X \leq 4)$
$= P(X = 4) + P(X = 3) + P(X = 2) + P(X = 1)$
$= 0.2 + 0.3 + 0.2 + 0.3 = 1$
Using all this information, the cumulative distribution function is:

x	1	2	3	4
F(x)	0.3	0.5	0.8	1

d) Add up the probabilities to work out the values of F(x):
F(2) = $P(X \leq 2) = P(X = 2) = \frac{1}{2}$
F(4) = $P(X \leq 4) = P(X = 4) + P(X = 2) = \frac{1}{4} + \frac{1}{2} = \frac{3}{4}$
F(8) = $P(X \leq 8) = P(X = 8) + P(X = 4) + P(X = 2)$
$= \frac{1}{8} + \frac{1}{4} + \frac{1}{2} = \frac{7}{8}$

$F(16) = P(X \le 16)$
$\quad = P(X = 16) + P(X = 8) + P(X = 4) + P(X = 2)$
$\quad = \frac{1}{16} + \frac{1}{8} + \frac{1}{4} + \frac{1}{2} = \frac{15}{16}$

$F(32) = P(X \le 32)$
$\quad = P(X = 32) + P(X = 16) + P(X = 8)$
$\quad\quad + P(X = 4) + P(X = 2)$
$\quad = \frac{1}{32} + \frac{1}{16} + \frac{1}{8} + \frac{1}{4} + \frac{1}{2} = \frac{31}{32}$

$F(64) = P(X \le 64)$
$\quad = P(X = 64) + P(X = 32) + P(X = 16)$
$\quad\quad + P(X = 8) + P(X = 4) + P(X = 2)$
$\quad = \frac{1}{32} + \frac{1}{32} + \frac{1}{16} + \frac{1}{8} + \frac{1}{4} + \frac{1}{2} = 1$

Using all this information, the cumulative distribution function is:

x	2	4	8	16	32	64
$F(x)$	$\frac{1}{2}$	$\frac{3}{4}$	$\frac{7}{8}$	$\frac{15}{16}$	$\frac{31}{32}$	1

Q2 a) You need to draw up a table showing the cumulative distribution function, so work out the values of $F(x)$:
$F(1) = P(X = 1) = 0.3$
$F(2) = P(X = 2) + P(X = 1) = 0.1 + 0.3 = 0.4$
$F(3) = P(X = 3) + P(X = 2) + P(X = 1)$
$\quad = 0.45 + 0.1 + 0.3 = 0.85$
$F(4) = P(X = 4) + P(X = 3) + P(X = 2) + P(X = 1)$
$\quad = 0.15 + 0.45 + 0.1 + 0.3 = 1$

So the cumulative distribution function looks like this:

x	1	2	3	4
$F(x)$	0.3	0.4	0.85	1

(i) $P(X \le 3) = F(3) = 0.85$
(ii) $P(1 < X \le 3) = P(X \le 3) - P(X \le 1)$
$\quad = 0.85 - 0.3 = 0.55$

b) Again, start by working out the values of $F(x)$:
$F(-2) = P(X = -2) = \frac{1}{10}$
$F(-1) = P(X = -1) + P(X = -2) = \frac{2}{5} + \frac{1}{10} = \frac{1}{2}$
$F(0) = P(X = 0) + P(X = -1) + P(X = -2)$
$\quad = \frac{1}{10} + \frac{2}{5} + \frac{1}{10} = \frac{3}{5}$
$F(1) = P(X = 1) + P(X = 0) + P(X = -1) + P(X = -2)$
$\quad = \frac{1}{5} + \frac{1}{10} + \frac{2}{5} + \frac{1}{10} = \frac{4}{5}$
$F(2) = P(X = 2) + P(X = 1) + P(X = 0)$
$\quad\quad + P(X = -1) + P(X = -2)$
$\quad = \frac{1}{5} + \frac{1}{5} + \frac{1}{10} + \frac{2}{5} + \frac{1}{10} = 1$

So the cumulative distribution function looks like this:

x	-2	-1	0	1	2
$F(x)$	$\frac{1}{10}$	$\frac{1}{2}$	$\frac{3}{5}$	$\frac{4}{5}$	1

(i) $P(X \le 0) = F(0) = \frac{3}{5}$
(ii) $P(X > 0) = 1 - F(0) = 1 - \frac{3}{5} = \frac{2}{5}$
Here you use the fact that $P(X \le O) + P(X > O) = 1$ (all the probabilities add up to 1).

Q3 a) Use the probability function to work out the values of $F(x)$.
$F(1) = P(X = 1) = \frac{1}{8}$
$F(2) = P(X = 2) + P(X = 1) = \frac{1}{8} + \frac{1}{8} = \frac{2}{8} = \frac{1}{4}$
$F(3) = P(X = 3) + P(X = 2) + P(X = 1)$
$\quad = \frac{1}{8} + \frac{1}{8} + \frac{1}{8} = \frac{3}{8}$

Because you are adding on a constant term of $\frac{1}{8}$ each time, the rest are easy to work out:
$F(4) = \frac{4}{8} = \frac{1}{2}$, $F(5) = \frac{5}{8}$, $F(6) = \frac{6}{8} = \frac{3}{4}$,
$F(7) = \frac{7}{8}$, $F(8) = \frac{8}{8} = 1$

So the cumulative distribution function looks like this:

x	1	2	3	4	5	6	7	8
$F(x)$	$\frac{1}{8}$	$\frac{1}{4}$	$\frac{3}{8}$	$\frac{1}{2}$	$\frac{5}{8}$	$\frac{3}{4}$	$\frac{7}{8}$	1

b) (i) $P(X \le 3) = F(3) = \frac{3}{8}$
(ii) $P(3 < X \le 7) = P(X \le 7) - P(X \le 3)$
$\quad = \frac{7}{8} - \frac{3}{8} = \frac{4}{8} = \frac{1}{2}$

Q4 a) $P(X = 5) = P(X \le 5) - P(X \le 4) = 1 - 0.9 = 0.1$
$P(X = 4) = P(X \le 4) - P(X \le 3) = 0.9 - 0.6 = 0.3$
$P(X = 3) = P(X \le 3) - P(X \le 2) = 0.6 - 0.3 = 0.3$
$P(X = 2) = P(X \le 2) - P(X \le 1) = 0.3 - 0.2 = 0.1$
$P(X = 1) = P(X \le 1) = 0.2$
So the probability distribution is:

x	1	2	3	4	5
$p(x)$	0.2	0.1	0.3	0.3	0.1

Always check that the probabilities add up to 1 — if they don't, you know for sure that you've gone wrong.

b) $P(X = 1) = P(X \le 1) - P(X \le 0) = 1 - 0.7 = 0.3$
$P(X = 0) = P(X \le 0) - P(X \le -1) = 0.7 - 0.2 = 0.5$
$P(X = -1) = P(X \le -1) - P(X \le -2) = 0.2 - 0.1 = 0.1$
$P(X = -2) = P(X \le -2) = 0.1$
So the probability distribution is:

x	-2	-1	0	1
$p(x)$	0.1	0.1	0.5	0.3

c) $P(X = 64) = P(X \le 64) - P(X \le 32) = 1 - \frac{3}{4} = \frac{1}{4}$
$P(X = 32) = P(X \le 32) - P(X \le 16) = \frac{3}{4} - \frac{1}{2} = \frac{1}{4}$
$P(X = 16) = P(X \le 16) - P(X \le 8) = \frac{1}{2} - \frac{1}{4} = \frac{1}{4}$
$P(X = 8) = P(X \le 8) - P(X \le 4) = \frac{1}{4} - \frac{1}{8} = \frac{1}{8}$
$P(X = 4) = P(X \le 4) - P(X \le 2) = \frac{1}{8} - \frac{1}{32} = \frac{3}{32}$
$P(X = 2) = P(X \le 2) = \frac{1}{32}$
So the probability distribution is:

x	2	4	8	16	32	64
$p(x)$	$\frac{1}{32}$	$\frac{3}{32}$	$\frac{1}{8}$	$\frac{1}{4}$	$\frac{1}{4}$	$\frac{1}{4}$

Q5 $P(X = 4) = P(X \le 4) - P(X \le 3) = 1 - 0.8 = 0.2$
$P(X = 3) = P(X \le 3) - P(X \le 2) = 0.8 - a$
$P(X = 2) = P(X \le 2) - P(X \le 1) = a - 0.3$
$P(X = 1) = P(X \le 1) = 0.3$
Now $P(X = 2) = P(X = 3)$ so $0.8 - a = a - 0.3$,
so $2a = 1.1$, so $a = 0.55$.
So $P(X = 2) = P(X = 3) = 0.25$
So the probability distribution is:

x	1	2	3	4
$p(x)$	0.3	0.25	0.25	0.2

Q6 a) $F(3) = P(X \le 3) = \sum_{\text{all } x} P(X = x) = 1$
So $\frac{(3 + k)^2}{25} = 1 \Rightarrow (3 + k)^2 = 25$
$\Rightarrow 3 + k = 5 \Rightarrow k = 2$

To find the probability distribution, you need to find the probability of each outcome:

$P(X = 3) = P(X \le 3) - P(X \le 2) = F(3) - F(2)$
$= \dfrac{(3+2)^2}{25} - \dfrac{(2+2)^2}{25} = \dfrac{25}{25} - \dfrac{16}{25} = \dfrac{9}{25}$

$P(X = 2) = P(X \le 2) - P(X \le 1) = F(2) - F(1)$
$= \dfrac{(2+2)^2}{25} - \dfrac{(1+2)^2}{25} = \dfrac{16}{25} - \dfrac{9}{25} = \dfrac{7}{25}$

$P(X = 1) = P(X \le 1) = F(1) = \dfrac{(1+2)^2}{25} = \dfrac{9}{25}$

So the table looks like:

x	1	2	3
$P(X = x)$	$\dfrac{9}{25}$	$\dfrac{7}{25}$	$\dfrac{9}{25}$

b) $F(3) = P(X \le 3) = \sum\limits_{\text{all } x} P(X = x) = 1$

So $\dfrac{(3+k)^3}{64} = 1 \implies (3+k)^3 = 64$
$\implies 3 + k = 4 \implies k = 1$

To find the probability distribution you need to find the probability of each outcome:

$P(X = 3) = P(X \le 3) - P(X \le 2) = F(3) - F(2)$
$= \dfrac{(3+1)^3}{64} - \dfrac{(2+1)^3}{64} = \dfrac{64}{64} - \dfrac{27}{64} = \dfrac{37}{64}$

$P(X = 2) = P(X \le 2) - P(X \le 1) = F(2) - F(1)$
$= \dfrac{(2+1)^3}{64} - \dfrac{(1+1)^3}{64} = \dfrac{27}{64} - \dfrac{8}{64} = \dfrac{19}{64}$

$P(X = 1) = P(X \le 1) = F(1) = \dfrac{(1+1)^3}{64} = \dfrac{8}{64} = \dfrac{1}{8}$

So the table looks like:

x	1	2	3
$P(X = x)$	$\dfrac{1}{8}$	$\dfrac{19}{64}$	$\dfrac{37}{64}$

c) $F(3) = P(X \le 3) = \sum\limits_{\text{all } x} P(X = x) = 1$

So $2^{(3 - k)} = 1$.
For 2 to the power of something to be equal to 1, the power must be 0, so $3 - k = 0 \implies k = 3$.

To find the probability distribution, you need to find the probability of each outcome:

$P(X = 3) = P(X \le 3) - P(X \le 2) = F(3) - F(2)$
$= 2^{(3-3)} - 2^{(2-3)} = 2^0 - 2^{-1}$
$= 1 - \dfrac{1}{2} = \dfrac{1}{2}$

$P(X = 2) = P(X \le 2) - P(X \le 1) = F(2) - F(1)$
$= 2^{(2-3)} - 2^{(1-3)} = 2^{-1} - 2^{-2}$
$= \dfrac{1}{2} - \dfrac{1}{4} = \dfrac{1}{4}$

$P(X = 1) = P(X \le 1) = F(1) = 2^{(1-3)} = 2^{-2} = \dfrac{1}{4}$

So the table looks like:

x	1	2	3
$P(X = x)$	$\dfrac{1}{4}$	$\dfrac{1}{4}$	$\dfrac{1}{2}$

Q7 a) $F(x)$ means the probability that the larger score on the dice is no larger than x. This means both dice must score no more than x, where $x = 1, 2, 3, 4, 5$ or 6. The probability that one dice will score no more than x is $\dfrac{x}{6}$, so the probability that both will score no more than x is $\dfrac{x}{6} \times \dfrac{x}{6} = \dfrac{x^2}{36}$.

Two dice rolls are completely independent, so the probabilities can just be multiplied together.

So $F(x) = \dfrac{x^2}{36}$, $x = 1, 2, 3, 4, 5, 6$.

b) To find the probability distribution you need to find the probability of each outcome:

$P(X = 6) = P(X \le 6) - P(X \le 5) = \dfrac{6^2}{36} - \dfrac{5^2}{36}$
$= \dfrac{36}{36} - \dfrac{25}{36} = \dfrac{11}{36}$

$P(X = 5) = P(X \le 5) - P(X \le 4) = \dfrac{5^2}{36} - \dfrac{4^2}{36}$
$= \dfrac{25}{36} - \dfrac{16}{36} = \dfrac{9}{36} = \dfrac{1}{4}$

$P(X = 4) = P(X \le 4) - P(X \le 3) = \dfrac{4^2}{36} - \dfrac{3^2}{36}$
$= \dfrac{16}{36} - \dfrac{9}{36} = \dfrac{7}{36}$

$P(X = 3) = P(X \le 3) - P(X \le 2) = \dfrac{3^2}{36} - \dfrac{2^2}{36}$
$= \dfrac{9}{36} - \dfrac{4}{36} = \dfrac{5}{36}$

$P(X = 2) = P(X \le 2) - P(X \le 1) = \dfrac{2^2}{36} - \dfrac{1^2}{36}$
$= \dfrac{4}{36} - \dfrac{1}{36} = \dfrac{3}{36} = \dfrac{1}{12}$

$P(X = 1) = P(X \le 1) = \dfrac{1^2}{36} = \dfrac{1}{36}$

So the table looks like:

x	1	2	3	4	5	6
$P(X = x)$	$\dfrac{1}{36}$	$\dfrac{1}{12}$	$\dfrac{5}{36}$	$\dfrac{7}{36}$	$\dfrac{1}{4}$	$\dfrac{11}{36}$

2. Binomial Distributions

Exercise 2.1 — Binomial coefficients

Q1 a) All 8 letters are different, so there are $8! = 40\ 320$ different arrangements.

b) If all 9 letters were different, there would be $9! = 362\ 880$ different arrangements. But since two of the letters are the same, you need to divide this by $2! = 2$. So there are $9! \div 2! = 181\ 440$ different arrangements.

c) If all 7 letters were different, there would be $7! = 5040$ different arrangements. But there are 2 Ts and 2 Rs, so you need to divide this by $2!$ twice. So there are $7! \div 2! \div 2! = 1260$ different arrangements.

Q2 $\dbinom{20}{11} = \dfrac{20!}{11!9!} = 167\ 960$ different ways

Q3 a) $\dbinom{10}{3} = \dbinom{10}{7} = \dfrac{10!}{3!7!} = 120$ ways

b) $\dbinom{10}{5} = \dfrac{10!}{5!5!} = 252$ ways

Q4 a) $\dbinom{11}{4} = \dbinom{11}{7} = \dfrac{11!}{4!7!} = 330$ ways

b) $\dbinom{11}{6} = \dbinom{11}{5} = \dfrac{11!}{6!5!} = 462$ ways

c) $\dbinom{11}{8} = \dbinom{11}{3} = \dfrac{11!}{8!3!} = 165$ ways

Exercise 2.2 — The binomial distribution

Q1 a) Not a binomial distribution — the number of trials is not fixed.

b) Here, X will follow a binomial distribution. $X \sim B(2000, 0.005)$.

c) Here, Y will follow a binomial distribution. $Y \sim B(10, 0.5)$.

Q2 The number of trials is fixed (i.e. the 15 acts), each trial can either succeed or fail, X is the total number of successes, and the probability of success is the same each time if the trials are independent. So to model this situation with a binomial distribution, you would need to assume that all the trials are independent.

Q3 The number of trials is fixed, each trial can either succeed or fail, and X is the total number of successes. To make the probability of success the same each time, the cards would need to be replaced, and to make each pick independent you could shuffle the pack after replacing the picked cards.
If this is done, then $X \sim B(10, \frac{3}{13})$.

Q4 The number of trials is fixed (650), each trial can either succeed or fail, X is the total number of successes, and the probability of each button falling off is the same if the trials are independent. So to model this situation with a binomial distribution, you would need to assume that all the trials are independent (i.e. the probability of each separate button falling off should not depend on whether any other button has fallen off).
If this assumption is satisfied, then $X \sim B(650, 0.001)$.

Exercise 2.3 — Using the binomial probability function

Q1 a) Use the binomial probability function with $n = 10$ and $p = 0.14$.

(i) $P(X = 2) = \binom{10}{2} \times 0.14^2 \times (1 - 0.14)^{10-2}$
$= \frac{10!}{2!8!} \times 0.14^2 \times 0.86^8 = 0.264$ (to 3 s.f.)

(ii) $P(X = 4) = \binom{10}{4} \times 0.14^4 \times (1 - 0.14)^{10-4}$
$= \frac{10!}{4!6!} \times 0.14^4 \times 0.86^6 = 0.0326$ (to 3 s.f.)

(iii) $P(X = 5) = \binom{10}{5} \times 0.14^5 \times (1 - 0.14)^{10-5}$
$= \frac{10!}{5!5!} \times 0.14^5 \times 0.86^5 = 0.00638$ (to 3 s.f.)

b) Use the binomial probability function with $n = 8$ and $p = 0.27$.

(i) $P(X = 3) = \binom{8}{3} \times 0.27^3 \times (1 - 0.27)^{8-3}$
$= \frac{8!}{3!5!} \times 0.27^3 \times 0.73^5 = 0.229$ (to 3 s.f.)

(ii) $P(X = 5) = \binom{8}{5} \times 0.27^5 \times (1 - 0.27)^{8-5}$
$= \frac{8!}{5!3!} \times 0.27^5 \times 0.73^3 = 0.0313$ (to 3 s.f.)

(iii) $P(X = 7) = \binom{8}{7} \times 0.27^7 \times (1 - 0.27)^{8-7}$
$= \frac{8!}{7!1!} \times 0.27^7 \times 0.73^1 = 0.000611$ (to 3 s.f.)

Q2 a) Use the binomial probability function with $n = 20$ and $p = 0.16$.

(i) $P(X < 2) = P(X = 0) + P(X = 1)$
$= \frac{20!}{0!20!} \times 0.16^0 \times 0.84^{20} + \frac{20!}{1!19!} \times 0.16^1 \times 0.84^{19}$
$= 0.03059... + 0.11653... = 0.147$ (to 3 s.f.)

(ii) $P(X \le 3) = P(X = 0) + P(X = 1) + P(X = 2) + P(X = 3)$
$= 0.03059... + 0.11653... + \frac{20!}{2!18!} \times 0.16^2 \times 0.84^{18}$
$+ \frac{20!}{3!17!} \times 0.16^3 \times 0.84^{17}$
$= 0.03059... + 0.11653... + 0.21087... + 0.24099...$
$= 0.599$ (to 3 s.f.)

(iii) $P(1 < X \le 4) = P(X = 2) + P(X = 3) + P(X = 4)$
$= 0.21087... + 0.24099... + \frac{20!}{4!16!} \times 0.16^4 \times 0.84^{16}$
$= 0.21087... + 0.24099... + 0.19509...$
$= 0.647$ (to 3 s.f.)

b) Use the binomial probability function with $n = 30$ and $p = 0.88$.

(i) $P(X > 28) = P(X = 29) + P(X = 30)$
$= \frac{30!}{29!1!} \times 0.88^{29} \times 0.12^1 + \frac{30!}{30!0!} \times 0.88^{30} \times 0.12^0$
$= 0.088369... + 0.021601...$
$= 0.110$ (to 3 s.f.)

(ii) $P(25 < X < 28) = P(X = 26) + P(X = 27)$
$= \frac{30!}{26!4!} \times 0.88^{26} \times 0.12^4 + \frac{30!}{27!3!} \times 0.88^{27} \times 0.12^3$
$= 0.204693... + 0.222383...$
$= 0.427$ (to 3 s.f.)

(iii) $P(X \ge 27) = P(X = 27) + P(X = 28)$
$+ P(X = 29) + P(X = 30)$
$= 0.222383... + \frac{30!}{28!2!} \times 0.88^{28} \times 0.12^2$
$+ 0.088369... + 0.021601...$
$= 0.222383... + 0.174729... + 0.088369...$
$+ 0.021601...$
$= 0.507$ (to 3 s.f.)

Q3 a) Use the binomial probability function with $n = 5$ and $p = \frac{1}{2}$.

(i) $P(X \le 4) = 1 - P(X > 4) = 1 - P(X = 5)$
$= 1 - \frac{5!}{5!0!} \times \left(\frac{1}{2}\right)^5 \times \left(\frac{1}{2}\right)^0 = 1 - 0.03125$
$= 0.969$ (to 3 s.f.)

(ii) $P(X > 1) = 1 - P(X \le 1) = 1 - P(X = 0) - P(X = 1)$
$= 1 - \frac{5!}{0!5!} \times \left(\frac{1}{2}\right)^0 \times \left(\frac{1}{2}\right)^5 - \frac{5!}{1!4!} \times \left(\frac{1}{2}\right)^1 \times \left(\frac{1}{2}\right)^4$
$= 1 - 0.03125 - 0.15625 = 0.813$ (to 3 s.f.)

(iii) $P(1 \le X \le 4) = 1 - P(X = 0) - P(X = 5)$
$= 1 - \frac{5!}{0!5!} \times \left(\frac{1}{2}\right)^0 \times \left(\frac{1}{2}\right)^5 - \frac{5!}{5!0!} \times \left(\frac{1}{2}\right)^5 \times \left(\frac{1}{2}\right)^0$
$= 1 - 0.03125 - 0.03125 = 0.938$ (to 3 s.f.)

b) Use the binomial probability function with $n = 8$ and $p = \frac{2}{3}$.

(i) $P(X < 7) = 1 - P(X \ge 7) = 1 - P(X = 7) - P(X = 8)$
$= 1 - \frac{8!}{7!1!} \times \left(\frac{2}{3}\right)^7 \times \left(\frac{1}{3}\right)^1 - \frac{8!}{8!0!} \times \left(\frac{2}{3}\right)^8 \times \left(\frac{1}{3}\right)^0$
$= 1 - 0.156073... - 0.039018... = 0.805$ (to 3 s.f.)

(ii) $P(X \ge 2) = 1 - P(X < 2) = 1 - P(X = 0) - P(X = 1)$
$= 1 - \frac{8!}{0!8!} \times \left(\frac{2}{3}\right)^0 \times \left(\frac{1}{3}\right)^8 - \frac{8!}{1!7!} \times \left(\frac{2}{3}\right)^1 \times \left(\frac{1}{3}\right)^7$
$= 1 - 0.00015241... - 0.00243865...$
$= 0.997$ (to 3 s.f.)

(iii) $P(0 \le X \le 8) = 1$
This must be 1, as X can only take values from 0 to 8.

Q4 $n = 5$ and $p = $ P(roll a six) $= \frac{1}{6}$, so

$$P(2 \text{ sixes}) = \binom{5}{2} \times \left(\frac{1}{6}\right)^2 \times \left(\frac{5}{6}\right)^3 = 0.161 \text{ (to 3 s.f.)}$$

Q5 a) There are 12 answers, which are either 'correct' or 'incorrect'. The student guesses at random so the questions are answered independently of each other and the probability of a correct answer is $\frac{1}{3}$.
So $X \sim $ B$(12, \frac{1}{3})$.

b) P$(X < 3) = $ P$(X = 0) + $ P$(X = 1) + $ P$(X = 2)$
$$= \frac{12!}{0!12!} \times \left(\frac{1}{3}\right)^0 \times \left(\frac{2}{3}\right)^{12} + \frac{12!}{1!11!} \times \left(\frac{1}{3}\right)^1 \times \left(\frac{2}{3}\right)^{11}$$
$$+ \frac{12!}{2!10!} \times \left(\frac{1}{3}\right)^2 \times \left(\frac{2}{3}\right)^{10}$$
$$= 0.00770... + 0.04624... + 0.12717...$$
$$= 0.181 \text{ (to 3 s.f.)}$$

Q6 Let X represent the number of defective items.
Then $X \sim $ B$(15, 0.05)$, and you need to find
P$(1 \leq X \leq 3)$.
P$(1 \leq X \leq 3) = $ P$(X = 1) + $ P$(X = 2) + $ P$(X = 3)$
$$= \frac{15!}{1!14!} \times 0.05^1 \times 0.95^{14} + \frac{15!}{2!13!} \times 0.05^2 \times 0.95^{13}$$
$$+ \frac{15!}{3!12!} \times 0.05^3 \times 0.95^{12}$$
$$= 0.36575... + 0.13475... + 0.03073... = 0.531 \text{ (to 3 s.f.)}$$

Q7 a) Let the random variable X represent the number of 'treble-20's the player gets in a set of 3 darts.
Then $X \sim $ B$(3, 0.75)$.
P$(X \geq 2) = $ P$(X = 2) + $ P$(X = 3)$
$$P(X = 2) = \binom{3}{2} \times 0.75^2 \times (1 - 0.75) = 0.421875$$
$$P(X = 3) = \binom{3}{3} \times 0.75^3 \times (1 - 0.75)^0 = 0.421875$$
So P$(X \geq 2) = 0.421875 + 0.421875$
$$= 0.84375 = 0.844 \text{ (to 3 s.f.)}$$

b) Now let X represent the number of 'treble-20's the player scores with 30 darts. Then $X \sim $ B$(30, 0.75)$.
You need to find P$(X \geq 26)$.
P$(X \geq 26) = $ P$(X = 26) + $ P$(X = 27) + $ P$(X = 28)$
$$+ P(X = 29) + P(X = 30)$$
$$= 0.06042... + 0.02685... + 0.00863...$$
$$+ 0.00178... + 0.00017...$$
$$= 0.0979 \text{ (to 3 s.f.)}$$

3. Using Binomial Tables

Exercise 3.1 — Using tables to find probabilities

Q1 a) P$(X \leq 2) = 0.5256$
b) P$(X \leq 7) = 0.9996$
c) P$(X \leq 9) = 1.0000$
d) P$(X < 5) = $ P$(X \leq 4) = 0.9219$
e) P$(X < 4) = $ P$(X \leq 3) = 0.7759$
f) P$(X < 6) = $ P$(X \leq 5) = 0.9803$

Q2 a) P$(X > 3) = 1 - $ P$(X \leq 3) = 1 - 0.0905 = 0.9095$
b) P$(X > 6) = 1 - $ P$(X \leq 6) = 1 - 0.6098 = 0.3902$
c) P$(X > 10) = 1 - $ P$(X \leq 10) = 1 - 0.9907 = 0.0093$
d) P$(X \geq 5) = 1 - $ P$(X < 5) = 1 - $ P$(X \leq 4)$
$$= 1 - 0.2173 = 0.7827$$

e) P$(X \geq 3) = 1 - $ P$(X < 3) = 1 - $ P$(X \leq 2)$
$$= 1 - 0.0271 = 0.9729$$
f) P$(X \geq 13) = 1 - $ P$(X < 13) = 1 - $ P$(X \leq 12)$
$$= 1 - 0.9997 = 0.0003$$

Q3 a) P$(X = 7) = $ P$(X \leq 7) - $ P$(X \leq 6)$
$$= 0.6010 - 0.4166 = 0.1844$$
b) P$(X = 12) = $ P$(X \leq 12) - $ P$(X \leq 11)$
$$= 0.9940 - 0.9804 = 0.0136$$
c) P$(2 < X \leq 4) = $ P$(X \leq 4) - $ P$(X \leq 2)$
$$= 0.1182 - 0.0121 = 0.1061$$
d) P$(10 < X \leq 15) = $ P$(X \leq 15) - $ P$(X \leq 10)$
$$= 1.0000 - 0.9468 = 0.0532$$
e) P$(7 \leq X \leq 10) = $ P$(X \leq 10) - $ P$(X \leq 6)$
$$= 0.9468 - 0.4166 = 0.5302$$
f) P$(3 \leq X < 11) = $ P$(X \leq 10) - $ P$(X \leq 2)$
$$= 0.9468 - 0.0121 = 0.9347$$

Q4 Define a new random variable $Y \sim $ B$(25, 0.2)$.
a) P$(X \geq 17) = $ P$(Y \leq 8) = 0.9532$
b) P$(X \geq 20) = $ P$(Y \leq 5) = 0.6167$
c) P$(X > 14) = $ P$(Y < 11) = $ P$(Y \leq 10) = 0.9944$
d) P$(X = 21) = $ P$(Y = 4) = $ P$(Y \leq 4) - $ P$(Y \leq 3)$
$$= 0.4207 - 0.2340 = 0.1867$$
e) P$(3 \leq X < 14) = $ P$(11 < Y \leq 22)$
$$= P(Y \leq 22) - P(Y \leq 11) = 1.0000 - 0.9985 = 0.0015$$
f) P$(12 \leq X < 18) = $ P$(7 < Y \leq 13)$
$$= P(Y \leq 13) - P(Y \leq 7) = 0.9999 - 0.8909 = 0.1090$$

Q5 Let X represent the number of children with green eyes.
Then $X \sim $ B$(30, 0.18)$.
Since $p = 0.18$ isn't a value in the binomial tables, use the c.d.f. on your calculator.
P$(X < 10) = $ P$(X \leq 9) = 0.96768... = 0.9677 \text{ (to 4 s.f.)}$

Q6 Let X represent the number of faulty items.
Then $X \sim $ B$(25, 0.05)$, so use the table for $n = 25$.
P$(X < 6) = $ P$(X \leq 5) = 0.9988$

Exercise 3.2 — Using binomial tables 'backwards'

Q1 a) Use the table for $n = 8$ and the column for $p = 0.35$.
Reading down the column tells you that
P$(X \leq 2) = 0.4278$, so $a = 2$.
b) P$(X < b) = 0.9747$, so P$(X \leq b - 1) = 0.9747$.
From the table, P$(X \leq 5) = 0.9747$.
So $b - 1 = 5$, which means that $b = 6$.
c) P$(X > c) = 0.8309$, so P$(X \leq c) = 1 - $ P$(X > c)$
$$= 1 - 0.8309 = 0.1691.$$
From the table, P$(X \leq 1) = 0.1691$,
which means that $c = 1$.
d) P$(X \geq d) = 0.1061$, so P$(X < d) = 1 - $ P$(X \geq d)$
$$= 1 - 0.1061 = 0.8939.$$
This means that P$(X \leq d - 1) = 0.8939$.
From the table, P$(X \leq 4) = 0.8939$, which means that $d - 1 = 4$, so $d = 5$.

Q2 a) Let X be the score of someone who guesses the answer to each question. Then $X \sim B(30, 0.25)$. Use the table for $n = 30$ and the column for $p = 0.25$. You need to find the minimum value m for which $P(X \geq m) \leq 0.1$. This is the minimum value m for which $P(X < m) \geq 0.9$, or $P(X \leq m - 1) \geq 0.9$. $P(X \leq 10) = 0.8943$, but $P(X \leq 11) = 0.9493$. This means that $m - 1 = 11$, so the pass mark should be at least 12.

b) This time you need to find the minimum value m for which $P(X \geq m) < 0.01$. This is the minimum value m for which $P(X < m) > 0.99$, or $P(X \leq m - 1) > 0.99$. $P(X \leq 12) = 0.9784$, but $P(X \leq 13) = 0.9918$. This means that $m - 1 = 13$, so the pass mark should be at least 14.

Q3 Here, $X \sim B(20, 0.5)$. You need $P(X \geq x) < 0.05$. This means $P(X < x) > 0.95$, or $P(X \leq x - 1) > 0.95$. Use the table for $n = 20$, and the column for $p = 0.5$. $P(X \leq 13) = 0.9423$, but $P(X \leq 14) = 0.9793$. This means that $x - 1 = 14$, so x should be at least 15.

4. Modelling Real Problems
Exercise 4.1 — Modelling real problems with B(n, p)

Q1 a) Each person who passes can be considered a separate trial, where 'success' means they take a leaflet, and 'failure' means they don't. Since there is a fixed number of independent trials (50), a constant probability of success (0.25), and X is the total number of successes, $X \sim B(50, 0.25)$.

b) $P(X > 4) = 1 - P(X \leq 4) = 1 - 0.0021 = 0.9979$

c) $P(X = 10) = P(X \leq 10) - P(X \leq 9)$
$= 0.2622 - 0.1637 = 0.0985$

Q2 a) Let X represent the number of plants in a tray with yellow flowers. Then $X \sim B(15, 0.35)$. Using binomial tables for $n = 15$ and $p = 0.35$: $P(X = 5) = P(X \leq 5) - P(X \leq 4)$ $= 0.5643 - 0.3519 = 0.2124$

b) P(more yellow flowers than white flowers)
$= P(X \geq 8) = 1 - P(X < 8) = 1 - P(X \leq 7)$
$= 1 - 0.8868 = 0.1132$

Q3 a) The probability of Simon being able to solve each crossword needs to remain the same, and all the outcomes need to be independent (i.e. Simon solving or not solving a puzzle one day should not affect whether he will be able to solve it on another day).

b) $P(X = 4) = \frac{18!}{4!14!} \times p^4 \times (1 - p)^{14}$

$P(X = 5) = \frac{18!}{5!13!} \times p^5 \times (1 - p)^{13}$

Putting these equal to each other gives:
$\frac{18!}{4!14!} \times p^4 \times (1 - p)^{14} = \frac{18!}{5!13!} \times p^5 \times (1 - p)^{13}$
Dividing by things that appear on both sides gives:
$\frac{1 - p}{14} = \frac{p}{5} \Rightarrow 5 = 19p \Rightarrow p = \frac{5}{19} = 0.263$ (3 s.f.)
You can divide both sides by p^4, $(1 - p)^{13}$ and 18! immediately. Write 14! as $14 \times 13!$ and 5! as $5 \times 4!$ to simplify further.

17. Statistical Hypothesis Testing
1. Hypothesis Tests
Exercise 1.1 — Null and alternative hypotheses

Q1 a) The probability that a seed germinates.

b) 0.9

c) Call the probability p. Then the null hypothesis is H_0: $p = 0.9$.

d) The alternative hypothesis is that the probability has increased, i.e. H_1: $p > 0.9$.

e) The test is one-tailed.

Q2 a) The probability that a mouse is caught each week.

b) 0.7.

c) Call the probability p. Then the null hypothesis is H_0: $p = 0.7$.

d) The alternative hypothesis is that the probability of catching a mouse has decreased, i.e. H_1: $p < 0.7$.

e) The test is one-tailed.

Q3 a) The team is interested in the population parameter p, the probability that a randomly selected teenager has the antibody present.

b) The null hypothesis is that the probability is the same, H_0: $p = 0.35$. The alternative hypothesis is that the probability is different, H_1: $p \neq 0.35$.

c) The test is two-tailed.

Q4 The council want to know if more than 16% of residents are now aware of the grants. Let p be the probability that a randomly selected resident knows about the grants. Then H_0: $p = 0.16$ and H_1: $p > 0.16$.

Q5 The owner wants to know if the proportion of customers buying a jar of chilli chutney has changed. Let p be the proportion of customers who buy a jar of chilli chutney. Then H_0: $p = 0.03$ and H_1: $p \neq 0.03$.

Q6 Boyd wants to know if the proportion of gym members that watch Australian soaps is higher than the claim of 40%. Let p be the probability that a randomly selected gym member watches Australian soaps. Then H_0: $p = 0.4$ and H_1: $p > 0.4$.

2. Hypothesis Tests for a Binomial Distribution
Exercise 2.1 — Testing for significance

Q1 a) If Charlotte cannot read minds, she would just be guessing a number between 1 and 5, and so the probability of getting it right would be 0.2. Let p be the probability of Charlotte guessing correctly. Then H_0: $p = 0.2$ and H_1: $p > 0.2$.

b) Let X be the number of times Charlotte guesses correctly in the sample. Then under H_0, $X \sim B(10, 0.2)$.

c) From the tables
$P(X \geq 4) = 1 - P(X \leq 3) = 1 - 0.8791 = 0.1209 > 0.05$.
So there is not significant evidence at the 5% level to reject H_0 in favour of Charlotte's claim.

Q2 Let p = the proportion of people who think chicken dinosaurs are good value. Then H_0: $p = 0.45$ and H_1: $p < 0.45$. The significance level $\alpha = 0.1$.
Let X be the number of students in the sample who think chicken dinosaurs are good value.
Then under H_0, $X \sim B(50, 0.45)$.
Now from the tables $P(X \leq 16) = 0.0427 < 0.1$.
So there is significant evidence at the 10% level to reject H_0 in favour of Ellen's claim that fewer people think chicken dinosaurs are good value.
In fact, there is even significant evidence at the 5% level to reject H_0 because $P(X \leq 16) = 0.0427 < 0.05$.

Q3 Let p = the proportion of John's pupils who gain distinctions. Then H_0: $p = 0.25$ and H_1: $p \neq 0.25$. The significance level $\alpha = 0.01$ but since it's a two-tailed test, you'll need $\frac{\alpha}{2} = 0.005$.
Let X = the number of John's exam candidates who get distinctions.
Then under H_0, $X \sim B(12, 0.25)$. So from the tables $P(X \geq 6) = 1 - P(X \leq 5) = 1 - 0.9456 = 0.0544 > 0.005$.
So there is not significant evidence at the 1% level to reject H_0 in favour of the alternative hypothesis that the number of distinctions has changed.

Q4 Let p = the proportion of the birds that are rare. Then H_0: $p = 0.15$ and H_1: $p \neq 0.15$. The significance level is $\alpha = 0.1$ but the test is two-tailed so you'll need $\frac{\alpha}{2} = 0.05$.
Let X be the number of rare birds in the sample.
Then under H_0, $X \sim B(40, 0.15)$.
Now from the tables, $P(X \leq 2) = 0.0486 < 0.05$.
So there is significant evidence at the 10% level to reject H_0 in favour of the alternative hypothesis that the number of rare birds is different with the new birdseed.

Q5 Let p = the proportion of customers who buy Pigeon Spotter Magazine. Then H_0: $p = 0.1$ and H_1: $p \neq 0.1$. The significance level is $\alpha = 0.05$ but the test is two-tailed so you'll need $\frac{\alpha}{2} = 0.025$. Let X = the number of customers who buy the magazine in the sample.
Then under H_0, $X \sim B(50, 0.1)$. Now from the tables $P(X \geq 8) = 1 - P(X \leq 7) = 1 - 0.8779 = 0.1221 > 0.025$.
So there is not significant evidence at the 5% level to reject H_0 in favour of the alternative hypothesis that the number of customers buying the magazine is different in the new shop.

Q6 Let p = the proportion of clients who pass the driving test first time. Then H_0: $p = 0.7$ and H_1: $p < 0.7$. The significance level is $\alpha = 0.01$. Let X be the number of people in the sample who passed their driving test on their first attempt. Then under H_0, $X \sim B(8, 0.7)$.
You'll need to use the tables to find $P(X \leq 4)$, but the probability is greater than 0.7, so you'll need to do the usual trick for this. Or you can find this probability using a calculator.

Let Y = the number of people in the sample who didn't pass first time, then $Y \sim B(8, 0.3)$. From the tables:
$P(X \leq 4) = P(Y \geq 4) = 1 - P(Y \leq 3)$
$\qquad\qquad = 1 - 0.8059 = 0.1941 > 0.01$
So there is not significant evidence at the 1% level to reject H_0 in favour of H_1, so Hati's claim is not upheld at the 1% level.

Exercise 2.2 — Critical regions

Q1 a) Let p = the proportion of pupils reaching the top reading level. So H_0: $p = 0.25$ and H_1: $p > 0.25$.
Let X be the number of pupils in the sample that are reaching the top reading level.
Then under H_0, $X \sim B(20, 0.25)$.
You're looking for the smallest value x such that $P(X \geq x) \leq 0.05$. Using the tables,
$P(X \geq 9) = 1 - P(X \leq 8) = 1 - 0.9591 = 0.0409$
$P(X \geq 8) = 1 - P(X \leq 7) = 1 - 0.8982 = 0.1018$
So the critical region is $X \geq 9$.

b) The actual significance level is 0.0409 or 4.09%.

Q2 Let p = the proportion of pupils giving up Miss Cackle's potion-making class after year 9.
So H_0: $p = 0.2$ and H_1: $p < 0.2$. Let X be the number of pupils in the class of 30 that give up potion-making after year 9. Then under H_0, $X \sim B(30, 0.2)$.
You're interested in the low values since you're looking for a decrease.
$P(X \leq 2) = 0.0442$ and $P(X \leq 3) = 0.1227$
This means the critical region is $X \leq 2$.

The actual significance level is 0.0442 or 4.42%.

Q3 Let p = proportion of southern local councils who provide weekly collections.
So H_0: $p = 0.4$ and H_1: $p \neq 0.4$. Let X be the number of southern councils in the sample that offer a weekly collection. Then under H_0, $X \sim B(25, 0.4)$.
Since this is a two-tailed test, you need to find two critical regions, one at each tail.
Lower tail: $P(X \leq 4) = 0.0095$ and $P(X \leq 5) = 0.0294$
The closest probability to 0.025 is 0.0294 so the critical region for this tail is $X \leq 5$. Upper tail:
$P(X \geq 15) = 1 - P(X \leq 14) = 1 - 0.9656 = 0.0344$
$P(X \geq 16) = 1 - P(X \leq 15) = 1 - 0.9868 = 0.0132$
The closest probability to 0.025 is 0.0344 so the critical region for this tail is $X \geq 15$.
So the critical region is $X \leq 5$ or $X \geq 15$.

The actual significance level is $0.0344 + 0.0294 = 0.0638$, or 6.38%.

Q4 a) Let p = the proportion of people who have booked their summer holiday before February 1st.
Then H_0: $p = 0.35$ and H_1: $p < 0.35$.
Let X be the number of people in the sample who have booked their holiday.
Then under H_0, $X \sim B(15, 0.35)$. Using the tables, $P(X \leq 1) = 0.0142$ and $P(X \leq 2) = 0.0617$.
This means the critical region is $X \leq 1$.

b) The actual significance level is 0.0142 or 1.42%.

c) 3 does not lie in the critical region so the result is not significant at the 5% level.

Q5 Let p = the proportion of people reporting an improvement in symptoms. Then H_0: $p = 0.15$ and H_1: $p > 0.15$. Let X be the number of people in the test who report an improvement in symptoms.
Then $X \sim B(50, 0.15)$ under H_0.
You're interested in the high values. From the tables:
$P(X \geq 15) = 1 - P(X \leq 14) = 1 - 0.9947 = 0.0053$
$P(X \geq 14) = 1 - P(X \leq 13) = 1 - 0.9868 = 0.0132$
The probability must be less than 0.01 so the critical region is $X \geq 15$.
The actual significance level is 0.0053 or 0.53%.

Q6 Let p = the proportion of five-year-old boys who believe they have magical powers.
Then H_0: $p = 0.05$ and H_1: $p \neq 0.05$.
Let X be the number of five-year-old boys in the sample who believe they have magical powers.
Then under H_0, $X \sim B(50, 0.05)$.
The test is two-tailed so you need to consider the upper and lower ends of the binomial distribution.
From the tables: $P(X \leq 0) = 0.0769$ — this is as close to 0.05 as you can possibly get so
the critical region for the lower tail is $X = 0$.
$P(X \geq 6) = 1 - P(X \leq 5) = 1 - 0.9622 = 0.0378$
$P(X \geq 5) = 1 - P(X \leq 4) = 1 - 0.8964 = 0.1036$
So the closest probability to 0.05 is 0.0378 and so the critical region for the higher tail is $X \geq 6$.
So the critical region is $X = 0$ or $X \geq 6$.
The actual significance level is $0.0769 + 0.0378 = 0.1147$

Q7 a) Let p = the proportion of customers the salesman can persuade to get a loyalty card.
Then H_0: $p = 0.6$ and H_1: $p > 0.6$. Let X be the number of customers he persuades in the sample.
Then $X \sim B(12, 0.6)$ under H_0.
This probability is higher than 0.5 so you need to introduce another random variable, Y. Let Y be the number of customers he doesn't persuade, then $Y \sim B(12, 0.4)$ under H_0.
Then you're looking for a value x such that $P(X \geq x) \leq 0.05$, i.e. $P(Y \leq y) \leq 0.05$,
where $y = 12 - x$.
$P(Y \leq 1) = 0.0196$ and $P(Y \leq 2) = 0.0834$
So the critical region is $Y \leq 1$, i.e. $X \geq 11$.

b) The actual significance level is 0.0196.

c) 10 doesn't lie in the critical region so this result is not significant at the 5% level.

Chapter 18: Quantities and Units in Mechanics

1. Understanding Units
Exercise 1.1 — S.I. units

Q1 a) metres $\times$ metres $\times$ metres $= \text{m}^3$
b) kilograms $\div \text{m}^3 = \text{kg m}^{-3}$ or kg/m^3
c) kilograms $\times \text{ms}^{-1} = \text{kg m s}^{-1}$ or kg m/s
d) Newtons $\times$ metres $= \text{kg m s}^{-2} \times \text{m}$
$= \text{kg m}^2\text{s}^{-2}$ or $\text{kg m}^2\text{/s}^2$
e) Newtons $\div \text{m}^2 = \text{kg m s}^{-2} \div \text{m}^2 = \text{kg m}^{-1}\text{s}^{-2}$ or $\text{kg/(m s}^2)$

2. Models in Mechanics
Exercise 2.1 — Modelling

Q1

Assumptions:
The apple is modelled as a particle.
The apple is initially at rest.
Air resistance can be ignored.
There are no other external forces acting.
The effect of gravity (g) is constant.

Q2

Assumptions:
The conker is modelled as a particle.
The shoelace is a light, inextensible string.
There are no other external forces acting.

Q3

Assumptions:
The sledge is modelled as a particle.
The surface of the slope is smooth (it's icy).
The rope is a light, inextensible string.
The rope is parallel to the slope.
No other external forces are acting.

Q4 a)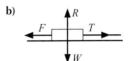

Assumptions:
The box is modelled as a particle.
The floor is smooth (it's polished).
There are no other external forces acting.

b)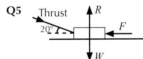

Assumptions:
The crate is modelled as a particle.
The rope is light and inextensible.
The floor is rough.
There are no other external forces acting.

Q5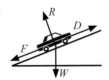

Assumptions:
The package is modelled as a particle.
The stick is light and rigid.
The ground is rough.
There are no other external forces acting.

Q6 a)

Assumptions:
The car is modelled as a particle.
The angle of the slope is constant.
The surface is rough.
There are no other external forces acting.

b)

Assumptions:
The car is modelled as a particle.
The angle of the slope is constant.
The surface is rough.
There are no other external forces acting.

Q7

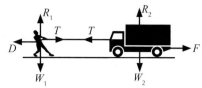

Assumptions:
The man and the lorry are both modelled as particles.
The rope is light and inextensible, and remains taut.
The road is rough.
No resistance forces slow the strongman's motion.
There are no other external forces acting.

Chapter 19: Kinematics

1. Motion Graphs

Exercise 1.1 — Displacement-time graphs

Q1 The velocity is given by the gradient of the graph.

First stage: $v = \text{gradient} = \frac{(40-0)\text{ km}}{(0.5-0)\text{ h}} = 80 \text{ kmh}^{-1}$

Second stage: $v = \frac{(60-40)\text{ km}}{(1-0.5)\text{ h}} = 40 \text{ kmh}^{-1}$

Third stage: $v = \frac{(60-60)\text{ km}}{(1.5-1)\text{ h}} = 0 \text{ kmh}^{-1}$

Fourth stage: $v = \frac{(0-60)\text{ km}}{(2-1.5)\text{ h}} = -120 \text{ kmh}^{-1}$

Q2 a) You need to calculate the time taken to travel between B and C. The coach travels 60 km at 40 kmh^{-1}, so the time taken is:
60 km ÷ 40 kmh^{-1} = 1.5 hours.

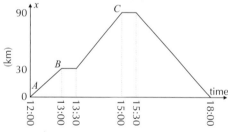

b) $v = -\frac{90\text{ km}}{2.5\text{ h}} = -36 \text{ kmh}^{-1}$

c) Total distance travelled =
30 km + 60 km + 90 km = 180 km
$\text{speed} = \frac{\text{distance}}{\text{time}} = \frac{180\text{ km}}{6\text{ h}} = 30 \text{ kmh}^{-1}$

Q3 The man travels 5 mph ÷ 1 h = 5 miles from 13:00 to 14:00, then 3 mph ÷ 1 h = 3 miles from 14:00 to 15:00.

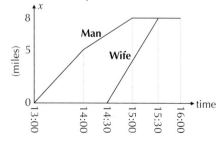

Q4 a) 500 m – 700 m + 600 m = 400 m
(The 700 m is subtracted because his velocity for that part of the journey is negative, so he is walking in the opposite direction.)

b)

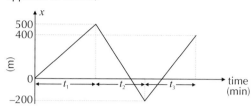

c) The gradient of each part of the graph is equal to the velocity during that stage. You already know the velocities, and the distances, for each stage, so you can use them to find the times.

$u = \frac{500}{t_1} \Rightarrow t_1 = \frac{500}{u}$

$-2u = \frac{-700}{t_2} \Rightarrow t_2 = \frac{350}{u}$

$1.5u = \frac{600}{t_3} \Rightarrow t_3 = \frac{400}{u}$

Total time = $t_1 + t_2 + t_3$
$= \frac{500}{u} + \frac{350}{u} + \frac{400}{u} = \frac{1250}{u}$ seconds

d) $\text{Average speed} = \frac{\text{total distance}}{\text{total time}}$
$= (500 + 700 + 600) \div \frac{1250}{u}$
$= \frac{36u}{25} \text{ ms}^{-1}$

Q5 a)

The $\frac{3}{2}t + 100$ comes from the fact that the car returns home at twice the speed that it travelled away from home, so must take half as long (i.e. $\frac{t}{2}$ seconds).
So the total time is: $t + 100 + \frac{t}{2} = \frac{3}{2}t + 100$

b) Total distance = speed × time
So distance covered in first part of journey = ut m
Car travels same distance in return journey, so total distance travelled = $2ut$ m.

c) $\text{Average speed} = \frac{\text{total distance}}{\text{total time}}$
$= \frac{2ut}{\frac{3}{2}t + 100} = \frac{4ut}{3t + 200} \text{ ms}^{-1}$

Exercise 1.2 — Velocity-time graphs

Q1 The bus accelerates uniformly from rest to a velocity of 20 kmh^{-1} in 2 min. It then travels at this speed for 18 min, before decelerating uniformly to 10 kmh^{-1} in 5 min. Finally, it decelerates uniformly to rest in 10 min.

Q2 a) Acceleration is given by the gradient of the graph.
$a = \text{gradient} = \frac{(15-0)\text{ ms}^{-1}}{(5-0)\text{ s}} = 3 \text{ ms}^{-2}$

b) $a = \frac{((-15)-0)\text{ ms}^{-1}}{(60-40)\text{ s}} = -0.75 \text{ ms}^{-2}$

c) $a = \frac{(0-(-15))\text{ ms}^{-1}}{(70-60)\text{ s}} = 1.5 \text{ ms}^{-2}$

Q3 a)

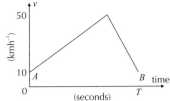

b) Split the area up into a rectangle and a triangle:

Area $= 10T + \dfrac{(50-10) \times T}{2} = 30T$

c) The gradient gives the acceleration, so considering the time the particle is accelerating:

$4 = \dfrac{(50-10)}{t_1} \Rightarrow t_1 = 10$

Now considering the time it is decelerating:

$-10 = \dfrac{(10-50)}{t_2} \Rightarrow t_2 = 4$

x is the area under the graph while the particle is accelerating:

$x = 10t_1 + \dfrac{(50-10) \times t_1}{2} = (10 \times 10) + \dfrac{40 \times 10}{2}$

$= 300$ m

y is the area under the graph while the particle is decelerating:

$y = 10t_2 + \dfrac{(50-10) \times t_2}{2} = (10 \times 4) + \dfrac{40 \times 4}{2} = 120$ m

T is just the sum of t_1 and t_2:

$T = 10 + 4 = 14$ s

Q4 a) The gradient gives the acceleration, so:

$a = 0.375 = \dfrac{15}{t} \Rightarrow t = 40$ s

So it takes the train 40 s to reach the signal box.

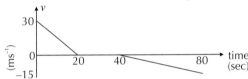

b) Gradient $= -\dfrac{30}{20} = -1.5$

So the train decelerates at a rate of 1.5 ms^{-2}

c) The distance is given by the area under the graph from $t = 0$ s to $t = 20$ s:

distance $= \dfrac{30 \times 20}{2} = 300$ m

You could also have found the area under the graph from t = 40 s to t = 80 s — the distance is the same.

Q5 a) Taking upwards as positive:

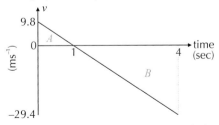

If you took downwards as positive, your graph should be the same as this, but flipped vertically, i.e. sloping upwards from −9.8 ms⁻¹ to 29.4 ms⁻¹.

b) (i) As the stone travels upwards, it will slow down until it reaches its highest point, where it will have velocity $v = 0$ ms^{-1}. The distance the stone travels from the cliff edge to its highest point is equal to its displacement during this time. This is given by the area marked A on the graph.

Area $A = \dfrac{1 \times 9.8}{2} = 4.9$

So distance from cliff to highest point is 4.9 m.

(ii) As the stone falls from its highest point to the sea, its speed will increase from 0 ms^{-1} to 29.4 ms^{-1}. The distance the stone travels from its highest point to the sea is equal to the magnitude of its displacement during this time. This is given by the area marked B on the graph.

Area $B = \dfrac{3 \times -29.4}{2} = -44.1$ m

So the stone travels 44.1 m downwards from its highest point to the sea.

(iii) The height of the cliff is equal to the magnitude of the stone's final displacement from its starting point. Find this by adding the areas of A and B:

$4.9 + (-44.1) = -39.2$ m

So the height of the cliff is 39.2 m

You can also think of the height of the cliff as being the difference between your answers to (i) and (ii):
44.1 − 4.9 = 39.2 m.

2. Constant Acceleration Equations

Exercise 2.1 — Constant acceleration equations

Q1 a) $u = 0, v = 12, a = a, t = 5$

$v = u + at$

$12 = 0 + 5a$

$a = 12 \div 5 = 2.4$ ms^{-2}

b) $s = s, u = 0, v = 12, t = 5$

$s = \left(\dfrac{u+v}{2}\right)t$

$s = \left(\dfrac{0+12}{2}\right) \times 5 = 30$ m

Q2 a) $18 \times 1000 \div 60^2 = 5$ ms^{-1}

b) $s = 50, u = 5, v = 0, t = t$

$s = \left(\dfrac{u+v}{2}\right)t$

$50 = \left(\dfrac{5+0}{2}\right)t$

$t = 50 \div 2.5 = 20$ s

c) $s = 50, u = 5, v = 0, a = a$

$v^2 = u^2 + 2as$

$0 = 5^2 + 2a \times 50$

$2a = -5^2 \div 50$

$a = -0.25$

So the cyclist decelerates at a rate of 0.25 ms^{-2}

Q3 a) $s = 60, u = 5, v = 25, a = a$

$v^2 = u^2 + 2as$

$25^2 = 5^2 + (2a \times 60)$

$625 = 25 + 120a$

$a = 600 \div 120 = 5$ ms^{-2}

b) Acceleration is constant.
The skier is modelled as a particle travelling in a straight line.

Q4 a) From the first post to the second post:

$s = 18, u = u, a = a, t = 2$

$s = ut + \frac{1}{2}at^2$

$18 = 2u + \frac{1}{2}a \times 2^2$

$18 = 2u + 2a$

$9 = u + a$

$\Rightarrow u = 9 - a$ ①

From the first post to the third post:

$s = 36, u = u, a = a, t = 3$

$s = ut + \frac{1}{2}at^2$

$36 = 3u + \frac{1}{2}a \times 3^2$

$36 = 3u + 4.5a$

$\Rightarrow 12 = u + 1.5a$ ②

Substituting ① into ②:

$12 = (9 - a) + 1.5a$

$3 = 0.5a \Rightarrow a = 6 \text{ ms}^{-2}$

b) Use expression for u from part a):

$u = 9 - a = 9 - 6 = 3 \text{ ms}^{-1}$

Q5

$U \text{ ms}^{-1}$ 20 ms^{-1} tunnel 20 ms^{-1} $U \text{ ms}^{-1}$

$t = 0$ $t = 15$ $t = 40$ $t = 70$

a) While the bus is in the tunnel,

$s = s, u = 20, a = 0, t = 25$.

$s = ut + \frac{1}{2}at^2$

$s = (20 \times 25) + 0 = 500 \text{ m}$

b) Before the tunnel:

$s = s_1, u = U, v = 20, t = 15$

$s_1 = \left(\frac{u+v}{2}\right)t$

$s_1 = \left(\frac{U+20}{2}\right) \times 15$

After tunnel:

$s = s_2, u = 20, v = U, t = 30$

$s_2 = \left(\frac{u+v}{2}\right)t$

$s_2 = \left(\frac{20+U}{2}\right) \times 30$

Total distance travelled $= s_1 + 500 + s_2$:

$1580 = 15\left(\frac{U+20}{2}\right) + 500 + 30\left(\frac{20+U}{2}\right)$

$1080 = 45\left(\frac{U+20}{2}\right)$

$48 = U + 20 \Rightarrow U = 28 \text{ ms}^{-1}$

Exercise 2.2 — Gravity

Q1 $s = s, u = 0, a = 9.8, t = 3$

$s = ut + \frac{1}{2}at^2$

$s = 0 + \frac{1}{2} \times 9.8 \times 3^2 = 44.1 \text{ m}$

Q2 a) $s = 5, u = 0, a = 9.8, t = t$

$s = ut + \frac{1}{2}at^2$

$5 = 0 + \frac{1}{2} \times 9.8 \times t^2$

$t^2 = 1.02...$

$t = 1.01 \text{ s (3 s.f.)}$

b) $s = 5, u = 0, v = v, a = 9.8$

$v^2 = u^2 + 2as$

$v^2 = 0 + 2 \times 9.8 \times 5$

$v^2 = 98$

$v = 9.90 \text{ ms}^{-1} \text{ (3 s.f.)}$

Q3 a) Taking upwards as positive:

$s = s, u = 30, v = 0, a = -9.8$

$v^2 = u^2 + 2as$

$0 = 30^2 + (2 \times -9.8 \times s)$

$s = 900 \div 19.6 = 45.918... = 45.9 \text{ m (3 s.f.)}$

b) $s = 0, u = 30, a = -9.8, t = t$

$s = ut + \frac{1}{2}at^2$

$0 = 30t + \frac{1}{2} \times -9.8t^2$

$0 = 30t - 4.9t^2$

$0 = t(30 - 4.9t)$

$t = 0 \text{ or } (30 - 4.9t) = 0$

$30 = 4.9t$

$t = 30 \div 4.9 = 6.1224... = 6.12 \text{ s (3 s.f.)}$

c) $u = 30, v = v, a = -9.8, t = 2$

$v = u + at$

$v = 30 + (-9.8 \times 2) = 10.4 \text{ ms}^{-1}$

v is positive, so the object is moving upwards.

Q4 a) Taking upwards as positive:

$u = u, v = -20, a = -9.8, t = 3$

$v = u + at$

$-20 = u - 9.8 \times 3$

$u = 9.4 \text{ ms}^{-1}$

b) $s = -d, v = -20, a = -9.8, t = 3$

$s = vt - \frac{1}{2}at^2$

$-d = (-20 \times 3) + (4.9 \times 9) \Rightarrow d = 15.9 \text{ m}$

Q5 a) Taking upwards as positive:

$s = s, u = 8, v = 0, a = -9.8$

$v^2 = u^2 + 2as$

$0 = 8^2 + (2 \times -9.8s)$

$s = 64 \div 19.6 = 3.265...$

Thrown from 5 m above ground,

so max height $= 3.265... + 5 = 8.27 \text{ m (3 s.f.)}$

b) $s = 8 - 5 = 3, u = 8, a = -9.8, t = t$

$s = ut + \frac{1}{2}at^2$

$3 = 8t + \frac{1}{2} \times -9.8t^2$

$4.9t^2 - 8t + 3 = 0$

Solve using the quadratic formula:

$t = \frac{8 \pm \sqrt{8^2 - (4 \times 4.9 \times 3)}}{9.8}$

$t = 0.583... \text{ or } t = 1.049...$

So required time is given by $1.049... - 0.583...$

$= 0.465 \text{ s (3 s.f.)}$

Q6 a) Taking upwards as positive:

$s = s, u = 12, v = 0, a = -9.8$

$v^2 = u^2 + 2as$

$0 = 12^2 - 2 \times 9.8s$

$s = 144 \div 19.6$

$s = 7.3469... = 7.35 \text{ m (3 s.f.)}$

b) $u = 12, v = 0, a = -9.8, t = t$

$v = u + at$

$0 = 12 - 9.8t$

$t = 12 \div 9.8 = 1.2244... = 1.22 \text{ s (3 s.f.)}$

c) Distance between 5th and 8th floors $= 7.3469...$

So distance between each floor $= 7.3469... \div 3$

Distance between ground and 5th floor $=$

$5(7.3469... \div 3) = 12.244...$

So $s = -12.244..., u = 12, v = v, a = -9.8$

$v^2 = u^2 + 2as = 12^2 + (2 \times -9.8 \times -12.244...)$

$v^2 = 384 \Rightarrow v = 19.595... = 19.6 \text{ ms}^{-1} \text{ (3 s.f.)}$

Q7 a) Take upwards as positive.
p is the time that the object is at its highest point.
So $u = 24.5$, $v = 0$, $a = -9.8$, $t = p$
$v = u + at$
$0 = 24.5 - 9.8p$
$p = 24.5 \div 9.8 = 2.5$ s

b) q is the time that the object lands. From the graph, this is 29.4 m below the point of projection.
$s = -29.4$, $u = 24.5$, $a = -9.8$, $t = q$
$s = ut + \frac{1}{2}at^2$
$-29.4 = 24.5q - \frac{1}{2}(9.8)q^2$
Dividing each term by 4.9, and rearranging:
$q^2 - 5q - 6 = 0$
$(q - 6)(q + 1) = 0$
So $q = 6$ or $q = -1$
q is a time, and must be positive, so $q = 6$ s

c) r is the object's max height.
$s = s$, $u = 24.5$, $v = 0$, $a = -9.8$
$v^2 = u^2 + 2as$
$0 = 24.5^2 + (2 \times -9.8s)$
$s = 24.5^2 \div 19.6 = 30.625$
The object was projected from 29.4 m above the ground, so: $r = 30.625 + 29.4 = 60.025$ m

Q8

a) Take upwards as positive. When the projectile is moving between the two targets:
$s = 120$, $u = u$, $a = -9.8$, $t = 3$
$s = ut + \frac{1}{2}at^2$
$120 = 3u + \frac{1}{2}(-9.8 \times 3^2)$
$3u = 164.1$
$u = 54.7$ ms^{-1} — this is the speed of the projectile as it passes the first target.
When the projectile is moving between the point of projection and the first target:
$s = 150$, $u = u$, $v = 54.7$, $a = -9.8$
$v^2 = u^2 + 2as$
$54.7^2 = u^2 + (2 \times -9.8 \times 150)$
$u^2 = 5932.09$
$u = 77.020...$
So the projectile is projected at 77.0 ms^{-1} (3 s.f.)

b) $s = s$, $u = 77.020...$, $v = 0$, $a = -9.8$
$v^2 = u^2 + 2as$
$0 = 77.020...^2 + (2 \times -9.8s)$
$s = 77.020...^2 \div 19.6 = 302.657...$
The projectile is projected from 50 m below ground, so the max height above ground is:
$302.657... - 50 = 252.657... = 253$ m (3 s.f.)

c) $u = 77.020...$, $v = 54.7$, $a = -9.8$, $t = t$
$v = u + at$
$54.7 = 77.020... - 9.8t$
$t = (77.020... - 54.7) \div 9.8 = 2.2775...$
$t = 2.28$ s (3 s.f.)

Exercise 2.3 — More complicated problems

Q1 a) $s = 28$, $u = 2$, $v = 6$, $t = t$
$s = \left(\frac{u + v}{2}\right)t$
$28 = \left(\frac{2 + 6}{2}\right)t$
$28 = 4t \Rightarrow t = 7$ s

b)
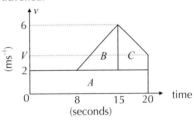

c) The area under the graph gives the total distance travelled.

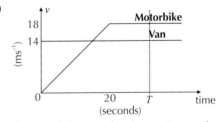

Area of $A = 20 \times 2 = 40$
Area of $B = \left(\frac{7 \times 4}{2}\right) = 14$
Area of $C = \left(\frac{4 + (V - 2)}{2}\right) \times 5 = 5 + 2.5V$
Total area $= 40 + 14 + 5 + 2.5V = 59 + 2.5V$
Total distance travelled is 67 m, so:
$59 + 2.5V = 67$
$2.5V = 8$
$V = 3.2$ ms^{-1}

Q2 a)

b) The motorbike overtakes the van T seconds after setting off. At this point, the two vehicles will have covered the same distance since $t = 0$, so the areas under the graphs up to this point will be the same.
Van area $= 14 \times T$
Motorbike area $= \left(\frac{T + (T - 20)}{2}\right) \times 18 = 18T - 180$
Making the two areas equal to each other:
$14T = 18T - 180$
$4T = 180$
$T = 45$ seconds

Q3 a) Write down the *suvat* variables for X and Y, considering the movement of each car separately. In each case, take the direction that the car moves as being positive.

$u_X = 15$, $a_X = 1$, $t_X = t$
$u_Y = 20$, $a_Y = 2$, $t_Y = t$

Using $s = ut + \frac{1}{2}at^2$:

$s_X = 15t + \frac{1}{2}t^2$
$s_Y = 20t + t^2$

They collide when $s_X + s_Y = 30$:

$15t + \frac{1}{2}t^2 + 20t + t^2 = 30$

$35t + \frac{3}{2}t^2 = 30$

Multiplying throughout by 2 and rearranging:
$3t^2 + 70t - 60 = 0$
Solve using the quadratic formula:

$$t = \frac{-70 \pm \sqrt{70^2 - (4 \times 3 \times (-60))}}{6}$$

$t = 0.8277...$ or $t = -24.161...$
So $t = 0.828$ s (3 s.f.)

b) Use $v = u + at$ on the two cars separately. Again, take the direction of motion as being positive for each car.

X: $v_X = 15 + 0.8277...$
$\quad v_X = 15.8$ ms⁻¹ (3 s.f.)
Y: $v_Y = 20 + 2(0.8277...)$
$\quad v_Y = 21.7$ ms⁻¹ (3 s.f.)

c) $s = ut + \frac{1}{2}at^2$

$s_X = (15 \times 0.8277...) + \frac{1}{2}(0.8277...)^2$

$s_X = 12.759... = 12.8$ m (3 s.f.)

Q4 a)

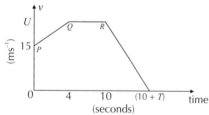

b) From P to Q: $u = 15$, $v = U$, $a = 3$, $t = 4$
$\quad v = u + at$
$\quad U = 15 + (3 \times 4) = 27$ ms⁻¹

c) The area under the graph from P to Q is:
$\frac{1}{2} \times (15 + 27) \times 4 = 84$
So the distance from P to Q is 84 m.
The area under the graph from Q to R is:
$27 \times 6 = 162$
So the distance from Q to R is 162 m.
The total distance travelled is 405 m, so the distance the particle travels in coming to rest is:
$405 - 162 - 84 = 159$ m
So, from R to rest: $s = 159$, $u = U = 27$, $v = 0$, $t = T$

$s = \left(\frac{u+v}{2}\right)t$

$159 = \left(\frac{27}{2}\right)T$

$\Rightarrow T = 11.777... = 11.8$ s (3 s.f.)
So the particle comes to rest $10 + 11.8$
$= 21.8$ s (3 s.f.) after passing P.

d) Gradient of graph $= \frac{0-U}{T} = \frac{-27}{11.777...} = -2.292...$
So it decelerates at a rate of 2.29 ms⁻² (3 s.f.)

Q5 a) Write down the *suvat* variables for the two balls:
$u_1 = 5$, $a_1 = -0.5$, $t_1 = t$
$u_2 = 4$, $a_2 = 0$, $t_2 = t - 3$

Using $s = ut + \frac{1}{2}at^2$:

First ball: $s_1 = 5t + \frac{1}{2}(-0.5)t^2$
$\quad\quad\quad s_1 = 5t - 0.25t^2$
Second ball: $s_2 = 4(t - 3) + 0$
$\quad\quad\quad\quad s_2 = 4t - 12$
They are level when $s_1 = s_2$: $5t - 0.25t^2 = 4t - 12$
Multiplying throughout by 4 and rearranging:
$t^2 - 4t - 48 = 0$
Solve using the quadratic formula or by completing the square:
$(t - 2)^2 - 52 = 0$
$t - 2 = \pm\sqrt{52}$
$t = 2 \pm \sqrt{52}$
$t = 9.2111...$ or $t = -5.2111...$
So the second ball passes the first ball
9.21 s (3 s.f.) after the first ball is rolled.

b) Using $s_2 = 4t - 12$ from part a):
$s_2 = (4 \times 9.2111...) - 12$
$\quad = 24.844... = 24.8$ m (3 s.f.)

c) Find the time that the first ball comes to rest using $v = u + at$ with $v = 0$:
$0 = 5 - 0.5t \Rightarrow t = 10$ s
Now find the distance the first ball travels in this time using $s = ut + \frac{1}{2}at^2$:

$s_1 = (5 \times 10) + \frac{1}{2}(-0.5 \times 10^2) = 25$ m
Find the distance the second ball travels in 15 s using $s = ut + \frac{1}{2}at^2$:

$s_2 = 4(15 - 3) + 0 = 48$ m
So the second ball is 48 m − 25 m = 23 m ahead.

Q6 a) Take upwards as the positive direction.
Find the time that B is at its highest point:
$u_B = 5$, $v_B = 0$, $a_B = -9.8$, $t_B = t$
Using $v = u + at$: $\quad 0 = 5 - 9.8t$
$\quad\quad\quad\quad\quad\quad \Rightarrow t = 5 \div 9.8 = 0.5102...$
Now find the displacement of A at this time (remembering that A is released 1 s before B):
$u_A = 0$, $a_A = -9.8$, $t_A = 1 + 0.5102... = 1.5102...$
Using $s = ut + \frac{1}{2}at^2$:

$s = 0 + \frac{1}{2}(-9.8 \times 1.5102...^2) = -11.1755...$
So A has travelled 11.2 m (3 s.f.)

b) Using $s = ut + \frac{1}{2}at^2$:
A: $u_A = 0$, $a_A = -9.8$, $t_A = t$

$\quad s = 0 + \frac{1}{2}(-9.8t^2)$

$\quad s = -4.9t^2$
B: $u_B = 5$, $a_B = -9.8$, $t_B = t - 1$

$\quad s = 5(t - 1) + \frac{1}{2} \times -9.8(t - 1)^2$

$\quad s = 5t - 5 - 4.9(t^2 - 2t + 1)$
$\quad s = 14.8t - 9.9 - 4.9t^2$
So A has moved $4.9t^2$ m down from a height of 40 m, and B has moved $(14.8t - 9.9 - 4.9t^2)$ m up from a height of 10 m.

A and *B* are at the same level when:
$40 - 4.9t^2 = 10 + 14.8t - 9.9 - 4.9t^2$
$\Rightarrow 39.9 = 14.8t$
$\Rightarrow t = 39.9 \div 14.8 = 2.6959...$
So they become level 2.70 seconds (3 s.f.)
after *A* is dropped.

c) Using $s = -4.9t^2$ (from part b)) for particle *A*:
$s = -4.9 \times (2.6959...)^2 = -35.6138...$
$40 - 35.6138... = 4.3861...$
So they are 4.39 m (3 s.f.) above the ground.

3. Non-Uniform Acceleration

Exercise 3.1 — Displacement with non-uniform acceleration

Q1 a) $s = 2(3)^3 - 4(3)^2 + 3 = 54 - 36 + 3 = 21$ m

b) $v = \dfrac{ds}{dt} = 6t^2 - 8t$

c) $v = 6(3)^2 - 8(3) = 54 - 24 = 30$ ms^{-1}

Q2 a) $v = \dfrac{ds}{dt} = t^4 - 8t^3 + 21t^2 - 20t + 5$
At $t = 0$, $v = 0^4 - 8(0)^3 + 21(0)^2 - 20(0) + 5 = 5$ ms^{-1}

b) $a = \dfrac{dv}{dt} = 4t^3 - 24t^2 + 42t - 20$
At $t = 2$, $a = 4(2)^3 - 24(2)^2 + 42(2) - 20$
$= 32 - 96 + 84 - 20 = 0$ ms^{-2}

Exercise 3.2 — Velocity and acceleration equations

Q1 a) $s = \int v\, dt = \int (1 + 6t + 6t^2 - 4t^3)\, dt$
$= t + 6\left(\dfrac{t^2}{2}\right) + 6\left(\dfrac{t^3}{3}\right) - 4\left(\dfrac{t^4}{4}\right) + C$
$= t + 3t^2 + 2t^3 - t^4 + C$
When $t = 0$, $s = 0$: $0 = 0 + 3(0)^2 + 2(0)^3 - 0^4 + C$
$\Rightarrow C = 0$
So $s = t + 3t^2 + 2t^3 - t^4$

b) At $t = 2$: $s = 2 + 3(2)^2 + 2(2)^3 - 2^4$
$= 2 + 12 + 16 - 16 = 14$ cm
$v = 1 + 6(2) + 6(2)^2 - 4(2)^3$
$= 1 + 12 + 24 - 32 = 5$ cms^{-1}

Q2 $v = \int a\, dt = \int (-3t^2 + 6t - 4)\, dt$
$= -3\left(\dfrac{t^3}{3}\right) + 6\left(\dfrac{t^2}{2}\right) - 4t + C_1$
$= -t^3 + 3t^2 - 4t + C_1$
When $t = 1$, $v = 0$: $0 = -(1)^3 + 3(1)^2 - 4(1) + C_1$
$C_1 = 1 - 3 + 4 = 2$
So $v = -t^3 + 3t^2 - 4t + 2$
$s = \int v\, dt = \int (-t^3 + 3t^2 - 4t + 2)\, dt$
$= -\left(\dfrac{t^4}{4}\right) + 3\left(\dfrac{t^3}{3}\right) - 4\left(\dfrac{t^2}{2}\right) + 2t + C_2$
$= -\dfrac{1}{4}t^4 + t^3 - 2t^2 + 2t + C_2$
When $t = 0$, $s = 2$:
$2 = -\dfrac{1}{4}(0)^4 + (0)^3 - 2(0)^2 + 2(0) + C_2$
$2 = C_2$
So $s = -\dfrac{1}{4}t^4 + t^3 - 2t^2 + 2t + 2$

Exercise 3.3 — Maximum and minimum points

Q1 a) $s = 2t^4 - 8t^3 + 8t^2$
At $t = 2$, $s = 2(2)^4 - 8(2)^3 + 8(2)^2 = 32 - 64 + 32 = 0$
So the yo-yo is released from $s = 0$ when $t = 0$,
and at time $t = 2$, the yo-yo returns to $s = 0$.

b) $\dfrac{ds}{dt} = 8t^3 - 24t^2 + 16t$
At maximum displacement, $\dfrac{ds}{dt} = 0$
$8t^3 - 24t^2 + 16t = 0$
$t^3 - 3t^2 + 2t = 0$
$t(t^2 - 3t + 2) = 0$
$t(t - 1)(t - 2) = 0$
So $t = 0$, $t = 1$ or $t = 2$
Check for negative $\dfrac{d^2s}{dt^2} = 24t^2 - 48t + 16$:
At $t = 0$, $\dfrac{d^2s}{dt^2} = 24(0)^2 - 48(0) + 16$
$= 16 > 0$ (local minimum)
At $t = 1$, $\dfrac{d^2s}{dt^2} = 24(1)^2 - 48(1) + 16$
$= -8 < 0$ (local maximum)
At $t = 2$, $\dfrac{d^2s}{dt^2} = 24(2)^2 - 48(2) + 16$
$= 16 > 0$ (local minimum)
So the maximum displacement must be at time $t = 1$:
$s = 2(1)^4 - 8(1)^3 + 8(1)^2 = 2$
So the maximum displacement (length of the string)
is 2 feet.

Q2 a) $v = t^3 - 6t^2 + 9t \Rightarrow \dfrac{dv}{dt} = 3t^2 - 12t + 9$
At maximum velocity, $\dfrac{dv}{dt} = 0$
$3t^2 - 12t + 9 = 0$
$t^2 - 4t + 3 = 0$
$(t - 1)(t - 3) = 0$
So $t = 1$ or $t = 3$
Check for negative $\dfrac{d^2v}{dt^2} = 6t - 12$:
When $t = 1$, $\dfrac{d^2v}{dt^2} = 6(1) - 12$
$= 6 - 12 = -6 < 0$ (local maximum)
When $t = 3$, $\dfrac{d^2v}{dt^2} = 6(3) - 12$
$= 18 - 12 = 6 > 0$ (local minimum)
So the cat reaches its maximum velocity
at time $t = 1$ s.

b) $s = \int v\, dt = \int (t^3 - 6t^2 + 9t)\, dt$
$= \left(\dfrac{t^4}{4}\right) - 6\left(\dfrac{t^3}{3}\right) + 9\left(\dfrac{t^2}{2}\right) + C$
$= \dfrac{1}{4}t^4 - 2t^3 + \dfrac{9}{2}t^2 + C$
At $t = 0$, $s = 5$: $5 = \dfrac{1}{4}(0)^4 - 2(0)^3 + \dfrac{9}{2}(0)^2 + C$
$C = 5$
Now find s at time $t = 2$:
$s = \dfrac{1}{4}t^4 - 2t^3 + \dfrac{9}{2}t^2 + 5$
$= \dfrac{1}{4}(2)^4 - 2(2)^3 + \dfrac{9}{2}(2)^2 + 5$
$= 4 - 16 + 18 + 5 = 11$ m

Q3 a) $s = 2 + 3t - 2t^2 \Rightarrow v = \dfrac{ds}{dt} = 3 - 4t$

$\dfrac{ds}{dt} = 0 \Rightarrow 3 - 4t = 0 \Rightarrow t = \dfrac{3}{4}$

$\dfrac{d^2s}{dt^2} = -4 < 0$ so $t = \dfrac{3}{4}$ must be a maximum.

At $t = \dfrac{3}{4}$, $s = 2 + 3\left(\dfrac{3}{4}\right) - 2\left(\dfrac{3}{4}\right)^2$

$= 2 + \dfrac{9}{4} - \dfrac{9}{8}$

$= 3\dfrac{1}{8} = 3.125$ m

So the maximum displacement is 3.125 m.

b) $s = t^2 + t^3 - 1.25t^4 \Rightarrow \dfrac{ds}{dt} = 2t + 3t^2 - 5t^3$

$\dfrac{ds}{dt} = 0 \Rightarrow 2t + 3t^2 - 5t^3 = 0$

$-t(5t^2 - 3t - 2) = 0$

$-t(5t + 2)(t - 1) = 0$

So $t = 0$, $t = -0.4$ or $t = 1$

We can ignore $t = -0.4$ as we are only interested in $t \geq 0$. Check for negative $\dfrac{d^2s}{dt^2} = 2 + 6t - 15t^2$:

At $t = 0$, $\dfrac{d^2s}{dt^2} = 2 + 6(0) - 15(0)^2$
$= 2 > 0$ (local minimum)

At $t = 1$, $\dfrac{d^2s}{dt^2} = 2 + 6(1) - 15(1)^2$
$= -7 < 0$ (local maximum)

So the maximum displacement happens at $t = 1$:
$s = 1 + 1 - 1.25(1) = 0.75$ m

c) $s = -3t^4 + 8t^3 - 6t^2 + 16 \Rightarrow \dfrac{ds}{dt} = -12t^3 + 24t^2 - 12t$

$\dfrac{ds}{dt} = 0 \Rightarrow -12t^3 + 24t^2 - 12t = 0$

$t^3 - 2t^2 + t = 0$

$t(t^2 - 2t + 1) = 0$

$t(t - 1)^2 = 0$

So $t = 0$ or $t = 1$

Check for negative $\dfrac{d^2s}{dt^2} = -36t^2 + 48t - 12$

At $t = 0$, $\dfrac{d^2s}{dt^2} = -36(0)^2 + 48(0) - 12$
$= -12 < 0$ (local maximum)

At $t = 1$, $\dfrac{d^2s}{dt^2} = -36(1)^2 + 48(1) - 12$
$= -36 + 48 - 12$
$= 0$ (could be max, min or inflection)

There are two possible local maximums, so check the value of s at both:

At $t = 0$, $s = -3(0)^4 + 8(0)^3 - 6(0)^2 + 16 = 16$ m

At $t = 1$, $s = -3(1)^4 + 8(1)^3 - 6(1)^2 + 16$
$= -3 + 8 - 6 + 16 = 15$ m

So the maximum displacement is 16 m.
It begins at its maximum displacement and moves towards the origin.

Q4 a) $s = 15t + 6t^2 - t^3 \Rightarrow v = \dfrac{ds}{dt} = 15 + 12t - 3t^2$

$\dfrac{dv}{dt} = 12 - 6t$

$\dfrac{dv}{dt} = 0 \Rightarrow 12 - 6t = 0 \Rightarrow t = 2$

$\dfrac{d^2v}{dt^2} = -6 < 0$ so $t = 2$ must give a maximum.

At $t = 2$, $v = 15 + 12(2) - 3(2)^2$
$= 15 + 24 - 12 = 27$

So the maximum velocity is 27 ms⁻¹.

b) $s = \dfrac{-t^5}{20} + \dfrac{t^4}{4} - \dfrac{t^3}{3} + 11t \Rightarrow v = \dfrac{ds}{dt} = -\dfrac{1}{4}t^4 + t^3 - t^2 + 11$

$\dfrac{dv}{dt} = -t^3 + 3t^2 - 2t$

$\dfrac{dv}{dt} = 0 \Rightarrow -t^3 + 3t^2 - 2t = 0$

$-t(t^2 - 3t + 2) = 0$

$-t(t - 1)(t - 2) = 0$

So $t = 0$, $t = 1$ or $t = 2$

Check for negative $\dfrac{d^2v}{dt^2} = -3t^2 + 6t - 2$

At $t = 0$, $\dfrac{d^2v}{dt^2} = -3(0)^2 + 6(0) - 2$
$= -2 < 0$ (local maximum)

At $t = 1$, $\dfrac{d^2v}{dt^2} = -3(1)^2 + 6(1) - 2$
$= 1 > 0$ (local minimum)

At $t = 2$, $\dfrac{d^2v}{dt^2} = -3(2)^2 + 6(2) - 2$
$= -2 < 0$ (local maximum)

There are two possible local maximums, so check the value of s at both.

At $t = 0$, $v = -\dfrac{1}{4}(0) + 0 - 0 + 11 = 11$ ms⁻¹

At $t = 2$, $v = -\dfrac{1}{4}(2)^4 + 2^3 - 2^2 + 11$
$= -4 + 8 - 4 + 11 = 11$ ms⁻¹

So the maximum velocity is 11 ms⁻¹ and it reaches this velocity twice: once at t = O and again at t = 2.

Q5 $s = \dfrac{1}{6}t^4 - 2t^3 + 5t^2 + 2t \Rightarrow v = \dfrac{ds}{dt} = \dfrac{2}{3}t^3 - 6t^2 + 10t + 2$

$\dfrac{dv}{dt} = 2t^2 - 12t + 10$

$\dfrac{dv}{dt} = 0 \Rightarrow 2t^2 - 12t + 10 = 0 \Rightarrow t^2 - 6t + 5 = 0$

$\Rightarrow (t - 1)(t - 5) = 0$

$\Rightarrow t = 1$ or $t = 5$

At $t = 1$, $v = \dfrac{2}{3}(1)^3 - 6(1)^2 + 10(1) + 2$

$= \dfrac{2}{3} - 6 + 10 + 2 = 6.67$ ms⁻¹ (3 s.f.)

At $t = 5$, $v = \dfrac{2}{3}(5)^3 - 6(5)^2 + 10(5) + 2$

$= \dfrac{250}{3} - 150 + 50 + 2 = -14.7$ ms⁻¹ (3 s.f.)

So its greatest speed is 14.7 ms⁻¹ in the negative direction.

Q6 $v = \int a \, dt = \int (6t - 4) \, dt$
$= 3t^2 - 4t + C$

The conditions both involve s, so you can't use them to find the value of C yet. But you can still integrate — just remember that C is a constant.

$s = \int v \, dt = \int (3t^2 - 4t + C) \, dt$
$= t^3 - 2t^2 + Ct + D$, where C and D are constants.

Now use your conditions to find C and D:

At $t = 0$, $s = 0$: $(0)^3 - 2(0)^2 + C(0) + D = 0$
$D = 0$

At $t = 1$, $s = 0$: $(1)^3 - 2(1)^2 + C(1) = 0$
$-1 + C = 0$
$C = 1$

So $s = t^3 - 2t^2 + t$ and $v = 3t^2 - 4t + 1$

The maximum displacement will occur when $v = 0$:

$v = 3t^2 - 4t + 1 = 0 \Rightarrow (3t - 1)(t - 1) = 0 \Rightarrow t = \dfrac{1}{3}$ or $t = 1$

Check for negative $\dfrac{d^2s}{dt^2} = a = 6t - 4$:

At $t = \dfrac{1}{3}$, $a = 6 \times \dfrac{1}{3} - 4 = -2 < 0$ (local maximum)

At $t = 1$, $a = 6 \times 1 - 4 = 2 > 0$ (local minimum)

So the maximum displacement happens at $t = \dfrac{1}{3}$,

and $s = \left(\dfrac{1}{3}\right)^3 - 2\left(\dfrac{1}{3}\right)^2 + \left(\dfrac{1}{3}\right) = \dfrac{4}{27} = 0.148$ m (3 s.f.)

Chapter 20: Forces and Newton's Laws

1. Forces

Exercise 1.1 — Treating forces as vectors

Q1 a) Magnitude = 7 N
Direction $\theta = 0°$

b) Magnitude = $\sqrt{2^2 + 2^2} = \sqrt{8} = 2.83$ N (3 s.f.)
Direction $\theta = \tan^{-1}\left(\frac{2}{2}\right) = \tan^{-1}(1) = 45°$

c) Magnitude = $\sqrt{3^2 + 4^2} = \sqrt{25} = 5$ N
Direction $\theta = \tan^{-1}\left(\frac{4}{3}\right) = 53.1°$ (3 s.f.)

d) Magnitude = $\sqrt{(-3)^2 + 4^2} = \sqrt{25} = 5$ N
Angle above the negative horizontal $\alpha = \tan^{-1}\left(\frac{4}{3}\right)$
$= 53.1...°$
So direction $\theta = 180° - \alpha = 127°$ (3 s.f.)

e) Magnitude = $\sqrt{12^2 + (-5)^2} = \sqrt{169} = 13$ kN
Angle below the positive horizontal $\alpha = \tan^{-1}\left(\frac{5}{12}\right)$
$= 22.6...°$
So direction $\theta = 360° - \alpha = 337°$ (3 s.f.)

f) Magnitude = $\sqrt{(-1)^2 + (-4)^2} = \sqrt{17} = 4.12$ N (3 s.f.)
Angle below the negative horizontal $\alpha = \tan^{-1}\left(\frac{4}{1}\right)$
$= 75.9...°$
So direction $\theta = 180° + \alpha = 256°$ (3 s.f.)

Q2 a) Magnitude = $\sqrt{3^2 + 1^2} = \sqrt{10} = 3.16$ N (3 s.f.)
Direction $\theta = \tan^{-1}\left(\frac{1}{3}\right) = 18.4°$ (3 s.f.)

b) Magnitude = $\sqrt{(-4)^2 + (-2)^2} = \sqrt{20} = 4.47$ N (3 s.f.)
Angle below the negative horizontal $\alpha = \tan^{-1}\left(\frac{2}{4}\right)$
$= 26.5...°$
So direction $\theta = 180° + \alpha = 207°$ (3 s.f.)

c) Magnitude = $\sqrt{12^2 + (-3)^2} = \sqrt{153} = 12.4$ N (3 s.f.)
Angle below the positive horizontal $\alpha = \tan^{-1}\left(\frac{3}{12}\right)$
$= 14.0...°$
So direction $\theta = 360° - \alpha = 346°$ (3 s.f.)

d) Magnitude = $\sqrt{(-0.5)^2 + 0.5^2} = 0.707$ kN (3 s.f.)
Angle above the negative horizontal $\alpha = \tan^{-1}\left(\frac{0.5}{0.5}\right)$
$= 45°$
So direction $\theta = 180° - \alpha = 135°$

e) Magnitude = 11 N
Direction $\theta = 270°$

f) Magnitude = $\sqrt{15^2 + 25^2} = \sqrt{850} = 29.2$ kN (3 s.f.)
Direction $\theta = \tan^{-1}\left(\frac{25}{15}\right) = 59.0°$ (3 s.f.)

Q3

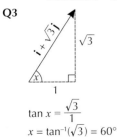

$\tan x = \frac{\sqrt{3}}{1}$
$x = \tan^{-1}(\sqrt{3}) = 60°$

Q4 Magnitude = $\sqrt{(56a)^2 + (-42a)^2} = \sqrt{4900a^2} = 70a$
$70a = 35 \implies a = 0.5$

Q5

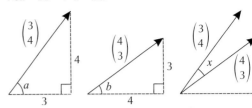

$a = \tan^{-1}\left(\frac{4}{3}\right) = 53.13...°$ $b = \tan^{-1}\left(\frac{3}{4}\right) = 36.86...°$
So the angle between the two forces
$x = a - b = 16.3°$ (to 3 s.f.)
You could also have used the method for finding the angle between two vectors from page 212.

Exercise 1.2 — Resultant forces and equilibrium

Q1 Since the object is in equilibrium, there is no resultant force.
Resolving vertically ($\uparrow$): $T - 8 = 0 \implies T = 8$ N

Q2 To find the resultant, add the components:
$(8\mathbf{i} + 5\mathbf{j}) + (3\mathbf{i} - 2\mathbf{j}) = (8 + 3)\mathbf{i} + (5 - 2)\mathbf{j} = 11\mathbf{i} + 3\mathbf{j}$

Q3 Resultant force = $(200 - 30)\mathbf{i} + ((-100) + (-50))\mathbf{j}$
$= 170\mathbf{i} - 150\mathbf{j}$

Q4 Since the object is in equilibrium, the resultant force has $\mathbf{i}$ and $\mathbf{j}$ components of zero.
Resolving in the $\mathbf{i}$ direction:
$3 + x - 5 = 0 \implies x = 2$

Q5 a)

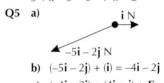

b) $(-5\mathbf{i} - 2\mathbf{j}) + (\mathbf{i}) = -4\mathbf{i} - 2\mathbf{j}$

c) $(-4\mathbf{i} - 2\mathbf{j}) + (4\mathbf{i} + \mathbf{j}) + \mathbf{F} = 0$
$-\mathbf{j} + \mathbf{F} = 0 \implies \mathbf{F} = \mathbf{j}$ N

2. Newton's Laws of Motion

Exercise 2.1 — Using Newton's laws

Q1 $F_{net} = ma$
$F_{net} = 15 \times 4 = 60$ N

Q2 a) $F_{net} = ma$
$10 = 5a \implies a = 2$ ms^{-2}

b) Use a constant acceleration equation.
$u = 0, v = v, a = 2, t = 8$
$v = u + at$
$v = 0 + (2 \times 8) = 16$ ms^{-1}

Q3

Resolving vertically ($\uparrow$):
$F_{net} = ma$
$T - 18g = 18 \times 0.4$
$T = 7.2 + 176.4 = 183.6$ N

Q4 a) $F_{net} = ma$
$18 = 5m \implies m = 18 \div 5 = 3.6$ kg

b) $u = 0$, $v = v$, $a = 5$, $t = 4$
$v = u + at$
$v = 0 + (5 \times 4) = 20$ ms^{-1}

c) $R - mg = 0 \Rightarrow R = 3.6 \times 9.8 = 35.28$ N

Q5 a) $u = 0$, $v = 2.5$, $a = a$, $t = 4$
$v = u + at$
$2.5 = 0 + 4a \Rightarrow a = 0.625$ ms^{-2}

b)

55g 120 N

Resolving vertically ($\uparrow$):
$F_{net} = ma$
$T - 120 - 55g = 55 \times 0.625$
$T = 34.375 + 120 + 539 = 693$ N (3 s.f.)

Q6

▲ 1.5 N

a ▼

▼ 0.3g

Resolving vertically ($\downarrow$):
$0.3g - 1.5 = 0.3a$
$a = 1.44 \div 0.3 = 4.8$ ms^{-2}
$u = 0$, $a = 4.8$, $s = s$, $t = 12$
$s = ut + \frac{1}{2}at^2$
$s = 0 + \left(\frac{1}{2} \times 4.8 \times 12^2\right) = 345.6$ m

Remember that if something is dropped, its initial velocity is zero.

Q7 a) $F_{net} = ma$
$8\mathbf{i} - 2\mathbf{j} = 10\mathbf{a}$
$\mathbf{a} = 0.8\mathbf{i} - 0.2\mathbf{j}$

b) $|\mathbf{a}| = \sqrt{0.8^2 + (-0.2)^2} = 0.8246...$
$= 0.825$ ms^{-2} (3 s.f.)

c) $u = 0$, $v = v$, $a = 0.8246...$, $t = 6$
$v = u + at$
$v = 0 + (0.8246... \times 6) = 4.947... = 4.95$ ms^{-1} (3 s.f.)

Q8 $\mathbf{u} = (0\mathbf{i} + 0\mathbf{j})$, $\mathbf{v} = (32\mathbf{i} + 24\mathbf{j})$, $\mathbf{a} = a$, $t = 2$
$\mathbf{v} = \mathbf{u} + \mathbf{a}t$
$(32\mathbf{i} + 24\mathbf{j}) = (0\mathbf{i} + 0\mathbf{j}) + 2\mathbf{a}$
$\Rightarrow \mathbf{a} = (16\mathbf{i} + 12\mathbf{j})$ ms^{-2}
$F_{net} = ma$
$(8\mathbf{i} + 6\mathbf{j}) = m(16\mathbf{i} + 12\mathbf{j})$
i: $8 = 16m \Rightarrow m = 8 \div 16 = 0.5$ kg
Check with **j:** $6 = 12m \Rightarrow m = 6 \div 12 = 0.5$ kg

Q9 a) $\mathbf{u} = (0\mathbf{i} + 0\mathbf{j})$, $\mathbf{v} = (30\mathbf{i} + 20\mathbf{j})$, $\mathbf{a} = a$, $t = 10$
$\mathbf{v} = \mathbf{u} + \mathbf{a}t$
$(30\mathbf{i} + 20\mathbf{j}) = (0\mathbf{i} + 0\mathbf{j}) + 10\mathbf{a}$
$\Rightarrow \mathbf{a} = (3\mathbf{i} + 2\mathbf{j})$ ms^{-2}
$F_{net} = ma = 2(3\mathbf{i} + 2\mathbf{j})$
$= (6\mathbf{i} + 4\mathbf{j})$ N

b) $(10\mathbf{i} - 3\mathbf{j}) + x = 6\mathbf{i} + 4\mathbf{j}$
$x = (6 - 10)\mathbf{i} + (4 + 3)\mathbf{j}$
$= (-4\mathbf{i} + 7\mathbf{j})$ N
$|x| = \sqrt{(-4)^2 + 7^2} = 8.062... = 8.06$ N (3 s.f.)

Exercise 2.2 — Connected particles

Q1 a)

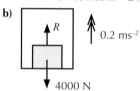

4000 N
2000g

$W = mg$
$4000 = m \times 9.8 \Rightarrow m = 408.16...$ kg
Resolving vertically ($\uparrow$) for the whole system:
$F_{net} = ma$
$T - 2000g - 4000 = (2000 + 408.16...) \times 0.2$
$T = 481.63... + 19\,600 + 4000$
$\Rightarrow T = 24\,081.63... = 24\,100$ N (3 s.f.)

b)

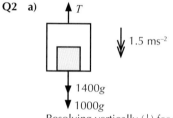

4000 N
Resolving vertically ($\uparrow$) for the load:
$F_{net} = ma$
$R - 4000 = (4000 \div 9.8) \times 0.2$
$\Rightarrow R = 4081.63... = 4080$ N (3 s.f.)

Q2 a)

T

1.5 ms^{-2}

1400g
1000g
Resolving vertically ($\downarrow$) for whole system:
$2400g - T = 2400 \times 1.5 \Rightarrow T = 19\,920$ N

b)

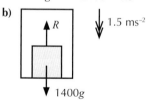

1.5 ms^{-2}

1400g
Resolving vertically ($\downarrow$) for the load:
$1400g - R = 1400 \times 1.5 \Rightarrow R = 11\,620$ N

c) The lift is now falling freely under gravity, so $a = g$:
$u = 0$, $v = v$, $a = 9.8$, $s = 30$
$v^2 = u^2 + 2as$
$v^2 = 2 \times 9.8 \times 30 = 588$
$v = 24.2$ ms^{-1} (3 s.f.)

Q3 a) Resolving horizontally for the whole system, taking the direction of acceleration as positive:
$F_{net} = ma$
$P = 3500 \times 0.3 = 1050$ N
The tractor and trailer are decelerating, so the acceleration (and the force P) are in the opposite direction to the motion of the system.

b) Resolving horizontally for the trailer:
$F_{net} = ma$
$T = 1500 \times 0.3 = 450$ N

c) E.g. The tractor and trailer are modelled as particles, there are no external forces (e.g. air resistance) acting, the coupling is horizontal, the braking force generated by the tractor is constant, the tractor and trailer are moving in a straight line on horizontal ground.

Q4 a)

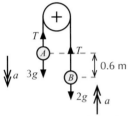

Resolving horizontally ($\rightarrow$) for the whole system:
$F_{net} = ma$
$P - 500 - 600 = 2000 \times 0.2 \Rightarrow P = 1500$ N

b) Resolving horizontally ($\rightarrow$) for the caravan:
$T - 500 = 800 \times 0.2 \Rightarrow T = 660$ N

c) $F_{net} = ma$
$-500 = 800a \Rightarrow a = -0.625$ ms^{-2}
$u = 20, v = 0, a = -0.625, t = t$
$v = u + at$
$0 = 20 - 0.625t \Rightarrow t = 32$ s

Exercise 2.3 — Pegs and pulleys

Q1 a)

b) Resolving vertically ($\downarrow$) for A:
$F_{net} = ma$
$3g - T = 3a$ ①
Resolving vertically ($\uparrow$) for B:
$F_{net} = ma$
$T - 2g = 2a$ ②
① + ②:
$g = 5a \Rightarrow a = 9.8 \div 5 = 1.96$ ms^{-2}
The particles will become level when they have each moved 0.3 m.
$u = 0, a = 1.96, s = 0.3, t = t$
$s = ut + \frac{1}{2}at^2$
$0.3 = \frac{1}{2} \times 1.96 \times t^2$
$t^2 = 0.306... \Rightarrow t = 0.5532... = 0.553$ s (3 s.f.)

Q2 a) $u = 0, a = a, s = 5, t = 2$
$s = ut + \frac{1}{2}at^2$
$5 = \frac{1}{2} \times a \times 2^2 \Rightarrow a = 5 \div 2 = 2.5$ ms^{-2}
Resolving vertically ($\downarrow$) for A:
$F_{net} = ma$
$35g - T = 35 \times 2.5 \Rightarrow T = 343 - 87.5 = 255.5$ N

b) Resolving vertically ($\uparrow$) for B:
$F_{net} = ma$
$T - Mg = 2.5M$
$255.5 = 12.3M \Rightarrow M = 20.8$ kg (3 s.f.)

Q3 a) Resolving horizontally ($\rightarrow$) for A:
$F_{net} = ma$
$T = 5a$ ①
Resolving vertically ($\downarrow$) for B:
$7g - T = 7a$ ②
Substituting ① into ②:
$7g - 5a = 7a$
$7g = 12a$
$a = 7g \div 12 = 5.716... = 5.72$ ms^{-2} (3 s.f.)

b) Using ①:
$T = 5a = 5 \times 5.716... = 28.583... = 28.6$ N (3 s.f.)

c) String is light and inextensible, pulley is fixed and smooth, horizontal surface is smooth, no other external forces are acting, A doesn't hit the pulley, B doesn't hit the floor, string doesn't break, pulley doesn't break, string between A and the pulley is horizontal, string is initially taut, acceleration due to gravity is constant at 9.8 ms^{-2}.

Q4 a)

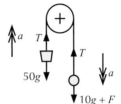

b) First find the acceleration.
$u = 0, s = 12, a = a, t = 20$
$s = ut + \frac{1}{2}at^2$
$12 = \frac{1}{2} \times a \times 20^2 \Rightarrow a = 0.06$ ms^{-2}
Now resolving vertically ($\uparrow$) for the bucket:
$F_{net} = ma$
$T - 50g = 50 \times 0.06 \Rightarrow T = 493$ N

c) Resolving vertically ($\downarrow$) for the counterweight:
$F_{net} = ma$
$10g + F - T = 10 \times 0.06$
$\Rightarrow F = 0.6 - 98 + 493 = 395.6$ N

d)

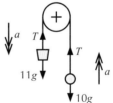

Resolving vertically ($\downarrow$) for the bucket:
$11g - T = 11a$ ①
Resolving vertically ($\uparrow$) for the counterweight:
$T - 10g = 10a$ ②
① + ②:
$g = 21a \Rightarrow a = 0.466...$ ms^{-2}
$u = 0, v = v, s = 12$
$v^2 = u^2 + 2as$
$v^2 = 2 \times 0.466... \times 12 = 11.2 \Rightarrow v = 3.35$ ms^{-1} (3 s.f.)

Q5 a) A has a greater mass than B, so A will accelerate downwards and B will accelerate upwards.

Resolving vertically ($\downarrow$) for A:

$15g - T = 15a$ ①

Resolving vertically ($\uparrow$) for B:

$T - 12g = 12a$ ②

①+②:

$3g = 27a \Rightarrow a = 1.088... = 1.09$ ms^{-2} (3 s.f.)

b) The force exerted on the pulley by the string is $2T$. Using ②:

$T = 12a + 12g = (12 \times 1.088...) + (12 \times 9.8)$

$T = 130.66...$

So $2T = 261.33... = 261$ N (3 s.f.)

c) First find the speed of the particles when A hits the ground:

$u = 0,\ v = v,\ a = 1.088...,\ s = 6$

$v^2 = u^2 + 2as$

$v^2 = 2 \times 1.088... \times 6 = 13.066... \Rightarrow v = 3.614...$

Now considering the motion of B as it moves freely under gravity, taking upwards as positive:

$u = 3.614...,\ v = 0,\ a = -9.8,\ t = t$

$v = u + at$

$0 = 3.614... - 9.8t \Rightarrow t = 0.368... = 0.369$ s (3 s.f.)

Q6 Split the motion into two parts. The first part is from the particles being released to P striking the pulley.

Resolving vertically ($\downarrow$) for Q:

$F_{net} = ma$

$10g - T = 10a$ ①

Resolving horizontally ($\rightarrow$) for P:

$F_{net} = ma$

$T = 8a$ ②

Substituting ② into ①:

$10g - 8a = 10a$

$10g = 18a \Rightarrow a = 5.444...$

Use this to find the time between the point that the particles are released and the point that P hits the pulley:

$u = 0,\ a = 5.444...,\ s = 4,\ t = t$

$s = ut + \frac{1}{2}at^2$

$4 = \frac{1}{2} \times 5.444... \times t^2$

$t^2 = 1.469... \Rightarrow t = 1.212...$

Also find the speed of the particles at this point:

$v = u + at$

$v = 0 + (5.444... \times 1.212...) = 6.599...$

Now consider the second part of the motion — Q falling freely under gravity:

$u = 6.599...,\ a = 9.8,\ s = 9 - 4 = 5,\ t = t$

$s = ut + \frac{1}{2}at^2$

$5 = (6.599...)t + 4.9t^2$

$4.9t^2 + (6.599...)t - 5 = 0$

Using the quadratic formula:

$$t = \frac{-6.599... \pm \sqrt{(6.599...)^2 - (4 \times 4.9 \times -5)}}{9.8}$$

So $t = 0.540...$ or $t = -1.887...$

t must be positive, so take $t = 0.540...$

So the total time taken is:

$1.212... + 0.540... = 1.752...$

$= 1.75$ s (3 s.f.)

Exercise 2.4 — Harder problems involving pegs and pulleys

Q1 a) Resolving horizontally ($\leftarrow$) for A:

$T - F = 6a \Rightarrow 6a = 12 - 10 = 2$

$\qquad\qquad a = 2 \div 6 = 0.333$ ms^{-2} (3 s.f.)

b) Resolving vertically ($\downarrow$) for B:

$Mg - T = Ma \Rightarrow Mg - Ma = 12$

$\qquad\qquad M(9.8 - 0.333...) = 12$

$\qquad\qquad M = 12 \div 9.466... = 1.27$ kg (3 s.f.)

Q2 a) $u = 0,\ v = 3,\ a = a,\ t = 5$

$v = u + at \Rightarrow 3 = 0 + 5a \Rightarrow a = 0.6$ ms^{-2}

Resolving vertically ($\uparrow$) for the crate:

$T - 250g = 250a \Rightarrow T = 250 \times 0.6 + 250 \times 9.8$

$\qquad\qquad\qquad = 150 + 2450 = 2600$ N

Resolving horizontally ($\leftarrow$) for the truck:

$D - T - F = 4000a \Rightarrow D = 4000 \times 0.6 + 2600 + 500$

$\qquad\qquad\qquad\qquad = 2400 + 3100 = 5500$ N

b) Resolving horizontally again ($\leftarrow$) for the truck:

$5500 - 500 = 4000a \Rightarrow a = 5000 \div 4000$

$\qquad\qquad\qquad\qquad = 1.25$ ms^{-2}

c) Take upwards ($\uparrow$) as the positive direction.

Find the height that the crate reaches before the rope snaps (i.e. its displacement during the first 5 seconds):

$s = s,\ u = 0,\ v = 3,\ a = 0.6,\ t = 5$

$s = \frac{1}{2}(u + v)t = 0.5 \times 3 \times 5 = 7.5$ m

You could've used one of the other suvat equations to find s.

After the rope snaps:

$s = -7.5,\ u = 3,\ a = -9.8,\ t = t$

$s = ut + \frac{1}{2}at^2 \Rightarrow -7.5 = 3t - 4.9t^2$

$\qquad\qquad\qquad\quad 4.9t^2 - 3t - 7.5 = 0$

Using the quadratic formula:

$$t = \frac{3 \pm \sqrt{(-3)^2 - (4 \times 4.9 \times (-7.5))}}{9.8}$$

$$= \frac{3 \pm \sqrt{9 + 147}}{9.8}$$

$t = -0.9683...$ ($t < 0$ so ignore) or $t = 1.5806...$

So the crate hits the ground 1.58 seconds (to 3 s.f.) after the rope snaps.

d) Some possible answers include:
- The pulley is assumed to be smooth, which is likely to be inaccurate. The model could be improved by accounting for the friction in the pulley.
- The driving force and the resistance force are given as constant, but it would be more accurate to assume that they vary with time and include that in the model.
- The falling crate would experience air resistance as it fell, so if the model were updated to include that, it would be more realistic.

Glossary

A

Acceleration
The rate of change of an object's **velocity** with respect to time.

Addition law
A **formula** linking the probability of two **events** both happening and the probability that at least one of them happens.

Algebraic division
Dividing one **algebraic expression** by another.

Algebraic expression
An **expression** which contains **constants** and / or **variables**.

Alternative hypothesis
The statement that you will accept instead if you decide to reject the **null hypothesis** in a **hypothesis test.** It gives a range of values for the **parameter** and is usually written H_1.

Assumption
A simplification of a real-life situation used in a **model**.

Asymptote
A line which a curve gets infinitely closer to, but never touches.

B

Base units
The basic **S.I. units** of measurement, which can be used to derive all other S.I. units.

Beam
A long, **thin**, straight body.

Bearing
A direction, given as an angle measured clockwise from north.

Biased sample
A **sample** which does not fairly represent the **population** it is taken from.

Binomial
A **polynomial** with only two terms e.g. $a + bx$.

Binomial coefficient
The number of orders in which x objects of one type and $(n - x)$ objects of a different type can be arranged.

Equal to $\binom{n}{x} = \dfrac{n!}{x!(n-x)!}$

Binomial distribution B(n, p)
A discrete **probability distribution** modelling the number of successes x in n independent trials when the probability of success in each trial is p.

Binomial expansion
The result of expanding a **binomial** raised to a power — e.g. $(a + bx)^n$.

Binomial formula
A formula which describes the general terms of a **binomial expansion**.

Bivariate data
Data that comes as an ordered pair of **variables** (x, y).

Boxplot
A diagram showing the **median**, **quartiles** and greatest/least values of a data set, as well as any **outliers**.

C

Census
A **survey** in which information is collected from every single member of the **population**.

Chord
A line joining two points which lie on the circumference of a circle.

Coding
Coding means transforming all the readings in a data set to make the numbers easier to work with.

Coefficient
The **constant** multiplying the **variable**(s) in an algebraic **term** e.g. 4 in the term $4x^2y$.

Collinear points
Three or more points are collinear if they all lie on the same straight line.

Common denominator
A denominator (i.e. bottom of a fraction) which is shared by all fractions in an **expression**.

Common factor
A factor which is shared by all the **terms** in an **expression**.

Complement (of an event A)
The group of all **outcomes** corresponding to event A not happening.

Completing the square
Rewriting a **quadratic** function as: $p(x + q)^2 + r$. Useful for solving equations or sketching curves.

Component
The effect of a **vector** in a given direction.

Compression
The **force** in a compressed **rod**. Another word for **thrust**.

Constant
A fixed numerical value in an **expression**.

Constant of integration
A constant term coming from an indefinite **integration** representing any number.

Correlation
A linear relationship between two **variables** showing that they change together to some extent.
(A correlation does not necessarily mean a causal relationship.)

Cosine rule
A rule for finding the missing sides or angles in a triangle when you know all of the sides, or two sides and the angle between them.

Critical region
The set of all values of the **test statistic** that would cause you to reject the **null hypothesis**.

Critical value
The value of the **test statistic** at the edge of the **critical region**.

Cubic equation
An **equation** that can be written $ax^3 + bx^2 + cx + d = 0$ (where $a \neq 0$).

Cumulative distribution function
A function, F(x), which gives the probability that a **random variable**, X, will be less than or equal to a particular value, x.

Cumulative frequency
The total frequency for all the classes in a data set up to and including a given class.

Cumulative frequency diagram
A graph plotting **cumulative frequency** of a data set.

Deceleration
An **acceleration** where the object's **speed** is decreasing.

Decreasing function
A function for which the **gradient** is always less than zero.

Definite integral
An **integral** which is evaluated over an interval given by two **limits**, representing the area under the curve between those limits.

Dependent variable
Another name for the **response variable**.

Derivative
The result you get when you **differentiate** something.

Derived units
Units of measurement which can be made by combining S.I. **base units**.

Differentiation
A method of finding the rate of change of a function with respect to a variable.
$\frac{dy}{dx}$ is 'derivative of y with respect to x'

Direct proportion
A relationship between two variables where multiplying one of them by any **constant** has the same effect on the other one.

Discrete random variable
A **random variable** with 'gaps' between its possible values.

Discriminant
The discriminant of a **quadratic** function $ax^2 + bx + c$ is the value of $b^2 - 4ac$.

Dispersion
Measures of dispersion describe how spread out data values are.

Displacement
A **vector** measurement of an object's distance from a particular point.

Disproof by counter-example
Finding one example of where a statement doesn't hold, hence showing that it is false.

Divisor
The number or expression you're dividing by in a division.

e
An **irrational number** for which the gradient of $y = e^x$ is equal to e^x.

Elimination
Method for solving linear **simultaneous equations**, by matching coefficients and then eliminating a variable.

Equation
A mathematical statement containing an '=' sign and at least one **variable** or **constant**.

Equilibrium
A state where there is no **resultant force** acting on a body, hence the body is at **rest** (or moving with constant **velocity**).

Event
An event is a 'group' of one or more possible **outcomes**.

Explanatory variable
In an experiment, the **variable** you can control, or the one that you think is affecting the other.

Exponential decay
Exponential decay happens when the rate of decay gets slower and slower as the amount gets smaller (negative **exponential growth**).

Exponential function
A function of the form $y = a^x$. $y = e^x$ is known as 'the' exponential function.

Exponential growth
Exponential growth happens when the rate of growth gets faster and faster as the amount gets bigger.

Expression
Any combination of numbers, variables, **functions** and operations ($+$, $-$, $\times$, $\div$ etc.) Unlike an **equation**, it doesn't have an equals sign.

Extrapolation
Predicting a value of y corresponding to a value of x outside the range for which you have data.

f'(x)
The **derivative** of f(x) with respect to x.

f''(x)
The **second order derivative** of f(x) with respect to x.

Factor
A factor of a **term** or **expression** is something which divides into it.

Factorial
n factorial, written $n!$, is the product of all **integers** from 1 to n.
So $n! = 1 \times 2 \times ... \times n$.

Factorising
The opposite of multiplying out brackets. Brackets are put in to write an expression as a product of its **factors**.

Factor Theorem
An extension of the **Remainder Theorem** that helps you factorise a polynomial. If f(a) = 0 then ($x - a$) is a **factor** of f(x).

Fence
If a data value lies outside a fence, then it is an **outlier**.

Finite population
A **population** for which it is possible and practical to count the members.

Force
An influence which can change the motion of a body (i.e. cause an **acceleration**).

Formula
A standard **equation** used to calculate a quantity or measure, e.g. volume.

Frequency density
The frequency of a class divided by its class width.

Friction
A frictional force is a resistive **force** due to **roughness** between a body and surface. It always acts against motion, or likely motion.

Function
A function gives different 'outputs' for different 'inputs'. They are usually defined by an **algebraic expression** — plugging in different input values for the **variable** produces different output values.

Function notation f(x)
Standard way of referring to **functions**. E.g. function g defined by $g(x) = x^2 + 5$.

Fundamental Theorem of Calculus
The fact that if differentiating takes you from one function to another, then integrating the second function will take you back to the first (with a constant of integration).
Written algebraically, this is:
$$\int f(x)\,dx = F(x) + C \iff f(x) = \frac{d}{dx}(F(x))$$

g
Acceleration due to gravity.
g is usually assumed to be 9.8 ms⁻².

Gradient
A number representing the steepness of a straight line or of a curve at a given point.

Gradient function
A **function** that can be used to find the **gradient** at any point on a curve.

Histogram
A diagram showing the frequencies with which a continuous variable falls in particular classes — the frequency of a class is proportional to the area of a bar.

Hypothesis
A statement that you want to test.

Hypothesis test
A method of testing a **hypothesis** using observed **sample** data.

i unit vector
The standard horizontal **unit vector** (i.e. along the x-axis).

Identity
An **equation** that is true for all values of the **variable**, denoted by the '≡' sign.

Increasing function
A function for which the **gradient** is always greater than zero.

Indefinite integral
An integral which includes a **constant of integration** that comes from integrating without **limits**.

Independent events
If the probability of an **event** B happening doesn't depend on whether or not an event A happens, events A and B are independent.

Independent variable
Another name for the **explanatory variable**.

Index
For a^n, n is the index and is often referred to as a **power**.

Inequality
An **expression** which contains one of the following symbols: >, <, ≥, ≤. Like an equation, but produces a range of solutions.

Inextensible
Describes a body which can't be stretched. (Usually a **string** or **wire**.)

Infinite population
A **population** for which it is impossible or impractical to count the members.

Integer
A positive or negative whole number (including 0).

Integral
The result you get when you **integrate** something.

Integration
Process for finding a function, given its **derivative** — the opposite of **differentiation**.

Intercept
The coordinates at which the graph of a function crosses one of the axes.

Interpercentile range
The difference between the values of two given **percentiles**.

Interpolation
Predicting a value of y corresponding to a value of x within the range for which you have data.

Interquartile range
A measure of **dispersion**. It's the difference between the **upper quartile** and the **lower quartile**.

Inverse function
An inverse function, e.g. $f^{-1}(x)$, reverses the effect of the function $f(x)$.

Inverse proportion
A relationship between two variables where multiplying one of them by any **constant** causes the other to be divided by the same constant.

Irrational number
A number that can't be expressed as the quotient (division) of two **integers**. Examples include **surds**, **e** and π.

j unit vector
The standard vertical **unit vector** (i.e. along the y-axis).

Kinematics
The study of the motion of objects.

Light
Describes a body which is modelled as having no mass.

Limits (integration)
The numbers between which you integrate to find a **definite integral**.

Linear factor
A **factor** of an algebraic expression of **degree** 1 — e.g. $ax + b$.

Linear inequality
An inequality that can be written as $ax + b > cx + d$.

Linear interpolation
Method of estimating the **median**, **quartiles** or **percentiles** of a grouped data set by assuming the readings within each class are evenly spread.

Linear regression
A method for finding the equation of a line of best fit on a **scatter diagram**.

Location
Measures of location show where the 'centre' of the data lies.

Logarithm
The logarithm to the base a of a number x (written $\log_a x$) is the **power** to which a must be raised to give that number.

Lower quartile
The value that 25% of data values in a data set are less than or equal to.

M

Magnitude
The size of a quantity. The magnitude of a **vector** is the distance between its start point and end point.

Maximum
The highest point on a graph, or on a section of a graph (this is a local maximum).

Mean
A measure of **location** — it's the sum of a set of data values, divided by the number of data values.

Median
A measure of **location** — it's the value in the middle of the data set when all the data values are in order of size.

Minimum
The lowest point on a graph or on a section of a graph (this is a local minimum).

Mode
A measure of **location** — it's the most frequently occurring data value.

Model
A mathematical description of a real-life situation, in which certain **assumptions** are made about the situation.

Mode of a discrete random variable
The value that the **random variable** is most likely to take — i.e. the one with the highest probability.

Modulus
The modulus of a number is its positive numerical value.
The modulus of a function, f(x), makes every value of f(x) positive by removing any minus signs.
The modulus of a **vector** is the same as its **magnitude**.

Mutually exclusive
Events are mutually exclusive (or just 'exclusive') if they have no **outcomes** in common, and so can't happen at the same time.

N

Natural logarithm
The **inverse function** of e^x, written as $\ln x$ or $\log_e x$.

^nC_r
The **binomial coefficient** of x^r in the **binomial expansion** of $(1 + x)^n$.
Also written $\binom{n}{r}$.

Normal
A straight line passing through a curve that is perpendicular (at right angles) to the curve at the point where it crosses the curve.

Normal reaction
The reaction **force** from a surface acting on an object. Acts at 90° to the surface.

Null hypothesis
A statement which gives a specific value to the **parameter** in a **hypothesis test**. Usually written H_0.

O

One-tailed test
A **hypothesis test** is 'one-tailed' if the **alternative hypothesis** is specific about whether the **parameter** is greater or less than the value specified by the **null hypothesis**.
E.g. it says $p < a$ or $p > a$ for a parameter p and constant a.

Opportunity sampling
A method of selecting a **sample** from a **population** in which a sample is selected at a time and place which is convenient for the sampler. Also known as convenience sampling.

Outcome
One of the possible results of a **trial** or experiment.

Outlier
A freak piece of data lying a long way from the majority of the values in a data set.

P

Parameter (statistics)
A quantity that describes a characteristic of a **population**.

Particle
A body whose mass is considered to act at a single point, so its dimensions don't matter.

Pascal's triangle
A triangle of numbers showing the **binomial coefficients**. Each term is the sum of the two above it.

Peg
A fixed support which a body can hang from or rest on.

Percentiles
The percentiles (P_1-P_{99}) divide an ordered data set into 100 parts.

Plane
A flat surface.

Point of inflection
A **stationary point** on a graph where the **gradient** doesn't change sign on either side of the point.

Polynomial
An algebraic expression made up of the sum of constant terms and variables raised to positive **integer** powers.

Population
The whole group of every single thing (person, animal, item etc.) that you want to investigate in a statistical test.

Position vector
The position of a point relative to a fixed origin, O, given in **vector** form.

Power
Another word for **index**.

Probability distribution for a discrete random variable
A table showing all the possible values that a **random variable** can take, plus the probability that it takes each value.

Probability function
A function that generates the probabilities of a **discrete random variable** taking each of its possible values.

Proof
Using mathematical arguments to show that a statement is true or false.

Proof by deduction
Using known facts to build up an argument to prove that a statement is true or false.

Proof by exhaustion
Splitting a situation into separate cases that cover all possible scenarios, then showing that the statement is true for each case, hence true overall.

Pulley
A wheel, usually modelled as fixed and **smooth**, over which a **string** passes.

Quadratic equation
An **equation** that can be written $ax^2 + bx + c = 0$ where $a \neq 0$.

Quadratic formula
A formula for solving a **quadratic equation** $ax^2 + bx + c = 0$ given by $x = \dfrac{-b \pm \sqrt{b^2 - 4ac}}{2a}$.

Quadratic inequality
An **inequality** that can be written as $ax^2 + bx + c \geq 0$, where $a \neq 0$. It can be solved by looking at the shape of the quadratic graph.

Qualitative variable
A **variable** that takes non-numerical values.

Quantitative variable
A **variable** that takes numerical values.

Quartiles
The three quartiles Q_1, Q_2 and Q_3 divide an ordered data set into four parts.

Quota sampling
A method of selecting a **sample** from a **population** by dividing it into categories and sampling a set number of individuals from each category, but not selecting them at random.

Random variable
A **variable** taking different values with different probabilities.

Range
A measure of **dispersion**. It's the difference between the highest value and the lowest value.

Rationalising the denominator
The process of removing **surds** from the denominator of a fraction.

Rational number
A number that can be written as the quotient (division) of two **integers**, where the denominator is non-zero.

Reciprocal function
A function of the form $y = \dfrac{k}{x^n}$ $(n > 0)$, where k is a constant.

Remainder
The expression that is left over following an **algebraic division** and that has a **degree** lower than the **divisor**.

Remainder Theorem
A method used to work out the remainder from an **algebraic division**, but without actually having to do the division. The **remainder** when f(x) is divided by $(x - a)$ is f(a).

Repeated root
If a quadratic (or cubic or quartic) when **factorised** has the same factor twice (or three times), this gives a repeated **root**.

Resistance
A **force** acting in the opposite direction to the movement of an object.

Resolving
Splitting a **vector** up into **components**.

Response variable
In an experiment, the **variable** you think is being affected.

Rest
Describes a body which is not moving. Often used to describe the initial state of a body.

Resultant (force or vector)
The single **force/vector** which has the same effect as two or more forces/vectors added together.

Rigid
Describes a body which does not bend.

Rod
A long, **thin**, straight, **rigid** body.

Root
The roots of a function f(x) are the values of x where f(x) = 0.

Rough
Describes a surface for which a **frictional force** will oppose the motion of a body in contact with the surface.

S.I. Units
System of measurements based on fixed scientific constants.

Sample
A selection of members from a **population**. Information from the sample is used to deduce information about the population as a whole.

Sample space
The set of all possible **outcomes** of a **trial**.

Scalar
A quantity which has a **magnitude** but not a direction.

Scatter diagram
Graph showing the two **variables** in a **bivariate** data set plotted against each other.

Second order derivative
The result of **differentiating** a function twice — it tells you the rate of change of the gradient of a function.
$\dfrac{d^2 y}{dx^2}$ means 'second order derivative of y with respect to x'.

Set
A collection of objects or numbers (called elements).

Significance level (α)
Determines how unlikely the observed value of the **test statistic** needs to be (under H_0) before rejecting the **null hypothesis** in a **hypothesis test**.

Significant result
The observed value of a **test statistic** is significant if, under H_0, it has a probability lower than the **significance level**.

Simple random sampling
A method of selecting a **sample** from a **population** in which every member is equally likely to be chosen and each selection is independent of every other selection.

Simultaneous equations
A set of **equations** containing two or more unknown quantities, often x and y, for which the same set of values satisfy each equation.

Sine rule
A rule for finding missing sides or angles in a triangle. It can be used if you know any two angles and a side, and in some cases, if you know two sides and an angle that isn't between them.

Smooth
Describes a surface for which there is no **friction** between the surface and a body in contact with it.

Solution
The value or values (usually of a **variable**) that satisfy a problem, e.g. an **equation** or **inequality**.

Speed
The **magnitude** of an object's **velocity**.

Standard deviation
A measure of **dispersion** calculated by taking the square root of the **variance**.

Static
Describes a body which is not moving. Often used to describe a body in **equilibrium**.

Stationary point
A point on a curve where the **gradient** is zero.

Statistic
A quantity that is calculated using only known observations from a **sample**.

Stratified sampling
A method of selecting a random **sample** from a **population** in which the population is divided into categories and the proportions of each category in the population are matched in the sample.

String
A **thin** body, usually modelled as being **light** and **inextensible**.

Substitution
Method for solving **simultaneous equations**, where you replace each occurrence of one unknown with an **expression** in terms of the other unknown.

Surd
A number that can only be expressed precisely by using a square root sign.

Survey
A way of collecting information about a **population** by questioning people or examining items.

Systematic sampling
A method of selecting a **sample** from a **population** in which every nth member is chosen from a full list of the population.

Tangent
A straight line which just touches a curve at a point. Its **gradient** is the same as the curve's gradient at that point.

Taut
Describes a **string** or **wire** which is experiencing a **tension force** and is tight and straight.

Tension
The **force** in a **taut wire** or **string**.

Term
A collection of numbers, **variables** and brackets all multiplied or divided together.

Test statistic
A **statistic** calculated from **sample** data which is used to decide whether or not to reject the **null hypothesis** in a **hypothesis test**.

Thin
Describes a body which is modelled as having no thickness, only length.

Thrust
The **force** in a compressed **rod**.

Tree diagram
Tree diagrams show probabilities for sequences of two or more **events**.

Trial
A process (e.g. an experiment) with different possible **outcomes**.

Turning point
A **stationary point** that is a (local) **maximum** or **minimum** point of a curve.

Two-tailed test
A **hypothesis test** is 'two-tailed' if the **alternative hypothesis** specifies only that the **parameter** doesn't equal the value specified by the **null hypothesis**. E.g. it says $p \neq a$ for a parameter p and constant a.

Two-way table
A way of representing a probability problem involving combinations of two **events** in a table, where each cell of the table represents a different combined event.

Unit vector
A **vector** of **magnitude** one unit.

Upper quartile
The value that 75% of data values in a data set are less than or equal to.

Variable
A letter in an expression representing an unknown which, unlike a **constant**, can take on different values.

Variance
A measure of **dispersion** from the **mean**.

Vector
A quantity which has both a **magnitude** and a direction.

Velocity
The rate of change of an object's **displacement** with respect to time.

Venn diagram
A Venn diagram shows how a collection of objects is split up into different groups, where everything in a group has something in common. In probability, the objects are **outcomes**, and the groups are **events**.

Vertex
Turning point of a graph — the **maximum** or **minimum** point for a **quadratic graph**.

Weight
The **force** due to a body's mass and the effect of gravity: $W = mg$.

Wire
A **thin**, **inextensible**, **rigid**, **light** body.

Index

MET51